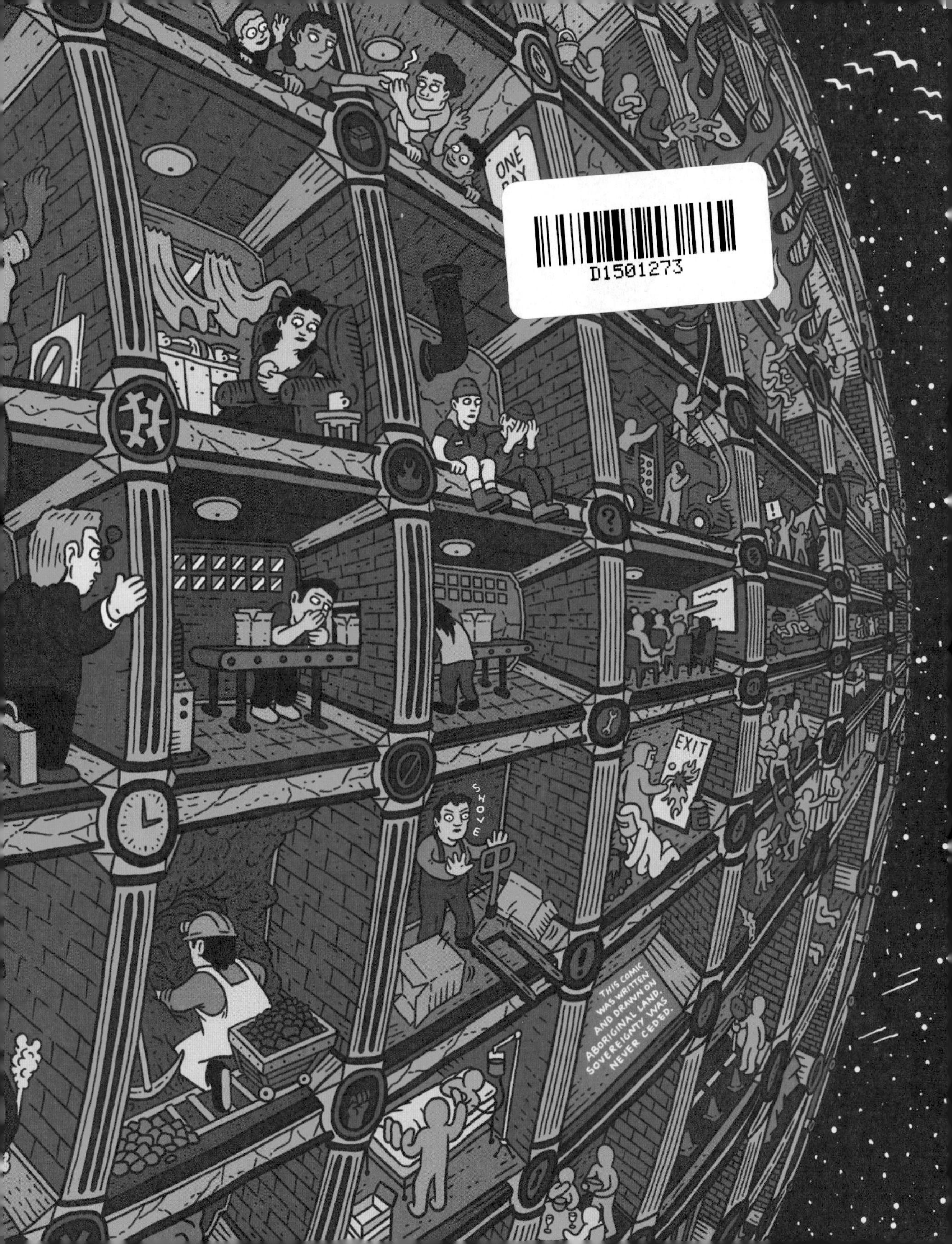
ONE DAY
SHOVE
EXIT
THIS COMIC WAS WRITTEN AND DRAWN ON ABORIGINAL LAND. SOVEREIGNTY WAS NEVER CEDED.

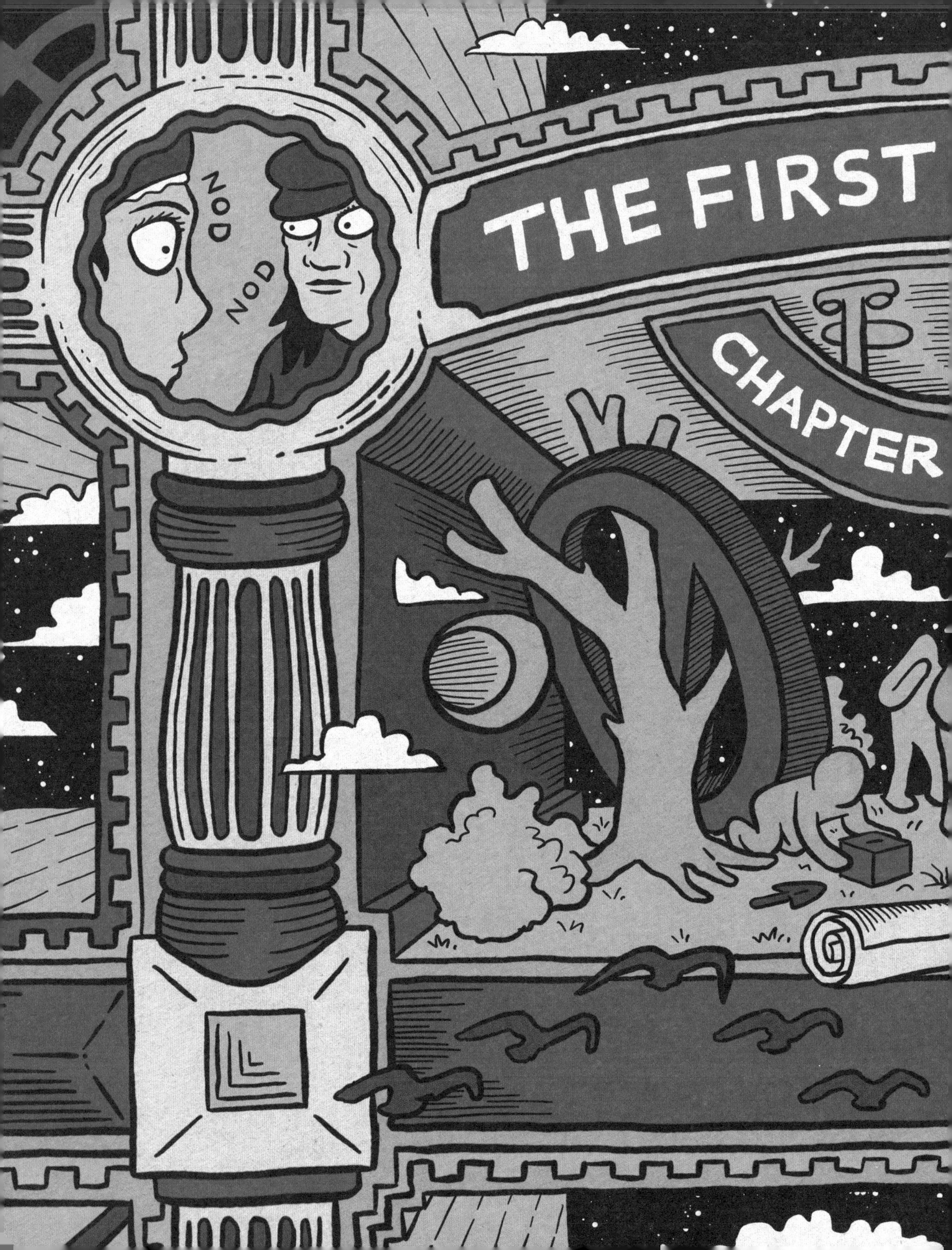

NOD
NOD
THE FIRST
CHAPTER

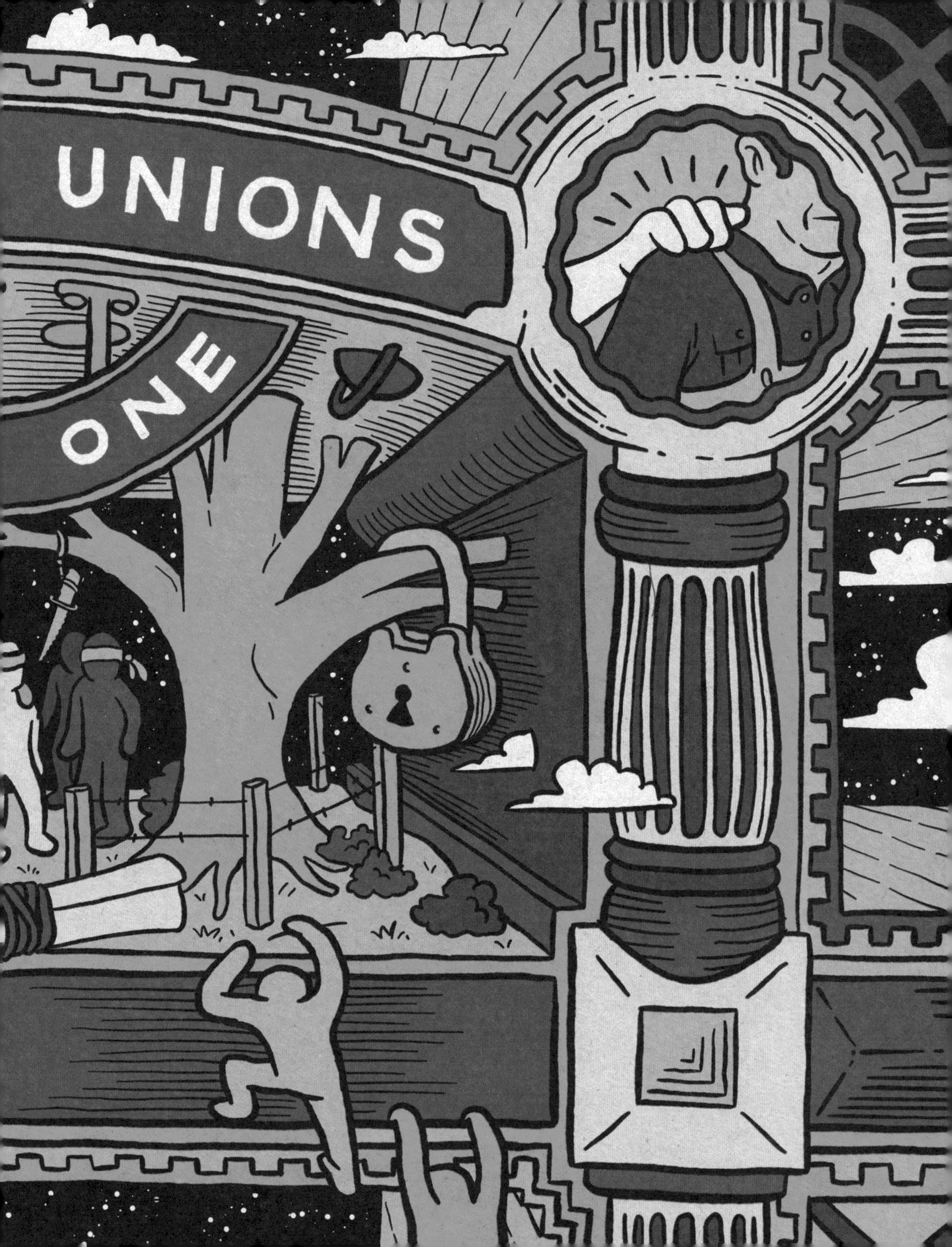
UNIONS
ONE

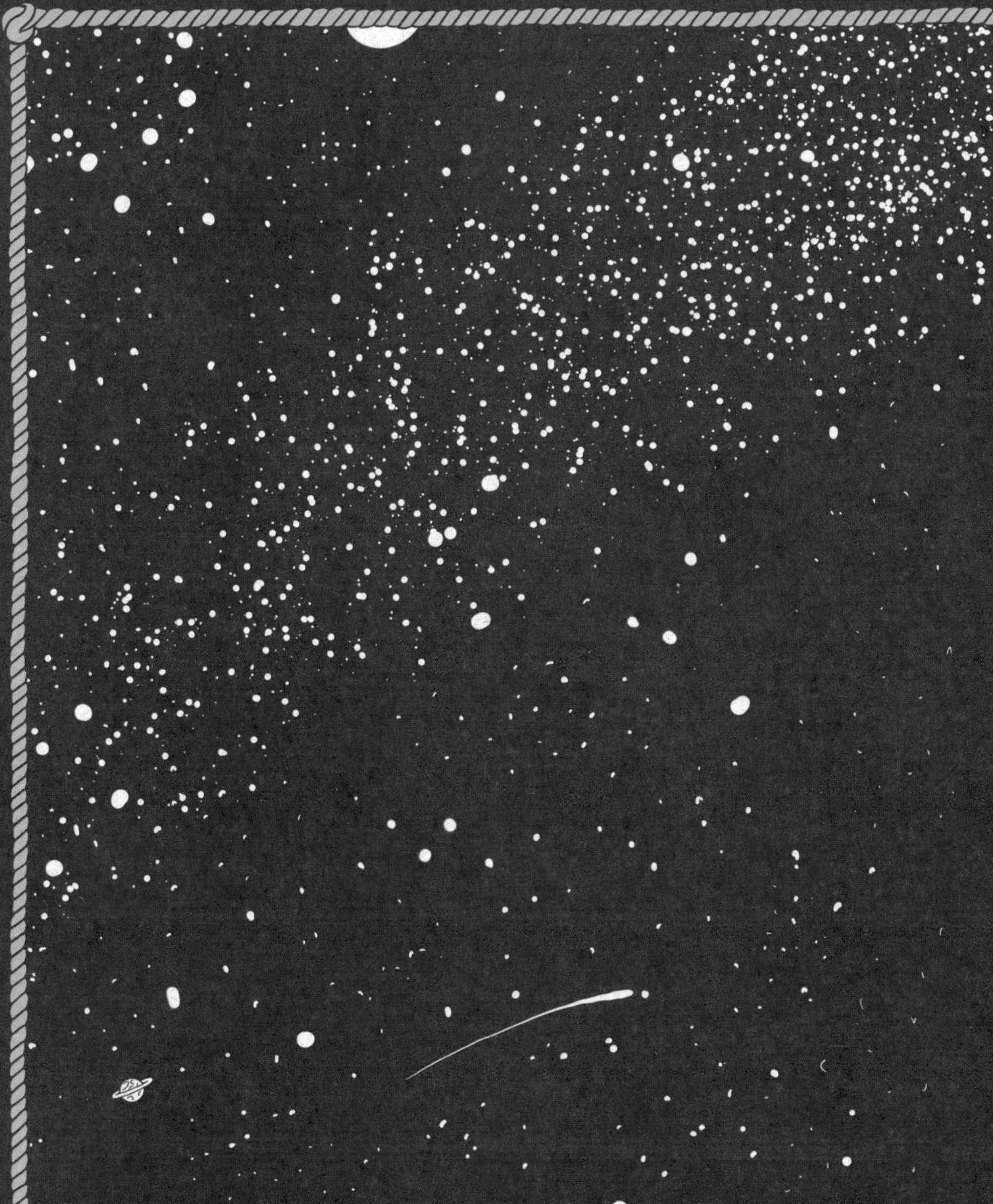

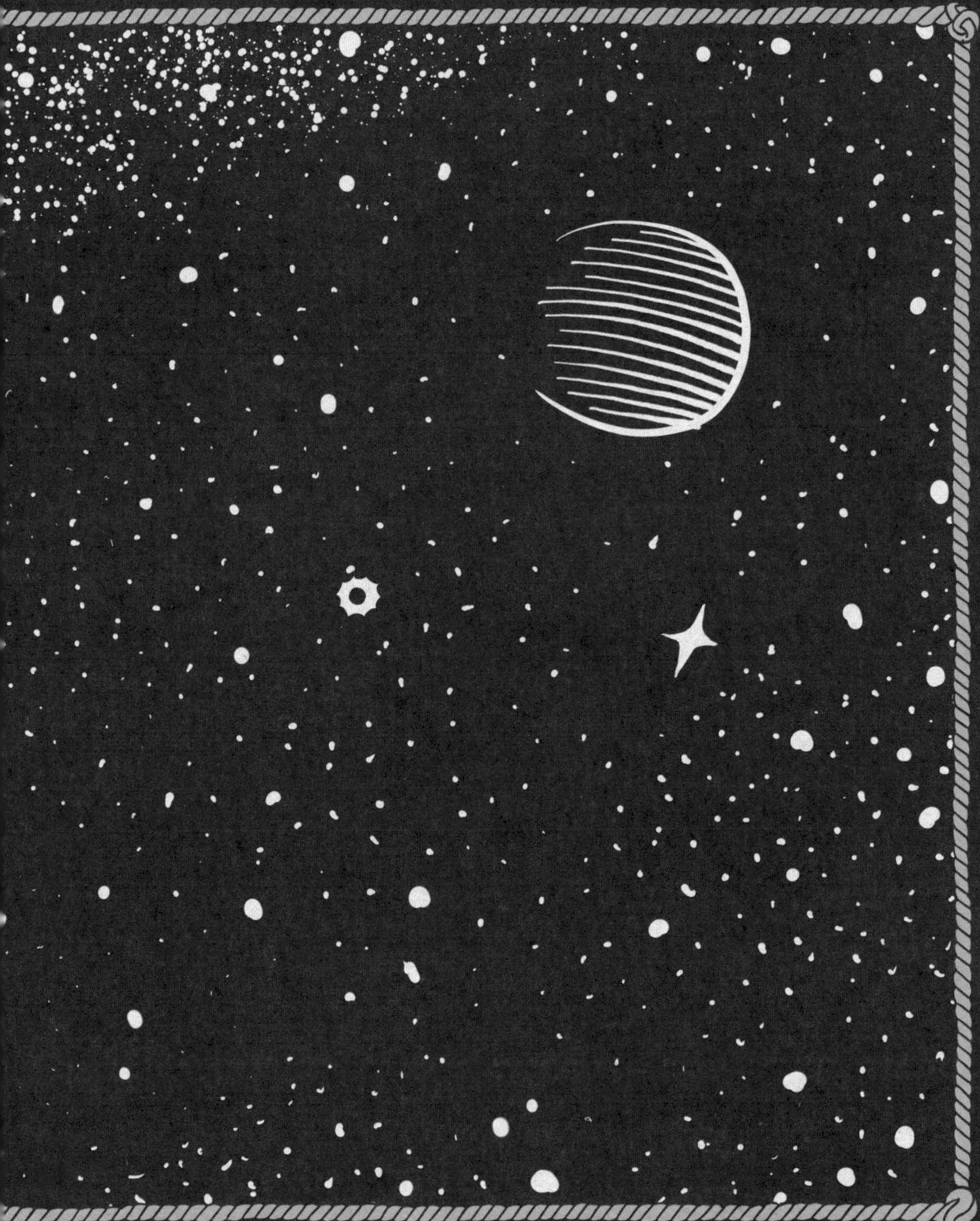

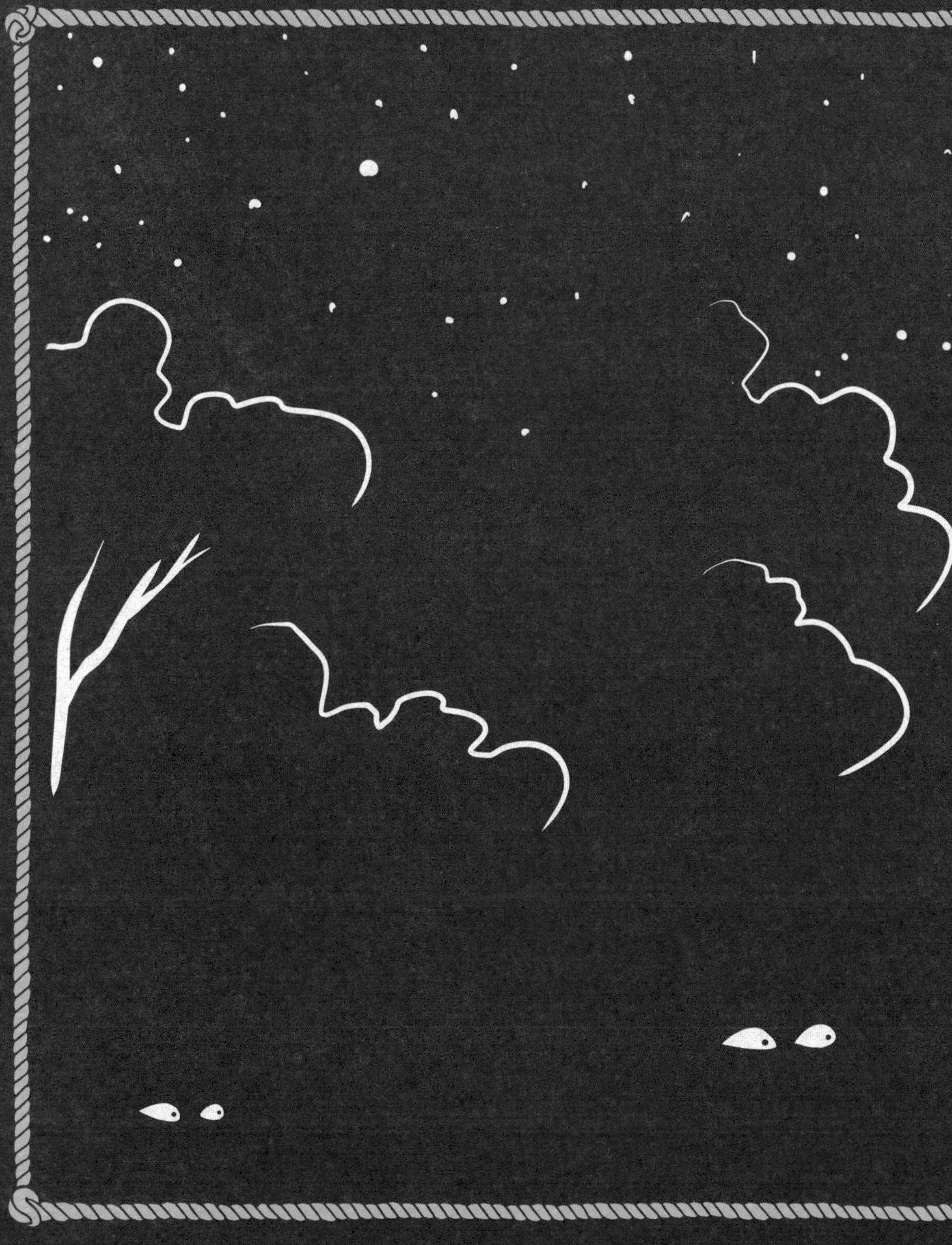

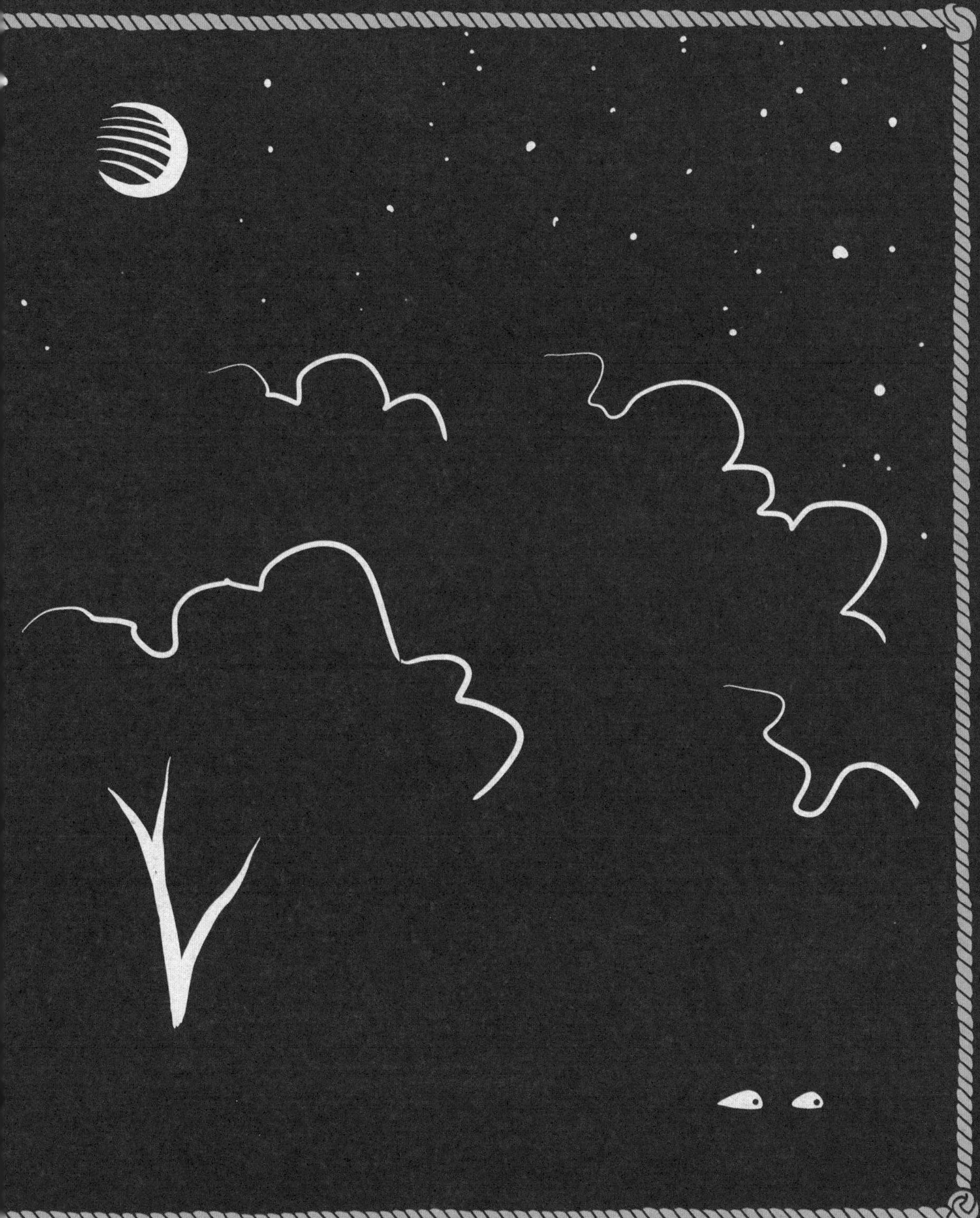

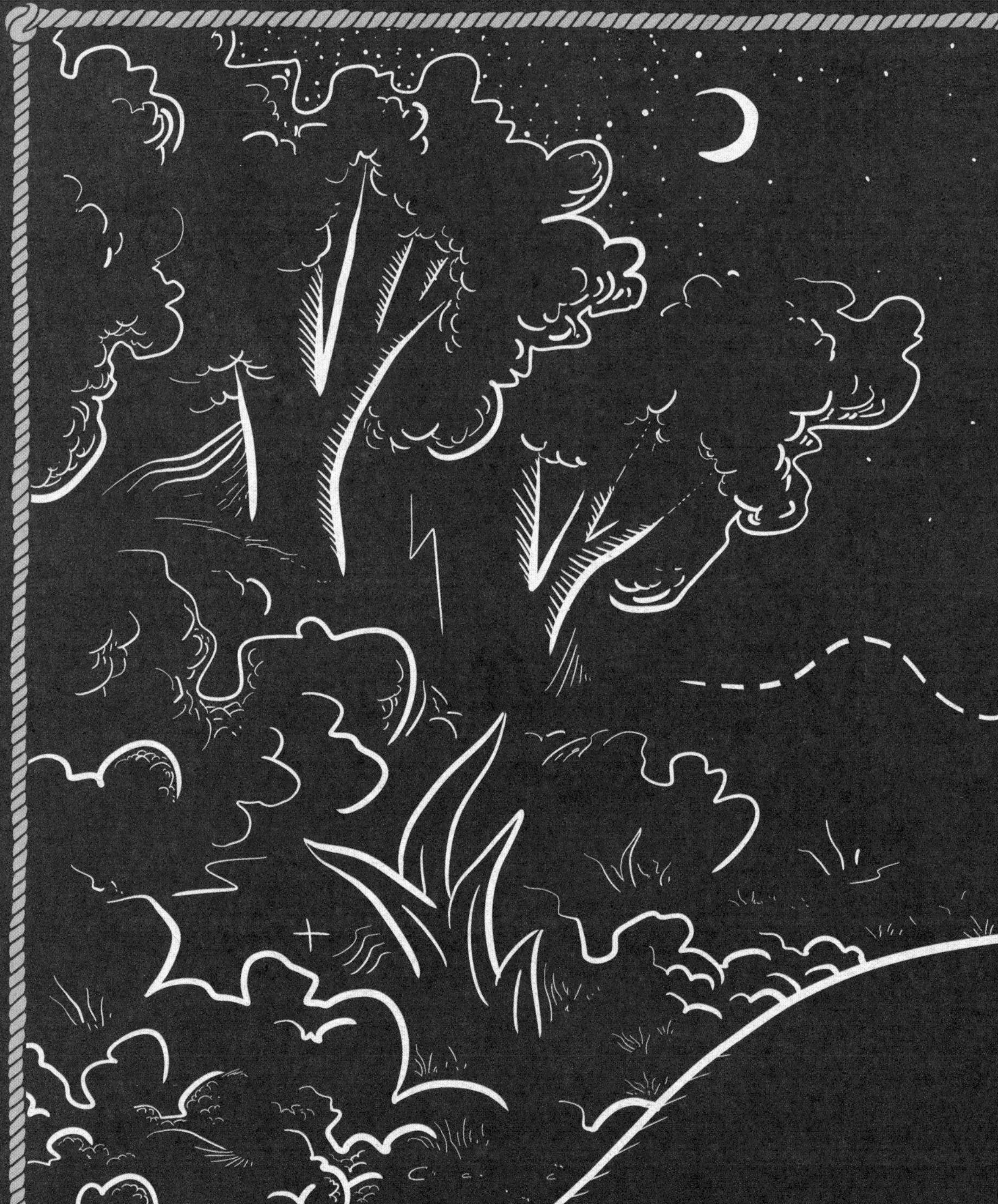

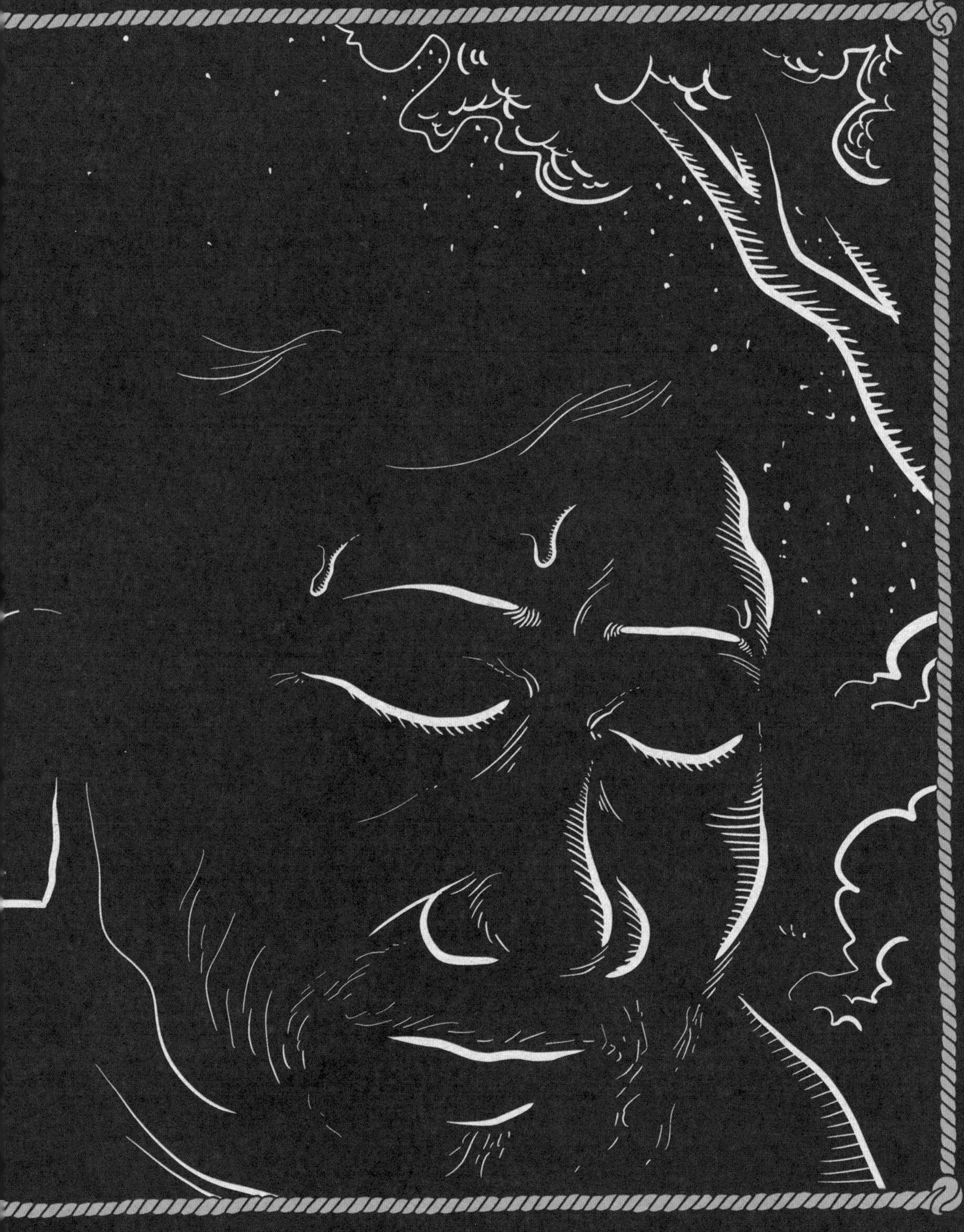

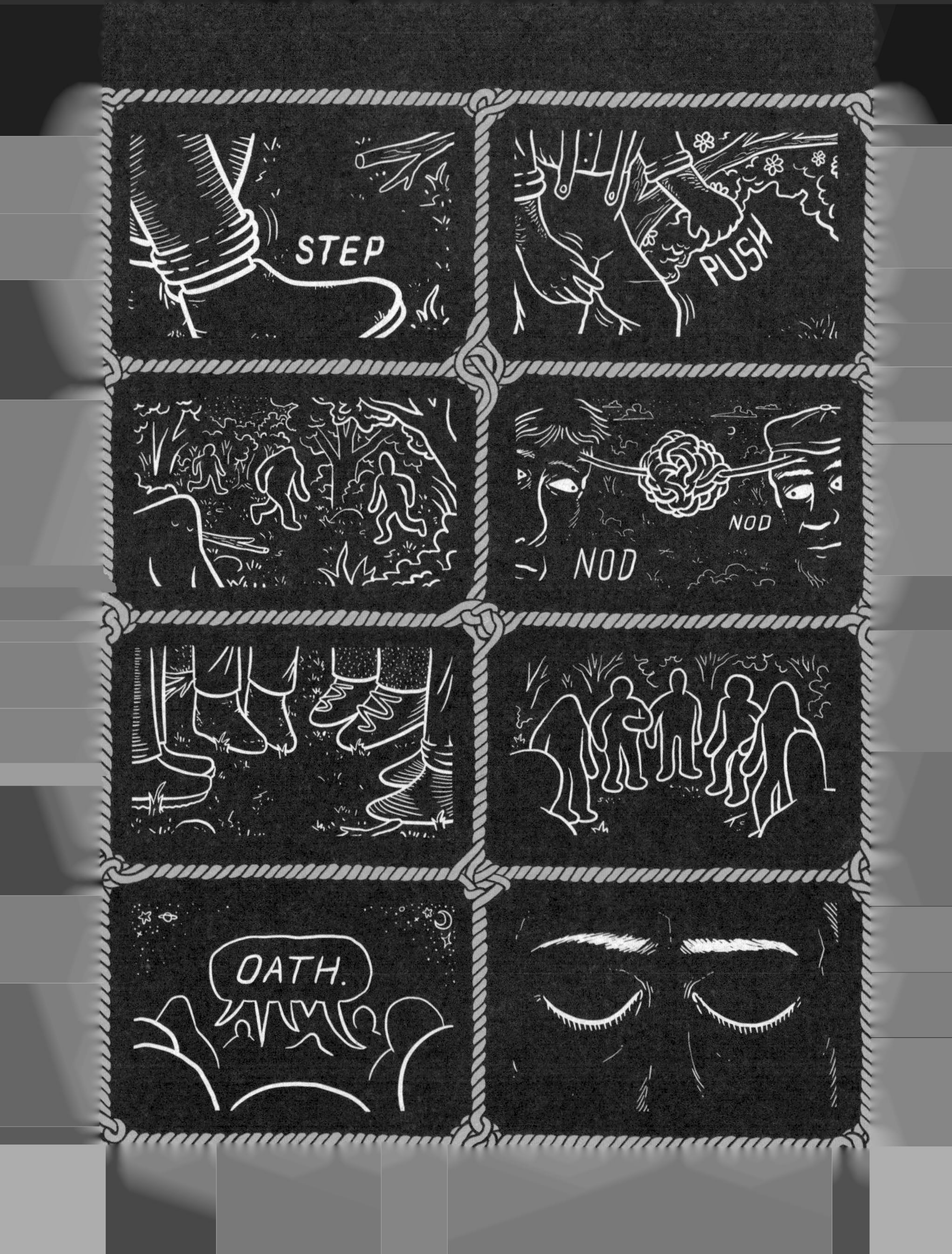
STEP
PUSH
NOD
NOD
OATH.

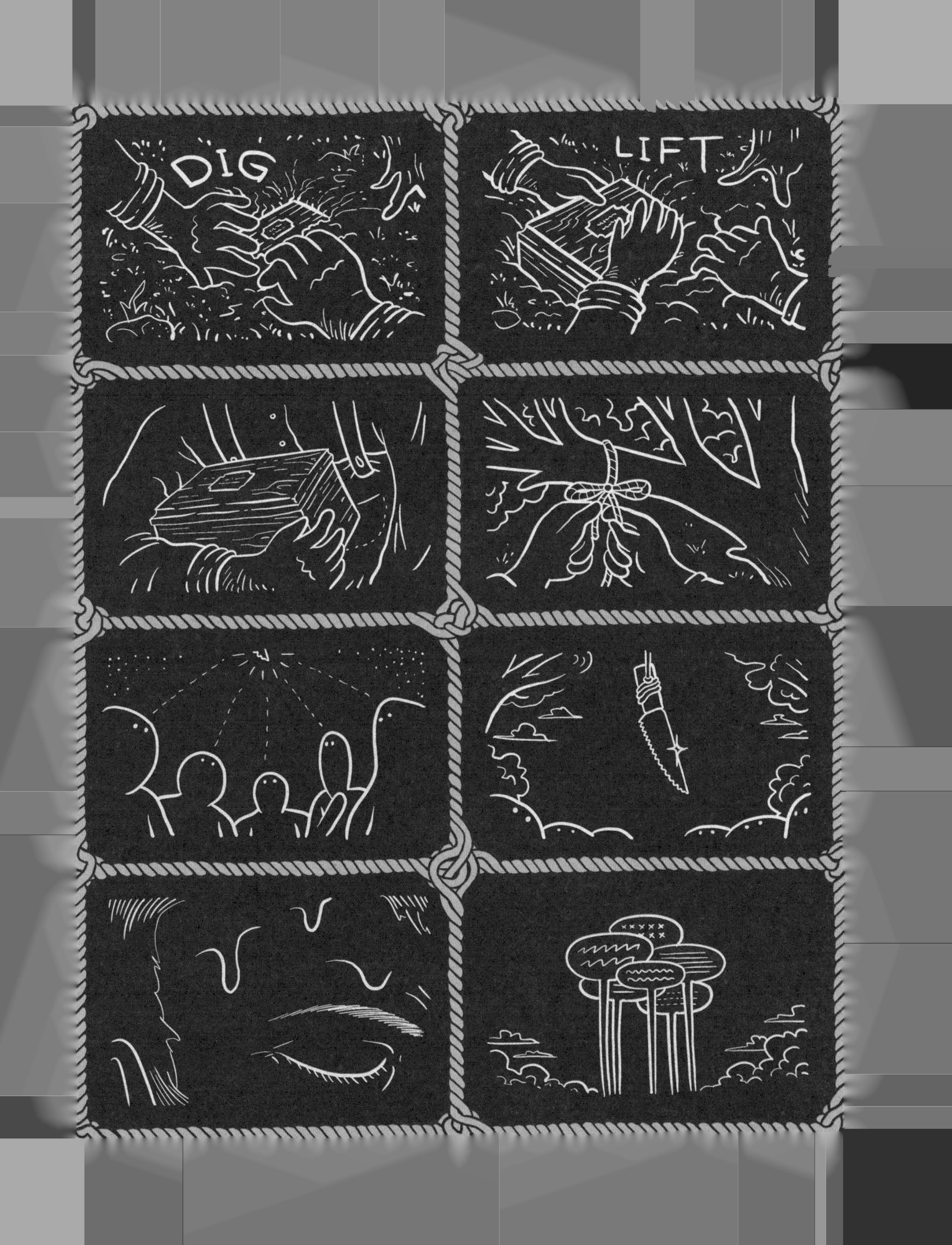
DIG
LIFT

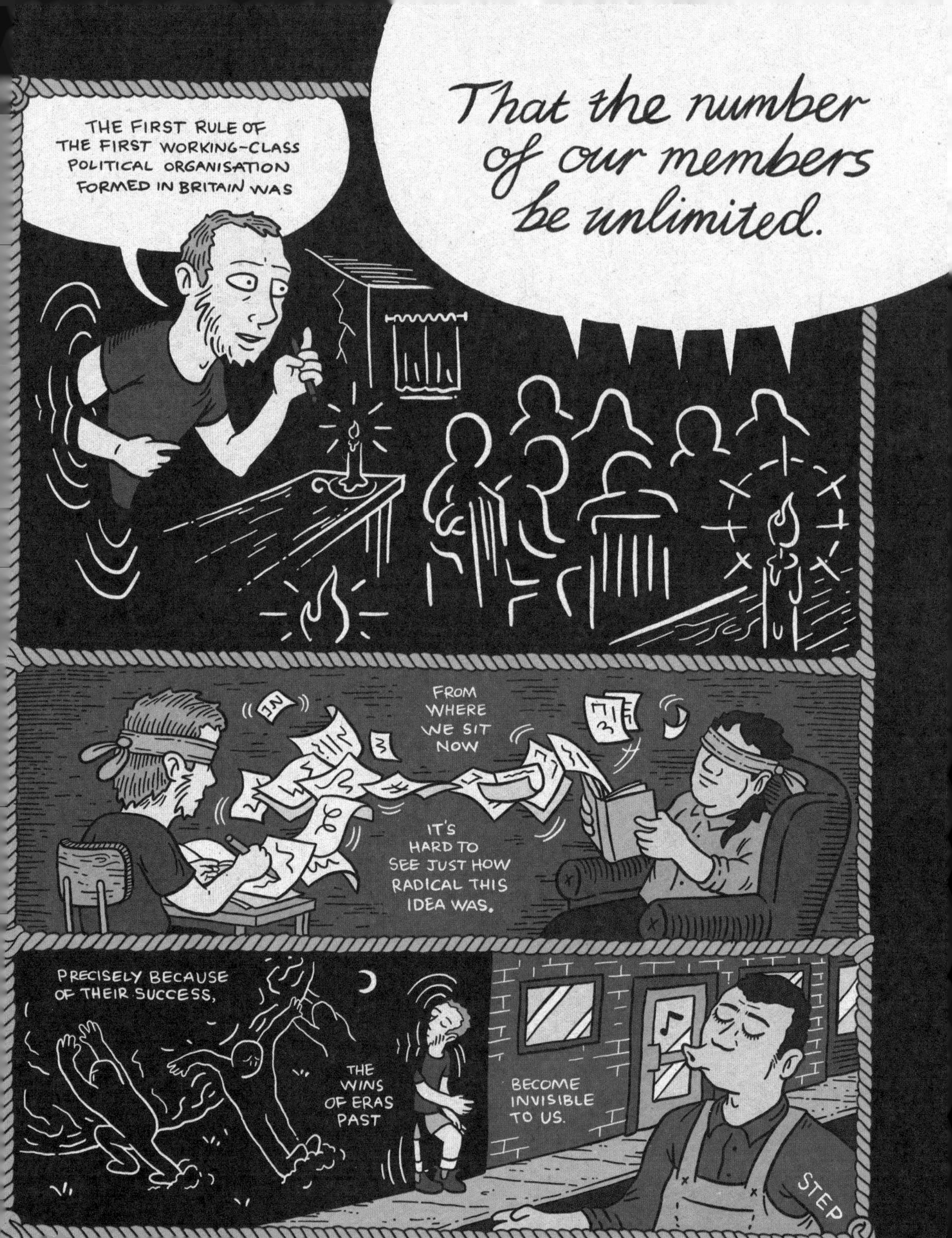
THE FIRST RULE OF THE FIRST WORKING-CLASS POLITICAL ORGANISATION FORMED IN BRITAIN WAS
That the number of our members be unlimited.
FROM WHERE WE SIT NOW
IT'S HARD TO SEE JUST HOW RADICAL THIS IDEA WAS.
PRECISELY BECAUSE OF THEIR SUCCESS,
THE WINS OF ERAS PAST
BECOME INVISIBLE TO US.
STEP

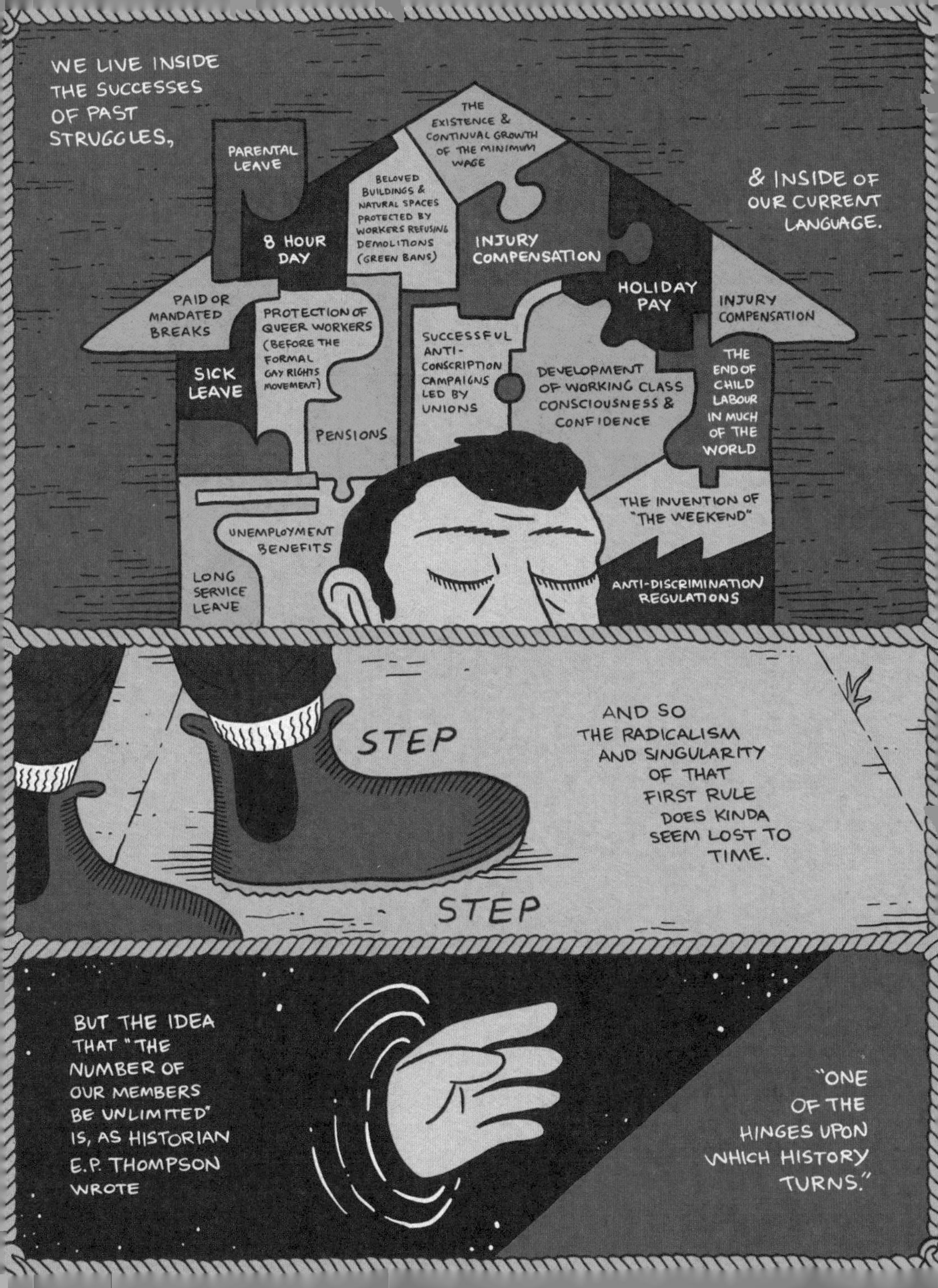
WE LIVE INSIDE THE SUCCESSES OF PAST STRUGGLES,
PARENTAL LEAVE
THE EXISTENCE & CONTINUAL GROWTH OF THE MINIMUM WAGE
BELOVED BUILDINGS & NATURAL SPACES PROTECTED BY WORKERS REFUSING DEMOLITIONS (GREEN BANS)
8 HOUR DAY
INJURY COMPENSATION
& INSIDE OF OUR CURRENT LANGUAGE.
PAID OR MANDATED BREAKS
PROTECTION OF QUEER WORKERS (BEFORE THE FORMAL GAY RIGHTS MOVEMENT)
HOLIDAY PAY
INJURY COMPENSATION
SUCCESSFUL ANTI-CONSCRIPTION CAMPAIGNS LED BY UNIONS
DEVELOPMENT OF WORKING CLASS CONSCIOUSNESS & CONFIDENCE
THE END OF CHILD LABOUR IN MUCH OF THE WORLD
SICK LEAVE
PENSIONS
THE INVENTION OF "THE WEEKEND"
UNEMPLOYMENT BENEFITS
LONG SERVICE LEAVE
ANTI-DISCRIMINATION REGULATIONS
STEP
AND SO THE RADICALISM AND SINGULARITY OF THAT FIRST RULE DOES KINDA SEEM LOST TO TIME.
STEP
BUT THE IDEA THAT "THE NUMBER OF OUR MEMBERS BE UNLIMITED" IS, AS HISTORIAN E.P. THOMPSON WROTE
"ONE OF THE HINGES UPON WHICH HISTORY TURNS."

THROUGH ORGANISATIONS LIKE THE FRIENDLY SOCIETY OF AGRICULTURAL LABOURERS, WORKERS DEVELOPED A POINTED SELF-AWARENESS,

AND AN UNDERSTANDING THAT IT WAS THEIR WORK THAT BOTH CONSTRUCTED THE WHEELS OF SOCIETY

AND ALSO MADE THOSE WHEELS TURN.

THESE WORKERS CAME TOGETHER IN ORDER TO FORGE THEIR LABOUR INTO A POLITICAL TOOL, IN AND OF ITSELF.

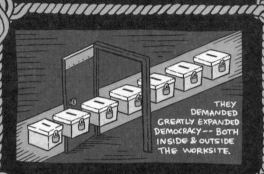

THEY DEMANDED GREATLY EXPANDED DEMOCRACY-- BOTH INSIDE & OUTSIDE THE WORKSITE.

INCREASED PAY,

REDUCED WORKING HOURS,

GREATER WORKPLACE SAFETY,

& MORE CONTROL OVER THE CONDITIONS OF THEIR LIVES.

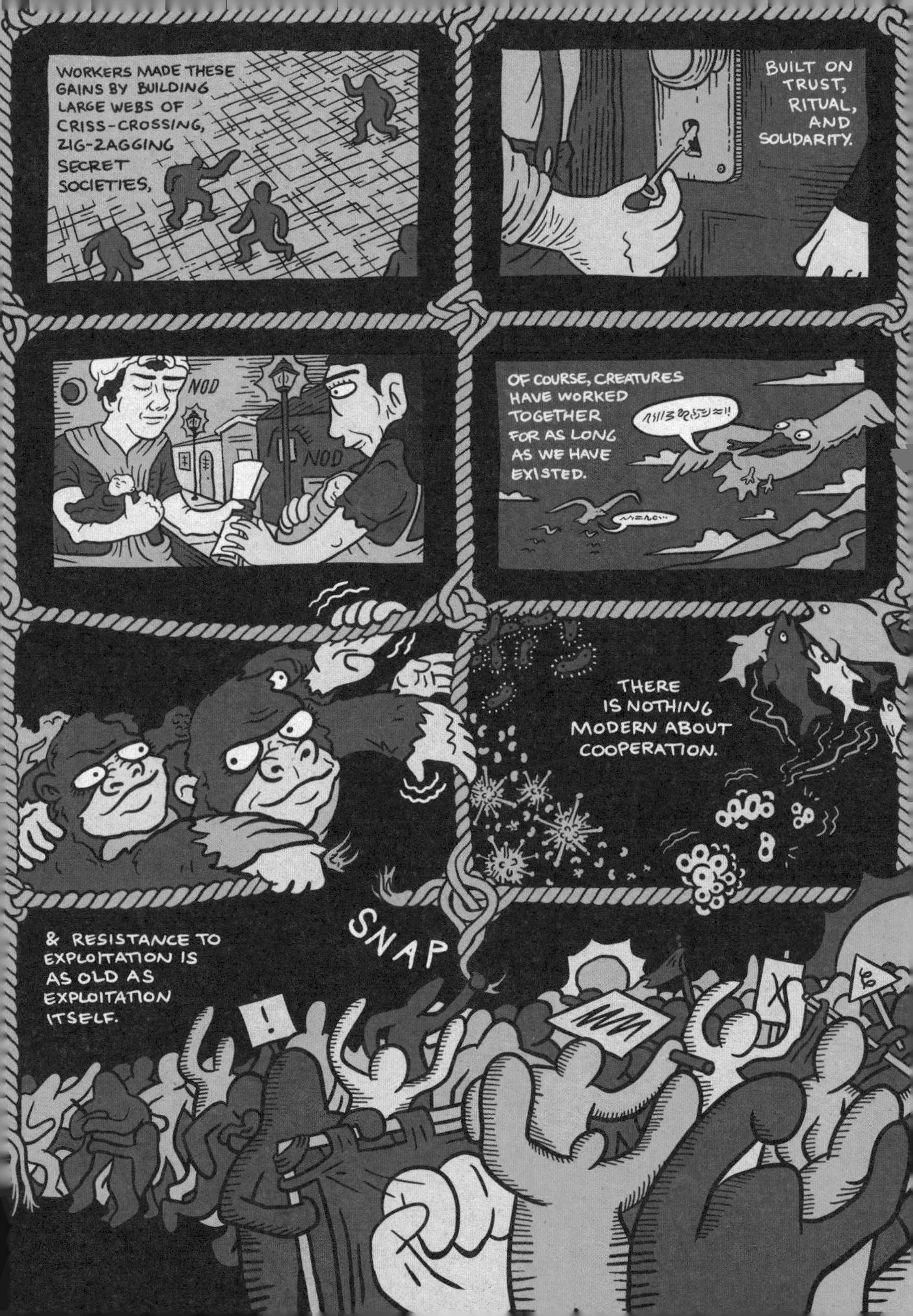
WORKERS MADE THESE GAINS BY BUILDING LARGE WEBS OF CRISS-CROSSING, ZIG-ZAGGING SECRET SOCIETIES,
BUILT ON TRUST, RITUAL, AND SOLIDARITY.
NOD
NOD
OF COURSE, CREATURES HAVE WORKED TOGETHER FOR AS LONG AS WE HAVE EXISTED.
THERE IS NOTHING MODERN ABOUT COOPERATION.
SNAP
& RESISTANCE TO EXPLOITATION IS AS OLD AS EXPLOITATION ITSELF.
!

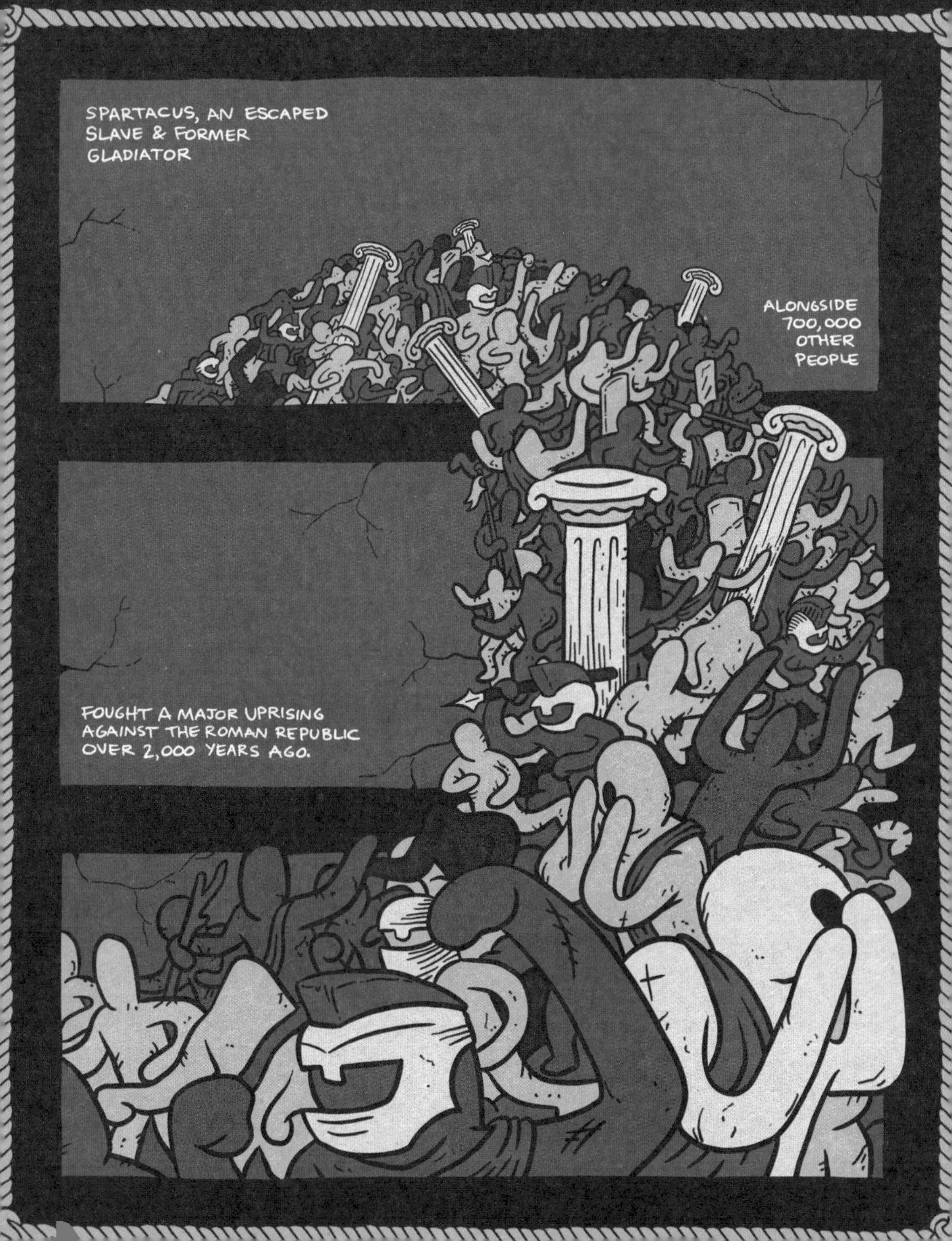
SPARTACUS, AN ESCAPED SLAVE & FORMER GLADIATOR
ALONGSIDE 700,000 OTHER PEOPLE
FOUGHT A MAJOR UPRISING AGAINST THE ROMAN REPUBLIC OVER 2,000 YEARS AGO.

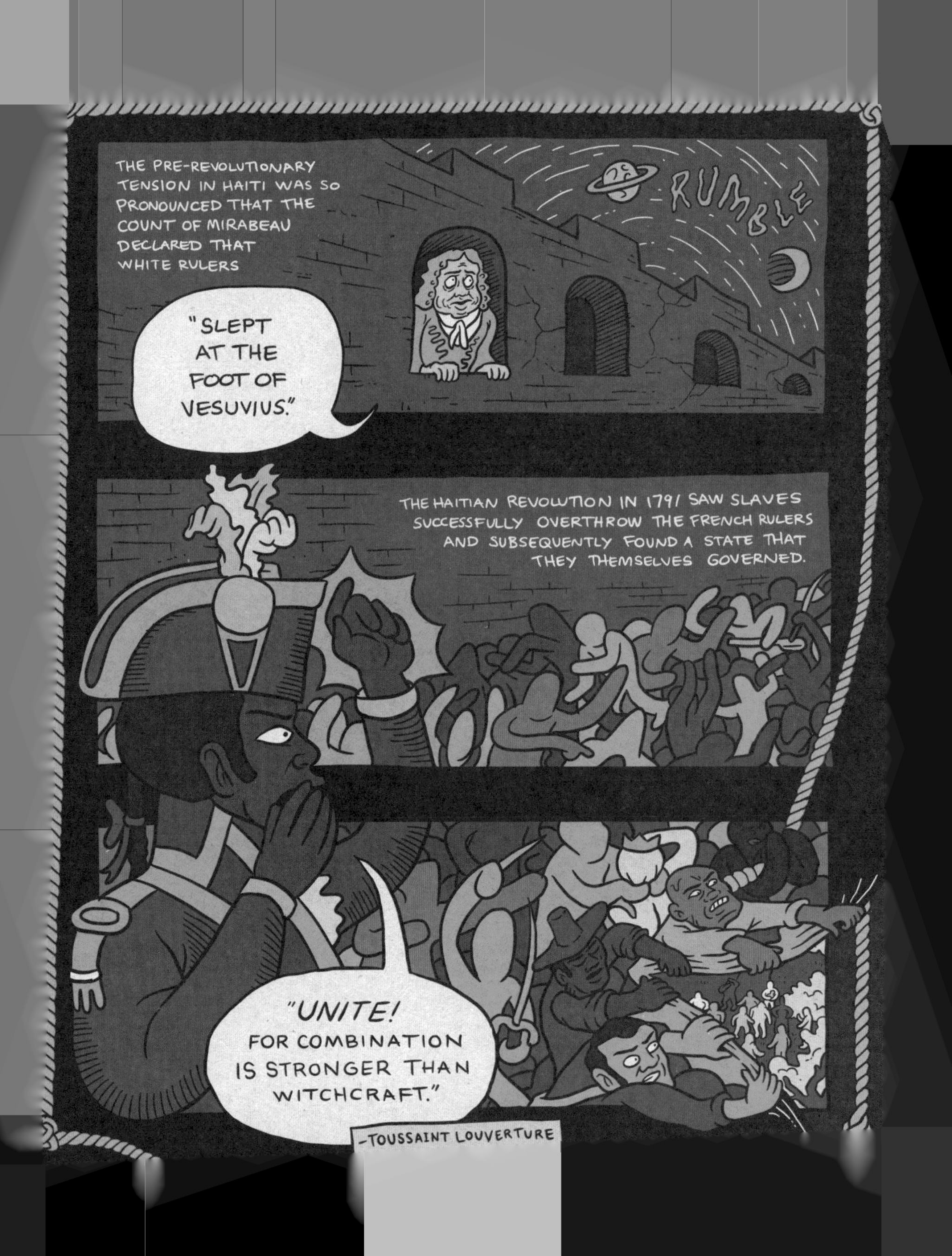
THE PRE-REVOLUTIONARY TENSION IN HAITI WAS SO PRONOUNCED THAT THE COUNT OF MIRABEAU DECLARED THAT WHITE RULERS
RUMBLE
"SLEPT AT THE FOOT OF VESUVIUS."
THE HAITIAN REVOLUTION IN 1791 SAW SLAVES SUCCESSFULLY OVERTHROW THE FRENCH RULERS AND SUBSEQUENTLY FOUND A STATE THAT THEY THEMSELVES GOVERNED.
"UNITE! FOR COMBINATION IS STRONGER THAN WITCHCRAFT."
-TOUSSAINT LOUVERTURE

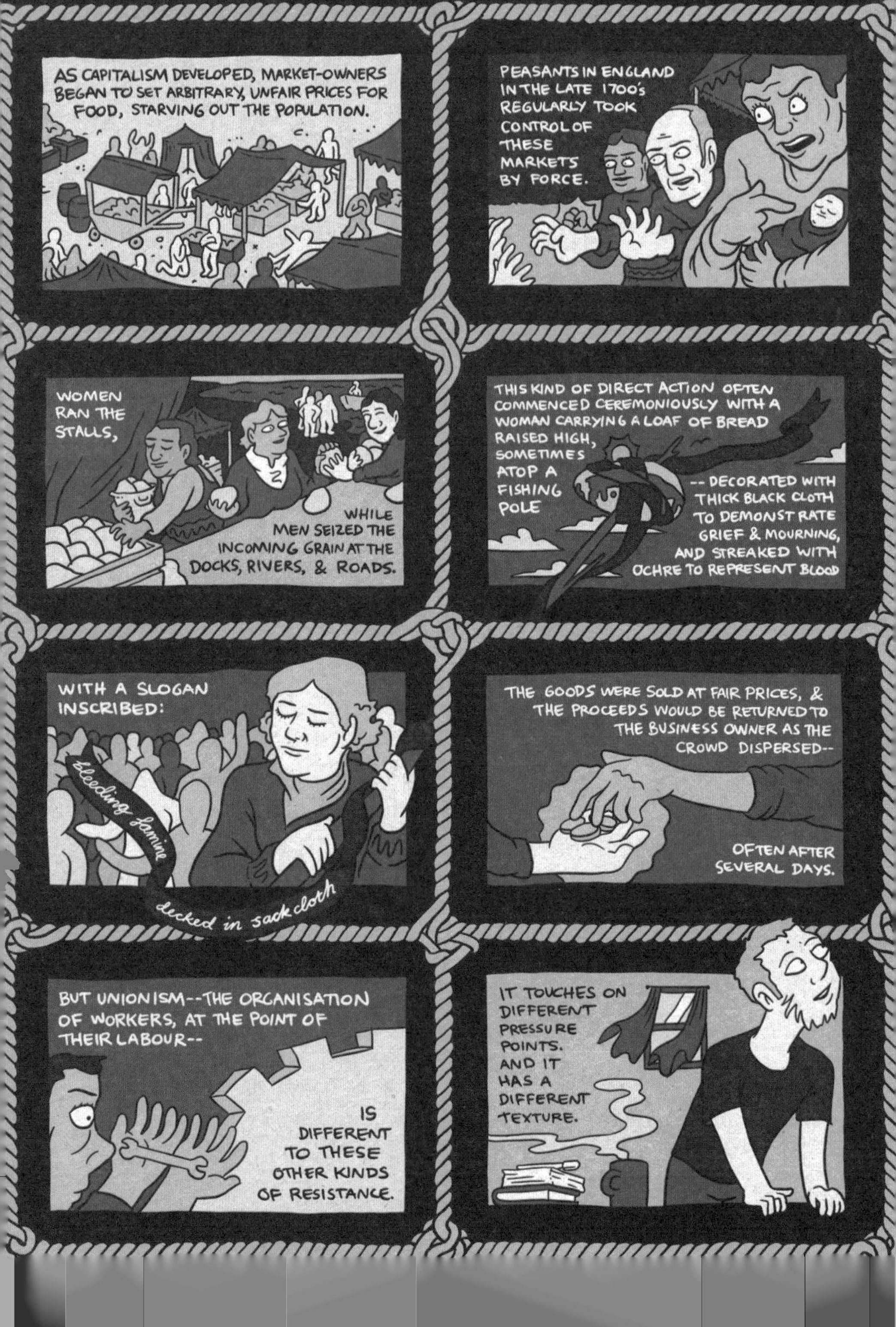

AS CAPITALISM DEVELOPED, MARKET-OWNERS BEGAN TO SET ARBITRARY, UNFAIR PRICES FOR FOOD, STARVING OUT THE POPULATION.
PEASANTS IN ENGLAND IN THE LATE 1700's REGULARLY TOOK CONTROL OF THESE MARKETS BY FORCE.
WOMEN RAN THE STALLS,
WHILE MEN SEIZED THE INCOMING GRAIN AT THE DOCKS, RIVERS, & ROADS.
THIS KIND OF DIRECT ACTION OFTEN COMMENCED CEREMONIOUSLY WITH A WOMAN CARRYING A LOAF OF BREAD RAISED HIGH, SOMETIMES ATOP A FISHING POLE
-- DECORATED WITH THICK BLACK CLOTH TO DEMONSTRATE GRIEF & MOURNING, AND STREAKED WITH OCHRE TO REPRESENT BLOOD
WITH A SLOGAN INSCRIBED:
bleeding famine
decked in sackcloth
THE GOODS WERE SOLD AT FAIR PRICES, & THE PROCEEDS WOULD BE RETURNED TO THE BUSINESS OWNER AS THE CROWD DISPERSED--
OFTEN AFTER SEVERAL DAYS.
BUT UNIONISM--THE ORGANISATION OF WORKERS, AT THE POINT OF THEIR LABOUR--
IS DIFFERENT TO THESE OTHER KINDS OF RESISTANCE.
IT TOUCHES ON DIFFERENT PRESSURE POINTS. AND IT HAS A DIFFERENT TEXTURE.

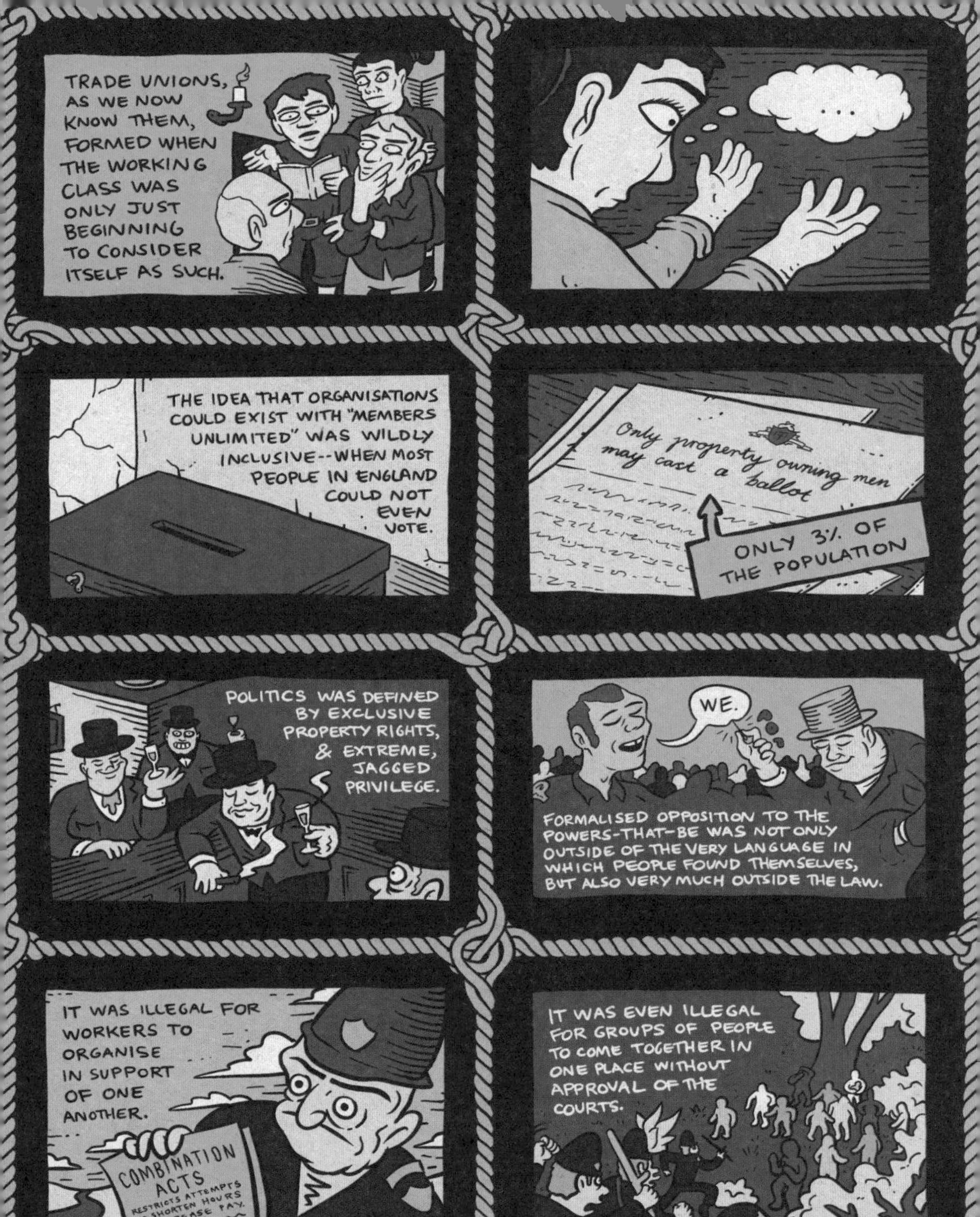

TRADE UNIONS, AS WE NOW KNOW THEM, FORMED WHEN THE WORKING CLASS WAS ONLY JUST BEGINNING TO CONSIDER ITSELF AS SUCH.
...
THE IDEA THAT ORGANISATIONS COULD EXIST WITH "MEMBERS UNLIMITED" WAS WILDLY INCLUSIVE--WHEN MOST PEOPLE IN ENGLAND COULD NOT EVEN VOTE.
Only property owning men may cast a ballot
ONLY 3% OF THE POPULATION
POLITICS WAS DEFINED BY EXCLUSIVE PROPERTY RIGHTS, & EXTREME, JAGGED PRIVILEGE.
WE.
FORMALISED OPPOSITION TO THE POWERS-THAT-BE WAS NOT ONLY OUTSIDE OF THE VERY LANGUAGE IN WHICH PEOPLE FOUND THEMSELVES, BUT ALSO VERY MUCH OUTSIDE THE LAW.
IT WAS ILLEGAL FOR WORKERS TO ORGANISE IN SUPPORT OF ONE ANOTHER.
COMBINATION ACTS
RESTRICTS ATTEMPTS TO SHORTEN HOURS OR INCREASE PAY.
IT WAS EVEN ILLEGAL FOR GROUPS OF PEOPLE TO COME TOGETHER IN ONE PLACE WITHOUT APPROVAL OF THE COURTS.

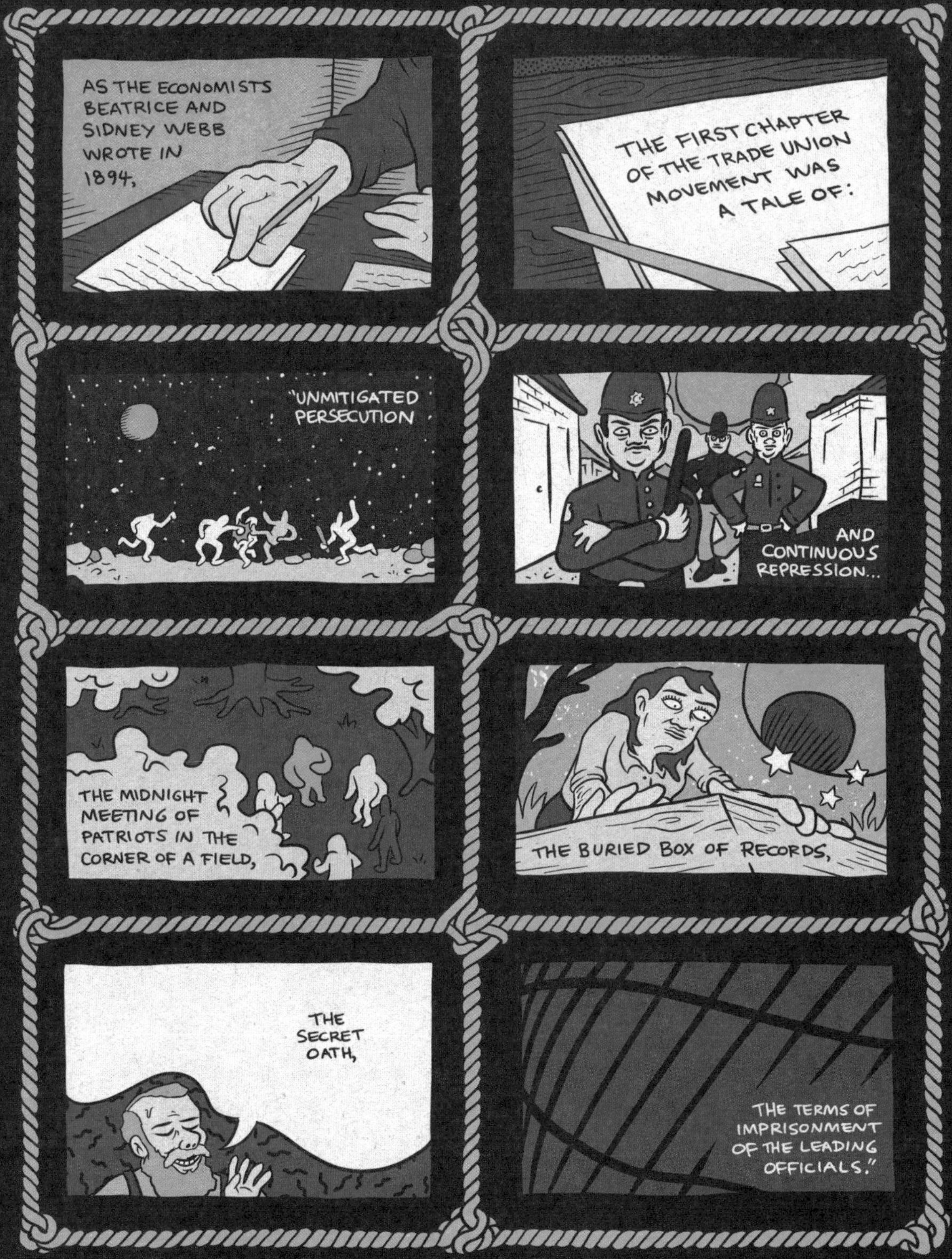
AS THE ECONOMISTS BEATRICE AND SIDNEY WEBB WROTE IN 1894,
THE FIRST CHAPTER OF THE TRADE UNION MOVEMENT WAS A TALE OF:
"UNMITIGATED PERSECUTION
AND CONTINUOUS REPRESSION...
THE MIDNIGHT MEETING OF PATRIOTS IN THE CORNER OF A FIELD,
THE BURIED BOX OF RECORDS,
THE SECRET OATH,
THE TERMS OF IMPRISONMENT OF THE LEADING OFFICIALS."

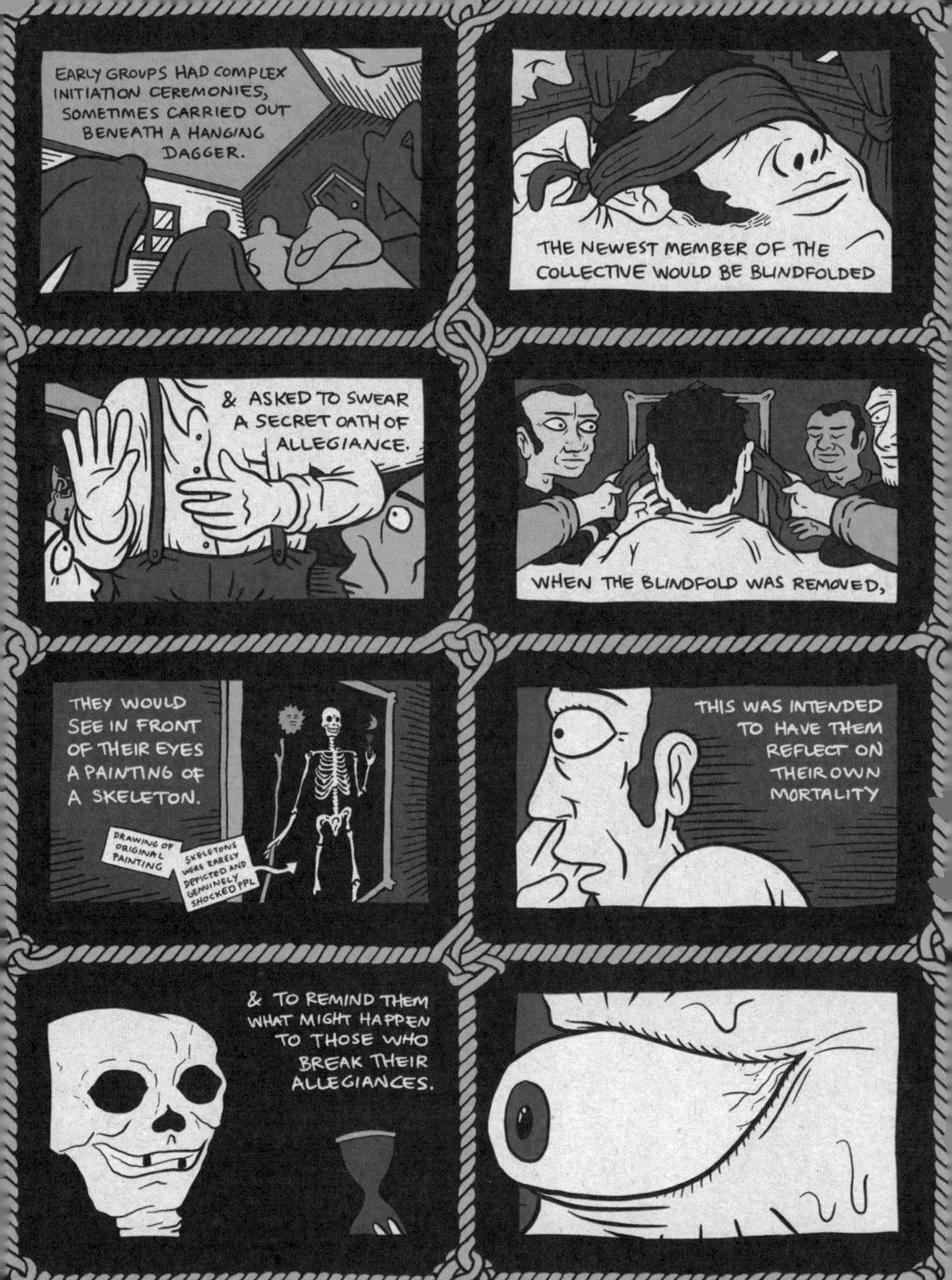
EARLY GROUPS HAD COMPLEX INITIATION CEREMONIES, SOMETIMES CARRIED OUT BENEATH A HANGING DAGGER.
THE NEWEST MEMBER OF THE COLLECTIVE WOULD BE BLINDFOLDED
& ASKED TO SWEAR A SECRET OATH OF ALLEGIANCE.
WHEN THE BLINDFOLD WAS REMOVED,
THEY WOULD SEE IN FRONT OF THEIR EYES A PAINTING OF A SKELETON.
DRAWING OF ORIGINAL PAINTING
SKELETONS WERE RARELY DEPICTED AND GENUINELY SHOCKED PPL
THIS WAS INTENDED TO HAVE THEM REFLECT ON THEIR OWN MORTALITY
& TO REMIND THEM WHAT MIGHT HAPPEN TO THOSE WHO BREAK THEIR ALLEGIANCES.

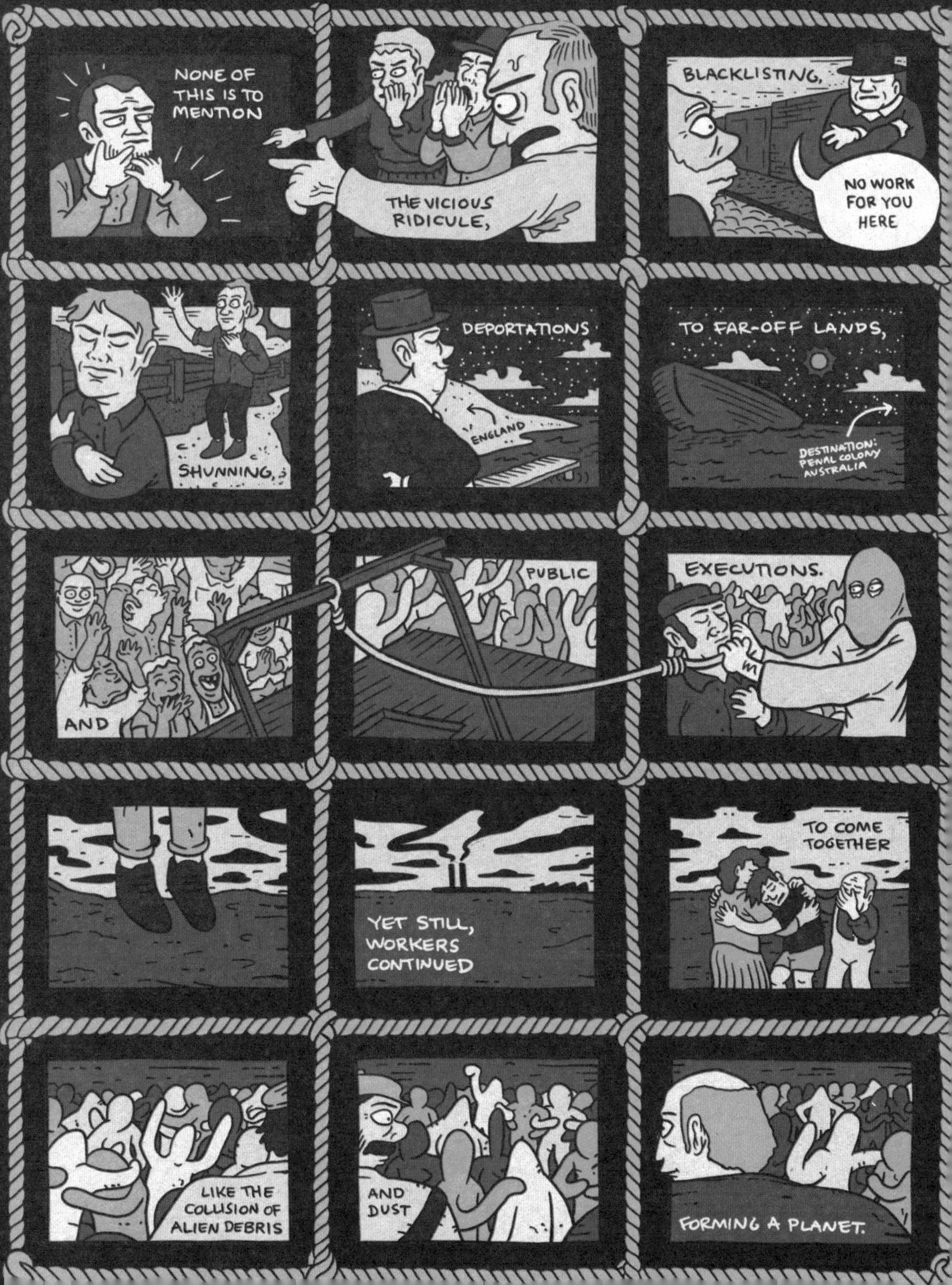
NONE OF THIS IS TO MENTION
THE VICIOUS RIDICULE,
BLACKLISTING,
NO WORK FOR YOU HERE
SHUNNING,
DEPORTATIONS
ENGLAND
TO FAR-OFF LANDS,
DESTINATION: PENAL COLONY AUSTRALIA
AND
PUBLIC
EXECUTIONS.
YET STILL, WORKERS CONTINUED
TO COME TOGETHER
LIKE THE COLLISION OF ALIEN DEBRIS
AND DUST
FORMING A PLANET.

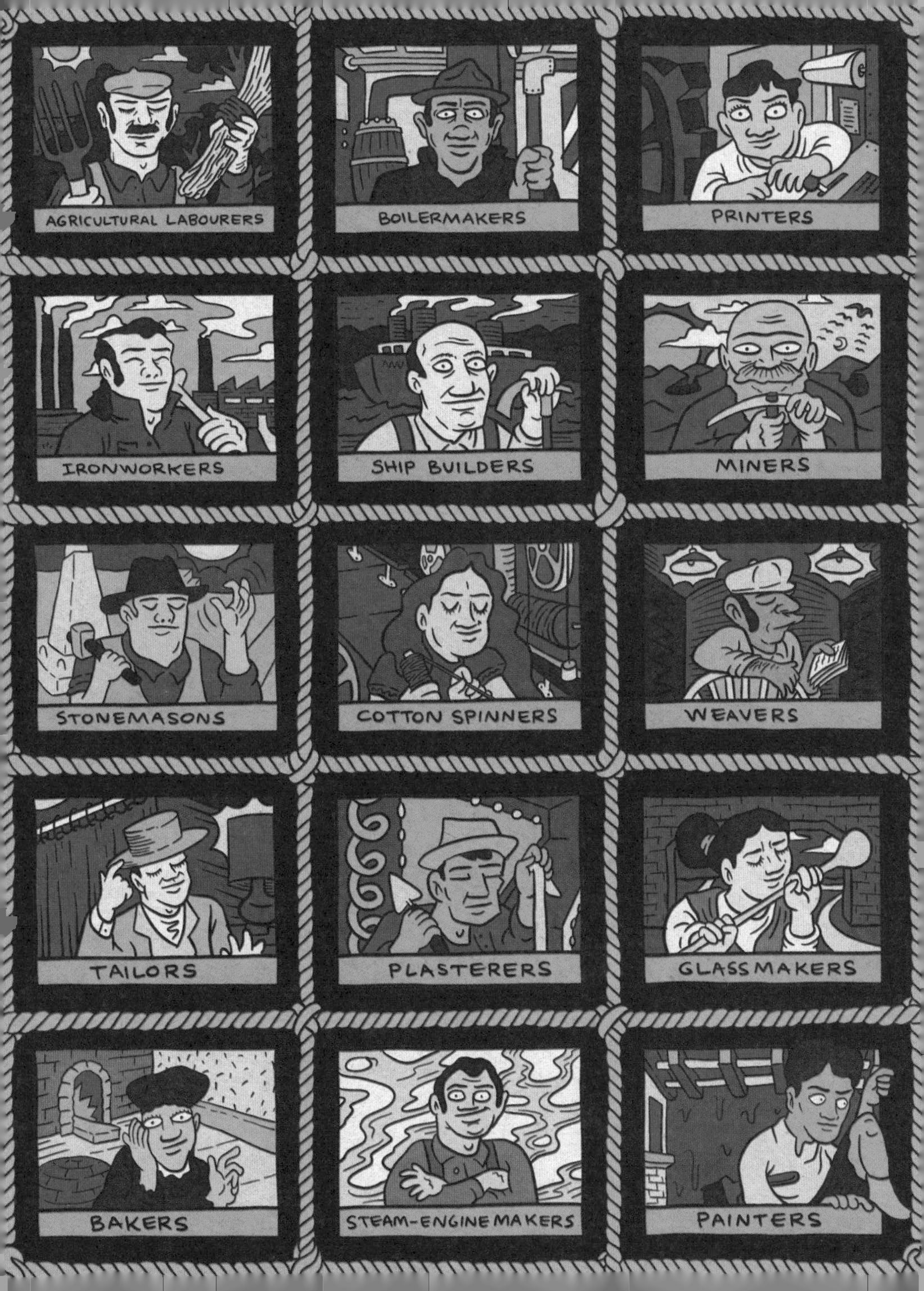
AGRICULTURAL LABOURERS
BOILERMAKERS
PRINTERS
IRONWORKERS
SHIP BUILDERS
MINERS
STONEMASONS
COTTON SPINNERS
WEAVERS
TAILORS
PLASTERERS
GLASSMAKERS
BAKERS
STEAM-ENGINE MAKERS
PAINTERS

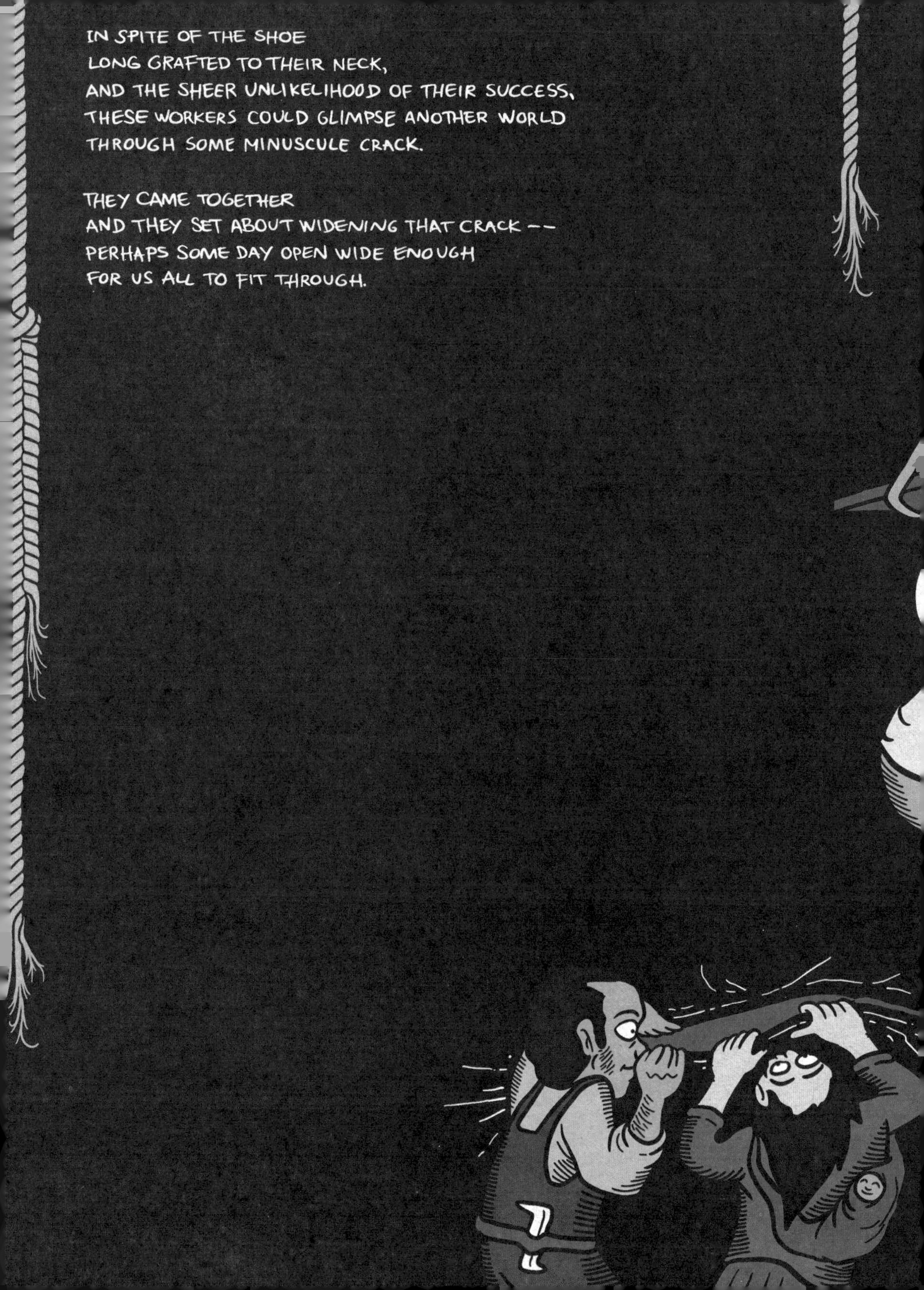
IN SPITE OF THE SHOE
LONG GRAFTED TO THEIR NECK,
AND THE SHEER UNLIKELIHOOD OF THEIR SUCCESS,
THESE WORKERS COULD GLIMPSE ANOTHER WORLD
THROUGH SOME MINUSCULE CRACK.
THEY CAME TOGETHER
AND THEY SET ABOUT WIDENING THAT CRACK --
PERHAPS SOME DAY OPEN WIDE ENOUGH
FOR US ALL TO FIT THROUGH.

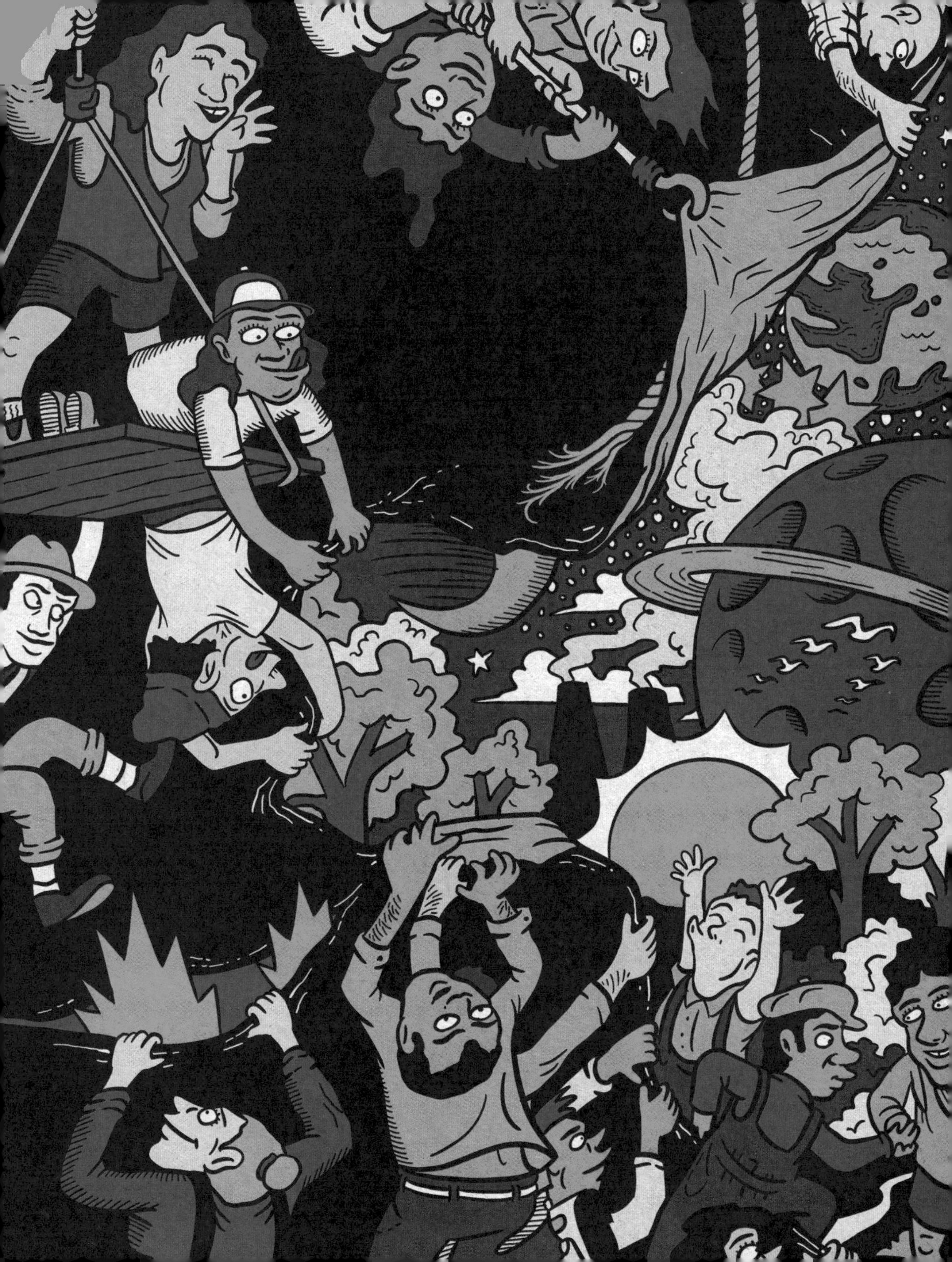

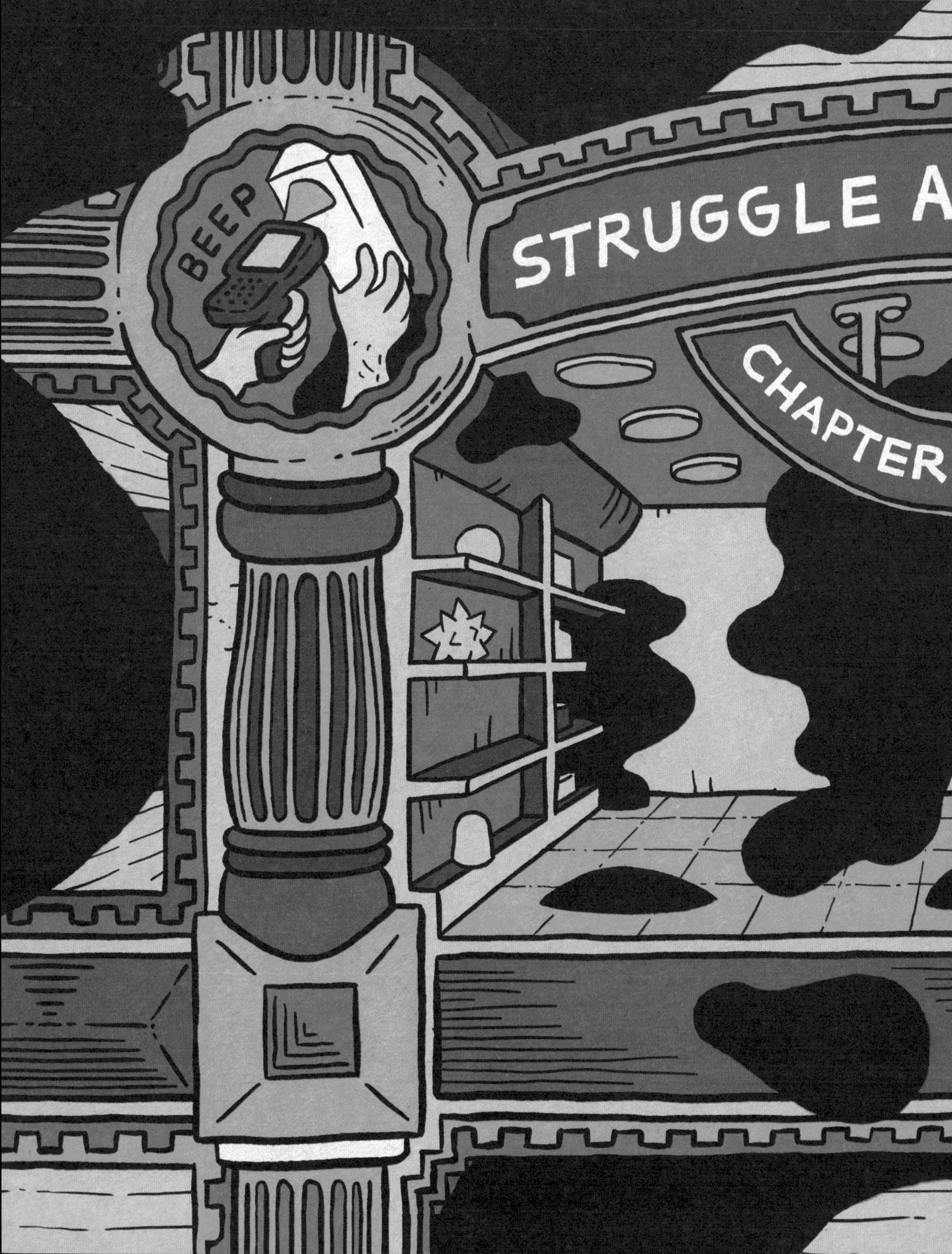
BEEP
STRUGGLE A
CHAPTER

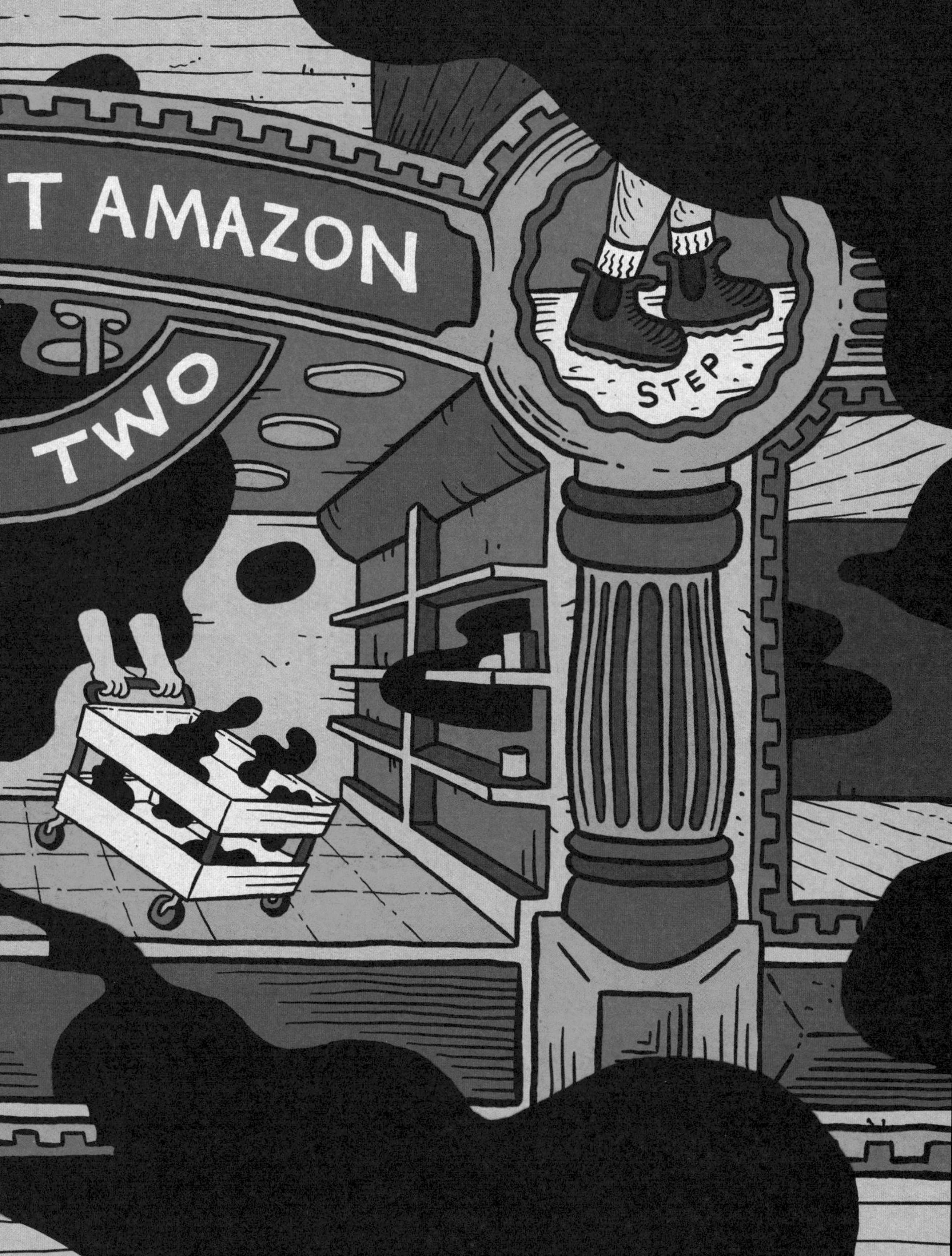
T AMAZON
TWO
STEP

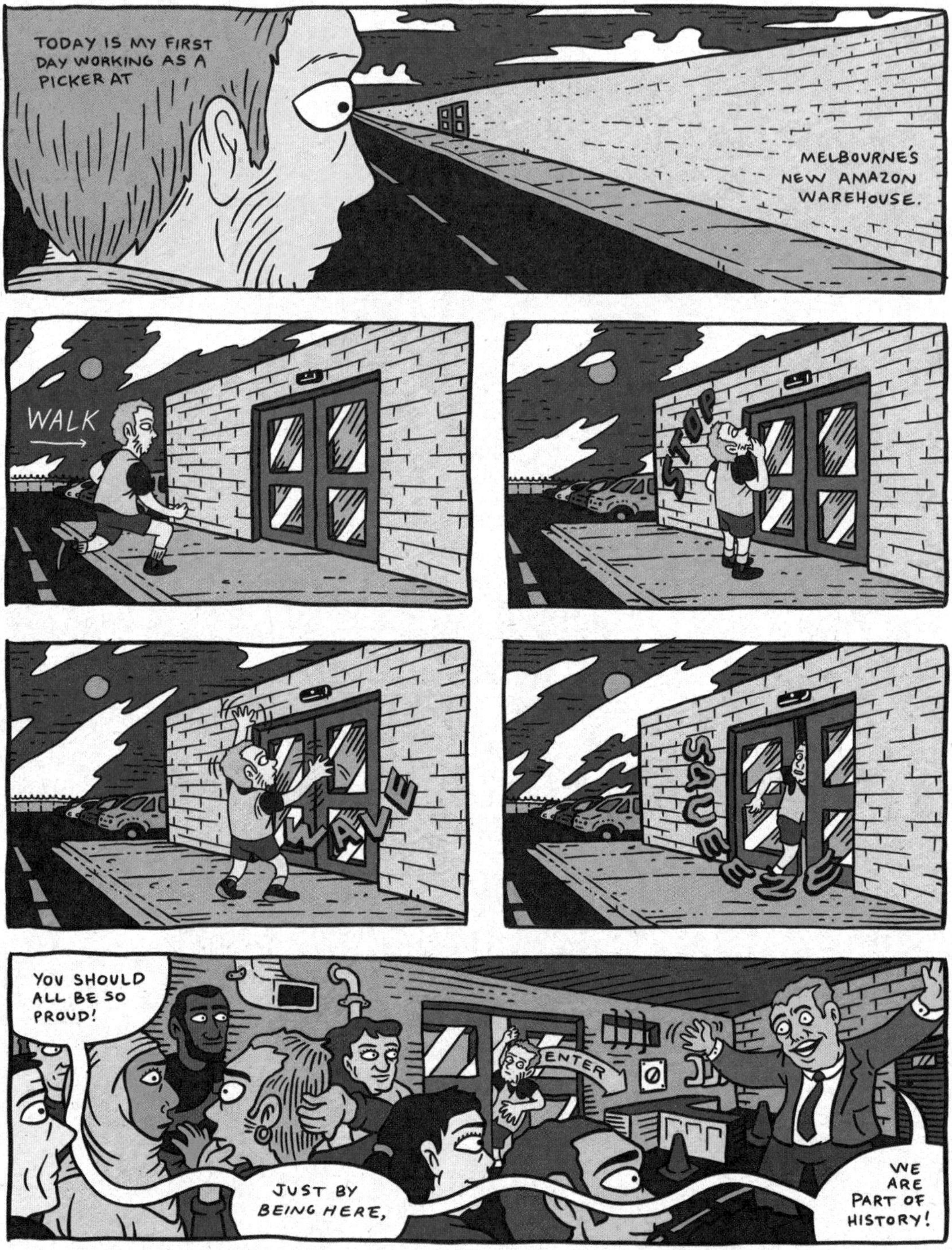
TODAY IS MY FIRST DAY WORKING AS A PICKER AT
MELBOURNE'S NEW AMAZON WAREHOUSE.
WALK
STOP
WAVE
SQUEEZE
YOU SHOULD ALL BE SO PROUD!
ENTER
JUST BY BEING HERE,
WE ARE PART OF HISTORY!

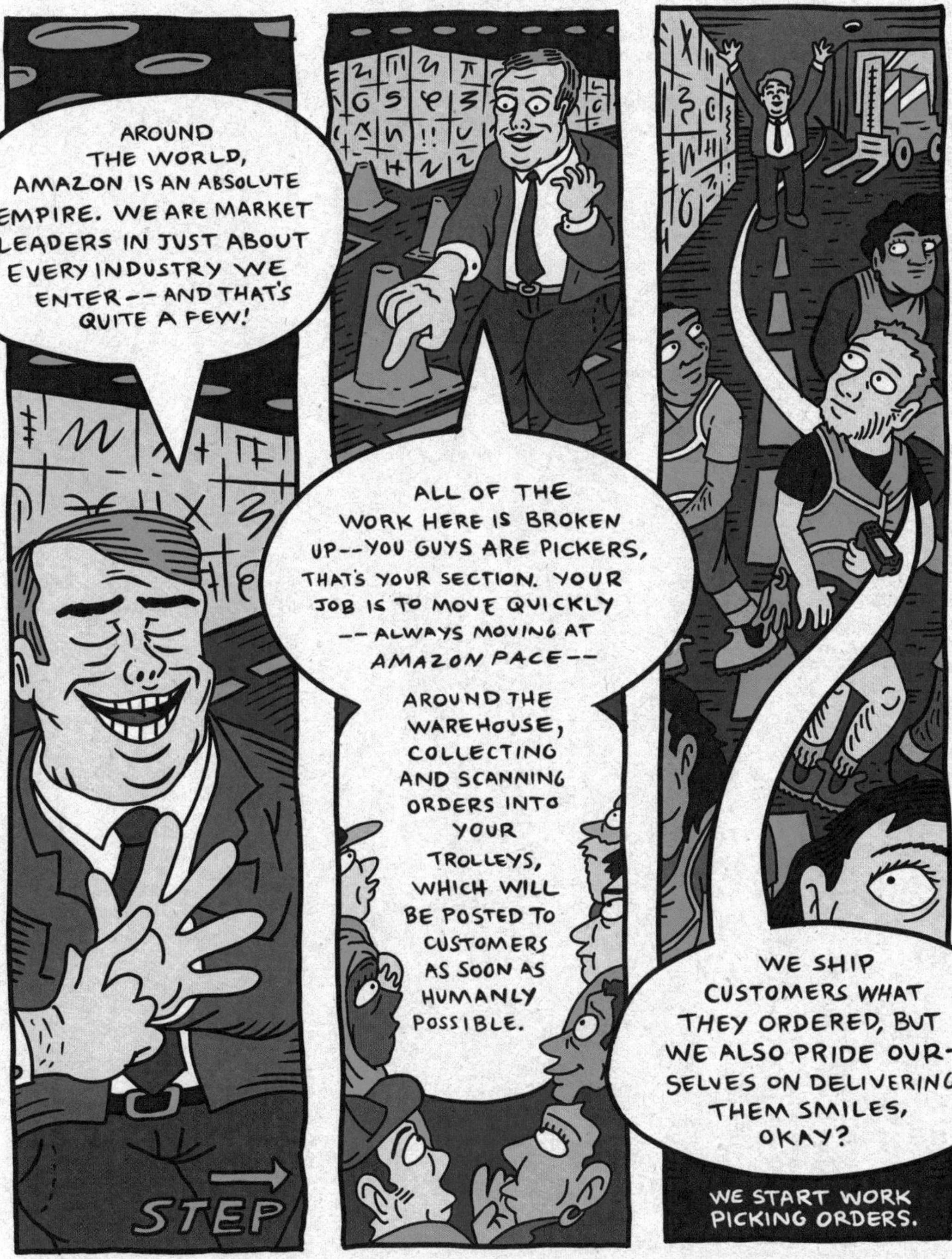
AROUND THE WORLD, AMAZON IS AN ABSOLUTE EMPIRE. WE ARE MARKET LEADERS IN JUST ABOUT EVERY INDUSTRY WE ENTER--AND THAT'S QUITE A FEW!
STEP
ALL OF THE WORK HERE IS BROKEN UP--YOU GUYS ARE PICKERS, THAT'S YOUR SECTION. YOUR JOB IS TO MOVE QUICKLY --ALWAYS MOVING AT AMAZON PACE--
AROUND THE WAREHOUSE, COLLECTING AND SCANNING ORDERS INTO YOUR TROLLEYS, WHICH WILL BE POSTED TO CUSTOMERS AS SOON AS HUMANLY POSSIBLE.
WE SHIP CUSTOMERS WHAT THEY ORDERED, BUT WE ALSO PRIDE OUR-SELVES ON DELIVERING THEM SMILES, OKAY?
WE START WORK PICKING ORDERS.

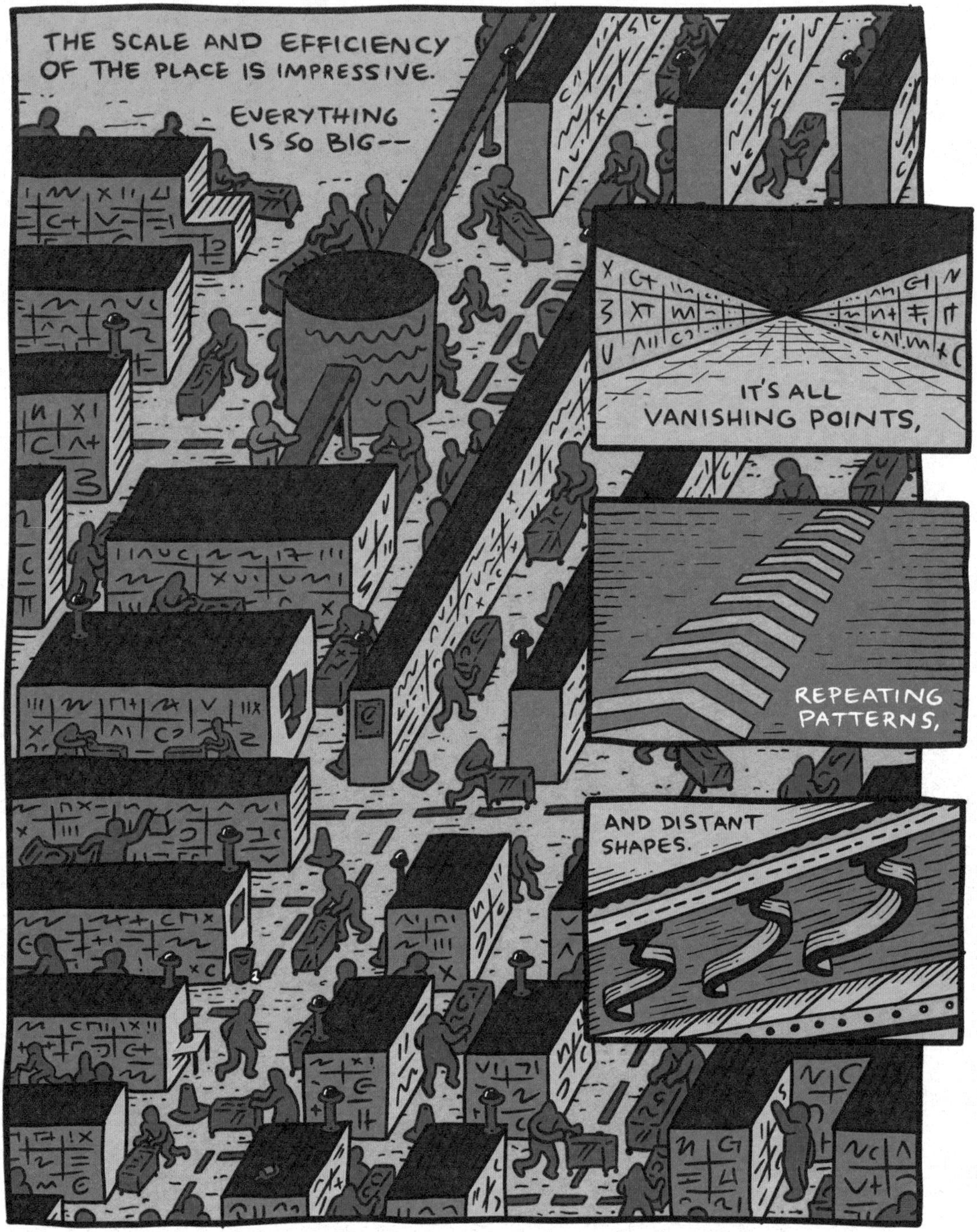
THE SCALE AND EFFICIENCY OF THE PLACE IS IMPRESSIVE.
EVERYTHING IS SO BIG--
IT'S ALL VANISHING POINTS,
REPEATING PATTERNS,
AND DISTANT SHAPES.

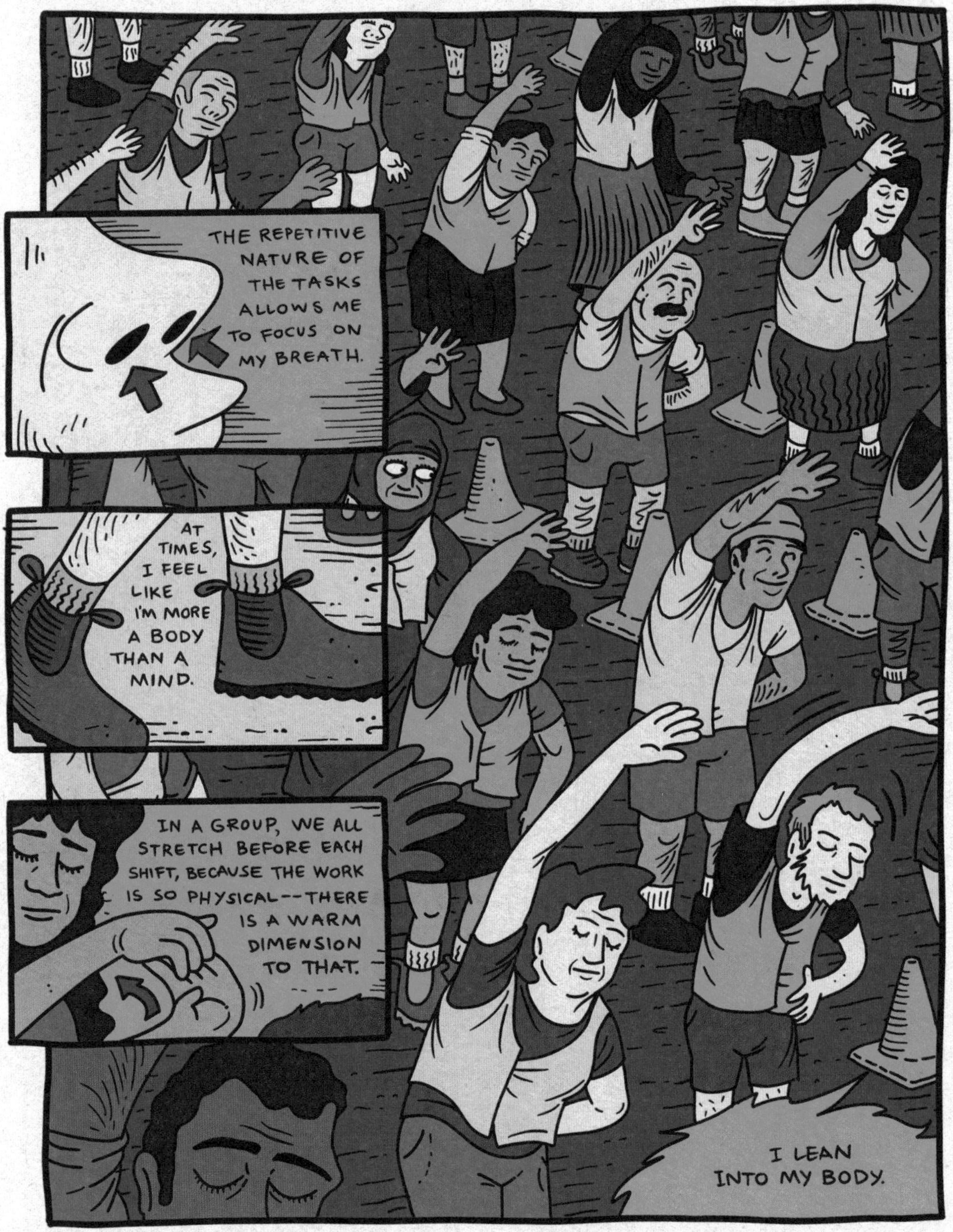
THE REPETITIVE NATURE OF THE TASKS ALLOWS ME TO FOCUS ON MY BREATH.
AT TIMES, I FEEL LIKE I'M MORE A BODY THAN A MIND.
IN A GROUP, WE ALL STRETCH BEFORE EACH SHIFT, BECAUSE THE WORK IS SO PHYSICAL--THERE IS A WARM DIMENSION TO THAT.
I LEAN INTO MY BODY.

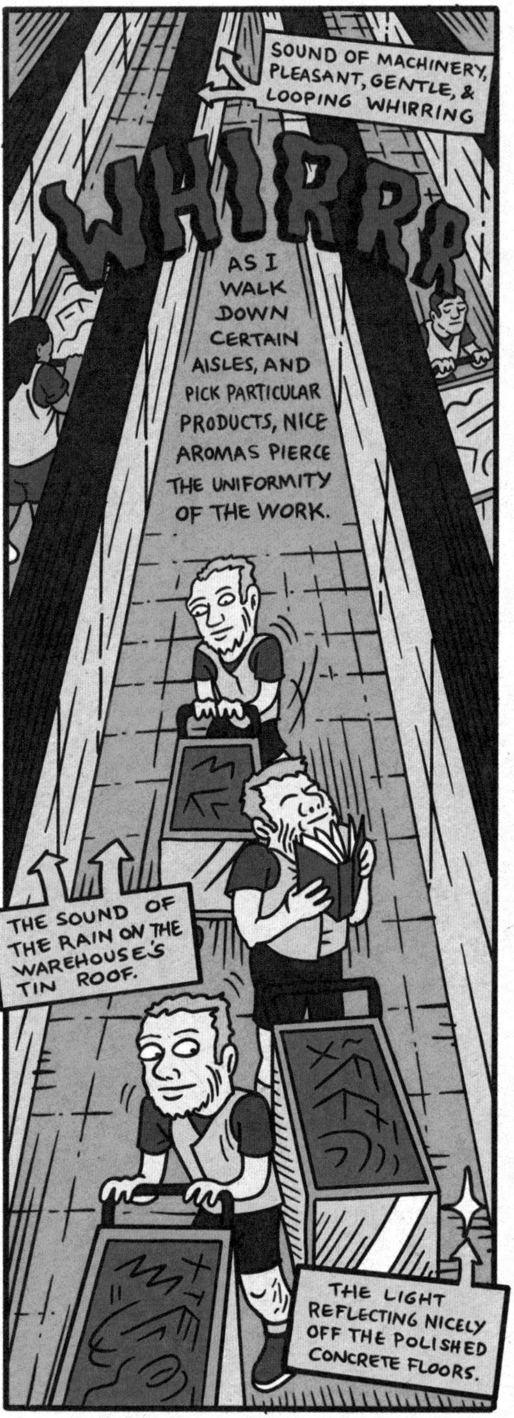
SOUND OF MACHINERY, PLEASANT, GENTLE, & LOOPING WHIRRING
WHIRRR
AS I WALK DOWN CERTAIN AISLES, AND PICK PARTICULAR PRODUCTS, NICE AROMAS PIERCE THE UNIFORMITY OF THE WORK.
THE SOUND OF THE RAIN ON THE WAREHOUSE'S TIN ROOF.
THE LIGHT REFLECTING NICELY OFF THE POLISHED CONCRETE FLOORS.

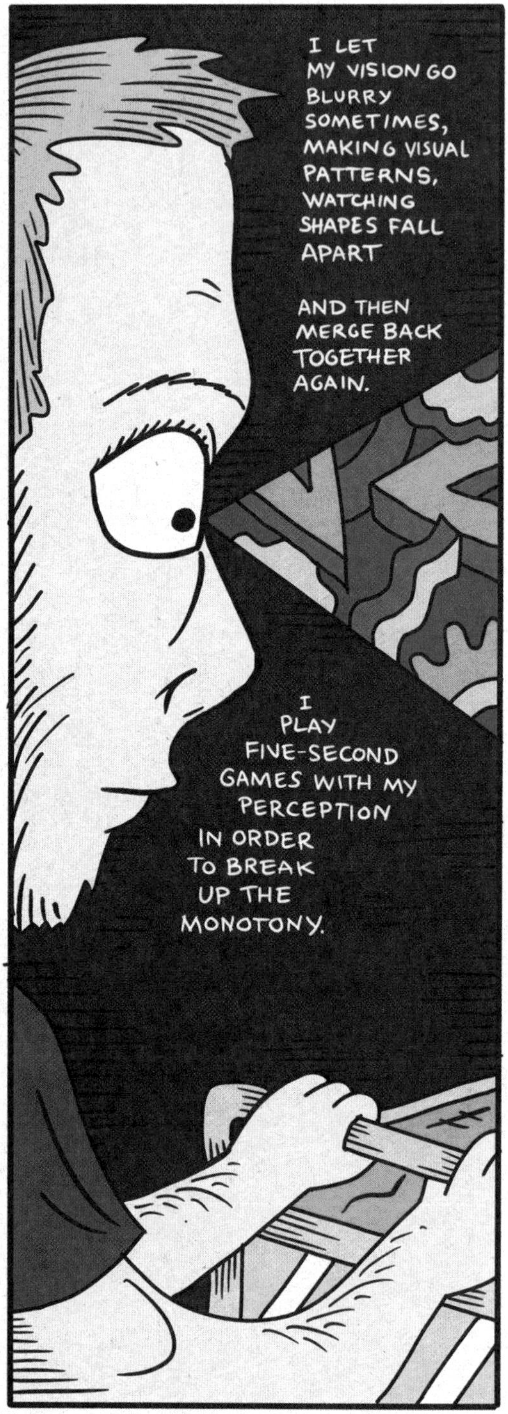
I LET MY VISION GO BLURRY SOMETIMES, MAKING VISUAL PATTERNS, WATCHING SHAPES FALL APART
AND THEN MERGE BACK TOGETHER AGAIN.
I PLAY FIVE-SECOND GAMES WITH MY PERCEPTION IN ORDER TO BREAK UP THE MONOTONY.

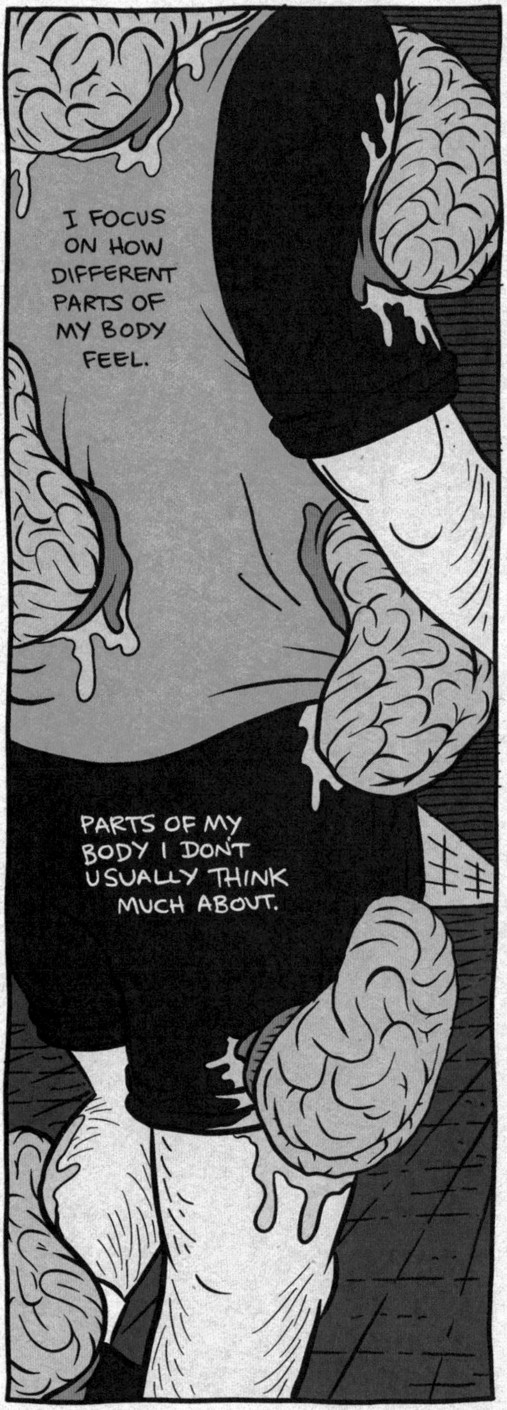
I FOCUS ON HOW DIFFERENT PARTS OF MY BODY FEEL.
PARTS OF MY BODY I DON'T USUALLY THINK MUCH ABOUT.

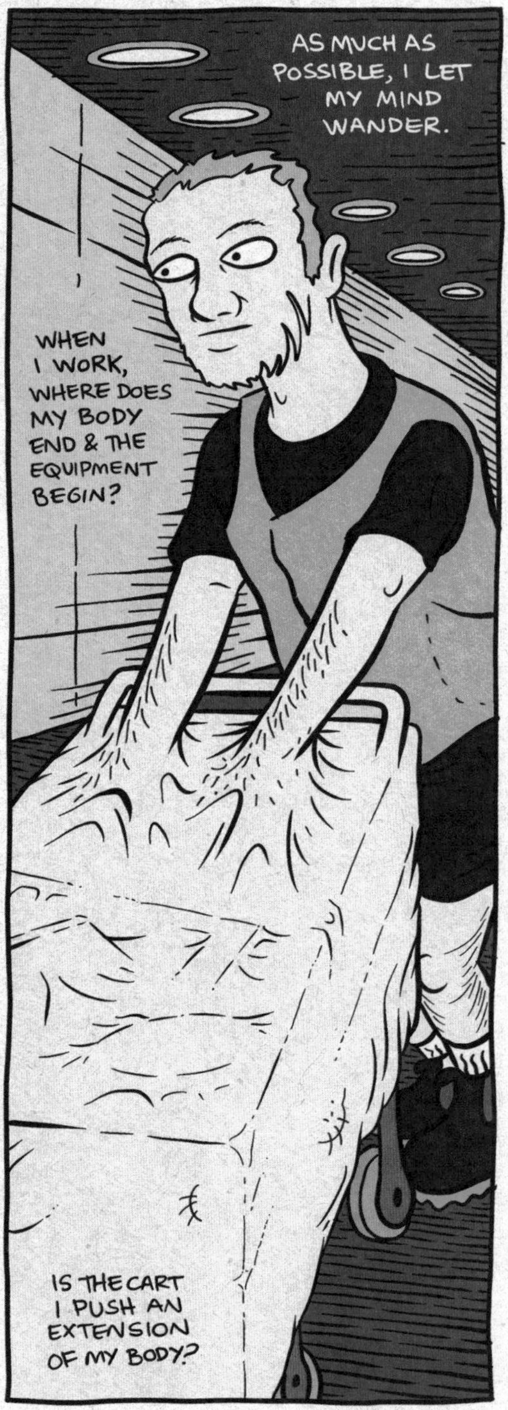
AS MUCH AS POSSIBLE, I LET MY MIND WANDER.
WHEN I WORK, WHERE DOES MY BODY END & THE EQUIPMENT BEGIN?
IS THE CART I PUSH AN EXTENSION OF MY BODY?

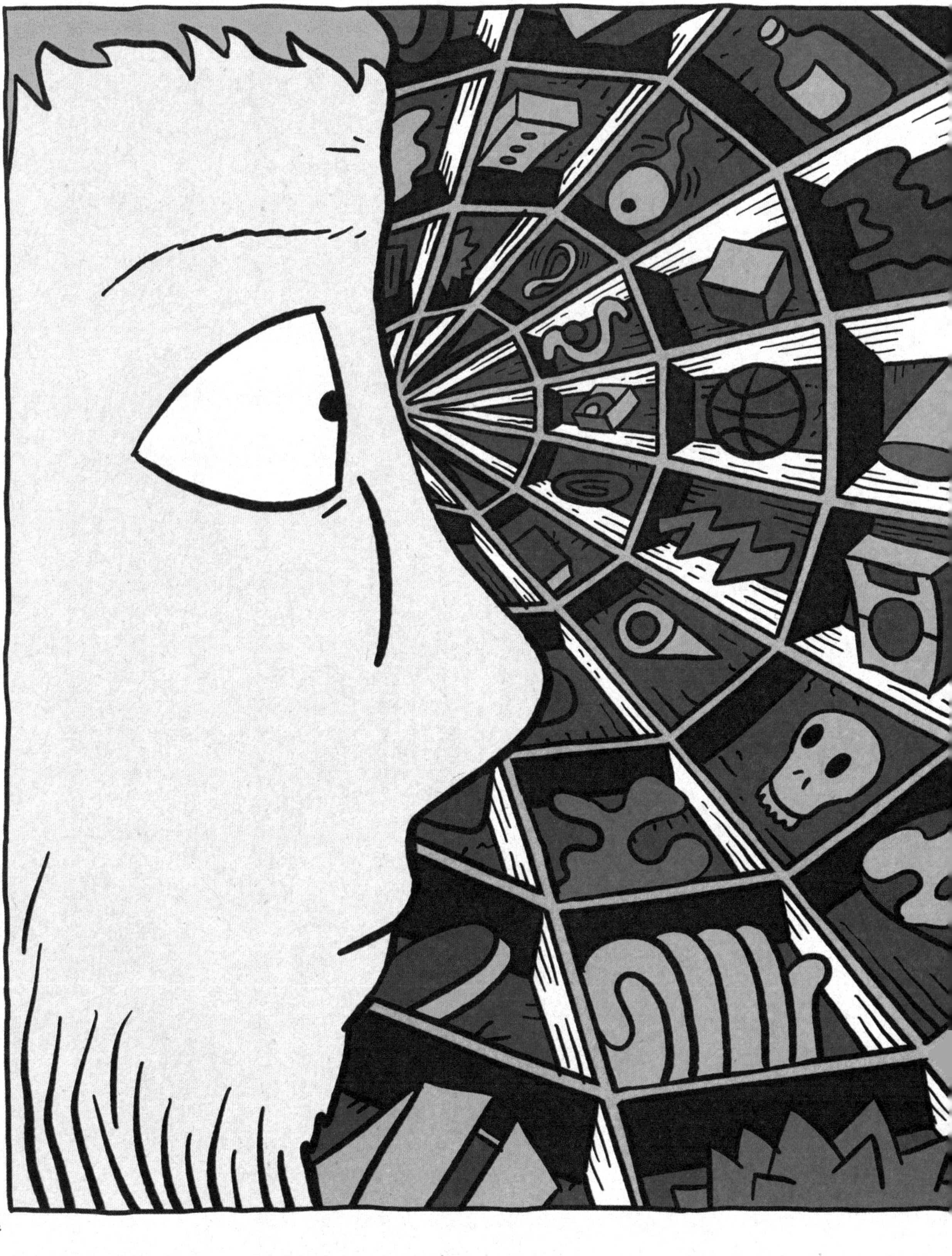

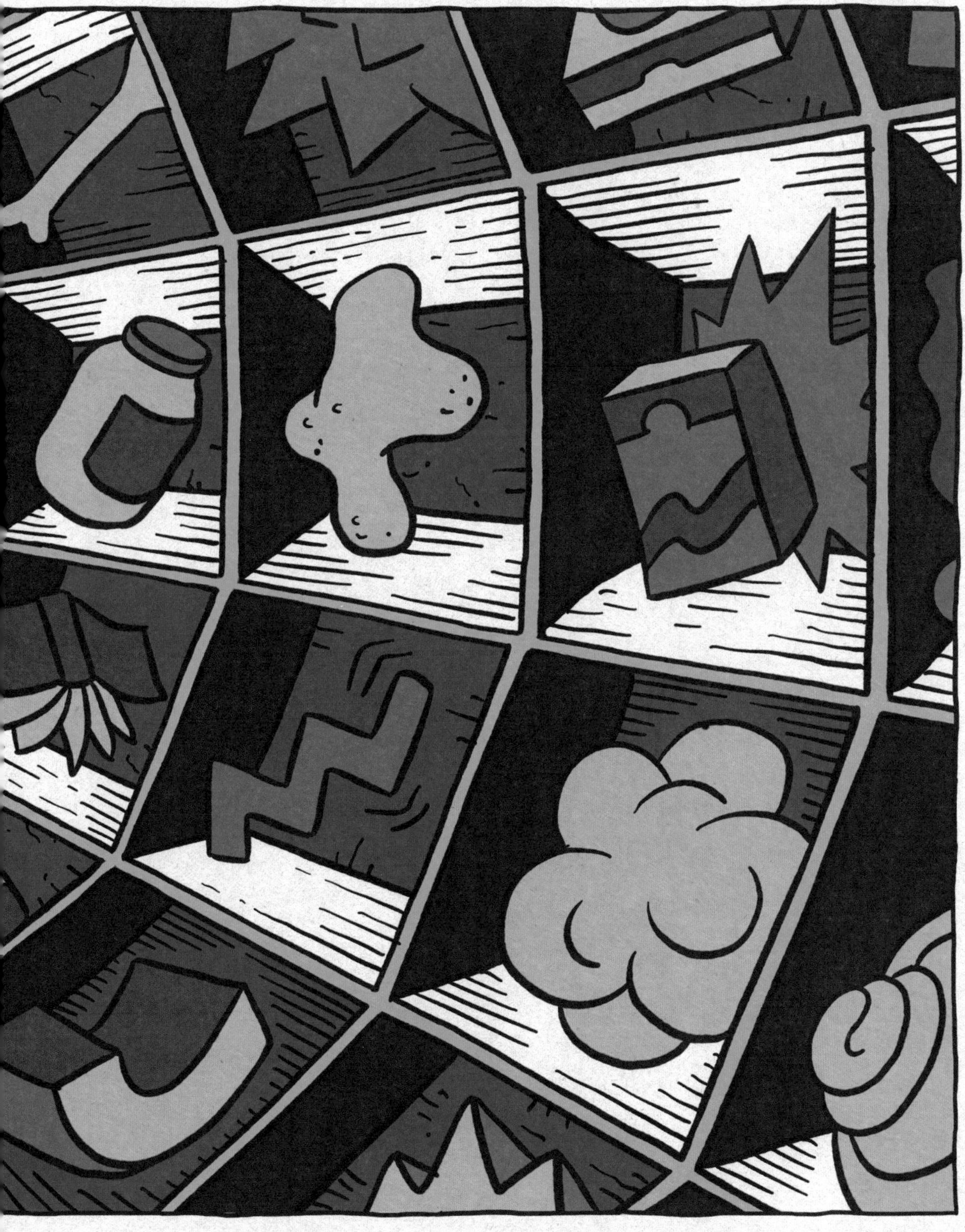

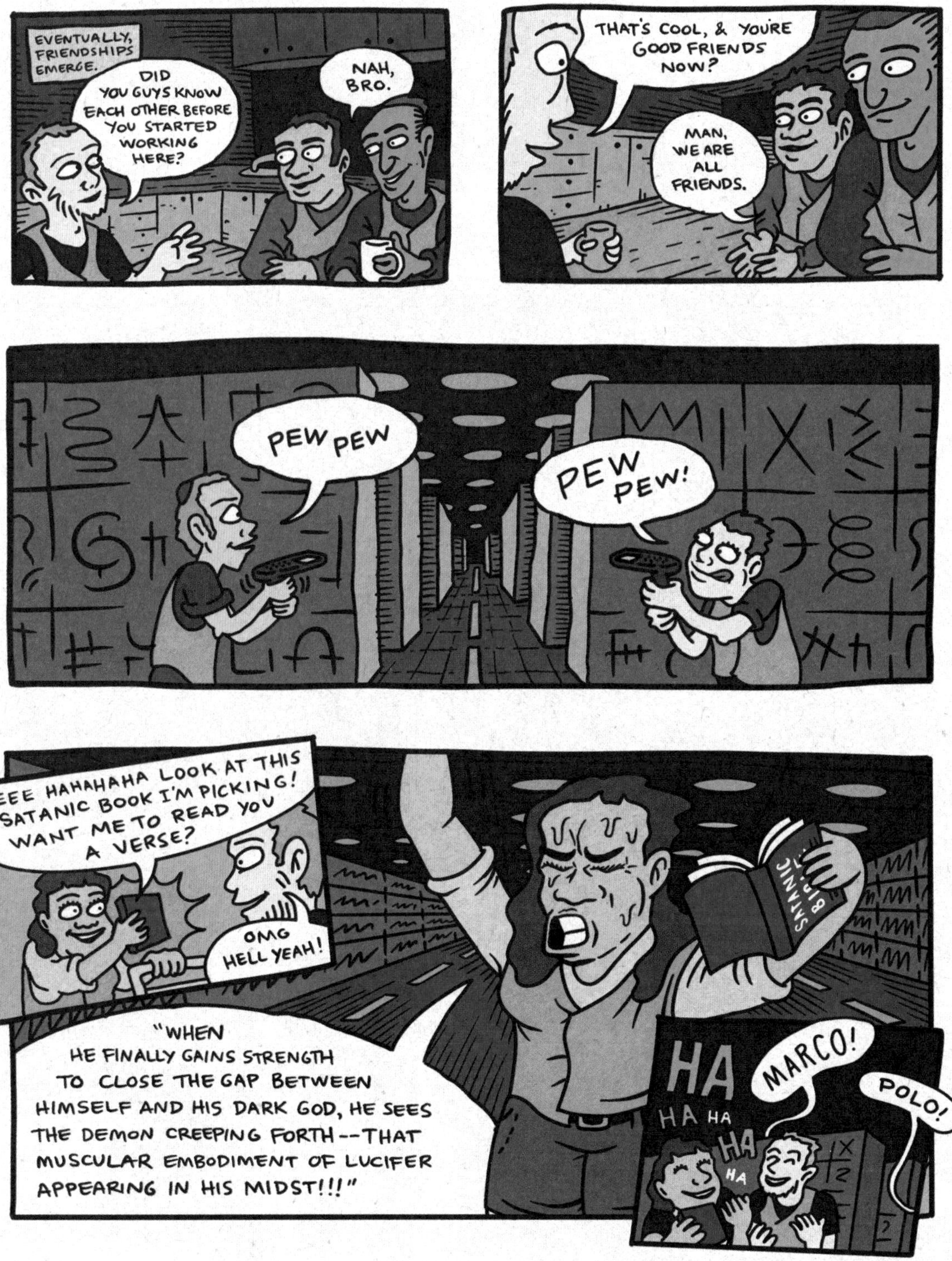
EVENTUALLY, FRIENDSHIPS EMERGE.
DID YOU GUYS KNOW EACH OTHER BEFORE YOU STARTED WORKING HERE?
NAH, BRO.
THAT'S COOL, & YOU'RE GOOD FRIENDS NOW?
MAN, WE ARE ALL FRIENDS.
PEW PEW
PEW PEW!
EEE HAHAHAHA LOOK AT THIS SATANIC BOOK I'M PICKING! WANT ME TO READ YOU A VERSE?
OMG HELL YEAH!
SATANIC BIBLE
"WHEN HE FINALLY GAINS STRENGTH TO CLOSE THE GAP BETWEEN HIMSELF AND HIS DARK GOD, HE SEES THE DEMON CREEPING FORTH--THAT MUSCULAR EMBODIMENT OF LUCIFER APPEARING IN HIS MIDST!!!"
HA HA HA HA HA
MARCO!
POLO!

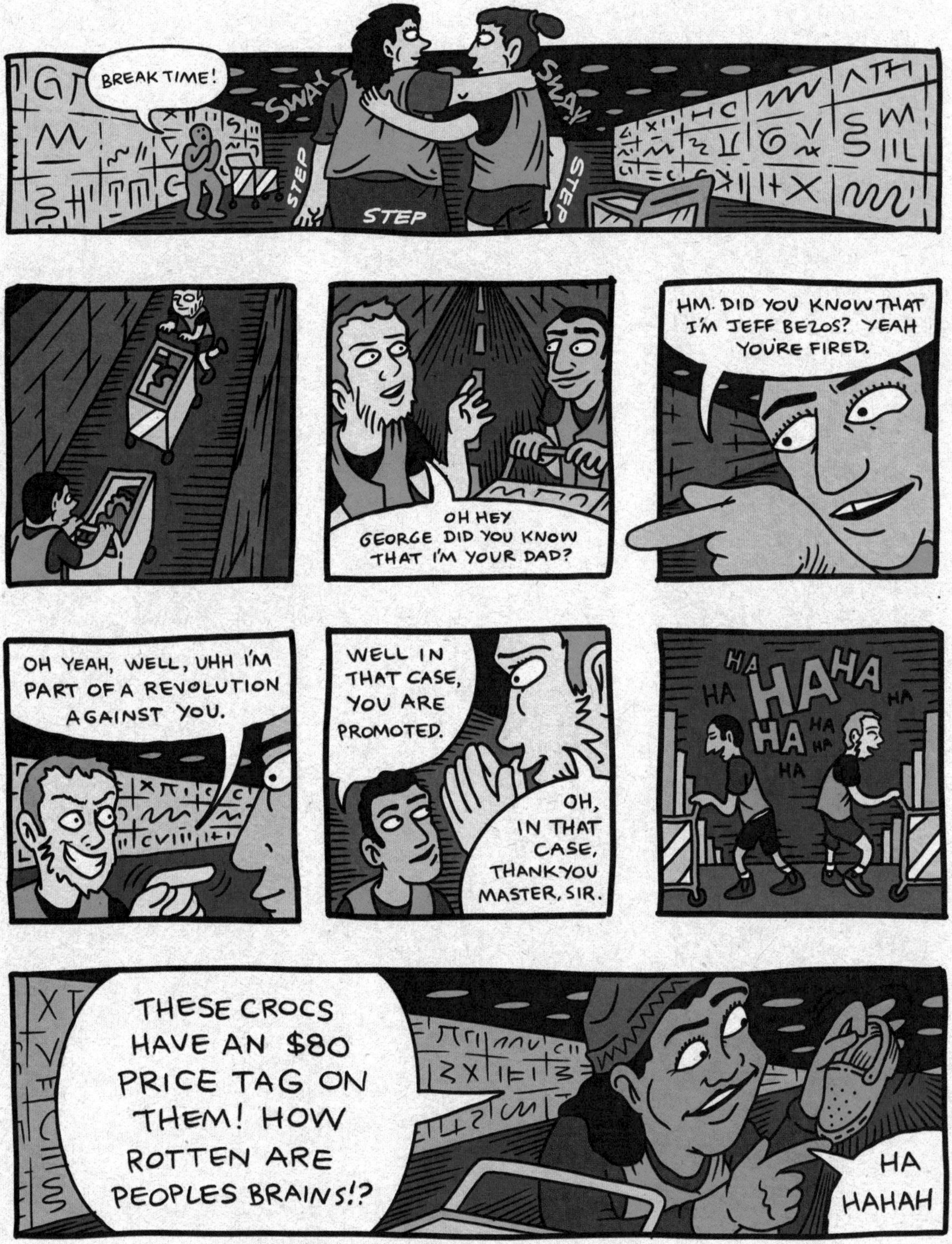
BREAK TIME!
SWAY
SWAY
STEP
STEP
STEP
OH HEY GEORGE DID YOU KNOW THAT I'M YOUR DAD?
HM. DID YOU KNOW THAT I'M JEFF BEZOS? YEAH YOU'RE FIRED.
OH YEAH, WELL, UHH I'M PART OF A REVOLUTION AGAINST YOU.
WELL IN THAT CASE, YOU ARE PROMOTED.
OH, IN THAT CASE, THANKYOU MASTER, SIR.
HA HA HAHA HA HA HA HA HA HA HA
THESE CROCS HAVE AN $80 PRICE TAG ON THEM! HOW ROTTEN ARE PEOPLES BRAINS!?
HA HAHAH

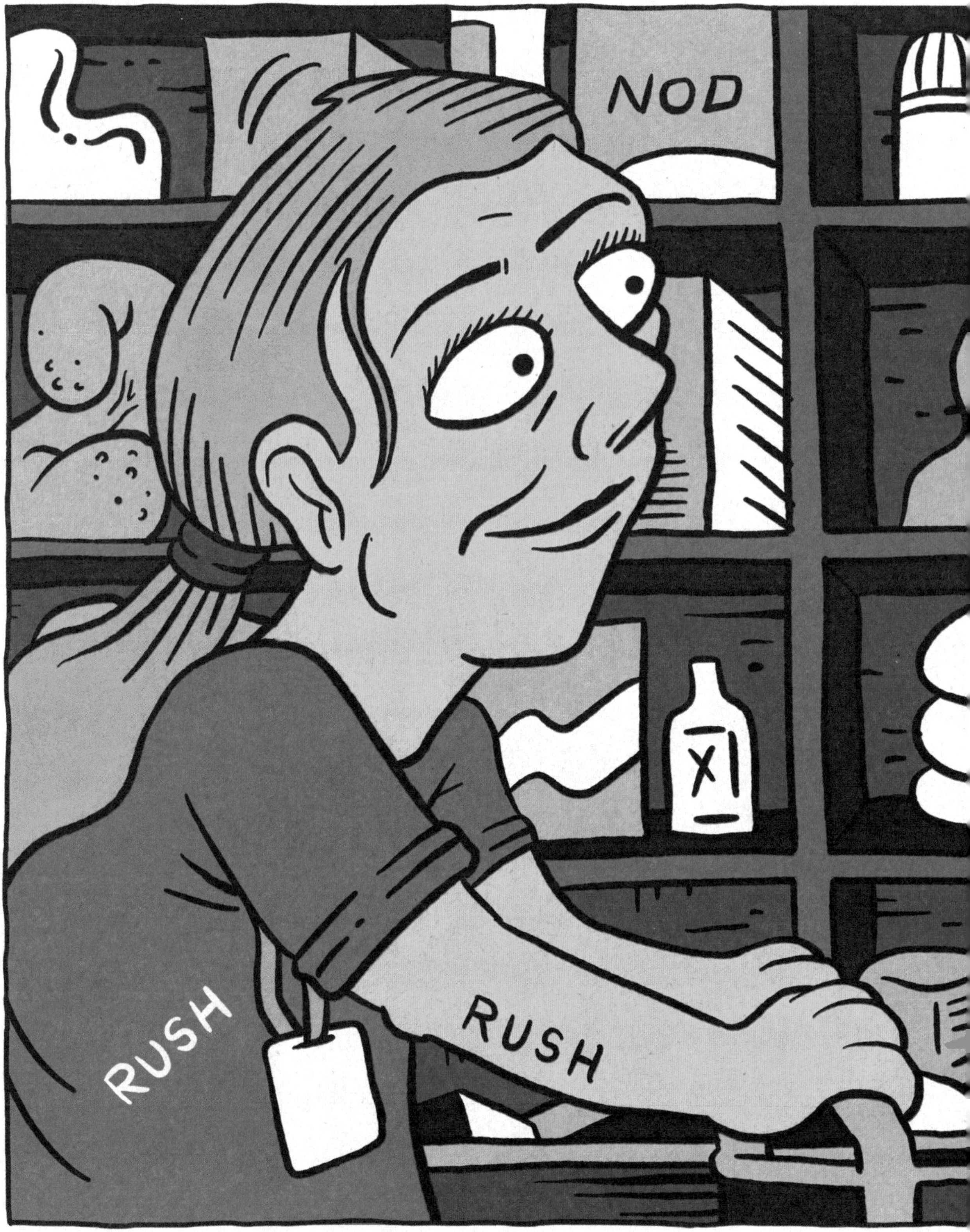
NOD
X
RUSH
RUSH

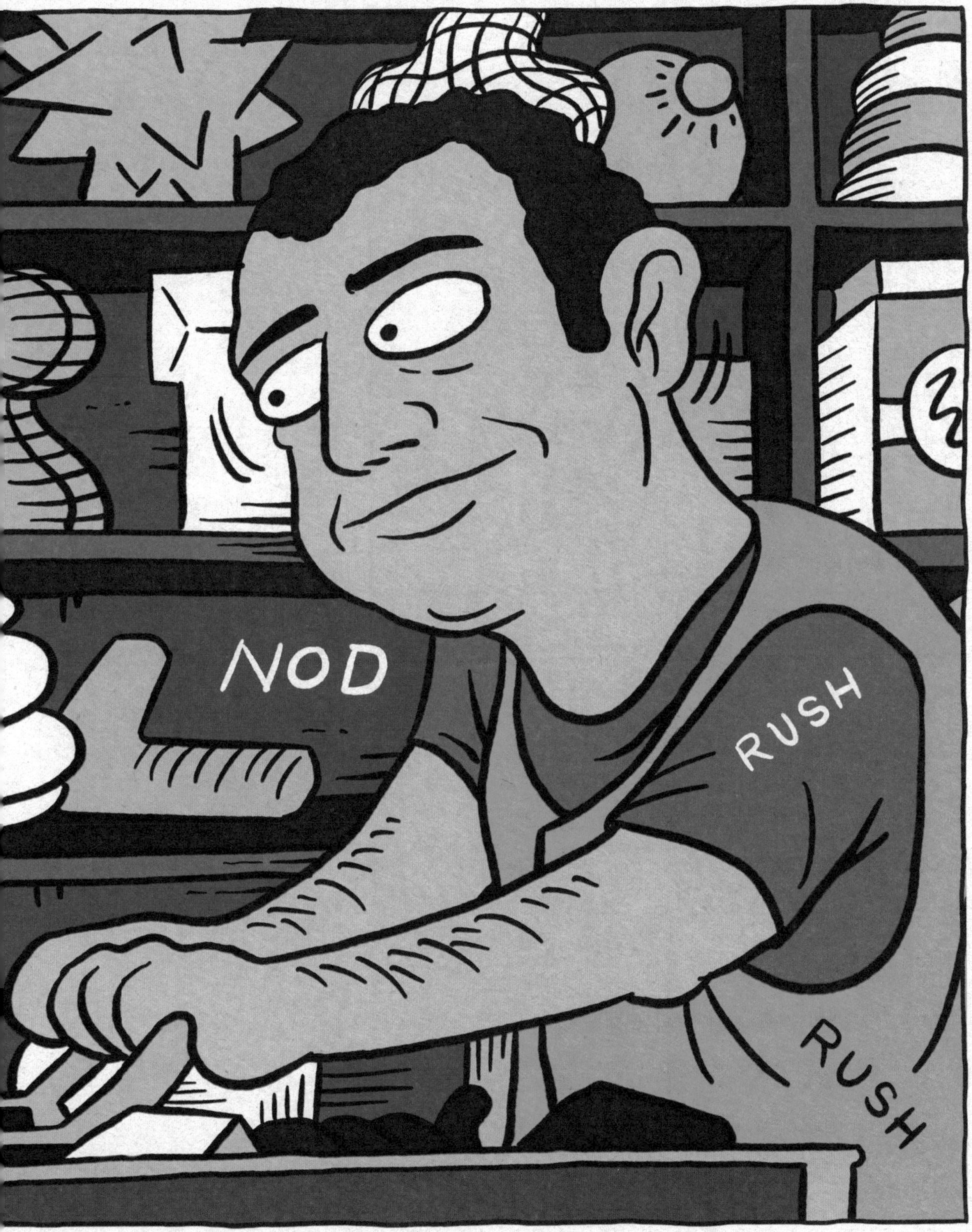
NOD
RUSH
RUSH

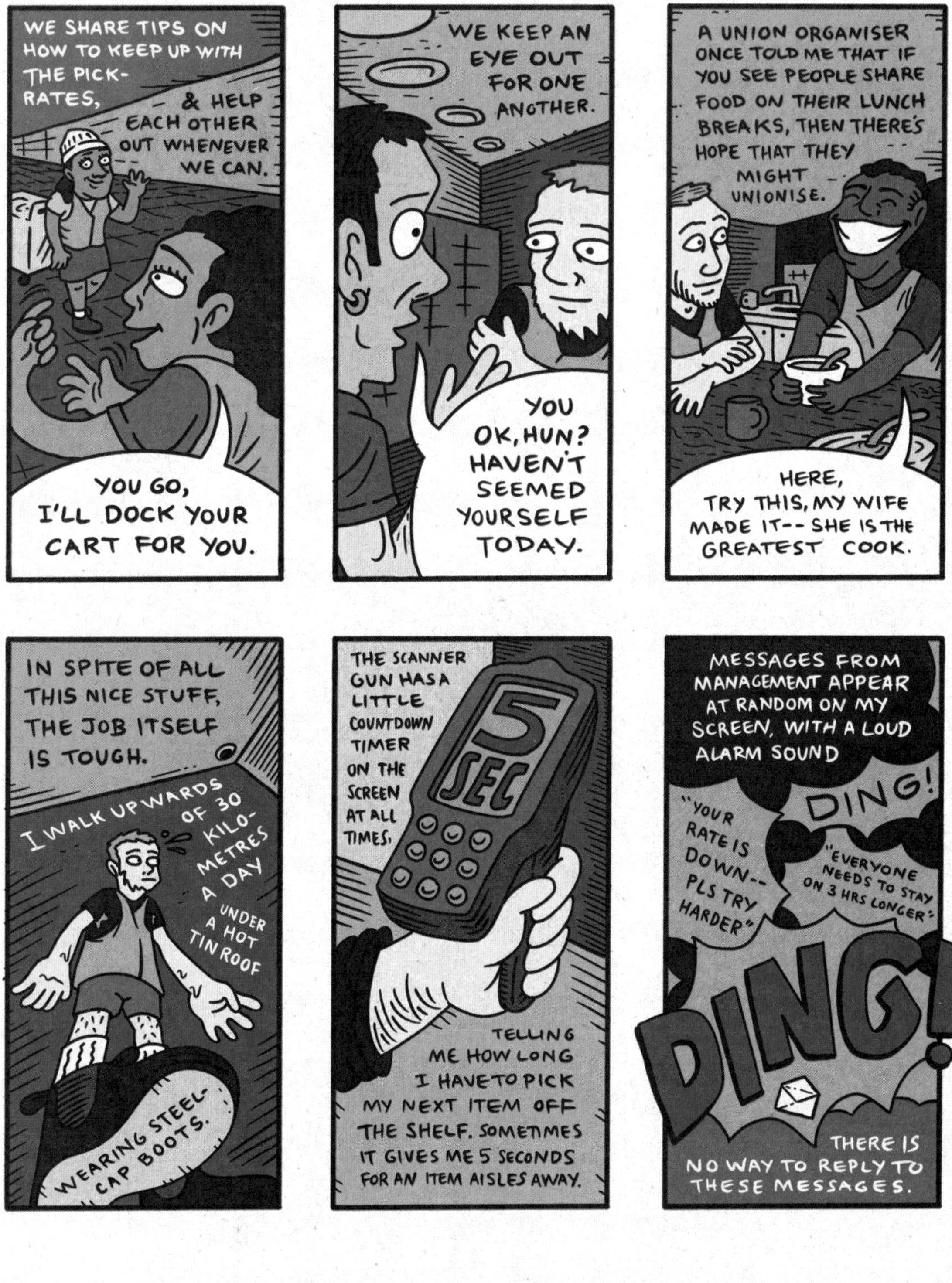
WE SHARE TIPS ON HOW TO KEEP UP WITH THE PICK-RATES,
& HELP EACH OTHER OUT WHENEVER WE CAN.
YOU GO, I'LL DOCK YOUR CART FOR YOU.
WE KEEP AN EYE OUT FOR ONE ANOTHER.
YOU OK, HUN? HAVEN'T SEEMED YOURSELF TODAY.
A UNION ORGANISER ONCE TOLD ME THAT IF YOU SEE PEOPLE SHARE FOOD ON THEIR LUNCH BREAKS, THEN THERE'S HOPE THAT THEY MIGHT UNIONISE.
HERE, TRY THIS, MY WIFE MADE IT-- SHE IS THE GREATEST COOK.
IN SPITE OF ALL THIS NICE STUFF, THE JOB ITSELF IS TOUGH.
I WALK UPWARDS OF 30 KILO-METRES A DAY
UNDER A HOT TIN ROOF
WEARING STEEL-CAP BOOTS.
THE SCANNER GUN HAS A LITTLE COUNTDOWN TIMER ON THE SCREEN AT ALL TIMES,
5 SEC
TELLING ME HOW LONG I HAVE TO PICK MY NEXT ITEM OFF THE SHELF. SOMETIMES IT GIVES ME 5 SECONDS FOR AN ITEM AISLES AWAY.
MESSAGES FROM MANAGEMENT APPEAR AT RANDOM ON MY SCREEN, WITH A LOUD ALARM SOUND
DING!
"YOUR RATE IS DOWN-- PLS TRY HARDER"
"EVERYONE NEEDS TO STAY ON 3 HRS LONGER"
DING!
THERE IS NO WAY TO REPLY TO THESE MESSAGES.

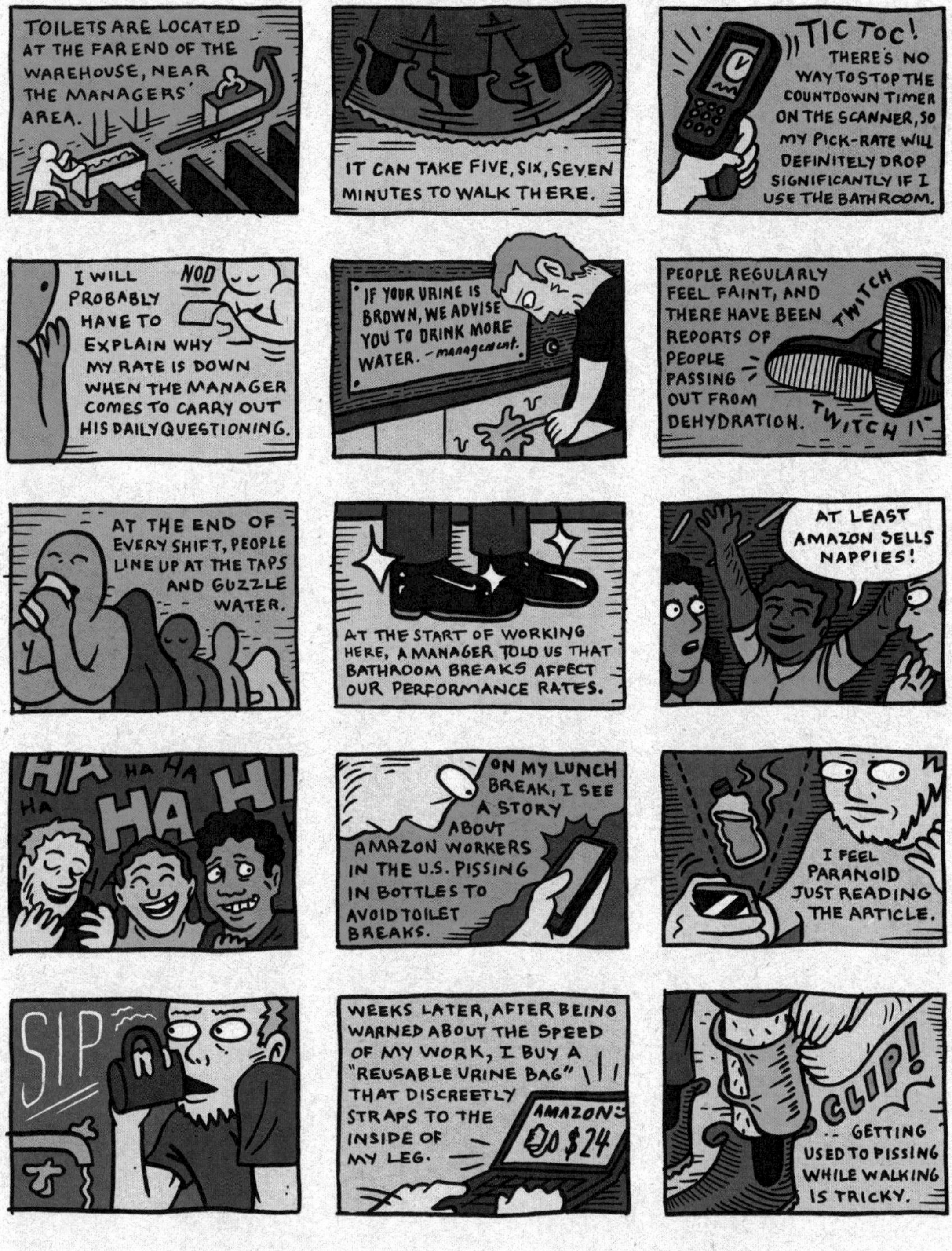
TOILETS ARE LOCATED AT THE FAR END OF THE WAREHOUSE, NEAR THE MANAGERS' AREA.
IT CAN TAKE FIVE, SIX, SEVEN MINUTES TO WALK THERE.
TIC TOC!
THERE'S NO WAY TO STOP THE COUNTDOWN TIMER ON THE SCANNER, SO MY PICK-RATE WILL DEFINITELY DROP SIGNIFICANTLY IF I USE THE BATHROOM.
I WILL PROBABLY HAVE TO EXPLAIN WHY MY RATE IS DOWN WHEN THE MANAGER COMES TO CARRY OUT HIS DAILY QUESTIONING.
NOD
IF YOUR URINE IS BROWN, WE ADVISE YOU TO DRINK MORE WATER. -management.
PEOPLE REGULARLY FEEL FAINT, AND THERE HAVE BEEN REPORTS OF PEOPLE PASSING OUT FROM DEHYDRATION.
TWITCH
TWITCH
AT THE END OF EVERY SHIFT, PEOPLE LINE UP AT THE TAPS AND GUZZLE WATER.
AT THE START OF WORKING HERE, A MANAGER TOLD US THAT BATHROOM BREAKS AFFECT OUR PERFORMANCE RATES.
AT LEAST AMAZON SELLS NAPPIES!
HA HA HA HA HA HA HA
ON MY LUNCH BREAK, I SEE A STORY ABOUT AMAZON WORKERS IN THE U.S. PISSING IN BOTTLES TO AVOID TOILET BREAKS.
I FEEL PARANOID JUST READING THE ARTICLE.
SIP
WEEKS LATER, AFTER BEING WARNED ABOUT THE SPEED OF MY WORK, I BUY A "REUSABLE URINE BAG" THAT DISCREETLY STRAPS TO THE INSIDE OF MY LEG.
AMAZON:
$24
CLIP!
GETTING USED TO PISSING WHILE WALKING IS TRICKY.

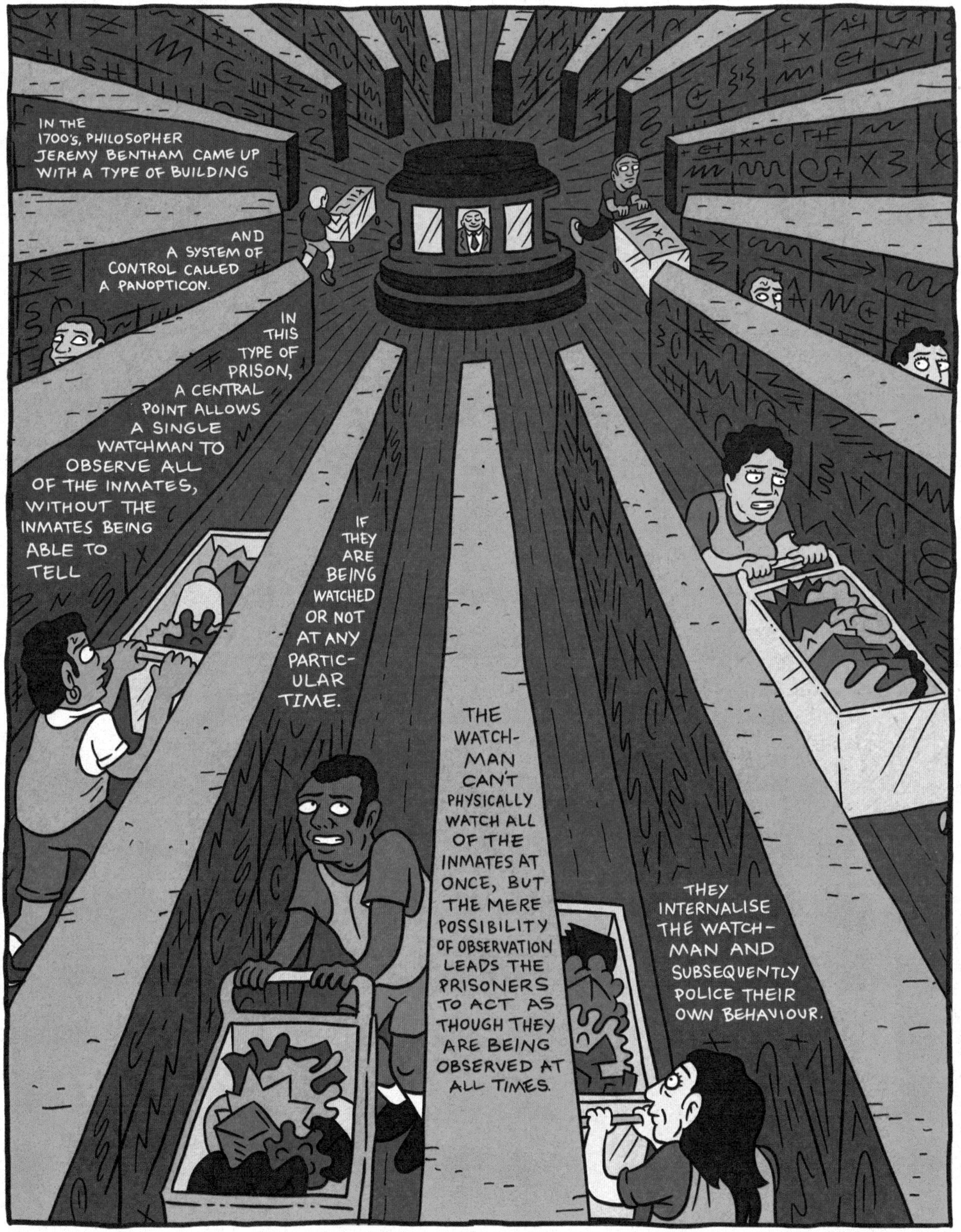
IN THE 1700's, PHILOSOPHER JEREMY BENTHAM CAME UP WITH A TYPE OF BUILDING
AND A SYSTEM OF CONTROL CALLED A PANOPTICON.
IN THIS TYPE OF PRISON, A CENTRAL POINT ALLOWS A SINGLE WATCHMAN TO OBSERVE ALL OF THE INMATES, WITHOUT THE INMATES BEING ABLE TO TELL
IF THEY ARE BEING WATCHED OR NOT AT ANY PARTIC-ULAR TIME.
THE WATCH-MAN CAN'T PHYSICALLY WATCH ALL OF THE INMATES AT ONCE, BUT THE MERE POSSIBILITY OF OBSERVATION LEADS THE PRISONERS TO ACT AS THOUGH THEY ARE BEING OBSERVED AT ALL TIMES.
THEY INTERNALISE THE WATCH-MAN AND SUBSEQUENTLY POLICE THEIR OWN BEHAVIOUR.

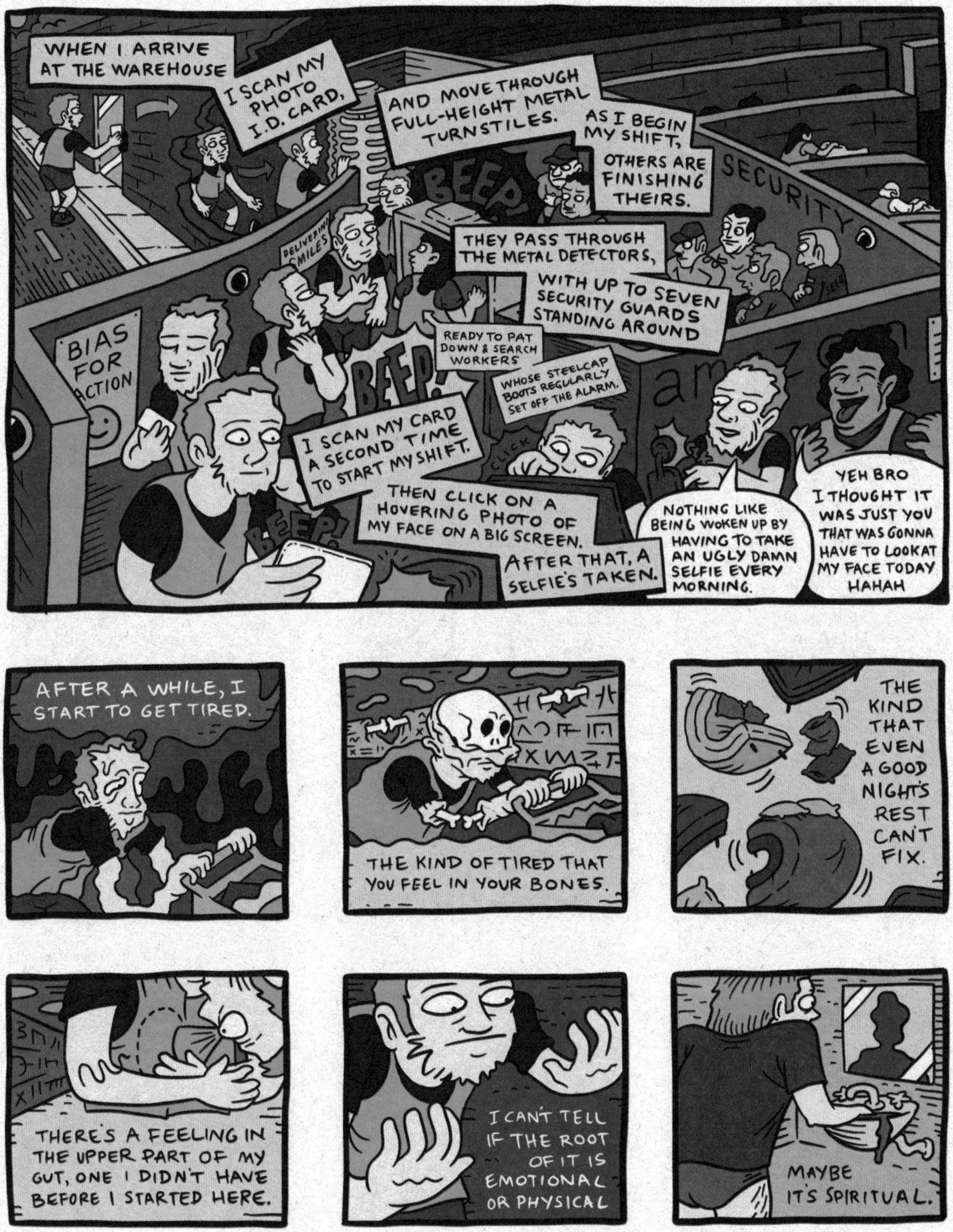
WHEN I ARRIVE AT THE WAREHOUSE
I SCAN MY PHOTO I.D. CARD,
AND MOVE THROUGH FULL-HEIGHT METAL TURNSTILES.
AS I BEGIN MY SHIFT,
OTHERS ARE FINISHING THEIRS.
BEEP!
SECURITY
THEY PASS THROUGH THE METAL DETECTORS,
WITH UP TO SEVEN SECURITY GUARDS STANDING AROUND
READY TO PAT DOWN & SEARCH WORKERS
WHOSE STEELCAP BOOTS REGULARLY SET OFF THE ALARM.
BIAS FOR ACTION
BEEP!
I SCAN MY CARD A SECOND TIME TO START MY SHIFT.
THEN CLICK ON A HOVERING PHOTO OF MY FACE ON A BIG SCREEN.
CLICK
BEEP!
AFTER THAT, A SELFIE'S TAKEN.
NOTHING LIKE BEING WOKEN UP BY HAVING TO TAKE AN UGLY DAMN SELFIE EVERY MORNING.
YEH BRO I THOUGHT IT WAS JUST YOU THAT WAS GONNA HAVE TO LOOK AT MY FACE TODAY HAHAH
AFTER A WHILE, I START TO GET TIRED.
THE KIND OF TIRED THAT YOU FEEL IN YOUR BONES.
THE KIND THAT EVEN A GOOD NIGHT'S REST CAN'T FIX.
THERE'S A FEELING IN THE UPPER PART OF MY GUT, ONE I DIDN'T HAVE BEFORE I STARTED HERE.
I CAN'T TELL IF THE ROOT OF IT IS EMOTIONAL OR PHYSICAL
MAYBE IT'S SPIRITUAL.

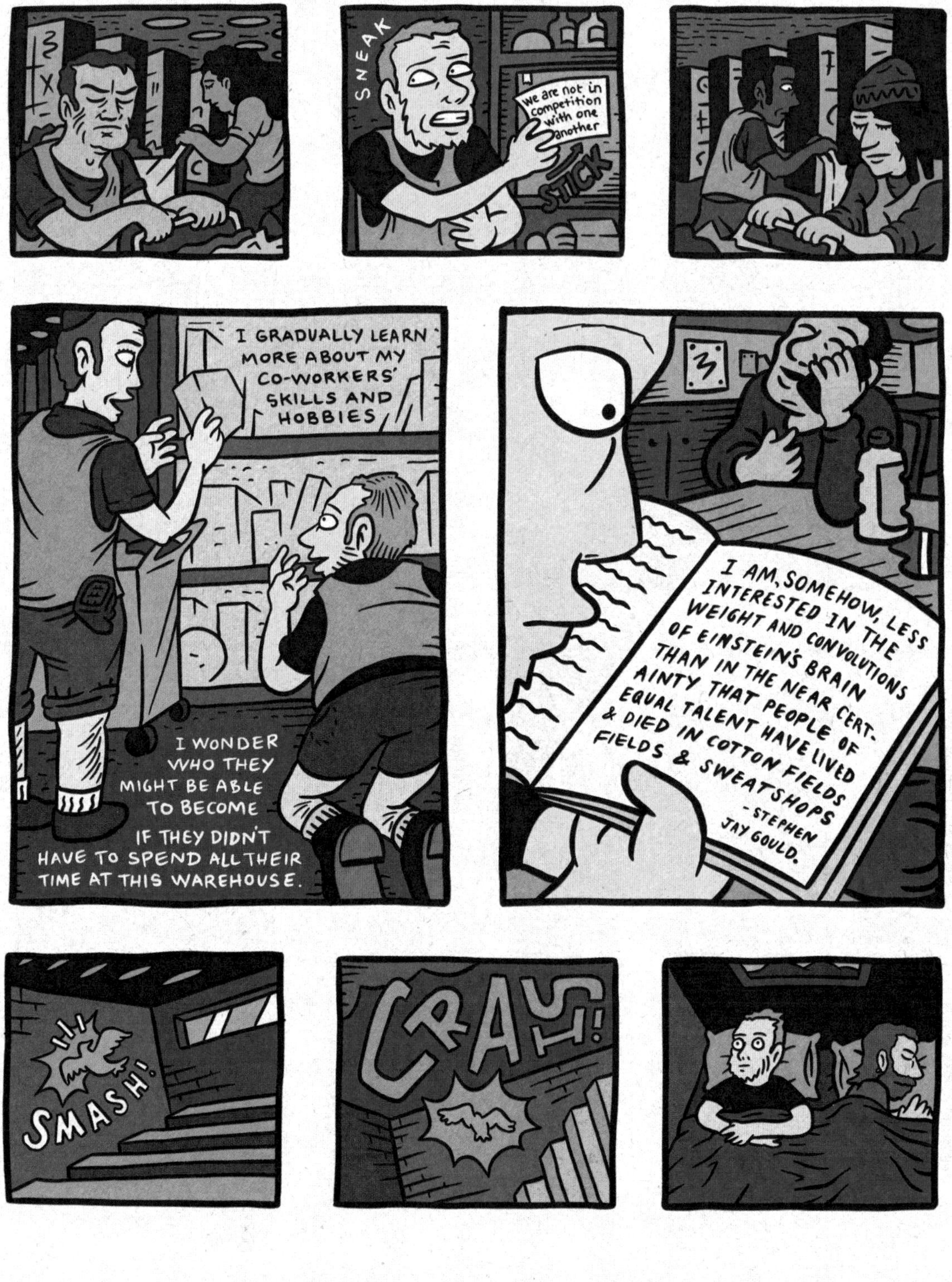
SNEAK
we are not in competition with one another
STICK
I GRADUALLY LEARN MORE ABOUT MY CO-WORKERS' SKILLS AND HOBBIES
I WONDER WHO THEY MIGHT BE ABLE TO BECOME
IF THEY DIDN'T HAVE TO SPEND ALL THEIR TIME AT THIS WAREHOUSE.
I AM, SOMEHOW, LESS INTERESTED IN THE WEIGHT AND CONVOLUTIONS OF EINSTEIN'S BRAIN THAN IN THE NEAR CERT-AINTY THAT PEOPLE OF EQUAL TALENT HAVE LIVED & DIED IN COTTON FIELDS & SWEATSHOPS
- STEPHEN JAY GOULD.
SMASH!
CRASH!

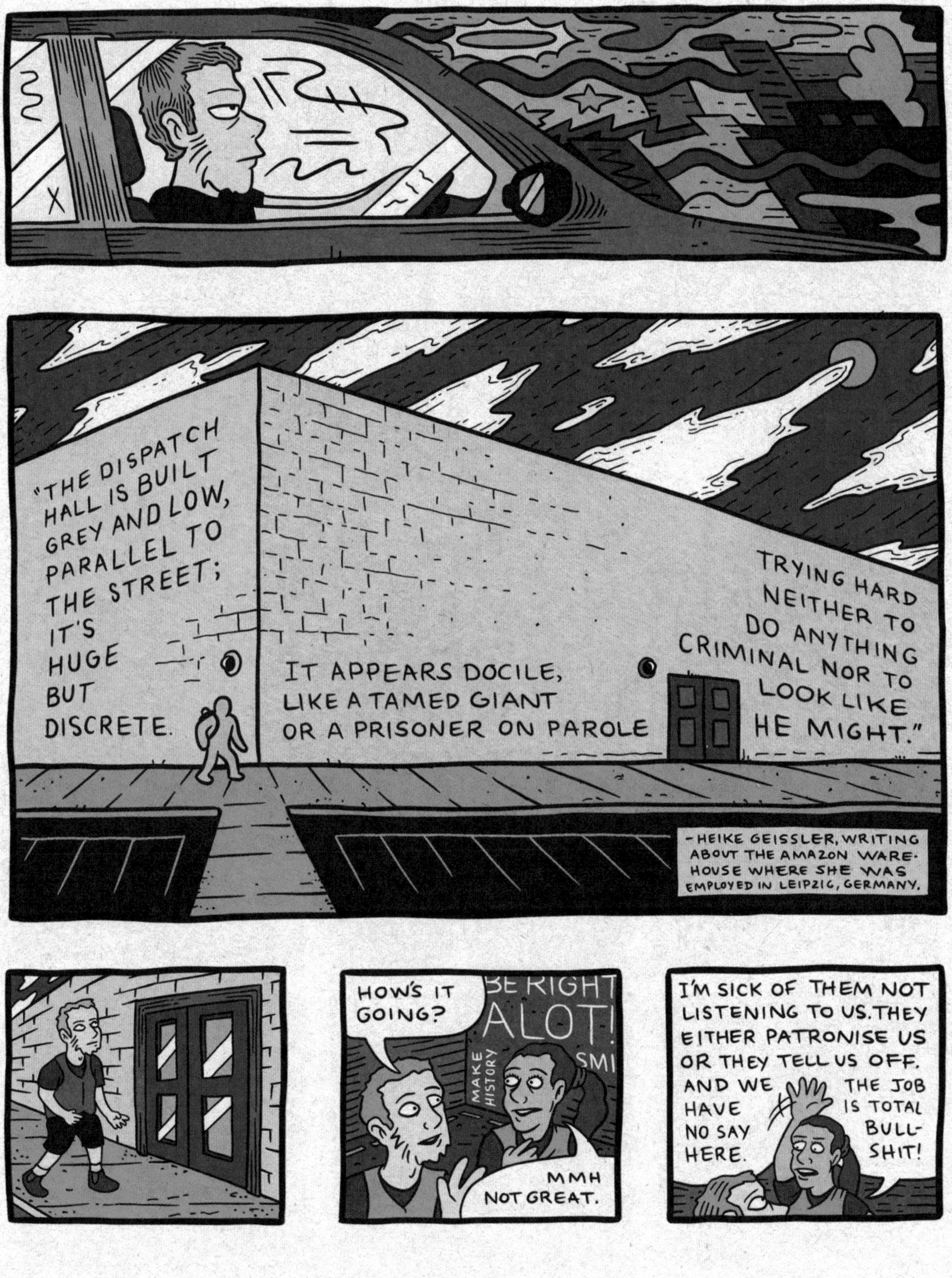
"THE DISPATCH HALL IS BUILT GREY AND LOW, PARALLEL TO THE STREET; IT'S HUGE BUT DISCRETE.
IT APPEARS DOCILE, LIKE A TAMED GIANT OR A PRISONER ON PAROLE
TRYING HARD NEITHER TO DO ANYTHING CRIMINAL NOR TO LOOK LIKE HE MIGHT."
-HEIKE GEISSLER, WRITING ABOUT THE AMAZON WAREHOUSE WHERE SHE WAS EMPLOYED IN LEIPZIG, GERMANY.
HOW'S IT GOING?
BE RIGHT
ALOT!
SMI
MAKE HISTORY
MMH NOT GREAT.
I'M SICK OF THEM NOT LISTENING TO US. THEY EITHER PATRONISE US OR THEY TELL US OFF. AND WE HAVE NO SAY HERE.
THE JOB IS TOTAL BULLSHIT!

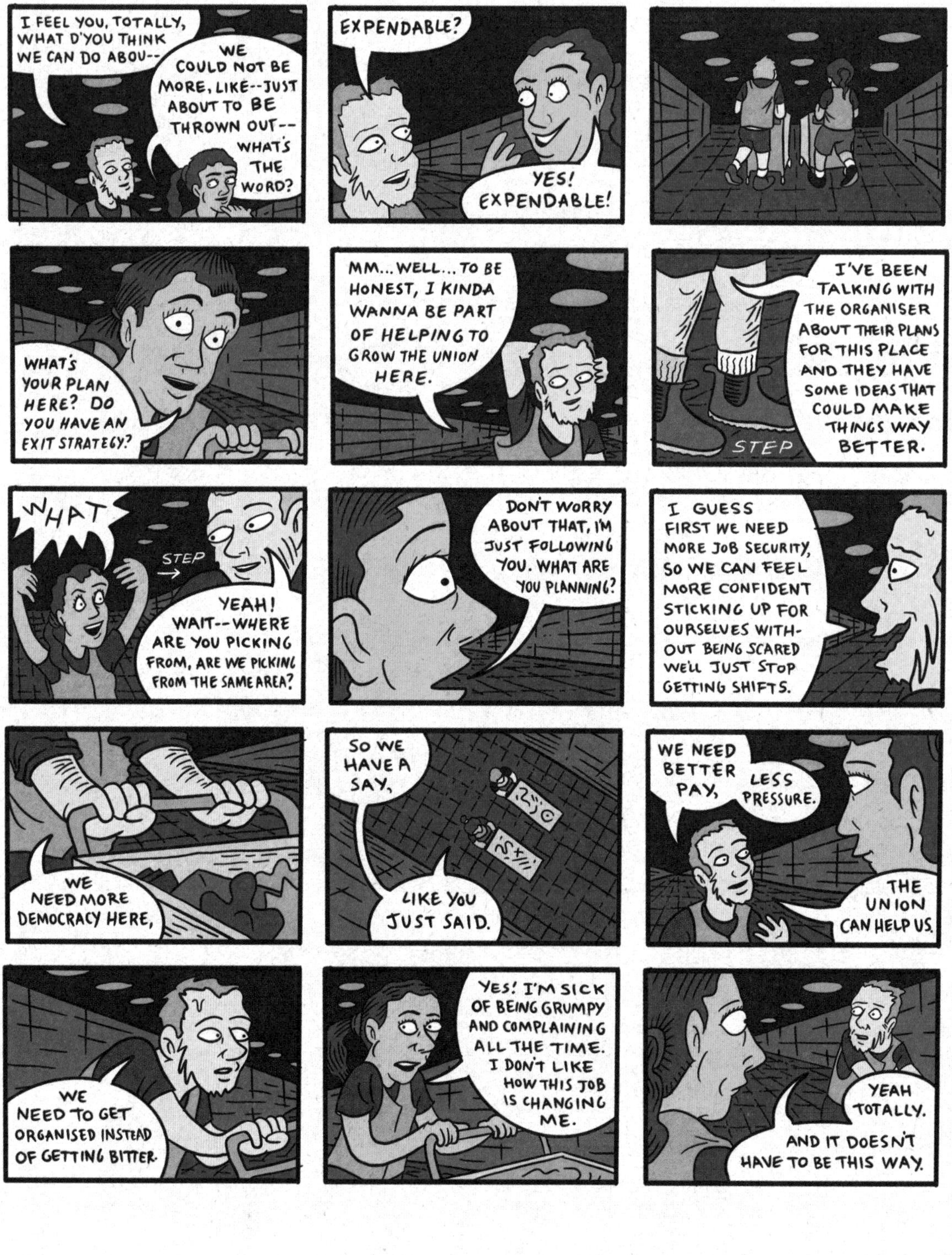
I FEEL YOU, TOTALLY, WHAT D'YOU THINK WE CAN DO ABOU--
WE COULD NOT BE MORE, LIKE--JUST ABOUT TO BE THROWN OUT-- WHAT'S THE WORD?
EXPENDABLE?
YES! EXPENDABLE!
WHAT'S YOUR PLAN HERE? DO YOU HAVE AN EXIT STRATEGY?
MM... WELL... TO BE HONEST, I KINDA WANNA BE PART OF HELPING TO GROW THE UNION HERE.
I'VE BEEN TALKING WITH THE ORGANISER ABOUT THEIR PLANS FOR THIS PLACE AND THEY HAVE SOME IDEAS THAT COULD MAKE THINGS WAY BETTER.
STEP
WHAT
STEP
YEAH! WAIT--WHERE ARE YOU PICKING FROM, ARE WE PICKING FROM THE SAME AREA?
DON'T WORRY ABOUT THAT, I'M JUST FOLLOWING YOU. WHAT ARE YOU PLANNING?
I GUESS FIRST WE NEED MORE JOB SECURITY, SO WE CAN FEEL MORE CONFIDENT STICKING UP FOR OURSELVES WITHOUT BEING SCARED WE'LL JUST STOP GETTING SHIFTS.
WE NEED MORE DEMOCRACY HERE,
SO WE HAVE A SAY,
LIKE YOU JUST SAID.
WE NEED BETTER PAY,
LESS PRESSURE.
THE UNION CAN HELP US.
WE NEED TO GET ORGANISED INSTEAD OF GETTING BITTER.
YES! I'M SICK OF BEING GRUMPY AND COMPLAINING ALL THE TIME. I DON'T LIKE HOW THIS JOB IS CHANGING ME.
YEAH TOTALLY.
AND IT DOESN'T HAVE TO BE THIS WAY.

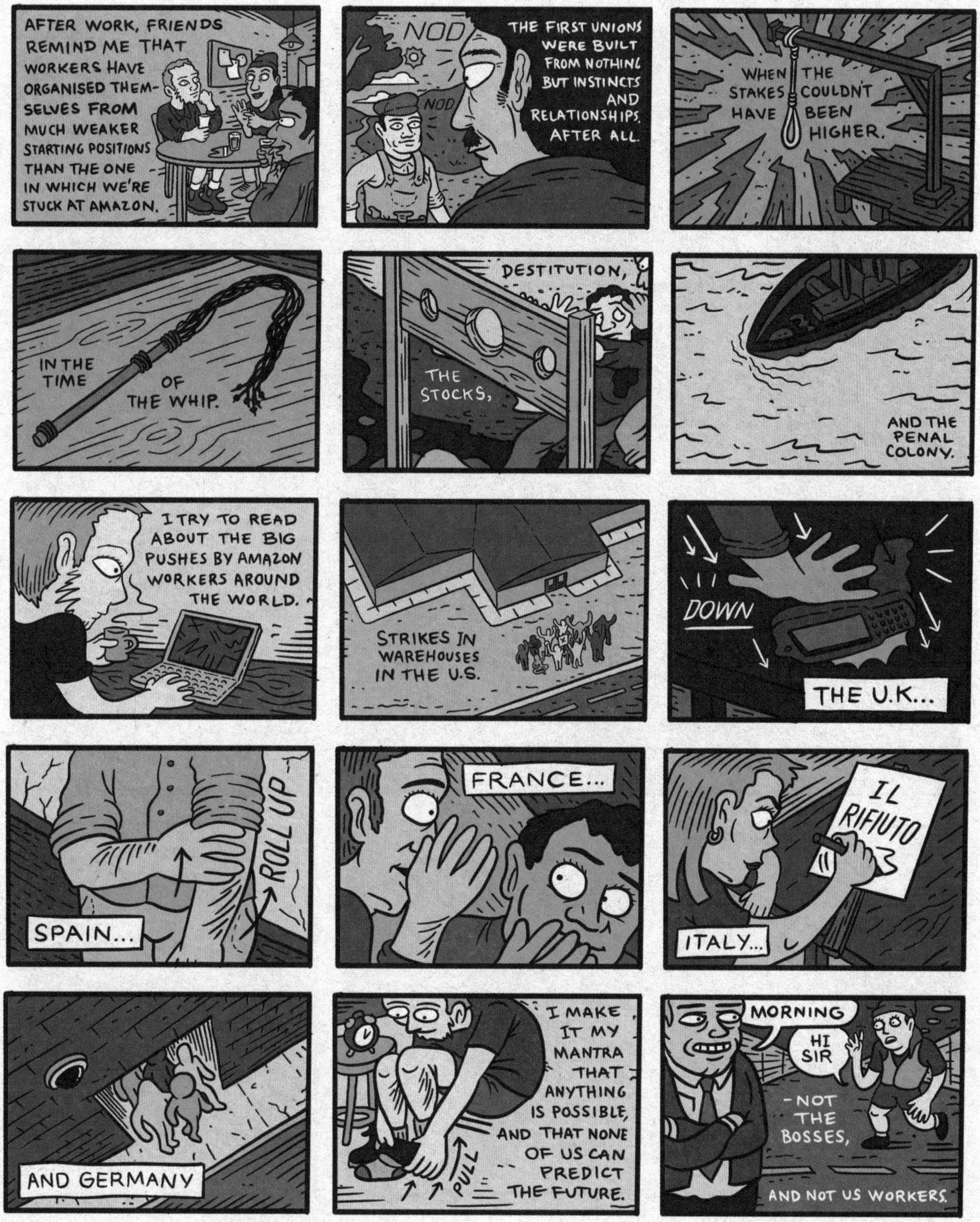

AFTER WORK, FRIENDS REMIND ME THAT WORKERS HAVE ORGANISED THEMSELVES FROM MUCH WEAKER STARTING POSITIONS THAN THE ONE IN WHICH WE'RE STUCK AT AMAZON.
NOD
NOD
THE FIRST UNIONS WERE BUILT FROM NOTHING BUT INSTINCTS AND RELATIONSHIPS, AFTER ALL.
WHEN THE STAKES COULDN'T HAVE BEEN HIGHER.
IN THE TIME OF THE WHIP.
DESTITUTION,
THE STOCKS,
AND THE PENAL COLONY.
I TRY TO READ ABOUT THE BIG PUSHES BY AMAZON WORKERS AROUND THE WORLD.
STRIKES IN WAREHOUSES IN THE U.S.
DOWN
THE U.K...
ROLL UP
SPAIN...
FRANCE...
IL RIFIUTO
ITALY...
AND GERMANY
I MAKE IT MY MANTRA THAT ANYTHING IS POSSIBLE, AND THAT NONE OF US CAN PREDICT THE FUTURE.
PULL
MORNING
HI SIR
-NOT THE BOSSES,
AND NOT US WORKERS.

SO WE SIGN UP A COUPLE OF DOZEN MEMBERS.

JOIN

HOPEFULLY THEY'LL BE HERE SOON.

BUT GETTING THE UNION GOING IS HARD — FOR A NUMBER OF REASONS.

OFF-SITE UNION MEETING

GRAB

NOT CONFIDENT IN MODERN UNIONS

UNAWARE OF

NOT ANTICON...

UNION DUES

INVESTED IN

MINDSET

LOW WAGES LEADING TO A

RELUCTANCE TO PAY

FEAR

WHAT UNIONS DO

THE JOB

MANAGEMENTS LIES

TRUSTS AMAZON

BRAND

PRECARITY

MONITORED CON...

VISA

INDIVIDUALISM

THE MAIN BARRIER IS THAT JUST ABOUT EVERY-ONE EITHER QUITS OR GETS FIRED.

I GOT A BETTER JOB!

NICE!

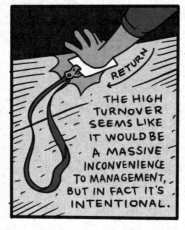

RETURN

THE HIGH TURNOVER SEEMS LIKE IT WOULD BE A MASSIVE INCONVENIENCE TO MANAGEMENT, BUT IN FACT IT'S INTENTIONAL.

HISTORICALLY, UNIONS HAVE GAINED STRONG FOOTHOLDS IN INDUSTRIES IN WHICH PEOPLE WORK FOR YEARS AND YEARS.

NOD

HOW ARE THE KIDS?

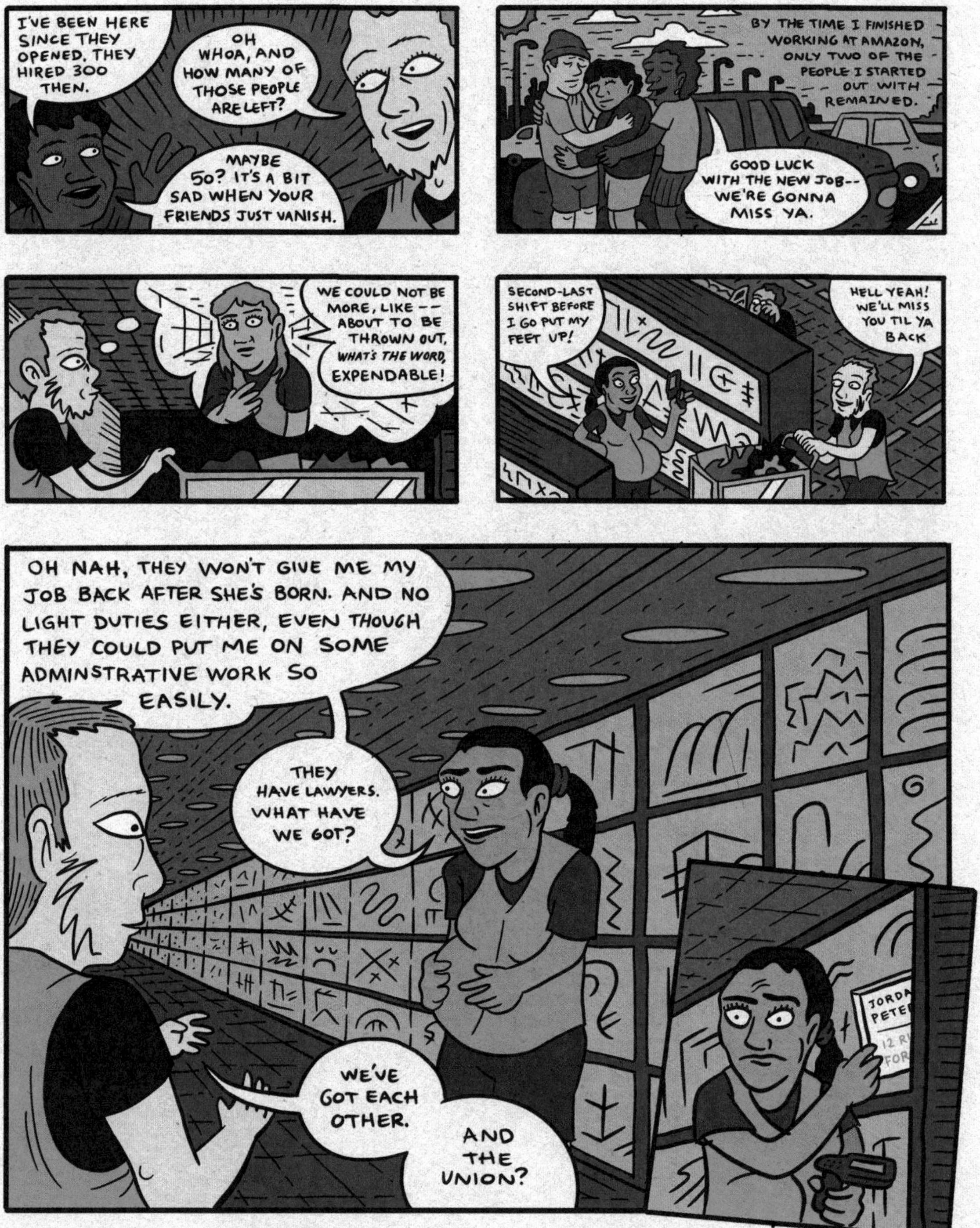

I'VE BEEN HERE SINCE THEY OPENED. THEY HIRED 300 THEN.
OH WHOA, AND HOW MANY OF THOSE PEOPLE ARE LEFT?
MAYBE 50? IT'S A BIT SAD WHEN YOUR FRIENDS JUST VANISH.
BY THE TIME I FINISHED WORKING AT AMAZON, ONLY TWO OF THE PEOPLE I STARTED OUT WITH REMAINED.
GOOD LUCK WITH THE NEW JOB-- WE'RE GONNA MISS YA.
WE COULD NOT BE MORE, LIKE -- ABOUT TO BE THROWN OUT, WHAT'S THE WORD, EXPENDABLE!
SECOND-LAST SHIFT BEFORE I GO PUT MY FEET UP!
HELL YEAH! WE'LL MISS YOU TIL YA BACK
OH NAH, THEY WON'T GIVE ME MY JOB BACK AFTER SHE'S BORN. AND NO LIGHT DUTIES EITHER, EVEN THOUGH THEY COULD PUT ME ON SOME ADMINSTRATIVE WORK SO EASILY.
THEY HAVE LAWYERS. WHAT HAVE WE GOT?
WE'VE GOT EACH OTHER.
AND THE UNION?

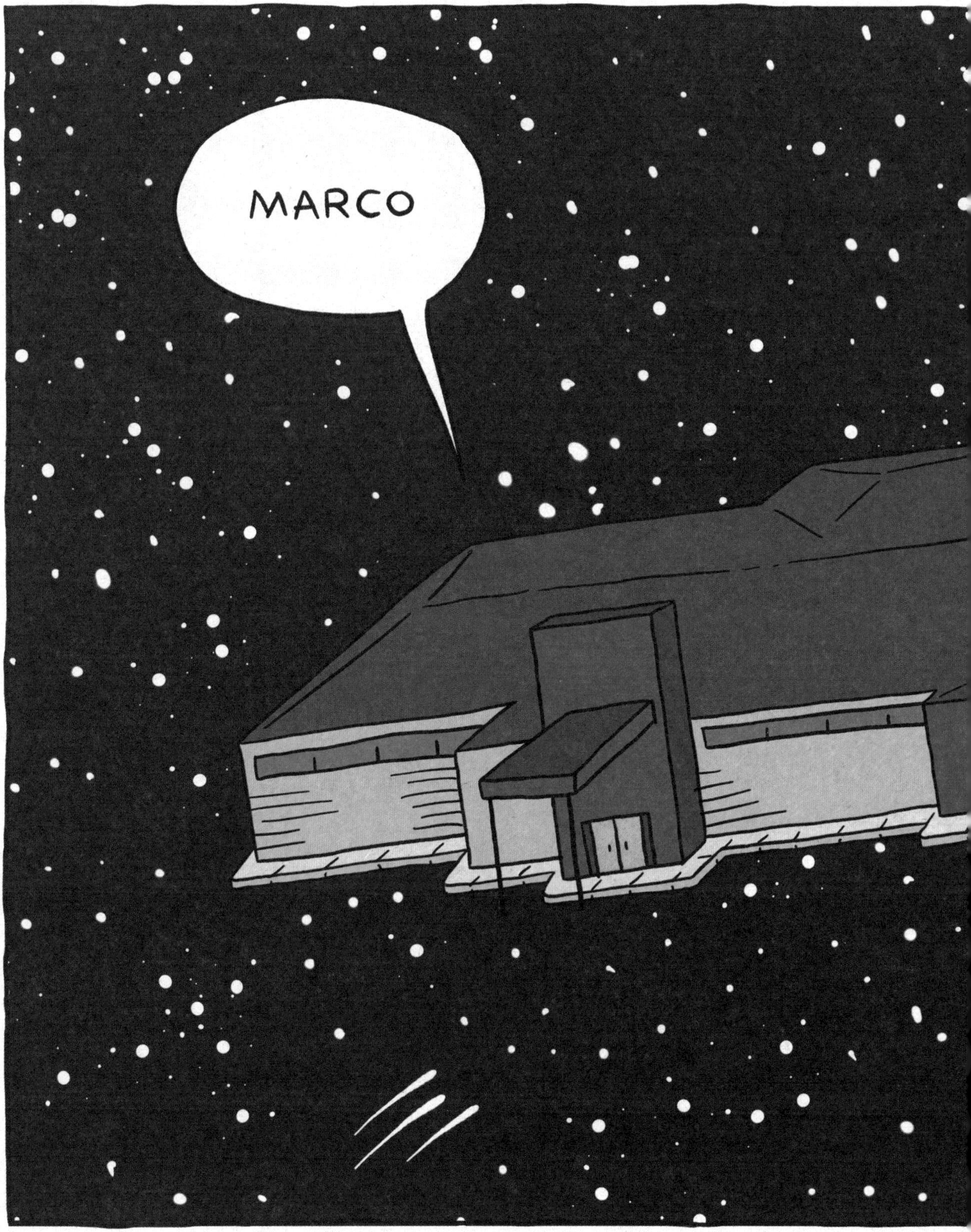
MARCO

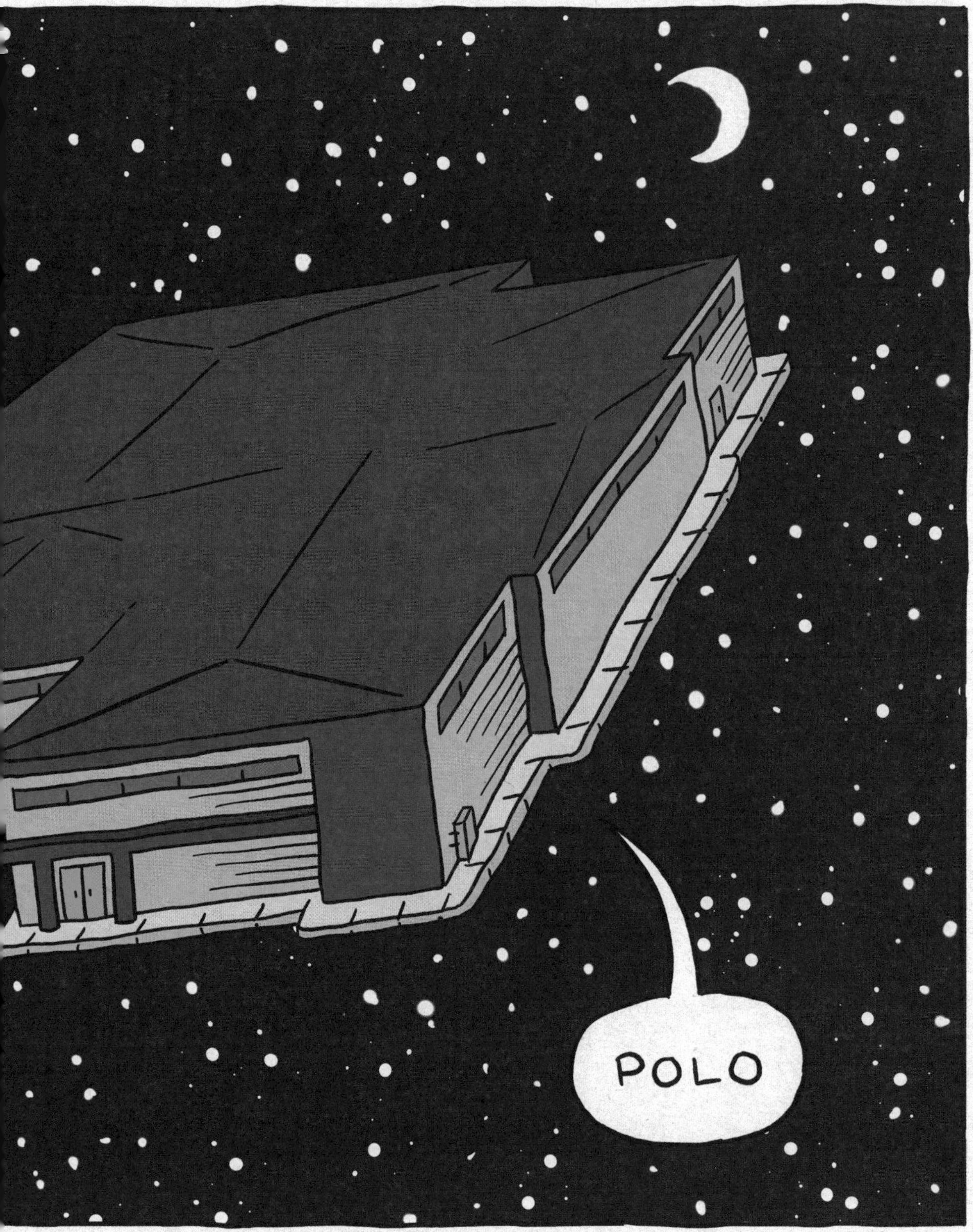
POLO

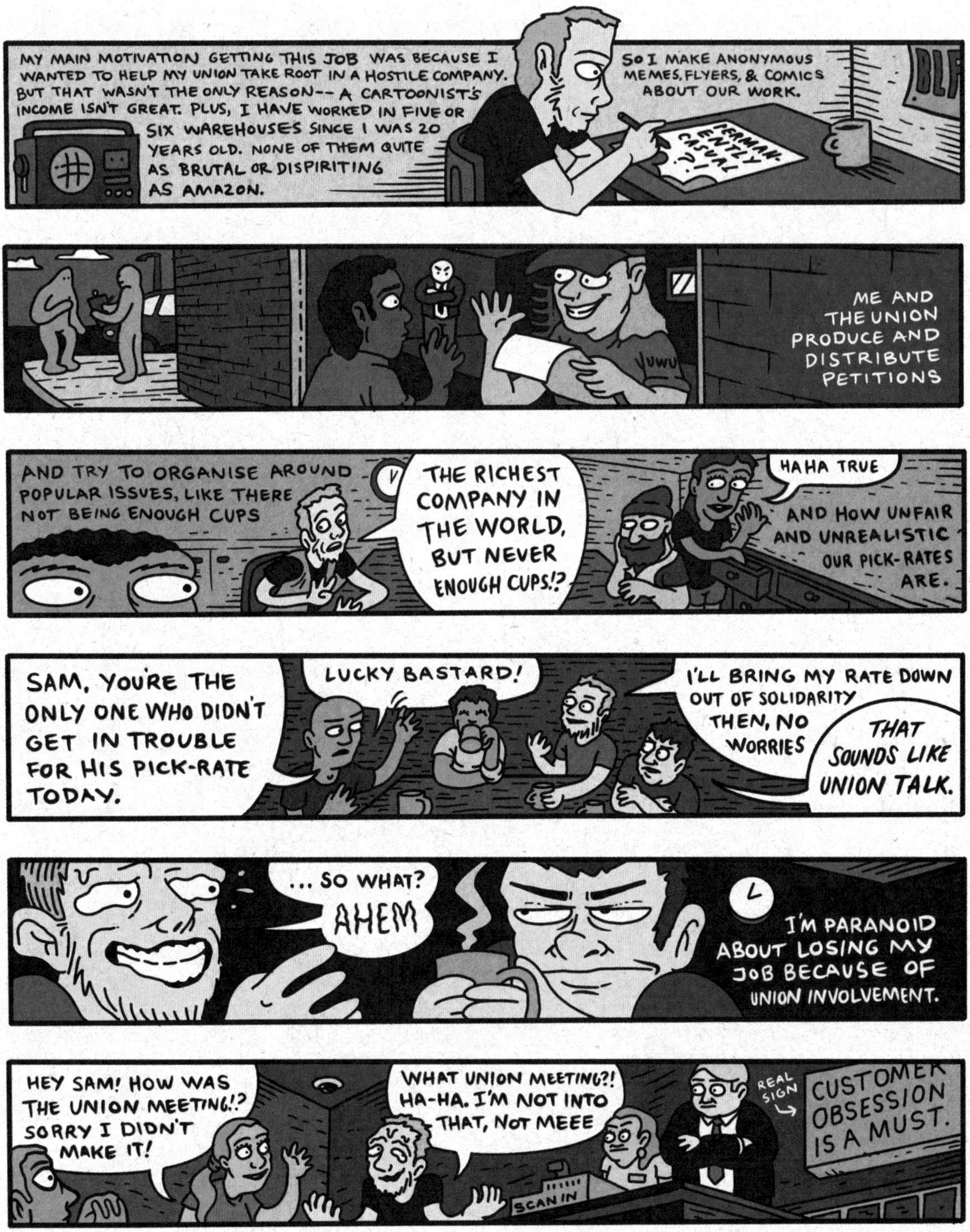

MY MAIN MOTIVATION GETTING THIS JOB WAS BECAUSE I WANTED TO HELP MY UNION TAKE ROOT IN A HOSTILE COMPANY. BUT THAT WASN'T THE ONLY REASON-- A CARTOONIST'S INCOME ISN'T GREAT. PLUS, I HAVE WORKED IN FIVE OR SIX WAREHOUSES SINCE I WAS 20 YEARS OLD. NONE OF THEM QUITE AS BRUTAL OR DISPIRITING AS AMAZON.
SO I MAKE ANONYMOUS MEMES, FLYERS, & COMICS ABOUT OUR WORK.
PERMANENTLY CASUAL ?!
ME AND THE UNION PRODUCE AND DISTRIBUTE PETITIONS
UWU
AND TRY TO ORGANISE AROUND POPULAR ISSUES, LIKE THERE NOT BEING ENOUGH CUPS
THE RICHEST COMPANY IN THE WORLD, BUT NEVER ENOUGH CUPS!?
HAHA TRUE
AND HOW UNFAIR AND UNREALISTIC OUR PICK-RATES ARE.
SAM, YOU'RE THE ONLY ONE WHO DIDN'T GET IN TROUBLE FOR HIS PICK-RATE TODAY.
LUCKY BASTARD!
I'LL BRING MY RATE DOWN OUT OF SOLIDARITY THEN, NO WORRIES
THAT SOUNDS LIKE UNION TALK.
... SO WHAT?
AHEM
I'M PARANOID ABOUT LOSING MY JOB BECAUSE OF UNION INVOLVEMENT.
HEY SAM! HOW WAS THE UNION MEETING!? SORRY I DIDN'T MAKE IT!
WHAT UNION MEETING?! HA-HA. I'M NOT INTO THAT, NOT MEEE
REAL SIGN
CUSTOMER OBSESSION IS A MUST.
SCAN IN

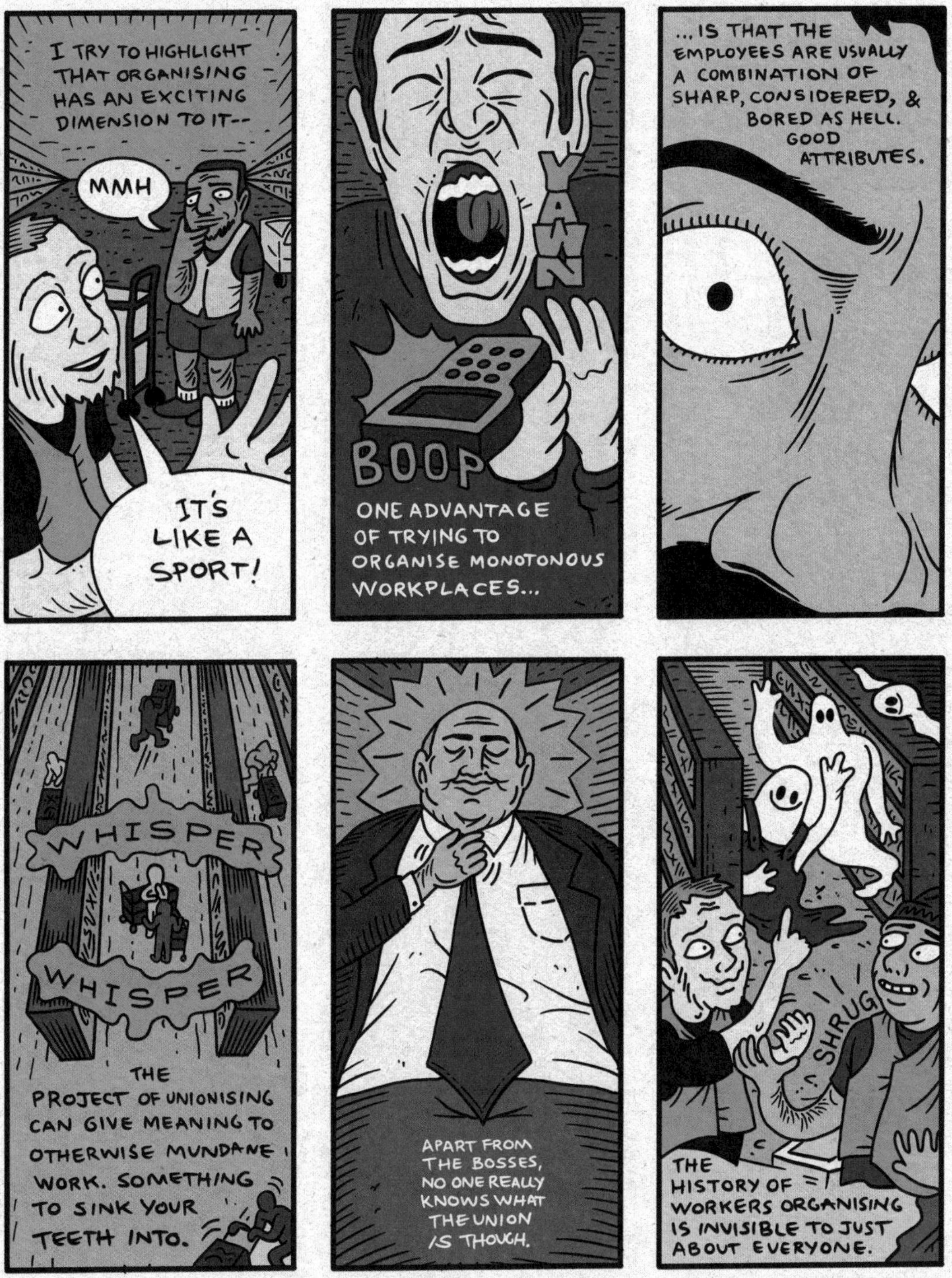

I TRY TO HIGHLIGHT THAT ORGANISING HAS AN EXCITING DIMENSION TO IT--
MMH
IT'S LIKE A SPORT!
YAWN
BOOP
ONE ADVANTAGE OF TRYING TO ORGANISE MONOTONOUS WORKPLACES...
...IS THAT THE EMPLOYEES ARE USUALLY A COMBINATION OF SHARP, CONSIDERED, & BORED AS HELL. GOOD ATTRIBUTES.
WHISPER
WHISPER
THE PROJECT OF UNIONISING CAN GIVE MEANING TO OTHERWISE MUNDANE WORK. SOMETHING TO SINK YOUR TEETH INTO.
APART FROM THE BOSSES, NO ONE REALLY KNOWS WHAT THE UNION IS THOUGH.
SHRUG
THE HISTORY OF WORKERS ORGANISING IS INVISIBLE TO JUST ABOUT EVERYONE.

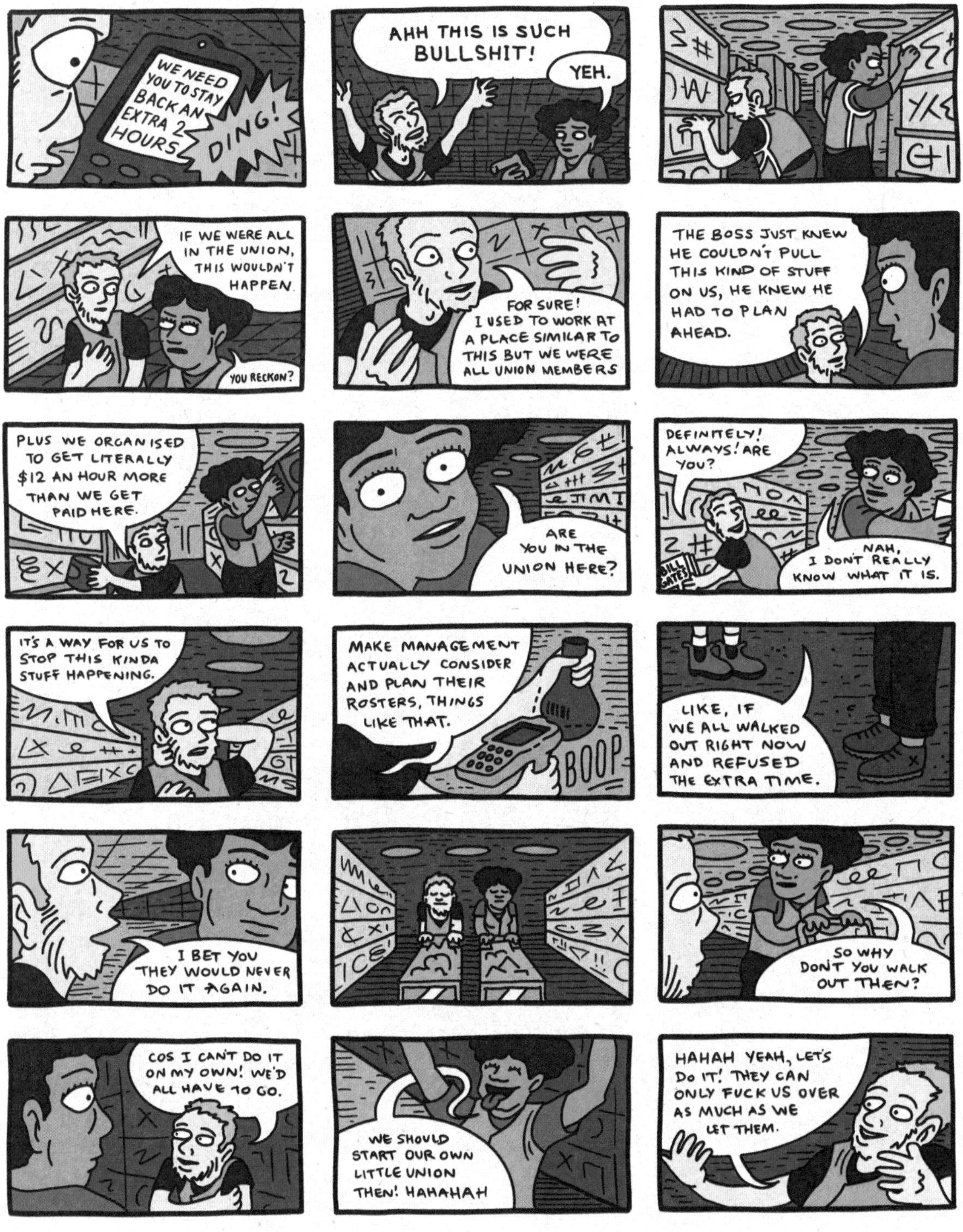
WE NEED YOU TO STAY BACK AN EXTRA 2 HOURS
DING!
AHH THIS IS SUCH BULLSHIT!
YEH.
IF WE WERE ALL IN THE UNION, THIS WOULDN'T HAPPEN.
YOU RECKON?
FOR SURE! I USED TO WORK AT A PLACE SIMILAR TO THIS BUT WE WERE ALL UNION MEMBERS
THE BOSS JUST KNEW HE COULDN'T PULL THIS KIND OF STUFF ON US, HE KNEW HE HAD TO PLAN AHEAD.
PLUS WE ORGANISED TO GET LITERALLY $12 AN HOUR MORE THAN WE GET PAID HERE.
ARE YOU IN THE UNION HERE?
DEFINITELY! ALWAYS! ARE YOU?
BILL GATES
NAH, I DON'T REALLY KNOW WHAT IT IS.
IT'S A WAY FOR US TO STOP THIS KINDA STUFF HAPPENING.
MAKE MANAGEMENT ACTUALLY CONSIDER AND PLAN THEIR ROSTERS, THINGS LIKE THAT.
BOOP
LIKE, IF WE ALL WALKED OUT RIGHT NOW AND REFUSED THE EXTRA TIME.
I BET YOU THEY WOULD NEVER DO IT AGAIN.
SO WHY DON'T YOU WALK OUT THEN?
COS I CAN'T DO IT ON MY OWN! WE'D ALL HAVE TO GO.
WE SHOULD START OUR OWN LITTLE UNION THEN! HAHAHAH
HAHAH YEAH, LET'S DO IT! THEY CAN ONLY FUCK US OVER AS MUCH AS WE LET THEM.

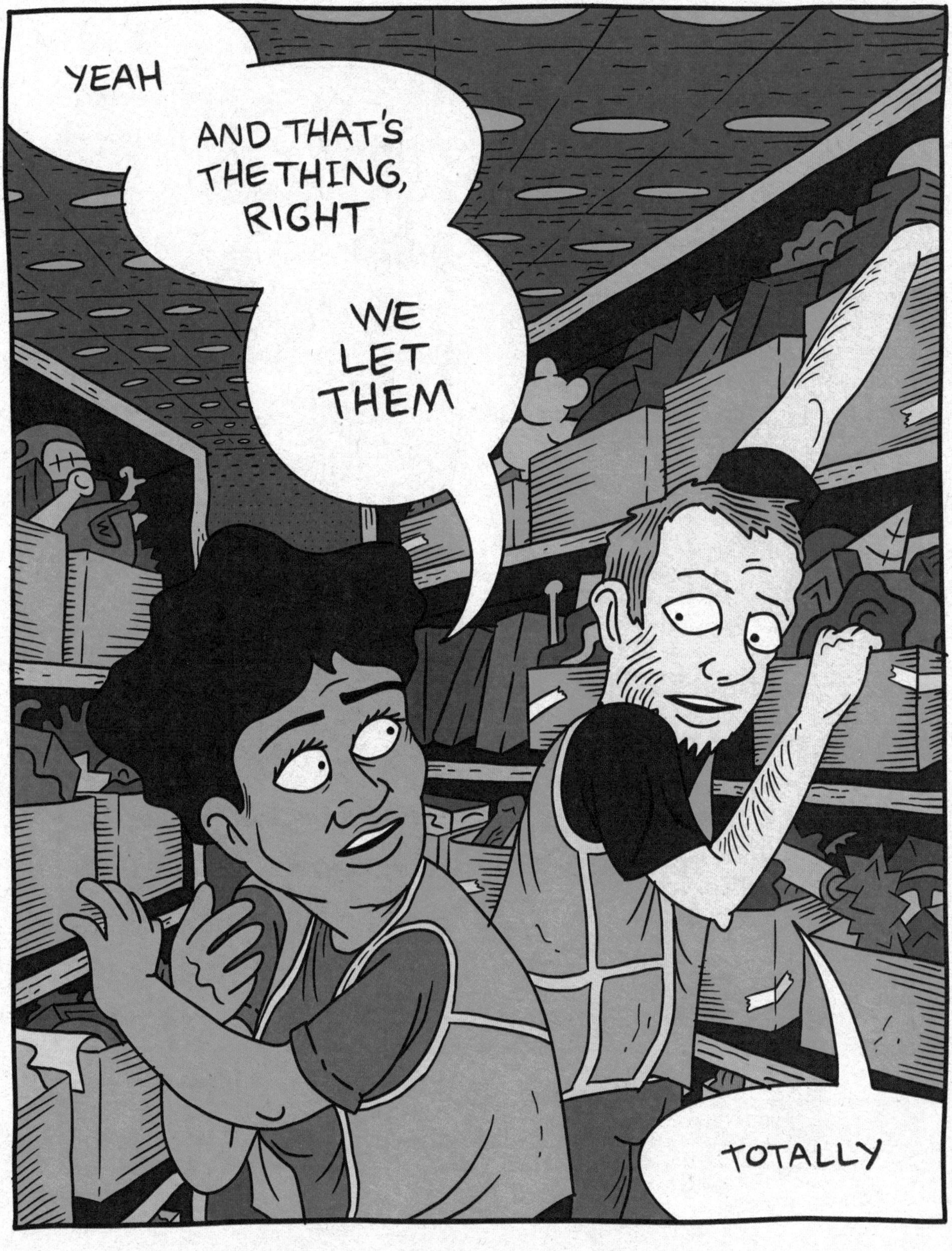
YEAH
AND THAT'S THE THING, RIGHT
WE LET THEM
TOTALLY

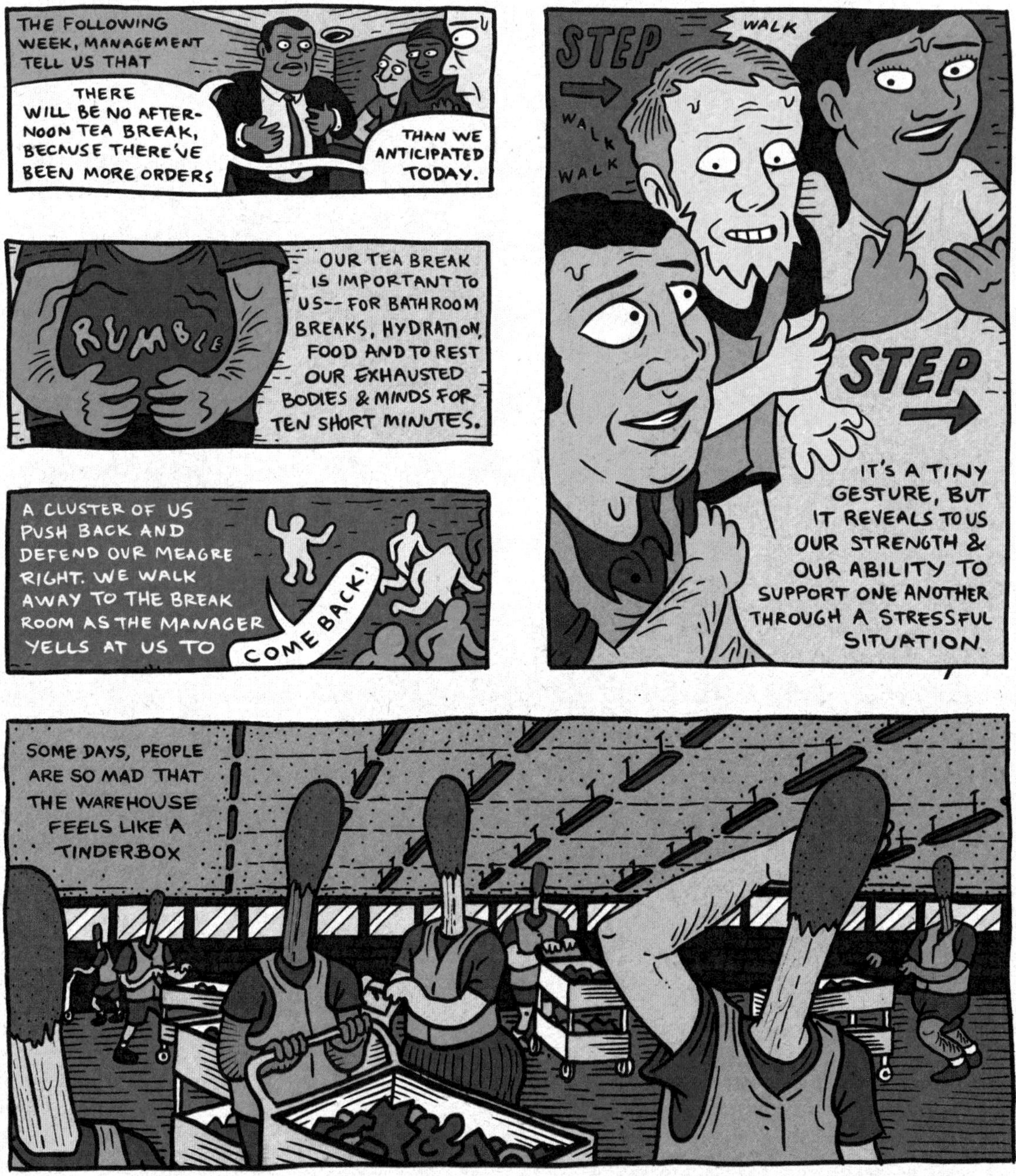
THE FOLLOWING WEEK, MANAGEMENT TELL US THAT
THERE WILL BE NO AFTER-NOON TEA BREAK, BECAUSE THERE'VE BEEN MORE ORDERS
THAN WE ANTICIPATED TODAY.
RUMBLE
OUR TEA BREAK IS IMPORTANT TO US-- FOR BATHROOM BREAKS, HYDRATION, FOOD AND TO REST OUR EXHAUSTED BODIES & MINDS FOR TEN SHORT MINUTES.
A CLUSTER OF US PUSH BACK AND DEFEND OUR MEAGRE RIGHT. WE WALK AWAY TO THE BREAK ROOM AS THE MANAGER YELLS AT US TO
COME BACK!
STEP
WALK
WALK
WALK
STEP
IT'S A TINY GESTURE, BUT IT REVEALS TO US OUR STRENGTH & OUR ABILITY TO SUPPORT ONE ANOTHER THROUGH A STRESSFUL SITUATION.
SOME DAYS, PEOPLE ARE SO MAD THAT THE WAREHOUSE FEELS LIKE A TINDERBOX
BUT MOST DAYS, EVERYONE IS JUST TRYING TO GET THROUGH ANOTHER SHIFT.
BACK TO HELL
STEP
WINK

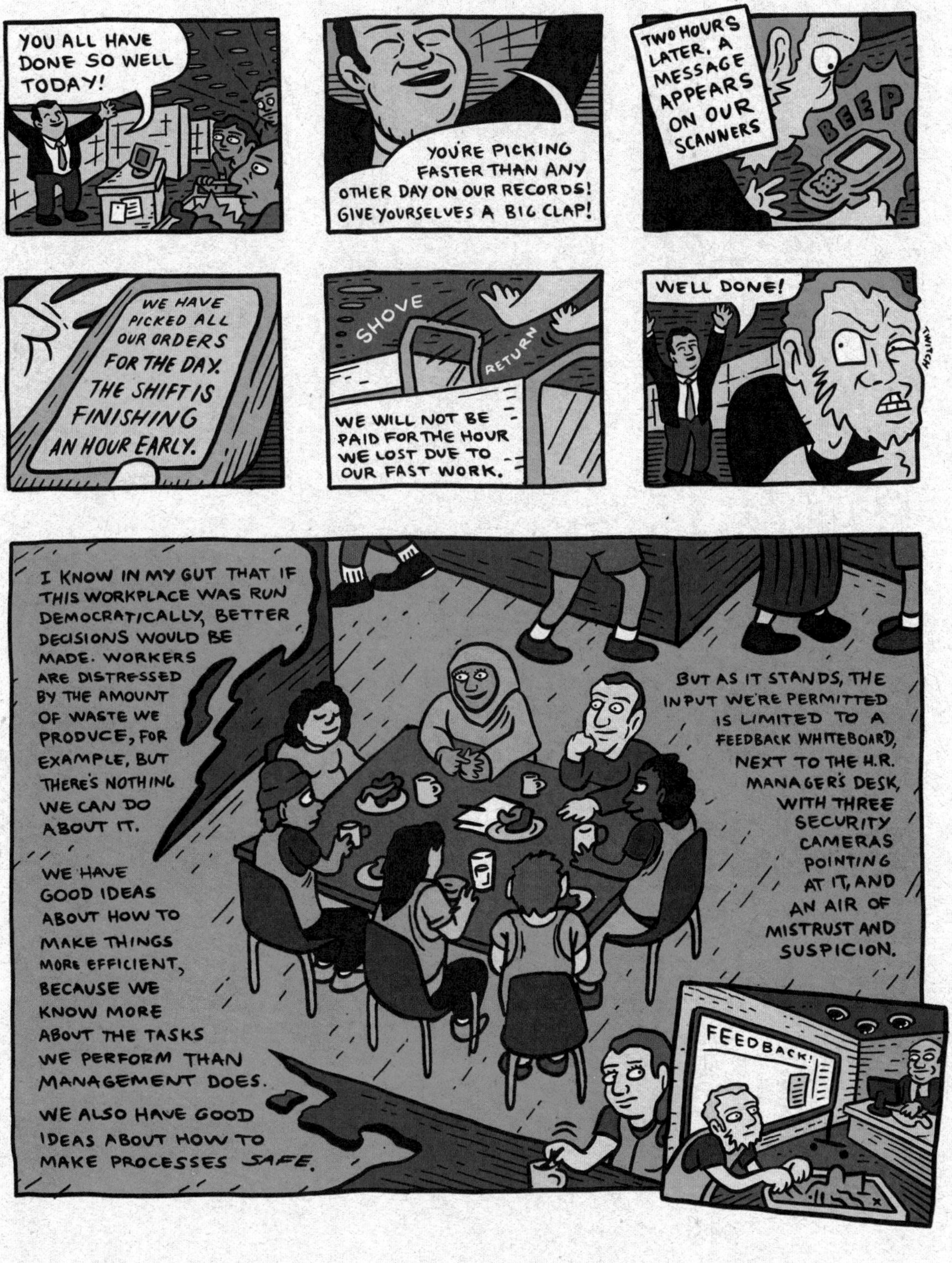

YOU ALL HAVE DONE SO WELL TODAY!
YOU'RE PICKING FASTER THAN ANY OTHER DAY ON OUR RECORDS! GIVE YOURSELVES A BIG CLAP!
TWO HOURS LATER, A MESSAGE APPEARS ON OUR SCANNERS
BEEP
WE HAVE PICKED ALL OUR ORDERS FOR THE DAY. THE SHIFT IS FINISHING AN HOUR EARLY.
SHOVE
RETURN
WE WILL NOT BE PAID FOR THE HOUR WE LOST DUE TO OUR FAST WORK.
WELL DONE!
TWITCH
I KNOW IN MY GUT THAT IF THIS WORKPLACE WAS RUN DEMOCRATICALLY, BETTER DECISIONS WOULD BE MADE. WORKERS ARE DISTRESSED BY THE AMOUNT OF WASTE WE PRODUCE, FOR EXAMPLE, BUT THERE'S NOTHING WE CAN DO ABOUT IT.
WE HAVE GOOD IDEAS ABOUT HOW TO MAKE THINGS MORE EFFICIENT, BECAUSE WE KNOW MORE ABOUT THE TASKS WE PERFORM THAN MANAGEMENT DOES.
WE ALSO HAVE GOOD IDEAS ABOUT HOW TO MAKE PROCESSES SAFE.
BUT AS IT STANDS, THE INPUT WE'RE PERMITTED IS LIMITED TO A FEEDBACK WHITEBOARD, NEXT TO THE H.R. MANAGER'S DESK, WITH THREE SECURITY CAMERAS POINTING AT IT, AND AN AIR OF MISTRUST AND SUSPICION.
FEEDBACK!

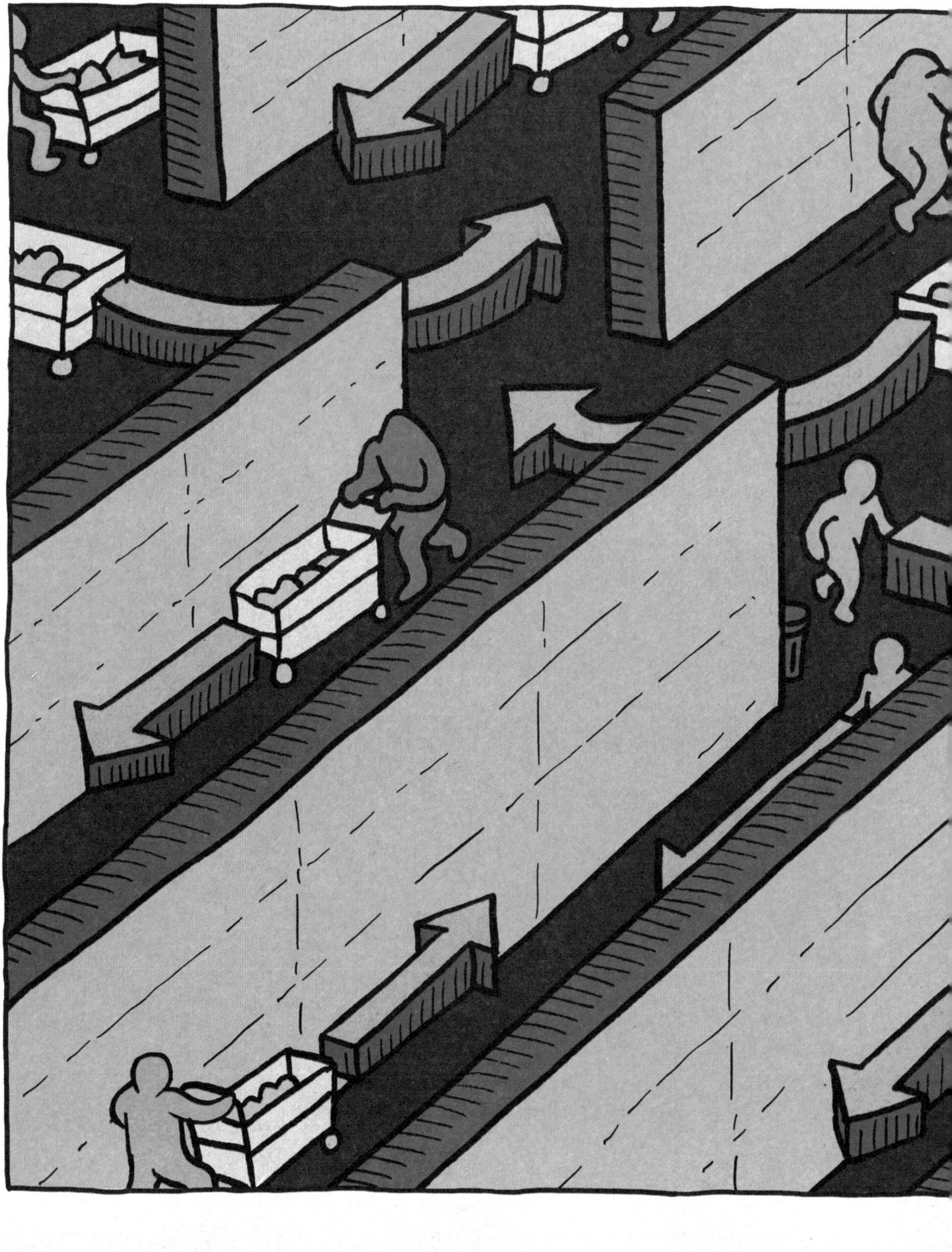

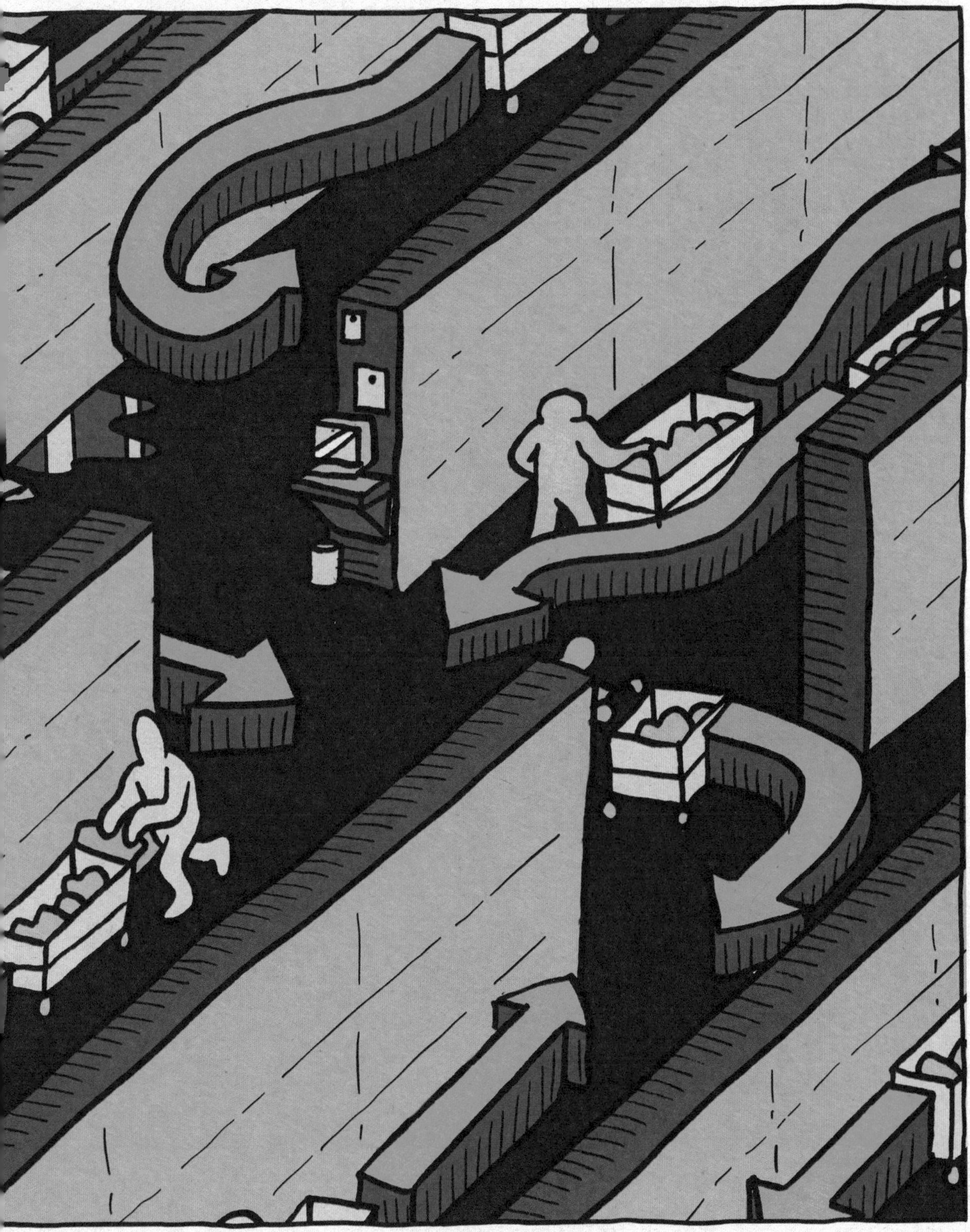

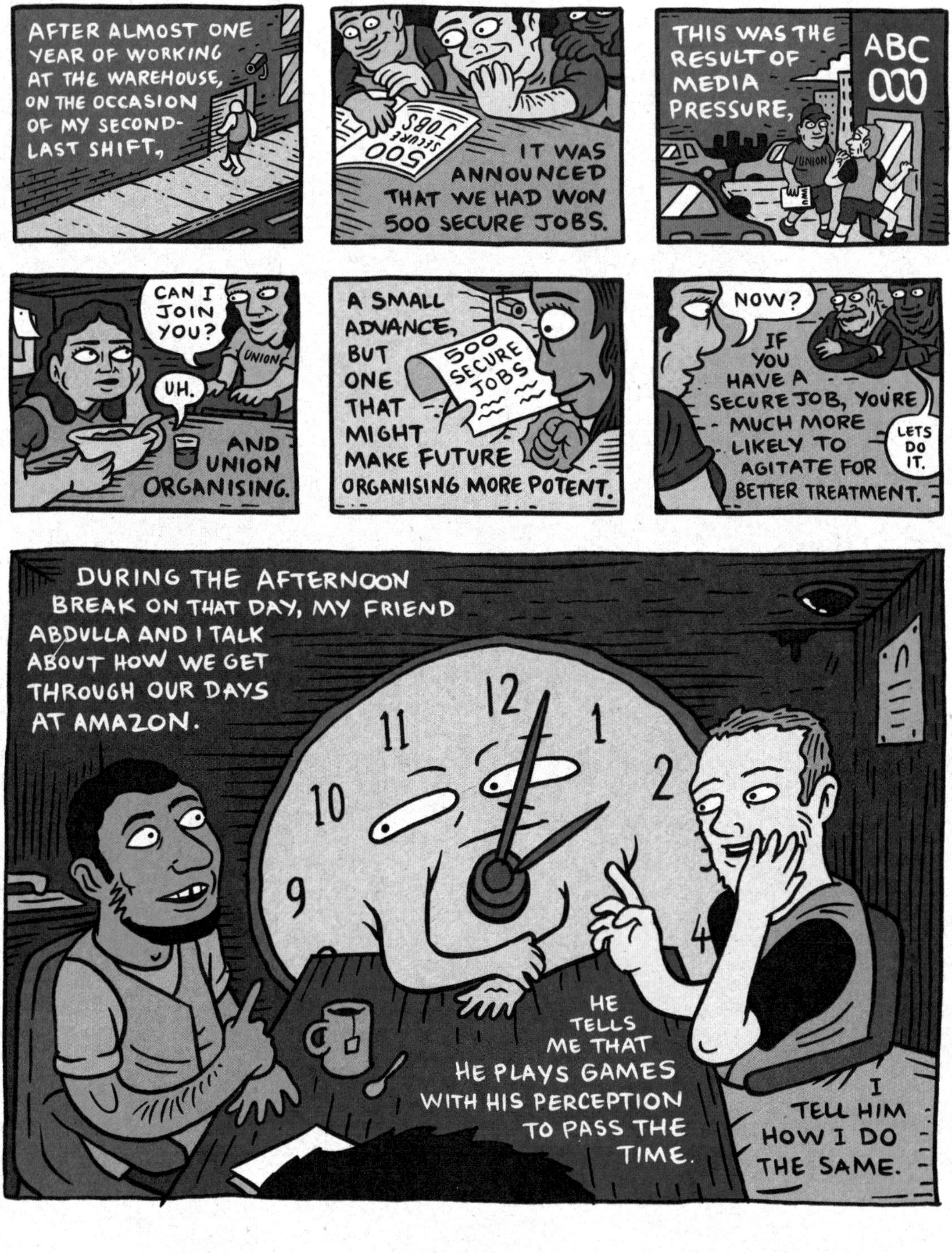

AFTER ALMOST ONE YEAR OF WORKING AT THE WAREHOUSE, ON THE OCCASION OF MY SECOND-LAST SHIFT,
500 SECURE JOBS
IT WAS ANNOUNCED THAT WE HAD WON 500 SECURE JOBS.
THIS WAS THE RESULT OF MEDIA PRESSURE,
ABC
UNION
CAN I JOIN YOU?
UNION
UH.
AND UNION ORGANISING.
A SMALL ADVANCE, BUT ONE THAT MIGHT MAKE FUTURE ORGANISING MORE POTENT.
500 SECURE JOBS
NOW?
IF YOU HAVE A SECURE JOB, YOU'RE MUCH MORE LIKELY TO AGITATE FOR BETTER TREATMENT.
LETS DO IT.
DURING THE AFTERNOON BREAK ON THAT DAY, MY FRIEND ABDULLA AND I TALK ABOUT HOW WE GET THROUGH OUR DAYS AT AMAZON.
HE TELLS ME THAT HE PLAYS GAMES WITH HIS PERCEPTION TO PASS THE TIME.
I TELL HIM HOW I DO THE SAME.

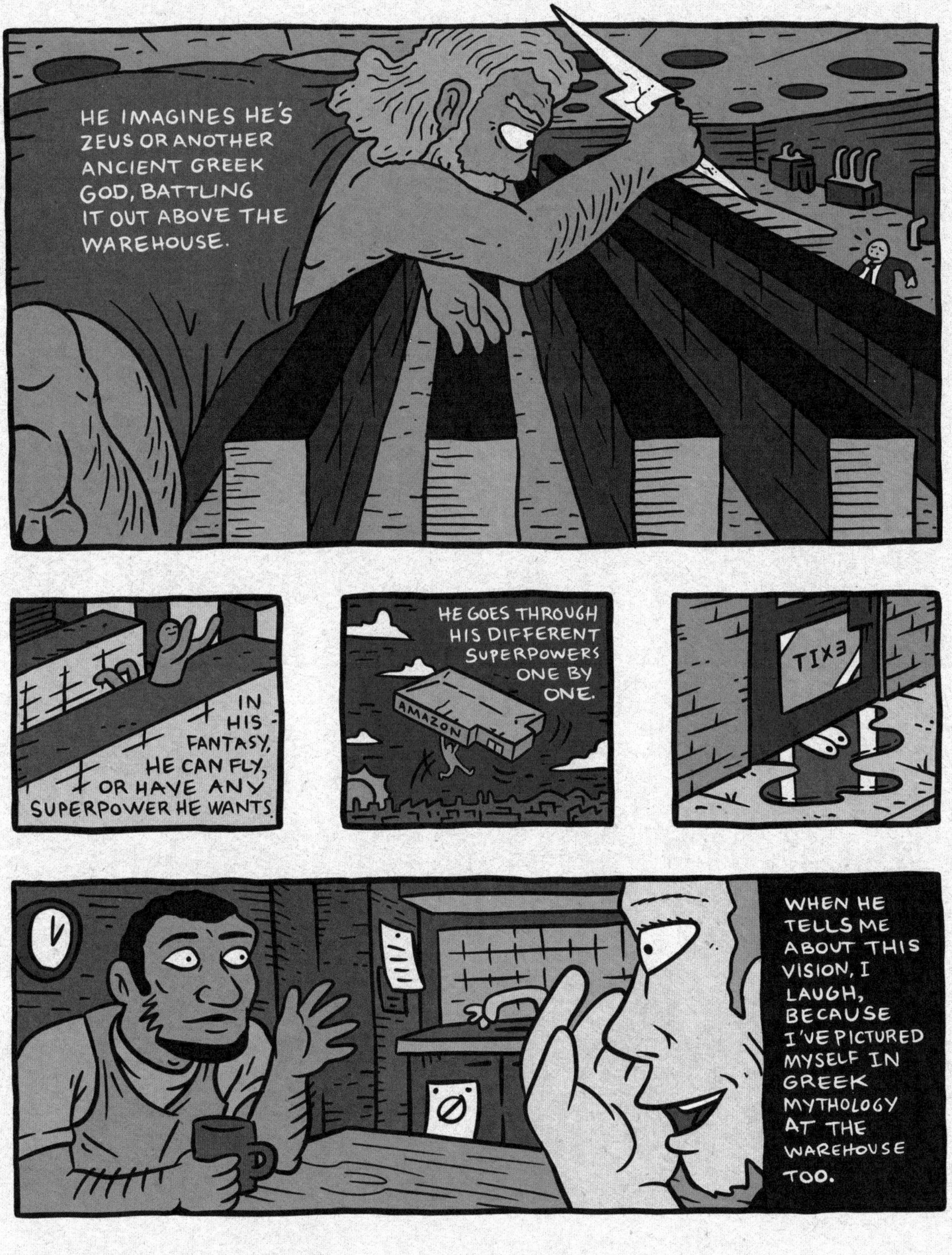
HE IMAGINES HE'S ZEUS OR ANOTHER ANCIENT GREEK GOD, BATTLING IT OUT ABOVE THE WAREHOUSE.
IN HIS FANTASY, HE CAN FLY, OR HAVE ANY SUPERPOWER HE WANTS.
HE GOES THROUGH HIS DIFFERENT SUPERPOWERS ONE BY ONE.
AMAZON
EXIT
WHEN HE TELLS ME ABOUT THIS VISION, I LAUGH, BECAUSE I'VE PICTURED MYSELF IN GREEK MYTHOLOGY AT THE WAREHOUSE TOO.

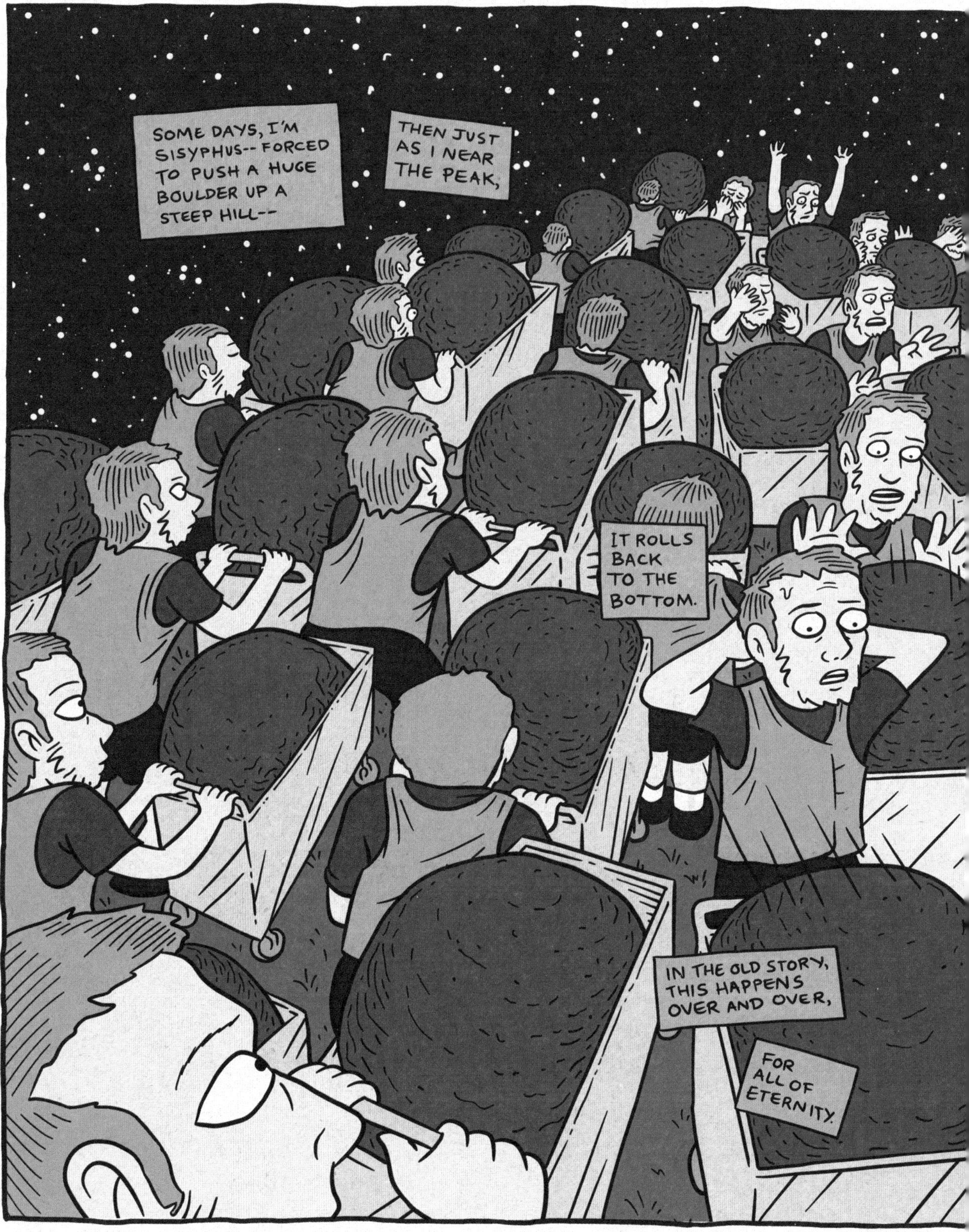
SOME DAYS, I'M SISYPHUS-- FORCED TO PUSH A HUGE BOULDER UP A STEEP HILL--
THEN JUST AS I NEAR THE PEAK,
IT ROLLS BACK TO THE BOTTOM.
IN THE OLD STORY, THIS HAPPENS OVER AND OVER,
FOR ALL OF ETERNITY.

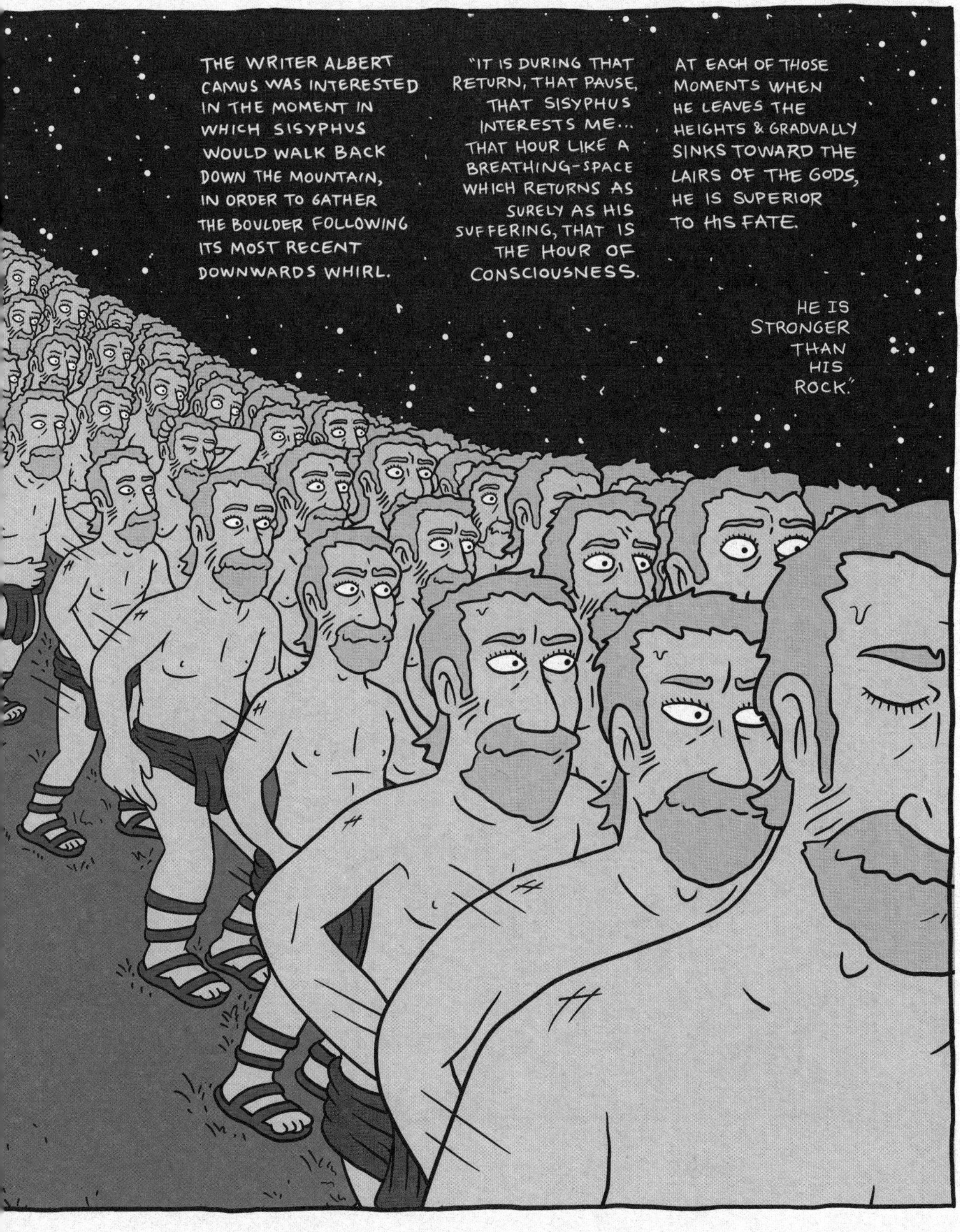
THE WRITER ALBERT CAMUS WAS INTERESTED IN THE MOMENT IN WHICH SISYPHUS WOULD WALK BACK DOWN THE MOUNTAIN, IN ORDER TO GATHER THE BOULDER FOLLOWING ITS MOST RECENT DOWNWARDS WHIRL.
"IT IS DURING THAT RETURN, THAT PAUSE, THAT SISYPHUS INTERESTS ME... THAT HOUR LIKE A BREATHING-SPACE WHICH RETURNS AS SURELY AS HIS SUFFERING, THAT IS THE HOUR OF CONSCIOUSNESS.
AT EACH OF THOSE MOMENTS WHEN HE LEAVES THE HEIGHTS & GRADUALLY SINKS TOWARD THE LAIRS OF THE GODS, HE IS SUPERIOR TO HIS FATE.
HE IS STRONGER THAN HIS ROCK."

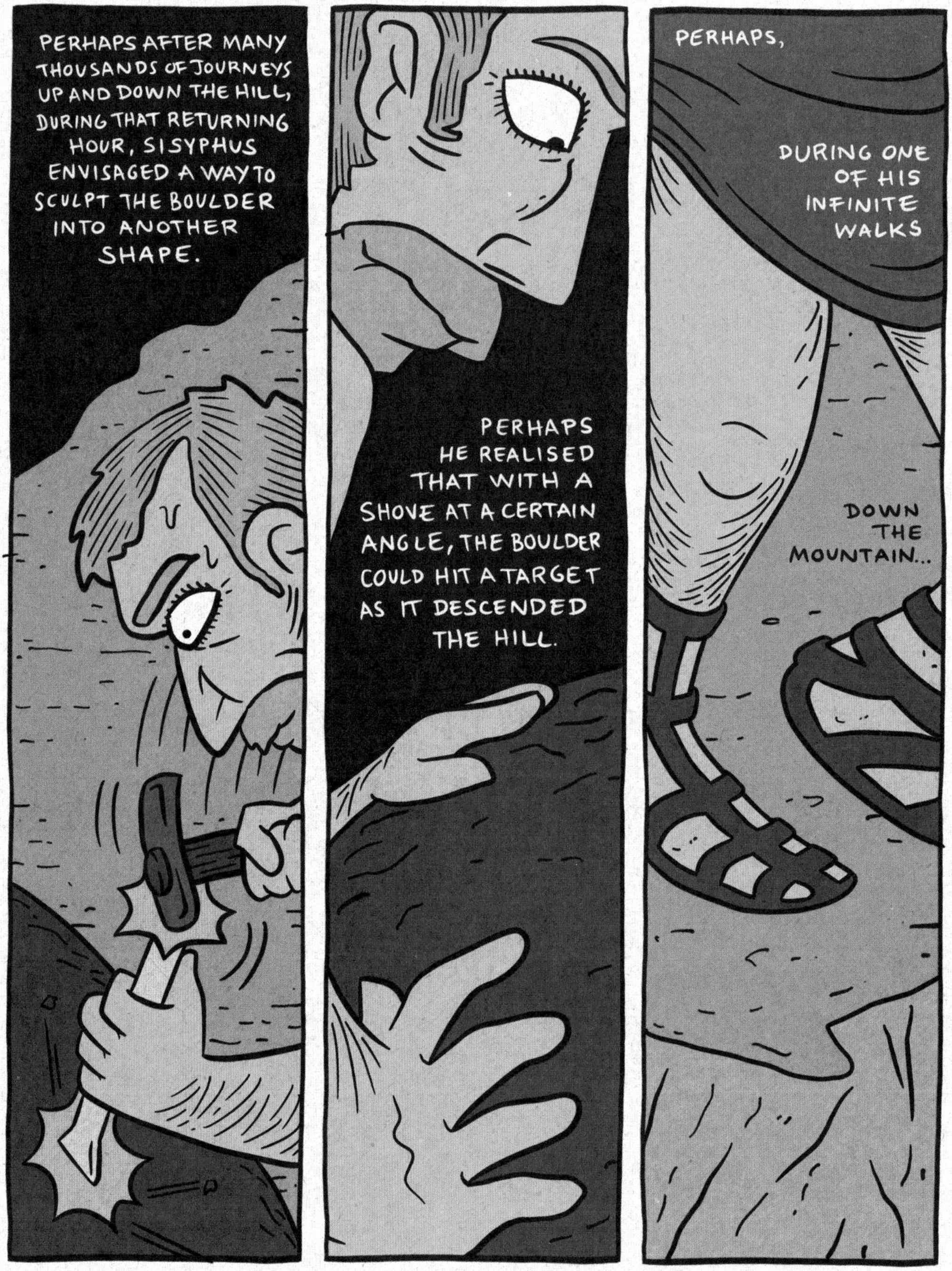
PERHAPS AFTER MANY THOUSANDS OF JOURNEYS UP AND DOWN THE HILL, DURING THAT RETURNING HOUR, SISYPHUS ENVISAGED A WAY TO SCULPT THE BOULDER INTO ANOTHER SHAPE.
PERHAPS HE REALISED THAT WITH A SHOVE AT A CERTAIN ANGLE, THE BOULDER COULD HIT A TARGET AS IT DESCENDED THE HILL.
PERHAPS,
DURING ONE OF HIS INFINITE WALKS
DOWN THE MOUNTAIN...

...MAYBE SISYPHUS CAME TO SEE THE BOULDER
NOT JUST AS A BOULDER, BUT AS A TOOL.
OR MAYBE ONE DAY SISYPHUS SAW CRACKS IN THE BOULDER
CRACKS HE'D NEVER NOTICED BEFORE.

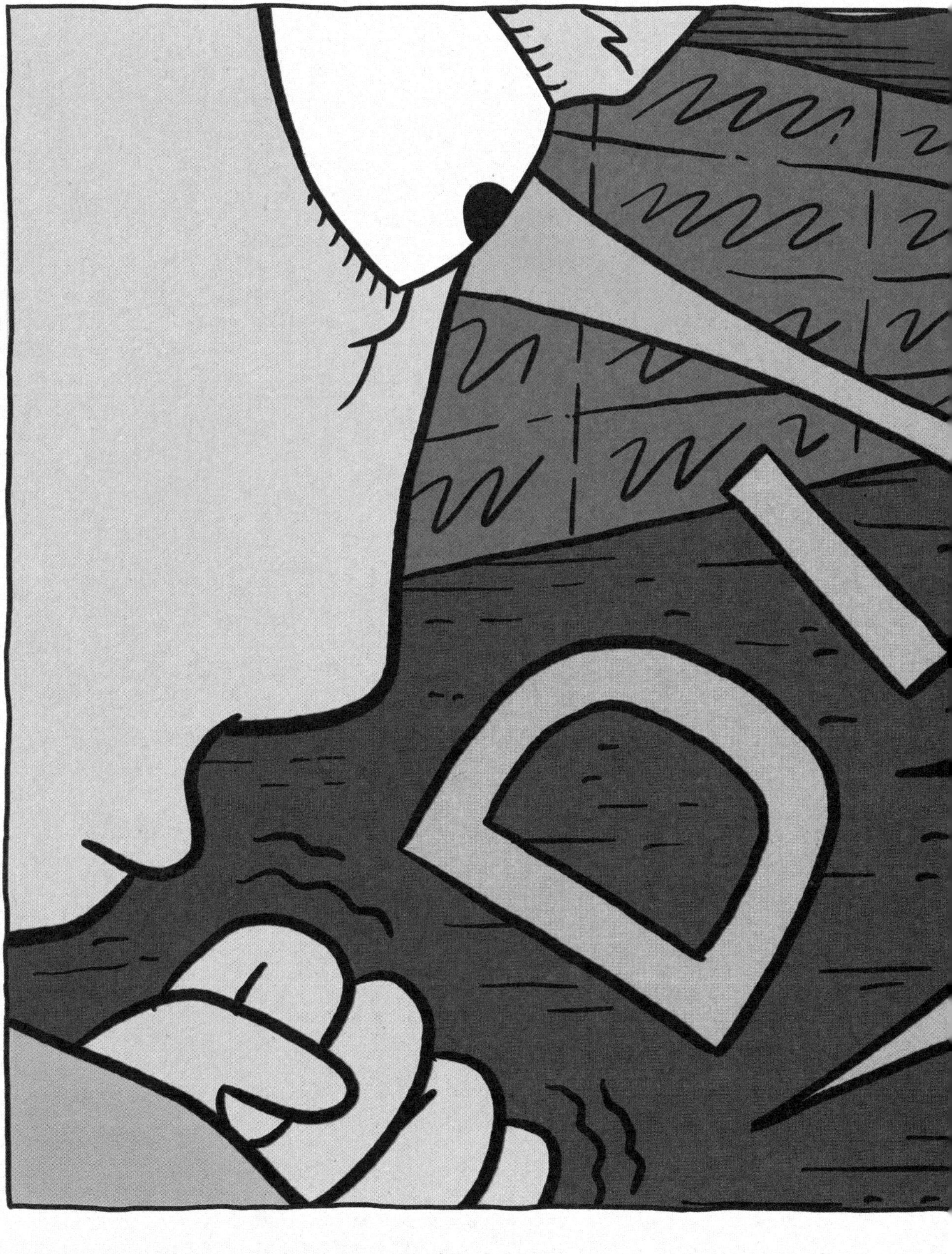

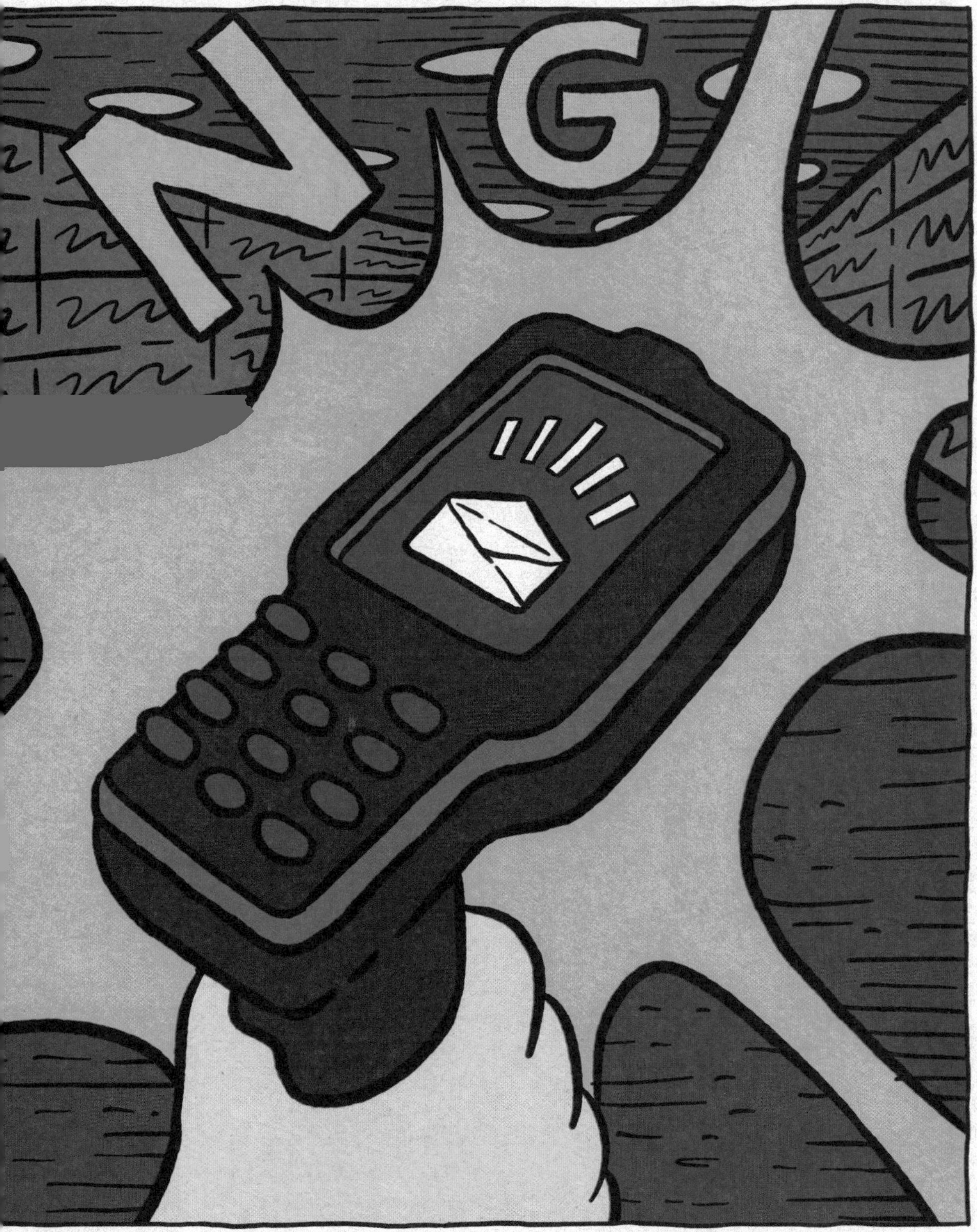
NG

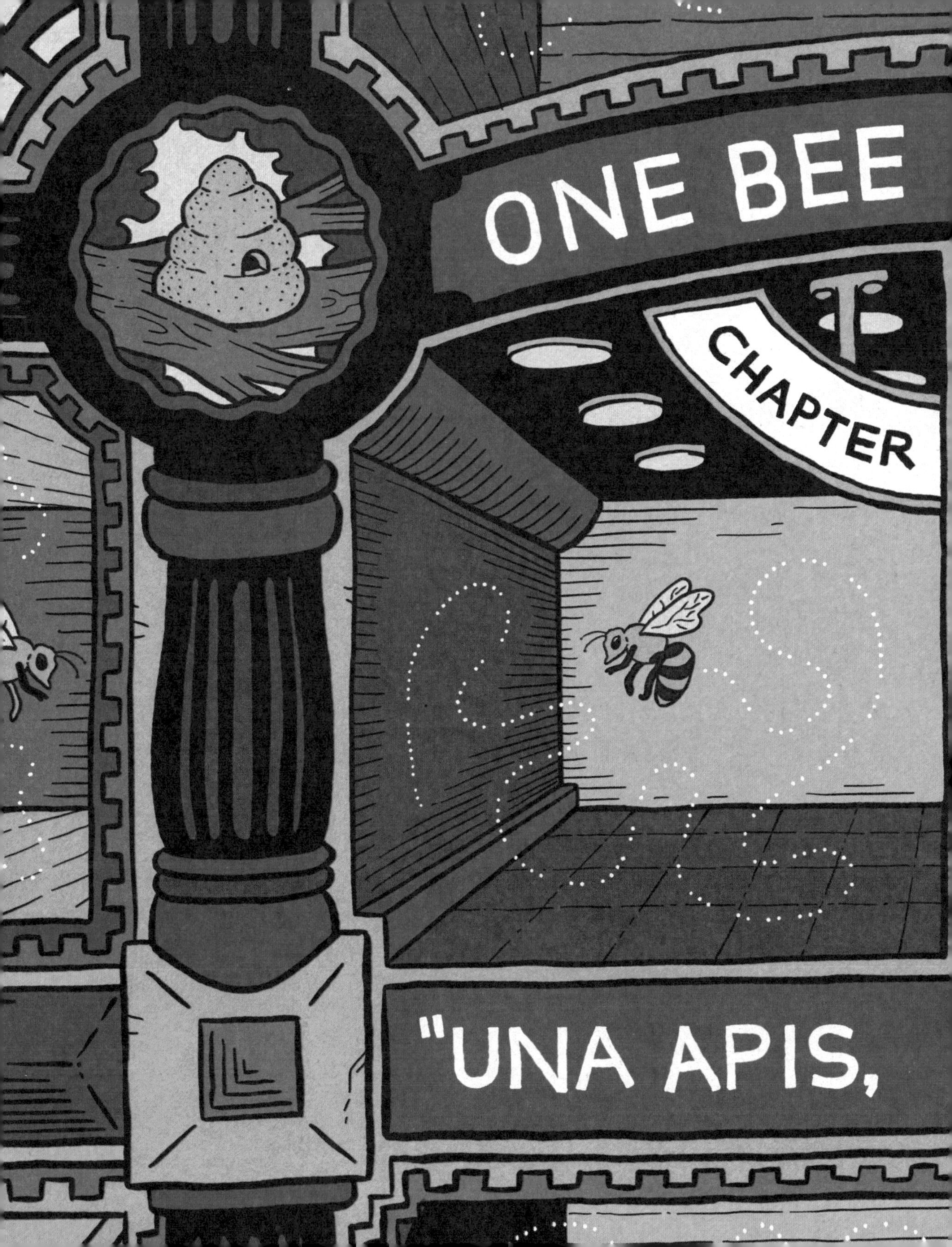
ONE BEE
CHAPTER
"UNA APIS,

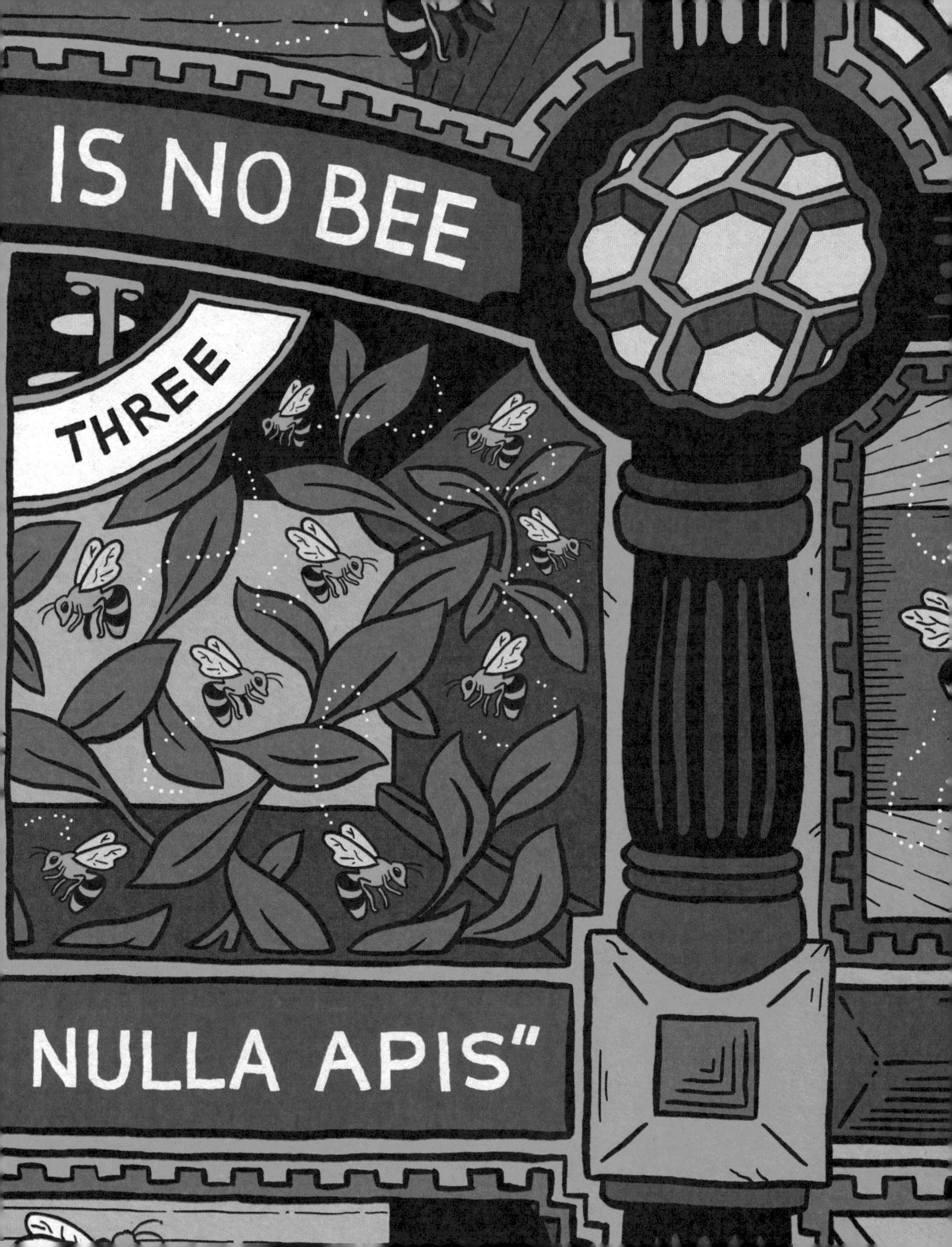
IS NO BEE
THREE
NULLA APIS"

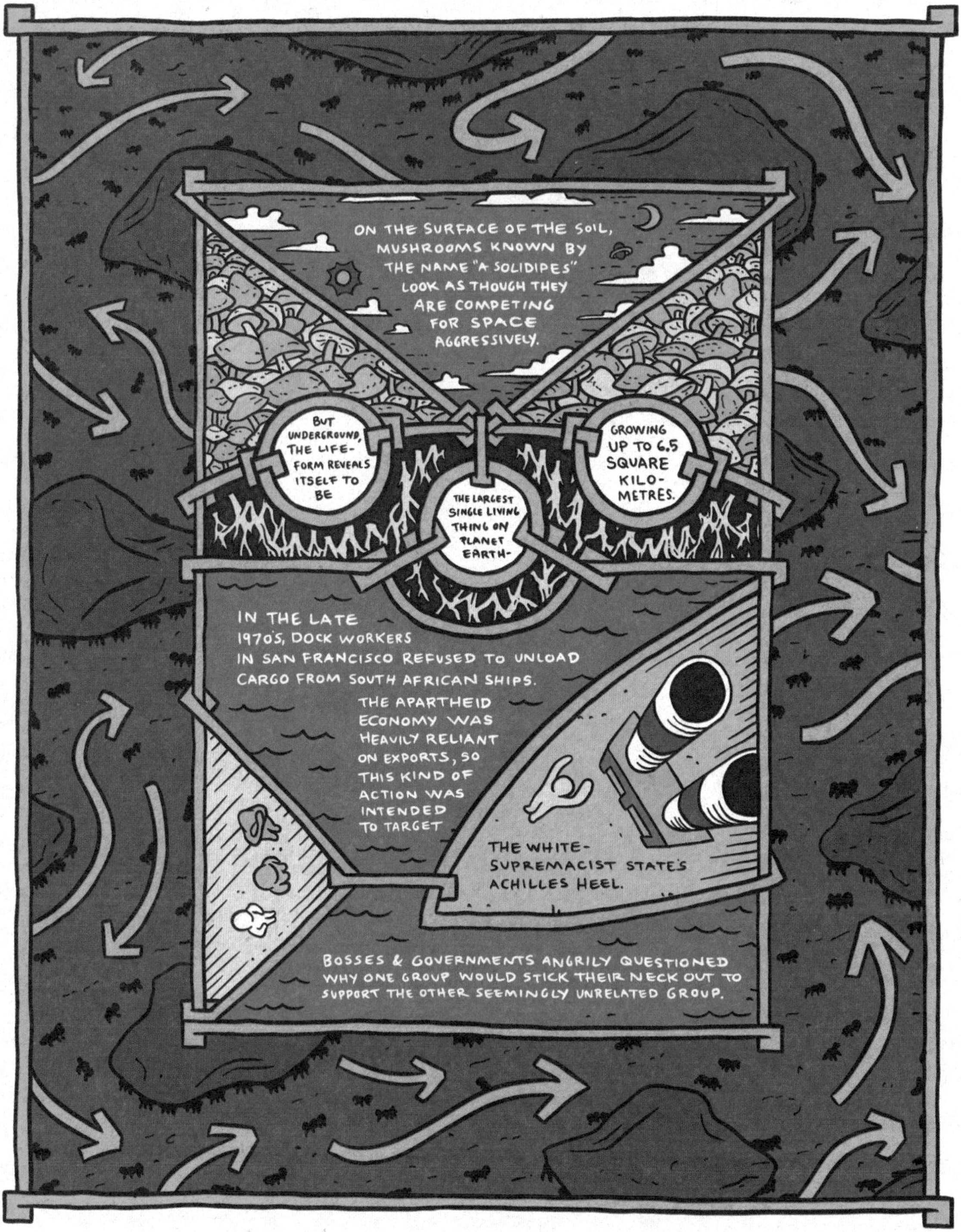
ON THE SURFACE OF THE SOIL, MUSHROOMS KNOWN BY THE NAME "A SOLIDIPES" LOOK AS THOUGH THEY ARE COMPETING FOR SPACE AGGRESSIVELY.
BUT UNDERGROUND, THE LIFE-FORM REVEALS ITSELF TO BE
THE LARGEST SINGLE LIVING THING ON PLANET EARTH-
GROWING UP TO 6.5 SQUARE KILO-METRES.
IN THE LATE 1970'S, DOCK WORKERS IN SAN FRANCISCO REFUSED TO UNLOAD CARGO FROM SOUTH AFRICAN SHIPS.
THE APARTHEID ECONOMY WAS HEAVILY RELIANT ON EXPORTS, SO THIS KIND OF ACTION WAS INTENDED TO TARGET
THE WHITE-SUPREMACIST STATE'S ACHILLES HEEL.
BOSSES & GOVERNMENTS ANGRILY QUESTIONED WHY ONE GROUP WOULD STICK THEIR NECK OUT TO SUPPORT THE OTHER SEEMINGLY UNRELATED GROUP.

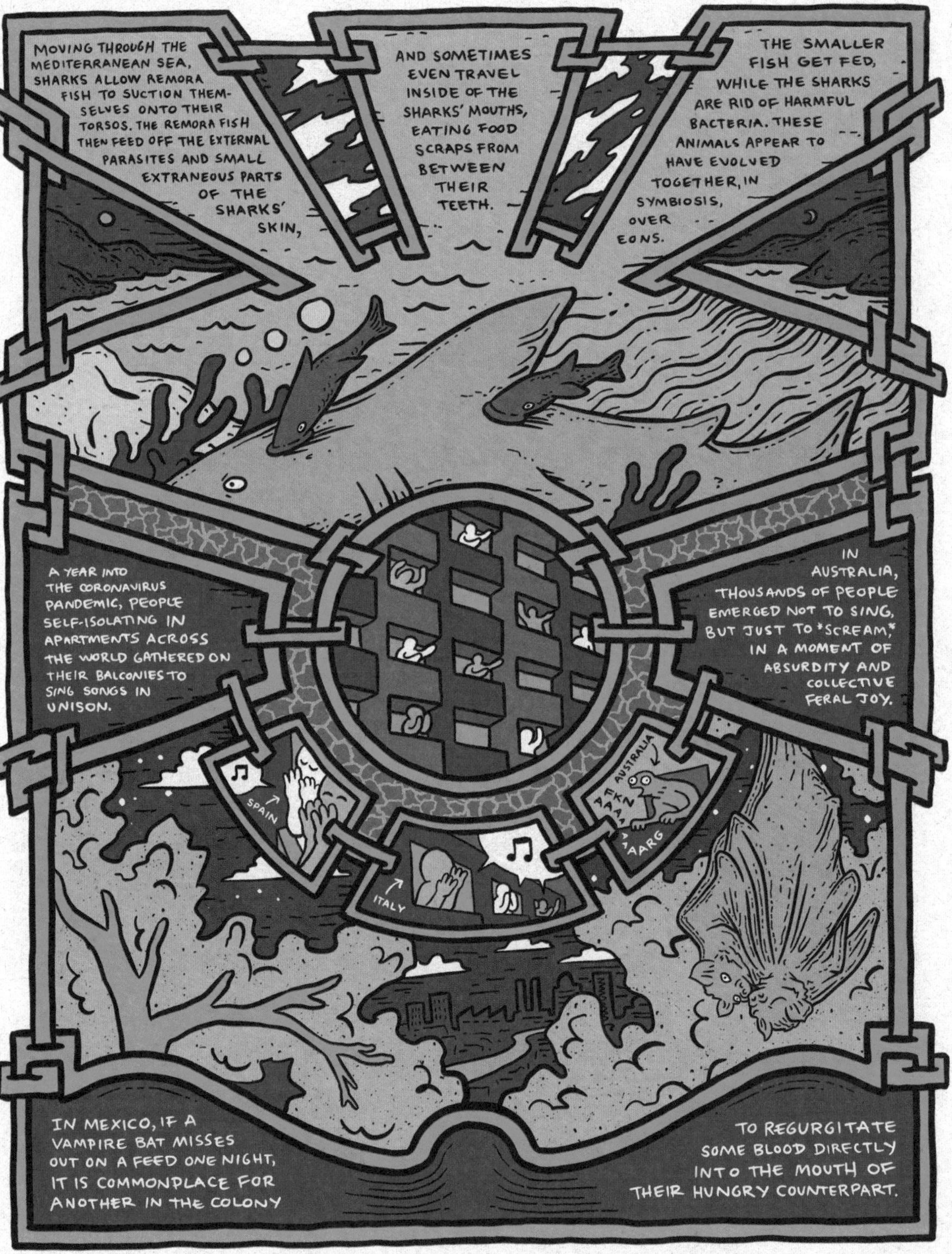
MOVING THROUGH THE MEDITERRANEAN SEA, SHARKS ALLOW REMORA FISH TO SUCTION THEMSELVES ONTO THEIR TORSOS. THE REMORA FISH THEN FEED OFF THE EXTERNAL PARASITES AND SMALL EXTRANEOUS PARTS OF THE SHARKS' SKIN,
AND SOMETIMES EVEN TRAVEL INSIDE OF THE SHARKS' MOUTHS, EATING FOOD SCRAPS FROM BETWEEN THEIR TEETH.
THE SMALLER FISH GET FED, WHILE THE SHARKS ARE RID OF HARMFUL BACTERIA. THESE ANIMALS APPEAR TO HAVE EVOLVED TOGETHER, IN SYMBIOSIS, OVER EONS.
A YEAR INTO THE CORONAVIRUS PANDEMIC, PEOPLE SELF-ISOLATING IN APARTMENTS ACROSS THE WORLD GATHERED ON THEIR BALCONIES TO SING SONGS IN UNISON.
SPAIN
ITALY
AUSTRALIA
FKN AAAA AAARG
IN AUSTRALIA, THOUSANDS OF PEOPLE EMERGED NOT TO SING, BUT JUST TO *SCREAM,* IN A MOMENT OF ABSURDITY AND COLLECTIVE FERAL JOY.
IN MEXICO, IF A VAMPIRE BAT MISSES OUT ON A FEED ONE NIGHT, IT IS COMMONPLACE FOR ANOTHER IN THE COLONY
TO REGURGITATE SOME BLOOD DIRECTLY INTO THE MOUTH OF THEIR HUNGRY COUNTERPART.

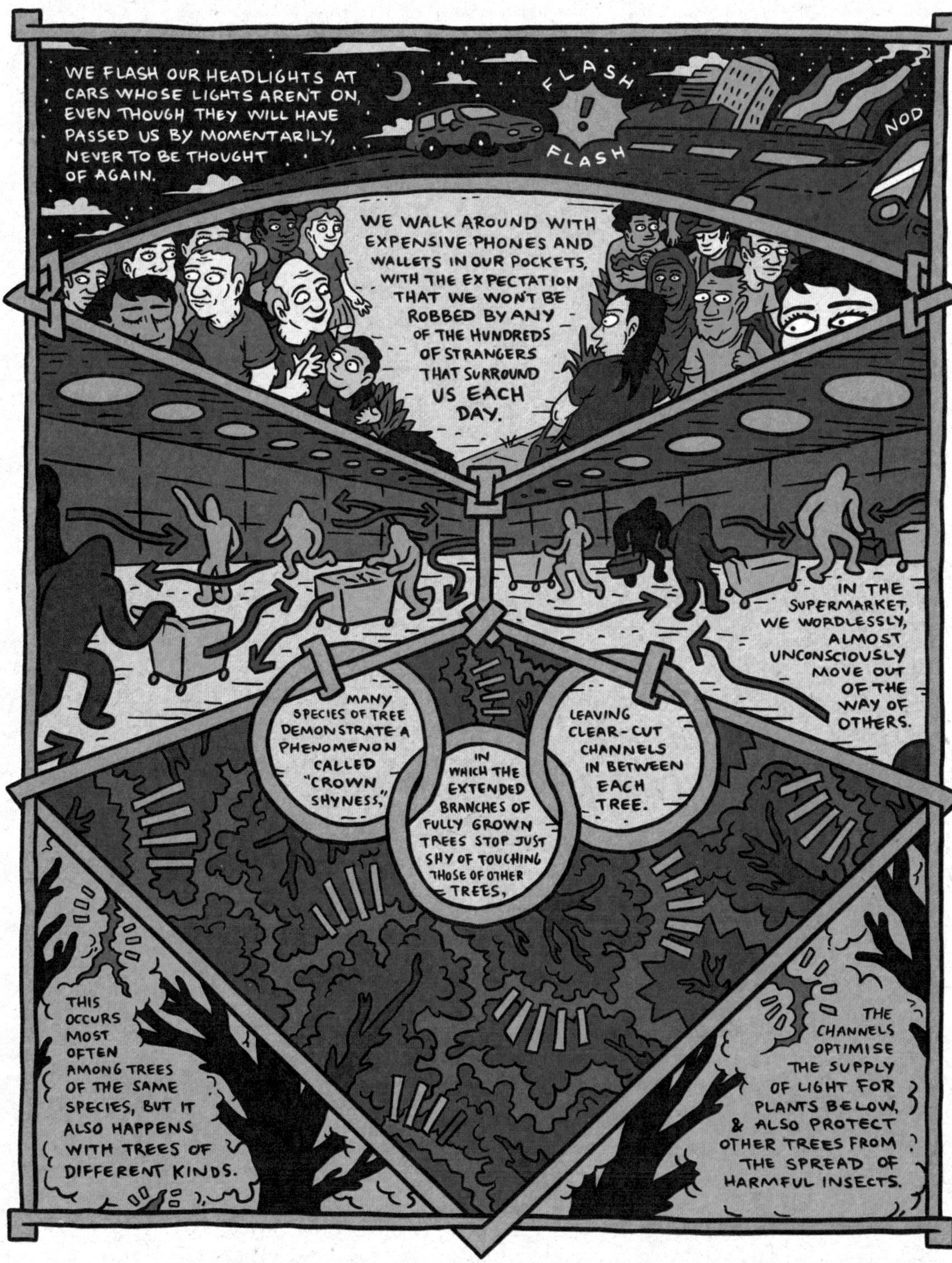

WE FLASH OUR HEADLIGHTS AT CARS WHOSE LIGHTS AREN'T ON, EVEN THOUGH THEY WILL HAVE PASSED US BY MOMENTARILY, NEVER TO BE THOUGHT OF AGAIN.
FLASH
!
FLASH
NOD
WE WALK AROUND WITH EXPENSIVE PHONES AND WALLETS IN OUR POCKETS, WITH THE EXPECTATION THAT WE WON'T BE ROBBED BY ANY OF THE HUNDREDS OF STRANGERS THAT SURROUND US EACH DAY.
IN THE SUPERMARKET, WE WORDLESSLY, ALMOST UNCONSCIOUSLY MOVE OUT OF THE WAY OF OTHERS.
MANY SPECIES OF TREE DEMONSTRATE A PHENOMENON CALLED "CROWN SHYNESS,"
IN WHICH THE EXTENDED BRANCHES OF FULLY GROWN TREES STOP JUST SHY OF TOUCHING THOSE OF OTHER TREES,
LEAVING CLEAR-CUT CHANNELS IN BETWEEN EACH TREE.
THIS OCCURS MOST OFTEN AMONG TREES OF THE SAME SPECIES, BUT IT ALSO HAPPENS WITH TREES OF DIFFERENT KINDS.
THE CHANNELS OPTIMISE THE SUPPLY OF LIGHT FOR PLANTS BELOW, & ALSO PROTECT OTHER TREES FROM THE SPREAD OF HARMFUL INSECTS.

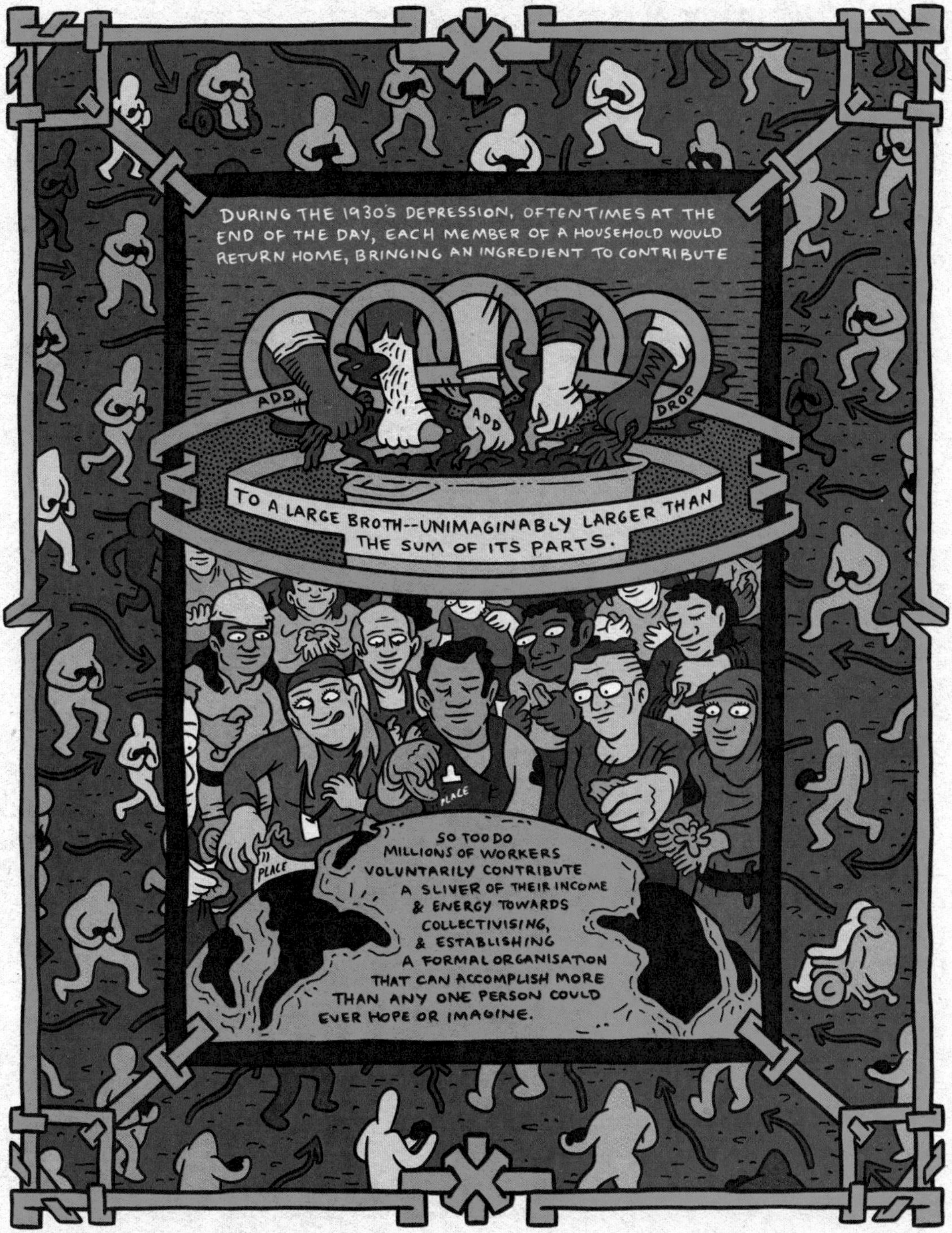
DURING THE 1930'S DEPRESSION, OFTENTIMES AT THE END OF THE DAY, EACH MEMBER OF A HOUSEHOLD WOULD RETURN HOME, BRINGING AN INGREDIENT TO CONTRIBUTE
ADD
ADD
DROP
TO A LARGE BROTH--UNIMAGINABLY LARGER THAN THE SUM OF ITS PARTS.
PLACE
PLACE
SO TOO DO MILLIONS OF WORKERS VOLUNTARILY CONTRIBUTE A SLIVER OF THEIR INCOME & ENERGY TOWARDS COLLECTIVISING, & ESTABLISHING A FORMAL ORGANISATION THAT CAN ACCOMPLISH MORE THAN ANY ONE PERSON COULD EVER HOPE OR IMAGINE.

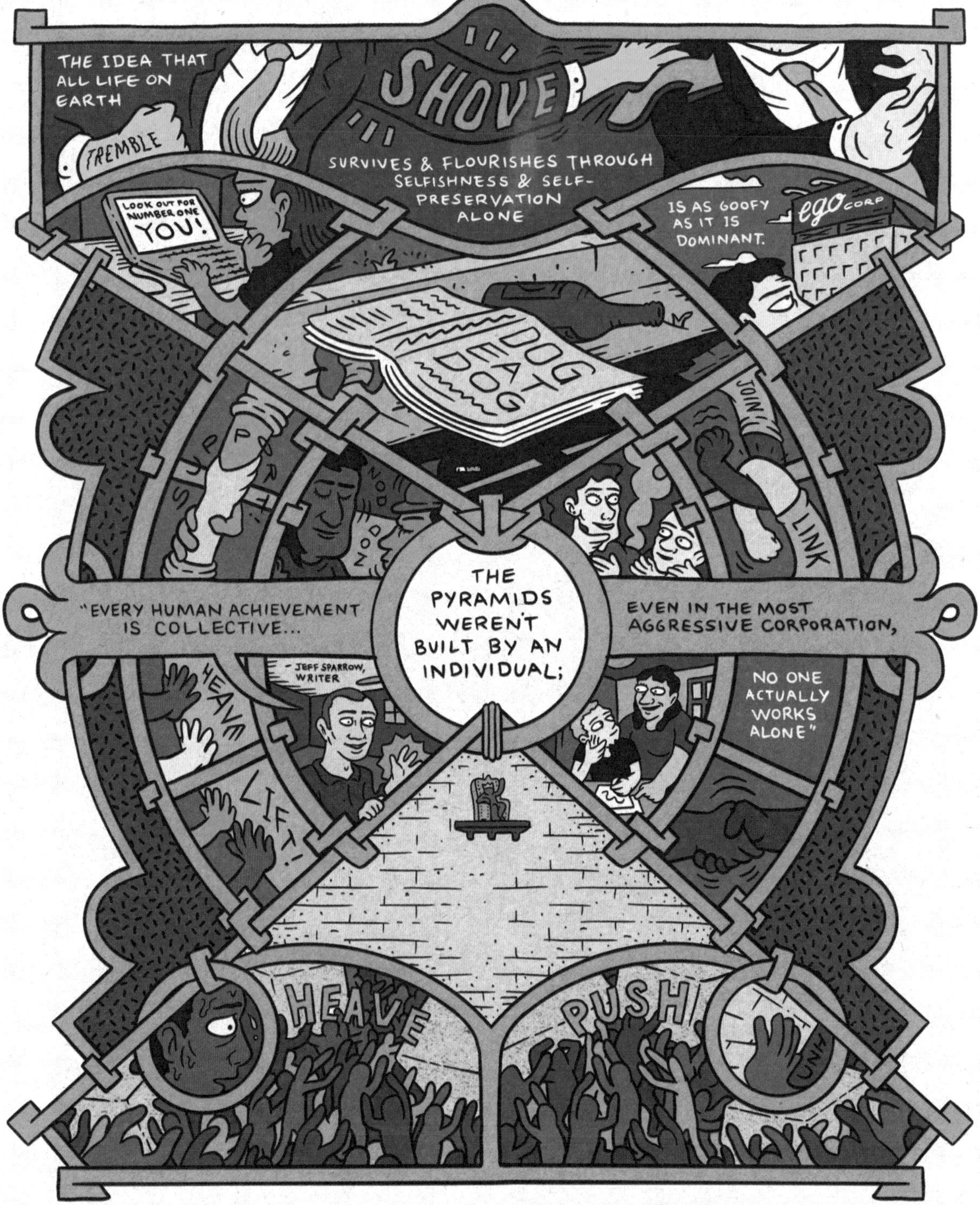

THE IDEA THAT ALL LIFE ON EARTH
TREMBLE
SHOVE
SURVIVES & FLOURISHES THROUGH SELFISHNESS & SELF-PRESERVATION ALONE
LOOK OUT FOR NUMBER ONE YOU!
IS AS GOOFY AS IT IS DOMINANT.
ego CORP
DOG EAT DOG
SUPPORT
NOD
JOIN
LINK
"EVERY HUMAN ACHIEVEMENT IS COLLECTIVE...
- JEFF SPARROW, WRITER
THE PYRAMIDS WEREN'T BUILT BY AN INDIVIDUAL;
EVEN IN THE MOST AGGRESSIVE CORPORATION,
NO ONE ACTUALLY WORKS ALONE"
HEAVE
LIFT
HEAVE
PUSH
UNITE

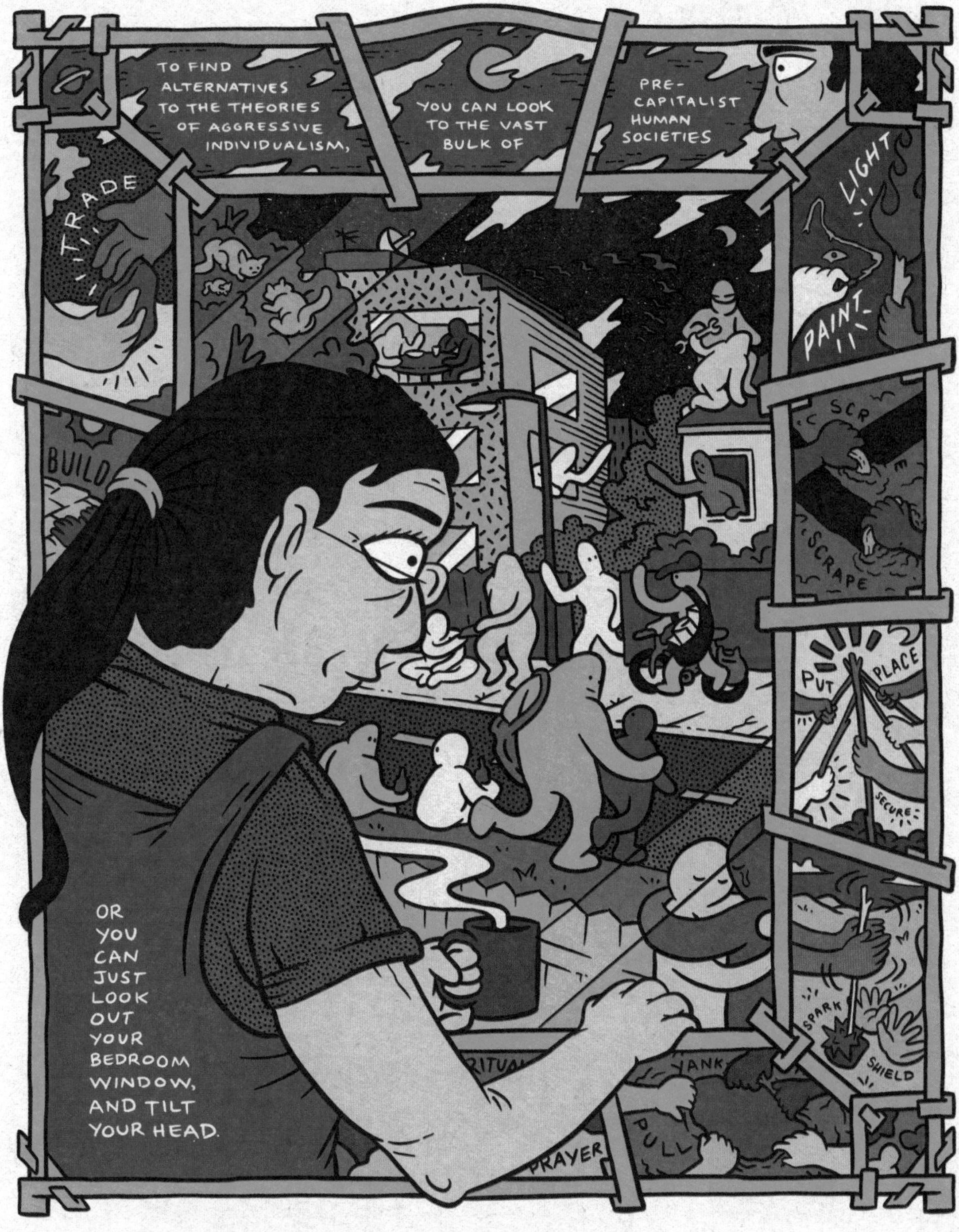

TO FIND ALTERNATIVES TO THE THEORIES OF AGGRESSIVE INDIVIDUALISM,
YOU CAN LOOK TO THE VAST BULK OF
PRE-CAPITALIST HUMAN SOCIETIES
TRADE
LIGHT
PAINT
BUILD
SCR
SCRAPE
PUT
PLACE
SECURE
SPARK
SHIELD
YANK
PULL
PRAYER
OR YOU CAN JUST LOOK OUT YOUR BEDROOM WINDOW, AND TILT YOUR HEAD.

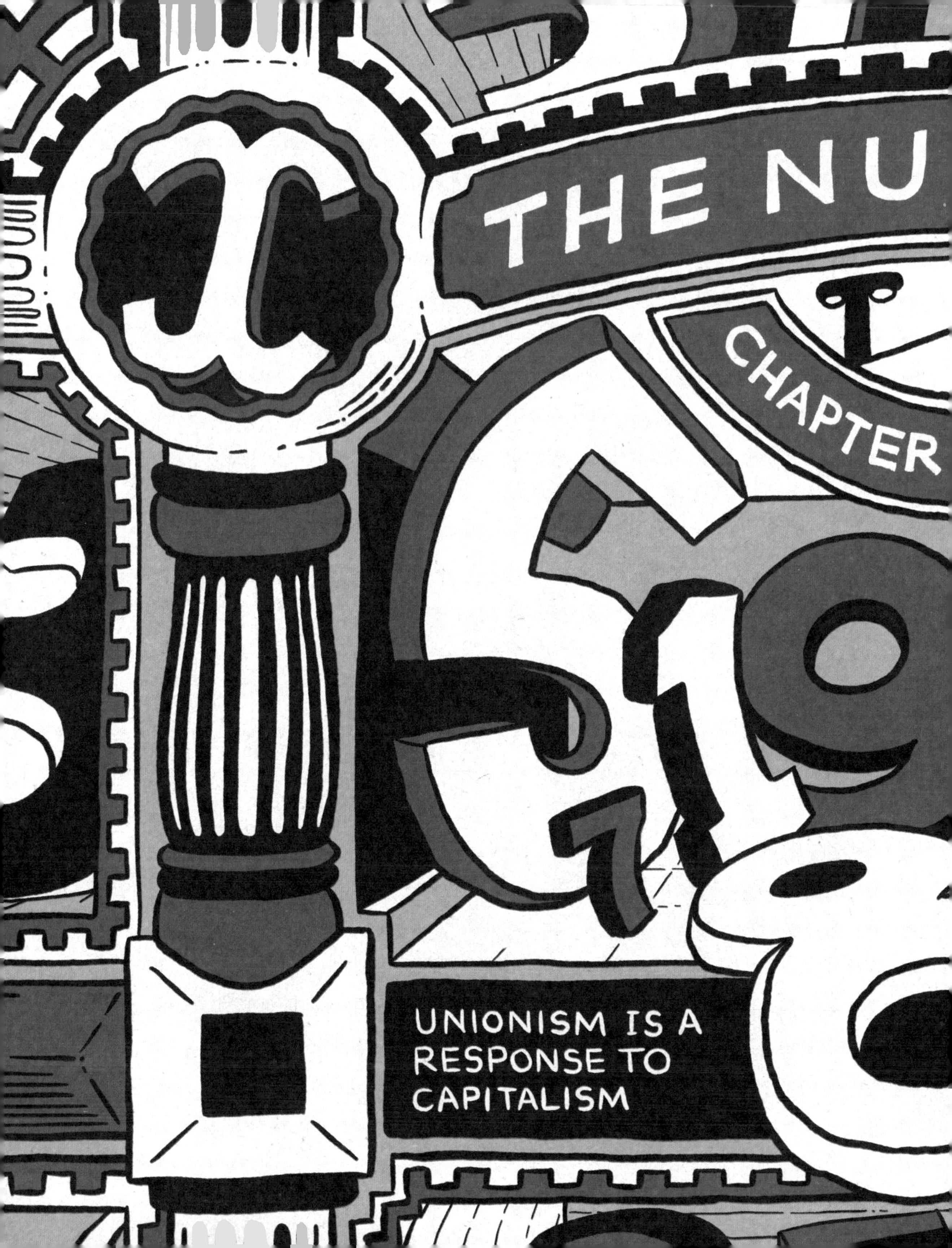
THE NU
CHAPTER
UNIONISM IS A
RESPONSE TO
CAPITALISM

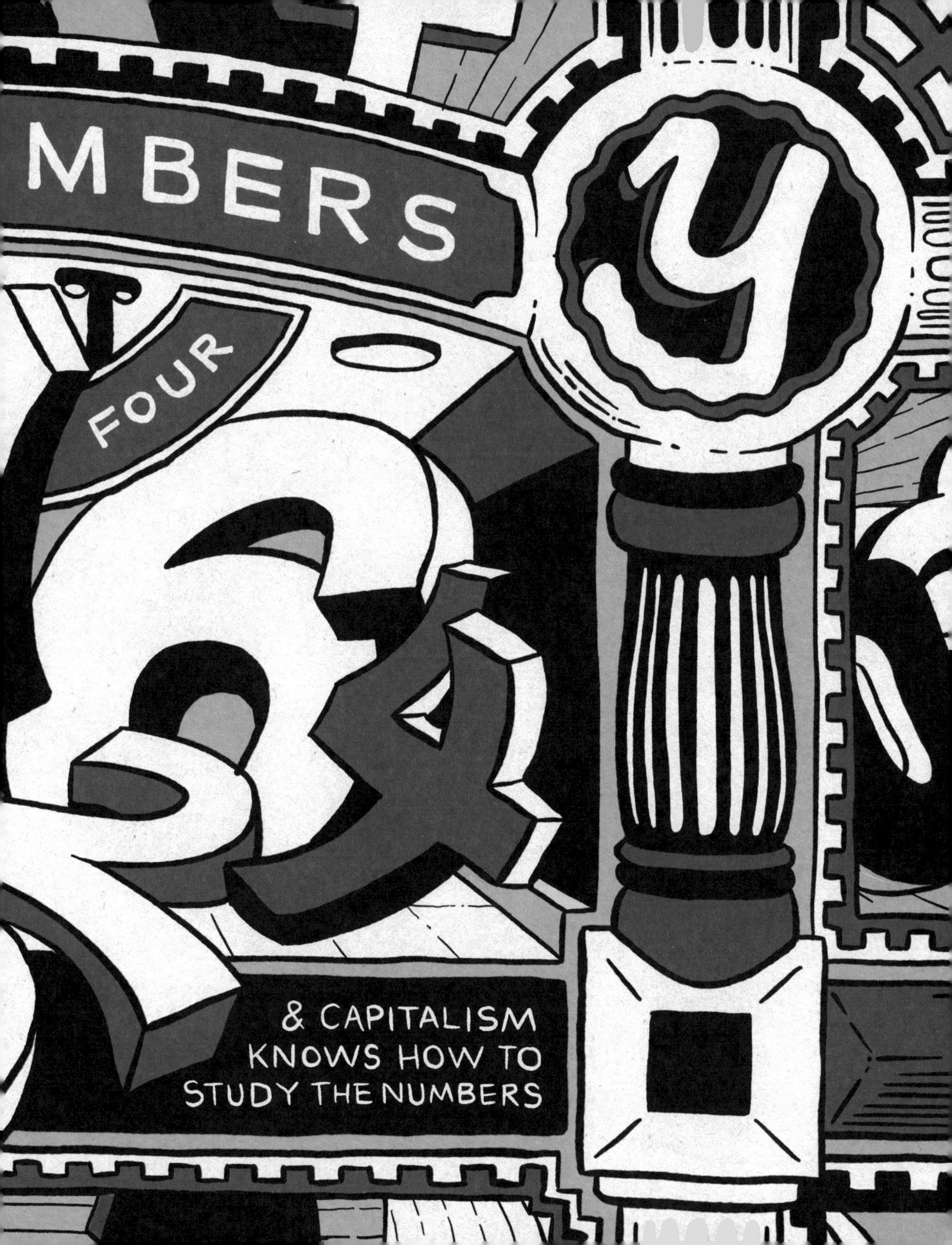
MBERS
FOUR
& CAPITALISM
KNOWS HOW TO
STUDY THE NUMBERS

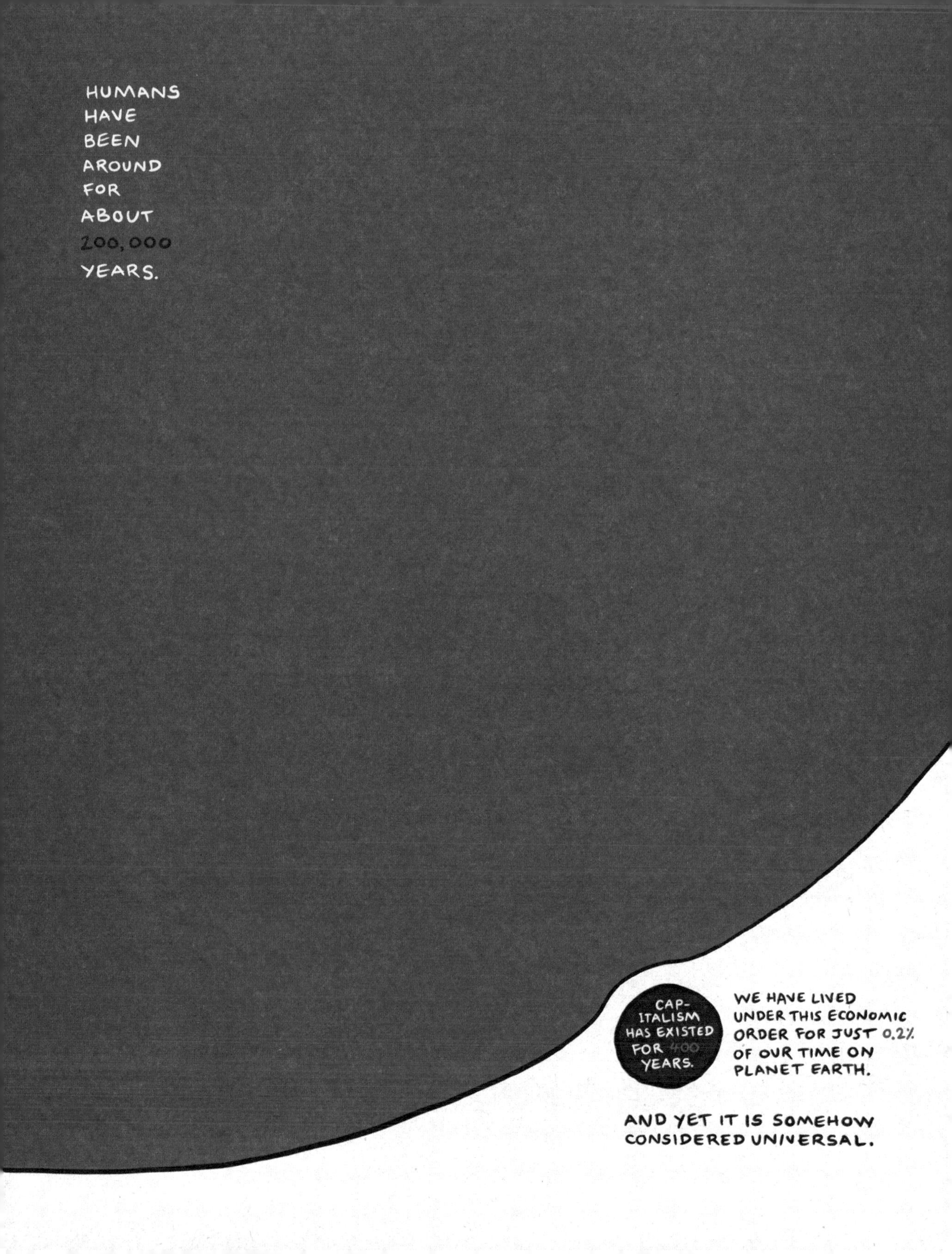
HUMANS HAVE BEEN AROUND FOR ABOUT 200,000 YEARS.
CAP-ITALISM HAS EXISTED FOR 400 YEARS.
WE HAVE LIVED UNDER THIS ECONOMIC ORDER FOR JUST 0.2% OF OUR TIME ON PLANET EARTH.
AND YET IT IS SOMEHOW CONSIDERED UNIVERSAL.

THE 1760's-1840's SAW PEOPLE SCRAPED
OFF THE LAND, OUT OF THEIR HOMES & SMALL
COMMUNITIES AND INTO THE CITIES, WHERE
MACHINERY, INDUSTRIALISATION, & URBAN
SQUALOR BECAME THE NEW NORM IN JUST
A FEW SHORT
YEARS.

IT'S HARD TO
OVERSTATE
THE SIGNIFICANCE
OF THIS SHIFT.

(THIS HISTORICAL
TURN REACHED
ONE MILESTONE
IN 2014, WHEN
OVER 50% OF
HUMANS CAME
TO LIVE IN CITIES,
RATHER THAN
MORE EARTH-
BASED SYSTEMS,
RURAL AREAS OR
SMALL TOWNS.)

WITH THE TURN
OF THE INDUSTRIAL
REVOLUTION, THE
SKILLED, HIGHLY
DEVELOPED CRAFT
OF MANY WORKERS
WAS NOW CARRIED
OUT BY MACHINES.

AUTOMATION
IS NO NEW
PHENOMENON.

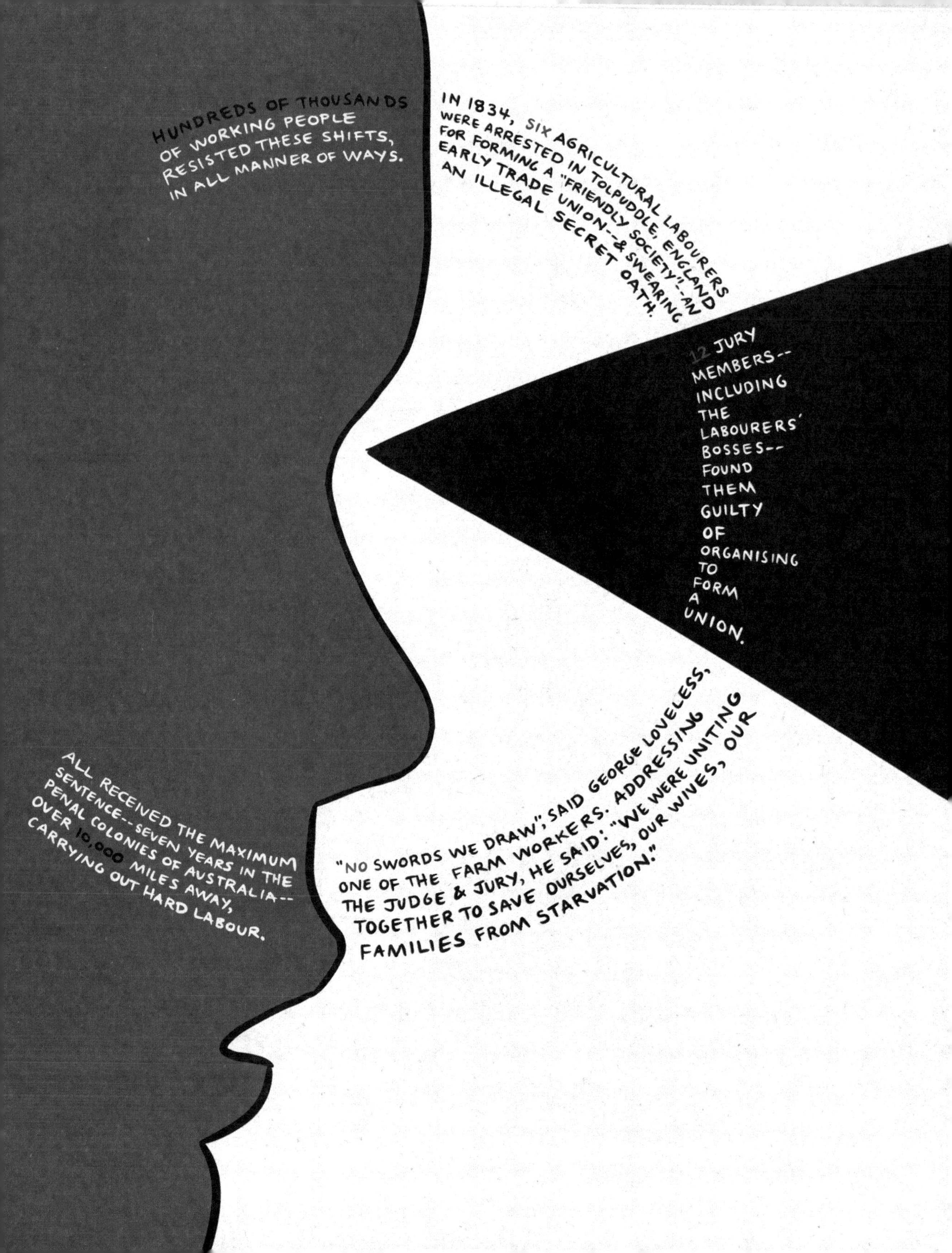
HUNDREDS OF THOUSANDS OF WORKING PEOPLE RESISTED THESE SHIFTS, IN ALL MANNER OF WAYS.
IN 1834, SIX AGRICULTURAL LABOURERS WERE ARRESTED IN TOLPUDDLE, ENGLAND FOR FORMING A "FRIENDLY SOCIETY"--AN EARLY TRADE UNION--& SWEARING AN ILLEGAL SECRET OATH.
12 JURY MEMBERS--INCLUDING THE LABOURERS' BOSSES--FOUND THEM GUILTY OF ORGANISING TO FORM A UNION.
ALL RECEIVED THE MAXIMUM SENTENCE--SEVEN YEARS IN THE PENAL COLONIES OF AUSTRALIA--OVER 10,000 MILES AWAY, CARRYING OUT HARD LABOUR.
"NO SWORDS WE DRAW," SAID GEORGE LOVELESS, ONE OF THE FARM WORKERS. ADDRESSING THE JUDGE & JURY, HE SAID: "WE WERE UNITING TOGETHER TO SAVE OURSELVES, OUR WIVES, OUR FAMILIES FROM STARVATION."

BACK IN ENGLAND, AN ASSEMBLY OF 100,000 CAME TOGETHER TO OPPOSE THE TOLPUDDLE MARTYRS' PERSECUTION.

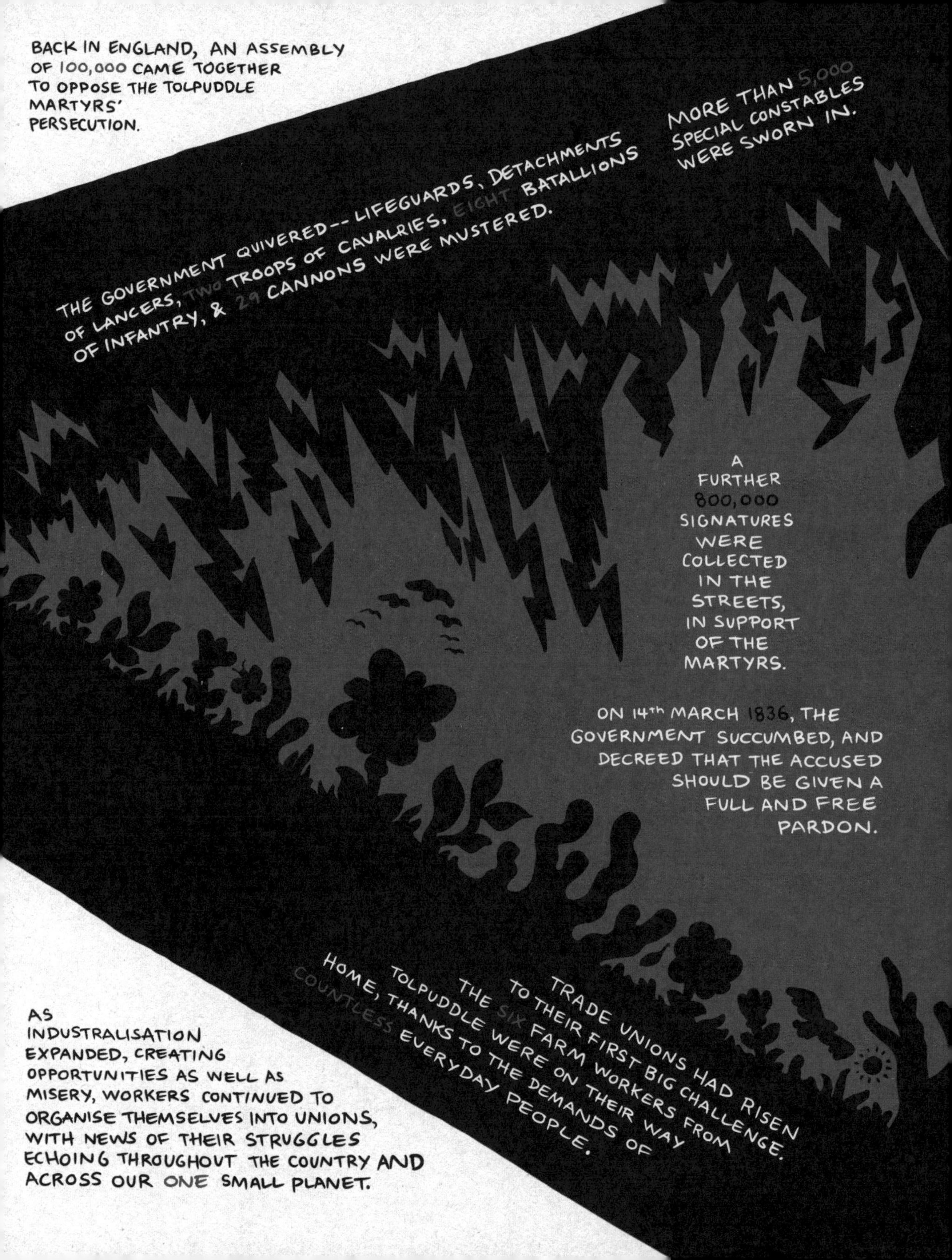
THE GOVERNMENT QUIVERED-- LIFEGUARDS, DETACHMENTS OF LANCERS, TWO TROOPS OF CAVALRIES, EIGHT BATALLIONS OF INFANTRY, & 29 CANNONS WERE MUSTERED.
MORE THAN 5,000 SPECIAL CONSTABLES WERE SWORN IN.
A FURTHER 800,000 SIGNATURES WERE COLLECTED IN THE STREETS, IN SUPPORT OF THE MARTYRS.
ON 14th MARCH 1836, THE GOVERNMENT SUCCUMBED, AND DECREED THAT THE ACCUSED SHOULD BE GIVEN A FULL AND FREE PARDON.
TRADE UNIONS HAD RISEN TO THEIR FIRST BIG CHALLENGE. THE SIX FARM WORKERS FROM TOLPUDDLE WERE ON THEIR WAY HOME, THANKS TO THE DEMANDS OF COUNTLESS EVERYDAY PEOPLE.

AS INDUSTRALISATION EXPANDED, CREATING OPPORTUNITIES AS WELL AS MISERY, WORKERS CONTINUED TO ORGANISE THEMSELVES INTO UNIONS, WITH NEWS OF THEIR STRUGGLES ECHOING THROUGHOUT THE COUNTRY AND ACROSS OUR ONE SMALL PLANET.

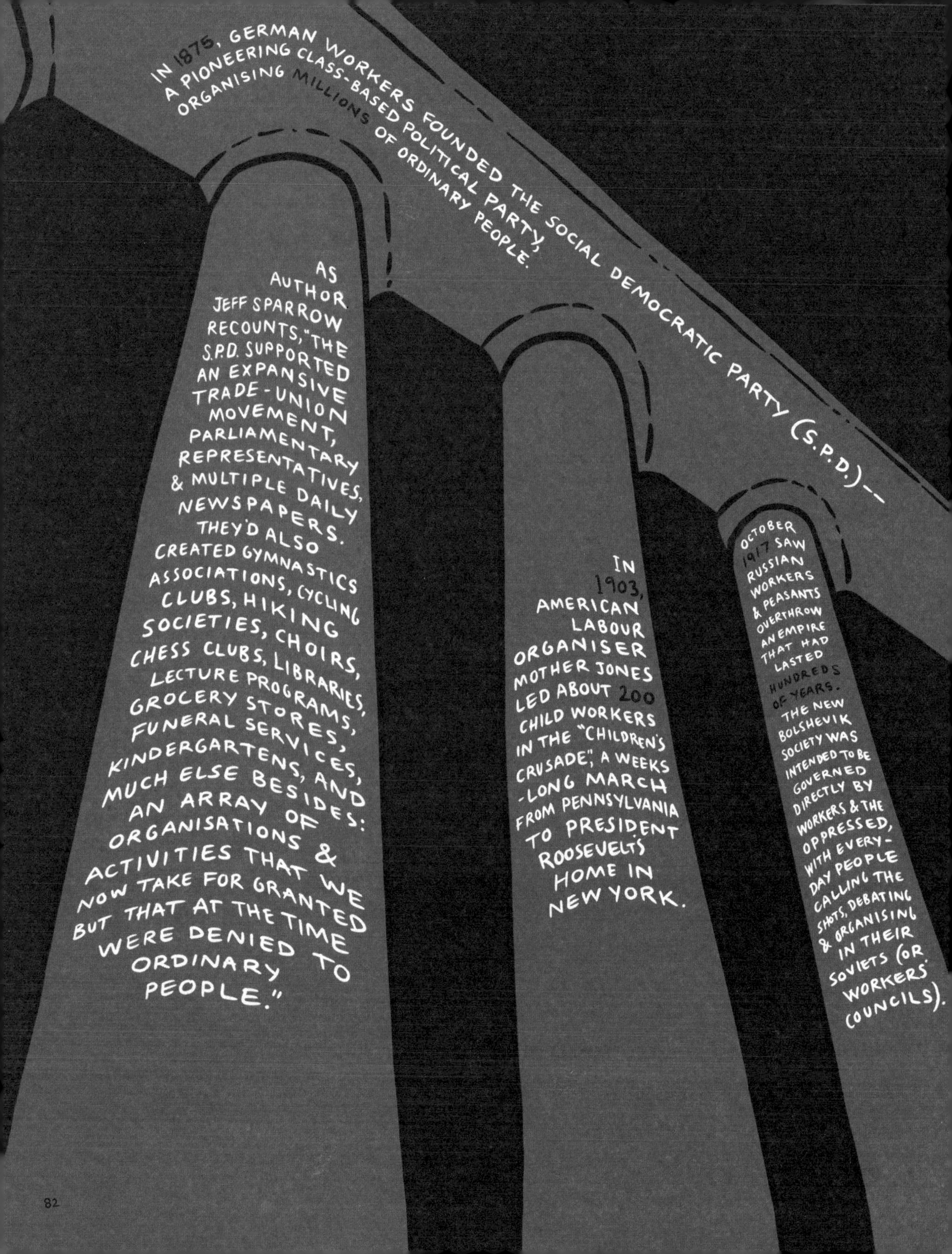
IN 1875, GERMAN WORKERS FOUNDED THE SOCIAL DEMOCRATIC PARTY (S.P.D.)--
A PIONEERING CLASS-BASED POLITICAL PARTY,
ORGANISING MILLIONS OF ORDINARY PEOPLE.
AS AUTHOR JEFF SPARROW RECOUNTS, "THE S.P.D. SUPPORTED AN EXPANSIVE TRADE-UNION MOVEMENT, PARLIAMENTARY REPRESENTATIVES, & MULTIPLE DAILY NEWSPAPERS. THEY'D ALSO CREATED GYMNASTICS ASSOCIATIONS, CYCLING CLUBS, HIKING SOCIETIES, CHOIRS, CHESS CLUBS, LIBRARIES, LECTURE PROGRAMS, GROCERY STORES, FUNERAL SERVICES, KINDERGARTENS, AND MUCH ELSE BESIDES: AN ARRAY OF ORGANISATIONS & ACTIVITIES THAT WE NOW TAKE FOR GRANTED BUT THAT AT THE TIME WERE DENIED TO ORDINARY PEOPLE."
IN 1903, AMERICAN LABOUR ORGANISER MOTHER JONES LED ABOUT 200 CHILD WORKERS IN THE "CHILDREN'S CRUSADE", A WEEKS-LONG MARCH FROM PENNSYLVANIA TO PRESIDENT ROOSEVELT'S HOME IN NEW YORK.
OCTOBER 1917 SAW RUSSIAN WORKERS & PEASANTS OVERTHROW AN EMPIRE THAT HAD LASTED HUNDREDS OF YEARS. THE NEW BOLSHEVIK SOCIETY WAS INTENDED TO BE GOVERNED DIRECTLY BY WORKERS & THE OPPRESSED, WITH EVERY-DAY PEOPLE CALLING THE SHOTS, DEBATING & ORGANISING IN THEIR SOVIETS (OR WORKERS' COUNCILS).

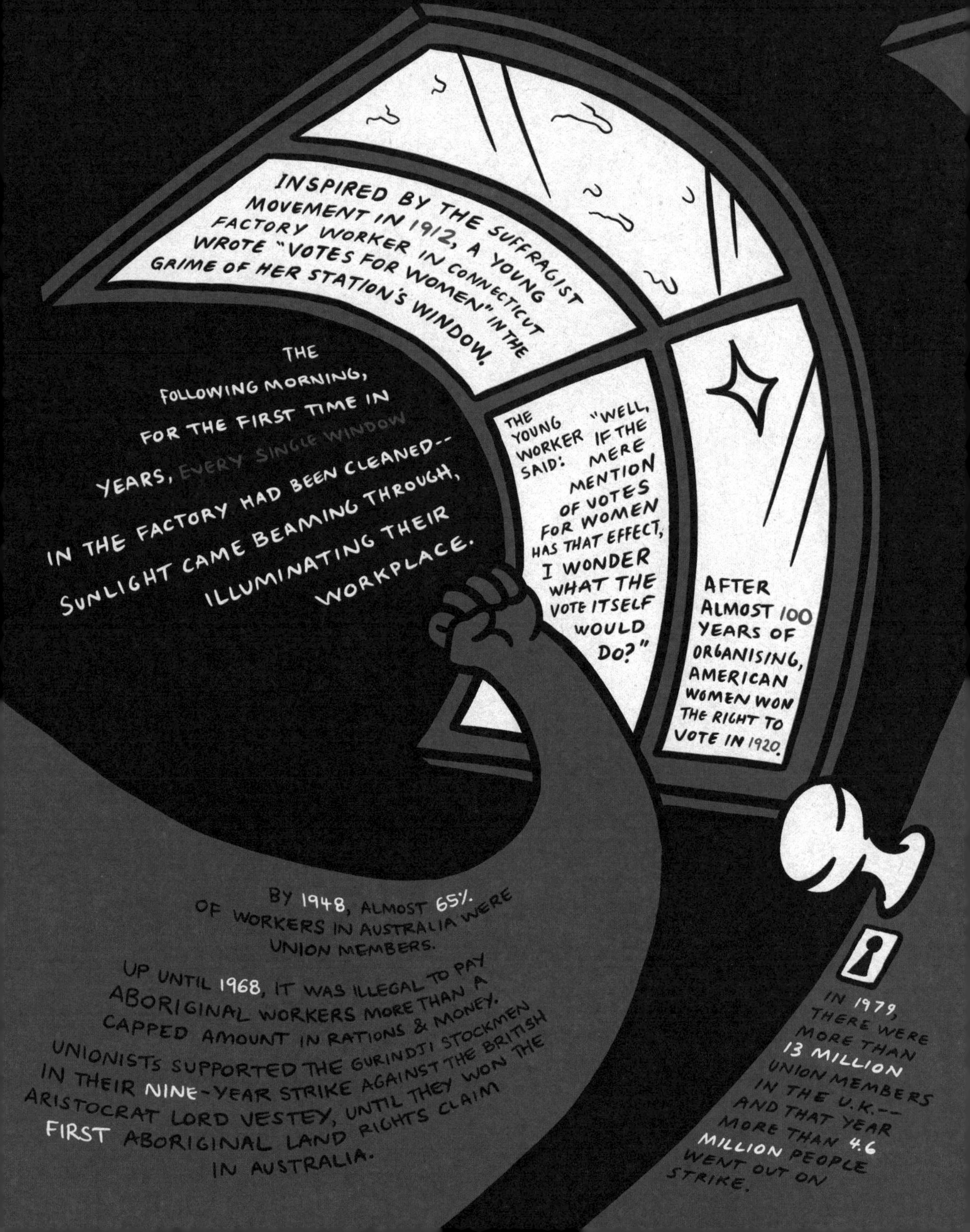

INSPIRED BY THE SUFFRAGIST MOVEMENT IN 1912, A YOUNG FACTORY WORKER IN CONNECTICUT WROTE "VOTES FOR WOMEN" IN THE GRIME OF HER STATION'S WINDOW.
THE FOLLOWING MORNING, FOR THE FIRST TIME IN YEARS, EVERY SINGLE WINDOW IN THE FACTORY HAD BEEN CLEANED-- SUNLIGHT CAME BEAMING THROUGH, ILLUMINATING THEIR WORKPLACE.
THE YOUNG WORKER SAID: "WELL, IF THE MERE MENTION OF VOTES FOR WOMEN HAS THAT EFFECT, I WONDER WHAT THE VOTE ITSELF WOULD DO?"
AFTER ALMOST 100 YEARS OF ORGANISING, AMERICAN WOMEN WON THE RIGHT TO VOTE IN 1920.
BY 1948, ALMOST 65% OF WORKERS IN AUSTRALIA WERE UNION MEMBERS.
UP UNTIL 1968, IT WAS ILLEGAL TO PAY ABORIGINAL WORKERS MORE THAN A CAPPED AMOUNT IN RATIONS & MONEY.
UNIONISTS SUPPORTED THE GURINDJI STOCKMEN IN THEIR NINE-YEAR STRIKE AGAINST THE BRITISH ARISTOCRAT LORD VESTEY, UNTIL THEY WON THE FIRST ABORIGINAL LAND RIGHTS CLAIM IN AUSTRALIA.
IN 1979, THERE WERE MORE THAN 13 MILLION UNION MEMBERS IN THE U.K.-- AND THAT YEAR MORE THAN 4.6 MILLION PEOPLE WENT OUT ON STRIKE.

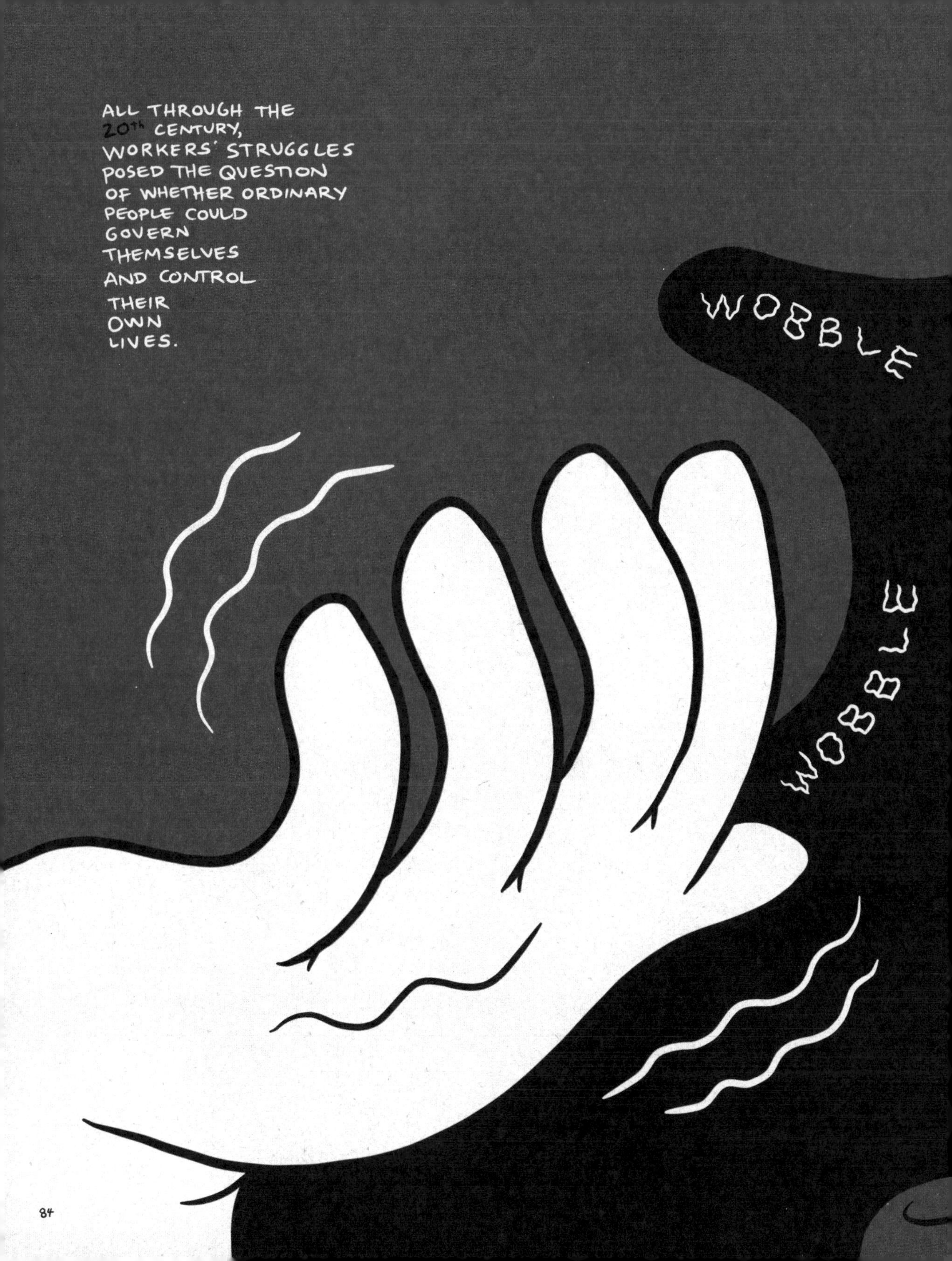
ALL THROUGH THE 20th CENTURY, WORKERS' STRUGGLES POSED THE QUESTION OF WHETHER ORDINARY PEOPLE COULD GOVERN THEMSELVES AND CONTROL THEIR OWN LIVES.
WOBBLE
WOBBLE

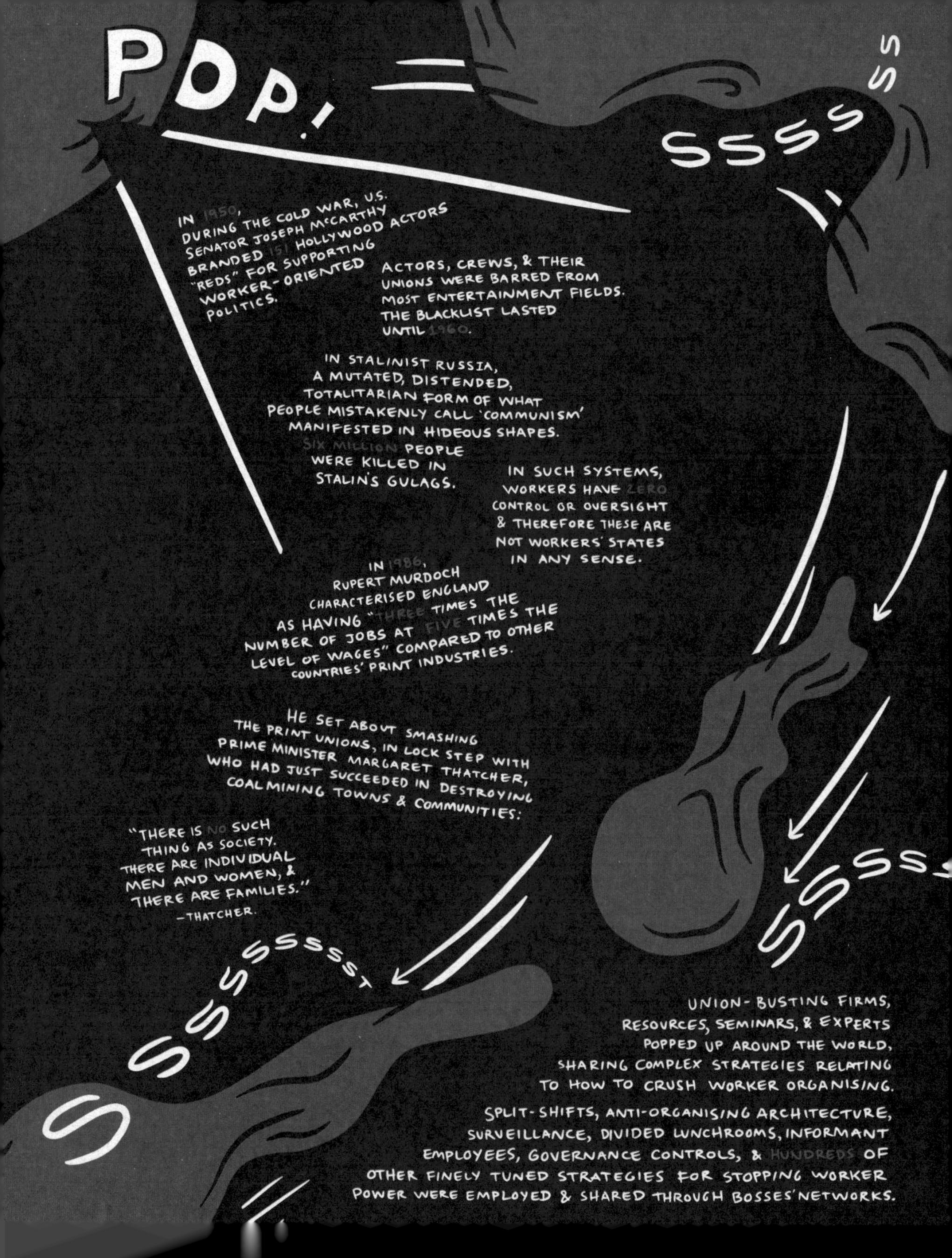
POP!
SSSSSSS
IN 1950, DURING THE COLD WAR, U.S. SENATOR JOSEPH McCARTHY BRANDED 151 HOLLYWOOD ACTORS "REDS" FOR SUPPORTING WORKER-ORIENTED POLITICS.
ACTORS, CREWS, & THEIR UNIONS WERE BARRED FROM MOST ENTERTAINMENT FIELDS. THE BLACKLIST LASTED UNTIL 1960.
IN STALINIST RUSSIA, A MUTATED, DISTENDED, TOTALITARIAN FORM OF WHAT PEOPLE MISTAKENLY CALL 'COMMUNISM' MANIFESTED IN HIDEOUS SHAPES. SIX MILLION PEOPLE WERE KILLED IN STALIN'S GULAGS.
IN SUCH SYSTEMS, WORKERS HAVE ZERO CONTROL OR OVERSIGHT & THEREFORE THESE ARE NOT WORKERS' STATES IN ANY SENSE.
IN 1986, RUPERT MURDOCH CHARACTERISED ENGLAND AS HAVING "THREE TIMES THE NUMBER OF JOBS AT FIVE TIMES THE LEVEL OF WAGES" COMPARED TO OTHER COUNTRIES' PRINT INDUSTRIES.
HE SET ABOUT SMASHING THE PRINT UNIONS, IN LOCK STEP WITH PRIME MINISTER MARGARET THATCHER, WHO HAD JUST SUCCEEDED IN DESTROYING COALMINING TOWNS & COMMUNITIES:
"THERE IS NO SUCH THING AS SOCIETY. THERE ARE INDIVIDUAL MEN AND WOMEN, & THERE ARE FAMILIES." —THATCHER.
SSSSSSSSST
SSSSS
SSSSS
UNION-BUSTING FIRMS, RESOURCES, SEMINARS, & EXPERTS POPPED UP AROUND THE WORLD, SHARING COMPLEX STRATEGIES RELATING TO HOW TO CRUSH WORKER ORGANISING.
SPLIT-SHIFTS, ANTI-ORGANISING ARCHITECTURE, SURVEILLANCE, DIVIDED LUNCHROOMS, INFORMANT EMPLOYEES, GOVERNANCE CONTROLS, & HUNDREDS OF OTHER FINELY TUNED STRATEGIES FOR STOPPING WORKER POWER WERE EMPLOYED & SHARED THROUGH BOSSES' NETWORKS.

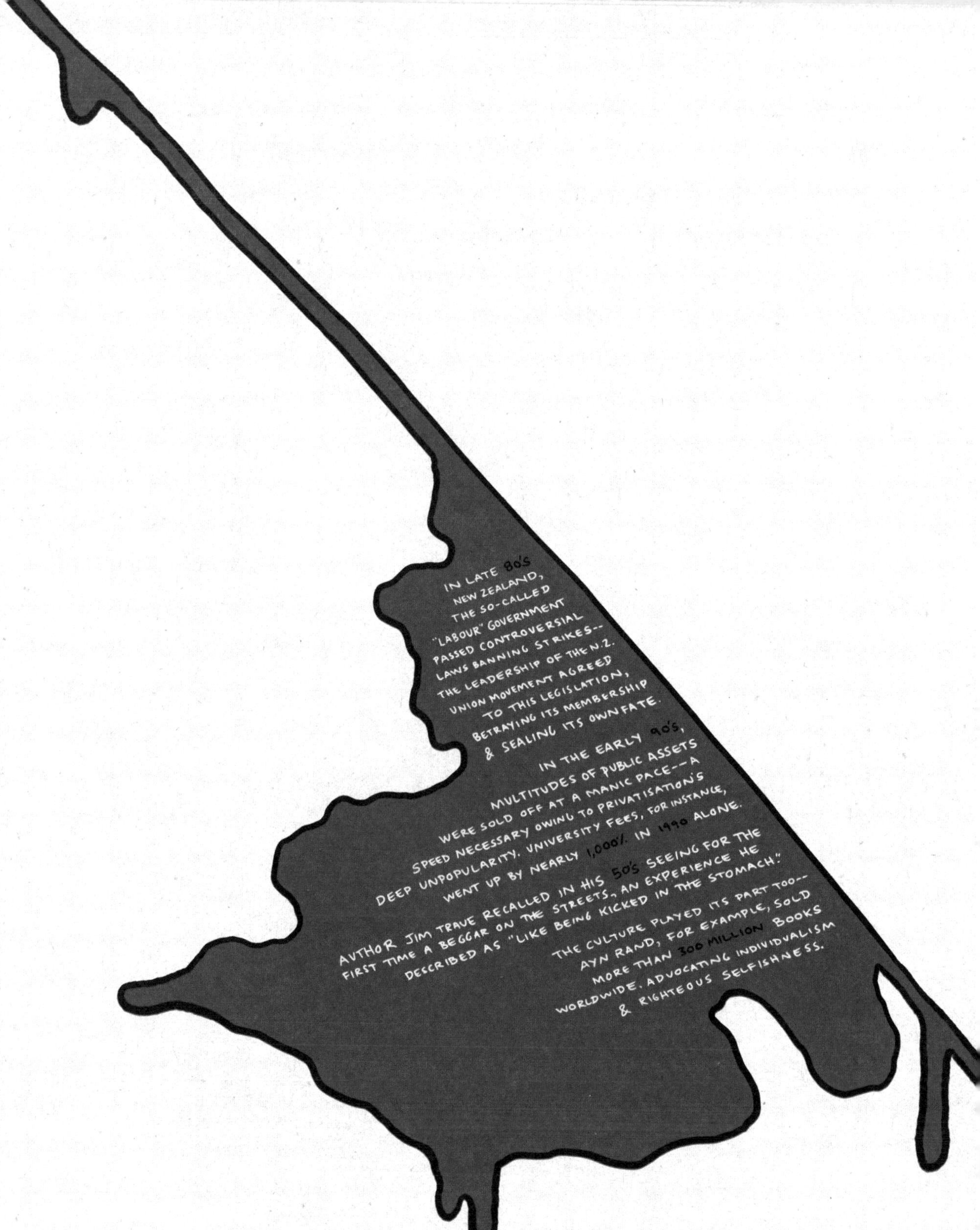
IN LATE 80'S NEW ZEALAND, THE SO-CALLED "LABOUR" GOVERNMENT PASSED CONTROVERSIAL LAWS BANNING STRIKES-- THE LEADERSHIP OF THE N.Z. UNION MOVEMENT AGREED TO THIS LEGISLATION, BETRAYING ITS MEMBERSHIP & SEALING ITS OWN FATE.
IN THE EARLY 90'S, MULTITUDES OF PUBLIC ASSETS WERE SOLD OFF AT A MANIC PACE--A SPEED NECESSARY OWING TO PRIVATISATION'S DEEP UNPOPULARITY. UNIVERSITY FEES, FOR INSTANCE, WENT UP BY NEARLY 1,000% IN 1990 ALONE.
AUTHOR JIM TRAVE RECALLED IN HIS 50'S SEEING FOR THE FIRST TIME A BEGGAR ON THE STREETS, AN EXPERIENCE HE DESCRIBED AS "LIKE BEING KICKED IN THE STOMACH."
THE CULTURE PLAYED ITS PART TOO-- AYN RAND, FOR EXAMPLE, SOLD MORE THAN 300 MILLION BOOKS WORLDWIDE, ADVOCATING INDIVIDUALISM & RIGHTEOUS SELFISHNESS.

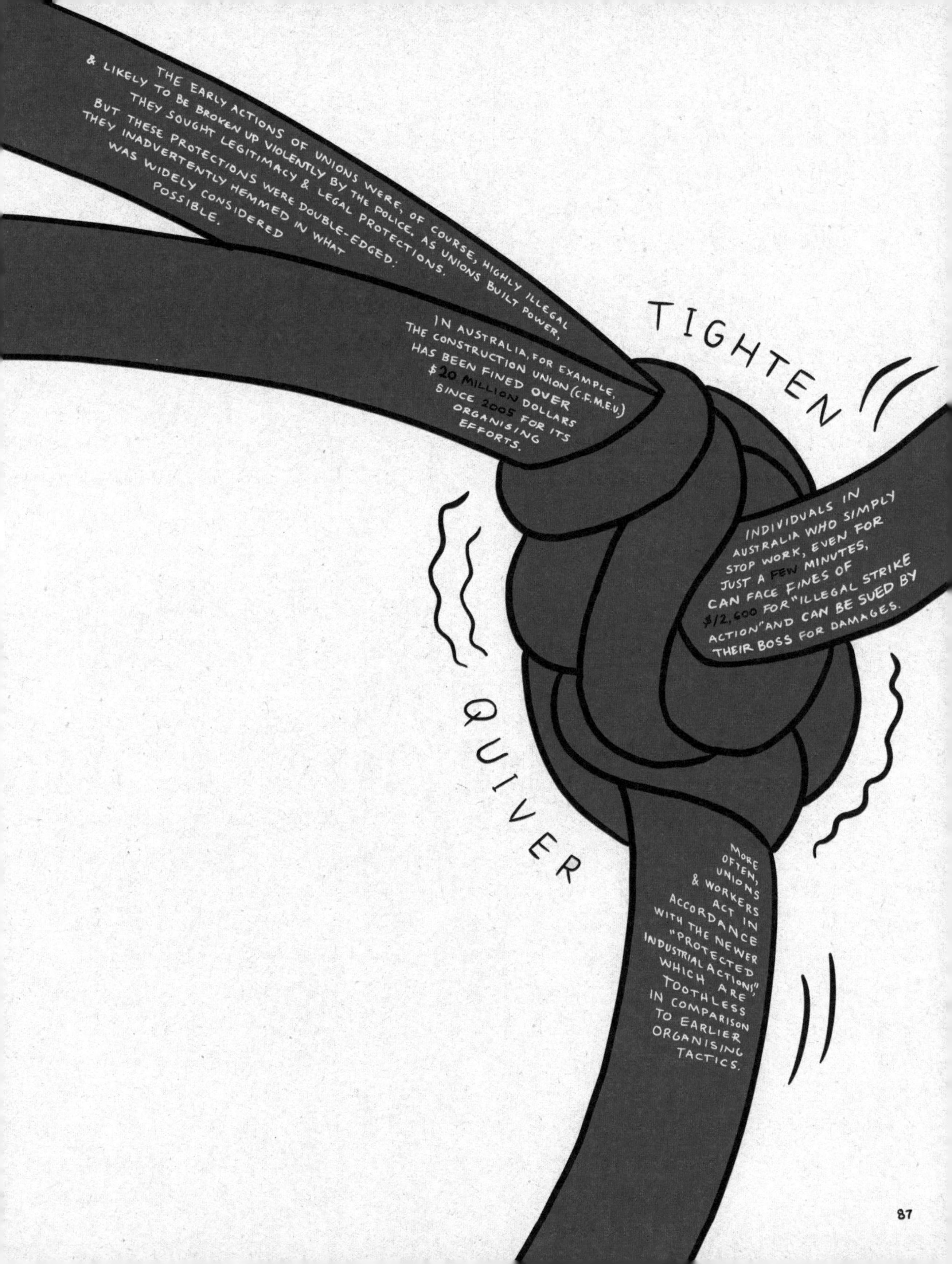
THE EARLY ACTIONS OF UNIONS WERE, OF COURSE, HIGHLY ILLEGAL & LIKELY TO BE BROKEN UP VIOLENTLY BY THE POLICE. AS UNIONS BUILT POWER, THEY SOUGHT LEGITIMACY & LEGAL PROTECTIONS. BUT THESE PROTECTIONS WERE DOUBLE-EDGED: THEY INADVERTENTLY HEMMED IN WHAT WAS WIDELY CONSIDERED POSSIBLE.
IN AUSTRALIA, FOR EXAMPLE, THE CONSTRUCTION UNION (C.F.M.E.U.) HAS BEEN FINED OVER $20 MILLION DOLLARS SINCE 2005 FOR ITS ORGANISING EFFORTS.
TIGHTEN
INDIVIDUALS IN AUSTRALIA WHO SIMPLY STOP WORK, EVEN FOR JUST A FEW MINUTES, CAN FACE FINES OF $12,600 FOR "ILLEGAL STRIKE ACTION" AND CAN BE SUED BY THEIR BOSS FOR DAMAGES.
QUIVER
MORE OFTEN, UNIONS & WORKERS ACT IN ACCORDANCE WITH THE NEWER "PROTECTED INDUSTRIAL ACTIONS," WHICH ARE TOOTHLESS IN COMPARISON TO EARLIER ORGANISING TACTICS.

THE INTERNATIONAL TRADE UNION CONFEDERATION'S 2021 GLOBAL RIGHTS INDEX SURVEYED 142 COUNTRIES. 87% OF THE COUNTRIES SURVEYED VIOLATED THEIR CITIZENS' RIGHT TO STRIKE.

64 OF THESE COUNTRIES DENY
OR CONSTRAIN FREEDOM
OF SPEECH & FREEDOM OF ASSEMBLY.

WORKERS INVOLVED IN ORGANISING WERE
EXPOSED TO PHYSICAL VIOLENCE IN
45 COUNTRIES.

2.5 BILLION WORKERS IN THE
GLOBAL WORKFORCE ARE EXCLUDED FROM
ANY PROTECTION UNDER LABOUR LAWS:
THOSE IN THE INFORMAL ECONOMY,
MIGRANT WORKERS,
THOSE IN PRECARIOUS WORK,
& THOSE WORKING FOR
PLATFORM OR APP
BUSINESSES.

ACCORDING TO THE STUDY,
UNION MEMBERS WERE MURDERED
IN AT LEAST 6 COUNTRIES IN 2021:
BRAZIL,
MYANMAR,
COLOMBIA,
GUATEMALA,
NIGERIA,
& THE PHILIPPINES.

IN COLOMBIA ALONE,
22 UNION MEMBERS
WERE MURDERED
DURING THAT ONE
YEAR.

IN
AUSTRALIA,
THE RELATIVE
FREQUENCY OF INDUSTRIAL
ACTION (MEASURED BY DAYS
LOST IN DISPUTES PER 1,000
WORKERS EMPLOYED) DECLINED
BY 97% FROM THE 1970'S TO
THE PRESENT DECADE.

THE NUMBER
OF WORKERS
WHO WENT ON
STRIKE IN
BRITAIN IN
2017 FELL TO
THE LOWEST
LEVEL SINCE
THE 1890's.

MEANWHILE,
8 MEN CONTROL THE SAME WEALTH AS THE
POOREST 50% OF THE GLOBAL POPULATION.

WHILE SOME PEOPLE
DIE FOR THE RIGHT TO
JOIN THEIR UNION,
OTHERS CONSIDER
THE $10 WEEKLY
FEE TOO STEEP,
OR PUT OFF
JOINING &
BECOMING
ACTIVE FOR
ANOTHER
DAY.

ON AVERAGE, UNIONISED
WORKERS TODAY EARN
$146 DOLLARS MORE PER
WEEK THAN NON UNION
MEMBERS.

WORKERS'
RIGHTS AND
PROTECTIONS MAY
BE DIMINISHING
AROUND THE WORLD,

BUT WE CAN TAKE SOME
COMFORT FROM THE FACT
THAT THE WINS OF THE PAST
WERE NOT ALL SECURED THROUGH
LEGAL OR CONVENTIONAL
METHODS.

IN CHINA, THERE IS ONLY ONE
LEGAL TRADE UNION, WHICH
REALLY ACTS AS AN EXTENSION
OF THE CHINESE STATE,
& IS THEREFORE FAR
FROM WORKERS'
CONTROL.

WORKERS IN
CHINA MOST OFTEN
ORGANISE OUTSIDE OF
THE COUNTRY'S
LEGAL FRAMEWORK,
WITH MILLIONS
AUTONOMOUSLY ORGANISING
UNOFFICIAL OR "WILDCAT"
STRIKES.

THESE ARE
ILLEGAL ACTIONS,
CARRIED OUT AT GREAT
RISK, & SO THE NUMBER
OF ACTIONS ARE HIDDEN,
ACTIVELY SUPPRESSED
BY THE STATE.

200 MILLION INDIAN
WORKERS WENT ON
STRIKE IN 2019,

MARKING THE
BIGGEST
STRIKE IN
HUMAN
HISTORY.

IN AUSTRALIA,
DESPITE THE DECLINE
IN MEMBERSHIP, UNIONS TODAY
STILL REPRESENT THE LARGEST VOLUNTARY
GROUPING OF PEOPLE IN THE COUNTRY.

THERE ARE ZERO
PEOPLE IN AUSTRALIA
WHOSE LIVES ARE
UNTOUCHED BY
UNIONISM.

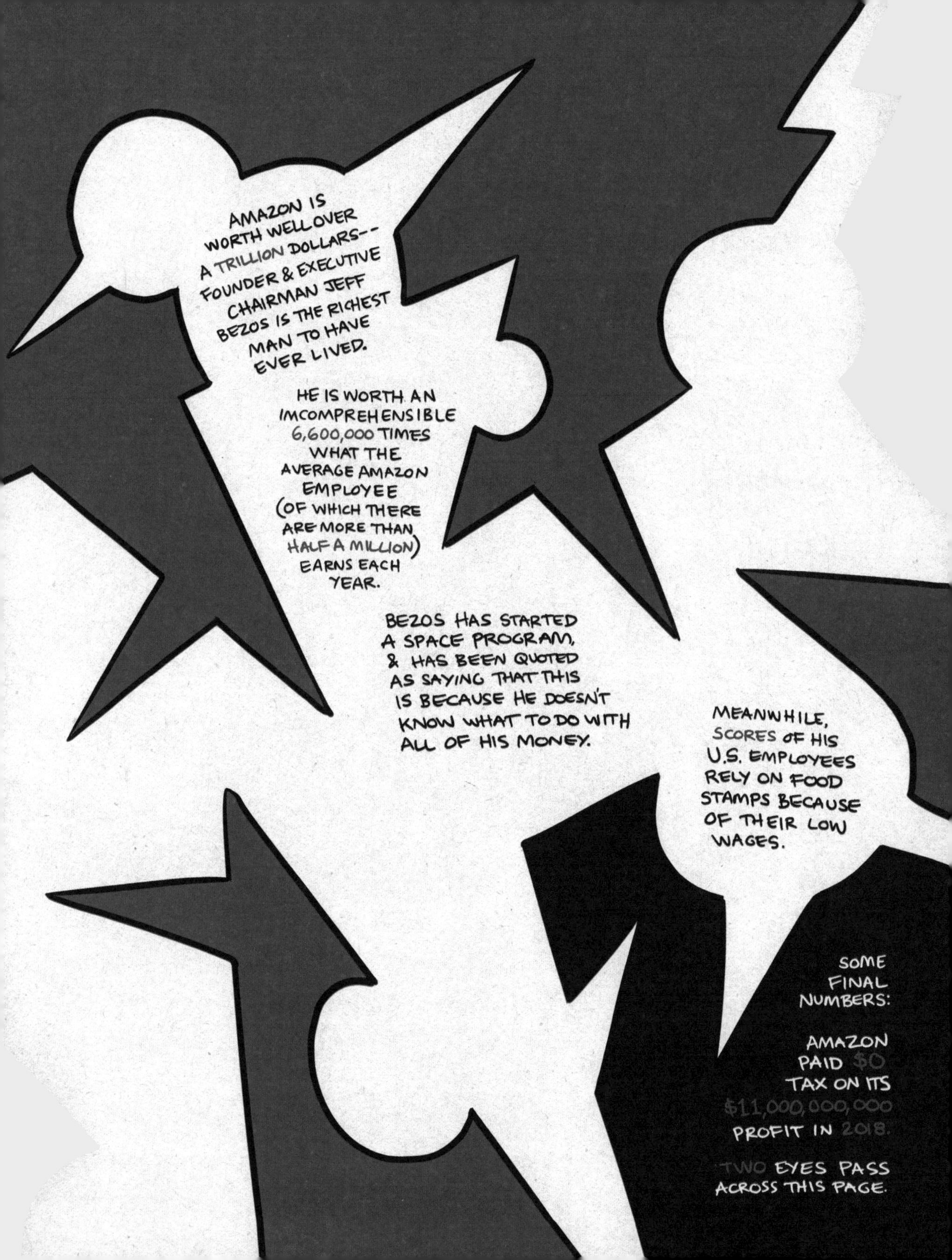
AMAZON IS WORTH WELL OVER A TRILLION DOLLARS-- FOUNDER & EXECUTIVE CHAIRMAN JEFF BEZOS IS THE RICHEST MAN TO HAVE EVER LIVED.
HE IS WORTH AN INCOMPREHENSIBLE 6,600,000 TIMES WHAT THE AVERAGE AMAZON EMPLOYEE (OF WHICH THERE ARE MORE THAN HALF A MILLION) EARNS EACH YEAR.
BEZOS HAS STARTED A SPACE PROGRAM, & HAS BEEN QUOTED AS SAYING THAT THIS IS BECAUSE HE DOESN'T KNOW WHAT TO DO WITH ALL OF HIS MONEY.
MEANWHILE, SCORES OF HIS U.S. EMPLOYEES RELY ON FOOD STAMPS BECAUSE OF THEIR LOW WAGES.
SOME FINAL NUMBERS:
AMAZON PAID $0 TAX ON ITS $11,000,000,000 PROFIT IN 2018.
TWO EYES PASS ACROSS THIS PAGE.

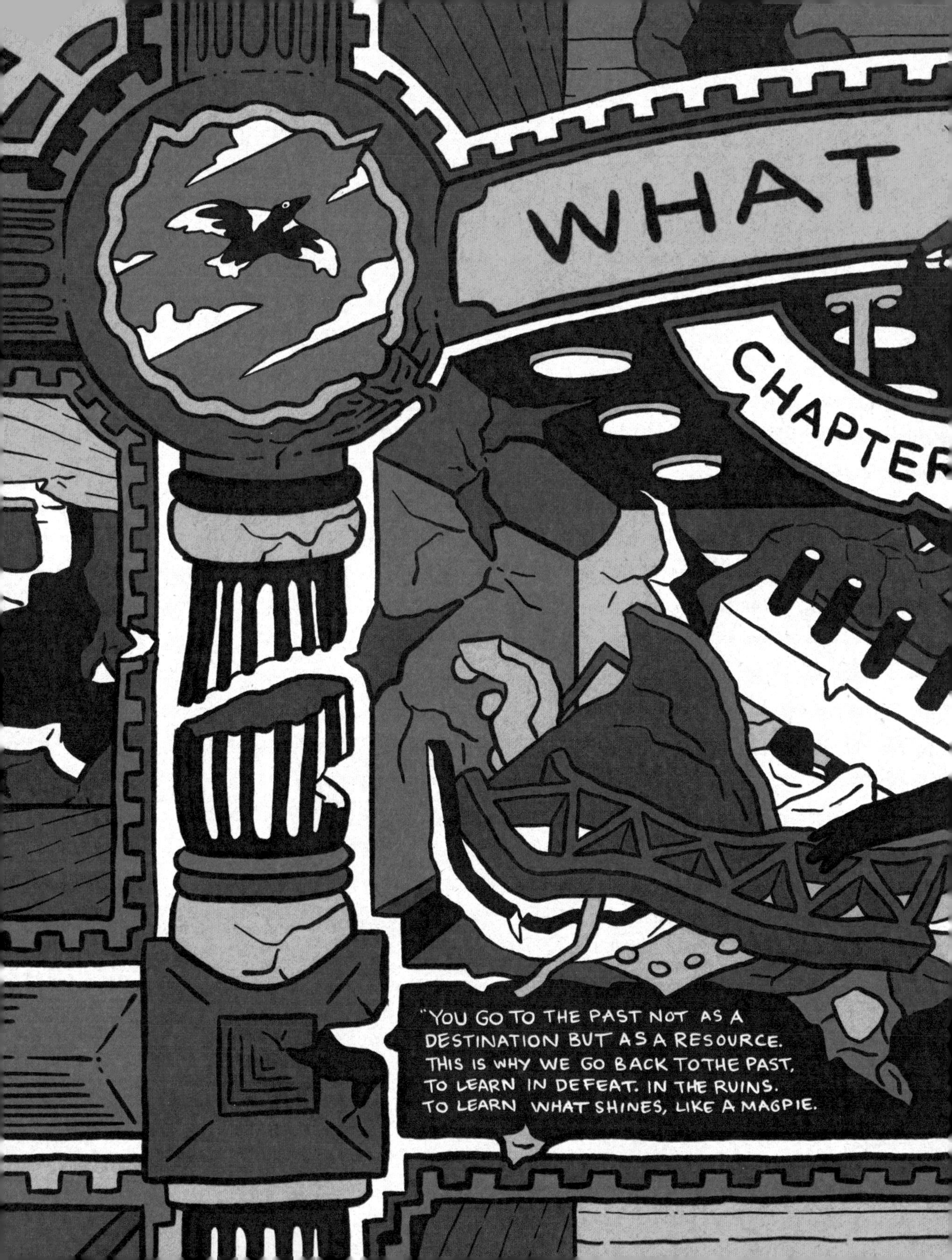
WHAT
CHAPTER
"YOU GO TO THE PAST NOT AS A DESTINATION BUT AS A RESOURCE. THIS IS WHY WE GO BACK TO THE PAST, TO LEARN IN DEFEAT. IN THE RUINS. TO LEARN WHAT SHINES, LIKE A MAGPIE.

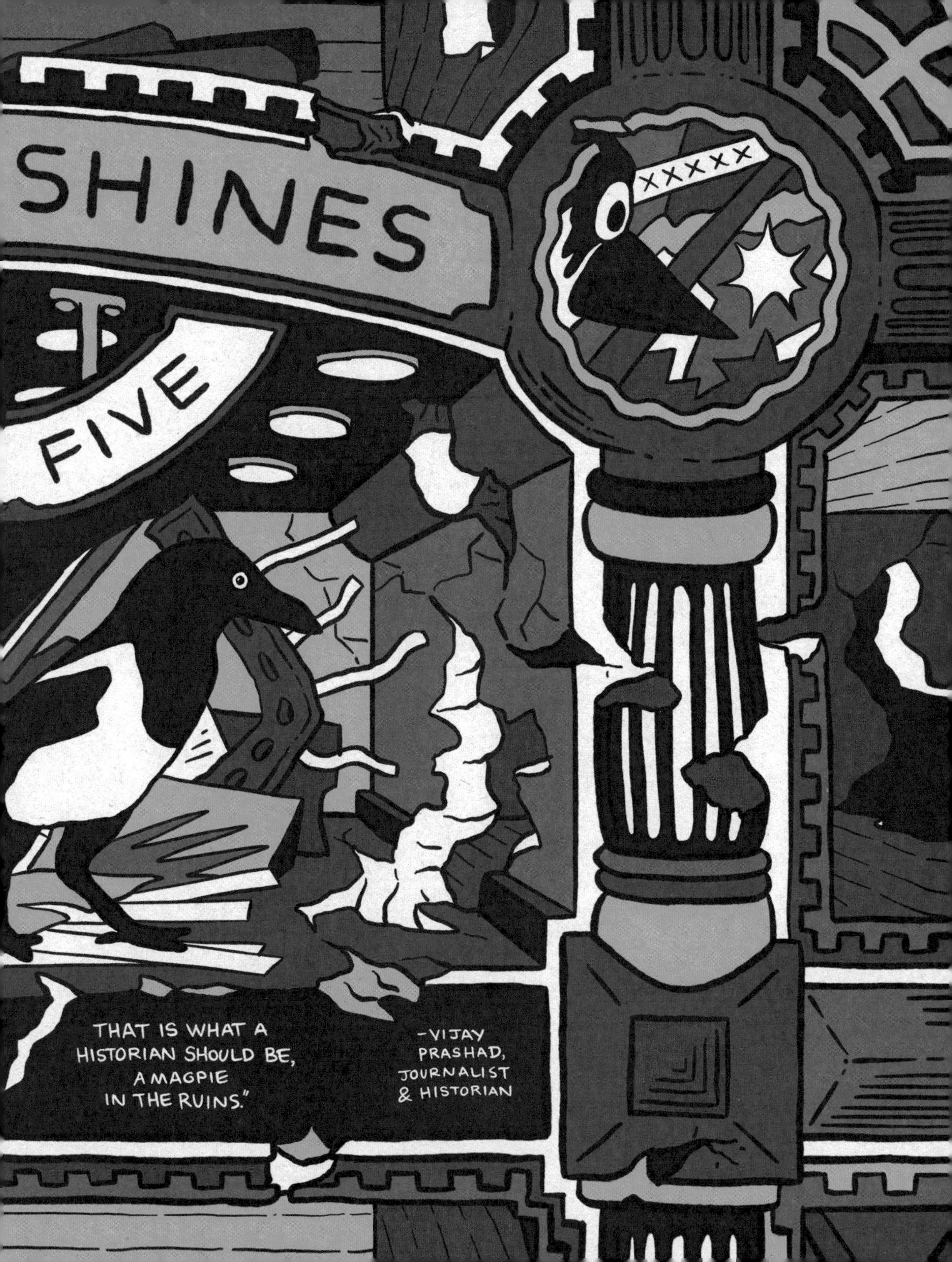
SHINES
FIVE
XXXXX
THAT IS WHAT A HISTORIAN SHOULD BE, A MAGPIE IN THE RUINS."
–VIJAY PRASHAD, JOURNALIST & HISTORIAN

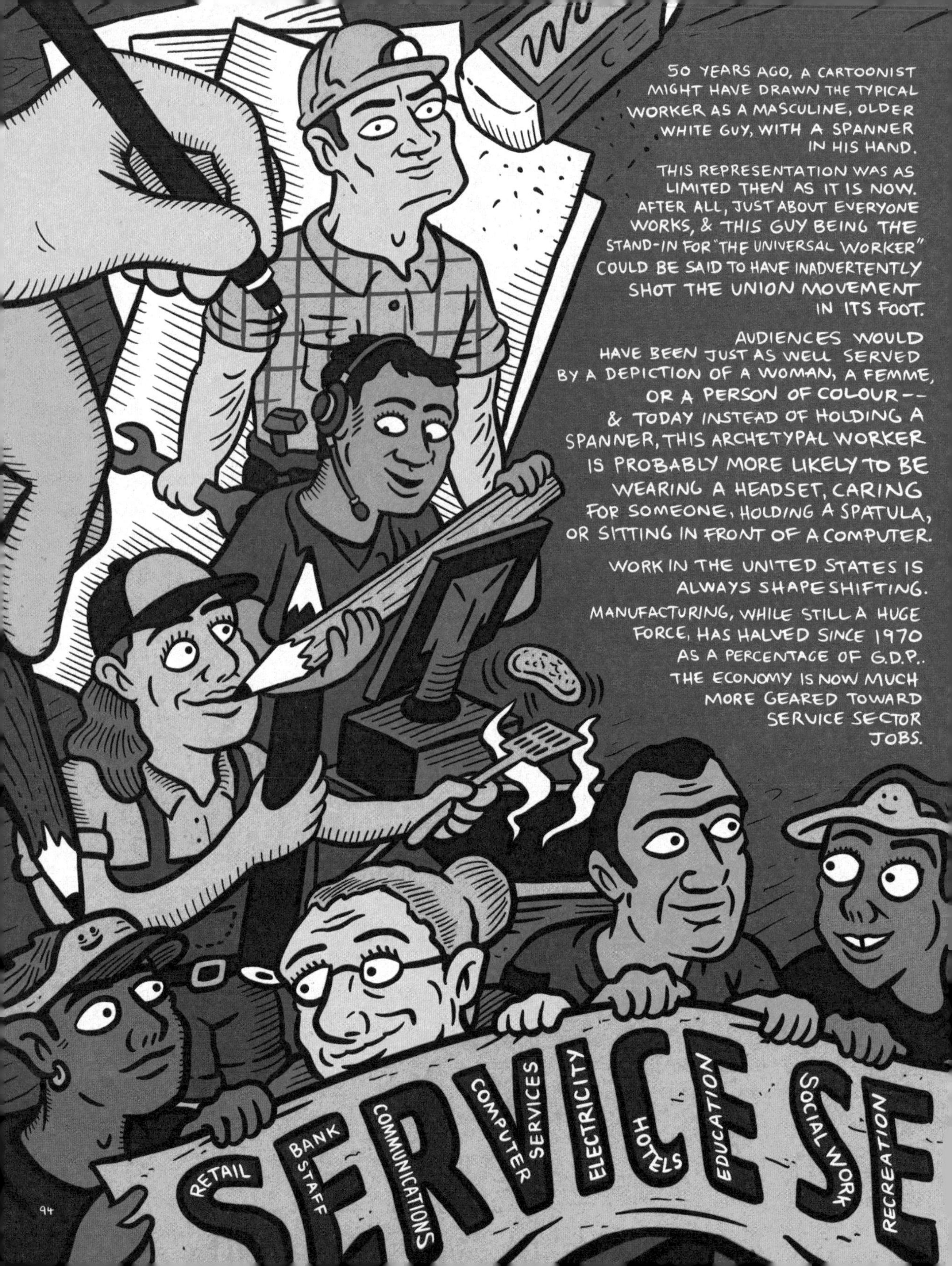
50 YEARS AGO, A CARTOONIST MIGHT HAVE DRAWN THE TYPICAL WORKER AS A MASCULINE, OLDER WHITE GUY, WITH A SPANNER IN HIS HAND.
THIS REPRESENTATION WAS AS LIMITED THEN AS IT IS NOW. AFTER ALL, JUST ABOUT EVERYONE WORKS, & THIS GUY BEING THE STAND-IN FOR "THE UNIVERSAL WORKER" COULD BE SAID TO HAVE INADVERTENTLY SHOT THE UNION MOVEMENT IN ITS FOOT.
AUDIENCES WOULD HAVE BEEN JUST AS WELL SERVED BY A DEPICTION OF A WOMAN, A FEMME, OR A PERSON OF COLOUR -- & TODAY INSTEAD OF HOLDING A SPANNER, THIS ARCHETYPAL WORKER IS PROBABLY MORE LIKELY TO BE WEARING A HEADSET, CARING FOR SOMEONE, HOLDING A SPATULA, OR SITTING IN FRONT OF A COMPUTER.
WORK IN THE UNITED STATES IS ALWAYS SHAPESHIFTING.
MANUFACTURING, WHILE STILL A HUGE FORCE, HAS HALVED SINCE 1970 AS A PERCENTAGE OF G.D.P.. THE ECONOMY IS NOW MUCH MORE GEARED TOWARD SERVICE SECTOR JOBS.
SERVICE SE
RETAIL
BANK STAFF
COMMUNICATIONS
COMPUTER SERVICES
ELECTRICITY
HOTELS
EDUCATION
SOCIAL WORK
RECREATION

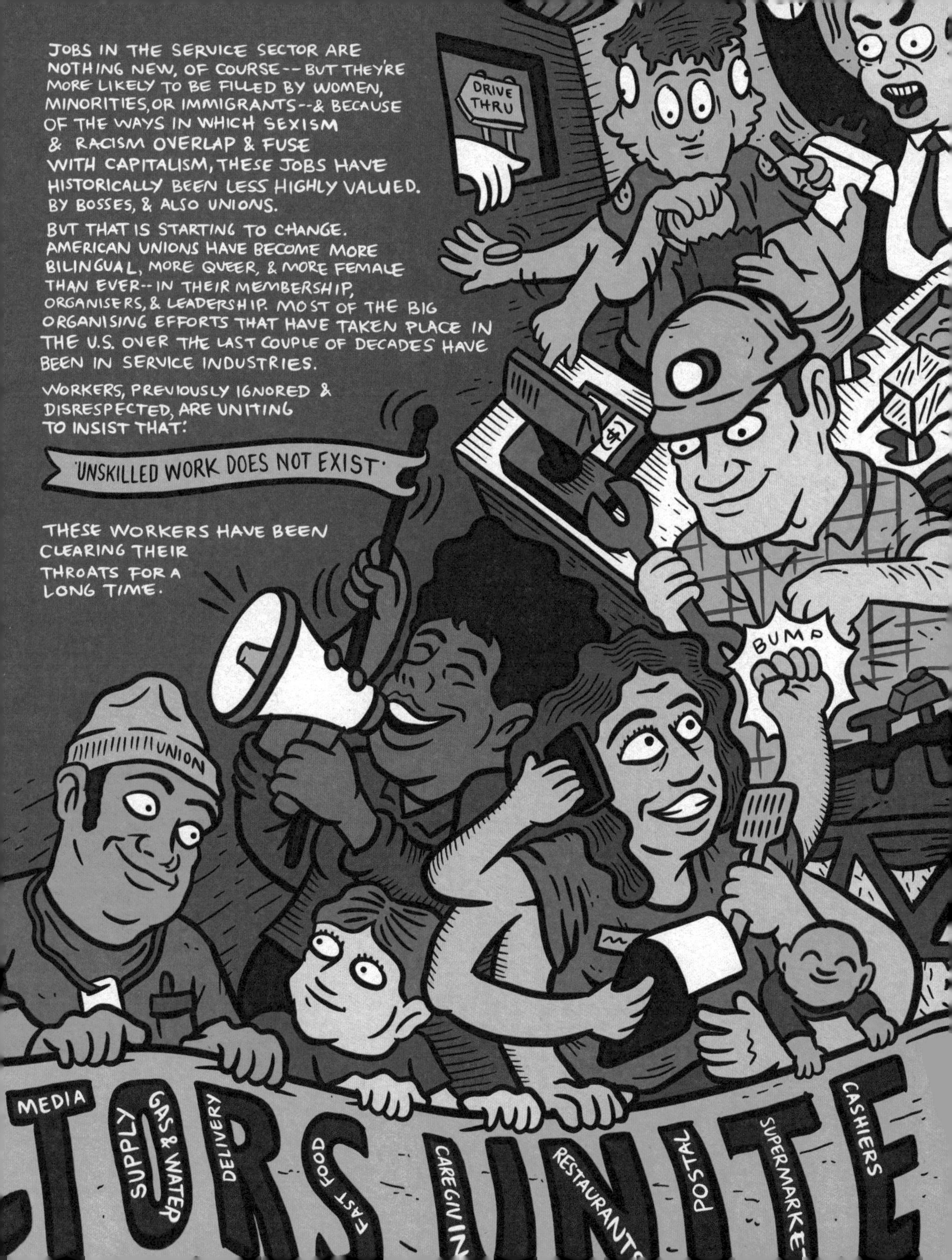
JOBS IN THE SERVICE SECTOR ARE NOTHING NEW, OF COURSE-- BUT THEY'RE MORE LIKELY TO BE FILLED BY WOMEN, MINORITIES, OR IMMIGRANTS--& BECAUSE OF THE WAYS IN WHICH SEXISM & RACISM OVERLAP & FUSE WITH CAPITALISM, THESE JOBS HAVE HISTORICALLY BEEN LESS HIGHLY VALUED. BY BOSSES, & ALSO UNIONS.
BUT THAT IS STARTING TO CHANGE. AMERICAN UNIONS HAVE BECOME MORE BILINGUAL, MORE QUEER, & MORE FEMALE THAN EVER-- IN THEIR MEMBERSHIP, ORGANISERS, & LEADERSHIP. MOST OF THE BIG ORGANISING EFFORTS THAT HAVE TAKEN PLACE IN THE U.S. OVER THE LAST COUPLE OF DECADES HAVE BEEN IN SERVICE INDUSTRIES.
WORKERS, PREVIOUSLY IGNORED & DISRESPECTED, ARE UNITING TO INSIST THAT:
'UNSKILLED WORK DOES NOT EXIST'
THESE WORKERS HAVE BEEN CLEARING THEIR THROATS FOR A LONG TIME.
DRIVE THRU
BUMP
UNION
MEDIA
SUPPLY
GAS & WATER
DELIVERY
FAST FOOD
POSTAL
CASHIERS

IN 1979, MELBOURNE UNIVERSITY STUDENT TERRY STOKES WAS ARRESTED FOR KISSING HIS LOVER, DARREN TURNER, OUTSIDE A PUB IN THE CITY. TERRY WAS EXPELLED FROM HIS HOUSING ON CAMPUS.

A MASS KISS-IN PROTEST OUTSIDE THE PUB FOLLOWED. THEN THE UNIVERSITY'S CAFETERIA WORKERS & THEIR UNION HELD A STOP-WORK MEETING-- AND THREATENED TO SHUT DOWN ALL OF THE UNIVERSITY'S FOOD SERVICE. WORKERS EXTENDED MEANINGFUL SOLIDARITY TO A PERSECUTED QUEER STUDENT WELL BEFORE THE AUSTRALIAN GAY-RIGHTS MOVEMENT TOOK HOLD.

THEY WON-- TERRY WAS INVITED TO RETURN, & THE WORKERS CONTINUED TO FEED THE CAMPUS.

THIS TACTIC WAS CONSISTENT WITH THE TIME. THROUGHOUT THE 1970'S, BUILDING & LABOURERS STEPPED OUTSIDE OF PURELY INDUSTRIAL ACTIVISM.

THEIR COMMUNIST-LED UNION HEEDED THE CALL OF ENVIRONMENTALISTS, HERITAGE ACTIVISTS, & PUBLIC-HOUSING RESIDENTS--STOPPING WORK ON CONSTRUCTION SITES THAT WOULD HAVE DAMAGING EFFECTS ON LOCAL GROUPS OF PEOPLE AND ECOSYSTEMS.

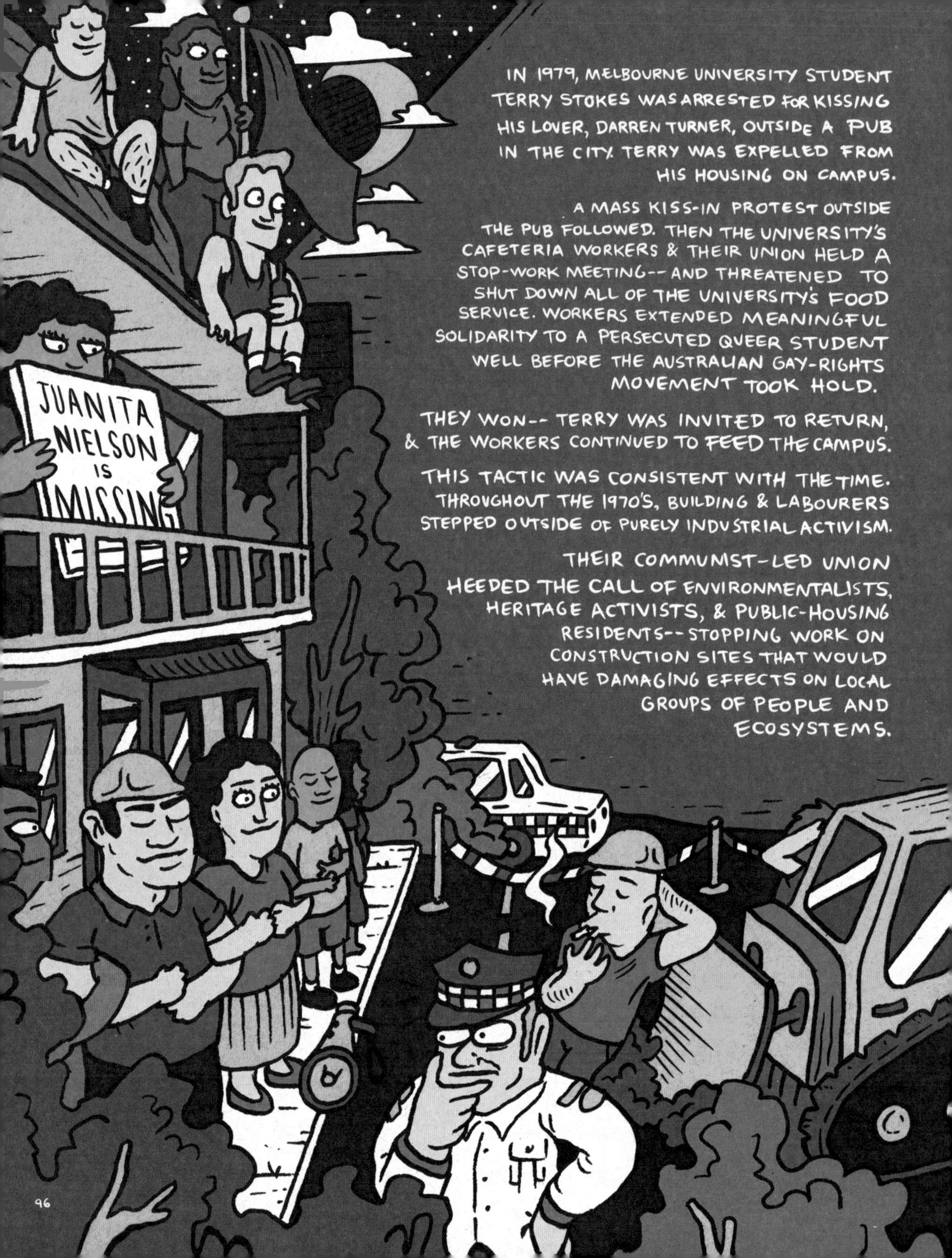
JUANITA NIELSON IS MISSING

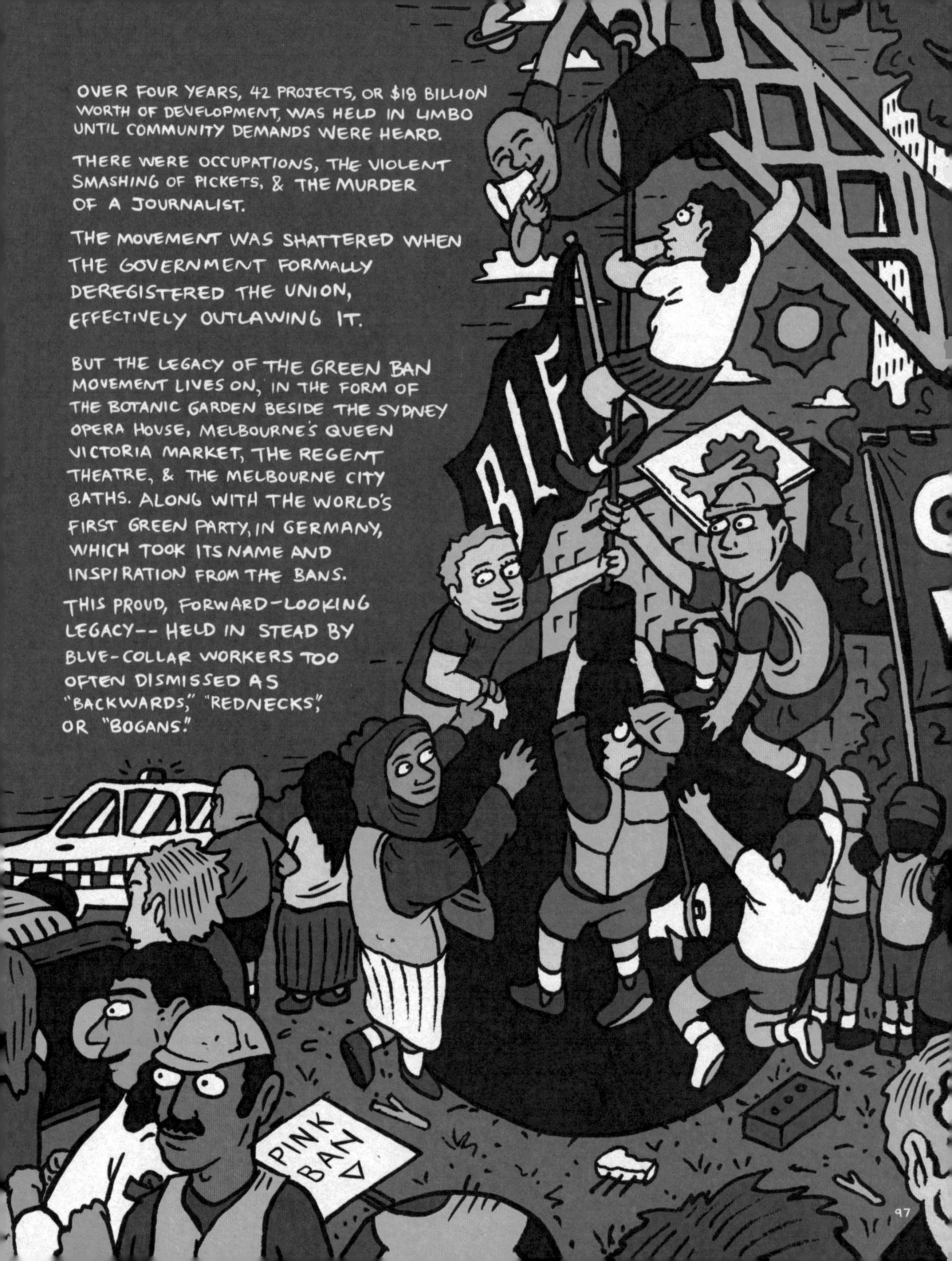
OVER FOUR YEARS, 42 PROJECTS, OR $18 BILLION WORTH OF DEVELOPMENT, WAS HELD IN LIMBO UNTIL COMMUNITY DEMANDS WERE HEARD.
THERE WERE OCCUPATIONS, THE VIOLENT SMASHING OF PICKETS, & THE MURDER OF A JOURNALIST.
THE MOVEMENT WAS SHATTERED WHEN THE GOVERNMENT FORMALLY DEREGISTERED THE UNION, EFFECTIVELY OUTLAWING IT.
BUT THE LEGACY OF THE GREEN BAN MOVEMENT LIVES ON, IN THE FORM OF THE BOTANIC GARDEN BESIDE THE SYDNEY OPERA HOUSE, MELBOURNE'S QUEEN VICTORIA MARKET, THE REGENT THEATRE, & THE MELBOURNE CITY BATHS. ALONG WITH THE WORLD'S FIRST GREEN PARTY, IN GERMANY, WHICH TOOK ITS NAME AND INSPIRATION FROM THE BANS.
THIS PROUD, FORWARD-LOOKING LEGACY-- HELD IN STEAD BY BLUE-COLLAR WORKERS TOO OFTEN DISMISSED AS "BACKWARDS," "REDNECKS," OR "BOGANS."
PINK BAN

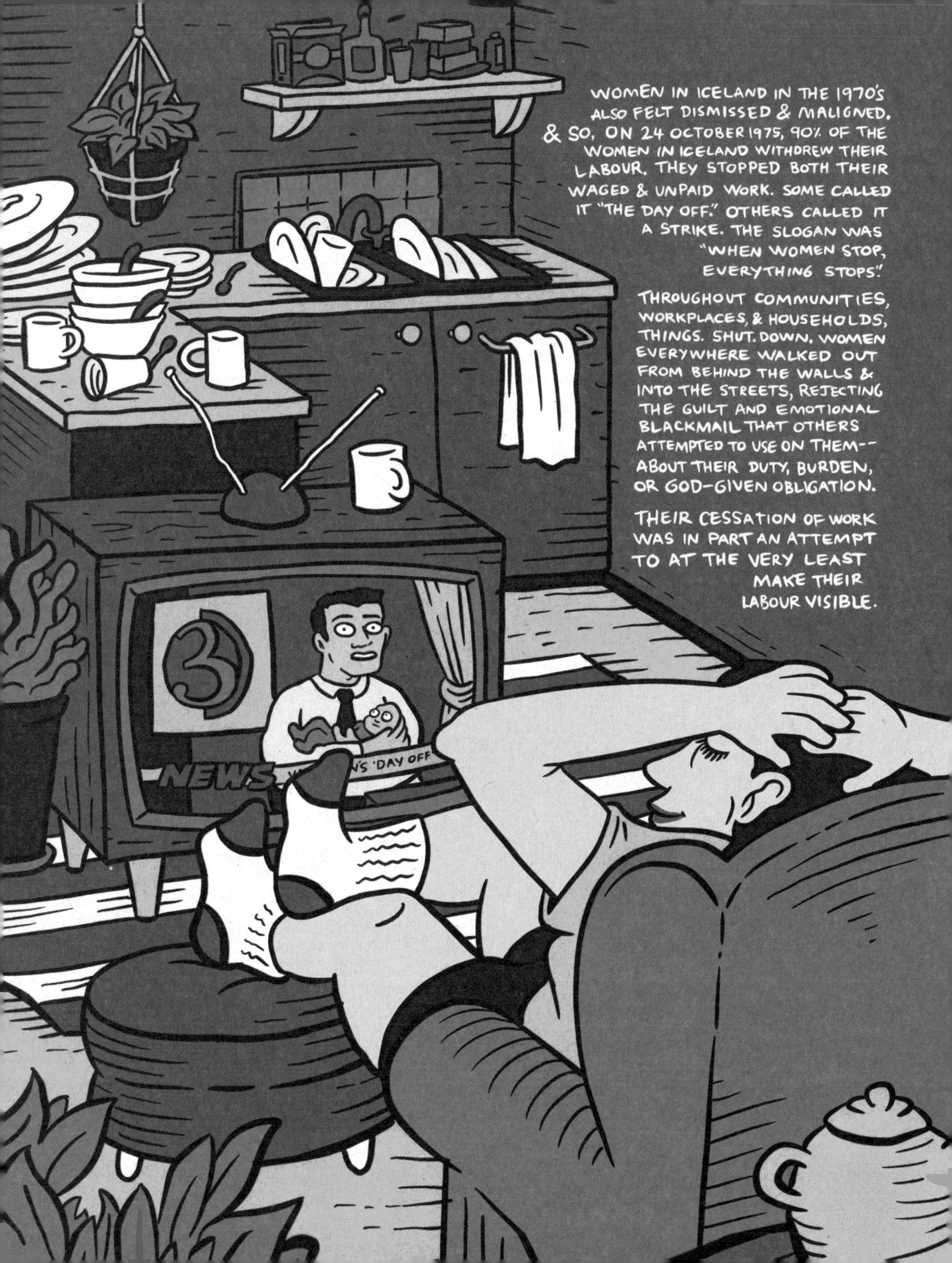
WOMEN IN ICELAND IN THE 1970'S ALSO FELT DISMISSED & MALIGNED. & SO, ON 24 OCTOBER 1975, 90% OF THE WOMEN IN ICELAND WITHDREW THEIR LABOUR. THEY STOPPED BOTH THEIR WAGED & UNPAID WORK. SOME CALLED IT "THE DAY OFF." OTHERS CALLED IT A STRIKE. THE SLOGAN WAS "WHEN WOMEN STOP, EVERYTHING STOPS."
THROUGHOUT COMMUNITIES, WORKPLACES, & HOUSEHOLDS, THINGS. SHUT. DOWN. WOMEN EVERYWHERE WALKED OUT FROM BEHIND THE WALLS & INTO THE STREETS, REJECTING THE GUILT AND EMOTIONAL BLACKMAIL THAT OTHERS ATTEMPTED TO USE ON THEM-- ABOUT THEIR DUTY, BURDEN, OR GOD-GIVEN OBLIGATION.
THEIR CESSATION OF WORK WAS IN PART AN ATTEMPT TO AT THE VERY LEAST MAKE THEIR LABOUR VISIBLE.
NEWS
'DAY OFF
3

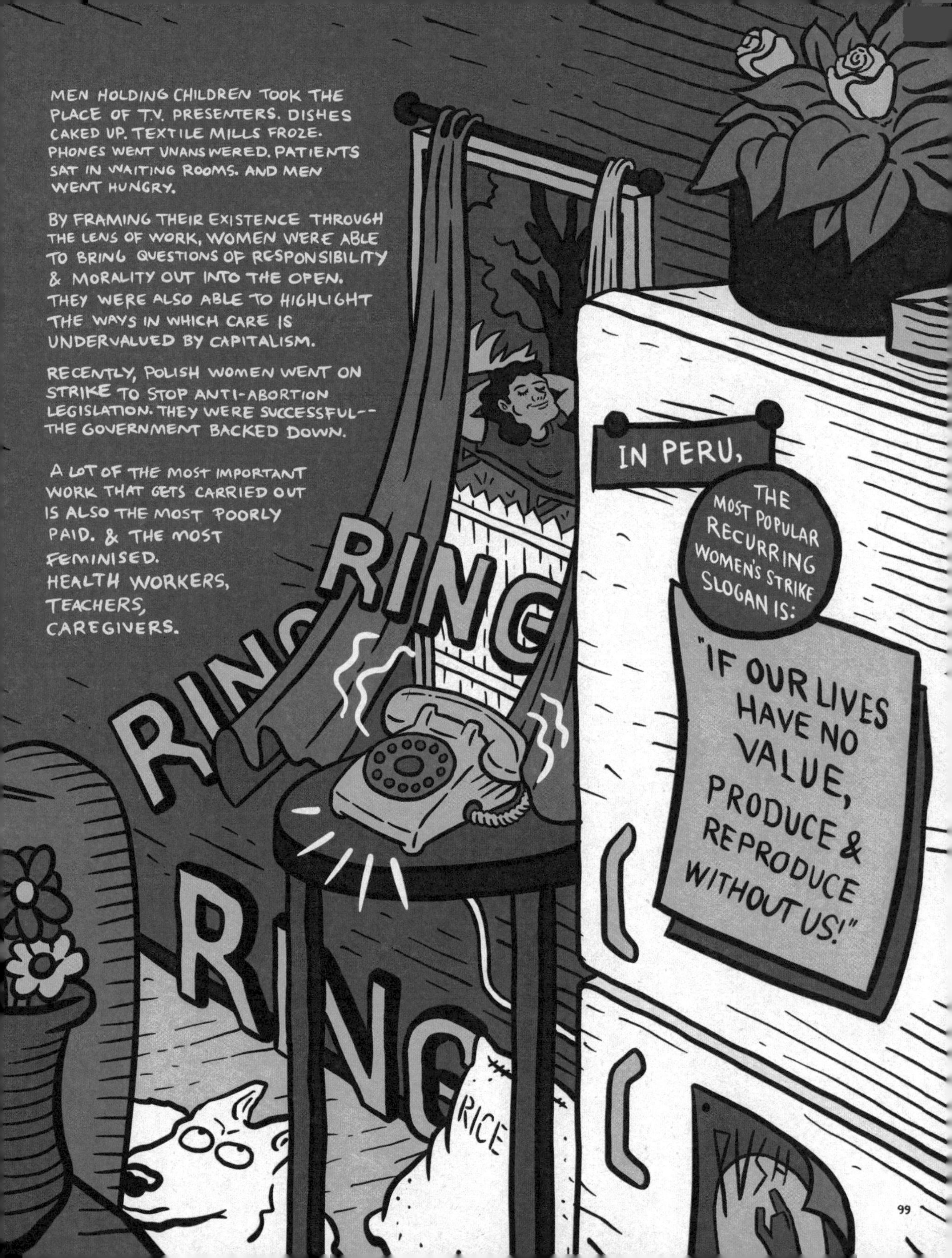
MEN HOLDING CHILDREN TOOK THE PLACE OF T.V. PRESENTERS. DISHES CAKED UP. TEXTILE MILLS FROZE. PHONES WENT UNANSWERED. PATIENTS SAT IN WAITING ROOMS. AND MEN WENT HUNGRY.
BY FRAMING THEIR EXISTENCE THROUGH THE LENS OF WORK, WOMEN WERE ABLE TO BRING QUESTIONS OF RESPONSIBILITY & MORALITY OUT INTO THE OPEN. THEY WERE ALSO ABLE TO HIGHLIGHT THE WAYS IN WHICH CARE IS UNDERVALUED BY CAPITALISM.
RECENTLY, POLISH WOMEN WENT ON STRIKE TO STOP ANTI-ABORTION LEGISLATION. THEY WERE SUCCESSFUL-- THE GOVERNMENT BACKED DOWN.
A LOT OF THE MOST IMPORTANT WORK THAT GETS CARRIED OUT IS ALSO THE MOST POORLY PAID. & THE MOST FEMINISED.
HEALTH WORKERS, TEACHERS, CAREGIVERS.
RING RING
RING
IN PERU,
THE MOST POPULAR RECURRING WOMEN'S STRIKE SLOGAN IS:
"IF OUR LIVES HAVE NO VALUE, PRODUCE & REPRODUCE WITHOUT US!"
RICE
PUSH

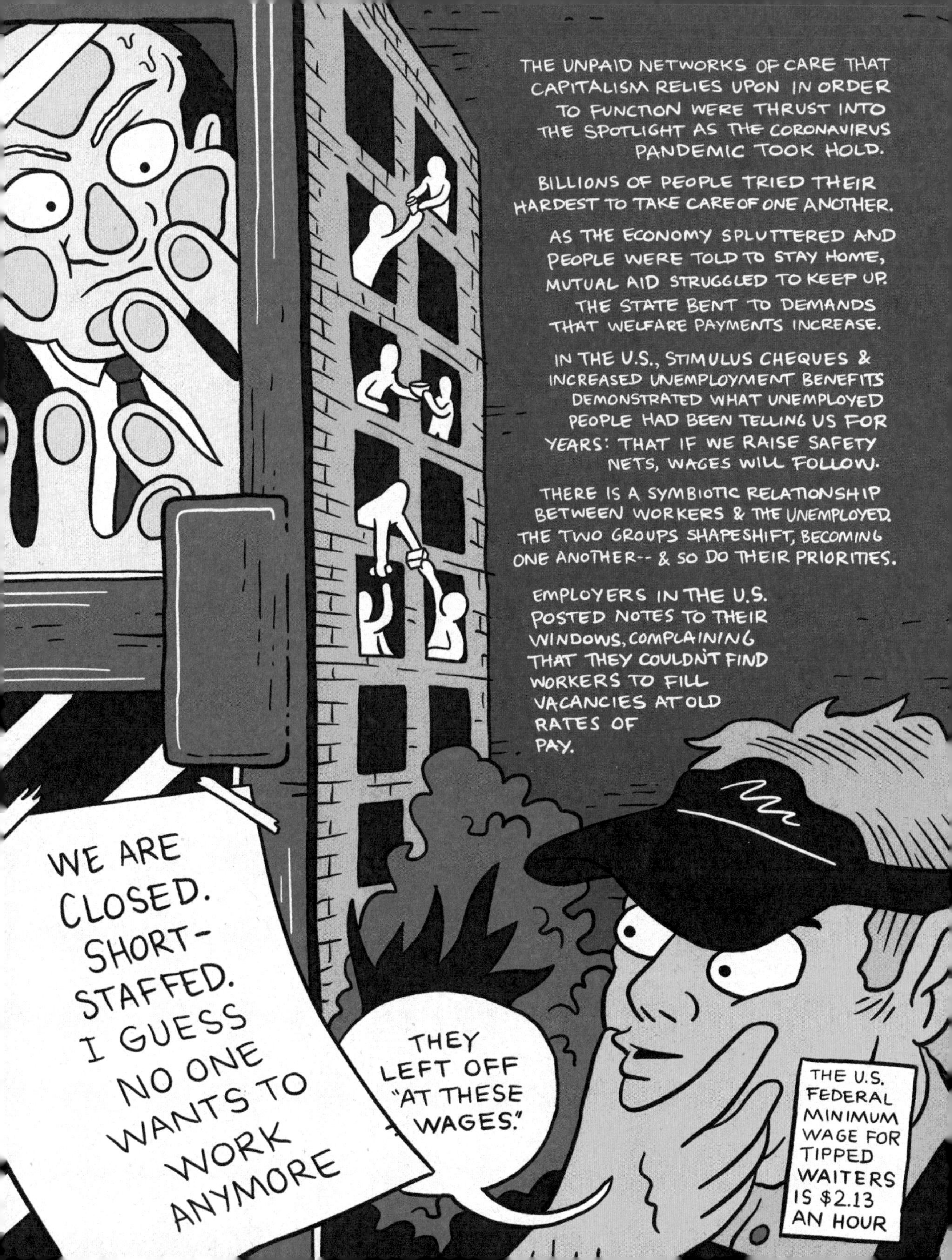

THE UNPAID NETWORKS OF CARE THAT CAPITALISM RELIES UPON IN ORDER TO FUNCTION WERE THRUST INTO THE SPOTLIGHT AS THE CORONAVIRUS PANDEMIC TOOK HOLD.
BILLIONS OF PEOPLE TRIED THEIR HARDEST TO TAKE CARE OF ONE ANOTHER.
AS THE ECONOMY SPLUTTERED AND PEOPLE WERE TOLD TO STAY HOME, MUTUAL AID STRUGGLED TO KEEP UP. THE STATE BENT TO DEMANDS THAT WELFARE PAYMENTS INCREASE.
IN THE U.S., STIMULUS CHEQUES & INCREASED UNEMPLOYMENT BENEFITS DEMONSTRATED WHAT UNEMPLOYED PEOPLE HAD BEEN TELLING US FOR YEARS: THAT IF WE RAISE SAFETY NETS, WAGES WILL FOLLOW.
THERE IS A SYMBIOTIC RELATIONSHIP BETWEEN WORKERS & THE UNEMPLOYED. THE TWO GROUPS SHAPESHIFT, BECOMING ONE ANOTHER-- & SO DO THEIR PRIORITIES.
EMPLOYERS IN THE U.S. POSTED NOTES TO THEIR WINDOWS, COMPLAINING THAT THEY COULDN'T FIND WORKERS TO FILL VACANCIES AT OLD RATES OF PAY.
WE ARE CLOSED. SHORT-STAFFED. I GUESS NO ONE WANTS TO WORK ANYMORE
THEY LEFT OFF "AT THESE WAGES."
THE U.S. FEDERAL MINIMUM WAGE FOR TIPPED WAITERS IS $2.13 AN HOUR

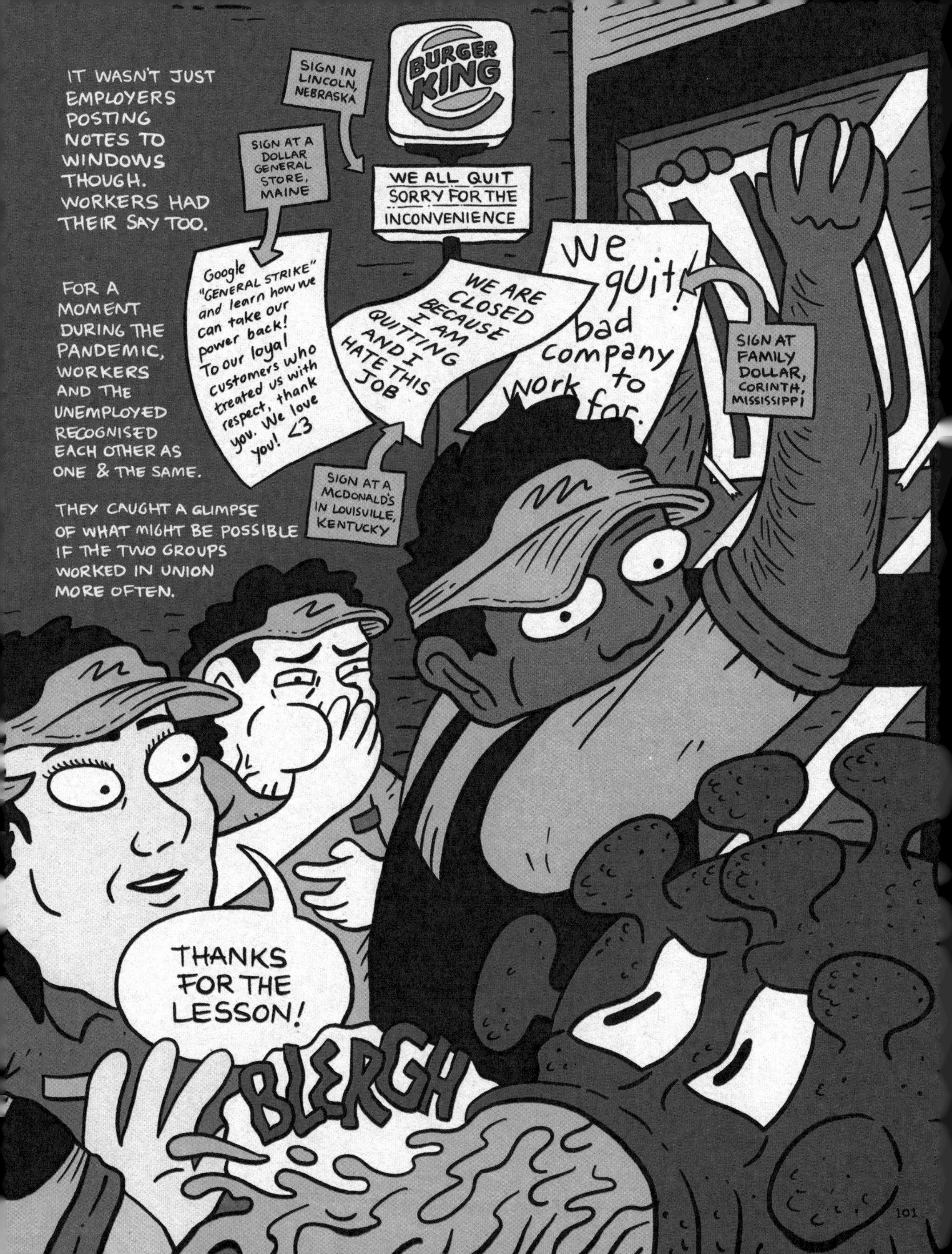

IT WASN'T JUST EMPLOYERS POSTING NOTES TO WINDOWS THOUGH. WORKERS HAD THEIR SAY TOO.
SIGN IN LINCOLN, NEBRASKA
BURGER KING
WE ALL QUIT SORRY FOR THE INCONVENIENCE
SIGN AT A DOLLAR GENERAL STORE, MAINE
Google "GENERAL STRIKE" and learn how we can take our power back! To our loyal customers who treated us with respect, thank you. We love you! <3
WE ARE CLOSED BECAUSE I AM QUITTING AND I HATE THIS JOB
SIGN AT A McDONALD'S IN LOUISVILLE, KENTUCKY
we quit! bad company to work for.
SIGN AT FAMILY DOLLAR, CORINTH, MISSISSIPPI
FOR A MOMENT DURING THE PANDEMIC, WORKERS AND THE UNEMPLOYED RECOGNISED EACH OTHER AS ONE & THE SAME.
THEY CAUGHT A GLIMPSE OF WHAT MIGHT BE POSSIBLE IF THE TWO GROUPS WORKED IN UNION MORE OFTEN.
THANKS FOR THE LESSON!
BLERGH

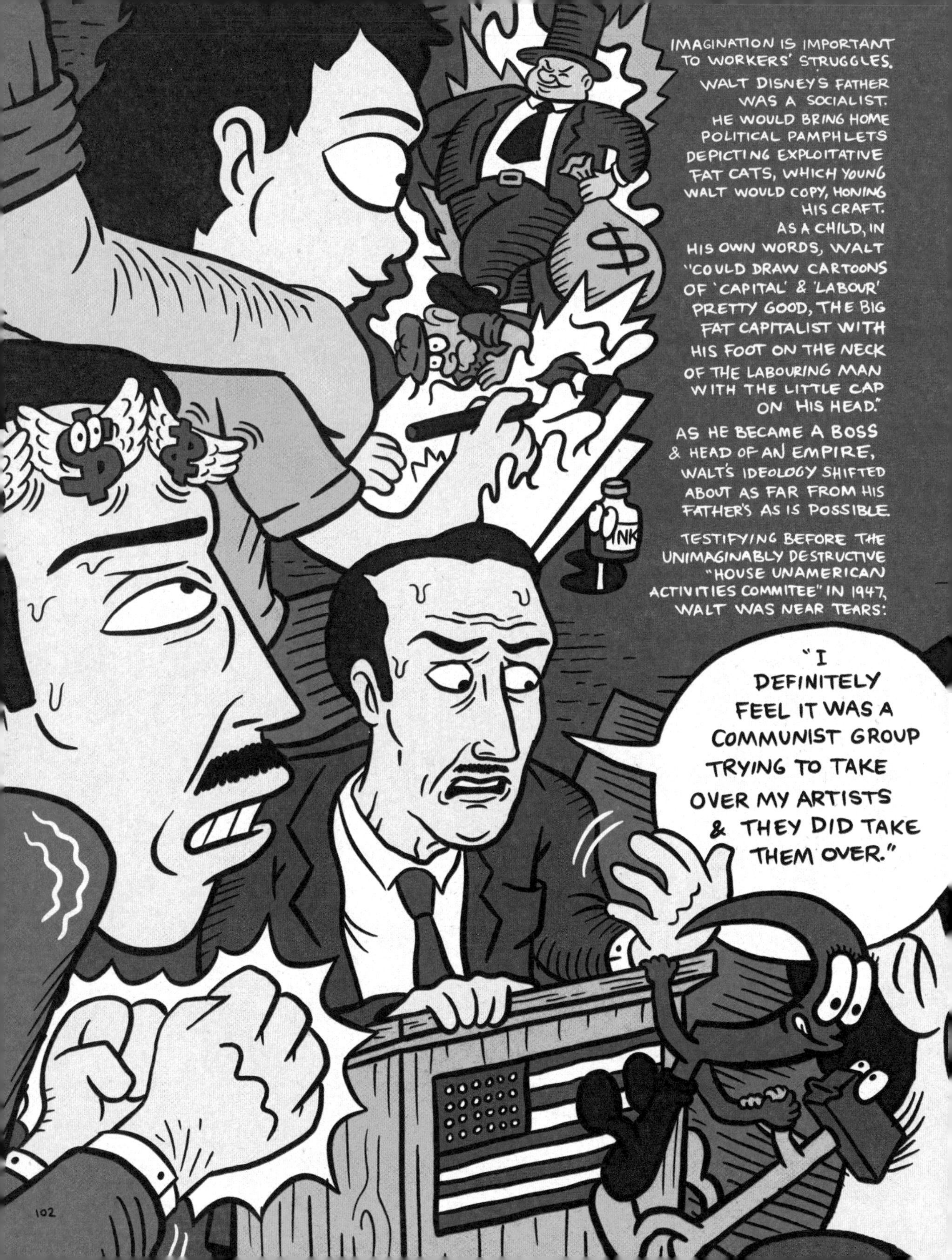

IMAGINATION IS IMPORTANT TO WORKERS' STRUGGLES.
WALT DISNEY'S FATHER WAS A SOCIALIST.
HE WOULD BRING HOME POLITICAL PAMPHLETS DEPICTING EXPLOITATIVE FAT CATS, WHICH YOUNG WALT WOULD COPY, HONING HIS CRAFT.
AS A CHILD, IN HIS OWN WORDS, WALT "COULD DRAW CARTOONS OF 'CAPITAL' & 'LABOUR' PRETTY GOOD, THE BIG FAT CAPITALIST WITH HIS FOOT ON THE NECK OF THE LABOURING MAN WITH THE LITTLE CAP ON HIS HEAD."
AS HE BECAME A BOSS & HEAD OF AN EMPIRE, WALT'S IDEOLOGY SHIFTED ABOUT AS FAR FROM HIS FATHER'S AS IS POSSIBLE.
TESTIFYING BEFORE THE UNIMAGINABLY DESTRUCTIVE "HOUSE UNAMERICAN ACTIVITIES COMMITEE" IN 1947, WALT WAS NEAR TEARS:
"I DEFINITELY FEEL IT WAS A COMMUNIST GROUP TRYING TO TAKE OVER MY ARTISTS & THEY DID TAKE THEM OVER."
$
INK

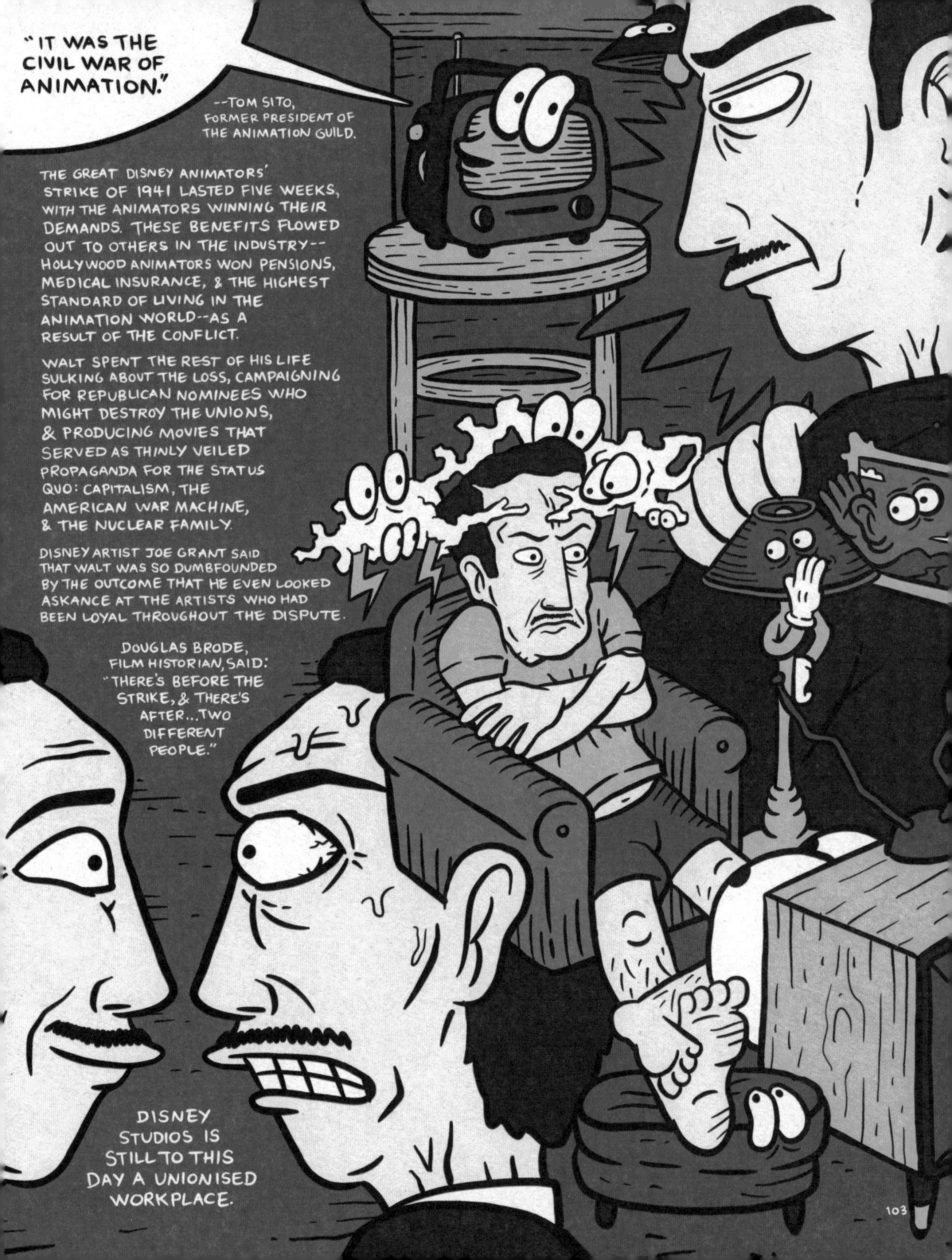

"IT WAS THE CIVIL WAR OF ANIMATION."
--TOM SITO, FORMER PRESIDENT OF THE ANIMATION GUILD.
THE GREAT DISNEY ANIMATORS' STRIKE OF 1941 LASTED FIVE WEEKS, WITH THE ANIMATORS WINNING THEIR DEMANDS. THESE BENEFITS FLOWED OUT TO OTHERS IN THE INDUSTRY--HOLLYWOOD ANIMATORS WON PENSIONS, MEDICAL INSURANCE, & THE HIGHEST STANDARD OF LIVING IN THE ANIMATION WORLD--AS A RESULT OF THE CONFLICT.
WALT SPENT THE REST OF HIS LIFE SULKING ABOUT THE LOSS, CAMPAIGNING FOR REPUBLICAN NOMINEES WHO MIGHT DESTROY THE UNIONS, & PRODUCING MOVIES THAT SERVED AS THINLY VEILED PROPAGANDA FOR THE STATUS QUO: CAPITALISM, THE AMERICAN WAR MACHINE, & THE NUCLEAR FAMILY.
DISNEY ARTIST JOE GRANT SAID THAT WALT WAS SO DUMBFOUNDED BY THE OUTCOME THAT HE EVEN LOOKED ASKANCE AT THE ARTISTS WHO HAD BEEN LOYAL THROUGHOUT THE DISPUTE.
DOUGLAS BRODE, FILM HISTORIAN, SAID: "THERE'S BEFORE THE STRIKE, & THERE'S AFTER...TWO DIFFERENT PEOPLE."
DISNEY STUDIOS IS STILL TO THIS DAY A UNIONISED WORKPLACE.

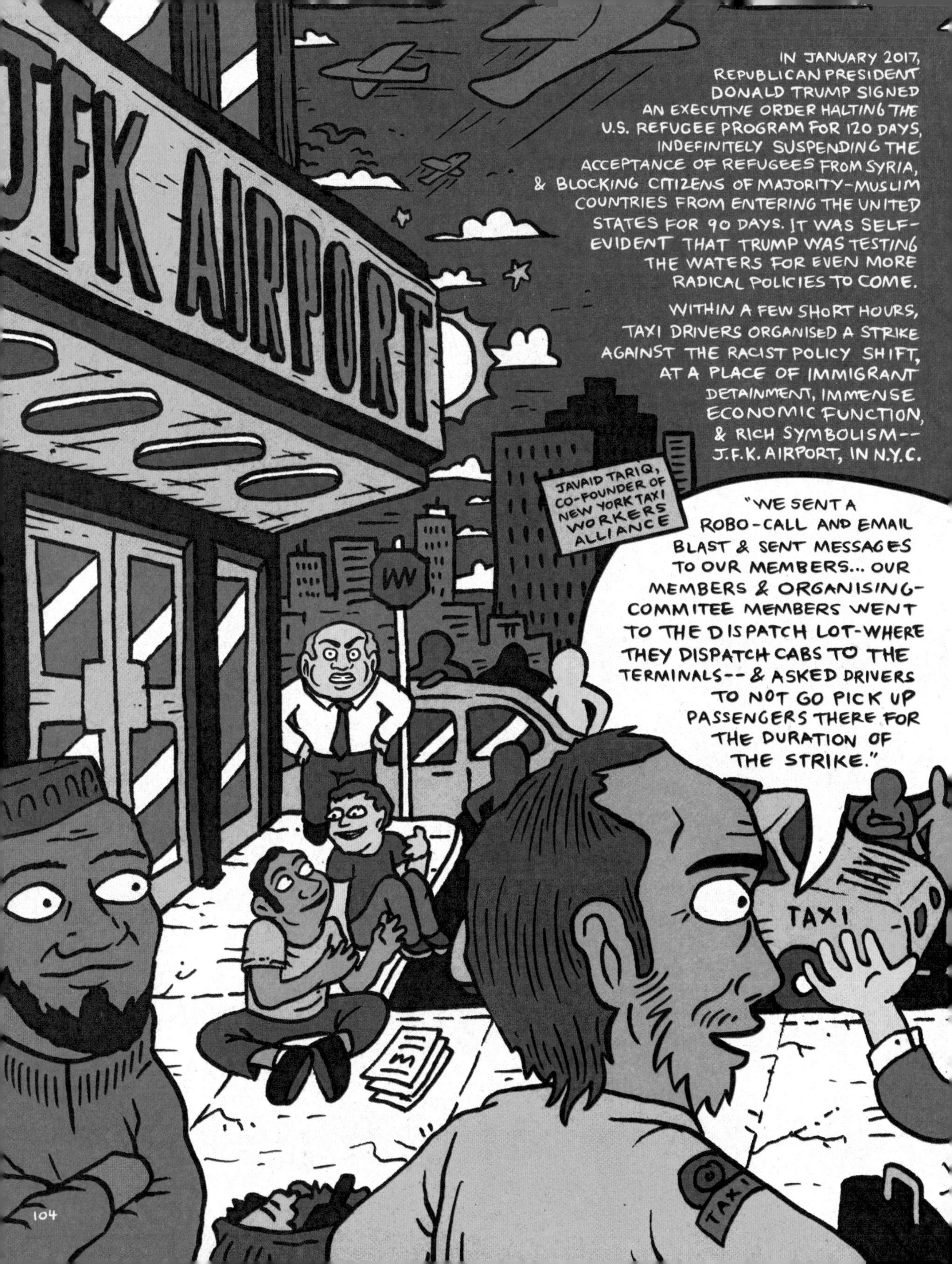
JFK AIRPORT
IN JANUARY 2017, REPUBLICAN PRESIDENT DONALD TRUMP SIGNED AN EXECUTIVE ORDER HALTING THE U.S. REFUGEE PROGRAM FOR 120 DAYS, INDEFINITELY SUSPENDING THE ACCEPTANCE OF REFUGEES FROM SYRIA, & BLOCKING CITIZENS OF MAJORITY-MUSLIM COUNTRIES FROM ENTERING THE UNITED STATES FOR 90 DAYS. IT WAS SELF-EVIDENT THAT TRUMP WAS TESTING THE WATERS FOR EVEN MORE RADICAL POLICIES TO COME.
WITHIN A FEW SHORT HOURS, TAXI DRIVERS ORGANISED A STRIKE AGAINST THE RACIST POLICY SHIFT, AT A PLACE OF IMMIGRANT DETAINMENT, IMMENSE ECONOMIC FUNCTION, & RICH SYMBOLISM-- J.F.K. AIRPORT, IN N.Y.C.
JAVAID TARIQ, CO-FOUNDER OF NEW YORK TAXI WORKERS ALLIANCE
"WE SENT A ROBO-CALL AND EMAIL BLAST & SENT MESSAGES TO OUR MEMBERS... OUR MEMBERS & ORGANISING-COMMITEE MEMBERS WENT TO THE DISPATCH LOT-WHERE THEY DISPATCH CABS TO THE TERMINALS-- & ASKED DRIVERS TO NOT GO PICK UP PASSENGERS THERE FOR THE DURATION OF THE STRIKE."
TAXI
TAXI

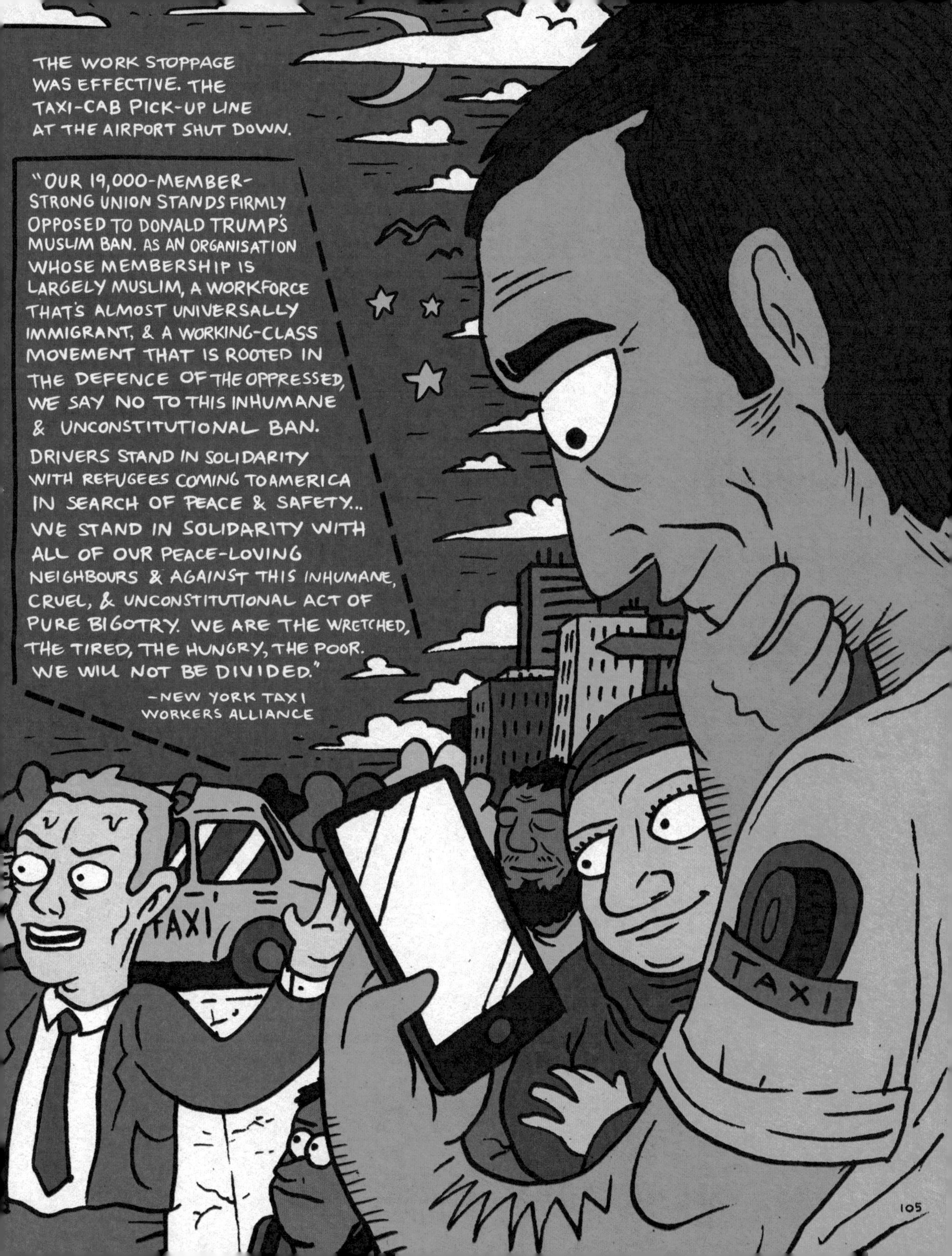
THE WORK STOPPAGE WAS EFFECTIVE. THE TAXI-CAB PICK-UP LINE AT THE AIRPORT SHUT DOWN.
"OUR 19,000-MEMBER-STRONG UNION STANDS FIRMLY OPPOSED TO DONALD TRUMP'S MUSLIM BAN. AS AN ORGANISATION WHOSE MEMBERSHIP IS LARGELY MUSLIM, A WORKFORCE THAT'S ALMOST UNIVERSALLY IMMIGRANT, & A WORKING-CLASS MOVEMENT THAT IS ROOTED IN THE DEFENCE OF THE OPPRESSED, WE SAY NO TO THIS INHUMANE & UNCONSTITUTIONAL BAN. DRIVERS STAND IN SOLIDARITY WITH REFUGEES COMING TO AMERICA IN SEARCH OF PEACE & SAFETY... WE STAND IN SOLIDARITY WITH ALL OF OUR PEACE-LOVING NEIGHBOURS & AGAINST THIS INHUMANE, CRUEL, & UNCONSTITUTIONAL ACT OF PURE BIGOTRY. WE ARE THE WRETCHED, THE TIRED, THE HUNGRY, THE POOR. WE WILL NOT BE DIVIDED."
-NEW YORK TAXI WORKERS ALLIANCE
TAXI
TAXI

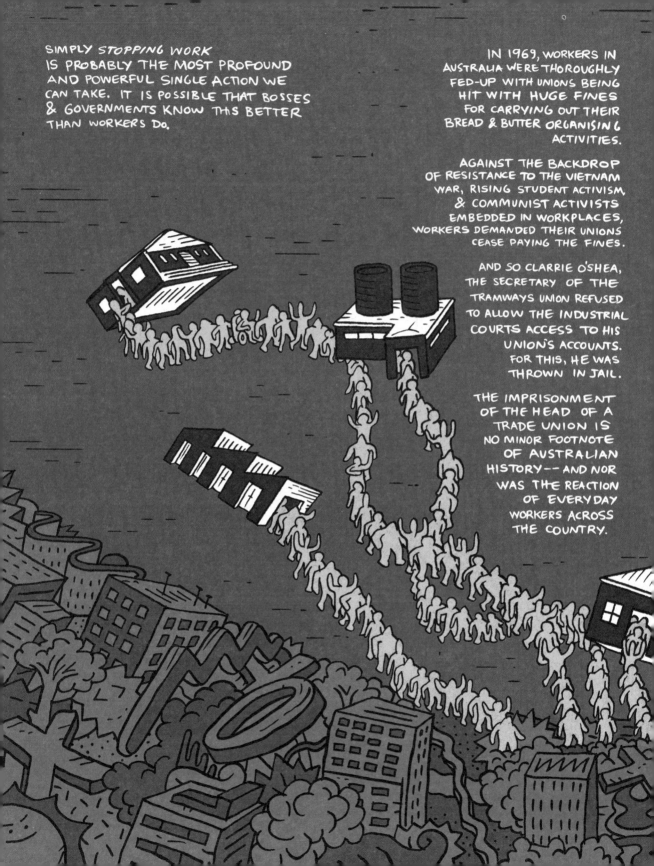

SIMPLY *STOPPING WORK* IS PROBABLY THE MOST PROFOUND AND POWERFUL SINGLE ACTION WE CAN TAKE. IT IS POSSIBLE THAT BOSSES & GOVERNMENTS KNOW THIS BETTER THAN WORKERS DO.

IN 1969, WORKERS IN AUSTRALIA WERE THOROUGHLY FED-UP WITH UNIONS BEING HIT WITH HUGE FINES FOR CARRYING OUT THEIR BREAD & BUTTER ORGANISING ACTIVITIES.

AGAINST THE BACKDROP OF RESISTANCE TO THE VIETNAM WAR, RISING STUDENT ACTIVISM, & COMMUNIST ACTIVISTS EMBEDDED IN WORKPLACES, WORKERS DEMANDED THEIR UNIONS CEASE PAYING THE FINES.

AND SO CLARRIE O'SHEA, THE SECRETARY OF THE TRAMWAYS UNION REFUSED TO ALLOW THE INDUSTRIAL COURTS ACCESS TO HIS UNION'S ACCOUNTS. FOR THIS, HE WAS THROWN IN JAIL.

THE IMPRISONMENT OF THE HEAD OF A TRADE UNION IS NO MINOR FOOTNOTE OF AUSTRALIAN HISTORY—AND NOR WAS THE REACTION OF EVERYDAY WORKERS ACROSS THE COUNTRY.

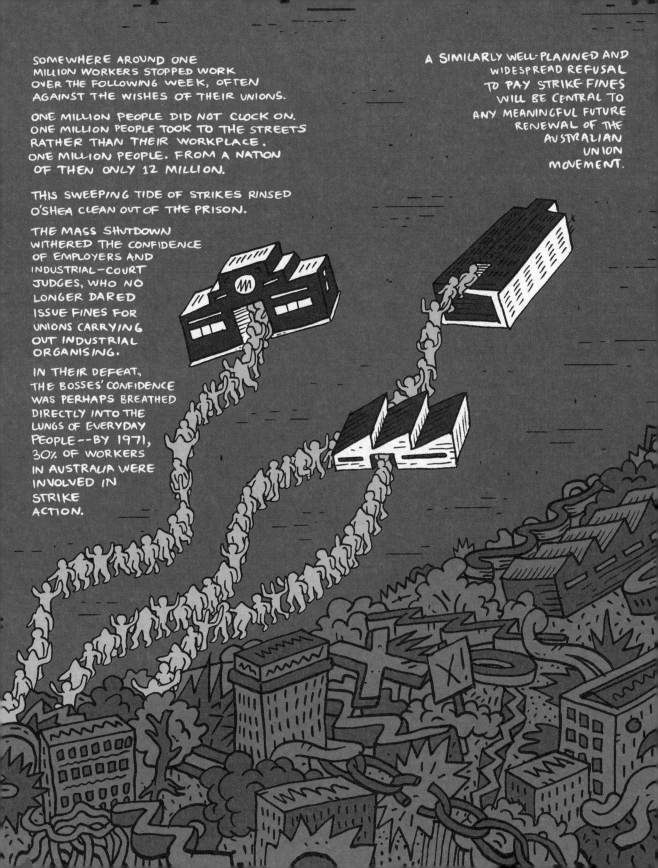

SOMEWHERE AROUND ONE MILLION WORKERS STOPPED WORK OVER THE FOLLOWING WEEK, OFTEN AGAINST THE WISHES OF THEIR UNIONS.

ONE MILLION PEOPLE DID NOT CLOCK ON. ONE MILLION PEOPLE TOOK TO THE STREETS RATHER THAN THEIR WORKPLACE. ONE MILLION PEOPLE. FROM A NATION OF THEN ONLY 12 MILLION.

THIS SWEEPING TIDE OF STRIKES RINSED O'SHEA CLEAN OUT OF THE PRISON.

THE MASS SHUTDOWN WITHERED THE CONFIDENCE OF EMPLOYERS AND INDUSTRIAL-COURT JUDGES, WHO NO LONGER DARED ISSUE FINES FOR UNIONS CARRYING OUT INDUSTRIAL ORGANISING.

IN THEIR DEFEAT, THE BOSSES' CONFIDENCE WAS PERHAPS BREATHED DIRECTLY INTO THE LUNGS OF EVERYDAY PEOPLE -- BY 1971, 30% OF WORKERS IN AUSTRALIA WERE INVOLVED IN STRIKE ACTION.

A SIMILARLY WELL-PLANNED AND WIDESPREAD REFUSAL TO PAY STRIKE FINES WILL BE CENTRAL TO ANY MEANINGFUL FUTURE RENEWAL OF THE AUSTRALIAN UNION MOVEMENT.

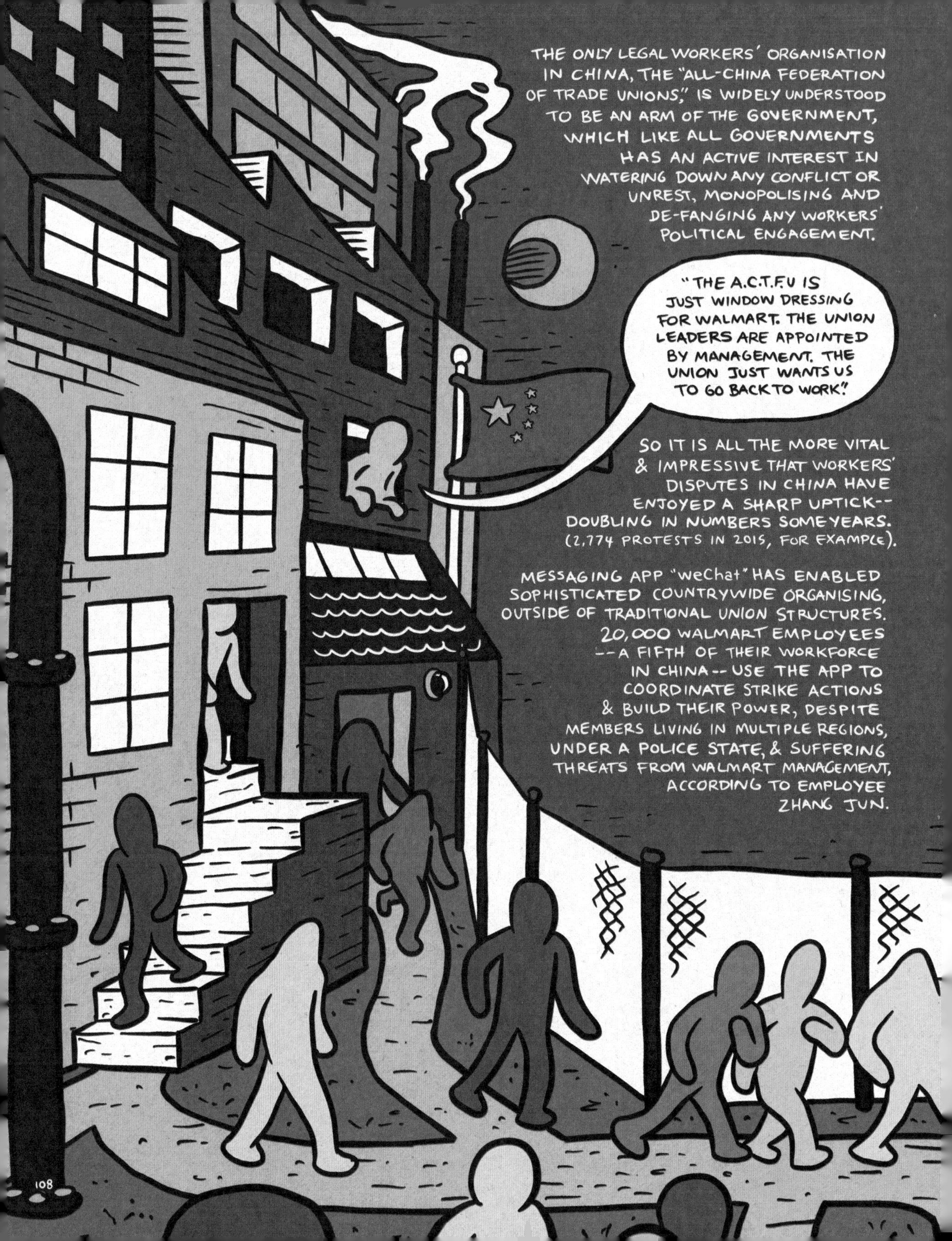
THE ONLY LEGAL WORKERS' ORGANISATION IN CHINA, THE "ALL-CHINA FEDERATION OF TRADE UNIONS," IS WIDELY UNDERSTOOD TO BE AN ARM OF THE GOVERNMENT, WHICH LIKE ALL GOVERNMENTS HAS AN ACTIVE INTEREST IN WATERING DOWN ANY CONFLICT OR UNREST, MONOPOLISING AND DE-FANGING ANY WORKERS' POLITICAL ENGAGEMENT.
"THE A.C.T.F.U IS JUST WINDOW DRESSING FOR WALMART. THE UNION LEADERS ARE APPOINTED BY MANAGEMENT. THE UNION JUST WANTS US TO GO BACK TO WORK!"
SO IT IS ALL THE MORE VITAL & IMPRESSIVE THAT WORKERS' DISPUTES IN CHINA HAVE ENJOYED A SHARP UPTICK-- DOUBLING IN NUMBERS SOME YEARS. (2,774 PROTESTS IN 2015, FOR EXAMPLE).
MESSAGING APP "weChat" HAS ENABLED SOPHISTICATED COUNTRYWIDE ORGANISING, OUTSIDE OF TRADITIONAL UNION STRUCTURES. 20,000 WALMART EMPLOYEES --A FIFTH OF THEIR WORKFORCE IN CHINA-- USE THE APP TO COORDINATE STRIKE ACTIONS & BUILD THEIR POWER, DESPITE MEMBERS LIVING IN MULTIPLE REGIONS, UNDER A POLICE STATE, & SUFFERING THREATS FROM WALMART MANAGEMENT, ACCORDING TO EMPLOYEE ZHANG JUN.

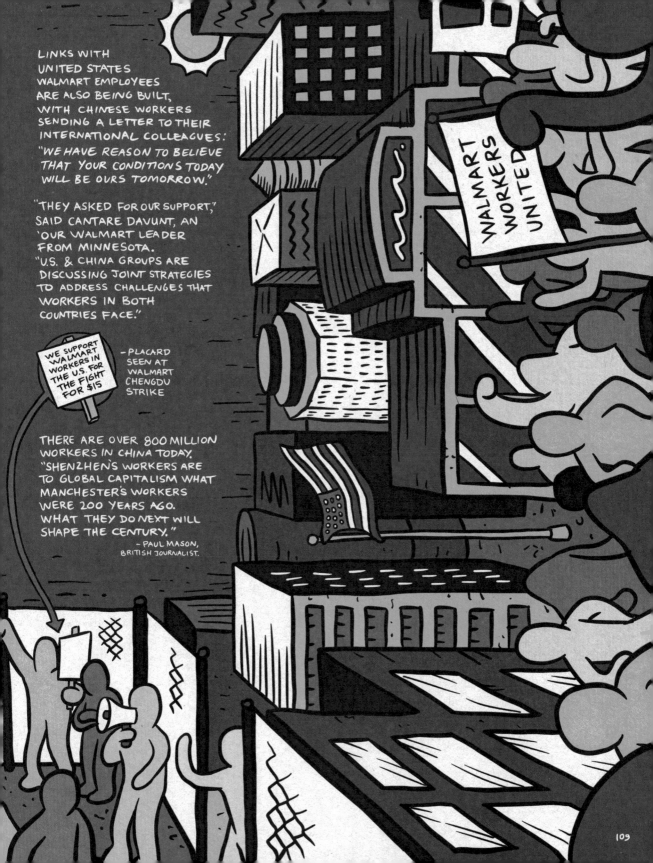

LINKS WITH UNITED STATES WALMART EMPLOYEES ARE ALSO BEING BUILT, WITH CHINESE WORKERS SENDING A LETTER TO THEIR INTERNATIONAL COLLEAGUES:

"WE HAVE REASON TO BELIEVE THAT YOUR CONDITIONS TODAY WILL BE OURS TOMORROW."

"THEY ASKED FOR OUR SUPPORT," SAID CANTARE DAVUNT, AN 'OUR WALMART LEADER FROM MINNESOTA. "U.S. & CHINA GROUPS ARE DISCUSSING JOINT STRATEGIES TO ADDRESS CHALLENGES THAT WORKERS IN BOTH COUNTRIES FACE."

WE SUPPORT WALMART WORKERS IN THE U.S. FOR THE FIGHT FOR $15

— PLACARD SEEN AT WALMART CHENGDU STRIKE

THERE ARE OVER 800 MILLION WORKERS IN CHINA TODAY. "SHENZHEN'S WORKERS ARE TO GLOBAL CAPITALISM WHAT MANCHESTER'S WORKERS WERE 200 YEARS AGO. WHAT THEY DO NEXT WILL SHAPE THE CENTURY."

— PAUL MASON, BRITISH JOURNALIST.

WALMART WORKERS UNITED

109

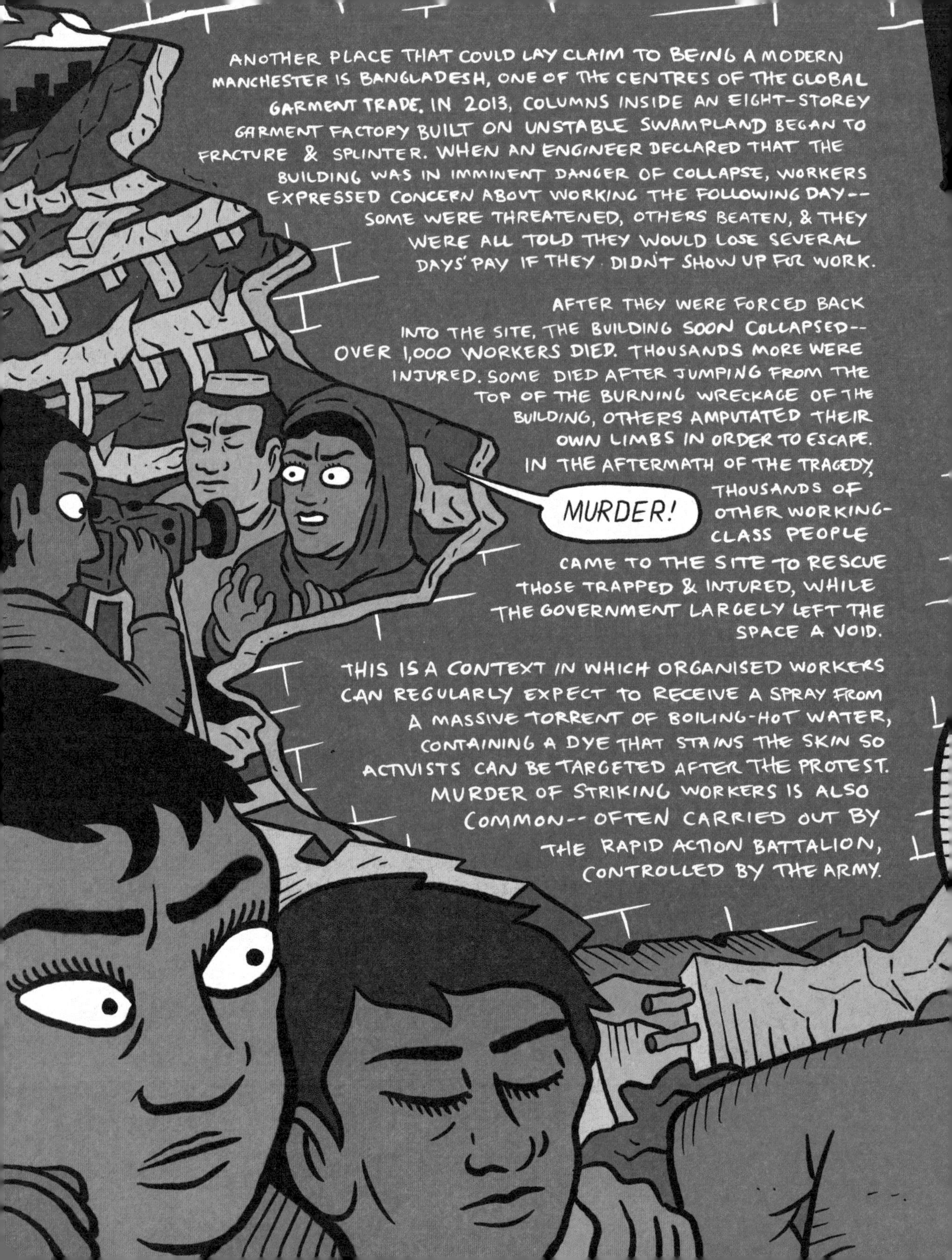
ANOTHER PLACE THAT COULD LAY CLAIM TO BEING A MODERN MANCHESTER IS BANGLADESH, ONE OF THE CENTRES OF THE GLOBAL GARMENT TRADE. IN 2013, COLUMNS INSIDE AN EIGHT-STOREY GARMENT FACTORY BUILT ON UNSTABLE SWAMPLAND BEGAN TO FRACTURE & SPLINTER. WHEN AN ENGINEER DECLARED THAT THE BUILDING WAS IN IMMINENT DANGER OF COLLAPSE, WORKERS EXPRESSED CONCERN ABOUT WORKING THE FOLLOWING DAY-- SOME WERE THREATENED, OTHERS BEATEN, & THEY WERE ALL TOLD THEY WOULD LOSE SEVERAL DAYS' PAY IF THEY DIDN'T SHOW UP FOR WORK.
AFTER THEY WERE FORCED BACK INTO THE SITE, THE BUILDING SOON COLLAPSED-- OVER 1,000 WORKERS DIED. THOUSANDS MORE WERE INJURED. SOME DIED AFTER JUMPING FROM THE TOP OF THE BURNING WRECKAGE OF THE BUILDING, OTHERS AMPUTATED THEIR OWN LIMBS IN ORDER TO ESCAPE. IN THE AFTERMATH OF THE TRAGEDY, THOUSANDS OF OTHER WORKING-CLASS PEOPLE CAME TO THE SITE TO RESCUE THOSE TRAPPED & INJURED, WHILE THE GOVERNMENT LARGELY LEFT THE SPACE A VOID.
MURDER!
THIS IS A CONTEXT IN WHICH ORGANISED WORKERS CAN REGULARLY EXPECT TO RECEIVE A SPRAY FROM A MASSIVE TORRENT OF BOILING-HOT WATER, CONTAINING A DYE THAT STAINS THE SKIN SO ACTIVISTS CAN BE TARGETED AFTER THE PROTEST. MURDER OF STRIKING WORKERS IS ALSO COMMON-- OFTEN CARRIED OUT BY THE RAPID ACTION BATTALION, CONTROLLED BY THE ARMY.

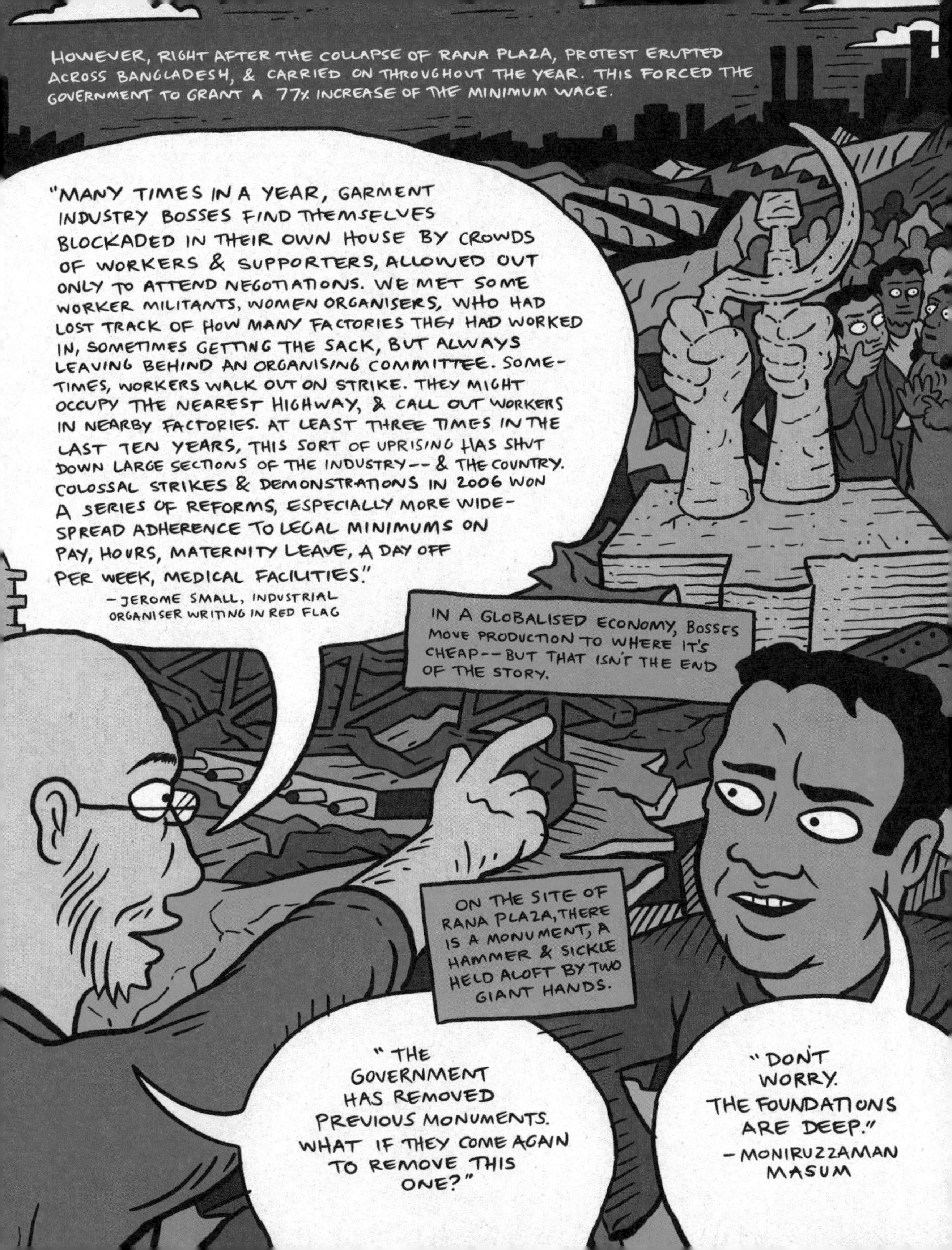
HOWEVER, RIGHT AFTER THE COLLAPSE OF RANA PLAZA, PROTEST ERUPTED ACROSS BANGLADESH, & CARRIED ON THROUGHOUT THE YEAR. THIS FORCED THE GOVERNMENT TO GRANT A 77% INCREASE OF THE MINIMUM WAGE.
"MANY TIMES IN A YEAR, GARMENT INDUSTRY BOSSES FIND THEMSELVES BLOCKADED IN THEIR OWN HOUSE BY CROWDS OF WORKERS & SUPPORTERS, ALLOWED OUT ONLY TO ATTEND NEGOTIATIONS. WE MET SOME WORKER MILITANTS, WOMEN ORGANISERS, WHO HAD LOST TRACK OF HOW MANY FACTORIES THEY HAD WORKED IN, SOMETIMES GETTING THE SACK, BUT ALWAYS LEAVING BEHIND AN ORGANISING COMMITTEE. SOMETIMES, WORKERS WALK OUT ON STRIKE. THEY MIGHT OCCUPY THE NEAREST HIGHWAY, & CALL OUT WORKERS IN NEARBY FACTORIES. AT LEAST THREE TIMES IN THE LAST TEN YEARS, THIS SORT OF UPRISING HAS SHUT DOWN LARGE SECTIONS OF THE INDUSTRY-- & THE COUNTRY. COLOSSAL STRIKES & DEMONSTRATIONS IN 2006 WON A SERIES OF REFORMS, ESPECIALLY MORE WIDESPREAD ADHERENCE TO LEGAL MINIMUMS ON PAY, HOURS, MATERNITY LEAVE, A DAY OFF PER WEEK, MEDICAL FACILITIES."
-JEROME SMALL, INDUSTRIAL ORGANISER WRITING IN RED FLAG
IN A GLOBALISED ECONOMY, BOSSES MOVE PRODUCTION TO WHERE IT'S CHEAP-- BUT THAT ISN'T THE END OF THE STORY.
ON THE SITE OF RANA PLAZA, THERE IS A MONUMENT, A HAMMER & SICKLE HELD ALOFT BY TWO GIANT HANDS.
" THE GOVERNMENT HAS REMOVED PREVIOUS MONUMENTS. WHAT IF THEY COME AGAIN TO REMOVE THIS ONE?"
"DON'T WORRY. THE FOUNDATIONS ARE DEEP."
-MONIRUZZAMAN MASUM

THROUGHOUT THE LATE 1800'S & EARLY 1900'S, JEWISH TAILORS & GENTILE DOCK WORKERS IN LONDON'S EAST END REGULARLY DISPLAYED SOLIDARITY & MATERIAL SUPPORT FOR ONE ANOTHER. IN 1889, DOCK WORKERS DONATED £100 TO SUPPORT A TAILORS' STRIKE. THE SUPPORT FLOWED BOTH WAYS--IN 1912, JEWISH UNION MEMBERS ORGANISED A SUPPORT COMMITTEE THAT LOOKED AFTER 300 DOCK-WORKER CHILDREN WHILE THEIR PARENTS STRUCK.

AND ON IT FLOWED-- TO 1936, WHEN SIR OSWALD MOSLEY'S BRITISH UNION OF FASCISTS HAD AROUND 40,000 MEMBERS. HE, ALONG WITH MULTIPLYING FASCIST ORGANISATIONS THE WORLD OVER, WERE ATTEMPTING TO MAKE A DEMON OF THE JEWISH PEOPLE. THE EAST END WAS HOME TO NEARLY HALF OF BRITAIN'S TOTAL JEWISH POPULATION, & SO IT BECAME A POINT OF MOSLEY'S FOCUS & ATTEMPTS TO BUILD POWER.

A FASCIST MARCH THROUGH THE EAST END WAS PLANNED. SO TOO WAS A PLAN TO BLOCK THE MARCH.

WORKER NEWSPAPERS SPRUIKED THE RALLY TO THOUSANDS IN THEIR WORKPLACES.

"OUR COMMUNICATIONS WERE THROUGH KNOCKS ON DOORS, NOTES THROUGH LETTERBOXES, THE POST, MEETINGS IN THE STREET, OR AT WORK, & BY WORD OF MOUTH... CHALKING SLOGANS ON WALLS & IN THE ROADS... WE CHALKED THOROUGHLY ALL THE ENTRANCES TO THE GREAT STANDARD TELEPHONES CABLE FACTORY IN NEW SOUTHGATE, WHERE 10,000 WENT TO WORK EVERY DAY."
-JOURNALIST RED WATSON.

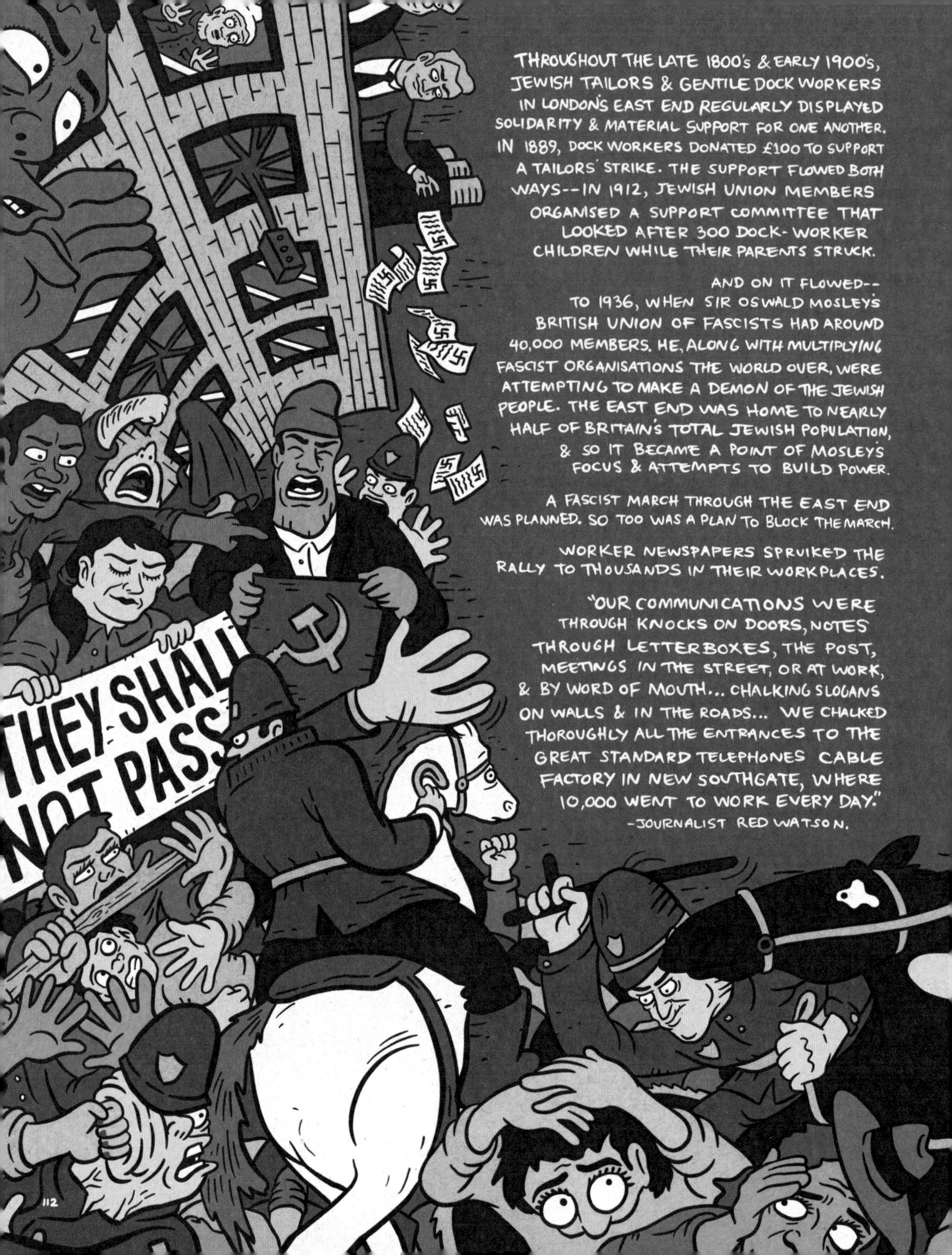
THEY SHALL NOT PASS

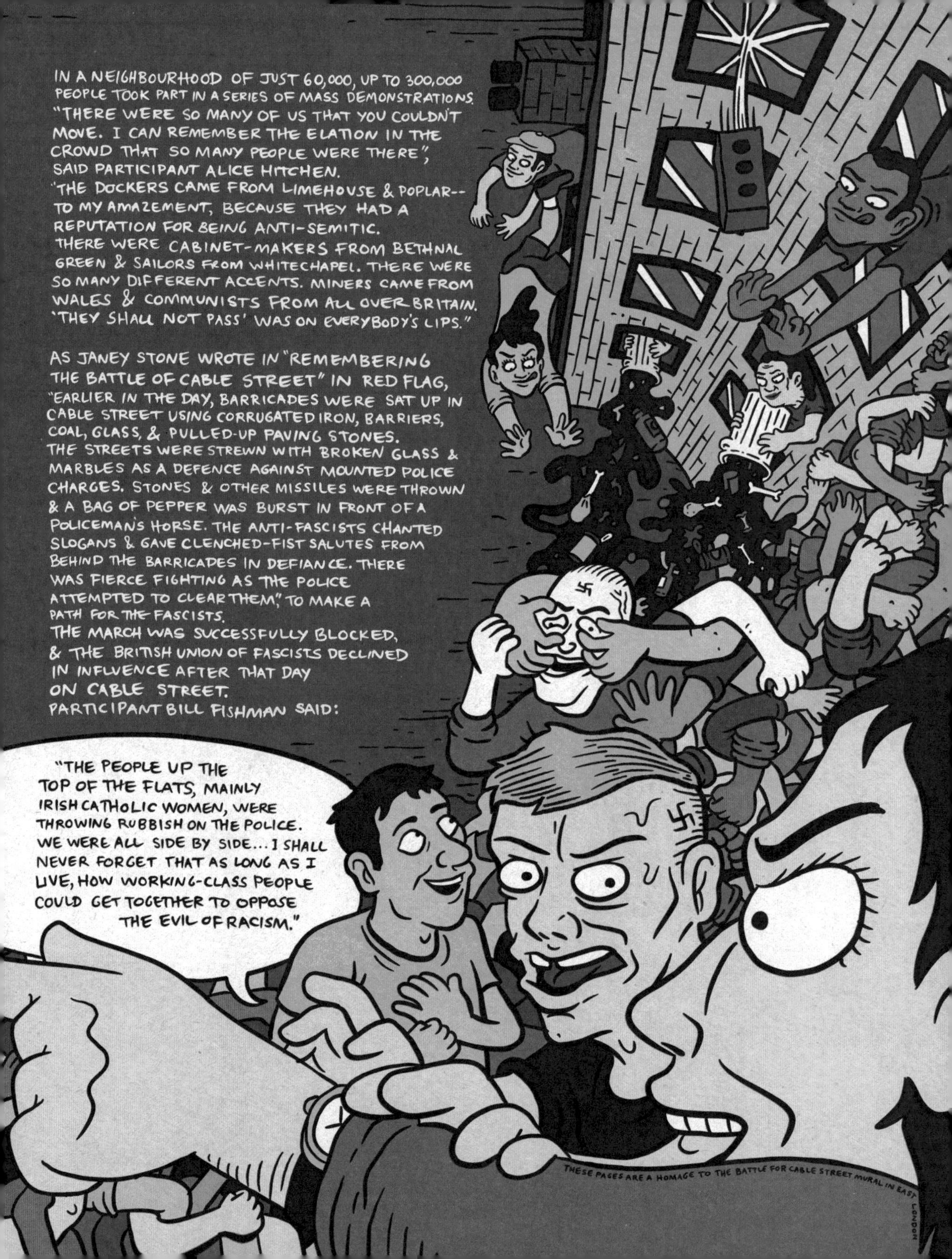
IN A NEIGHBOURHOOD OF JUST 60,000, UP TO 300,000 PEOPLE TOOK PART IN A SERIES OF MASS DEMONSTRATIONS. "THERE WERE SO MANY OF US THAT YOU COULDN'T MOVE. I CAN REMEMBER THE ELATION IN THE CROWD THAT SO MANY PEOPLE WERE THERE", SAID PARTICIPANT ALICE HITCHEN. "THE DOCKERS CAME FROM LIMEHOUSE & POPLAR-- TO MY AMAZEMENT, BECAUSE THEY HAD A REPUTATION FOR BEING ANTI-SEMITIC. THERE WERE CABINET-MAKERS FROM BETHNAL GREEN & SAILORS FROM WHITECHAPEL. THERE WERE SO MANY DIFFERENT ACCENTS. MINERS CAME FROM WALES & COMMUNISTS FROM ALL OVER BRITAIN. 'THEY SHALL NOT PASS' WAS ON EVERYBODY'S LIPS."
AS JANEY STONE WROTE IN "REMEMBERING THE BATTLE OF CABLE STREET" IN RED FLAG, "EARLIER IN THE DAY, BARRICADES WERE SAT UP IN CABLE STREET USING CORRUGATED IRON, BARRIERS, COAL, GLASS, & PULLED-UP PAVING STONES. THE STREETS WERE STREWN WITH BROKEN GLASS & MARBLES AS A DEFENCE AGAINST MOUNTED POLICE CHARGES. STONES & OTHER MISSILES WERE THROWN & A BAG OF PEPPER WAS BURST IN FRONT OF A POLICEMAN'S HORSE. THE ANTI-FASCISTS CHANTED SLOGANS & GAVE CLENCHED-FIST SALUTES FROM BEHIND THE BARRICADES IN DEFIANCE. THERE WAS FIERCE FIGHTING AS THE POLICE ATTEMPTED TO CLEAR THEM", TO MAKE A PATH FOR THE FASCISTS. THE MARCH WAS SUCCESSFULLY BLOCKED, & THE BRITISH UNION OF FASCISTS DECLINED IN INFLUENCE AFTER THAT DAY ON CABLE STREET. PARTICIPANT BILL FISHMAN SAID:
"THE PEOPLE UP THE TOP OF THE FLATS, MAINLY IRISH CATHOLIC WOMEN, WERE THROWING RUBBISH ON THE POLICE. WE WERE ALL SIDE BY SIDE... I SHALL NEVER FORGET THAT AS LONG AS I LIVE, HOW WORKING-CLASS PEOPLE COULD GET TOGETHER TO OPPOSE THE EVIL OF RACISM."
THESE PAGES ARE A HOMAGE TO THE BATTLE FOR CABLE STREET MURAL IN EAST LONDON

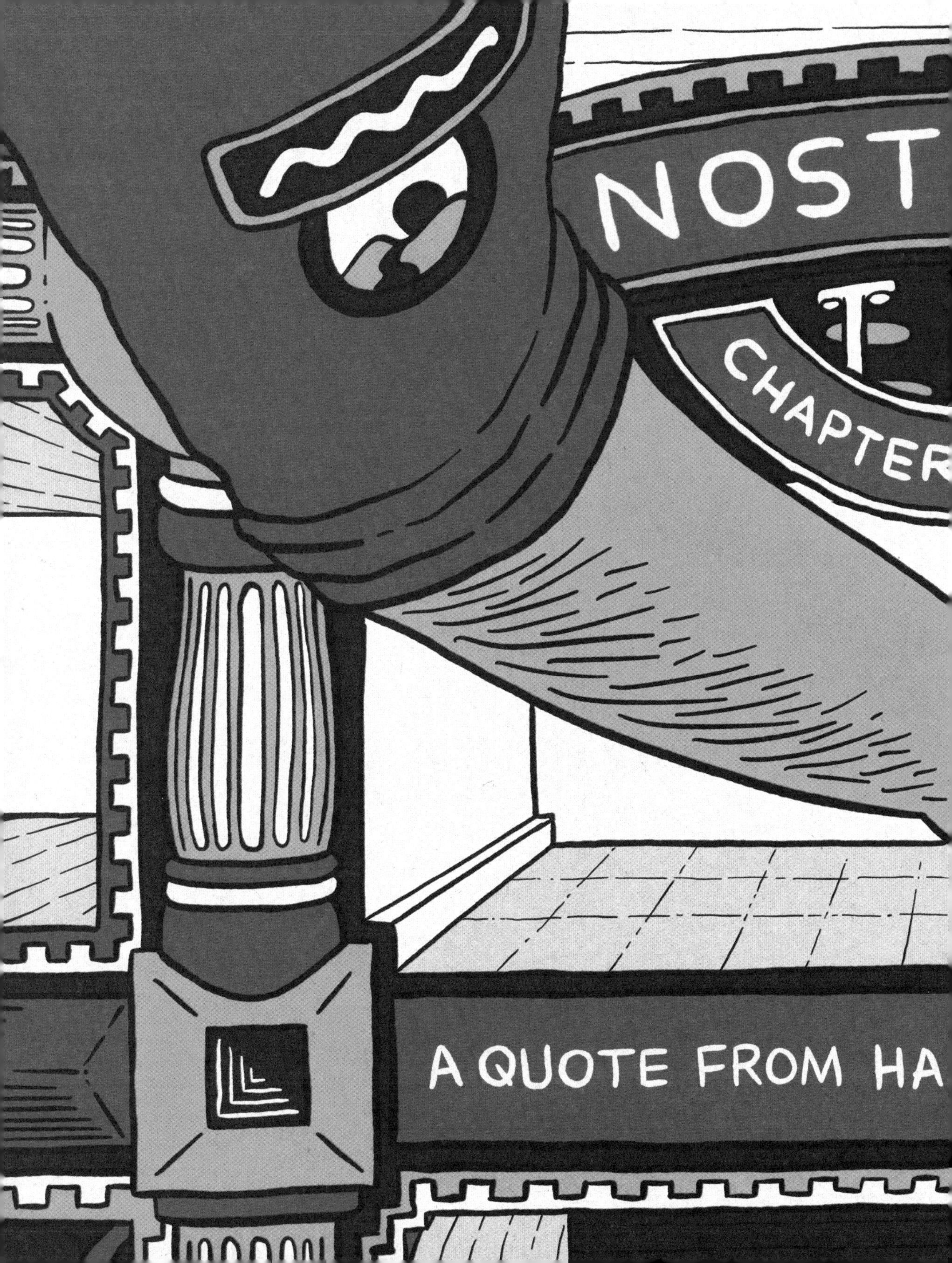

NOST
CHAPTER
A QUOTE FROM HA

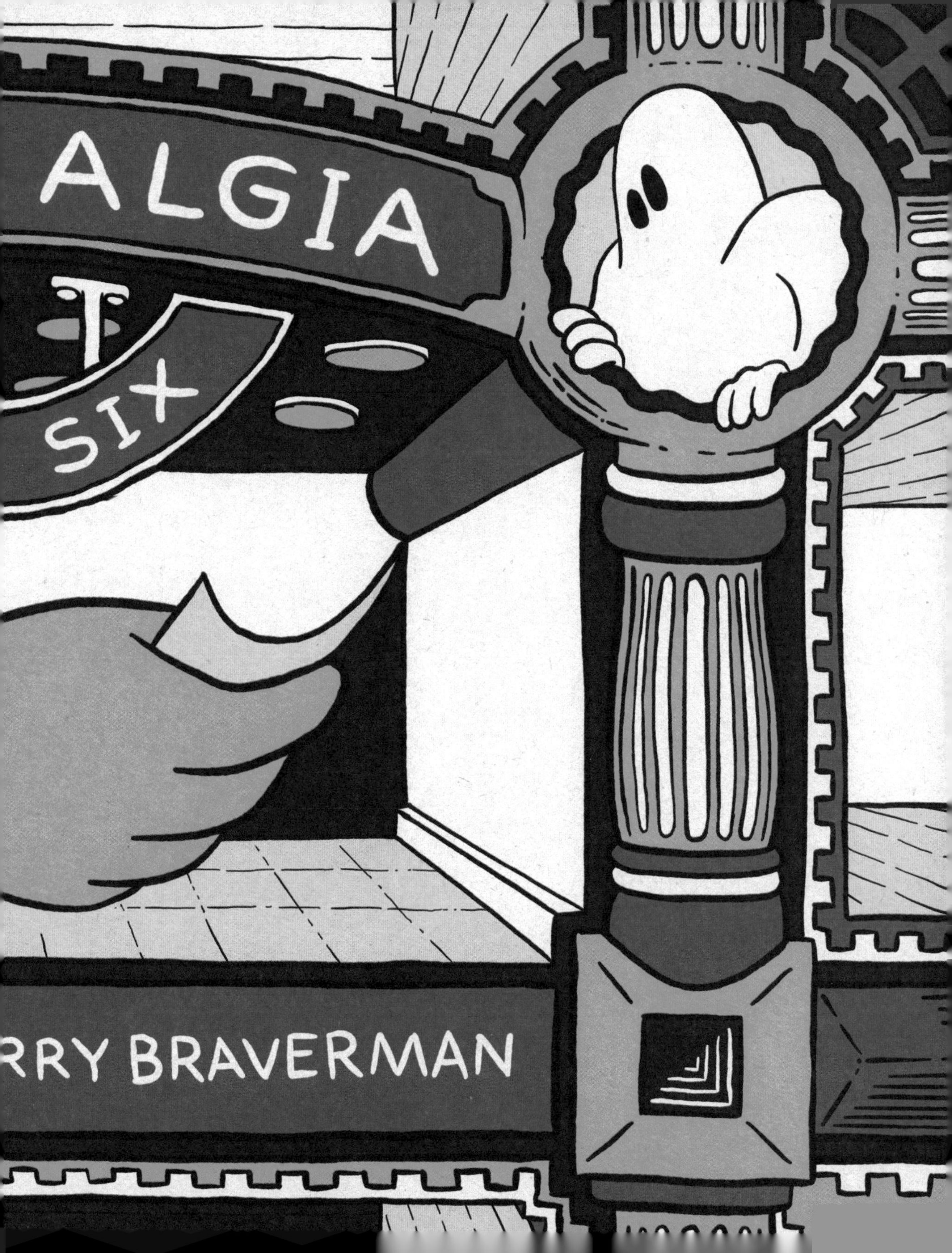
ALGIA
SIX
RRY BRAVERMAN

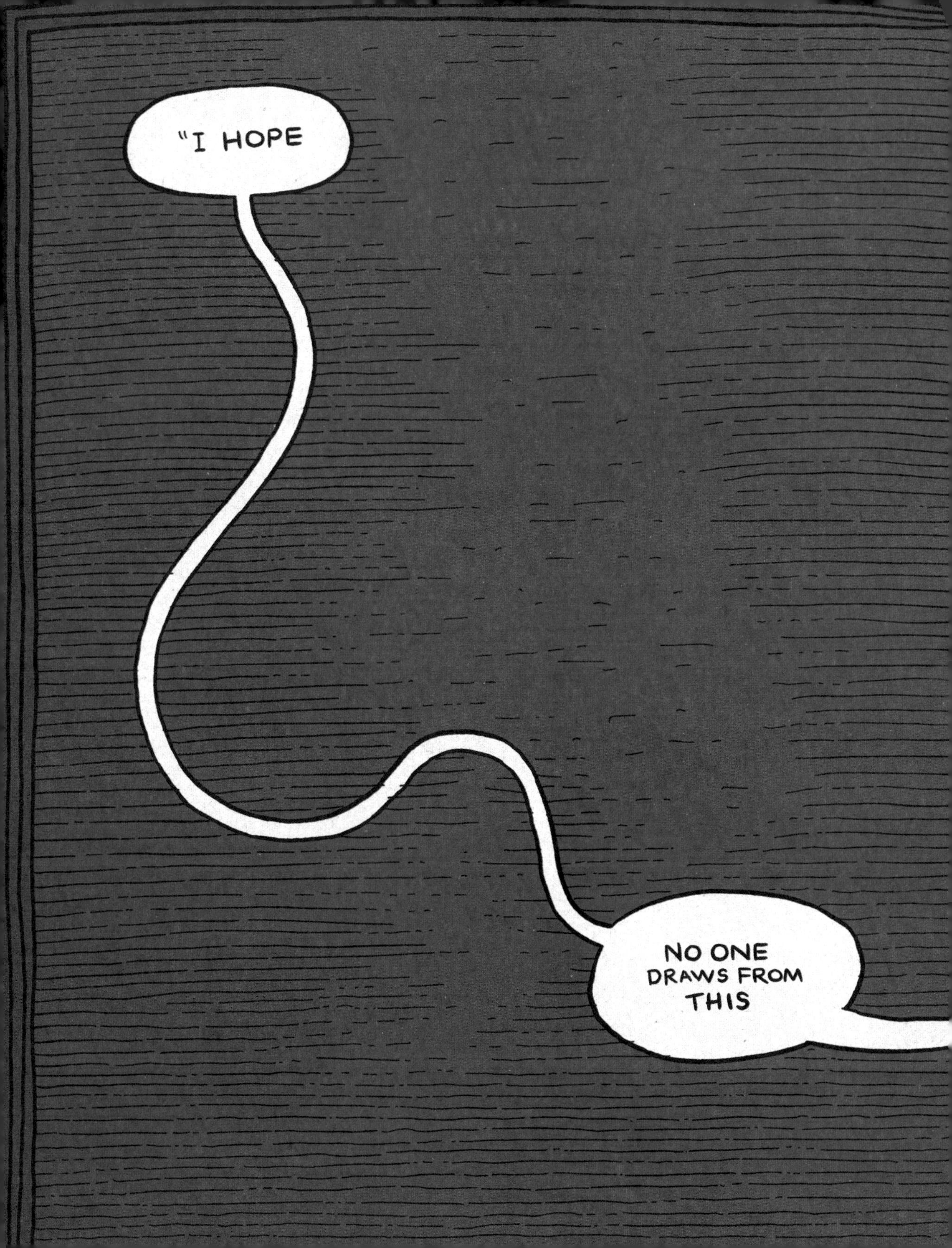
"I HOPE
NO ONE DRAWS FROM THIS

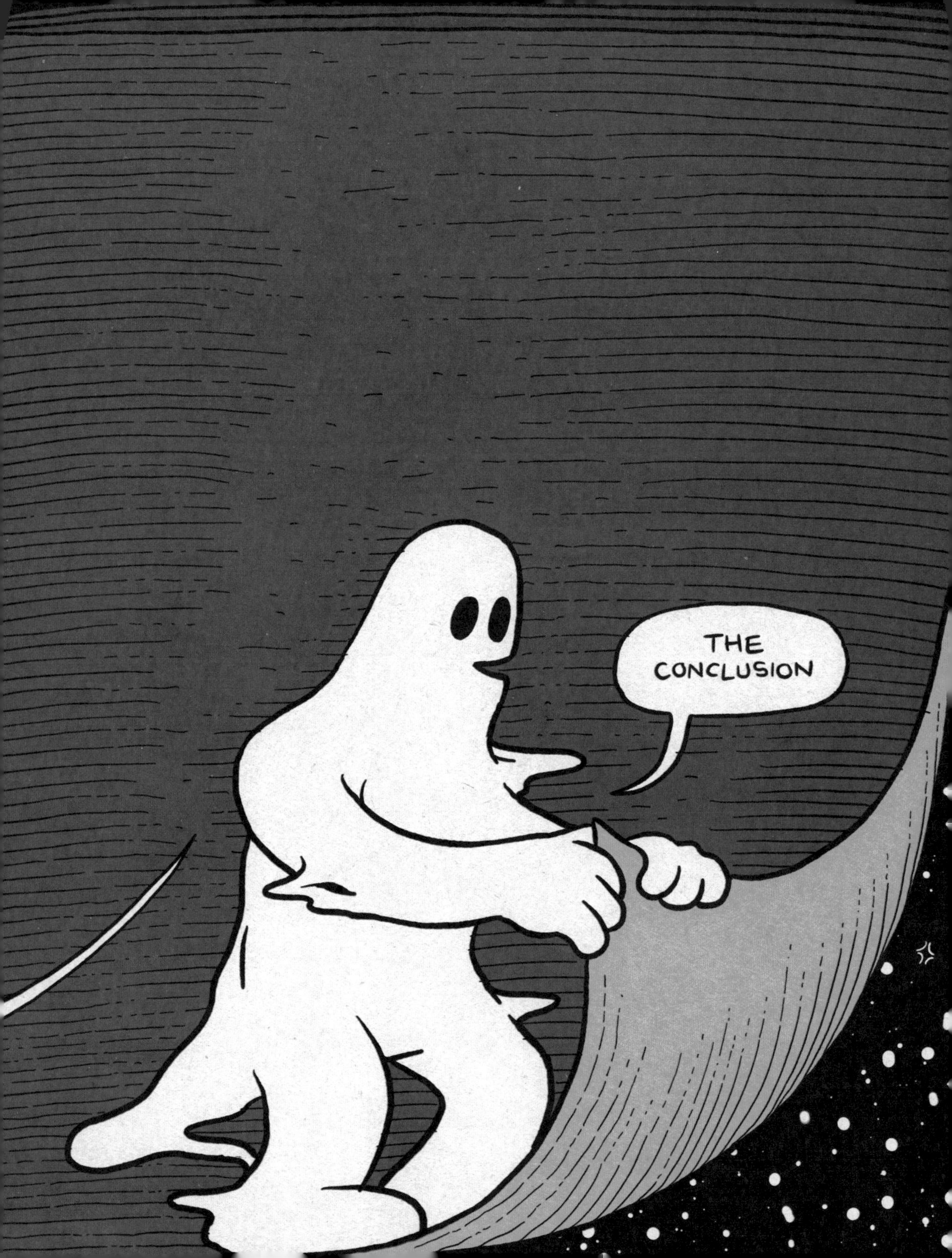
THE CONCLUSION

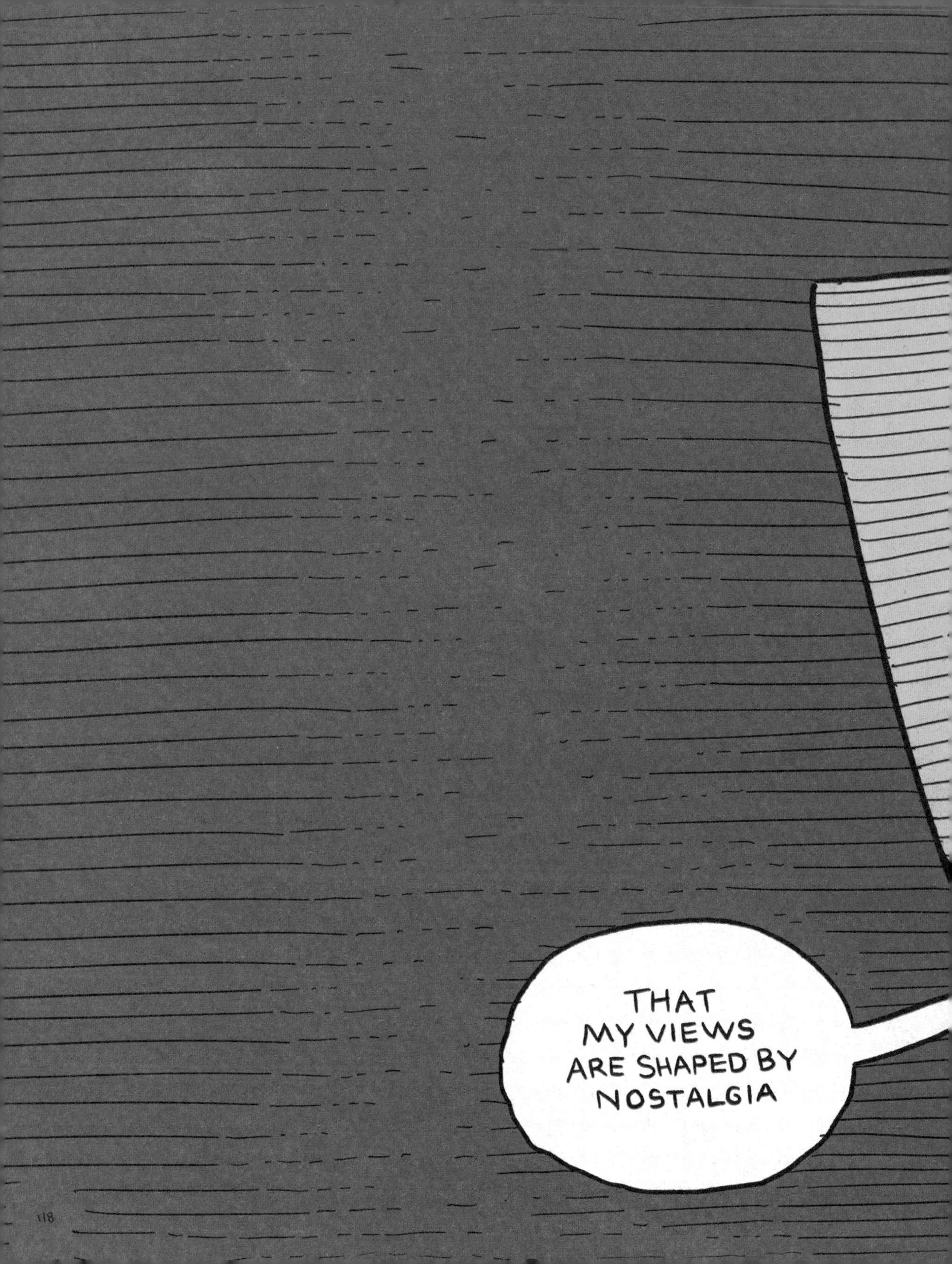
THAT MY VIEWS ARE SHAPED BY NOSTALGIA

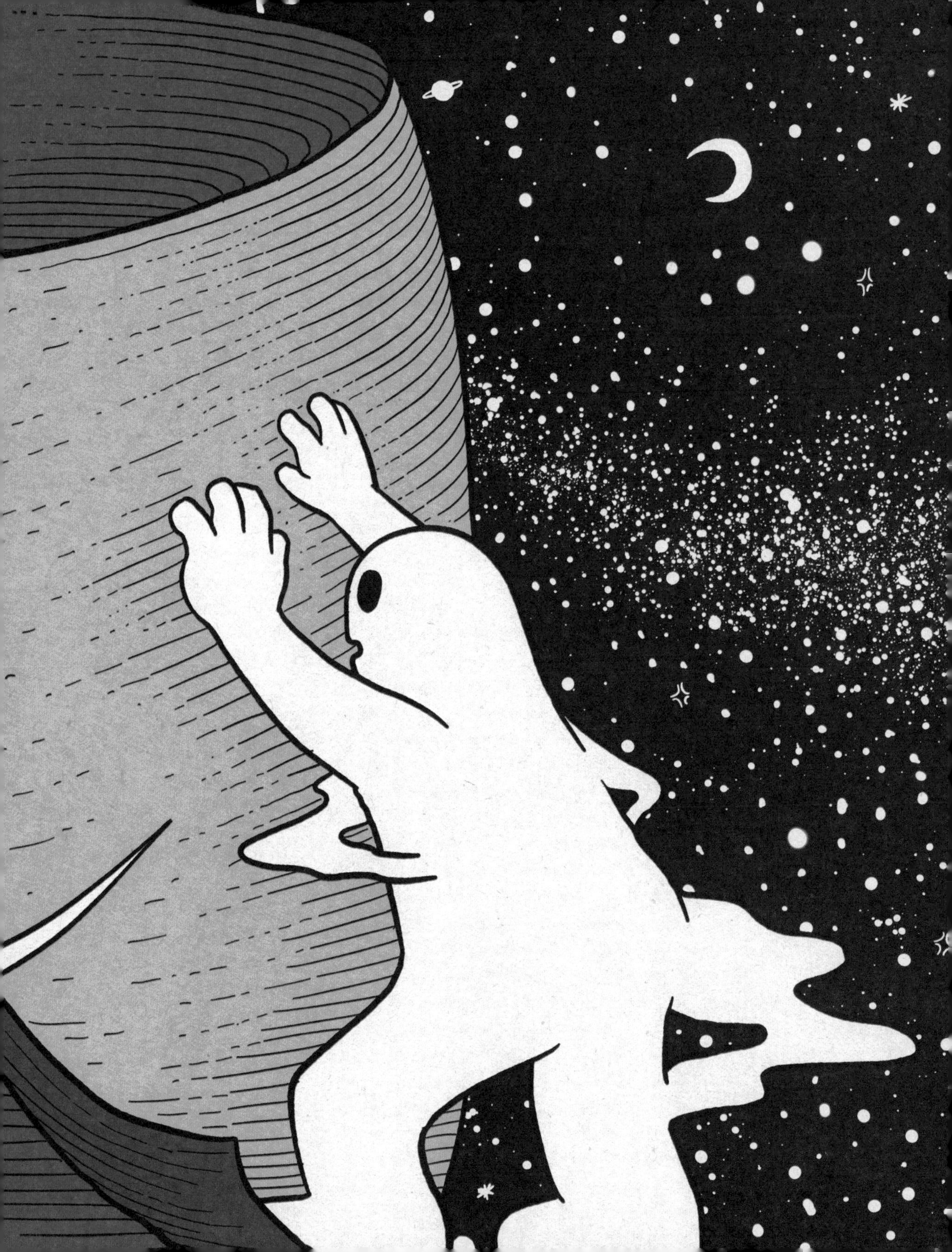

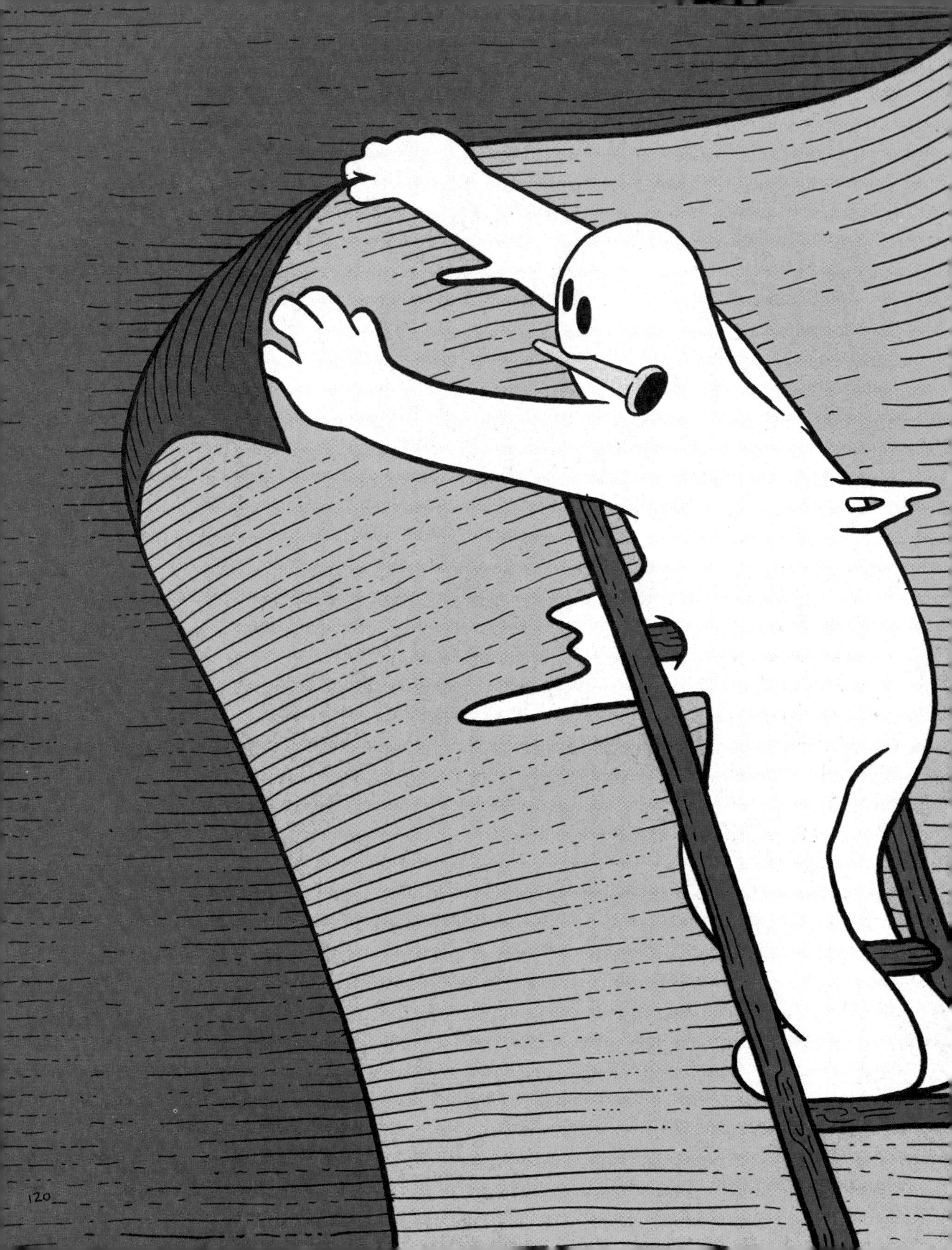

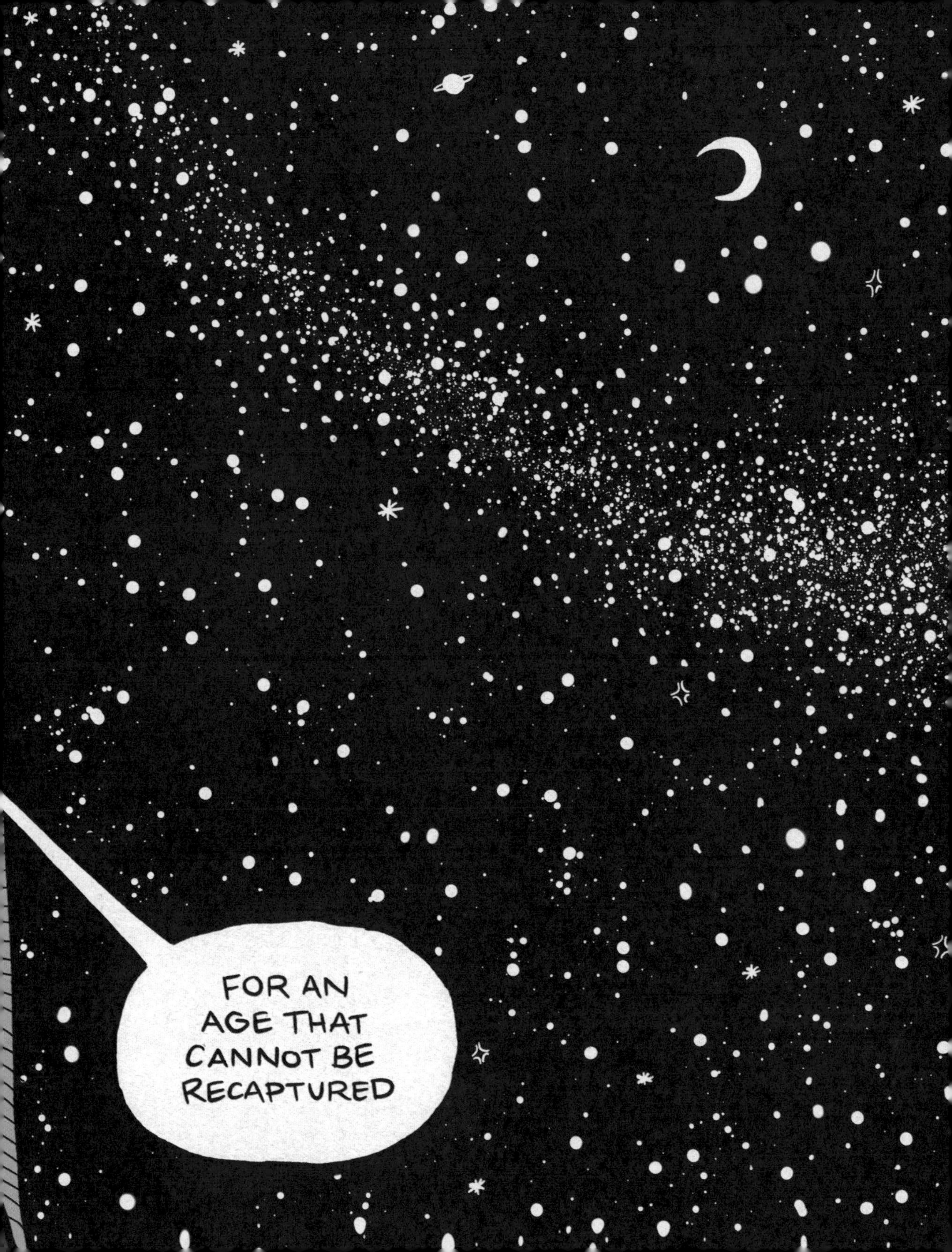
FOR AN AGE THAT CANNOT BE RECAPTURED

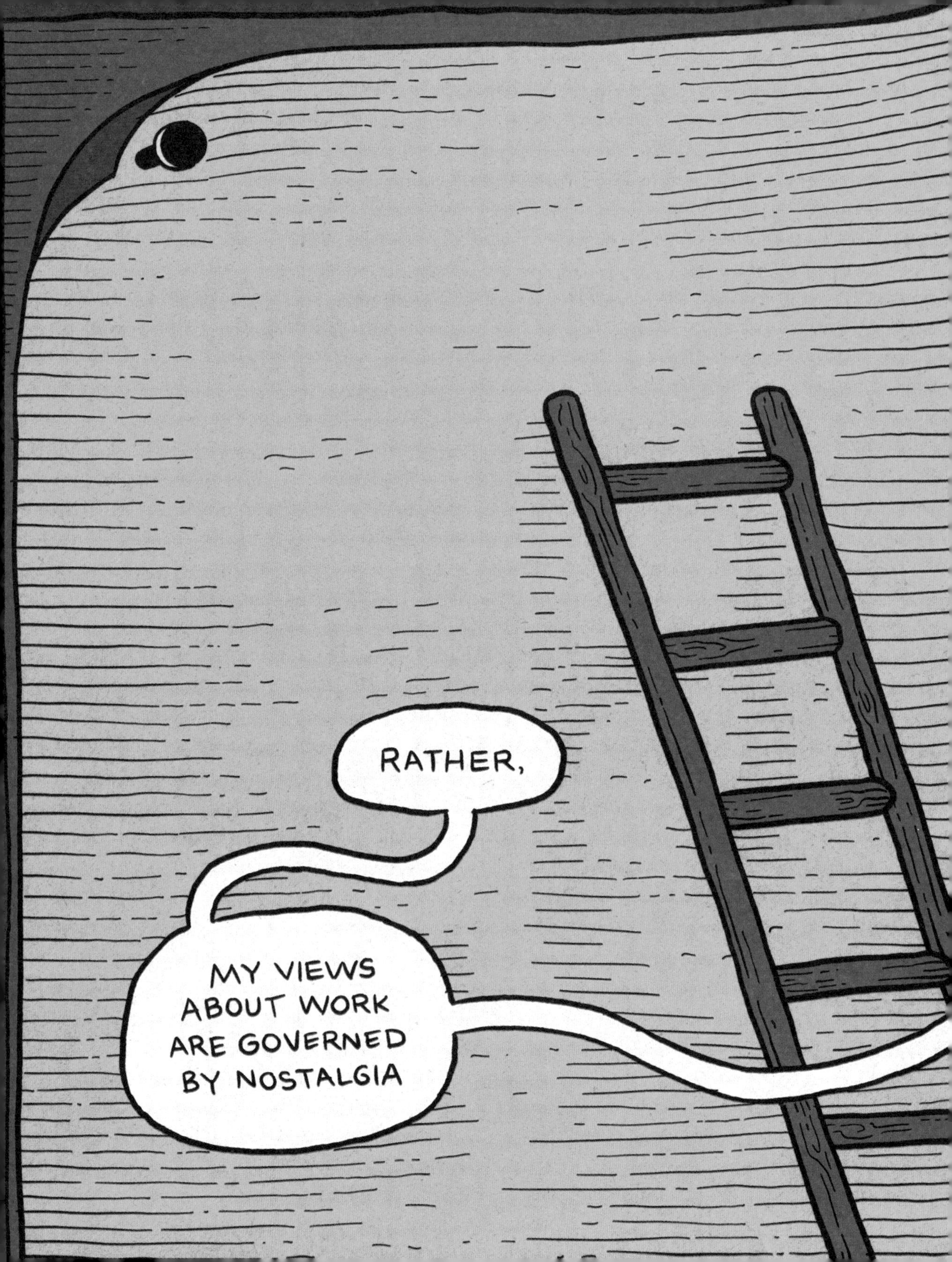
RATHER,
MY VIEWS ABOUT WORK ARE GOVERNED BY NOSTALGIA

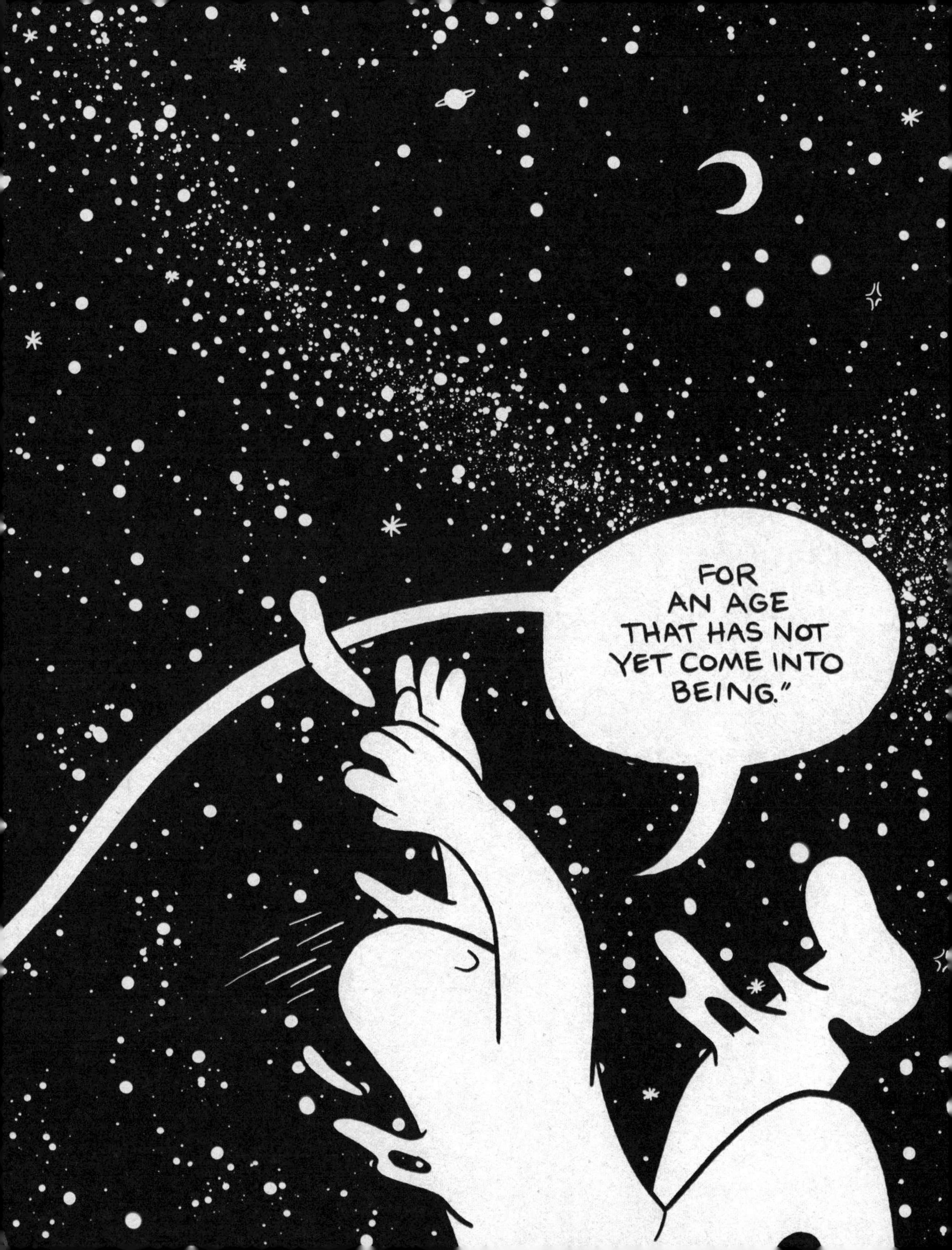
FOR AN AGE THAT HAS NOT YET COME INTO BEING."

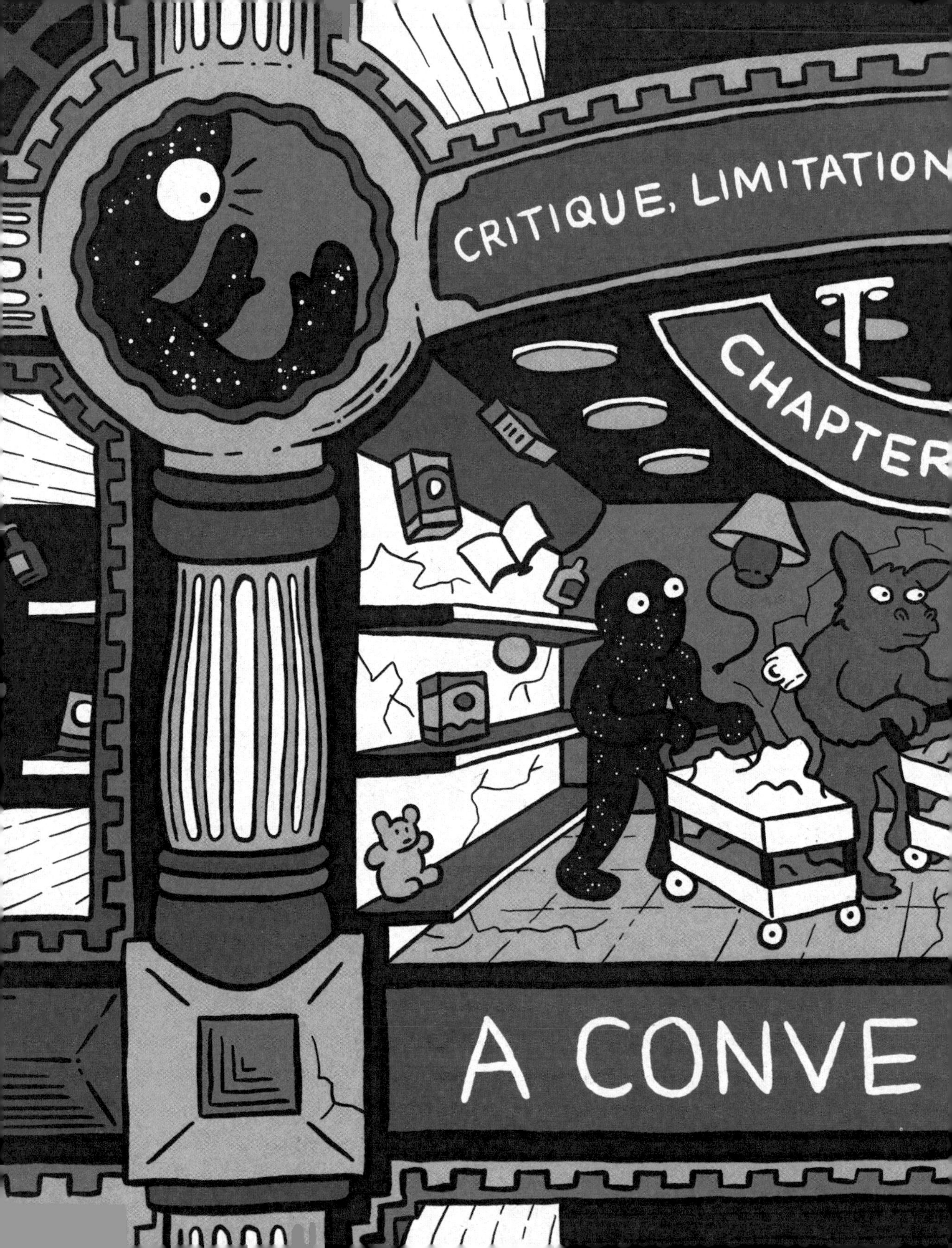
CRITIQUE, LIMITATION
CHAPTER
A CONVE

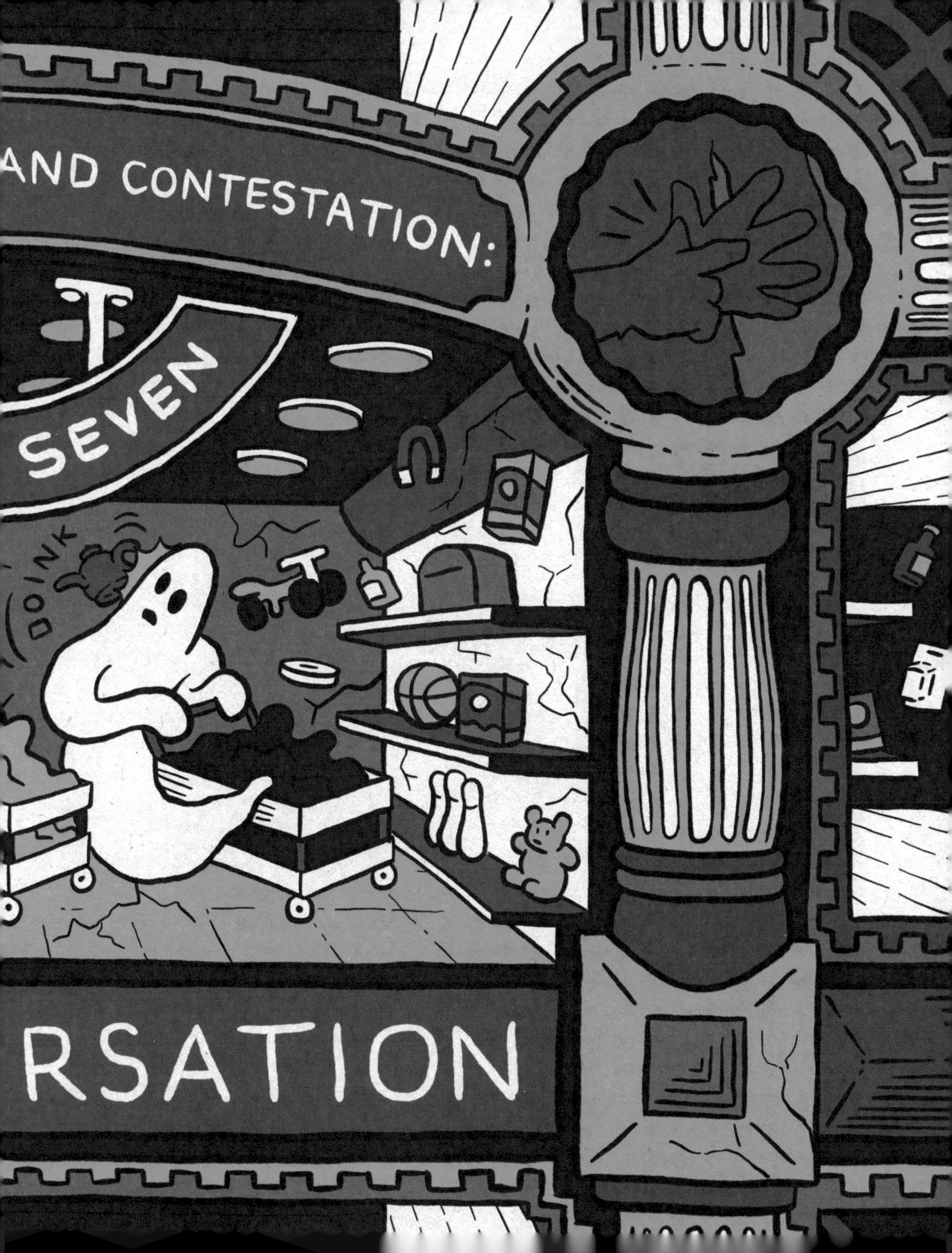
AND CONTESTATION:
SEVEN
DOINK
RSATION

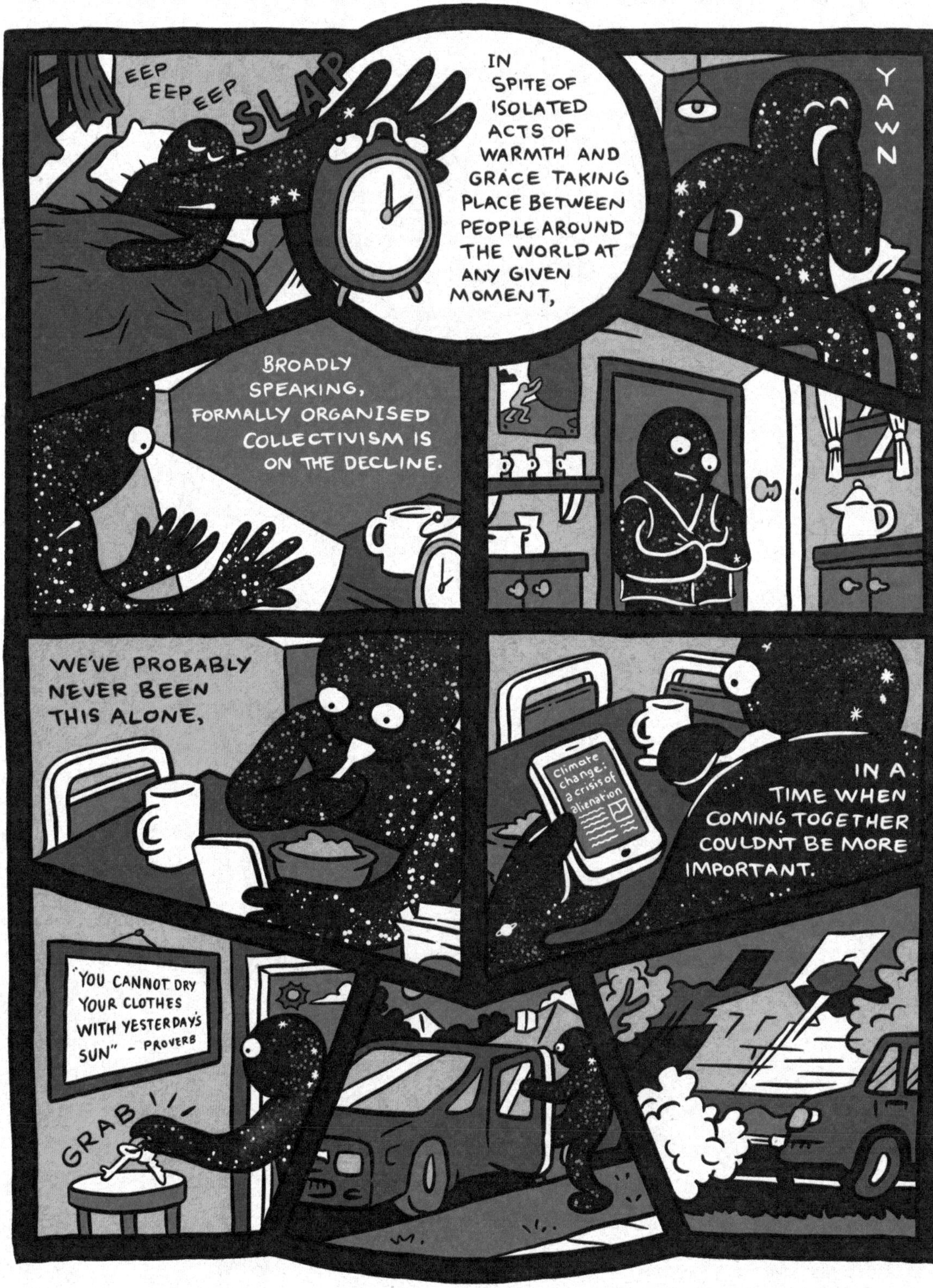

EEP EEP EEP EEP
SLAP
IN SPITE OF ISOLATED ACTS OF WARMTH AND GRACE TAKING PLACE BETWEEN PEOPLE AROUND THE WORLD AT ANY GIVEN MOMENT,
YAWN
BROADLY SPEAKING, FORMALLY ORGANISED COLLECTIVISM IS ON THE DECLINE.
WE'VE PROBABLY NEVER BEEN THIS ALONE,
Climate change: a crisis of alienation
IN A TIME WHEN COMING TOGETHER COULDNT BE MORE IMPORTANT.
"YOU CANNOT DRY YOUR CLOTHES WITH YESTERDAY'S SUN" - PROVERB
GRAB

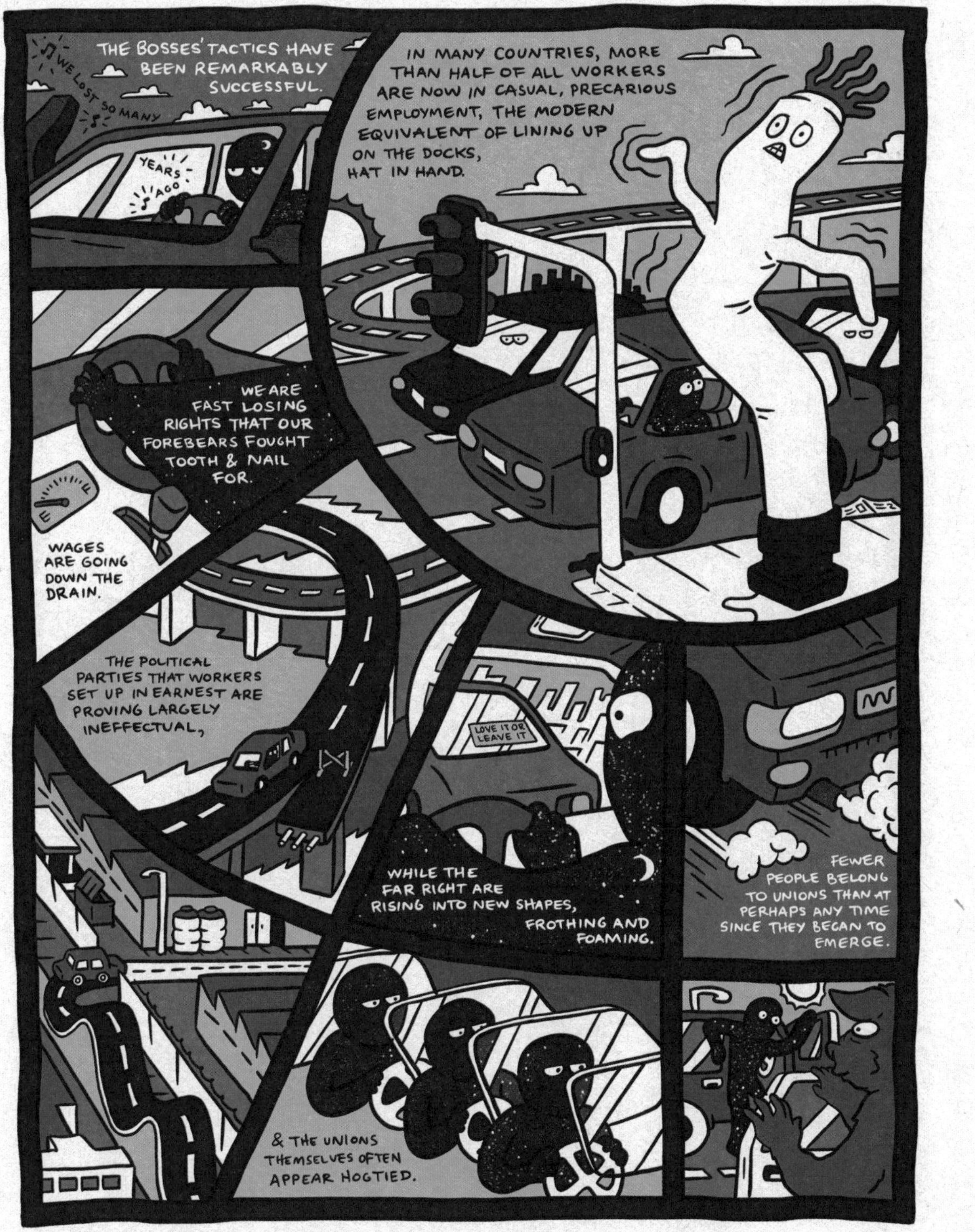
THE BOSSES' TACTICS HAVE BEEN REMARKABLY SUCCESSFUL.
WE LOST SO MANY
YEARS AGO
IN MANY COUNTRIES, MORE THAN HALF OF ALL WORKERS ARE NOW IN CASUAL, PRECARIOUS EMPLOYMENT, THE MODERN EQUIVALENT OF LINING UP ON THE DOCKS, HAT IN HAND.
WE ARE FAST LOSING RIGHTS THAT OUR FOREBEARS FOUGHT TOOTH & NAIL FOR.
WAGES ARE GOING DOWN THE DRAIN.
THE POLITICAL PARTIES THAT WORKERS SET UP IN EARNEST ARE PROVING LARGELY INEFFECTUAL,
LOVE IT OR LEAVE IT
WHILE THE FAR RIGHT ARE RISING INTO NEW SHAPES, FROTHING AND FOAMING.
FEWER PEOPLE BELONG TO UNIONS THAN AT PERHAPS ANY TIME SINCE THEY BEGAN TO EMERGE.
& THE UNIONS THEMSELVES OFTEN APPEAR HOGTIED.

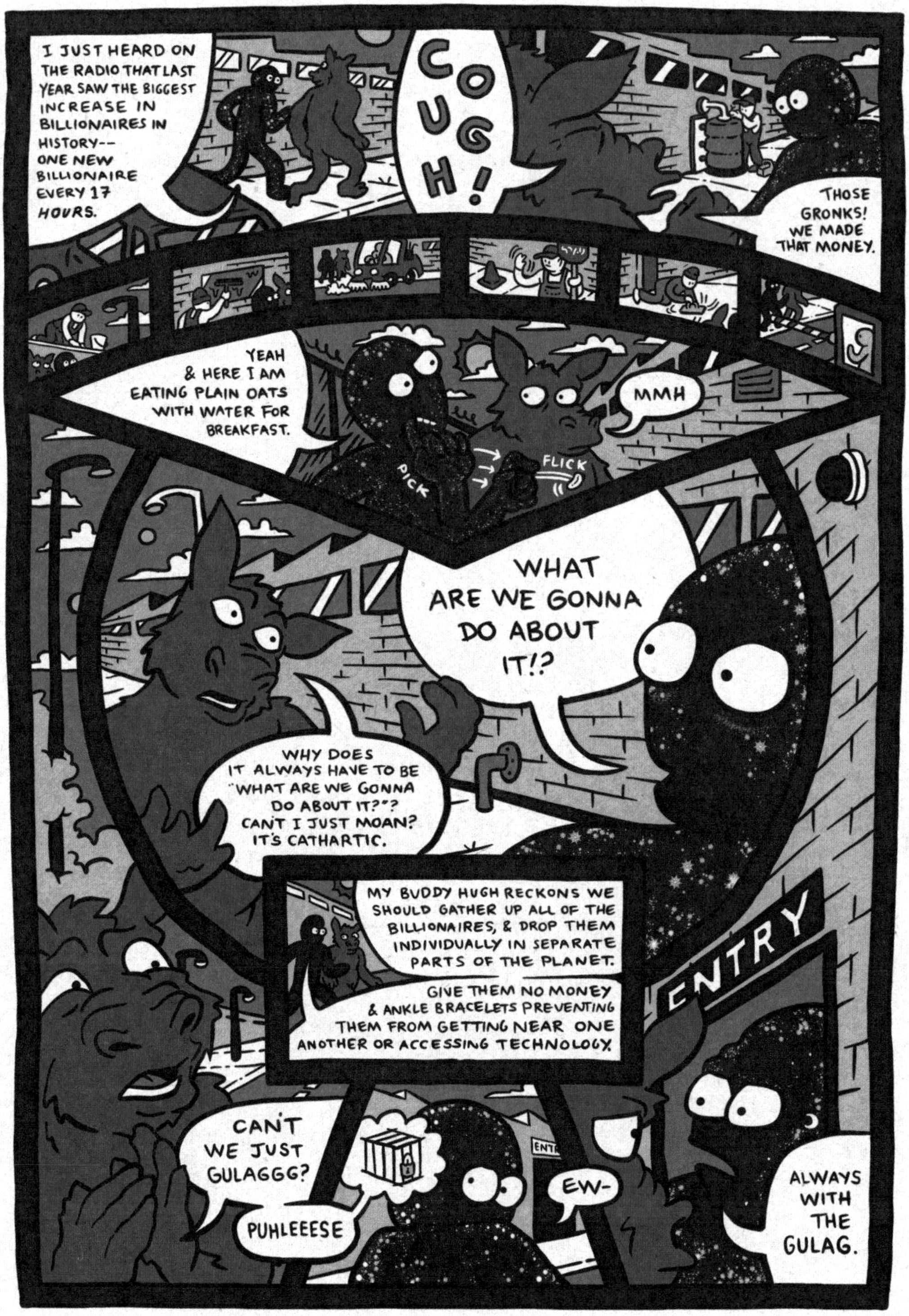
I JUST HEARD ON THE RADIO THAT LAST YEAR SAW THE BIGGEST INCREASE IN BILLIONAIRES IN HISTORY-- ONE NEW BILLIONAIRE EVERY 17 HOURS.
COUGH!
THOSE GRONKS! WE MADE THAT MONEY.
YEAH & HERE I AM EATING PLAIN OATS WITH WATER FOR BREAKFAST.
MMH
PICK
FLICK
WHAT ARE WE GONNA DO ABOUT IT!?
WHY DOES IT ALWAYS HAVE TO BE "WHAT ARE WE GONNA DO ABOUT IT?"? CAN'T I JUST MOAN? IT'S CATHARTIC.
MY BUDDY HUGH RECKONS WE SHOULD GATHER UP ALL OF THE BILLIONAIRES, & DROP THEM INDIVIDUALLY IN SEPARATE PARTS OF THE PLANET.
GIVE THEM NO MONEY & ANKLE BRACELETS PREVENTING THEM FROM GETTING NEAR ONE ANOTHER OR ACCESSING TECHNOLOGY.
ENTRY
CAN'T WE JUST GULAGGG?
PUHLEEESE
EW-
ALWAYS WITH THE GULAG.

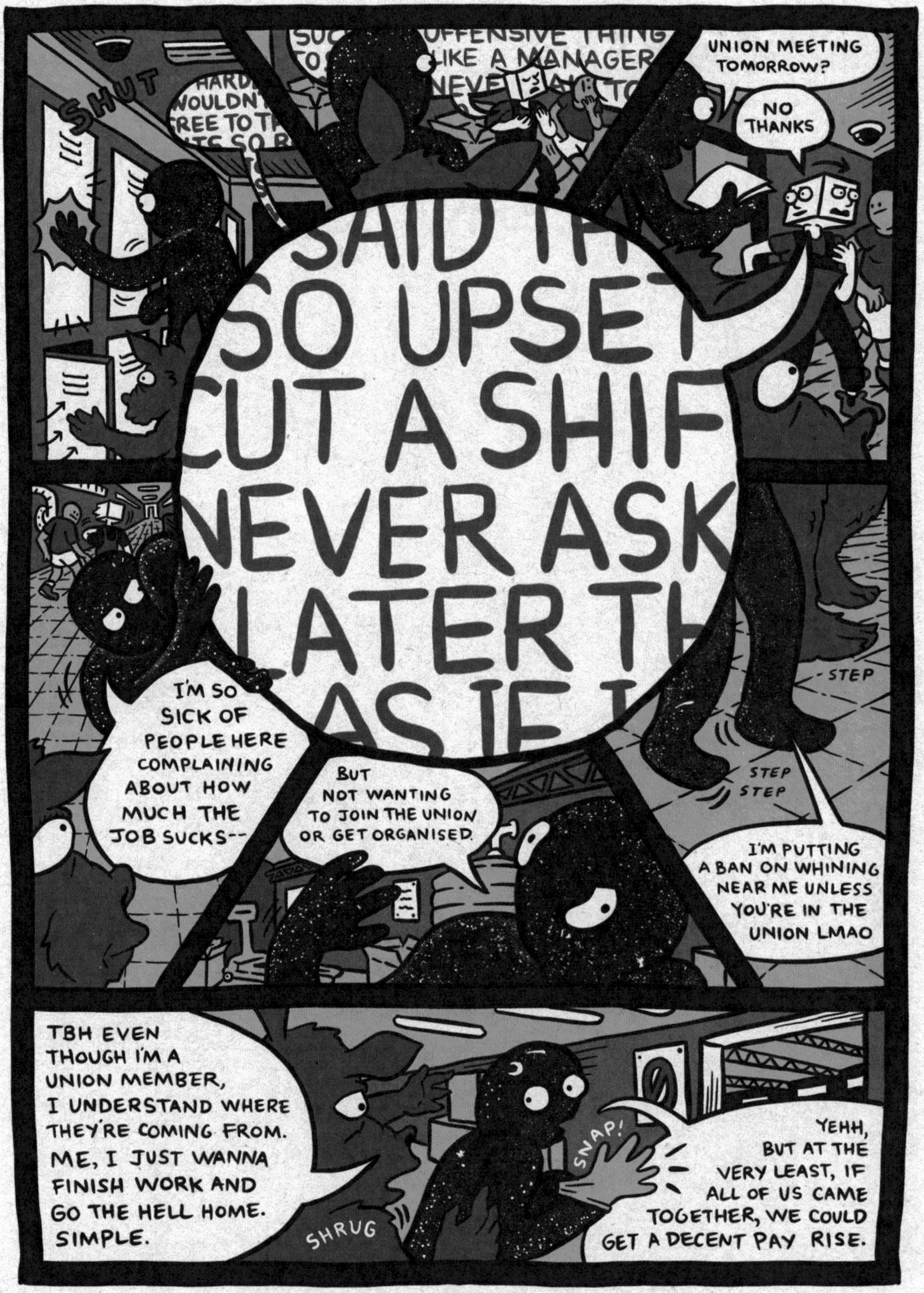
SHUT
LIKE A MANAGER
UNION MEETING TOMORROW?
NO THANKS
SAID TH
SO UPSET
CUT A SHIF
NEVER ASK
LATER TH
I'M SO SICK OF PEOPLE HERE COMPLAINING ABOUT HOW MUCH THE JOB SUCKS--
BUT NOT WANTING TO JOIN THE UNION OR GET ORGANISED.
STEP
STEP STEP
I'M PUTTING A BAN ON WHINING NEAR ME UNLESS YOU'RE IN THE UNION LMAO
TBH EVEN THOUGH I'M A UNION MEMBER, I UNDERSTAND WHERE THEY'RE COMING FROM. ME, I JUST WANNA FINISH WORK AND GO THE HELL HOME. SIMPLE.
SHRUG
SNAP!
YEHH, BUT AT THE VERY LEAST, IF ALL OF US CAME TOGETHER, WE COULD GET A DECENT PAY RISE.

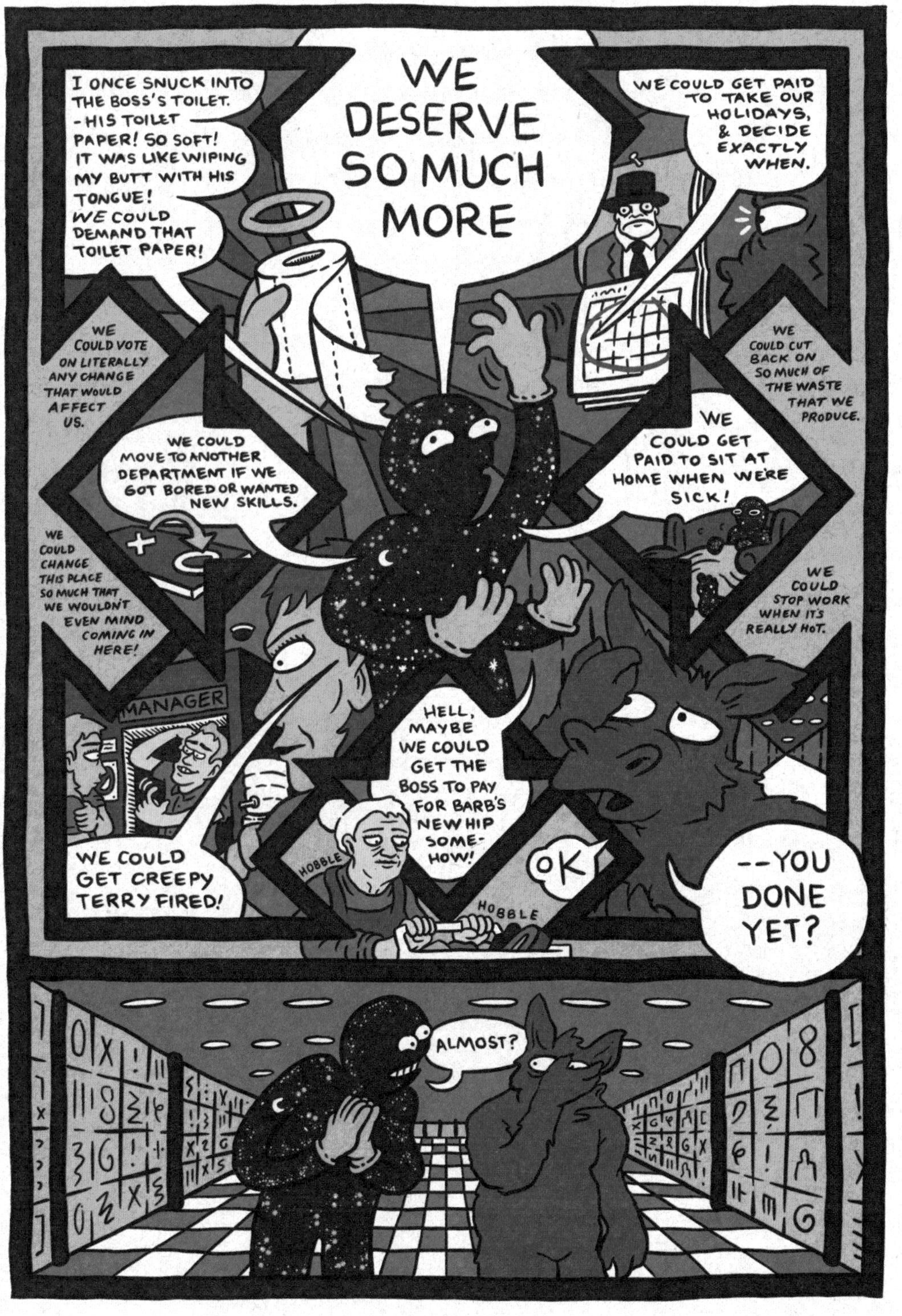
I ONCE SNUCK INTO THE BOSS'S TOILET. -HIS TOILET PAPER! SO SOFT! IT WAS LIKE WIPING MY BUTT WITH HIS TONGUE! WE COULD DEMAND THAT TOILET PAPER!
WE DESERVE SO MUCH MORE
WE COULD GET PAID TO TAKE OUR HOLIDAYS, & DECIDE EXACTLY WHEN.
WE COULD VOTE ON LITERALLY ANY CHANGE THAT WOULD AFFECT US.
WE COULD CUT BACK ON SO MUCH OF THE WASTE THAT WE PRODUCE.
WE COULD MOVE TO ANOTHER DEPARTMENT IF WE GOT BORED OR WANTED NEW SKILLS.
WE COULD GET PAID TO SIT AT HOME WHEN WE'RE SICK!
WE COULD CHANGE THIS PLACE SO MUCH THAT WE WOULDN'T EVEN MIND COMING IN HERE!
WE COULD STOP WORK WHEN IT'S REALLY HOT.
MANAGER
HELL, MAYBE WE COULD GET THE BOSS TO PAY FOR BARB'S NEW HIP SOME-HOW!
WE COULD GET CREEPY TERRY FIRED!
HOBBLE
OK
HOBBLE
--YOU DONE YET?
ALMOST?

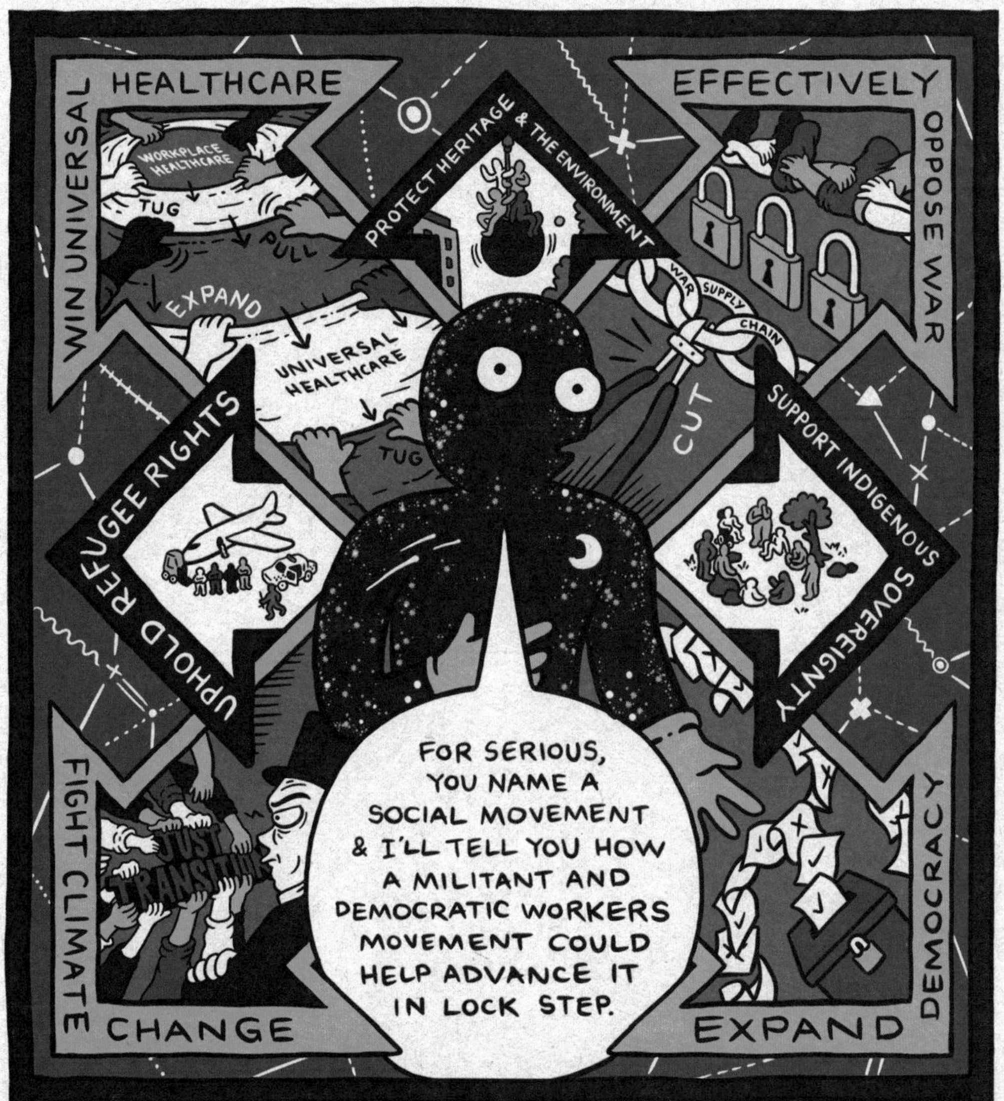
WIN UNIVERSAL HEALTHCARE
WORKPLACE HEALTHCARE
TUG
PULL
EXPAND
UNIVERSAL HEALTHCARE
TUG
PROTECT HERITAGE & THE ENVIRONMENT
EFFECTIVELY OPPOSE WAR
WAR SUPPLY CHAIN
CUT
UPHOLD REFUGEE RIGHTS
SUPPORT INDIGENOUS SOVEREIGNTY
FIGHT CLIMATE CHANGE
JUST TRANSITION
EXPAND DEMOCRACY
FOR SERIOUS, YOU NAME A SOCIAL MOVEMENT & I'LL TELL YOU HOW A MILITANT AND DEMOCRATIC WORKERS MOVEMENT COULD HELP ADVANCE IT IN LOCK STEP.

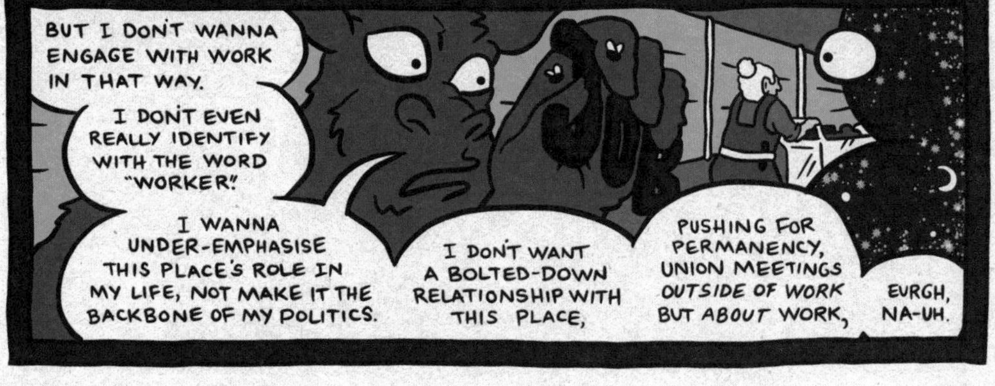
BUT I DON'T WANNA ENGAGE WITH WORK IN THAT WAY.
I DON'T EVEN REALLY IDENTIFY WITH THE WORD "WORKER."
I WANNA UNDER-EMPHASISE THIS PLACE'S ROLE IN MY LIFE, NOT MAKE IT THE BACKBONE OF MY POLITICS.
I DON'T WANT A BOLTED-DOWN RELATIONSHIP WITH THIS PLACE,
PUSHING FOR PERMANENCY, UNION MEETINGS *OUTSIDE OF WORK* BUT *ABOUT* WORK,
EURGH, NA-UH.

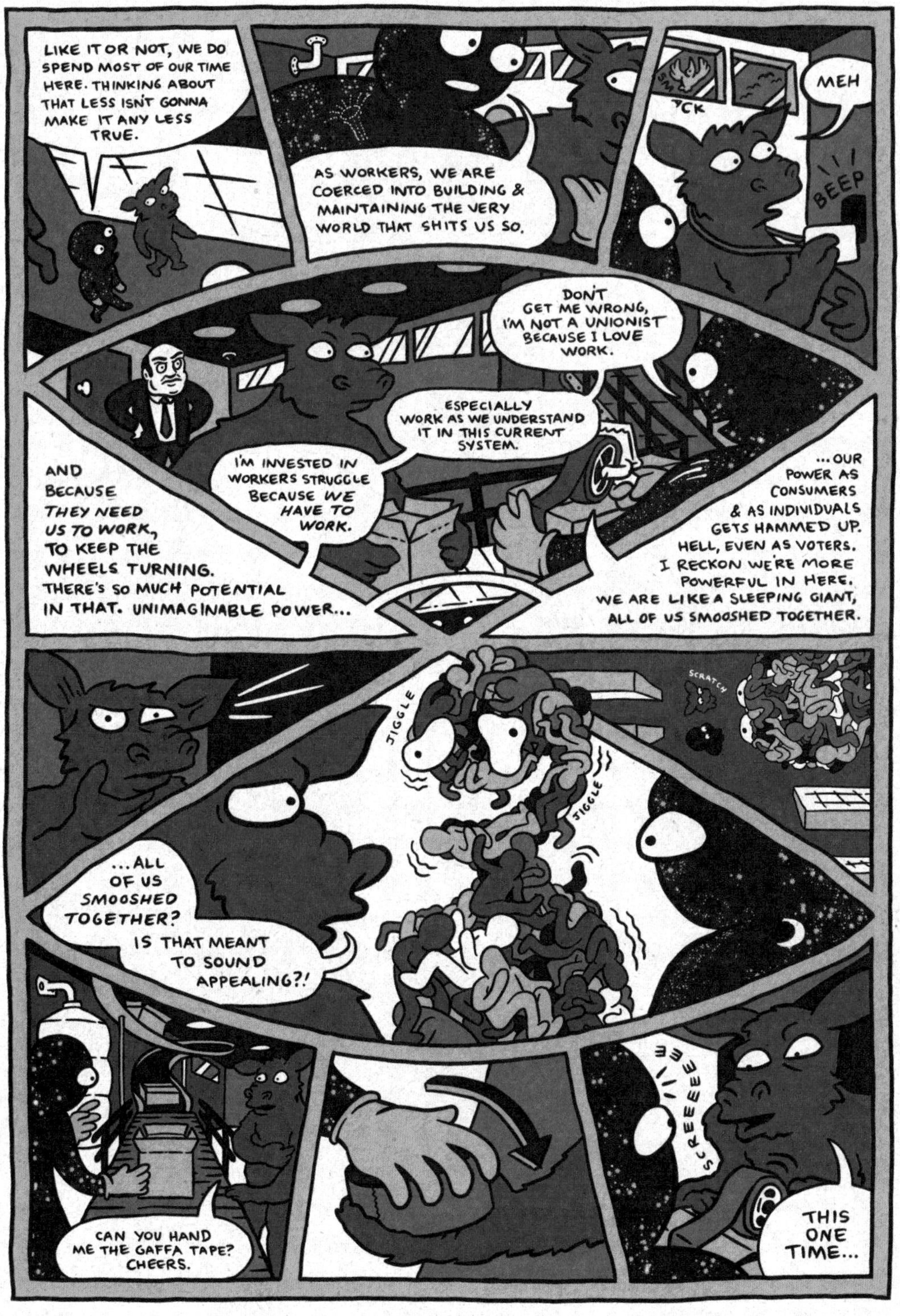
LIKE IT OR NOT, WE DO SPEND MOST OF OUR TIME HERE. THINKING ABOUT THAT LESS ISN'T GONNA MAKE IT ANY LESS TRUE.
AS WORKERS, WE ARE COERCED INTO BUILDING & MAINTAINING THE VERY WORLD THAT SHITS US SO.
SMACK
MEH
BEEP
DON'T GET ME WRONG, I'M NOT A UNIONIST BECAUSE I LOVE WORK.
ESPECIALLY WORK AS WE UNDERSTAND IT IN THIS CURRENT SYSTEM.
I'M INVESTED IN WORKERS STRUGGLE BECAUSE WE HAVE TO WORK.
AND BECAUSE THEY NEED US TO WORK, TO KEEP THE WHEELS TURNING. THERE'S SO MUCH POTENTIAL IN THAT. UNIMAGINABLE POWER...
...OUR POWER AS CONSUMERS & AS INDIVIDUALS GETS HAMMED UP. HELL, EVEN AS VOTERS. I RECKON WE'RE MORE POWERFUL IN HERE. WE ARE LIKE A SLEEPING GIANT, ALL OF US SMOOSHED TOGETHER.
JIGGLE
JIGGLE
SCRATCH
...ALL OF US SMOOSHED TOGETHER?
IS THAT MEANT TO SOUND APPEALING?!
CAN YOU HAND ME THE GAFFA TAPE? CHEERS.
SCREEEEEEE
THIS ONE TIME...

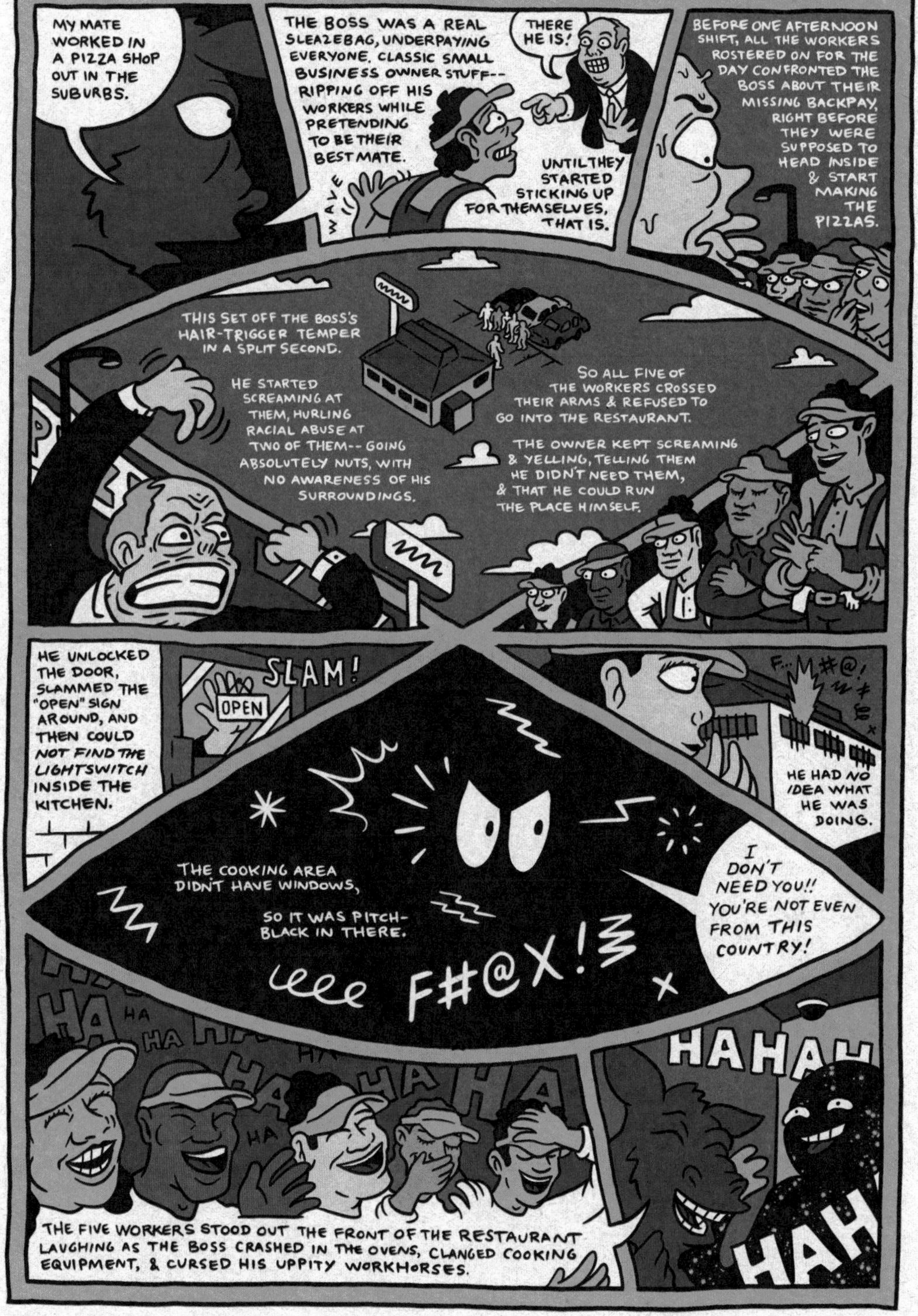
MY MATE WORKED IN A PIZZA SHOP OUT IN THE SUBURBS.
THE BOSS WAS A REAL SLEAZEBAG, UNDERPAYING EVERYONE. CLASSIC SMALL BUSINESS OWNER STUFF-- RIPPING OFF HIS WORKERS WHILE PRETENDING TO BE THEIR BEST MATE.
THERE HE IS!
WAVE
UNTIL THEY STARTED STICKING UP FOR THEMSELVES, THAT IS.
BEFORE ONE AFTERNOON SHIFT, ALL THE WORKERS ROSTERED ON FOR THE DAY CONFRONTED THE BOSS ABOUT THEIR MISSING BACKPAY, RIGHT BEFORE THEY WERE SUPPOSED TO HEAD INSIDE & START MAKING THE PIZZAS.
THIS SET OFF THE BOSS'S HAIR-TRIGGER TEMPER IN A SPLIT SECOND.
HE STARTED SCREAMING AT THEM, HURLING RACIAL ABUSE AT TWO OF THEM-- GOING ABSOLUTELY NUTS, WITH NO AWARENESS OF HIS SURROUNDINGS.
SO ALL FIVE OF THE WORKERS CROSSED THEIR ARMS & REFUSED TO GO INTO THE RESTAURANT.
THE OWNER KEPT SCREAMING & YELLING, TELLING THEM HE DIDN'T NEED THEM, & THAT HE COULD RUN THE PLACE HIMSELF.
HE UNLOCKED THE DOOR, SLAMMED THE "OPEN" SIGN AROUND, AND THEN COULD *NOT FIND THE LIGHTSWITCH* INSIDE THE KITCHEN.
SLAM!
OPEN
HE HAD *NO IDEA* WHAT HE WAS DOING.
THE COOKING AREA DIDN'T HAVE WINDOWS,
SO IT WAS PITCH-BLACK IN THERE.
I DON'T NEED YOU!! YOU'RE NOT EVEN FROM THIS COUNTRY!
F#@X!
HA HA HA HA HA
HAHAH
HAH
THE FIVE WORKERS STOOD OUT THE FRONT OF THE RESTAURANT LAUGHING AS THE BOSS CRASHED IN THE OVENS, CLANGED COOKING EQUIPMENT, & CURSED HIS UPPITY WORKHORSES.

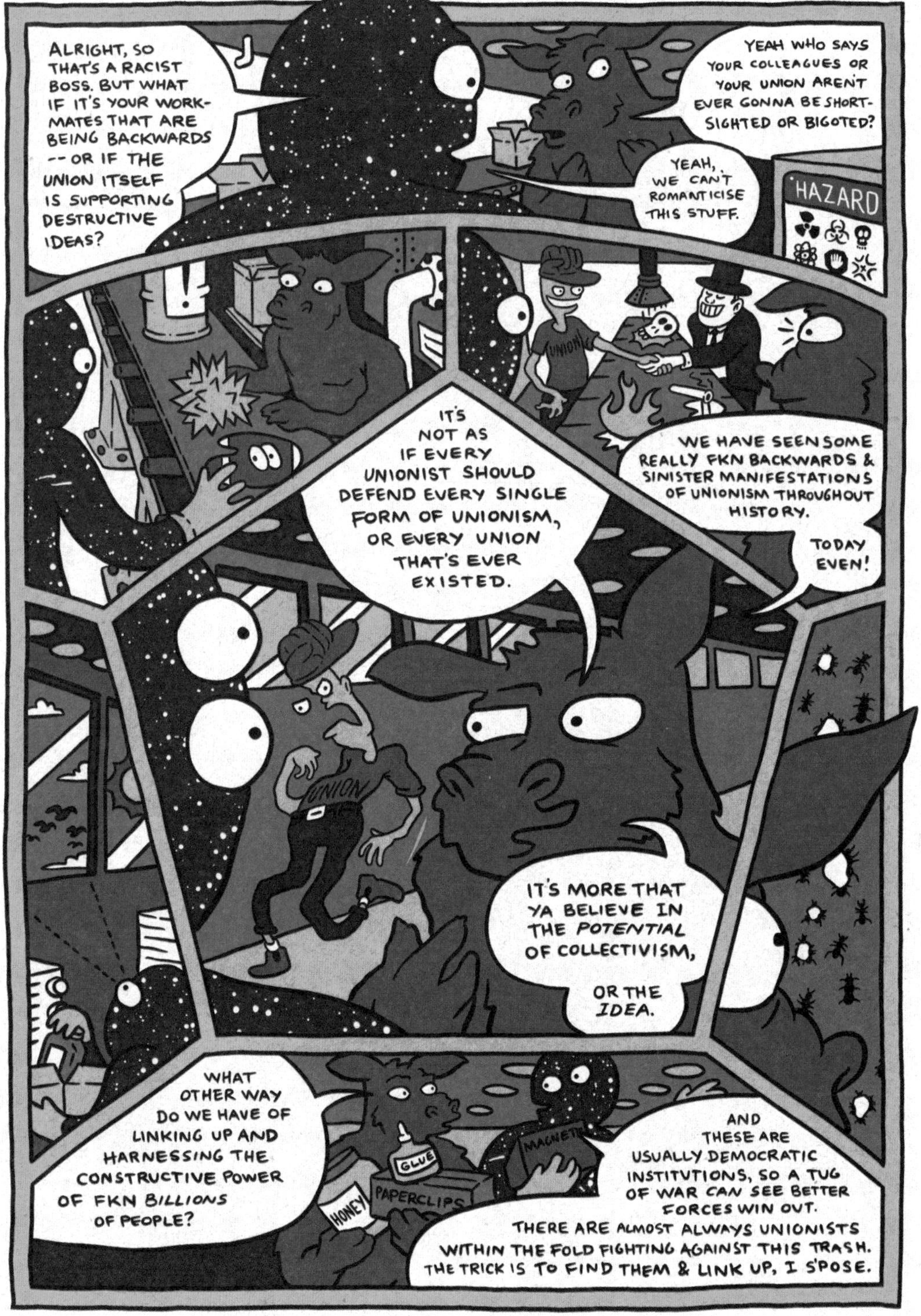
ALRIGHT, SO THAT'S A RACIST BOSS. BUT WHAT IF IT'S YOUR WORKMATES THAT ARE BEING BACKWARDS -- OR IF THE UNION ITSELF IS SUPPORTING DESTRUCTIVE IDEAS?
YEAH WHO SAYS YOUR COLLEAGUES OR YOUR UNION AREN'T EVER GONNA BE SHORT-SIGHTED OR BIGOTED?
YEAH, WE CAN'T ROMANTICISE THIS STUFF.
HAZARD
UNION
IT'S NOT AS IF EVERY UNIONIST SHOULD DEFEND EVERY SINGLE FORM OF UNIONISM, OR EVERY UNION THAT'S EVER EXISTED.
WE HAVE SEEN SOME REALLY FKN BACKWARDS & SINISTER MANIFESTATIONS OF UNIONISM THROUGHOUT HISTORY.
TODAY EVEN!
UNION
IT'S MORE THAT YA BELIEVE IN THE *POTENTIAL* OF COLLECTIVISM,
OR THE *IDEA*.
WHAT OTHER WAY DO WE HAVE OF LINKING UP AND HARNESSING THE CONSTRUCTIVE POWER OF FKN *BILLIONS* OF PEOPLE?
GLUE
HONEY
PAPERCLIPS
MAGNETS
AND THESE ARE USUALLY DEMOCRATIC INSTITUTIONS, SO A TUG OF WAR *CAN* SEE BETTER FORCES WIN OUT.
THERE ARE ALMOST ALWAYS UNIONISTS WITHIN THE FOLD FIGHTING AGAINST THIS TRASH. THE TRICK IS TO FIND THEM & LINK UP, I S'POSE.

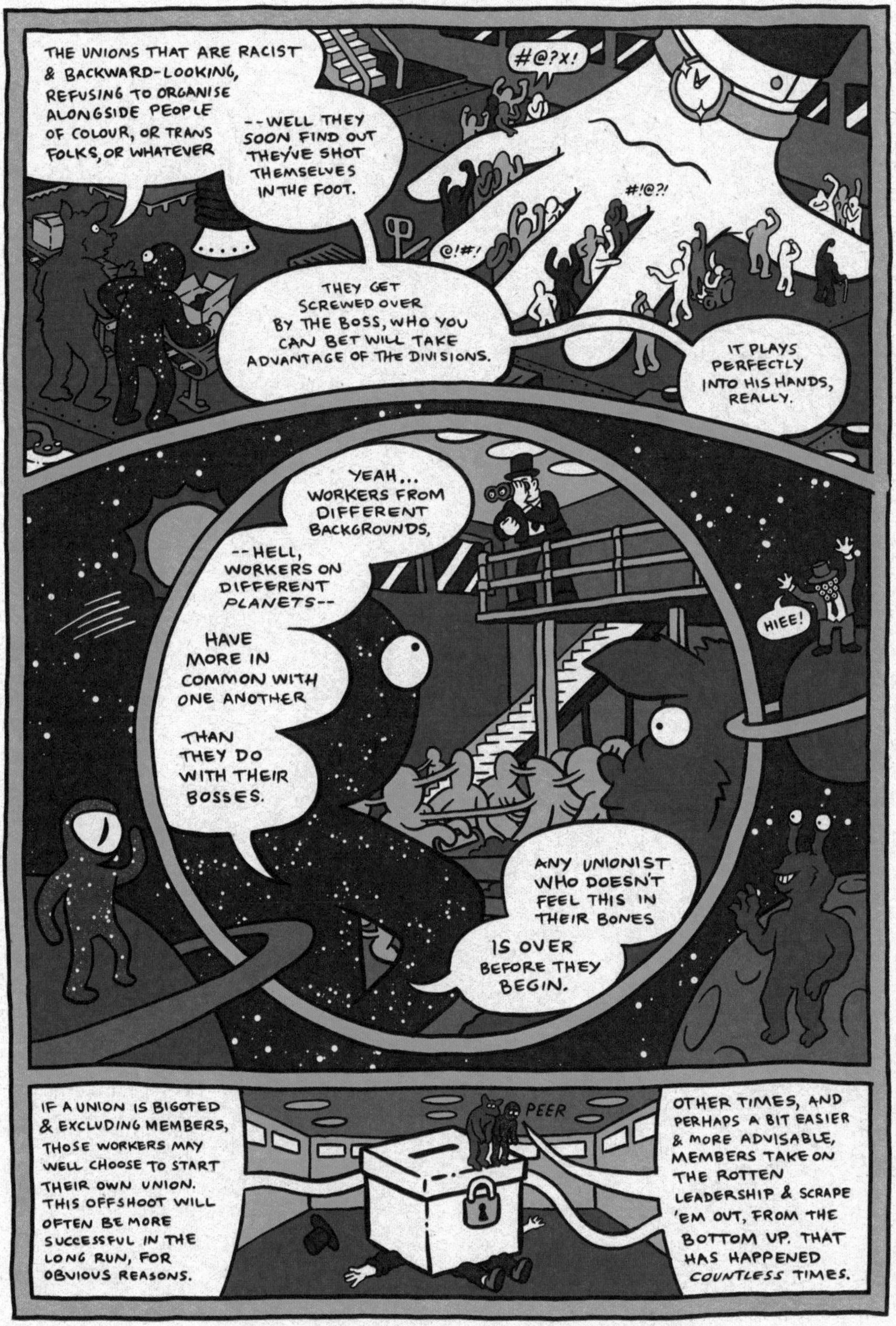

THE UNIONS THAT ARE RACIST & BACKWARD-LOOKING, REFUSING TO ORGANISE ALONGSIDE PEOPLE OF COLOUR, OR TRANS FOLKS, OR WHATEVER
--WELL THEY SOON FIND OUT THEY'VE SHOT THEMSELVES IN THE FOOT.
#@?X!
#!@?!
@!#!
THEY GET SCREWED OVER BY THE BOSS, WHO YOU CAN BET WILL TAKE ADVANTAGE OF THE DIVISIONS.
IT PLAYS PERFECTLY INTO HIS HANDS, REALLY.
YEAH... WORKERS FROM DIFFERENT BACKGROUNDS,
--HELL, WORKERS ON DIFFERENT *PLANETS*--
HAVE MORE IN COMMON WITH ONE ANOTHER
THAN THEY DO WITH THEIR BOSSES.
HIEE!
ANY UNIONIST WHO DOESN'T FEEL THIS IN THEIR BONES
IS OVER BEFORE THEY BEGIN.
IF A UNION IS BIGOTED & EXCLUDING MEMBERS, THOSE WORKERS MAY WELL CHOOSE TO START THEIR OWN UNION. THIS OFFSHOOT WILL OFTEN BE MORE SUCCESSFUL IN THE LONG RUN, FOR OBVIOUS REASONS.
PEER
OTHER TIMES, AND PERHAPS A BIT EASIER & MORE ADVISABLE, MEMBERS TAKE ON THE ROTTEN LEADERSHIP & SCRAPE 'EM OUT, FROM THE BOTTOM UP. THAT HAS HAPPENED *COUNTLESS* TIMES.

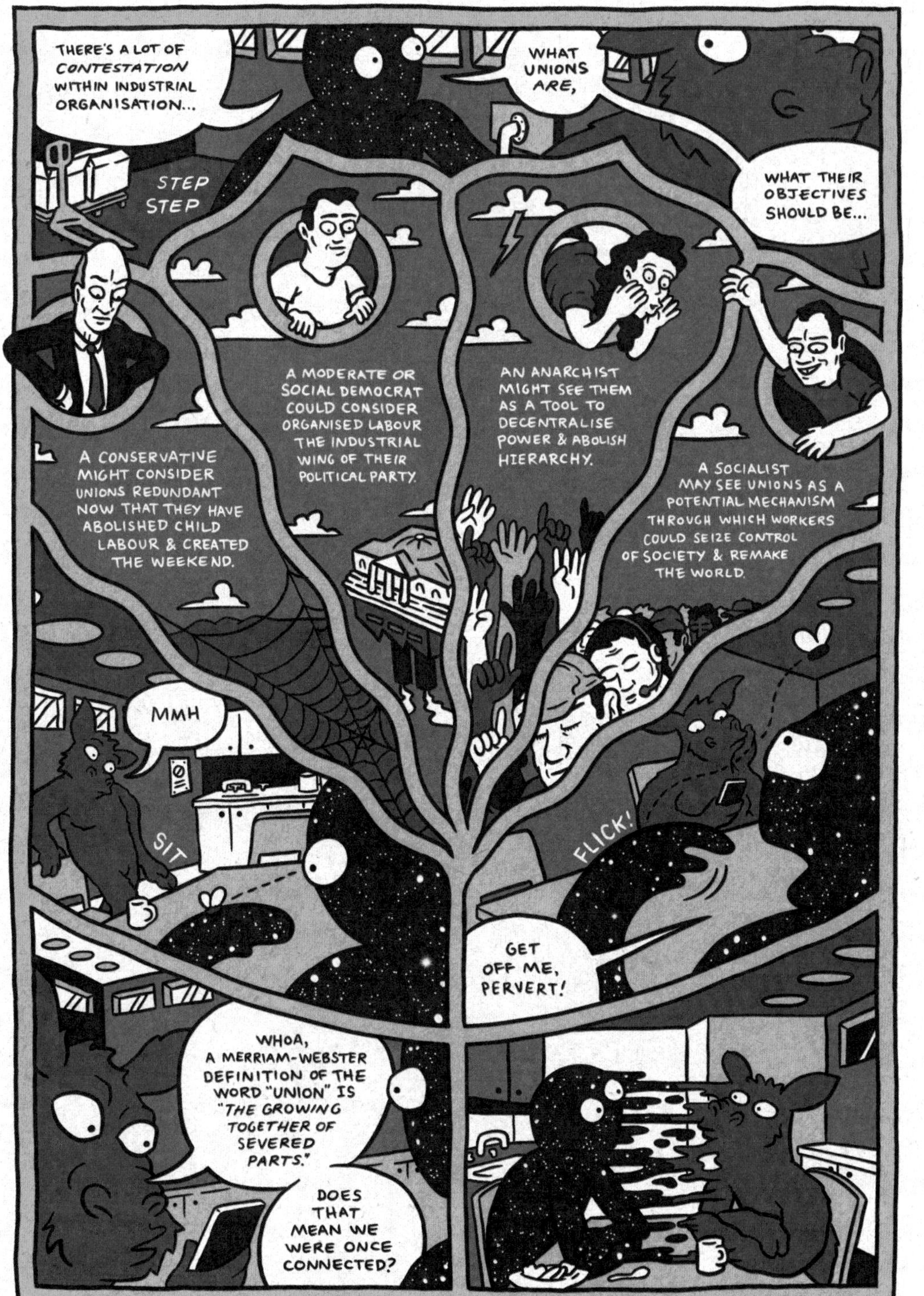
THERE'S A LOT OF CONTESTATION WITHIN INDUSTRIAL ORGANISATION...
WHAT UNIONS ARE,
WHAT THEIR OBJECTIVES SHOULD BE...
STEP STEP
A CONSERVATIVE MIGHT CONSIDER UNIONS REDUNDANT NOW THAT THEY HAVE ABOLISHED CHILD LABOUR & CREATED THE WEEKEND.
A MODERATE OR SOCIAL DEMOCRAT COULD CONSIDER ORGANISED LABOUR THE INDUSTRIAL WING OF THEIR POLITICAL PARTY.
AN ANARCHIST MIGHT SEE THEM AS A TOOL TO DECENTRALISE POWER & ABOLISH HIERARCHY.
A SOCIALIST MAY SEE UNIONS AS A POTENTIAL MECHANISM THROUGH WHICH WORKERS COULD SEIZE CONTROL OF SOCIETY & REMAKE THE WORLD.
MMH
SIT
FLICK!
GET OFF ME, PERVERT!
WHOA, A MERRIAM-WEBSTER DEFINITION OF THE WORD "UNION" IS "THE GROWING TOGETHER OF SEVERED PARTS."
DOES THAT MEAN WE WERE ONCE CONNECTED?

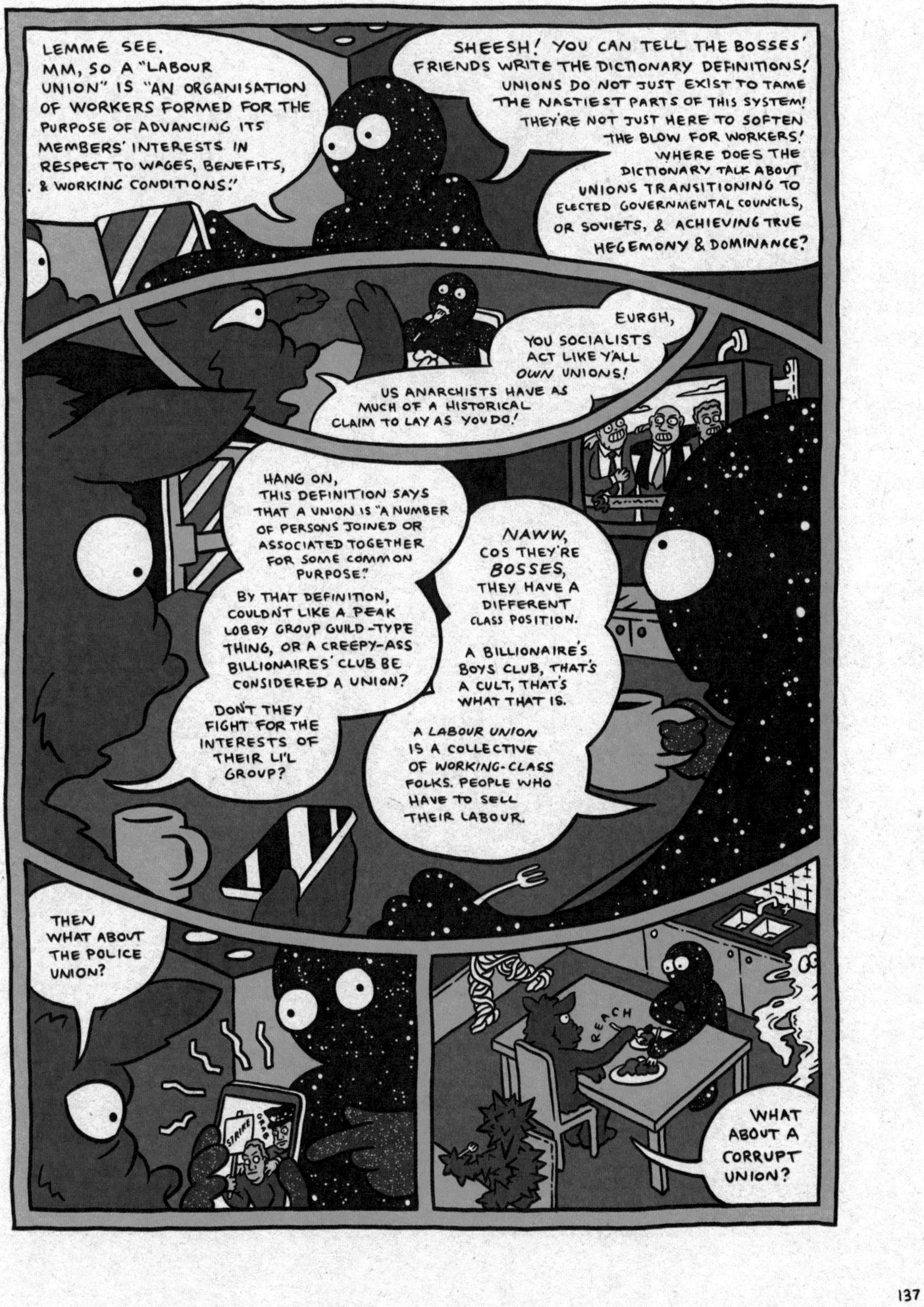
LEMME SEE. MM, SO A "LABOUR UNION" IS "AN ORGANISATION OF WORKERS FORMED FOR THE PURPOSE OF ADVANCING ITS MEMBERS' INTERESTS IN RESPECT TO WAGES, BENEFITS, & WORKING CONDITIONS."
SHEESH! YOU CAN TELL THE BOSSES' FRIENDS WRITE THE DICTIONARY DEFINITIONS! UNIONS DO NOT JUST EXIST TO TAME THE NASTIEST PARTS OF THIS SYSTEM! THEY'RE NOT JUST HERE TO SOFTEN THE BLOW FOR WORKERS! WHERE DOES THE DICTIONARY TALK ABOUT UNIONS TRANSITIONING TO ELECTED GOVERNMENTAL COUNCILS, OR SOVIETS, & ACHIEVING TRUE HEGEMONY & DOMINANCE?
EURGH, YOU SOCIALISTS ACT LIKE Y'ALL *OWN* UNIONS!
US ANARCHISTS HAVE AS MUCH OF A HISTORICAL CLAIM TO LAY AS YOU DO!
HANG ON, THIS DEFINITION SAYS THAT A UNION IS "A NUMBER OF PERSONS JOINED OR ASSOCIATED TOGETHER FOR SOME COMMON PURPOSE."
BY THAT DEFINITION, COULDN'T LIKE A PEAK LOBBY GROUP GUILD-TYPE THING, OR A CREEPY-ASS BILLIONAIRES' CLUB BE CONSIDERED A UNION?
DON'T THEY FIGHT FOR THE INTERESTS OF THEIR LI'L GROUP?
NAWW, COS THEY'RE *BOSSES,* THEY HAVE A DIFFERENT CLASS POSITION.
A BILLIONAIRE'S BOYS CLUB, THAT'S A CULT, THAT'S WHAT THAT IS.
A *LABOUR UNION* IS A COLLECTIVE OF WORKING-CLASS FOLKS. PEOPLE WHO HAVE TO SELL THEIR LABOUR.
THEN WHAT ABOUT THE POLICE UNION?
STRIKE
REACH
WHAT ABOUT A CORRUPT UNION?

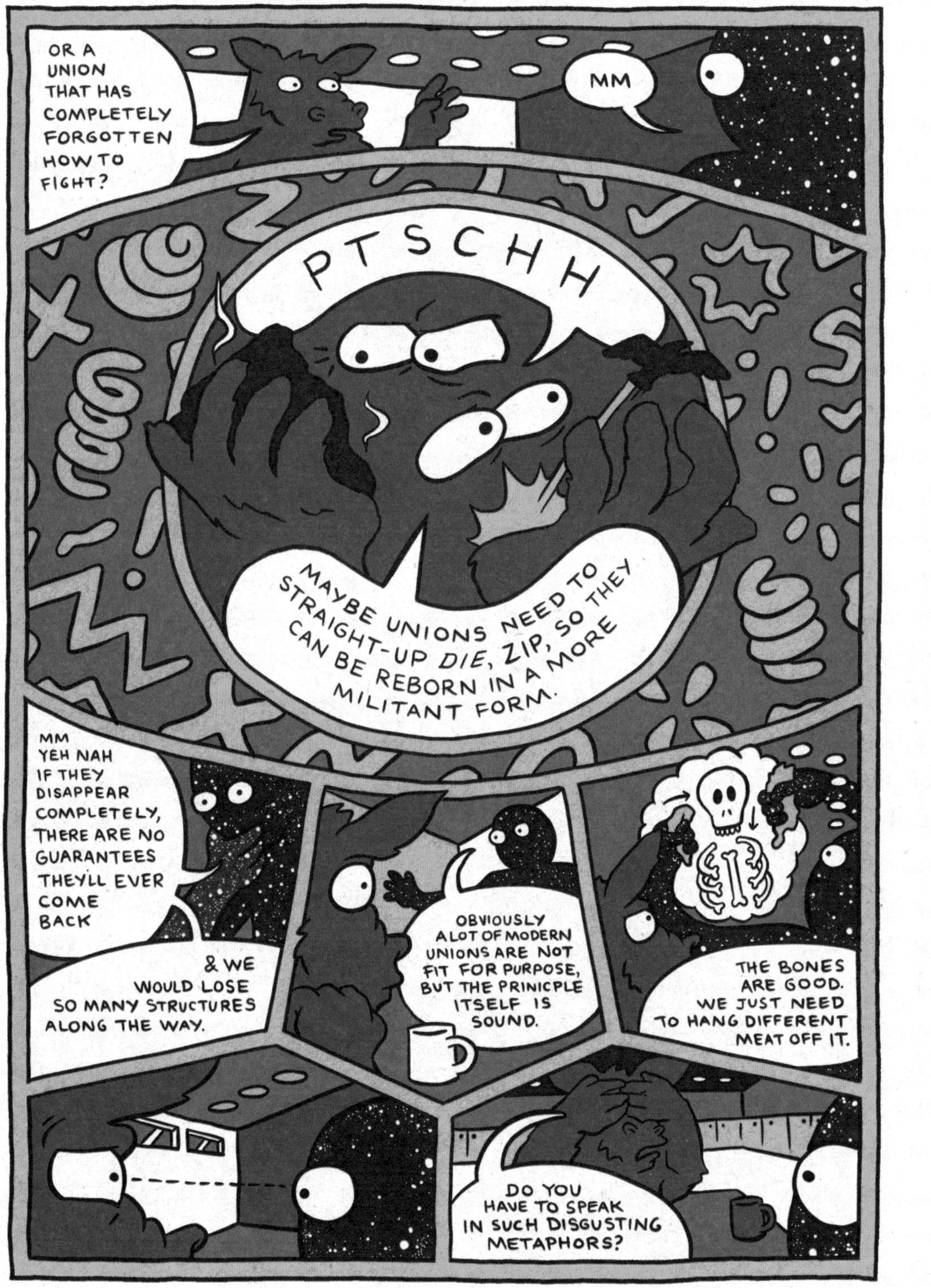

OR A UNION THAT HAS COMPLETELY FORGOTTEN HOW TO FIGHT?
MM
PTSCHH
MAYBE UNIONS NEED TO STRAIGHT-UP *DIE*, ZIP, SO THEY CAN BE REBORN IN A MORE MILITANT FORM.
MM YEH NAH IF THEY DISAPPEAR COMPLETELY, THERE ARE NO GUARANTEES THEY'LL EVER COME BACK
& WE WOULD LOSE SO MANY STRUCTURES ALONG THE WAY.
OBVIOUSLY ALOT OF MODERN UNIONS ARE NOT FIT FOR PURPOSE, BUT THE PRINICPLE ITSELF IS SOUND.
THE BONES ARE GOOD. WE JUST NEED TO HANG DIFFERENT MEAT OFF IT.
DO YOU HAVE TO SPEAK IN SUCH DISGUSTING METAPHORS?

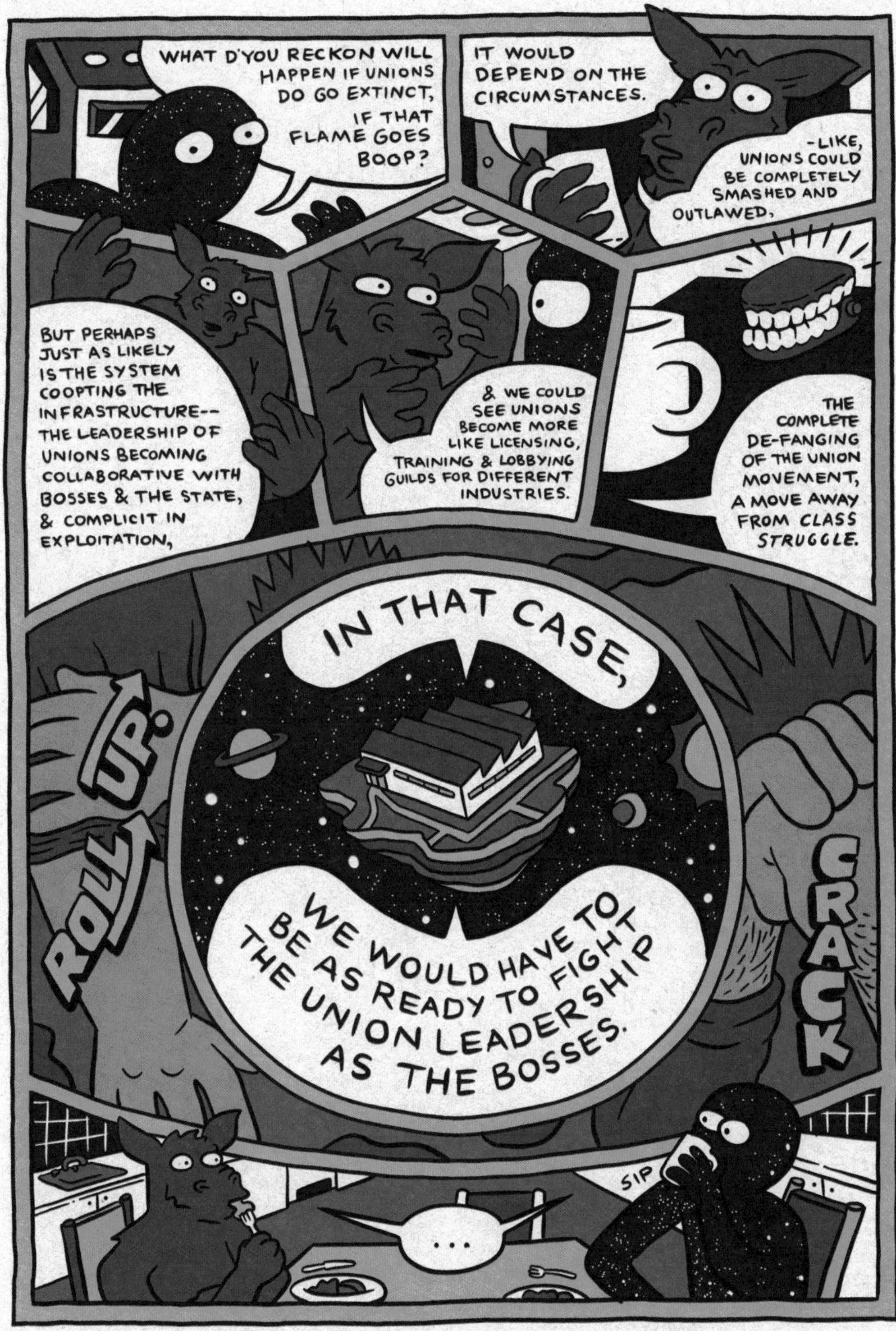
WHAT D'YOU RECKON WILL HAPPEN IF UNIONS DO GO EXTINCT, IF THAT FLAME GOES BOOP?
IT WOULD DEPEND ON THE CIRCUMSTANCES.
-LIKE, UNIONS COULD BE COMPLETELY SMASHED AND OUTLAWED,
BUT PERHAPS JUST AS LIKELY IS THE SYSTEM COOPTING THE INFRASTRUCTURE-- THE LEADERSHIP OF UNIONS BECOMING COLLABORATIVE WITH BOSSES & THE STATE, & COMPLICIT IN EXPLOITATION,
& WE COULD SEE UNIONS BECOME MORE LIKE LICENSING, TRAINING & LOBBYING GUILDS FOR DIFFERENT INDUSTRIES.
THE COMPLETE DE-FANGING OF THE UNION MOVEMENT, A MOVE AWAY FROM CLASS STRUGGLE.
IN THAT CASE,
WE WOULD HAVE TO BE AS READY TO FIGHT THE UNION LEADERSHIP AS THE BOSSES.
ROLL UP.
CRACK
SIP
...

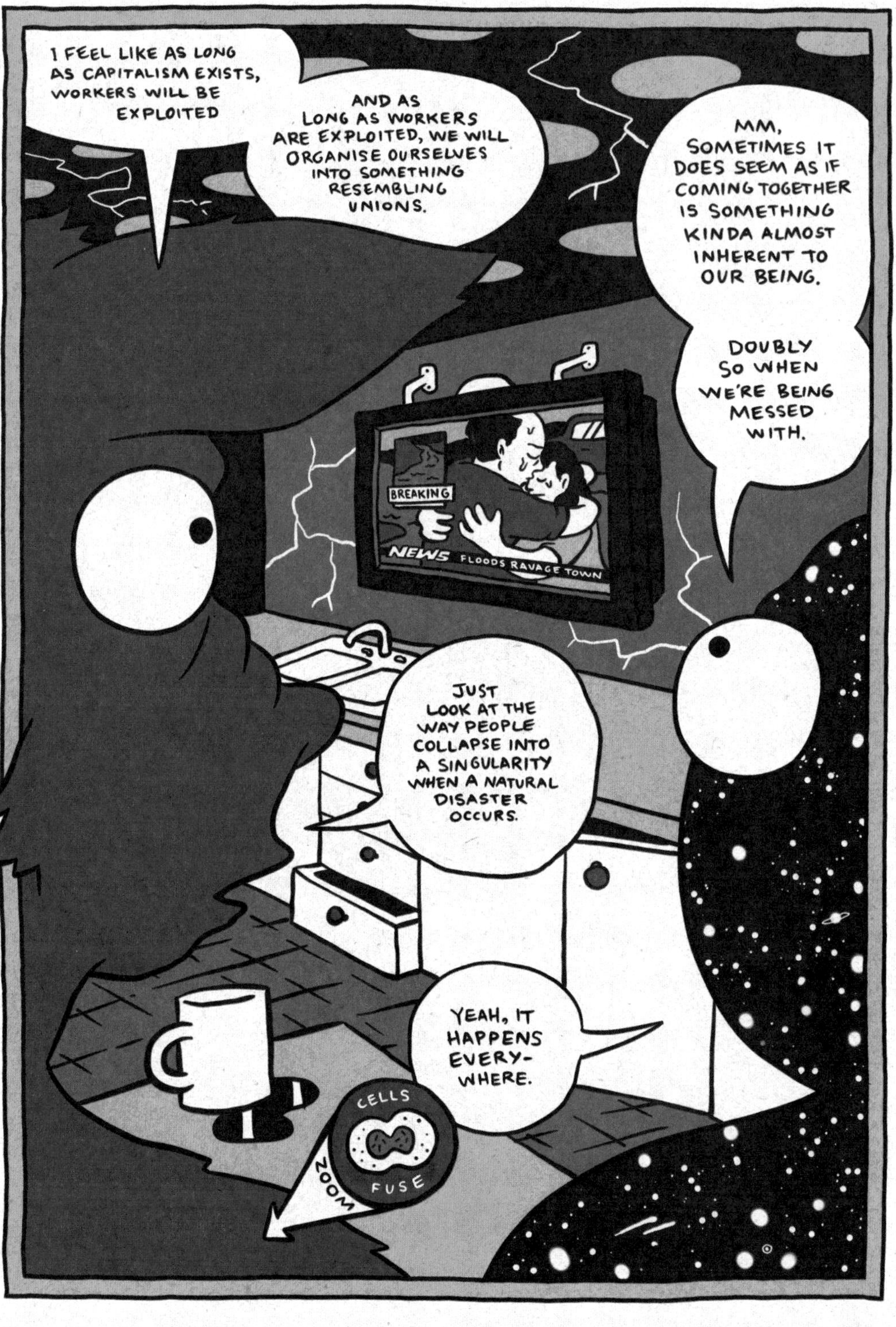
I FEEL LIKE AS LONG AS CAPITALISM EXISTS, WORKERS WILL BE EXPLOITED
AND AS LONG AS WORKERS ARE EXPLOITED, WE WILL ORGANISE OURSELVES INTO SOMETHING RESEMBLING UNIONS.
MM, SOMETIMES IT DOES SEEM AS IF COMING TOGETHER IS SOMETHING KINDA ALMOST INHERENT TO OUR BEING.
DOUBLY SO WHEN WE'RE BEING MESSED WITH.
BREAKING
NEWS FLOODS RAVAGE TOWN
JUST LOOK AT THE WAY PEOPLE COLLAPSE INTO A SINGULARITY WHEN A NATURAL DISASTER OCCURS.
YEAH, IT HAPPENS EVERY-WHERE.
CELLS FUSE
ZOOM

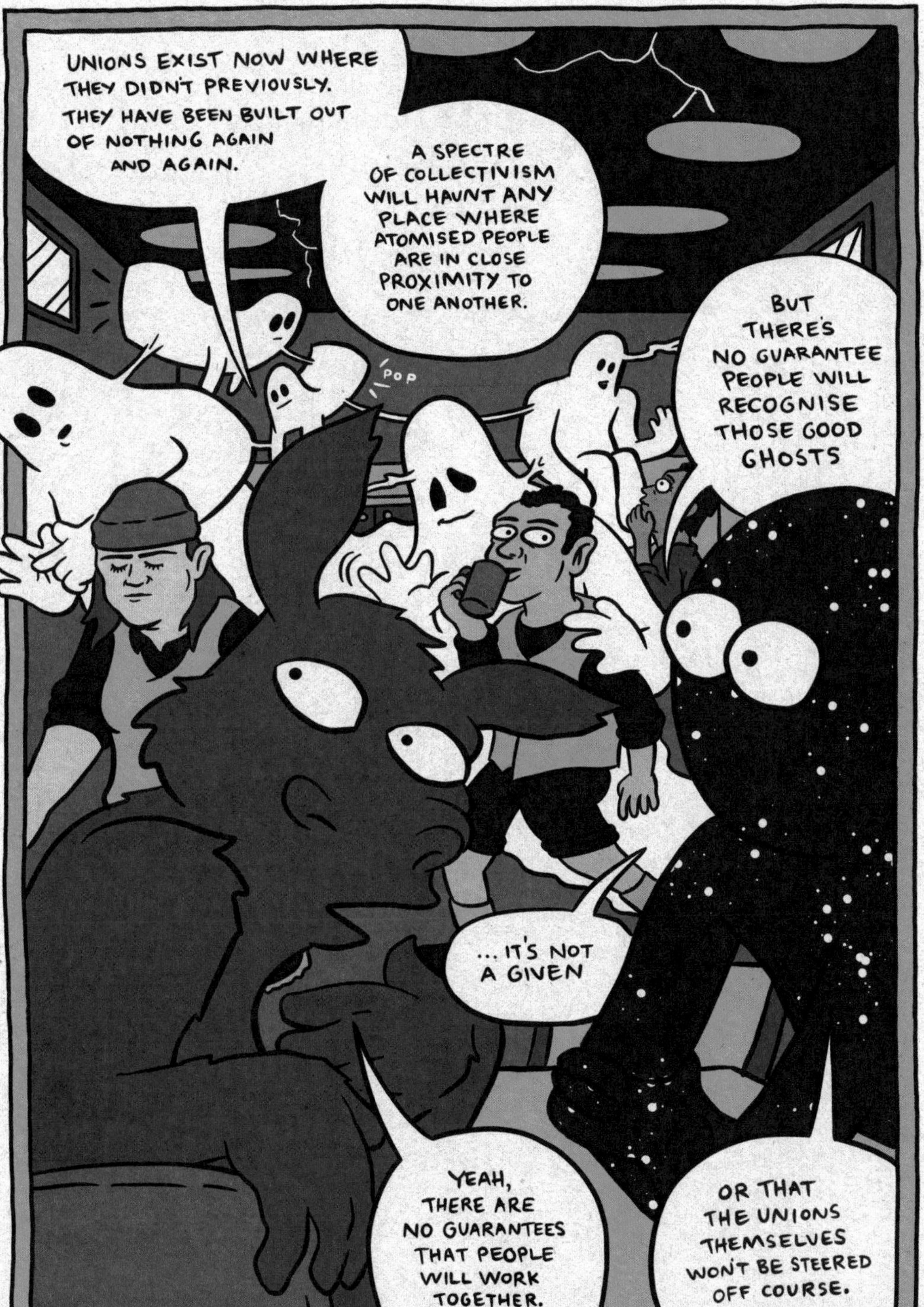
UNIONS EXIST NOW WHERE THEY DIDN'T PREVIOUSLY. THEY HAVE BEEN BUILT OUT OF NOTHING AGAIN AND AGAIN.
A SPECTRE OF COLLECTIVISM WILL HAUNT ANY PLACE WHERE ATOMISED PEOPLE ARE IN CLOSE PROXIMITY TO ONE ANOTHER.
POP
BUT THERE'S NO GUARANTEE PEOPLE WILL RECOGNISE THOSE GOOD GHOSTS
... IT'S NOT A GIVEN
YEAH, THERE ARE NO GUARANTEES THAT PEOPLE WILL WORK TOGETHER.
OR THAT THE UNIONS THEMSELVES WON'T BE STEERED OFF COURSE.

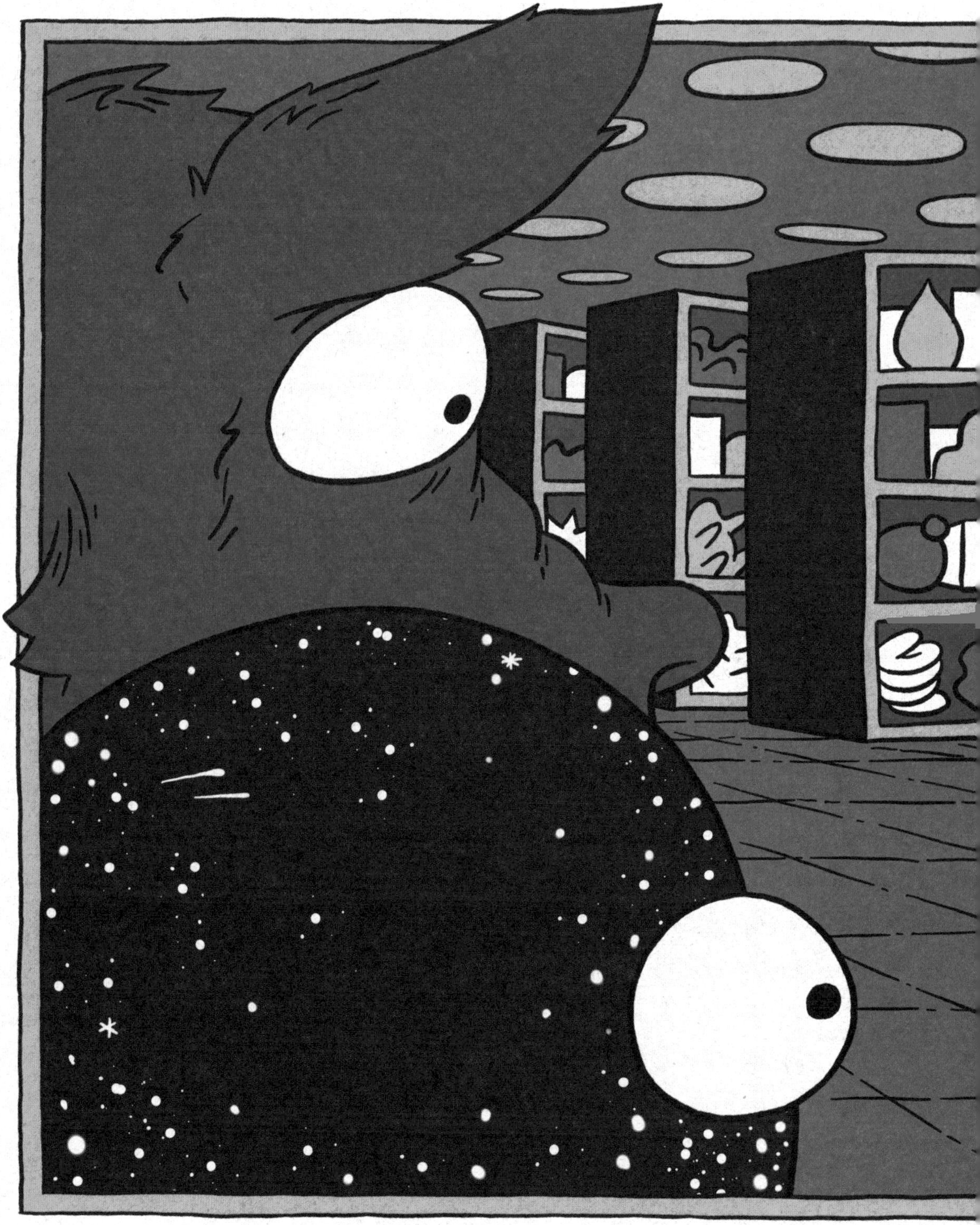

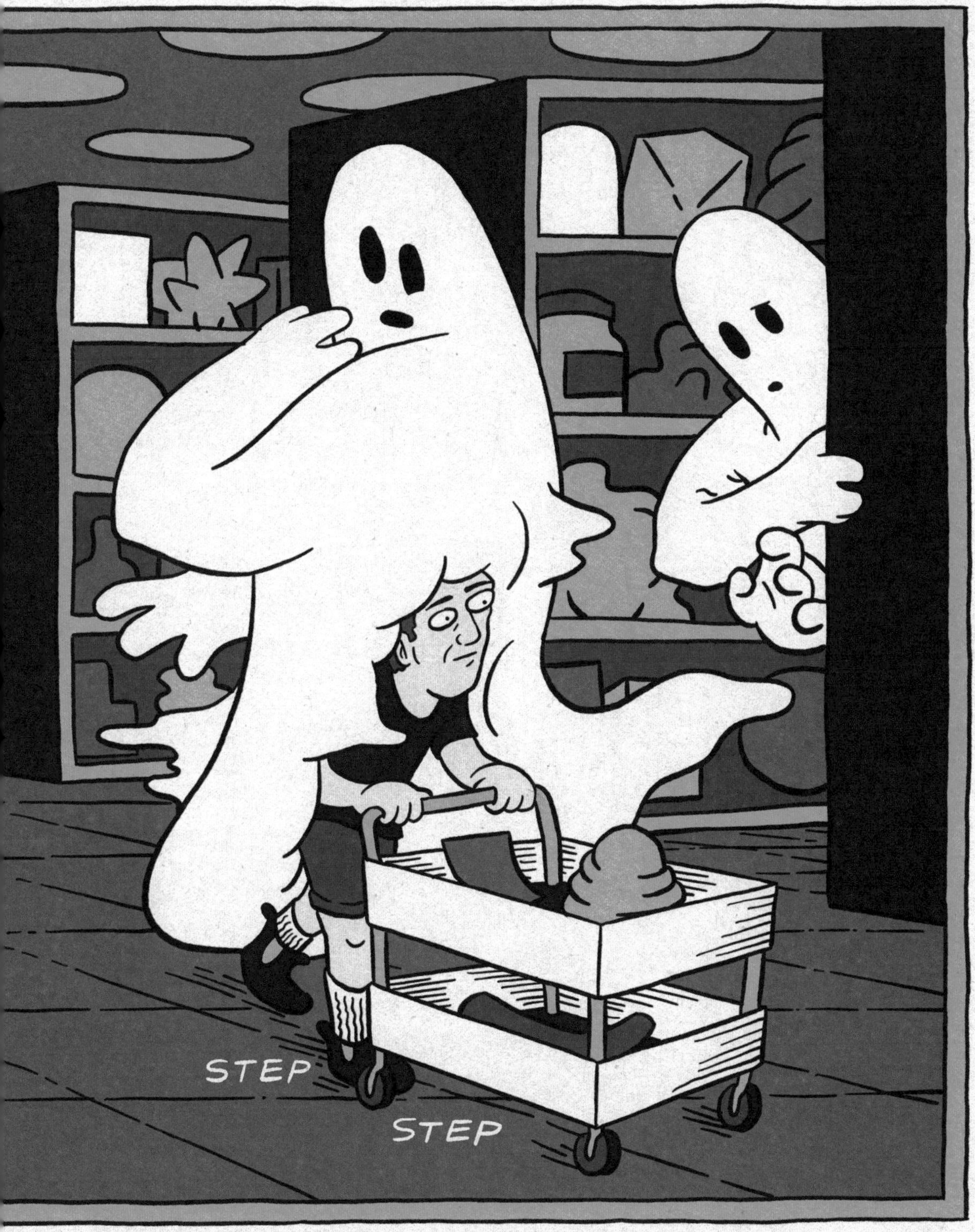
STEP
STEP

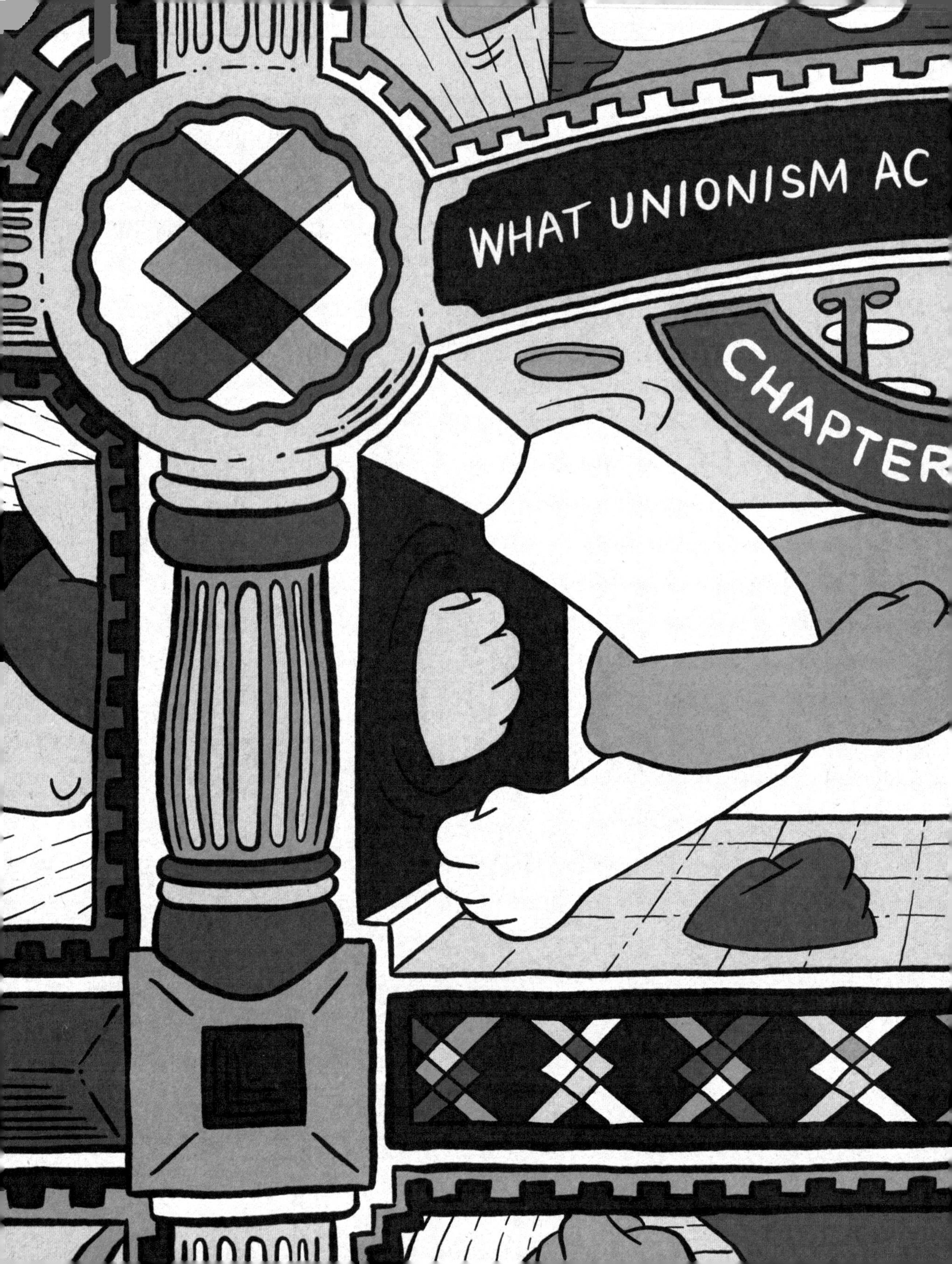
WHAT UNIONISM AC
CHAPTER

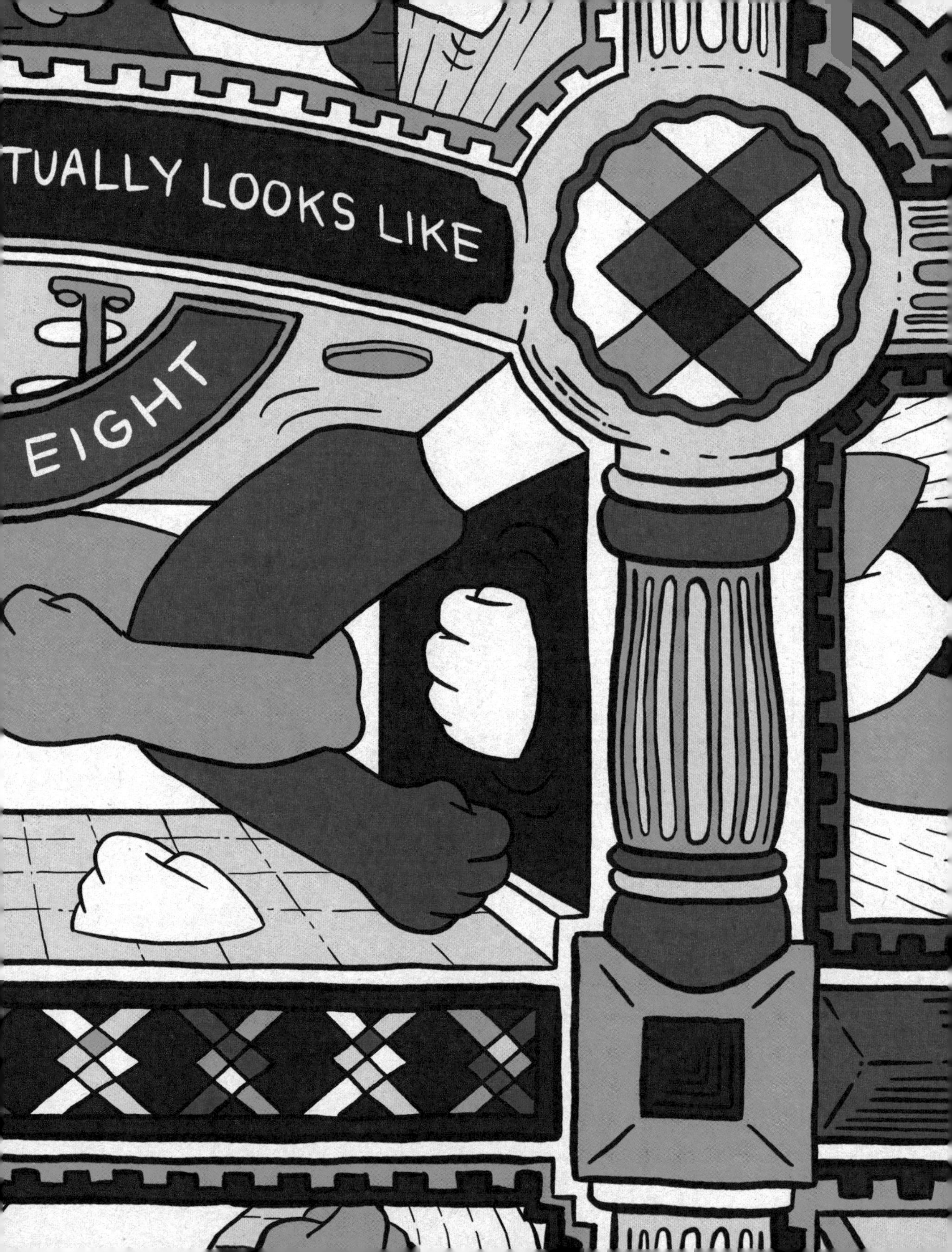
TUALLY LOOKS LIKE
EIGHT

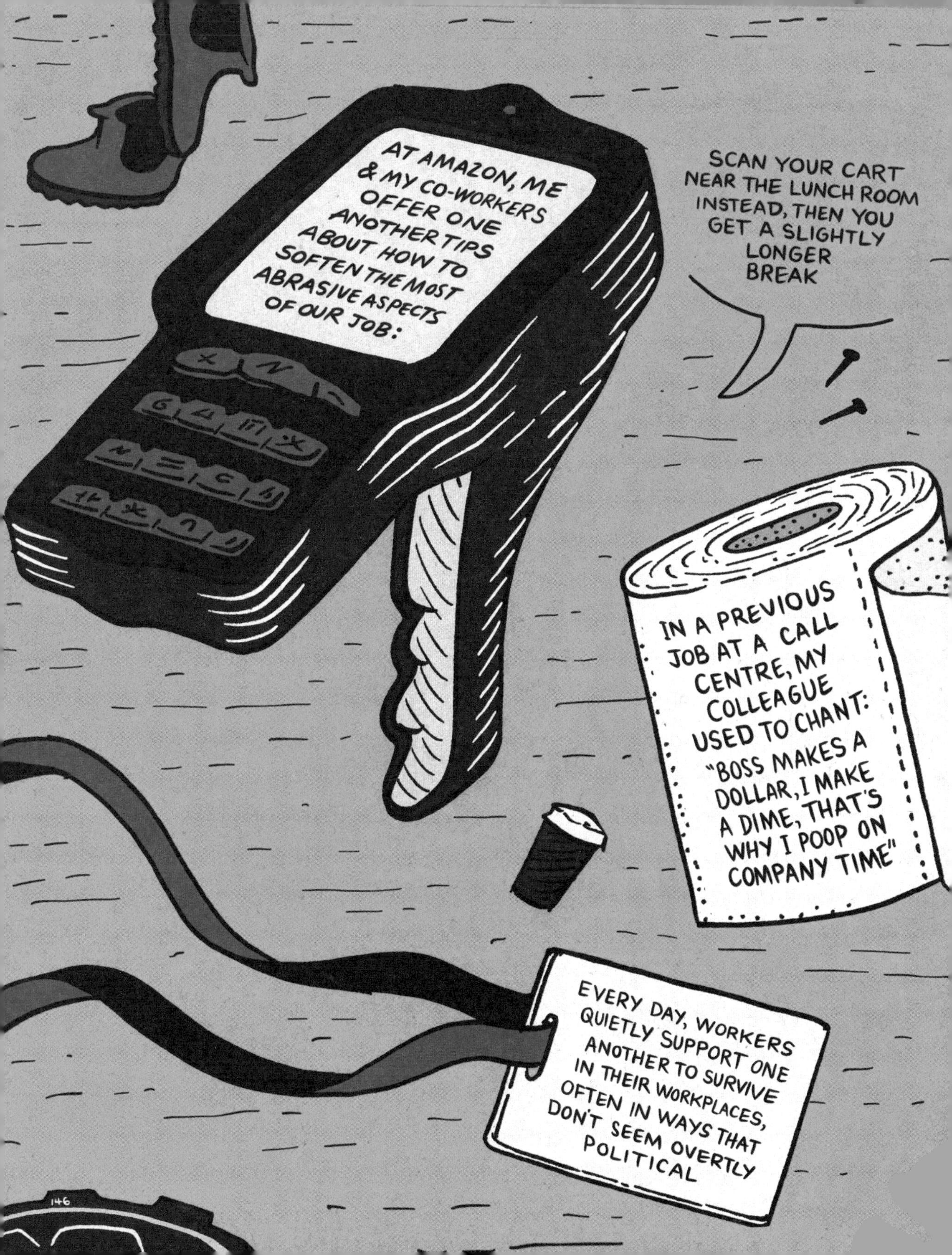
AT AMAZON, ME & MY CO-WORKERS OFFER ONE ANOTHER TIPS ABOUT HOW TO SOFTEN THE MOST ABRASIVE ASPECTS OF OUR JOB:
SCAN YOUR CART NEAR THE LUNCH ROOM INSTEAD, THEN YOU GET A SLIGHTLY LONGER BREAK
IN A PREVIOUS JOB AT A CALL CENTRE, MY COLLEAGUE USED TO CHANT: "BOSS MAKES A DOLLAR, I MAKE A DIME, THAT'S WHY I POOP ON COMPANY TIME"
EVERY DAY, WORKERS QUIETLY SUPPORT ONE ANOTHER TO SURVIVE IN THEIR WORKPLACES, OFTEN IN WAYS THAT DON'T SEEM OVERTLY POLITICAL

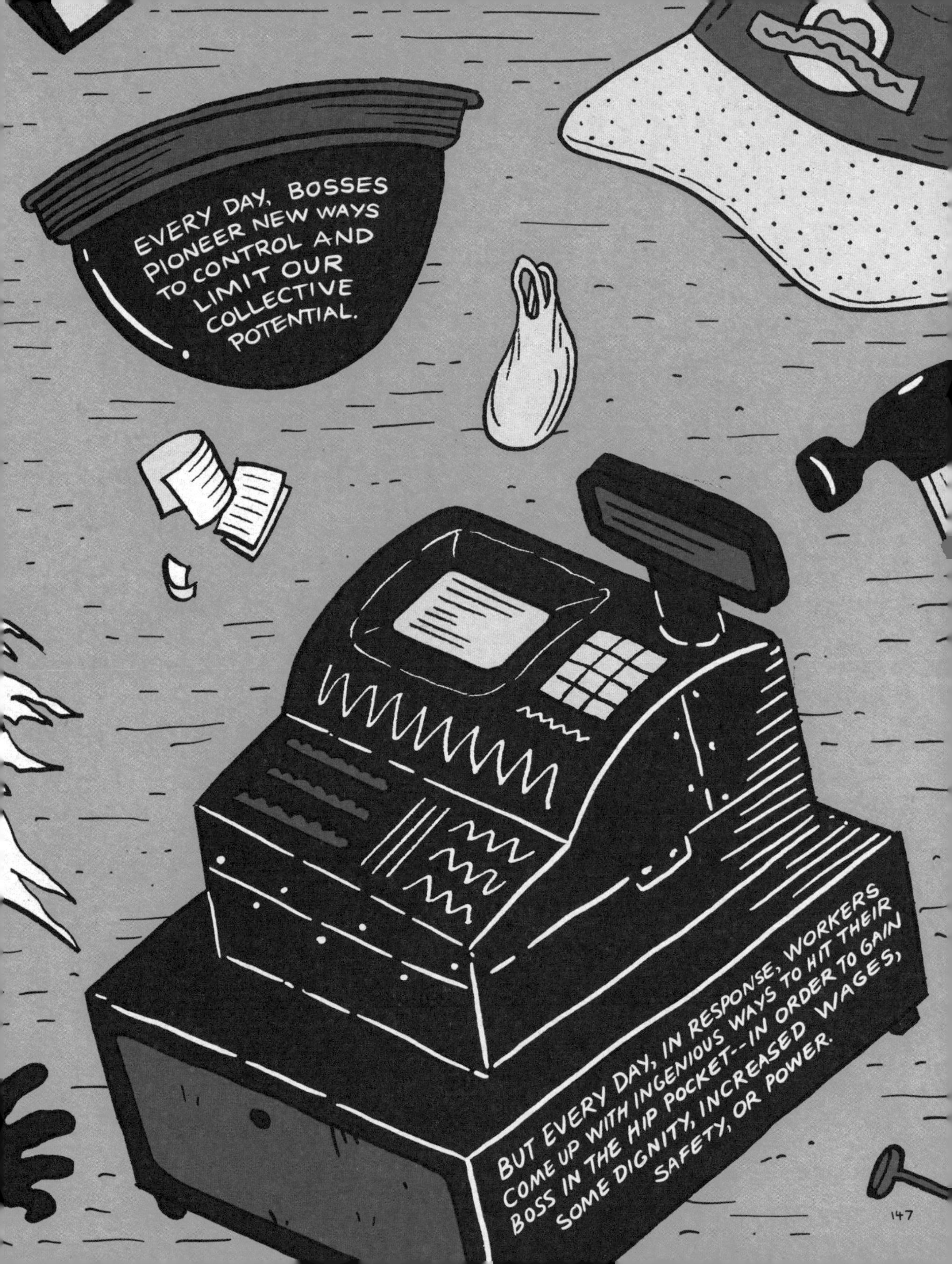
EVERY DAY, BOSSES PIONEER NEW WAYS TO CONTROL AND LIMIT OUR COLLECTIVE POTENTIAL.
BUT EVERY DAY, IN RESPONSE, WORKERS COME UP WITH INGENIOUS WAYS TO HIT THEIR BOSS IN THE HIP POCKET--IN ORDER TO GAIN SOME DIGNITY, INCREASED WAGES, SAFETY, OR POWER.

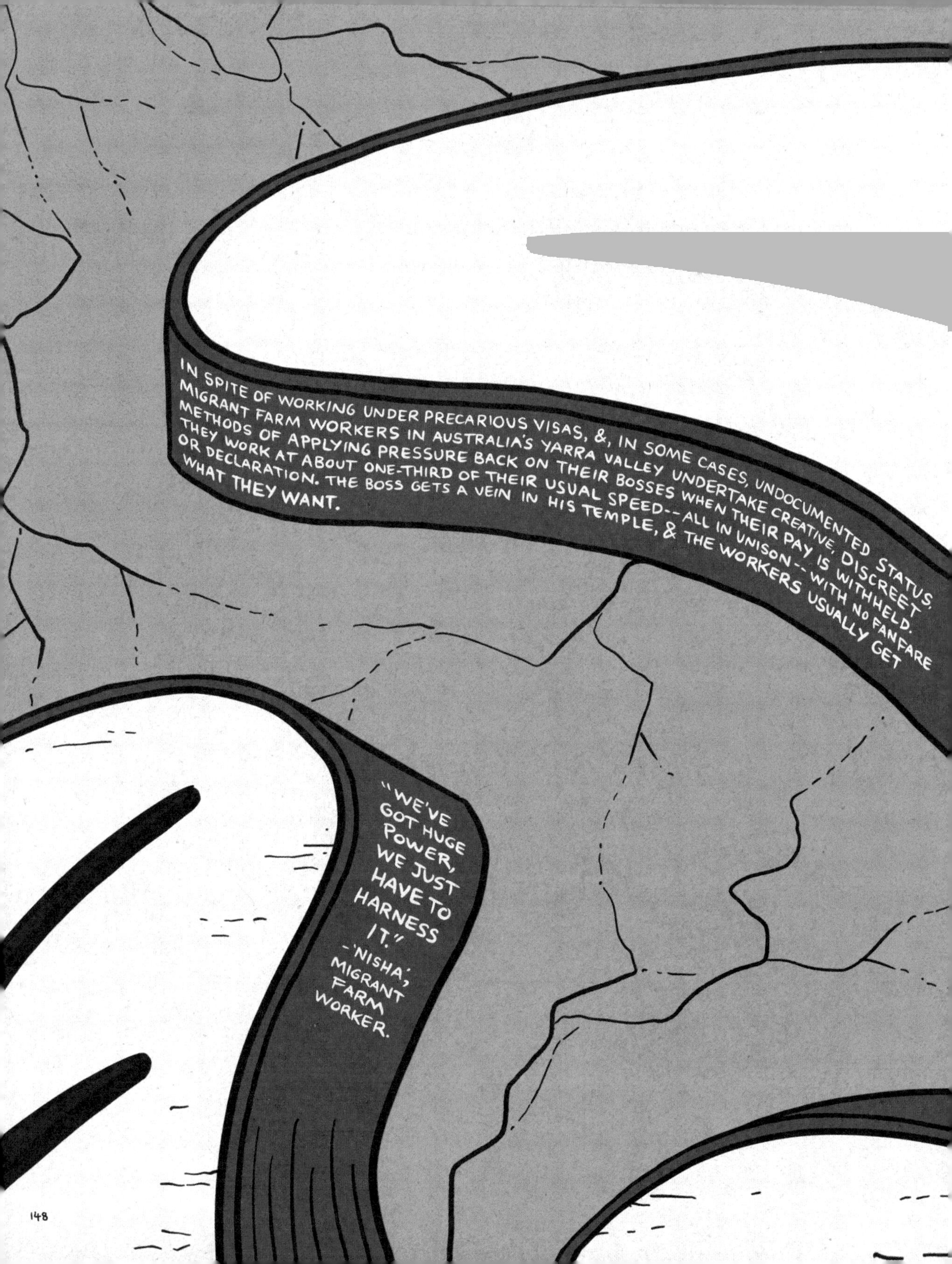
IN SPITE OF WORKING UNDER PRECARIOUS VISAS, &, IN SOME CASES, UNDOCUMENTED STATUS, MIGRANT FARM WORKERS IN AUSTRALIA'S YARRA VALLEY UNDERTAKE CREATIVE, DISCREET METHODS OF APPLYING PRESSURE BACK ON THEIR BOSSES WHEN THEIR PAY IS WITHHELD. THEY WORK AT ABOUT ONE-THIRD OF THEIR USUAL SPEED--ALL IN UNISON--WITH NO FANFARE OR DECLARATION. THE BOSS GETS A VEIN IN HIS TEMPLE, & THE WORKERS USUALLY GET WHAT THEY WANT.
"WE'VE GOT HUGE POWER, WE JUST HAVE TO HARNESS IT." -'NISHA', MIGRANT FARM WORKER.

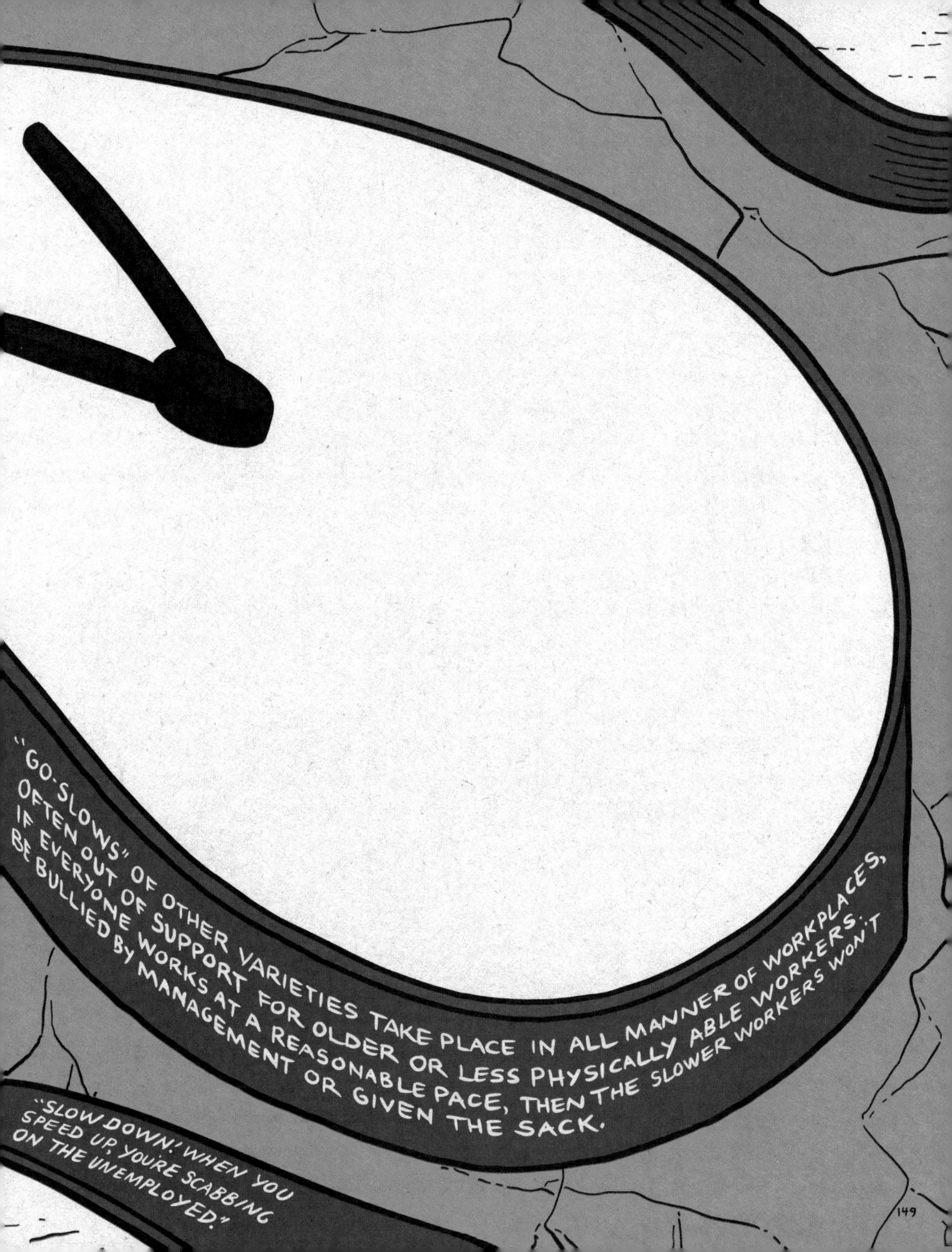
"GO-SLOWS" OF OTHER VARIETIES TAKE PLACE IN ALL MANNER OF WORKPLACES, OFTEN OUT OF SUPPORT FOR OLDER OR LESS PHYSICALLY ABLE WORKERS. IF EVERYONE WORKS AT A REASONABLE PACE, THEN THE SLOWER WORKERS WON'T BE BULLIED BY MANAGEMENT OR GIVEN THE SACK.
"SLOW DOWN! WHEN YOU SPEED UP, YOU'RE SCABBING ON THE UNEMPLOYED."

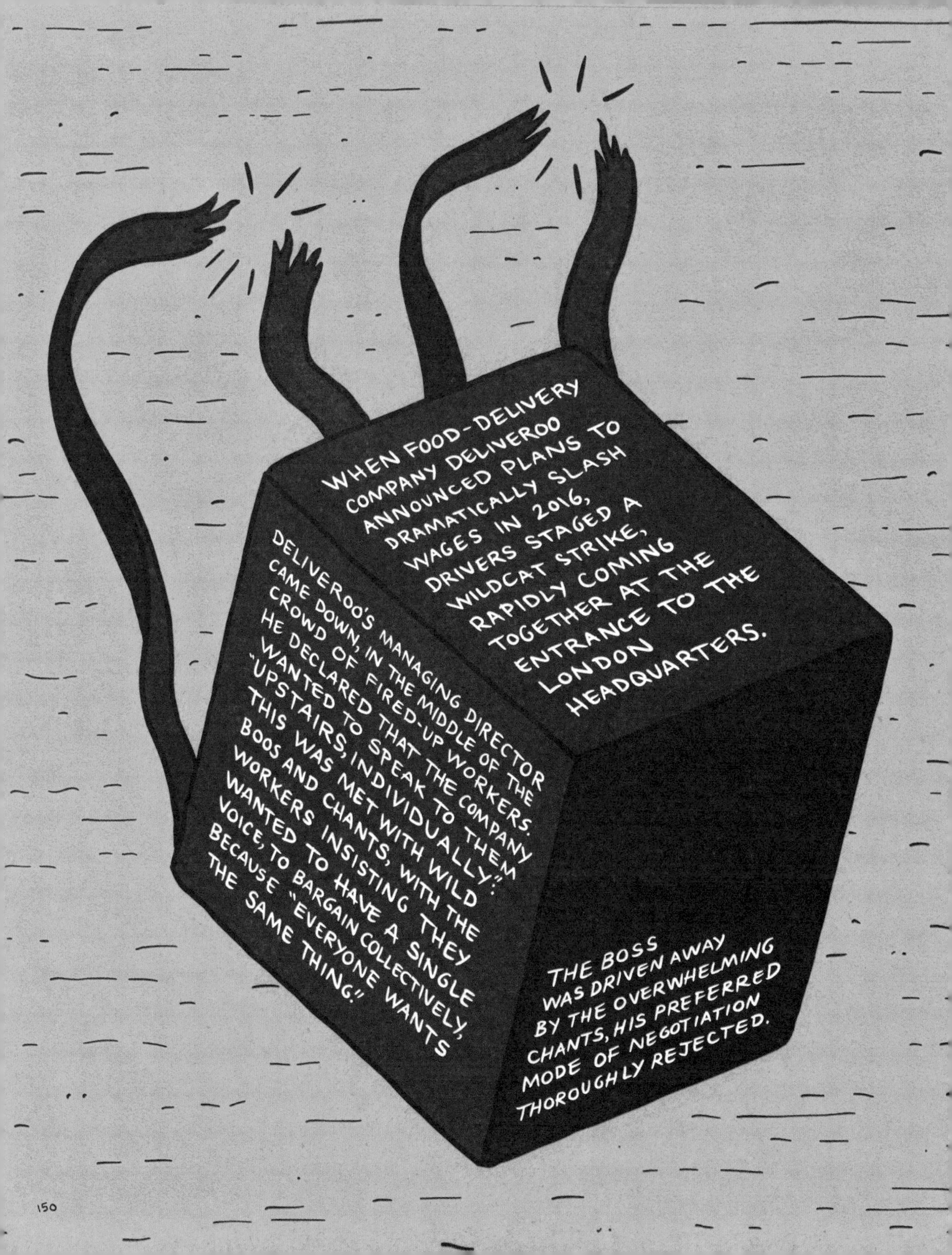

WHEN FOOD-DELIVERY COMPANY DELIVEROO ANNOUNCED PLANS TO DRAMATICALLY SLASH WAGES IN 2016, DRIVERS STAGED A WILDCAT STRIKE, RAPIDLY COMING TOGETHER AT THE ENTRANCE TO THE LONDON HEADQUARTERS.
DELIVEROO'S MANAGING DIRECTOR CAME DOWN, IN THE MIDDLE OF THE CROWD OF FIRED-UP WORKERS. HE DECLARED THAT THE COMPANY WANTED TO SPEAK TO THEM "UPSTAIRS, INDIVIDUALLY." THIS WAS MET WITH WILD BOOS AND CHANTS, WITH THE WORKERS INSISTING THEY WANTED TO HAVE A SINGLE VOICE, TO BARGAIN COLLECTIVELY, BECAUSE "EVERYONE WANTS THE SAME THING."
THE BOSS WAS DRIVEN AWAY BY THE OVERWHELMING CHANTS, HIS PREFERRED MODE OF NEGOTIATION THOROUGHLY REJECTED.

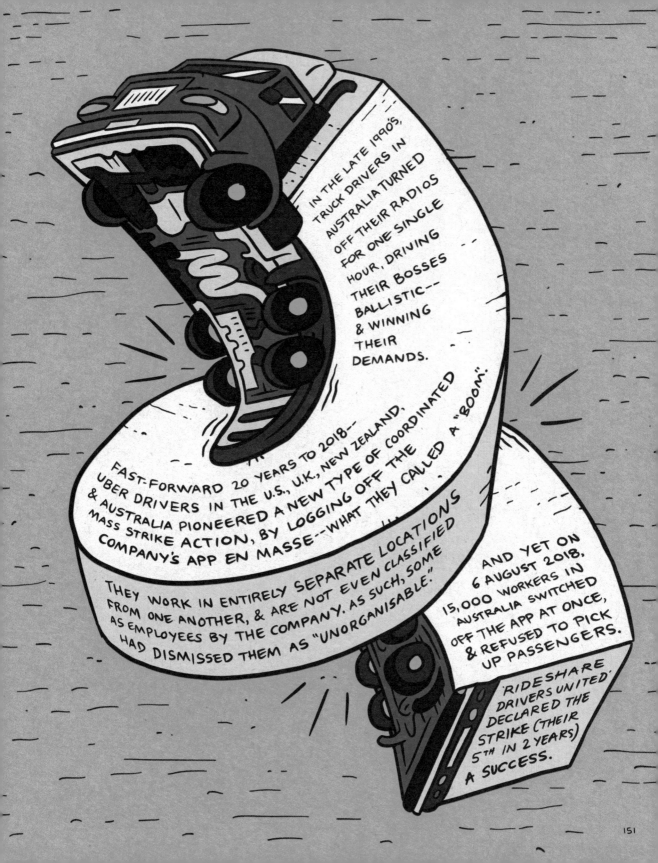

IN THE LATE 1990's, TRUCK DRIVERS IN AUSTRALIA TURNED OFF THEIR RADIOS FOR ONE SINGLE HOUR, DRIVING THEIR BOSSES BALLISTIC-- & WINNING THEIR DEMANDS.

FAST-FORWARD 20 YEARS TO 2018-- UBER DRIVERS IN THE U.S., U.K., NEW ZEALAND, & AUSTRALIA PIONEERED A NEW TYPE OF COORDINATED MASS STRIKE ACTION, BY LOGGING OFF THE COMPANY'S APP EN MASSE--WHAT THEY CALLED A "BOOM."

THEY WORK IN ENTIRELY SEPARATE LOCATIONS FROM ONE ANOTHER, & ARE NOT EVEN CLASSIFIED AS EMPLOYEES BY THE COMPANY. AS SUCH, SOME HAD DISMISSED THEM AS "UNORGANISABLE."

AND YET ON 6 AUGUST 2018, 15,000 WORKERS IN AUSTRALIA SWITCHED OFF THE APP AT ONCE, & REFUSED TO PICK UP PASSENGERS.

'RIDESHARE DRIVERS UNITED' DECLARED THE STRIKE (THEIR 5TH IN 2 YEARS) A SUCCESS.

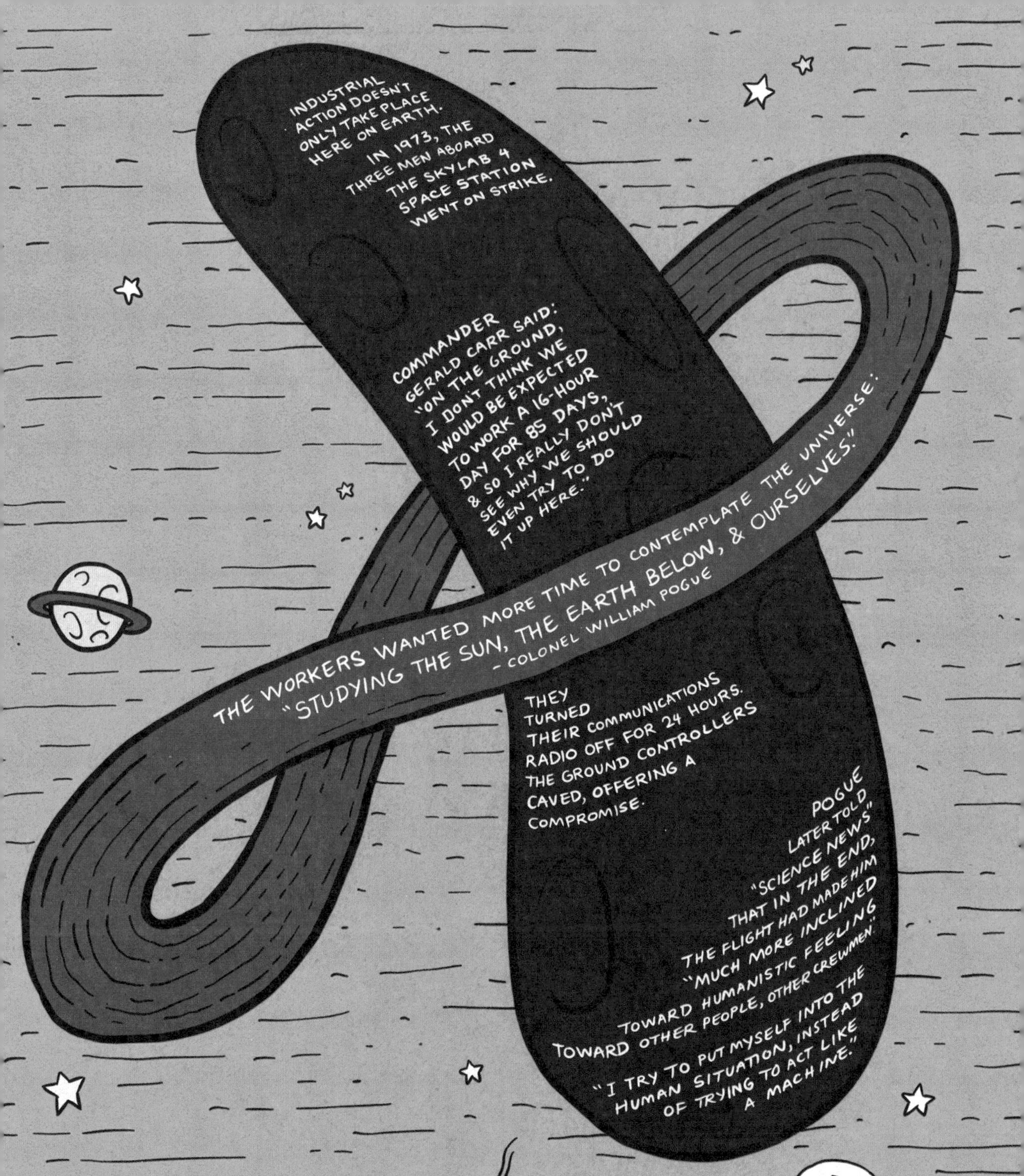
INDUSTRIAL ACTION DOESN'T ONLY TAKE PLACE HERE ON EARTH.
IN 1973, THE THREE MEN ABOARD THE SKYLAB 4 SPACE STATION WENT ON STRIKE.
COMMANDER GERALD CARR SAID: "ON THE GROUND, I DON'T THINK WE WOULD BE EXPECTED TO WORK A 16-HOUR DAY FOR 85 DAYS, & SO I REALLY DON'T SEE WHY WE SHOULD EVEN TRY TO DO IT UP HERE."
THE WORKERS WANTED MORE TIME TO CONTEMPLATE THE UNIVERSE:
"STUDYING THE SUN, THE EARTH BELOW, & OURSELVES."
- COLONEL WILLIAM POGUE
THEY TURNED THEIR COMMUNICATIONS RADIO OFF FOR 24 HOURS. THE GROUND CONTROLLERS CAVED, OFFERING A COMPROMISE.
POGUE LATER TOLD "SCIENCE NEWS" THAT IN THE END, THE FLIGHT HAD MADE HIM "MUCH MORE INCLINED TOWARD HUMANISTIC FEELING TOWARD OTHER PEOPLE, OTHER CREWMEN."
"I TRY TO PUT MYSELF INTO THE HUMAN SITUATION, INSTEAD OF TRYING TO ACT LIKE A MACHINE."
WORKERS HAD WON THE FIRST INDUSTRIAL DISPUTE IN SPACE.
THE FIRST THAT YOU KNOW OF, DICKHEAD!

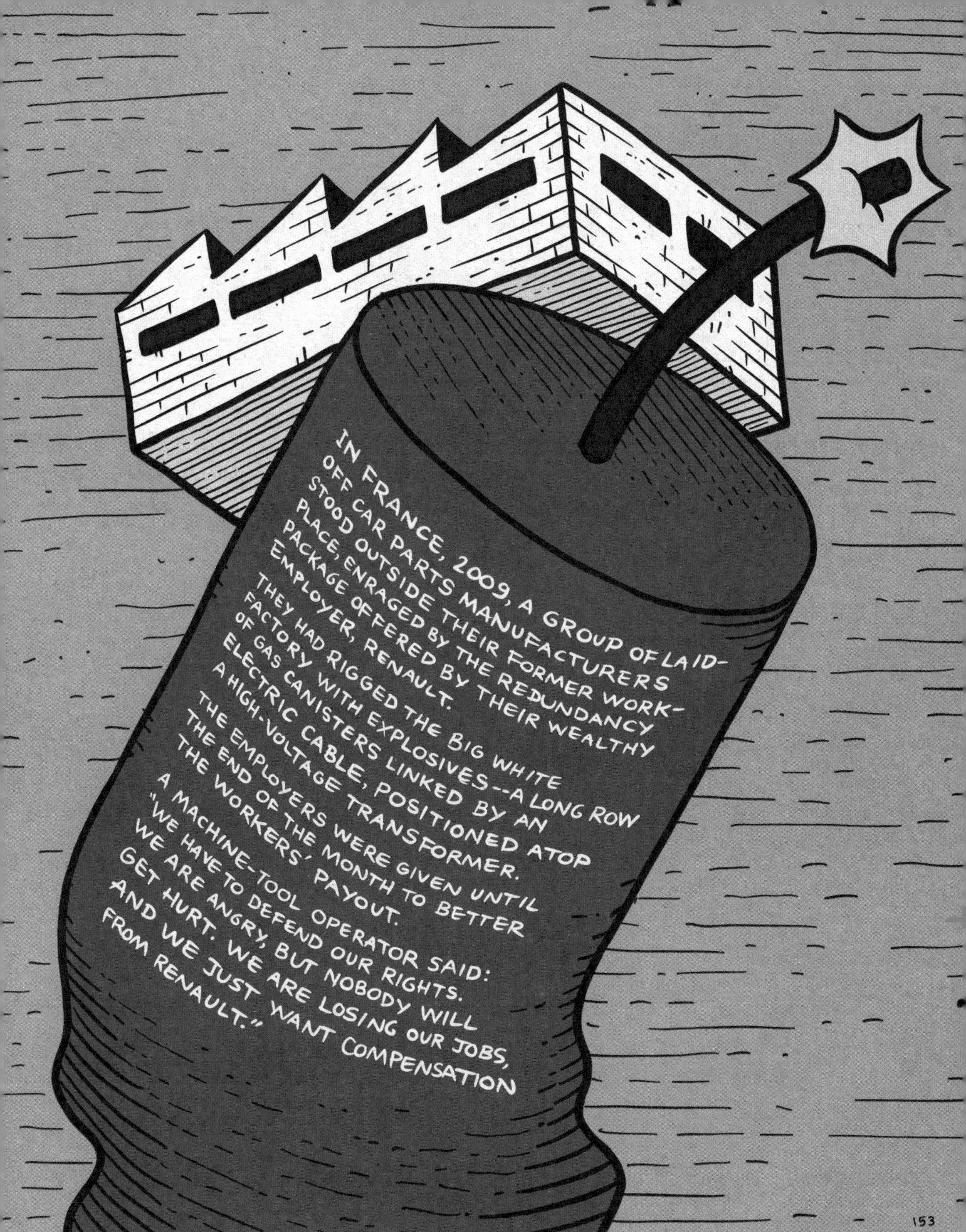
IN FRANCE, 2009, A GROUP OF LAID-
OFF CAR PARTS MANUFACTURERS
STOOD OUTSIDE THEIR FORMER WORK-
PLACE, ENRAGED BY THE REDUNDANCY
PACKAGE OFFERED BY THEIR WEALTHY
EMPLOYER, RENAULT.
THEY HAD RIGGED THE BIG WHITE
FACTORY WITH EXPLOSIVES--A LONG ROW
OF GAS CANISTERS LINKED BY AN
ELECTRIC CABLE, POSITIONED ATOP
A HIGH-VOLTAGE TRANSFORMER.
THE EMPLOYERS WERE GIVEN UNTIL
THE END OF THE MONTH TO BETTER
THE WORKERS' PAYOUT.
A MACHINE-TOOL OPERATOR SAID:
"WE HAVE TO DEFEND OUR RIGHTS.
WE ARE ANGRY, BUT NOBODY WILL
GET HURT. WE ARE LOSING OUR JOBS,
AND WE JUST WANT COMPENSATION
FROM RENAULT."

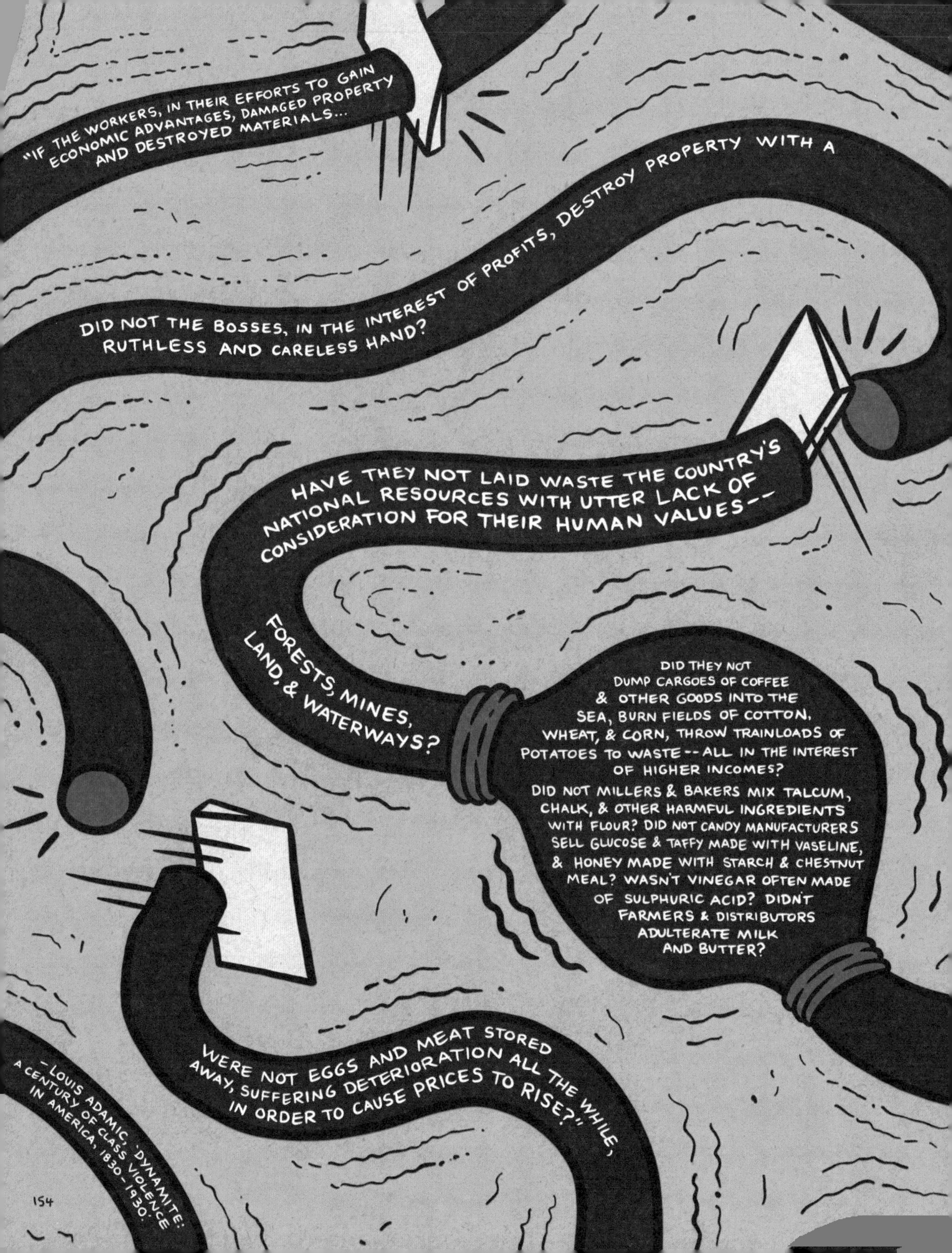

"IF THE WORKERS, IN THEIR EFFORTS TO GAIN ECONOMIC ADVANTAGES, DAMAGED PROPERTY AND DESTROYED MATERIALS...
DID NOT THE BOSSES, IN THE INTEREST OF PROFITS, DESTROY PROPERTY WITH A RUTHLESS AND CARELESS HAND?
HAVE THEY NOT LAID WASTE THE COUNTRY'S NATIONAL RESOURCES WITH UTTER LACK OF CONSIDERATION FOR THEIR HUMAN VALUES--
FORESTS, MINES, LAND, & WATERWAYS?
DID THEY NOT DUMP CARGOES OF COFFEE & OTHER GOODS INTO THE SEA, BURN FIELDS OF COTTON, WHEAT, & CORN, THROW TRAINLOADS OF POTATOES TO WASTE -- ALL IN THE INTEREST OF HIGHER INCOMES?
DID NOT MILLERS & BAKERS MIX TALCUM, CHALK, & OTHER HARMFUL INGREDIENTS WITH FLOUR? DID NOT CANDY MANUFACTURERS SELL GLUCOSE & TAFFY MADE WITH VASELINE, & HONEY MADE WITH STARCH & CHESTNUT MEAL? WASN'T VINEGAR OFTEN MADE OF SULPHURIC ACID? DIDN'T FARMERS & DISTRIBUTORS ADULTERATE MILK AND BUTTER?
WERE NOT EGGS AND MEAT STORED AWAY, SUFFERING DETERIORATION ALL THE WHILE, IN ORDER TO CAUSE PRICES TO RISE?"
-LOUIS ADAMIC, DYNAMITE: A CENTURY OF CLASS VIOLENCE IN AMERICA, 1830-1930.

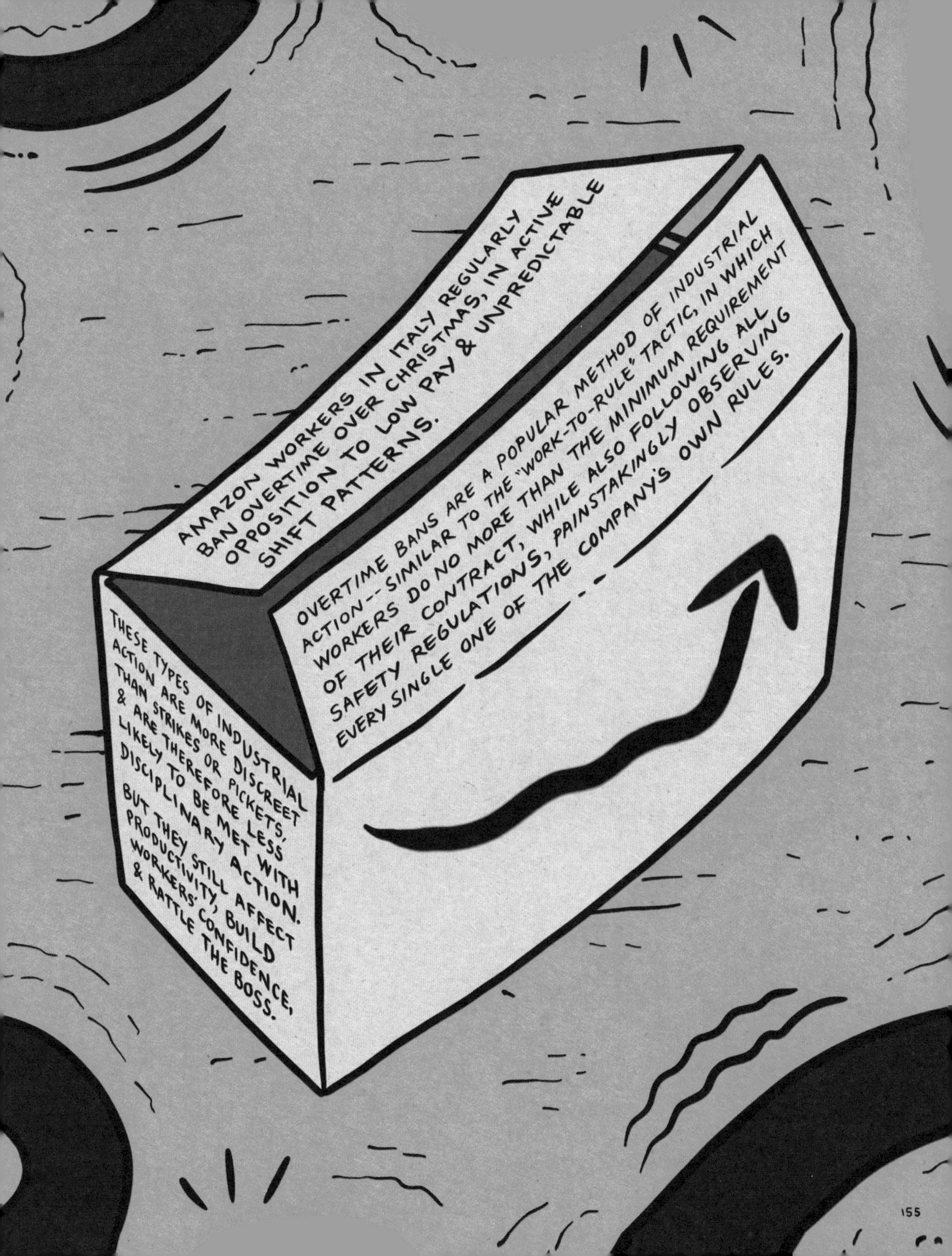
AMAZON WORKERS IN ITALY REGULARLY BAN OVERTIME OVER CHRISTMAS, IN ACTIVE OPPOSITION TO LOW PAY & UNPREDICTABLE SHIFT PATTERNS.
OVERTIME BANS ARE A POPULAR METHOD OF INDUSTRIAL ACTION--SIMILAR TO THE "WORK-TO-RULE" TACTIC, IN WHICH WORKERS DO NO MORE THAN THE MINIMUM REQUIREMENT OF THEIR CONTRACT, WHILE ALSO FOLLOWING ALL SAFETY REGULATIONS, PAINSTAKINGLY OBSERVING EVERY SINGLE ONE OF THE COMPANY'S OWN RULES.
THESE TYPES OF INDUSTRIAL ACTION ARE MORE DISCREET THAN STRIKES OR PICKETS, & ARE THEREFORE LESS LIKELY TO BE MET WITH DISCIPLINARY ACTION. BUT THEY STILL AFFECT PRODUCTIVITY, BUILD WORKERS' CONFIDENCE, & RATTLE THE BOSS.

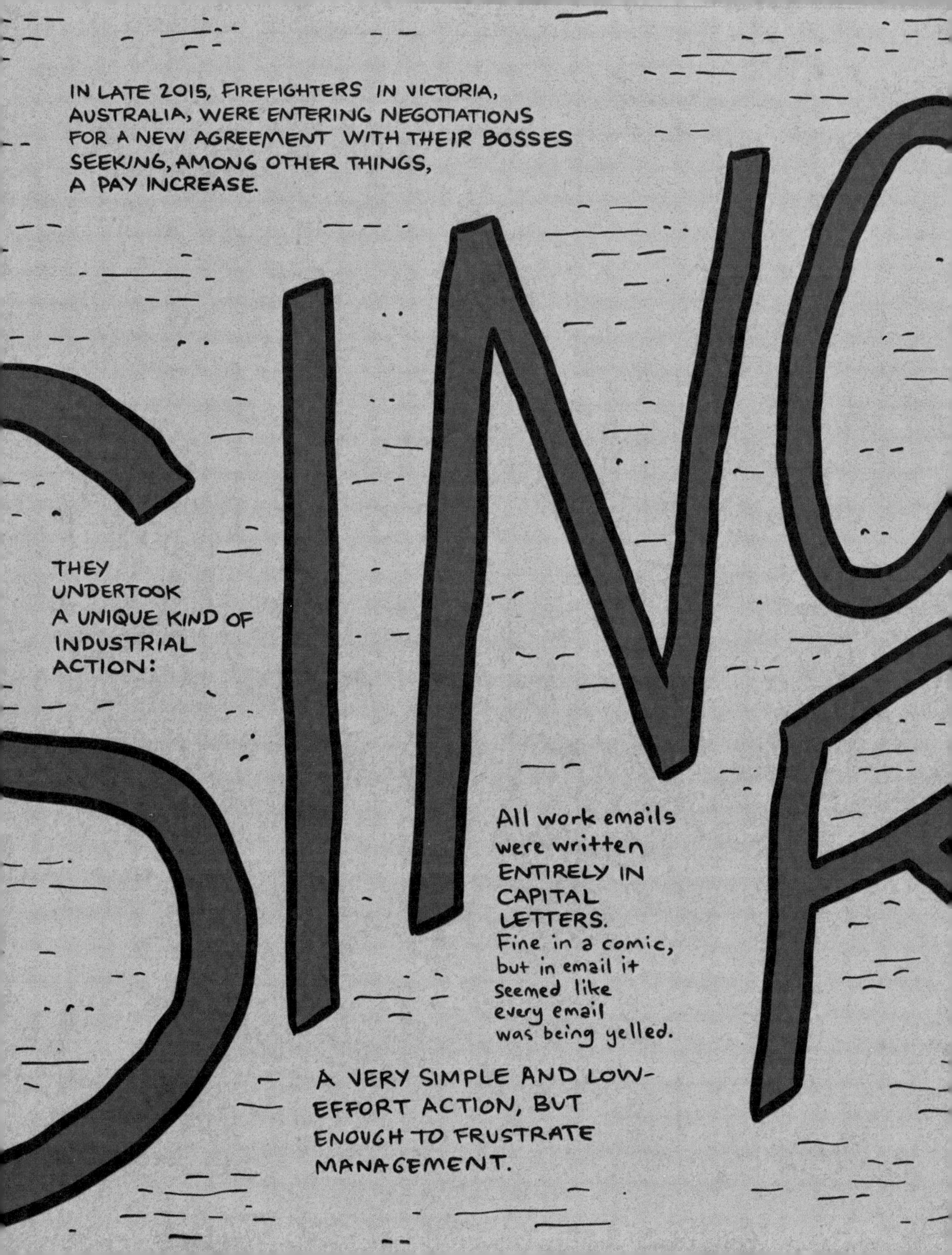
IN LATE 2015, FIREFIGHTERS IN VICTORIA, AUSTRALIA, WERE ENTERING NEGOTIATIONS FOR A NEW AGREEMENT WITH THEIR BOSSES SEEKING, AMONG OTHER THINGS, A PAY INCREASE.
THEY UNDERTOOK A UNIQUE KIND OF INDUSTRIAL ACTION:
All work emails were written ENTIRELY IN CAPITAL LETTERS. Fine in a comic, but in email it seemed like every email was being yelled.
A VERY SIMPLE AND LOW-EFFORT ACTION, BUT ENOUGH TO FRUSTRATE MANAGEMENT.

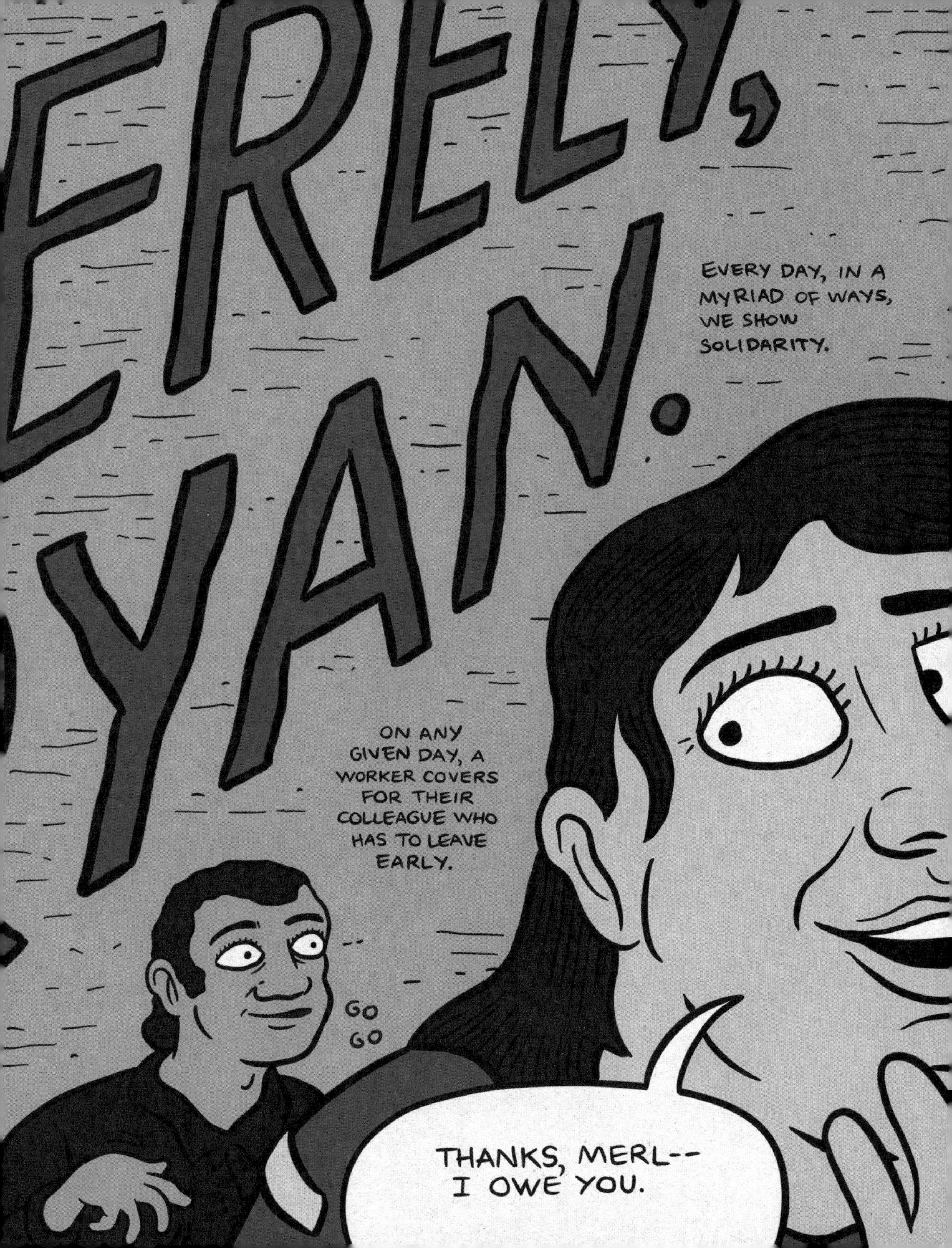
ERELY,
YAN.
EVERY DAY, IN A MYRIAD OF WAYS, WE SHOW SOLIDARITY.
ON ANY GIVEN DAY, A WORKER COVERS FOR THEIR COLLEAGUE WHO HAS TO LEAVE EARLY.
GO GO
THANKS, MERL-- I OWE YOU.

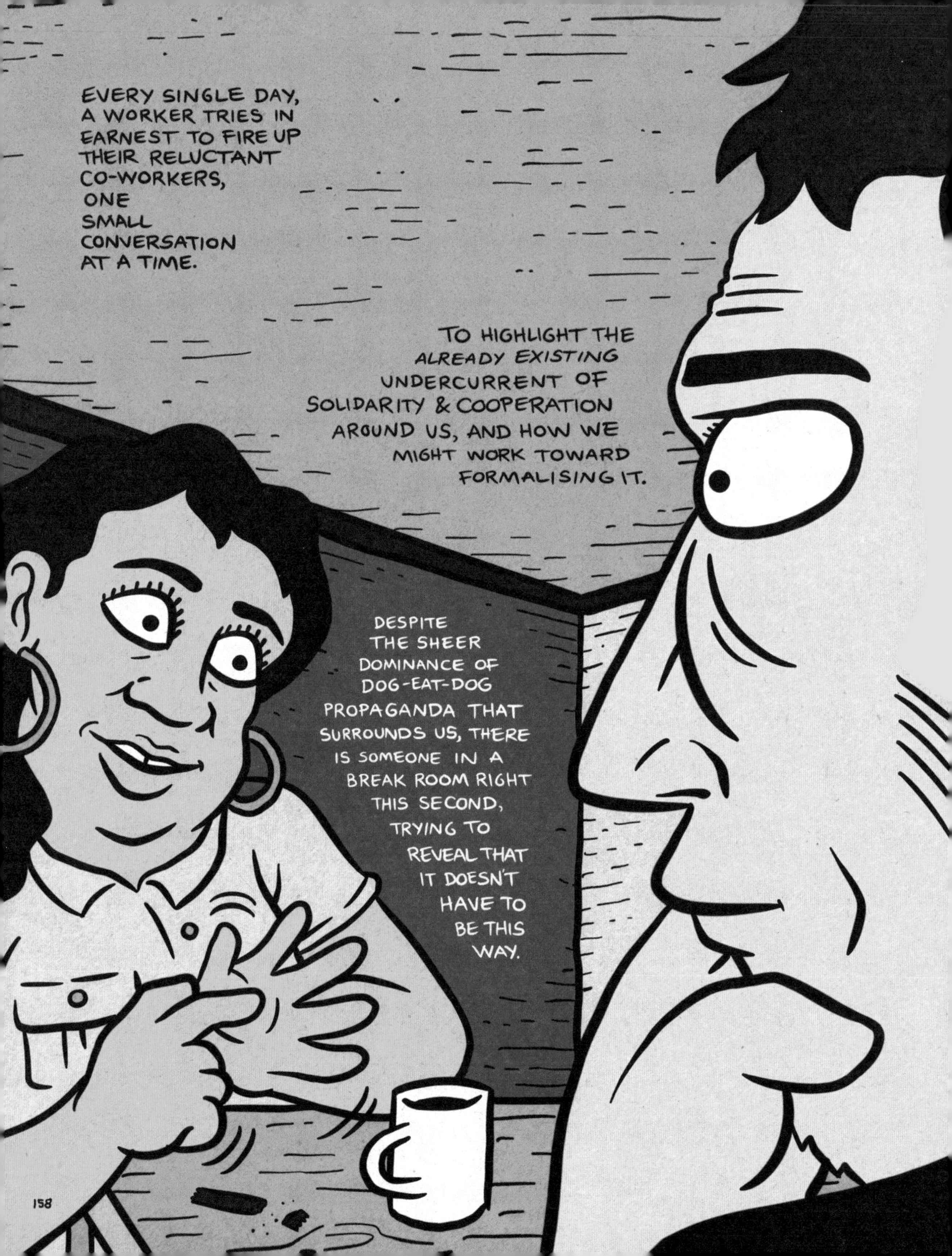
EVERY SINGLE DAY, A WORKER TRIES IN EARNEST TO FIRE UP THEIR RELUCTANT CO-WORKERS, ONE SMALL CONVERSATION AT A TIME.
TO HIGHLIGHT THE *ALREADY EXISTING* UNDERCURRENT OF SOLIDARITY & COOPERATION AROUND US, AND HOW WE MIGHT WORK TOWARD FORMALISING IT.
DESPITE THE SHEER DOMINANCE OF DOG-EAT-DOG PROPAGANDA THAT SURROUNDS US, THERE IS SOMEONE IN A BREAK ROOM RIGHT THIS SECOND, TRYING TO REVEAL THAT IT DOESN'T HAVE TO BE THIS WAY.

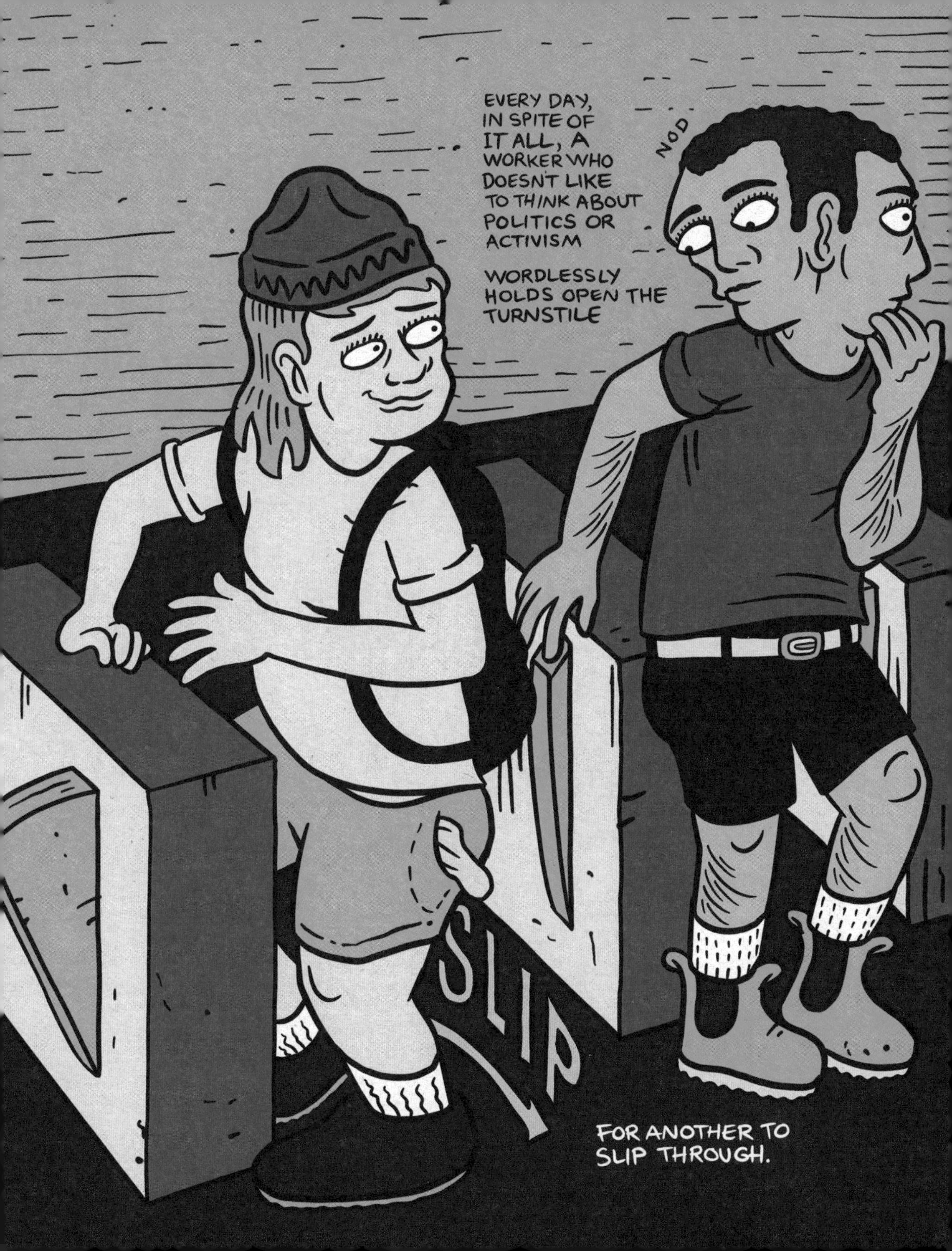
EVERY DAY, IN SPITE OF IT ALL, A WORKER WHO DOESN'T LIKE TO THINK ABOUT POLITICS OR ACTIVISM
WORDLESSLY HOLDS OPEN THE TURNSTILE
NOD
SLIP
FOR ANOTHER TO SLIP THROUGH.

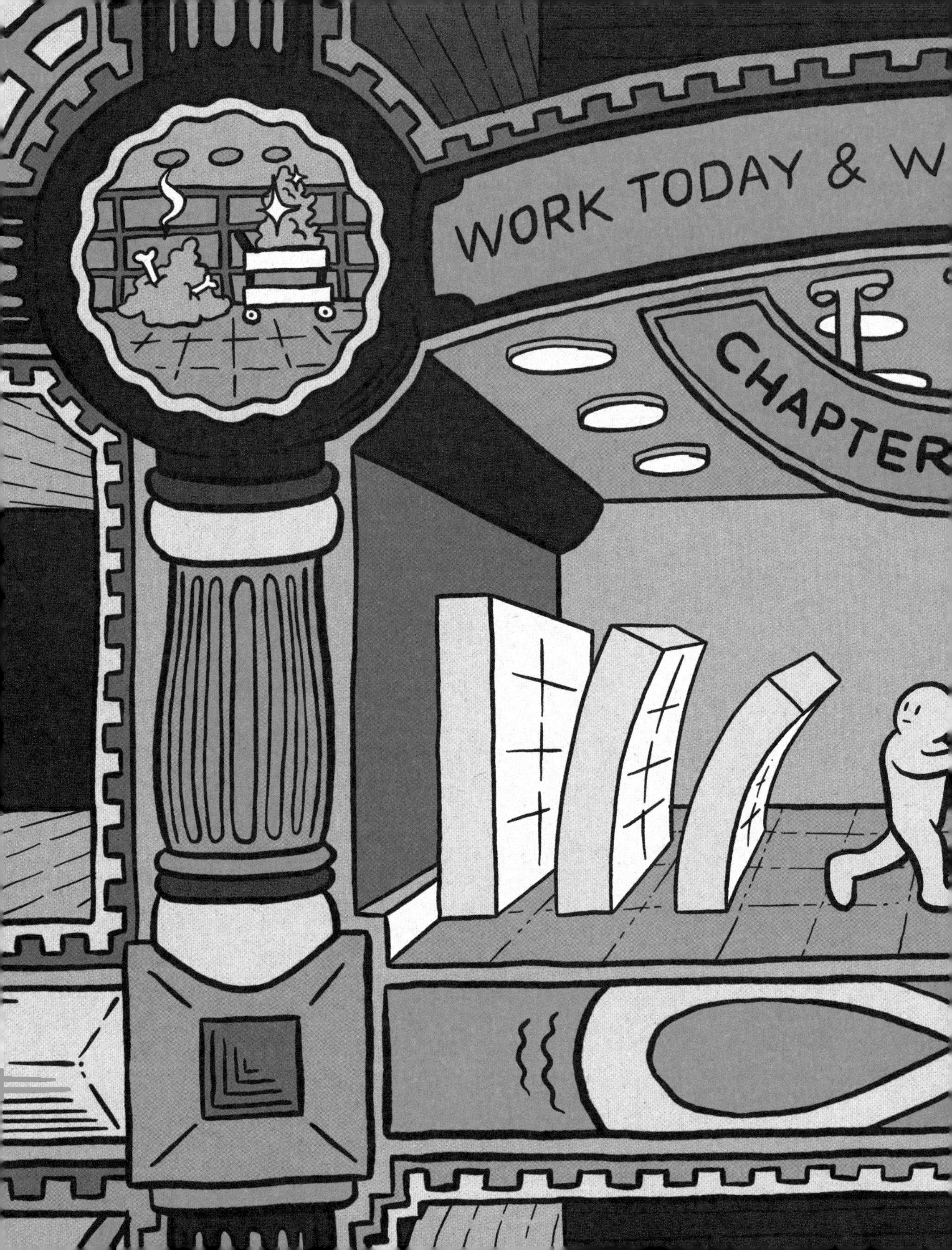
WORK TODAY & W
CHAPTER

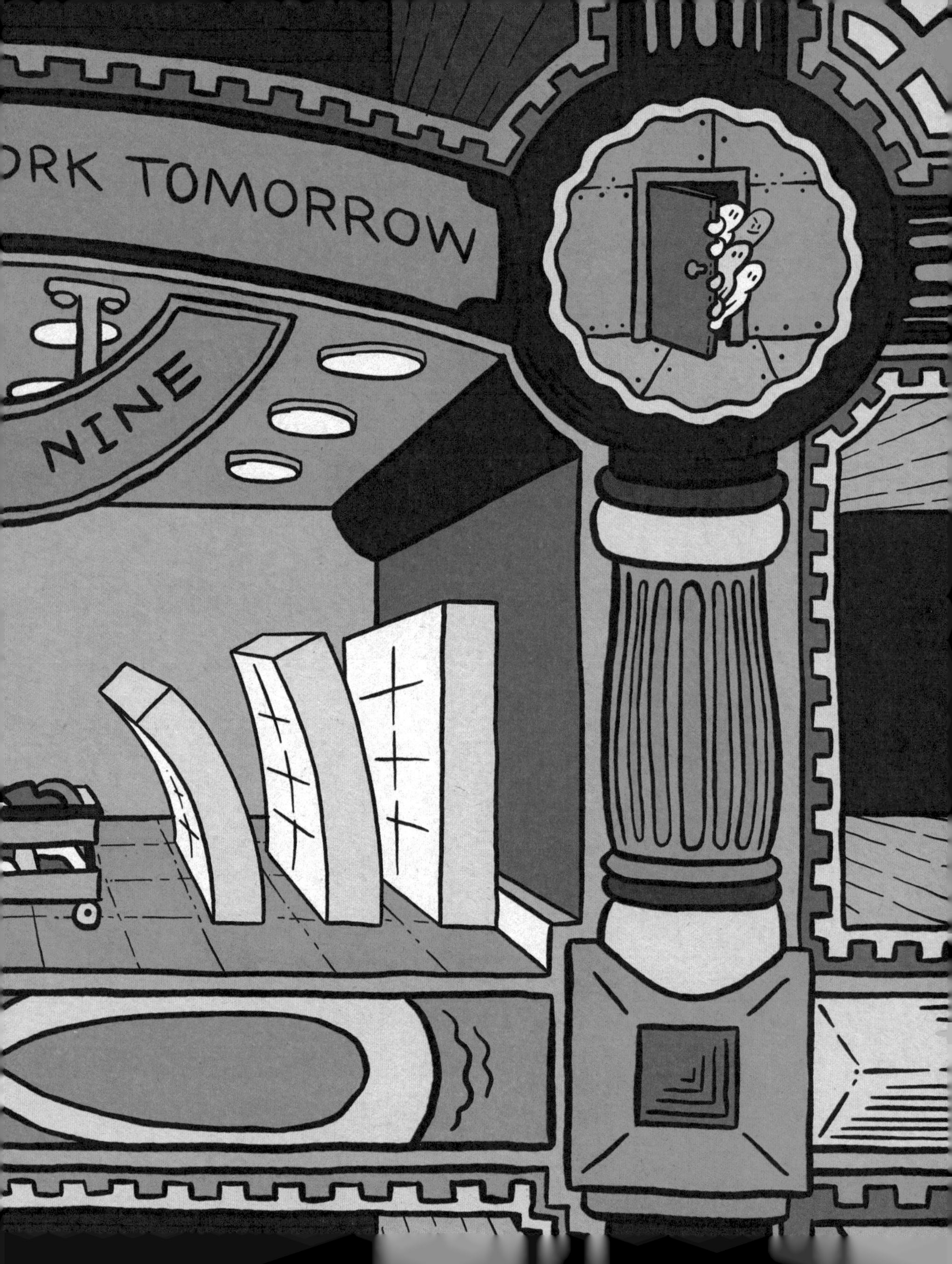

ORK TOMORROW
NINE

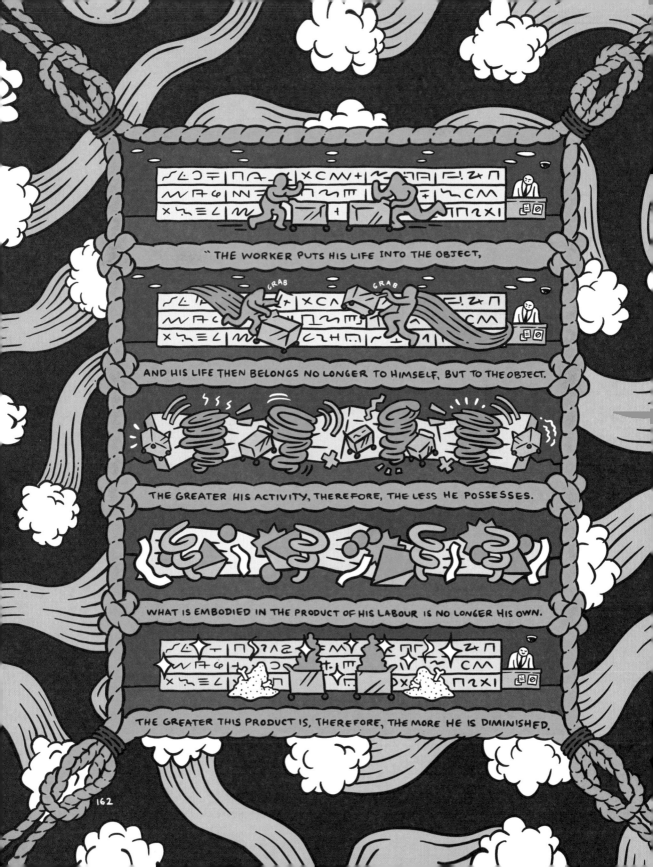

"THE WORKER PUTS HIS LIFE INTO THE OBJECT,

AND HIS LIFE THEN BELONGS NO LONGER TO HIMSELF, BUT TO THE OBJECT.

THE GREATER HIS ACTIVITY, THEREFORE, THE LESS HE POSSESSES.

WHAT IS EMBODIED IN THE PRODUCT OF HIS LABOUR IS NO LONGER HIS OWN.

THE GREATER THIS PRODUCT IS, THEREFORE, THE MORE HE IS DIMINISHED.

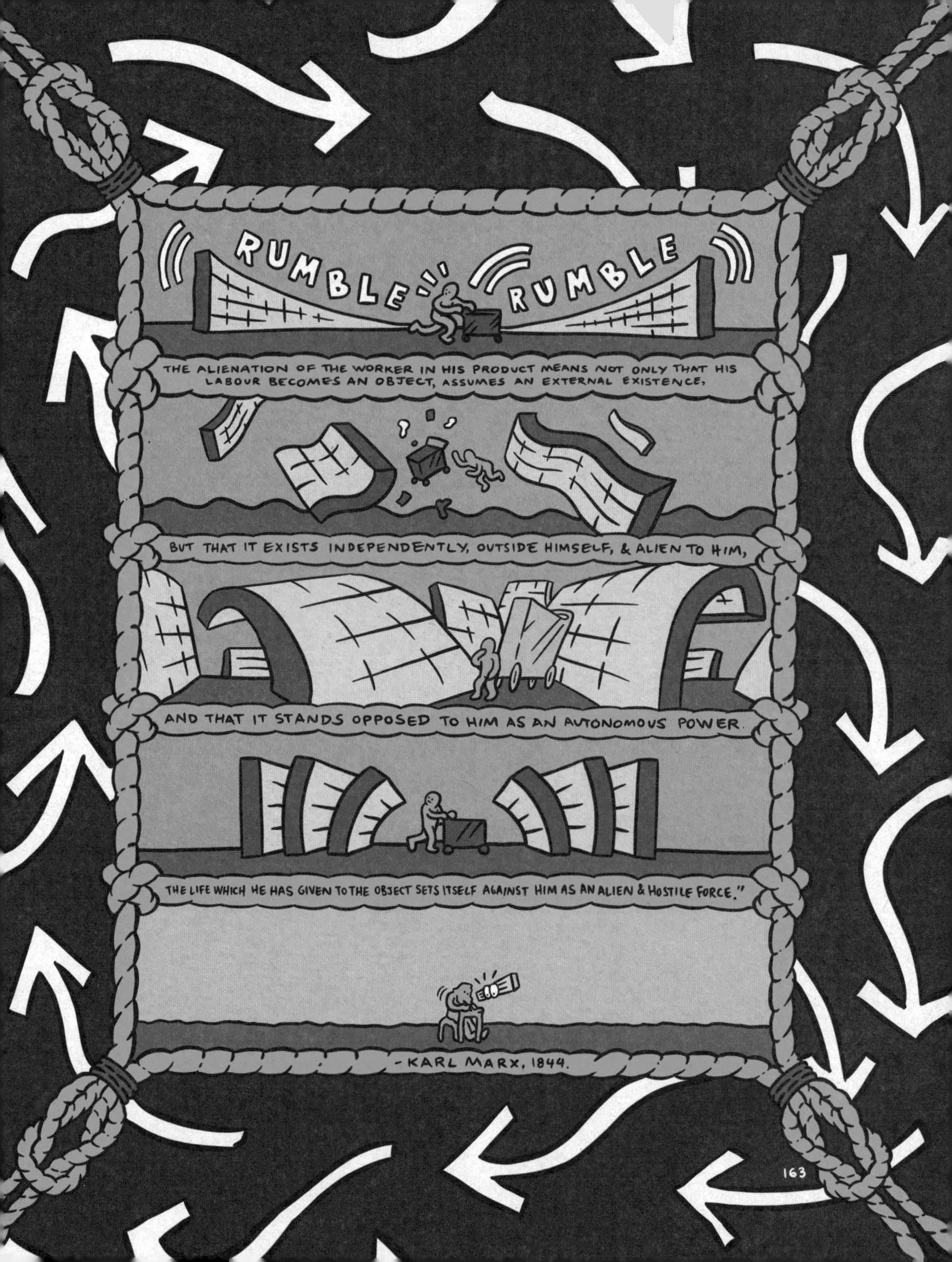
RUMBLE RUMBLE
THE ALIENATION OF THE WORKER IN HIS PRODUCT MEANS NOT ONLY THAT HIS LABOUR BECOMES AN OBJECT, ASSUMES AN EXTERNAL EXISTENCE,
BUT THAT IT EXISTS INDEPENDENTLY, OUTSIDE HIMSELF, & ALIEN TO HIM,
AND THAT IT STANDS OPPOSED TO HIM AS AN AUTONOMOUS POWER.
THE LIFE WHICH HE HAS GIVEN TO THE OBJECT SETS ITSELF AGAINST HIM AS AN ALIEN & HOSTILE FORCE."
-KARL MARX, 1844.

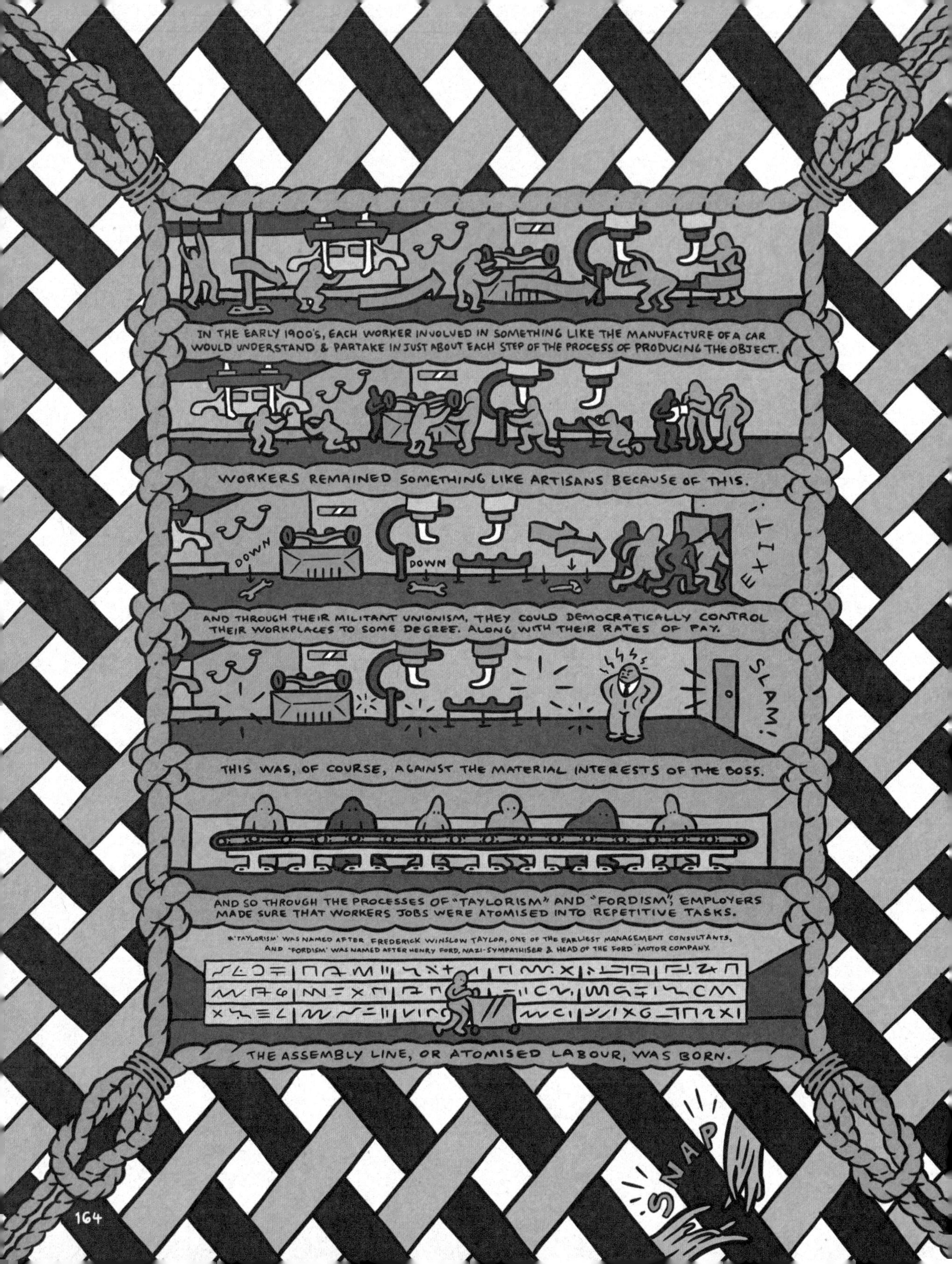
IN THE EARLY 1900'S, EACH WORKER INVOLVED IN SOMETHING LIKE THE MANUFACTURE OF A CAR WOULD UNDERSTAND & PARTAKE IN JUST ABOUT EACH STEP OF THE PROCESS OF PRODUCING THE OBJECT.
WORKERS REMAINED SOMETHING LIKE ARTISANS BECAUSE OF THIS.
DOWN
DOWN
EXIT!
AND THROUGH THEIR MILITANT UNIONISM, THEY COULD DEMOCRATICALLY CONTROL THEIR WORKPLACES TO SOME DEGREE. ALONG WITH THEIR RATES OF PAY.
SLAM!
THIS WAS, OF COURSE, AGAINST THE MATERIAL INTERESTS OF THE BOSS.
AND SO THROUGH THE PROCESSES OF "TAYLORISM" AND "FORDISM"* EMPLOYERS MADE SURE THAT WORKERS JOBS WERE ATOMISED INTO REPETITIVE TASKS.
* 'TAYLORISM' WAS NAMED AFTER FREDERICK WINSLOW TAYLOR, ONE OF THE EARLIEST MANAGEMENT CONSULTANTS, AND 'FORDISM' WAS NAMED AFTER HENRY FORD, NAZI-SYMPATHISER & HEAD OF THE FORD MOTOR COMPANY.
THE ASSEMBLY LINE, OR ATOMISED LABOUR, WAS BORN.
SNAP

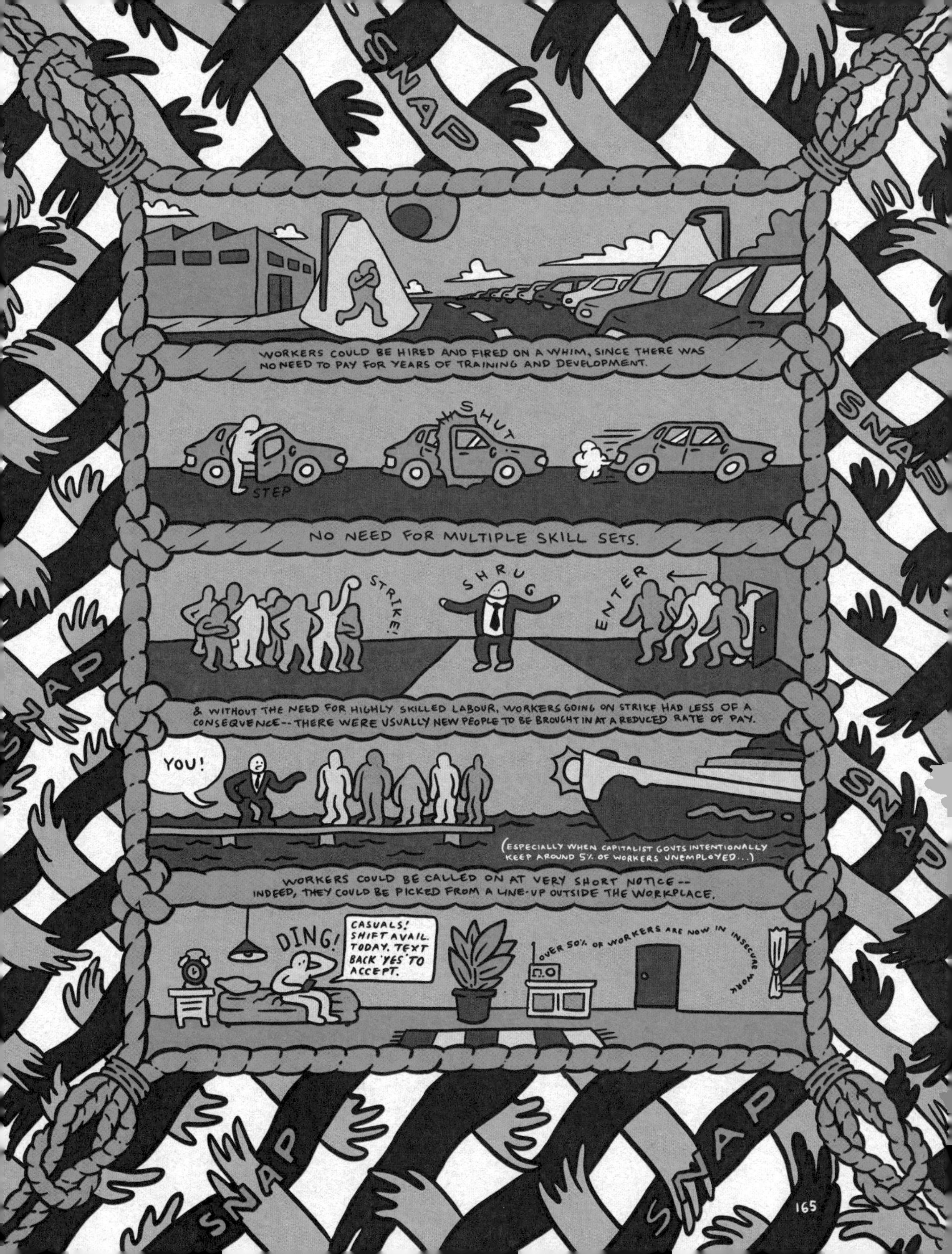
SNAP
WORKERS COULD BE HIRED AND FIRED ON A WHIM, SINCE THERE WAS NO NEED TO PAY FOR YEARS OF TRAINING AND DEVELOPMENT.
STEP
SHUT
NO NEED FOR MULTIPLE SKILL SETS.
STRIKE!
SHRUG
ENTER
& WITHOUT THE NEED FOR HIGHLY SKILLED LABOUR, WORKERS GOING ON STRIKE HAD LESS OF A CONSEQUENCE-- THERE WERE USUALLY NEW PEOPLE TO BE BROUGHT IN AT A REDUCED RATE OF PAY.
YOU!
(ESPECIALLY WHEN CAPITALIST GOVTS INTENTIONALLY KEEP AROUND 5% OF WORKERS UNEMPLOYED...)
WORKERS COULD BE CALLED ON AT VERY SHORT NOTICE-- INDEED, THEY COULD BE PICKED FROM A LINE-UP OUTSIDE THE WORKPLACE.
DING!
CASUALS! SHIFT AVAIL. TODAY. TEXT BACK 'YES' TO ACCEPT.
OVER 50% OF WORKERS ARE NOW IN INSECURE WORK

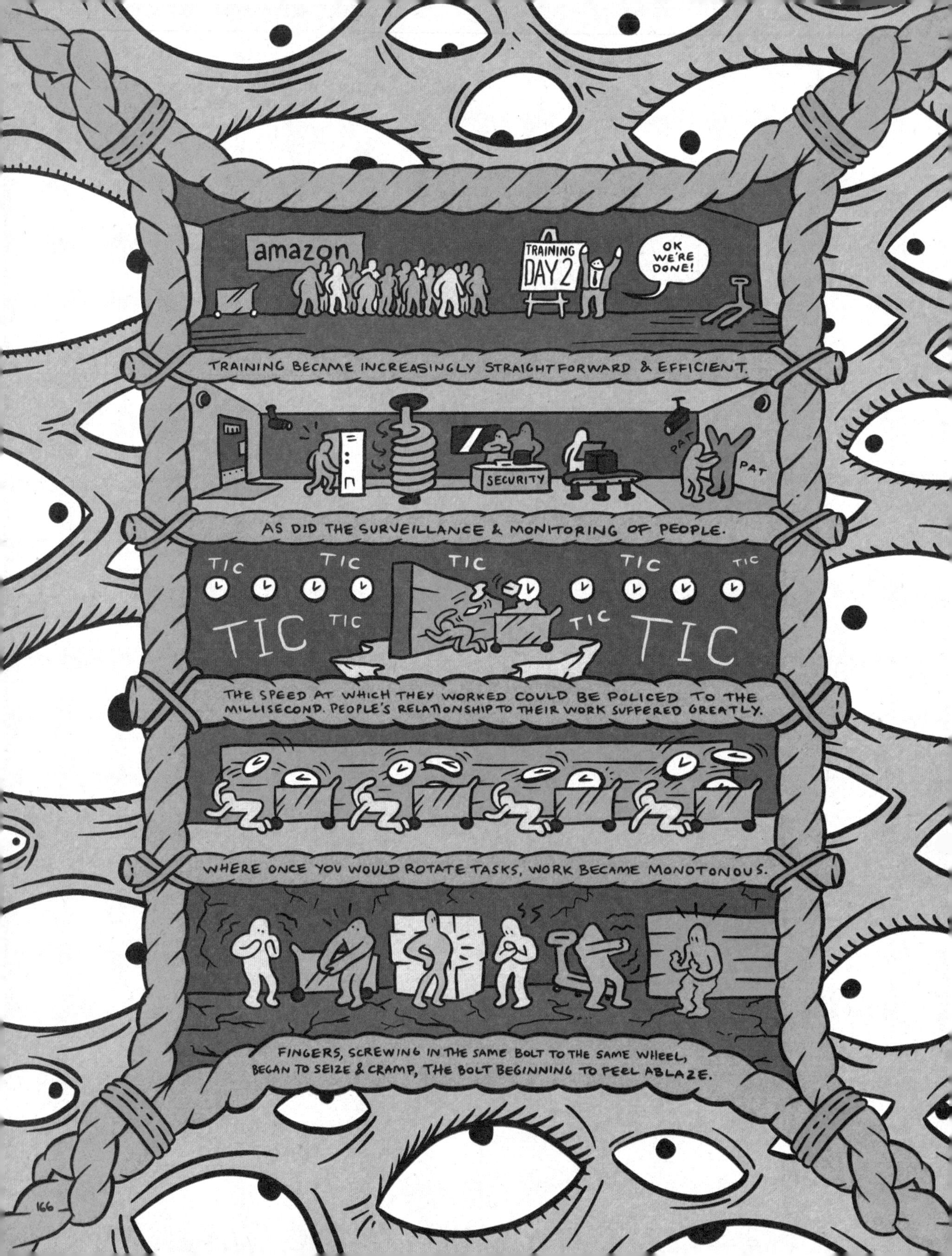
amazon
TRAINING DAY 2
OK WE'RE DONE!
TRAINING BECAME INCREASINGLY STRAIGHTFORWARD & EFFICIENT.
SECURITY
PAT
PAT
AS DID THE SURVEILLANCE & MONITORING OF PEOPLE.
TIC
TIC
TIC
TIC
TIC
TIC
TIC
TIC
TIC
THE SPEED AT WHICH THEY WORKED COULD BE POLICED TO THE MILLISECOND. PEOPLE'S RELATIONSHIP TO THEIR WORK SUFFERED GREATLY.
WHERE ONCE YOU WOULD ROTATE TASKS, WORK BECAME MONOTONOUS.
FINGERS, SCREWING IN THE SAME BOLT TO THE SAME WHEEL, BEGAN TO SEIZE & CRAMP, THE BOLT BEGINNING TO FEEL ABLAZE.

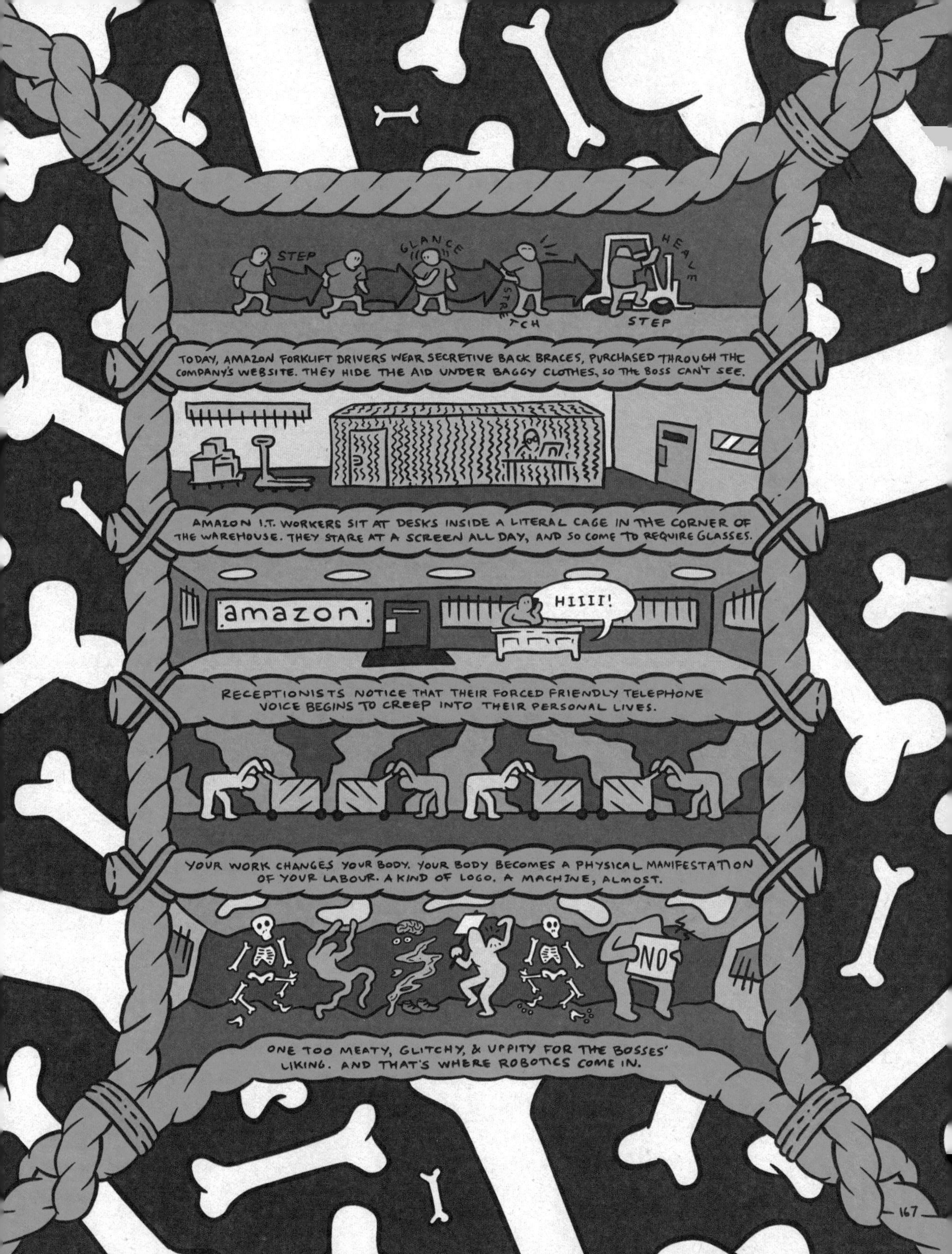

STEP
GLANCE
STRETCH
HEAVE
STEP
TODAY, AMAZON FORKLIFT DRIVERS WEAR SECRETIVE BACK BRACES, PURCHASED THROUGH THE COMPANY'S WEBSITE. THEY HIDE THE AID UNDER BAGGY CLOTHES, SO THE BOSS CAN'T SEE.
AMAZON I.T. WORKERS SIT AT DESKS INSIDE A LITERAL CAGE IN THE CORNER OF THE WAREHOUSE. THEY STARE AT A SCREEN ALL DAY, AND SO COME TO REQUIRE GLASSES.
amazon
HIIII!
RECEPTIONISTS NOTICE THAT THEIR FORCED FRIENDLY TELEPHONE VOICE BEGINS TO CREEP INTO THEIR PERSONAL LIVES.
YOUR WORK CHANGES YOUR BODY. YOUR BODY BECOMES A PHYSICAL MANIFESTATION OF YOUR LABOUR. A KIND OF LOGO. A MACHINE, ALMOST.
NO
ONE TOO MEATY, GLITCHY, & UPPITY FOR THE BOSSES' LIKING. AND THAT'S WHERE ROBOTICS COME IN.

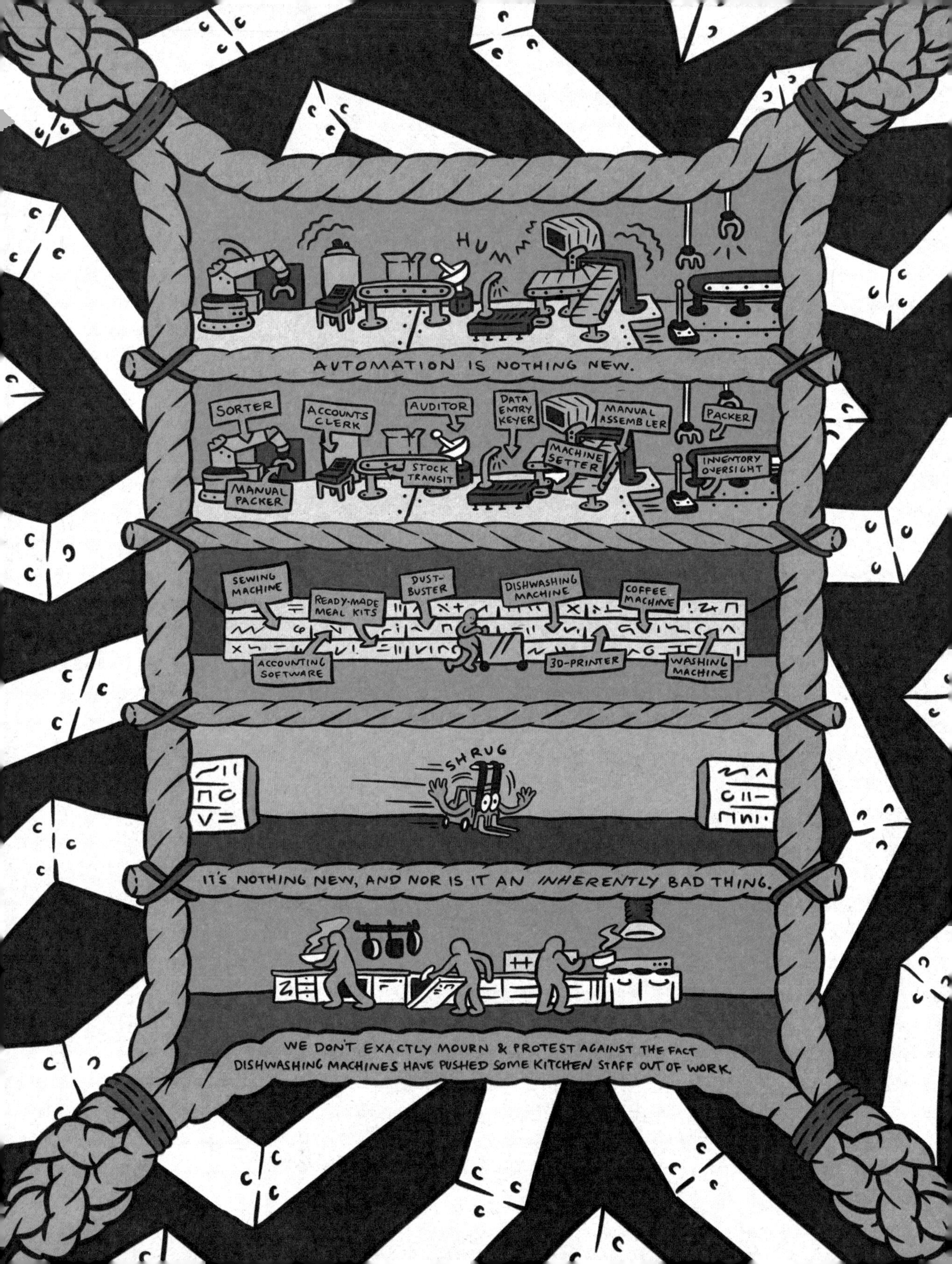
HUMM
AUTOMATION IS NOTHING NEW.
SORTER
ACCOUNTS CLERK
AUDITOR
DATA ENTRY KEYER
MANUAL ASSEMBLER
PACKER
MACHINE SETTER
INVENTORY OVERSIGHT
STOCK TRANSIT
MANUAL PACKER
SEWING MACHINE
READY-MADE MEAL KITS
DUST-BUSTER
DISHWASHING MACHINE
COFFEE MACHINE
ACCOUNTING SOFTWARE
3D-PRINTER
WASHING MACHINE
SHRUG
IT'S NOTHING NEW, AND NOR IS IT AN *INHERENTLY* BAD THING.
WE DON'T EXACTLY MOURN & PROTEST AGAINST THE FACT DISHWASHING MACHINES HAVE PUSHED SOME KITCHEN STAFF OUT OF WORK.

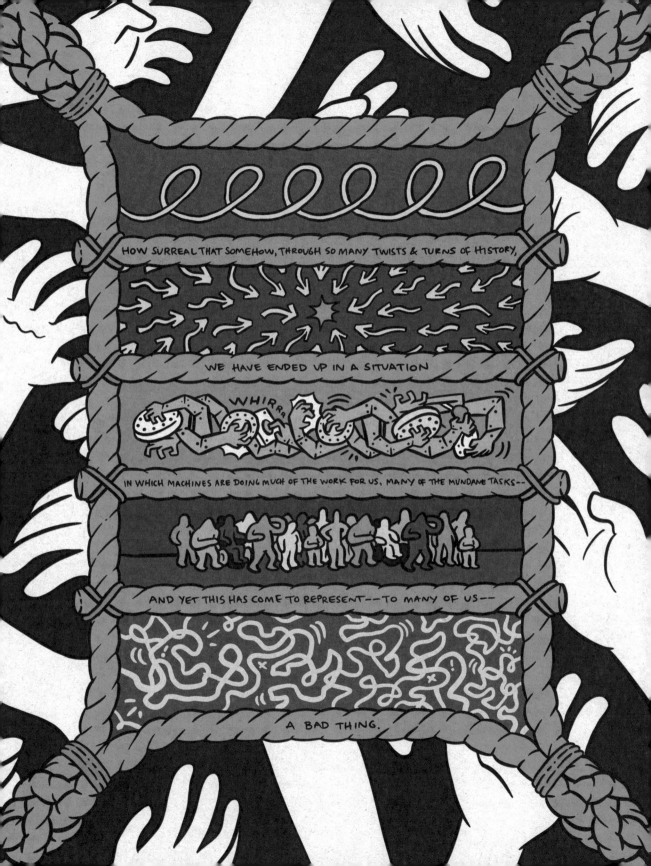

HOW SURREAL THAT SOMEHOW, THROUGH SO MANY TWISTS & TURNS OF HISTORY,

WE HAVE ENDED UP IN A SITUATION

WHIRRR

IN WHICH MACHINES ARE DOING MUCH OF THE WORK FOR US, MANY OF THE MUNDANE TASKS--

AND YET THIS HAS COME TO REPRESENT--TO MANY OF US--

A BAD THING.

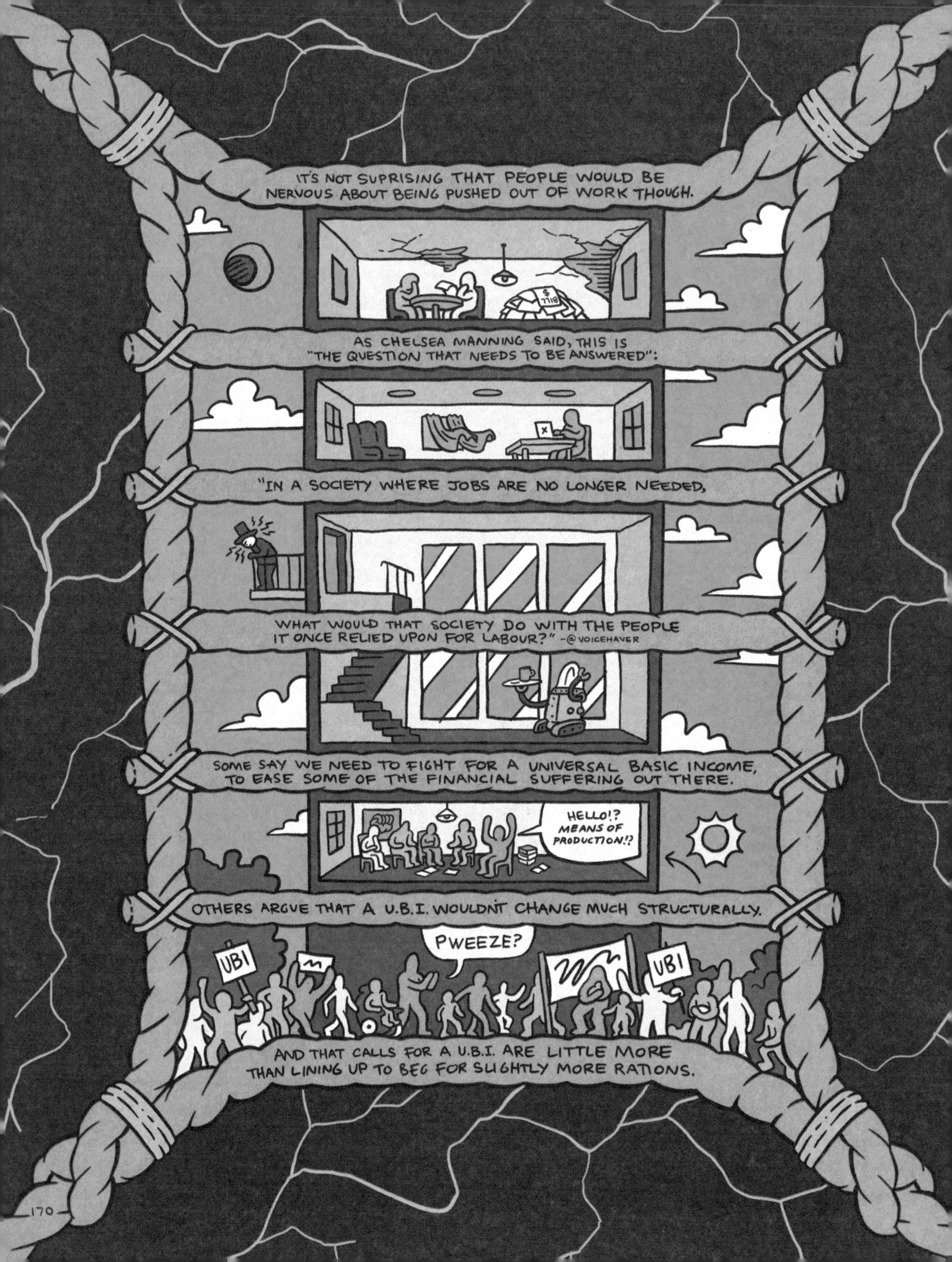
IT'S NOT SUPRISING THAT PEOPLE WOULD BE NERVOUS ABOUT BEING PUSHED OUT OF WORK THOUGH.
$ BILL
AS CHELSEA MANNING SAID, THIS IS "THE QUESTION THAT NEEDS TO BE ANSWERED":
"IN A SOCIETY WHERE JOBS ARE NO LONGER NEEDED,
WHAT WOULD THAT SOCIETY DO WITH THE PEOPLE IT ONCE RELIED UPON FOR LABOUR?" -@VOICEHAVER
SOME SAY WE NEED TO FIGHT FOR A UNIVERSAL BASIC INCOME, TO EASE SOME OF THE FINANCIAL SUFFERING OUT THERE.
HELLO!? MEANS OF PRODUCTION!?
OTHERS ARGUE THAT A U.B.I. WOULDN'T CHANGE MUCH STRUCTURALLY.
PWEEZE?
UBI
UBI
AND THAT CALLS FOR A U.B.I. ARE LITTLE MORE THAN LINING UP TO BEG FOR SLIGHTLY MORE RATIONS.

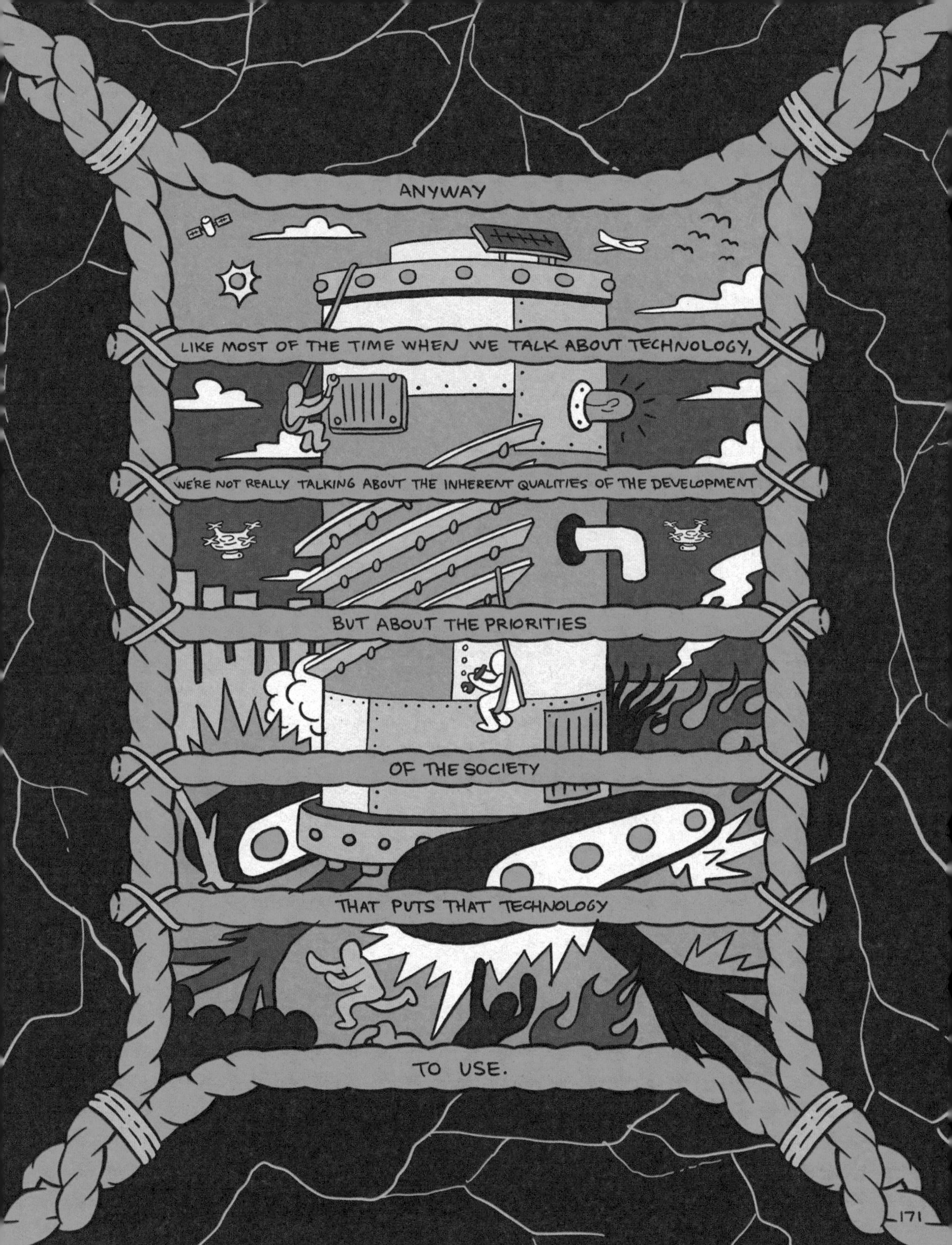
ANYWAY
LIKE MOST OF THE TIME WHEN WE TALK ABOUT TECHNOLOGY,
WE'RE NOT REALLY TALKING ABOUT THE INHERENT QUALITIES OF THE DEVELOPMENT
BUT ABOUT THE PRIORITIES
OF THE SOCIETY
THAT PUTS THAT TECHNOLOGY
TO USE.

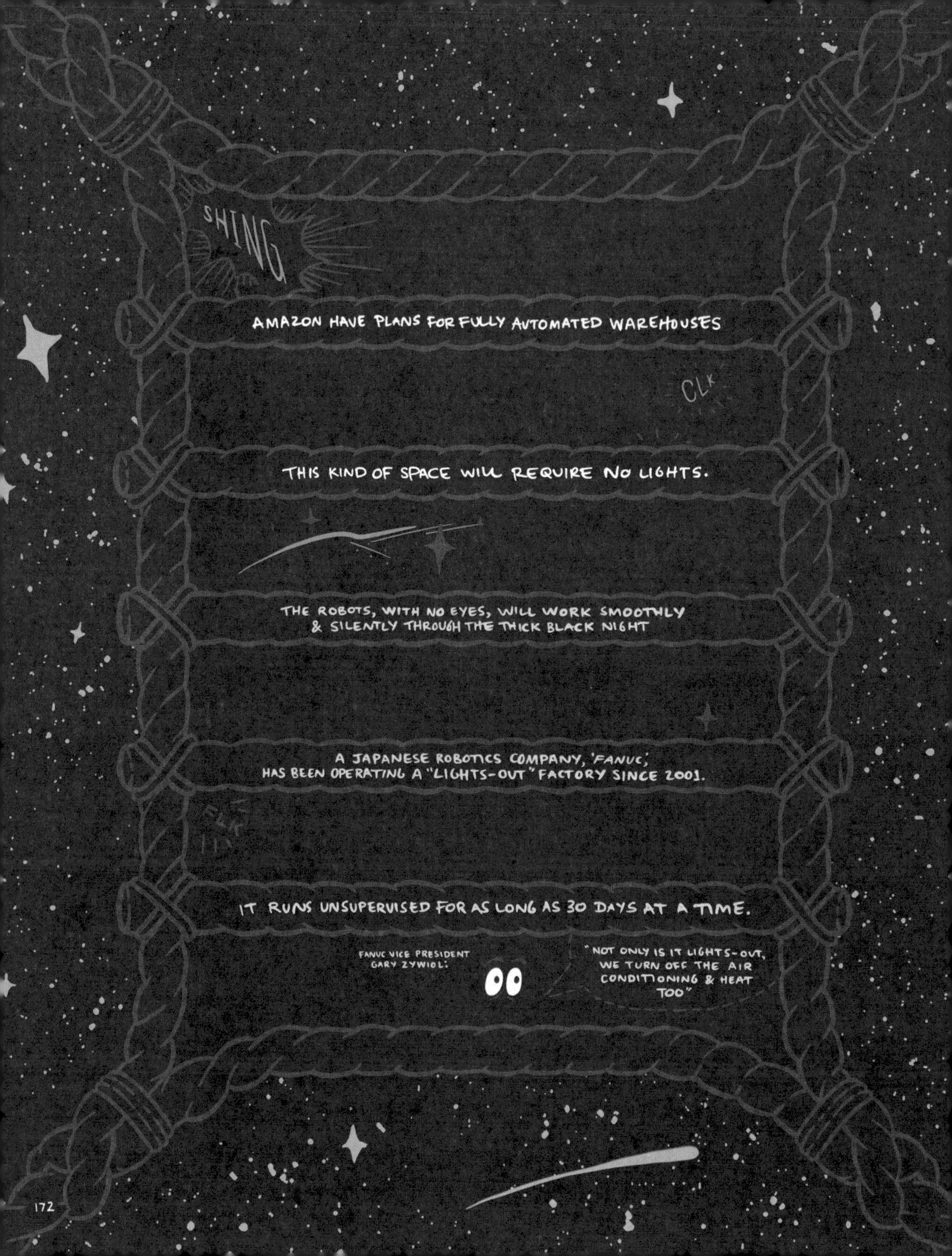
SHING
AMAZON HAVE PLANS FOR FULLY AUTOMATED WAREHOUSES
CLK
THIS KIND OF SPACE WILL REQUIRE NO LIGHTS.
THE ROBOTS, WITH NO EYES, WILL WORK SMOOTHLY & SILENTLY THROUGH THE THICK BLACK NIGHT
A JAPANESE ROBOTICS COMPANY, 'FANUC,' HAS BEEN OPERATING A "LIGHTS-OUT" FACTORY SINCE 2001.
IT RUNS UNSUPERVISED FOR AS LONG AS 30 DAYS AT A TIME.
FANUC VICE PRESIDENT GARY ZYWIOL:
"NOT ONLY IS IT LIGHTS-OUT, WE TURN OFF THE AIR CONDITIONING & HEAT TOO"

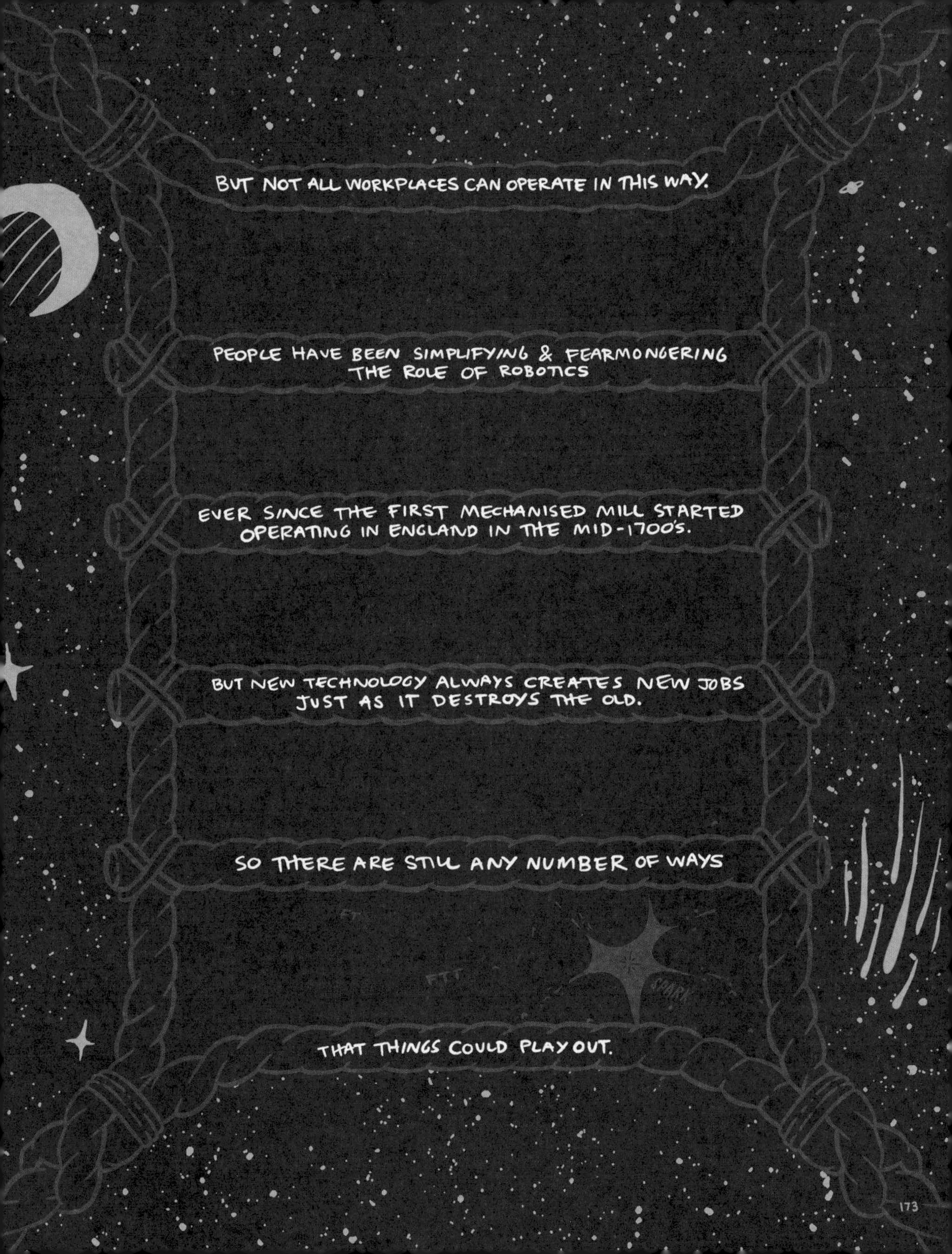
BUT NOT ALL WORKPLACES CAN OPERATE IN THIS WAY.
PEOPLE HAVE BEEN SIMPLIFYING & FEARMONGERING THE ROLE OF ROBOTICS
EVER SINCE THE FIRST MECHANISED MILL STARTED OPERATING IN ENGLAND IN THE MID-1700'S.
BUT NEW TECHNOLOGY ALWAYS CREATES NEW JOBS JUST AS IT DESTROYS THE OLD.
SO THERE ARE STILL ANY NUMBER OF WAYS
THAT THINGS COULD PLAY OUT.

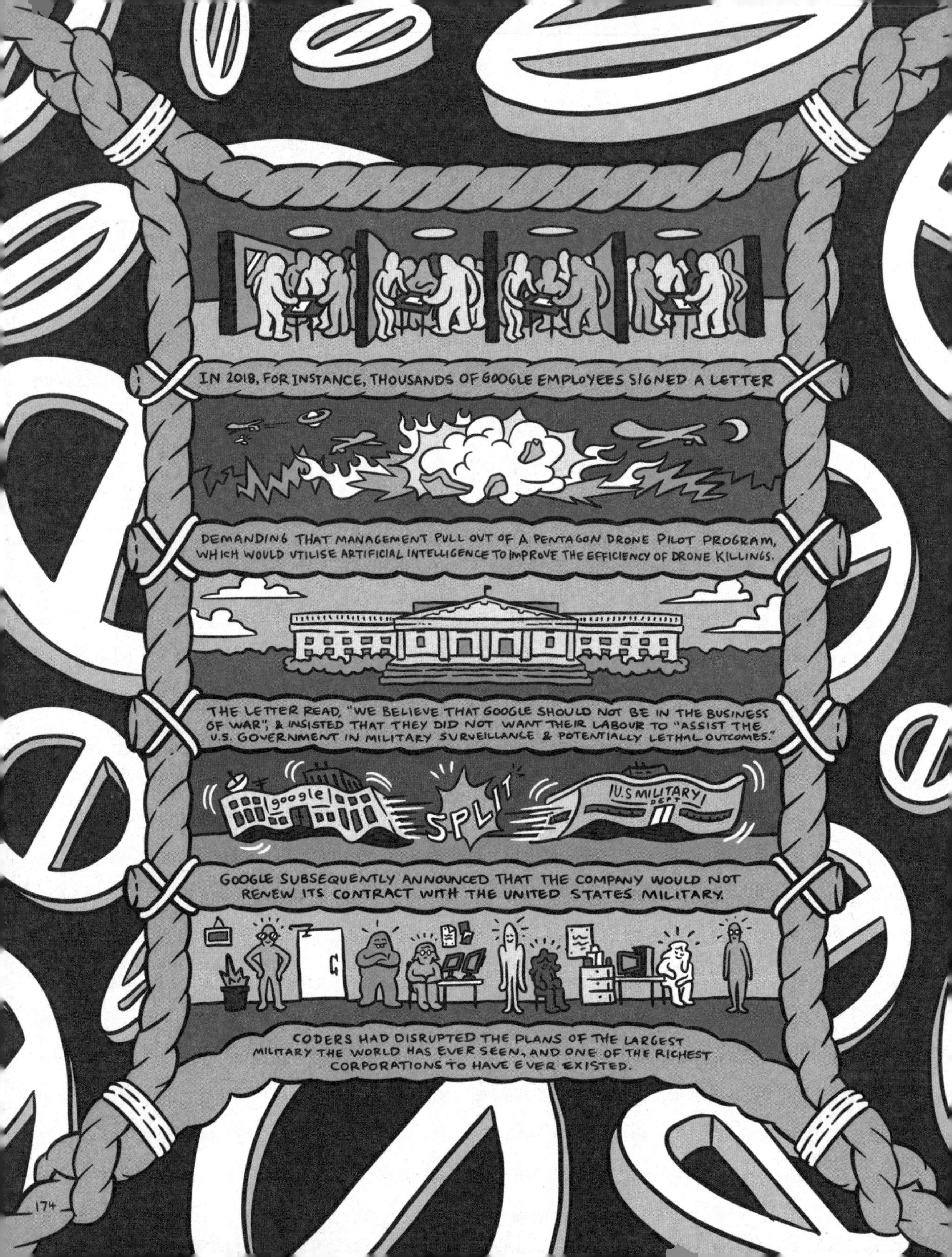
IN 2018, FOR INSTANCE, THOUSANDS OF GOOGLE EMPLOYEES SIGNED A LETTER
DEMANDING THAT MANAGEMENT PULL OUT OF A PENTAGON DRONE PILOT PROGRAM, WHICH WOULD UTILISE ARTIFICIAL INTELLIGENCE TO IMPROVE THE EFFICIENCY OF DRONE KILLINGS.
THE LETTER READ, "WE BELIEVE THAT GOOGLE SHOULD NOT BE IN THE BUSINESS OF WAR", & INSISTED THAT THEY DID NOT WANT THEIR LABOUR TO "ASSIST THE U.S. GOVERNMENT IN MILITARY SURVEILLANCE & POTENTIALLY LETHAL OUTCOMES."
google
SPLIT
U.S MILITARY DEPT
GOOGLE SUBSEQUENTLY ANNOUNCED THAT THE COMPANY WOULD NOT RENEW ITS CONTRACT WITH THE UNITED STATES MILITARY.
CODERS HAD DISRUPTED THE PLANS OF THE LARGEST MILITARY THE WORLD HAS EVER SEEN, AND ONE OF THE RICHEST CORPORATIONS TO HAVE EVER EXISTED.

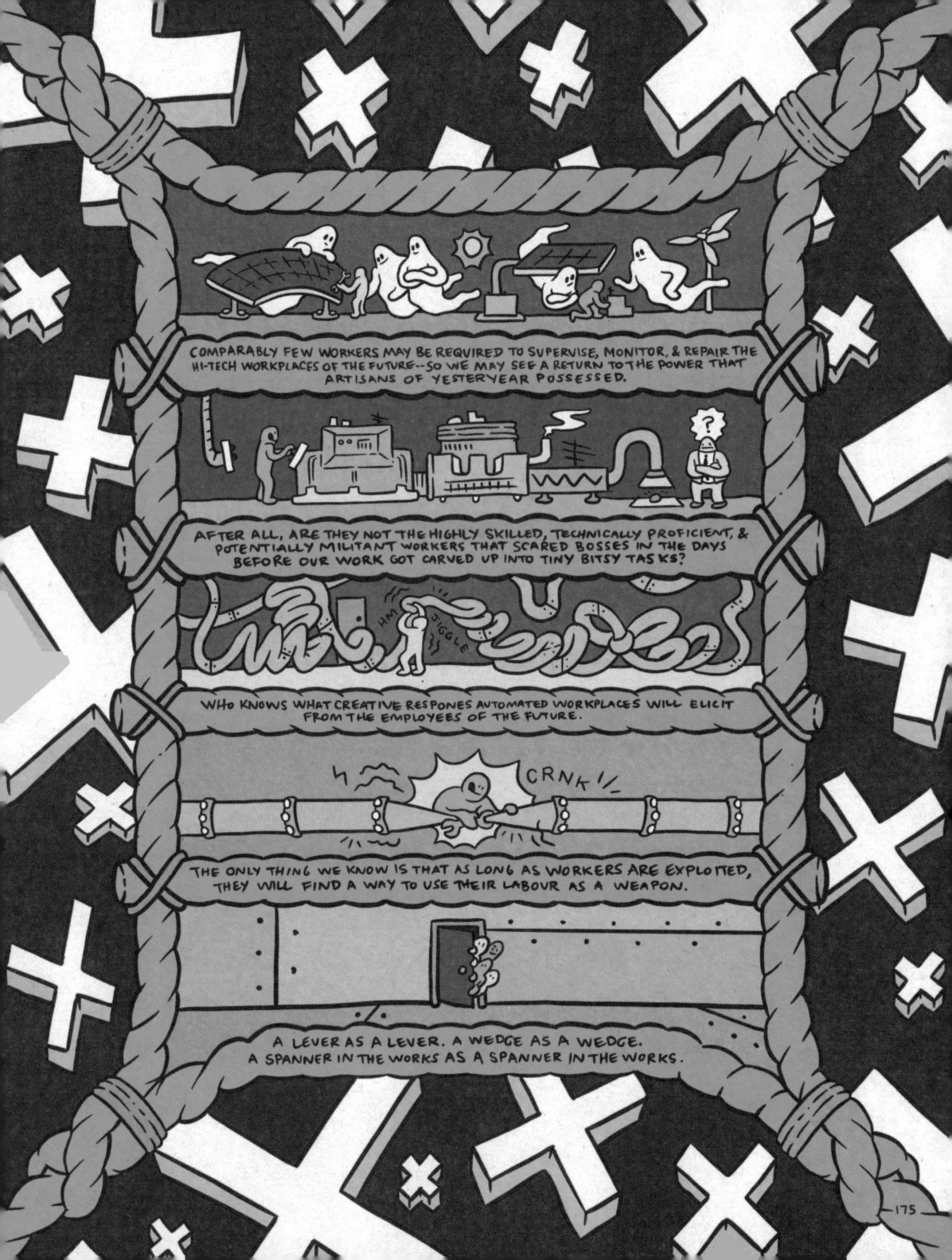

COMPARABLY FEW WORKERS MAY BE REQUIRED TO SUPERVISE, MONITOR, & REPAIR THE HI-TECH WORKPLACES OF THE FUTURE--SO WE MAY SEE A RETURN TO THE POWER THAT ARTISANS OF YESTERYEAR POSSESSED.
?
AFTER ALL, ARE THEY NOT THE HIGHLY SKILLED, TECHNICALLY PROFICIENT, & POTENTIALLY MILITANT WORKERS THAT SCARED BOSSES IN THE DAYS BEFORE OUR WORK GOT CARVED UP INTO TINY BITSY TASKS?
HM
JIGGLE
WHO KNOWS WHAT CREATIVE RESPONES AUTOMATED WORKPLACES WILL ELICIT FROM THE EMPLOYEES OF THE FUTURE.
CRNK
THE ONLY THING WE KNOW IS THAT AS LONG AS WORKERS ARE EXPLOITED, THEY WILL FIND A WAY TO USE THEIR LABOUR AS A WEAPON.
A LEVER AS A LEVER. A WEDGE AS A WEDGE.
A SPANNER IN THE WORKS AS A SPANNER IN THE WORKS.

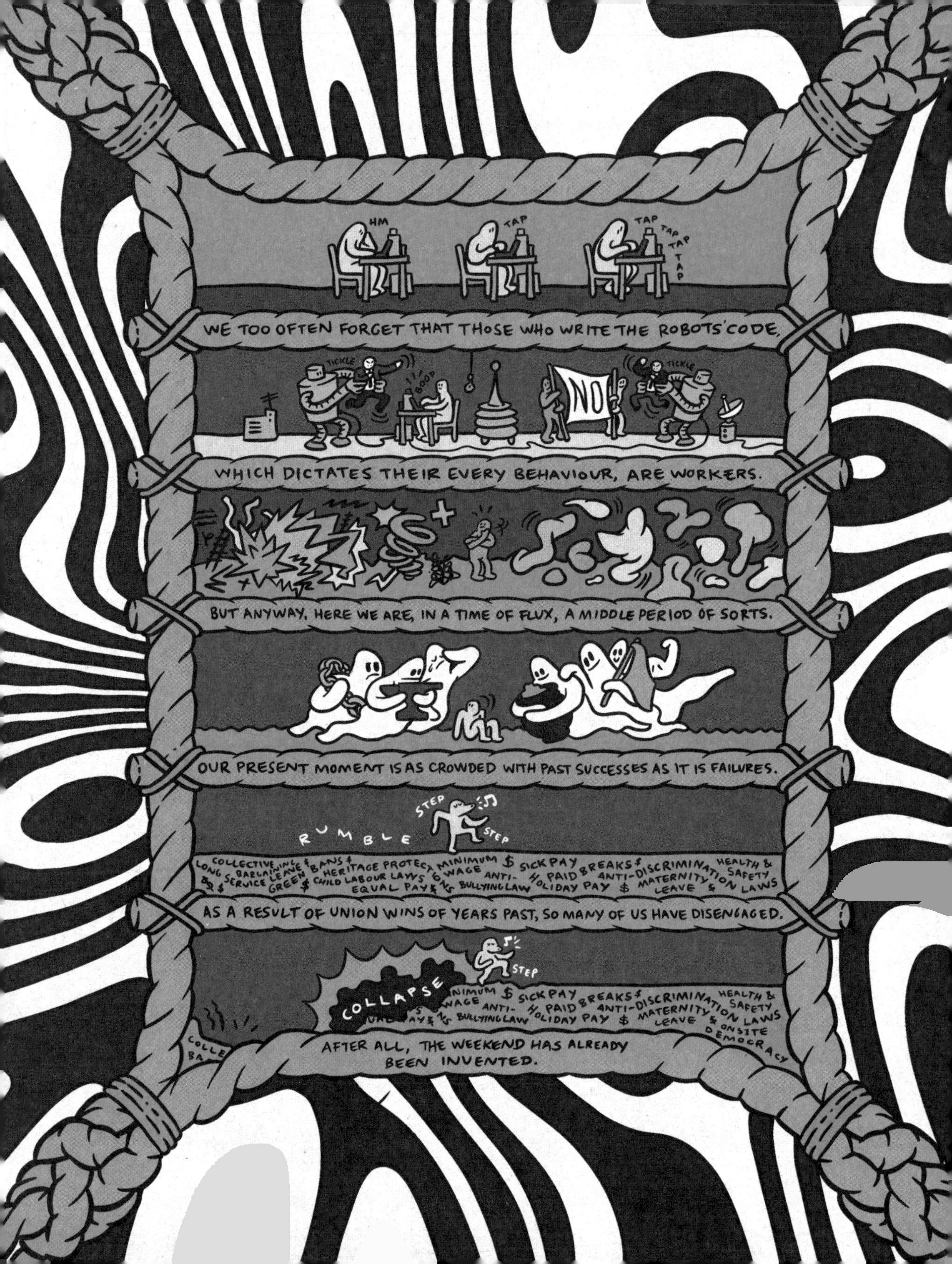
HM
TAP
TAP TAP TAP TAP TAP
WE TOO OFTEN FORGET THAT THOSE WHO WRITE THE ROBOTS' CODE,
TICKLE
BOOP
NO
TICKLE
WHICH DICTATES THEIR EVERY BEHAVIOUR, ARE WORKERS.
BUT ANYWAY, HERE WE ARE, IN A TIME OF FLUX, A MIDDLE PERIOD OF SORTS.
OUR PRESENT MOMENT IS AS CROWDED WITH PAST SUCCESSES AS IT IS FAILURES.
STEP
RUMBLE
STEP
COLLECTIVE BARGAINING
LONG SERVICE LEAVE
BANS
GREEN BANS
HERITAGE PROTECTIONS
CHILD LABOUR LAWS
EQUAL PAY
MINIMUM WAGE
ANTI-BULLYING LAW
SICK PAY
HOLIDAY PAY
PAID BREAKS
ANTI-DISCRIMINATION
MATERNITY LEAVE
HEALTH & SAFETY LAWS
AS A RESULT OF UNION WINS OF YEARS PAST, SO MANY OF US HAVE DISENGAGED.
STEP
COLLAPSE
ONSITE DEMOCRACY
AFTER ALL, THE WEEKEND HAS ALREADY BEEN INVENTED.

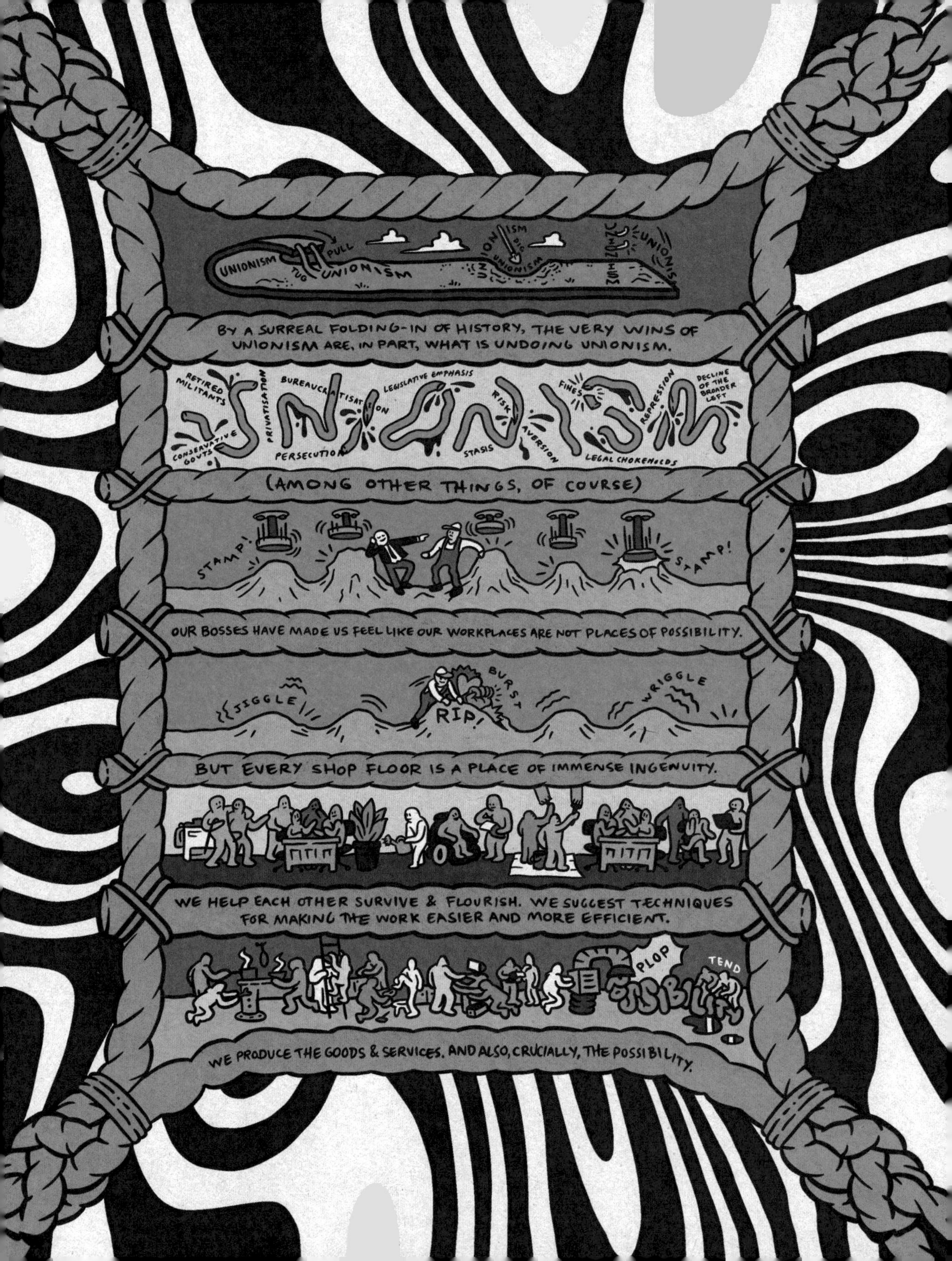

UNIONISM
PULL
TUG
UNIONISM
ISM
DIG
UNIONISM
UNIONISM
UNIONISM
BY A SURREAL FOLDING-IN OF HISTORY, THE VERY WINS OF UNIONISM ARE, IN PART, WHAT IS UNDOING UNIONISM.
RETIRED MILITANTS
CONSERVATIVE GOVTS
PRIVATISATION
BUREAUCRATISATION
PERSECUTION
LEGISLATIVE EMPHASIS
STASIS
RISK AVERSION
FINES
LEGAL CHOKEHOLDS
REPRESSION
DECLINE OF THE BROADER LEFT
(AMONG OTHER THINGS, OF COURSE)
STAMP!
STAMP!
OUR BOSSES HAVE MADE US FEEL LIKE OUR WORKPLACES ARE NOT PLACES OF POSSIBILITY.
JIGGLE
BURST
RIP!
WRIGGLE
BUT EVERY SHOP FLOOR IS A PLACE OF IMMENSE INGENUITY.
WE HELP EACH OTHER SURVIVE & FLOURISH. WE SUGGEST TECHNIQUES FOR MAKING THE WORK EASIER AND MORE EFFICIENT.
PLOP
TEND
POSSIBILITY
WE PRODUCE THE GOODS & SERVICES. AND ALSO, CRUCIALLY, THE POSSIBILITY.

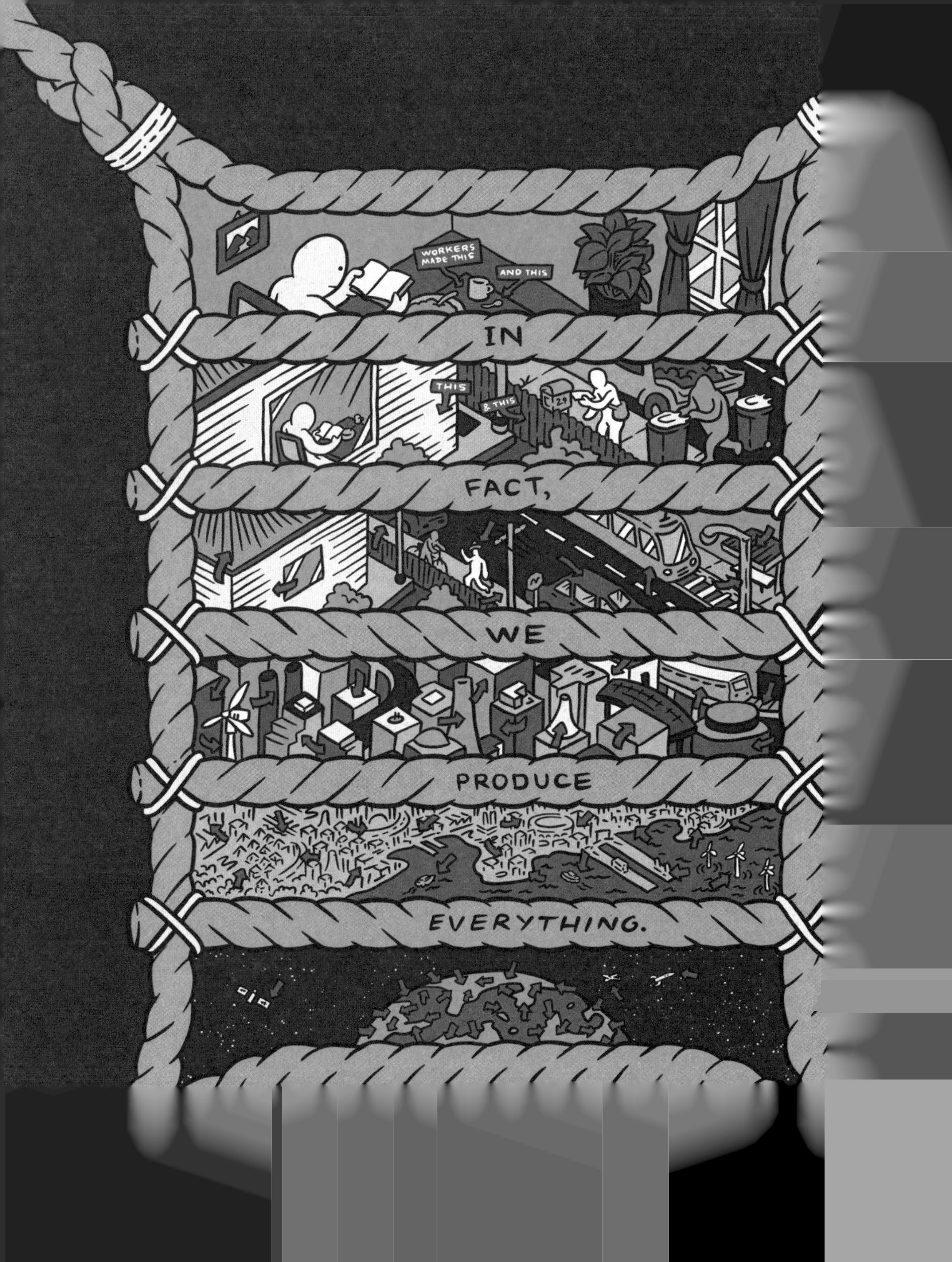
WORKERS MADE THIS
AND THIS
IN
THIS
& THIS
FACT,
WE
PRODUCE
EVERYTHING.

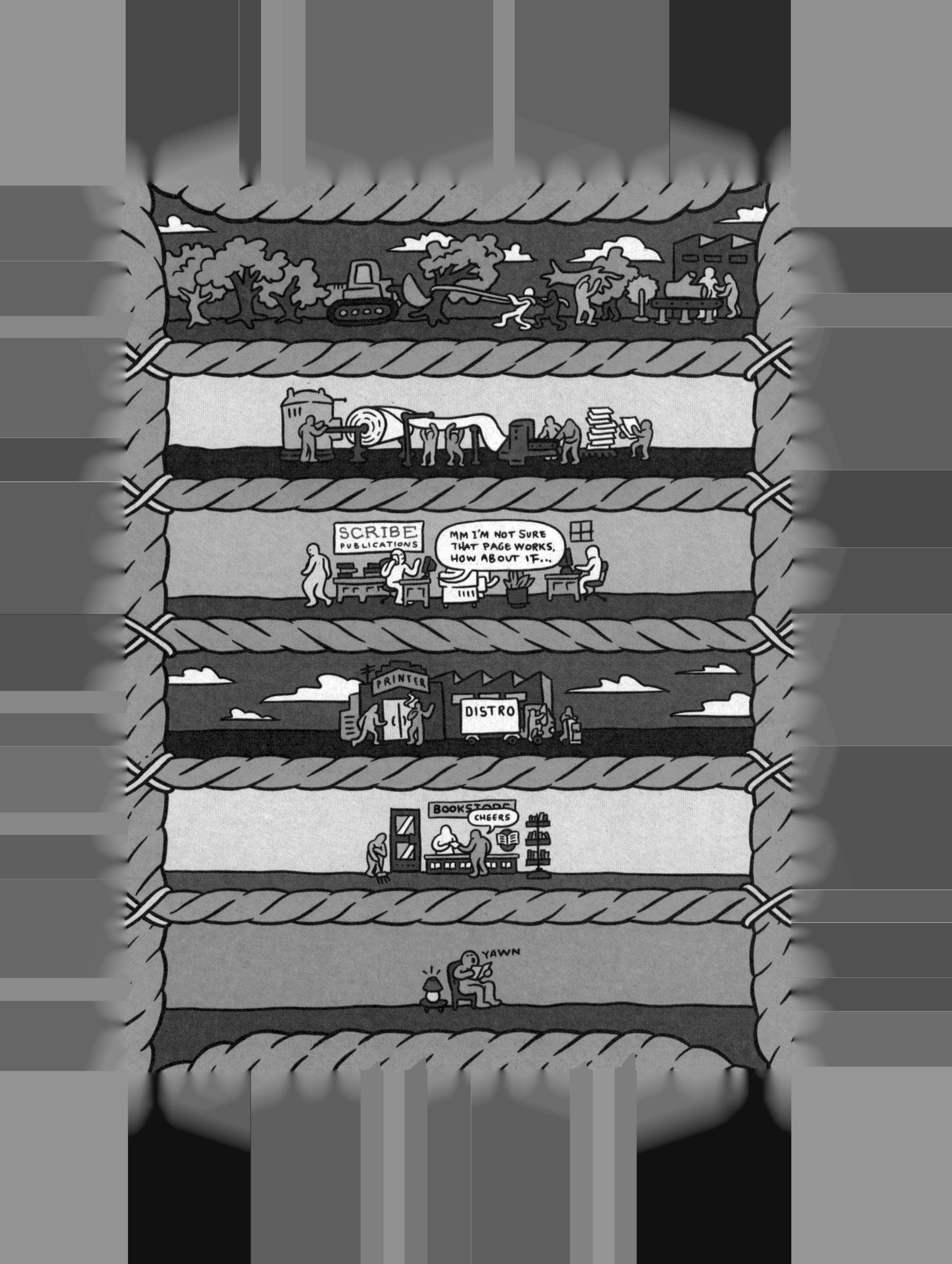
SCRIBE PUBLICATIONS
MM I'M NOT SURE THAT PAGE WORKS, HOW ABOUT IF...
PRINTER
DISTRO
CHEERS
YAWN

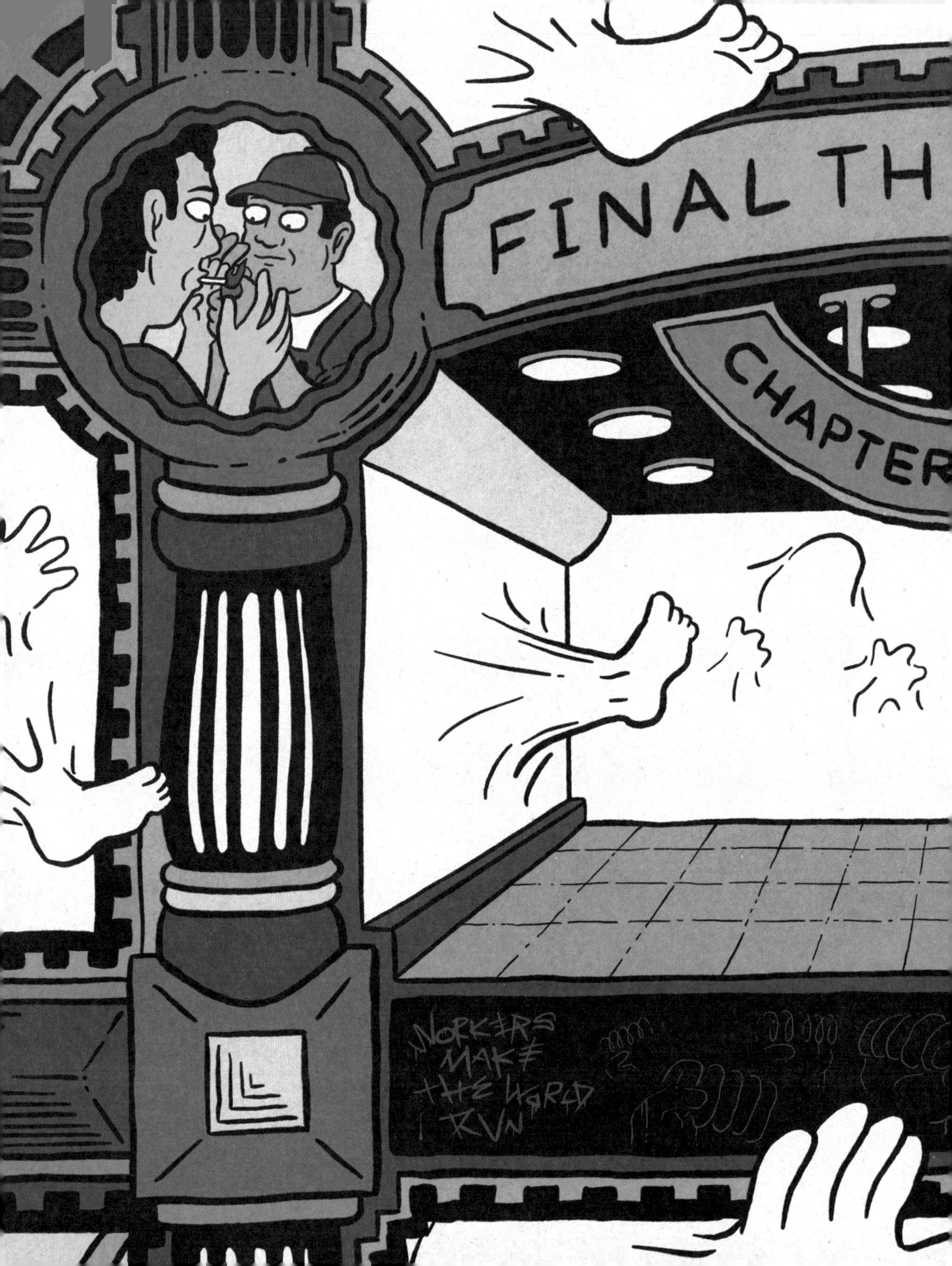

FINAL TH
CHAPTER
WORKERS MAKE THE WORLD RUN

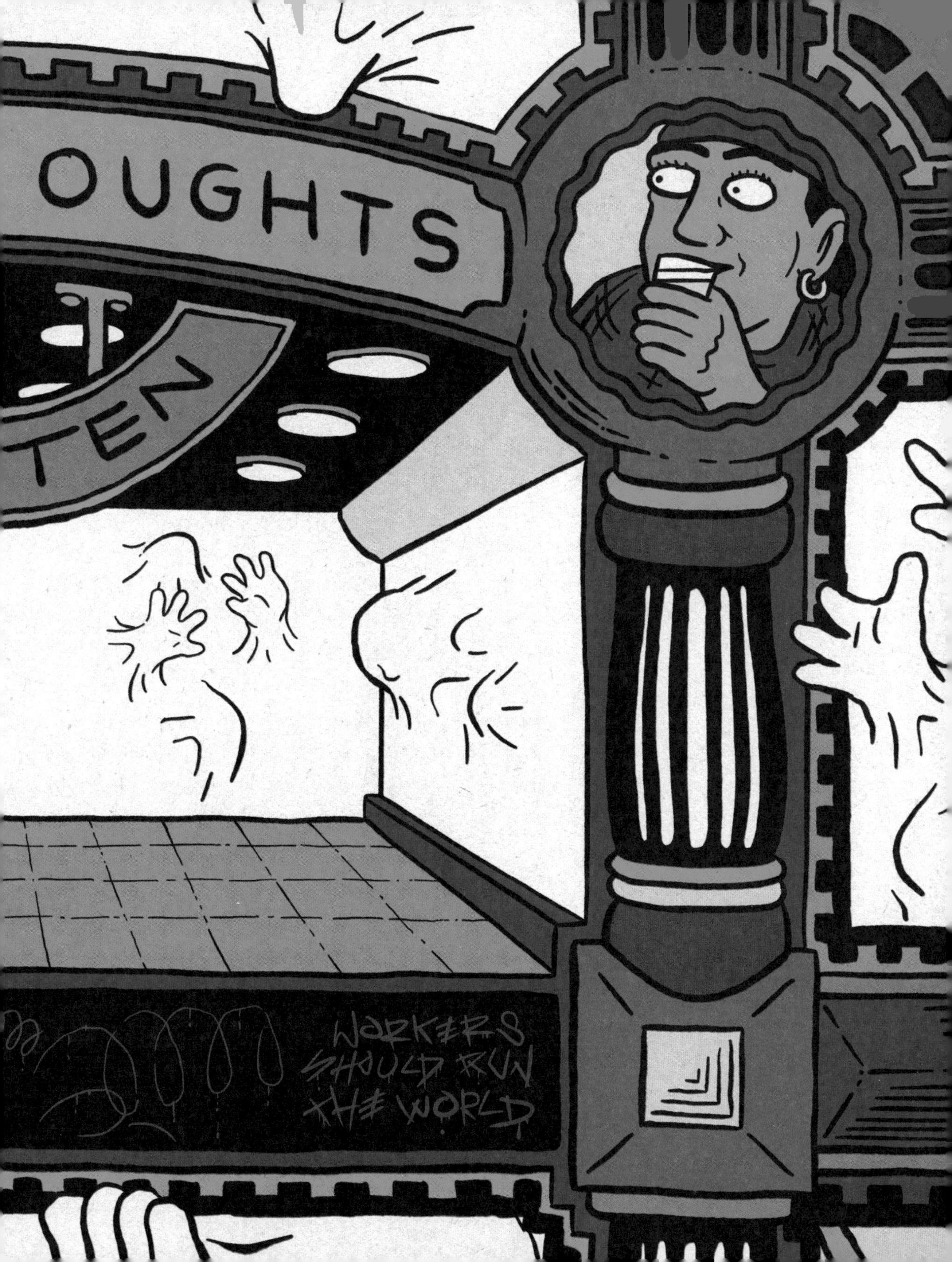
OUGHTS
TEN
WORKERS SHOULD RUN THE WORLD

"TOO LONG HAVE
THE WORKERS OF
THE WORLD

WAITED

FOR SOME MOSES
TO LEAD THEM OUT
OF BONDAGE.

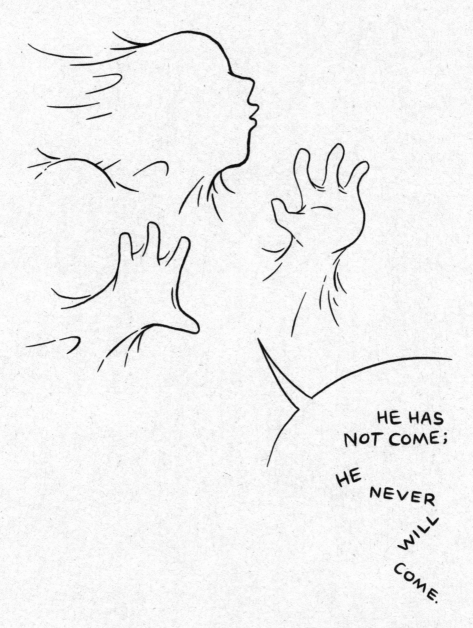

HE HAS
NOT COME;

HE NEVER
WILL
COME.

I WOULD NOT LEAD
YOU OUT IF I COULD;

FOR IF YOU COULD BE LED OUT,
YOU COULD BE LED BACK AGAIN.

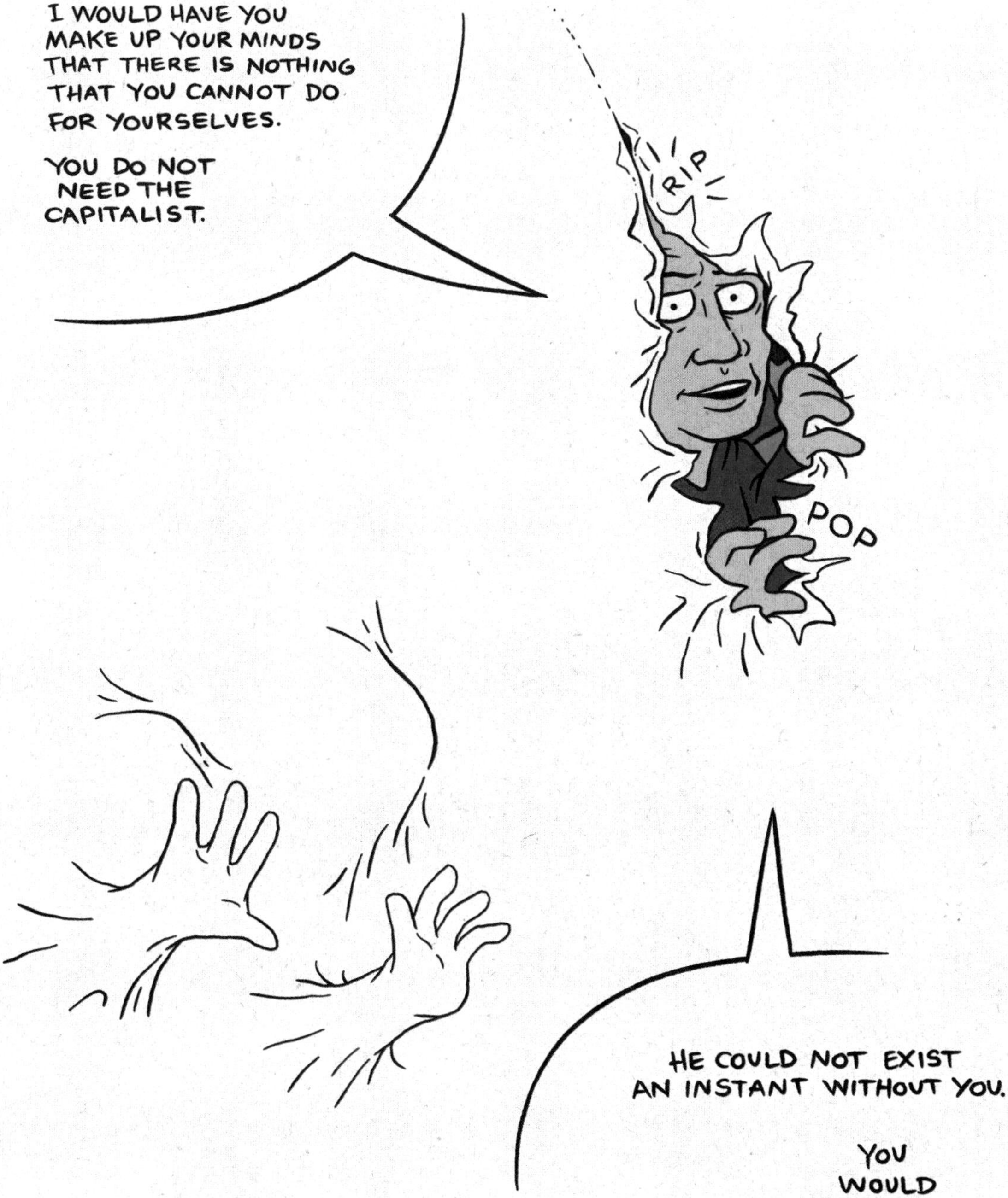
I WOULD HAVE YOU MAKE UP YOUR MINDS THAT THERE IS NOTHING THAT YOU CANNOT DO FOR YOURSELVES.
YOU DO NOT NEED THE CAPITALIST.
RIP
POP
HE COULD NOT EXIST AN INSTANT WITHOUT YOU.
YOU WOULD JUST BEGIN TO LIVE WITHOUT HIM.

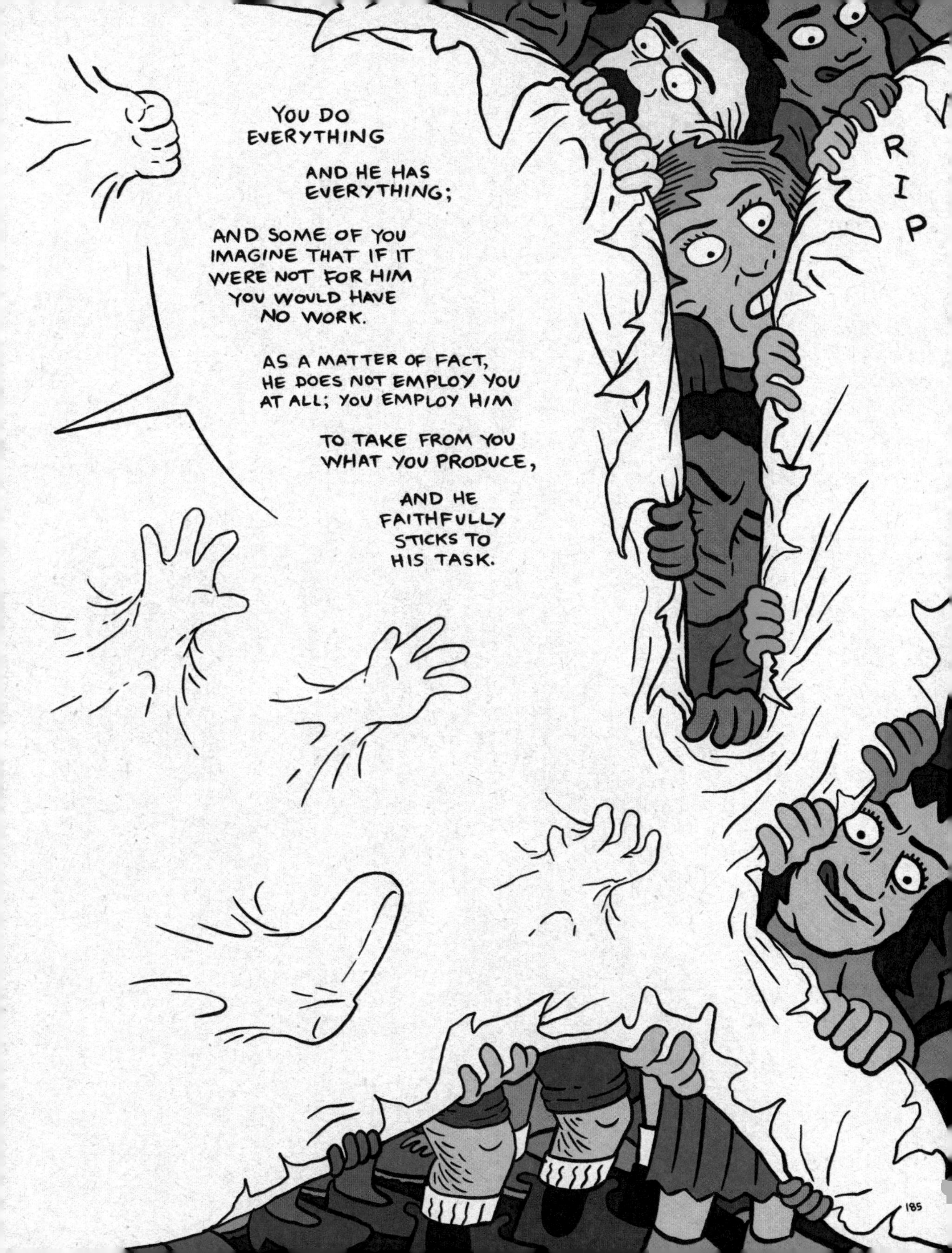
YOU DO EVERYTHING
AND HE HAS EVERYTHING;
AND SOME OF YOU IMAGINE THAT IF IT WERE NOT FOR HIM YOU WOULD HAVE NO WORK.
AS A MATTER OF FACT, HE DOES NOT EMPLOY YOU AT ALL; YOU EMPLOY HIM
TO TAKE FROM YOU WHAT YOU PRODUCE,
AND HE FAITHFULLY STICKS TO HIS TASK.
RIP

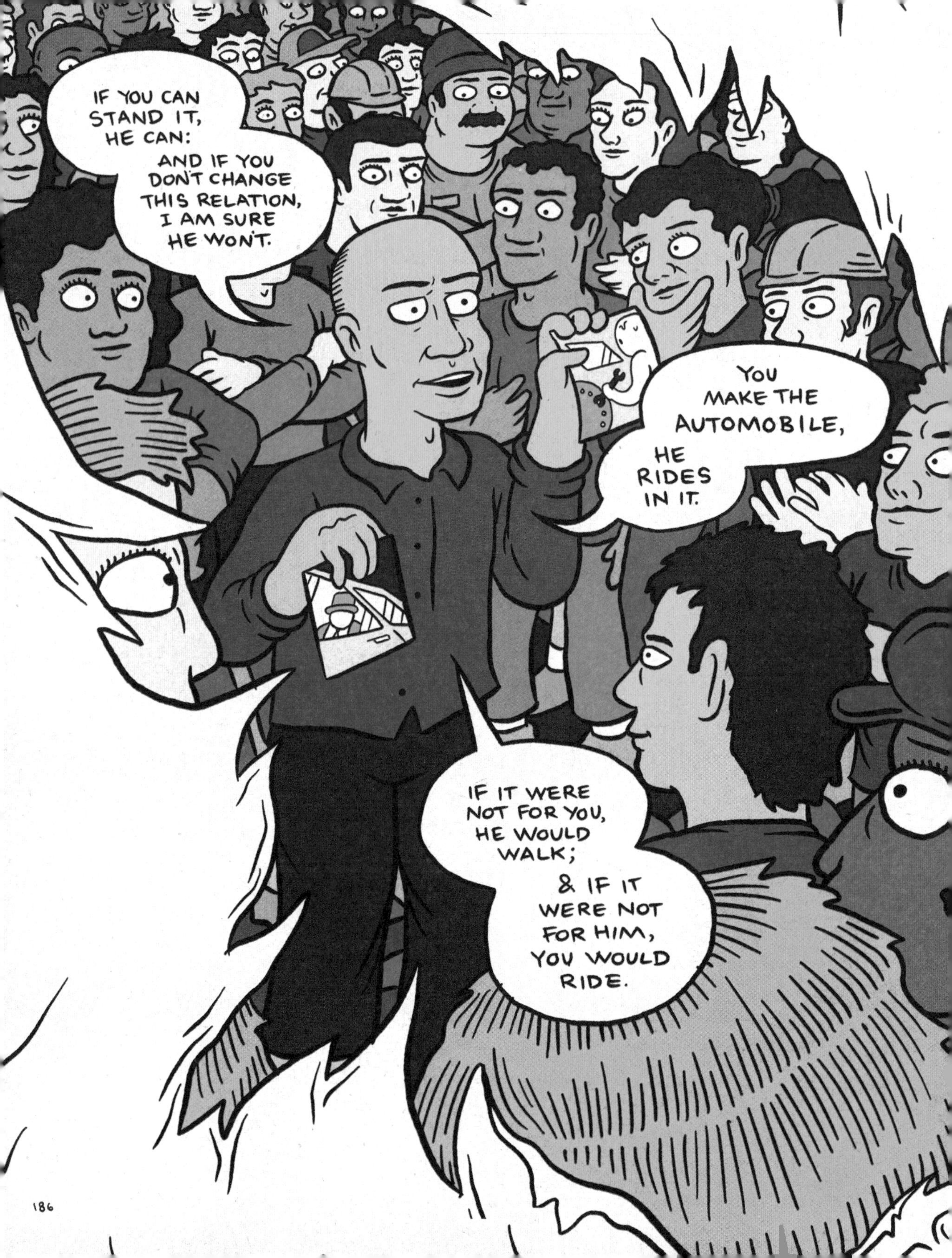
IF YOU CAN STAND IT, HE CAN:
AND IF YOU DON'T CHANGE THIS RELATION, I AM SURE HE WON'T.
YOU MAKE THE AUTOMOBILE,
HE RIDES IN IT.
IF IT WERE NOT FOR YOU, HE WOULD WALK;
& IF IT WERE NOT FOR HIM, YOU WOULD RIDE.

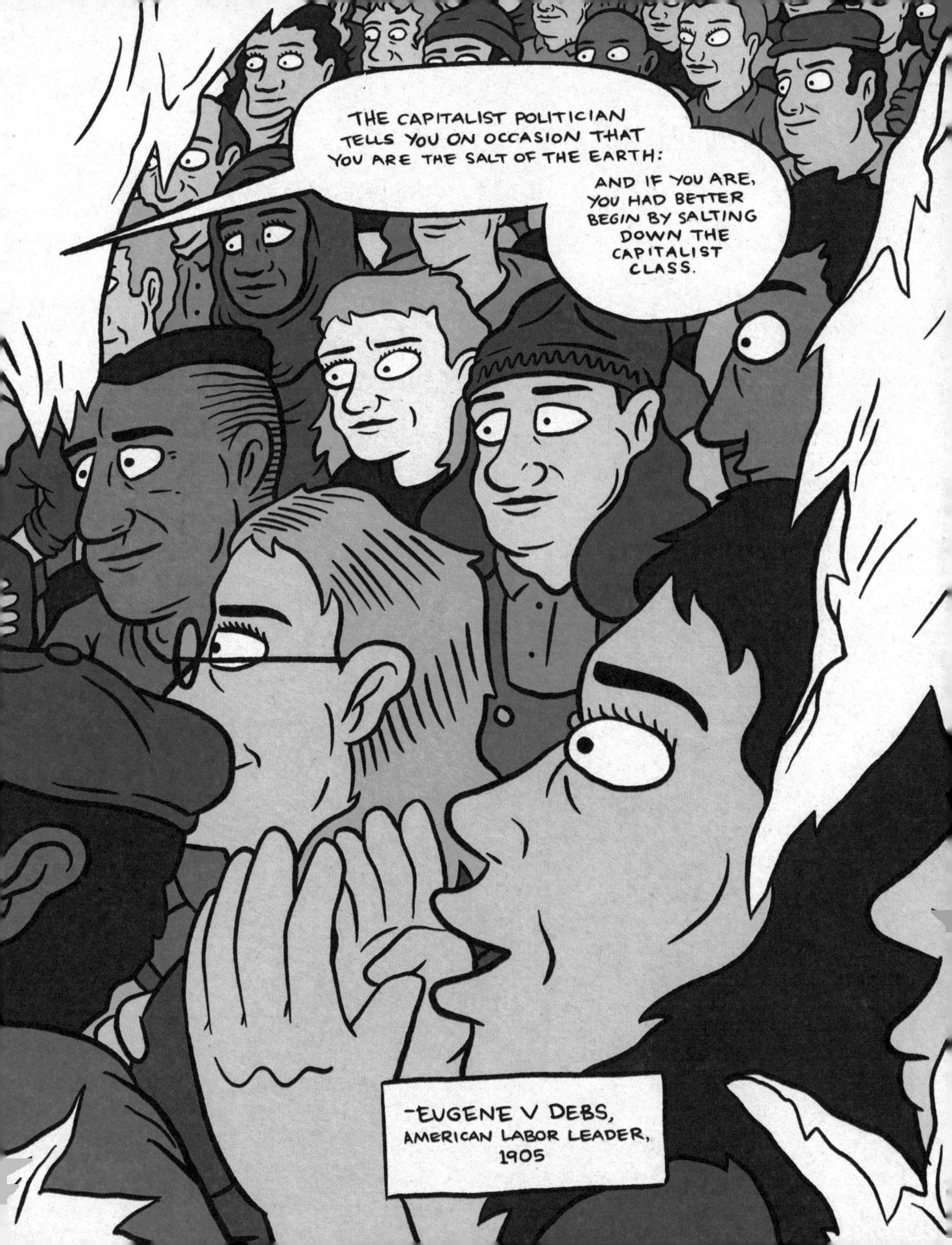
THE CAPITALIST POLITICIAN TELLS YOU ON OCCASION THAT YOU ARE THE SALT OF THE EARTH:
AND IF YOU ARE, YOU HAD BETTER BEGIN BY SALTING DOWN THE CAPITALIST CLASS.
–EUGENE V DEBS, AMERICAN LABOR LEADER, 1905

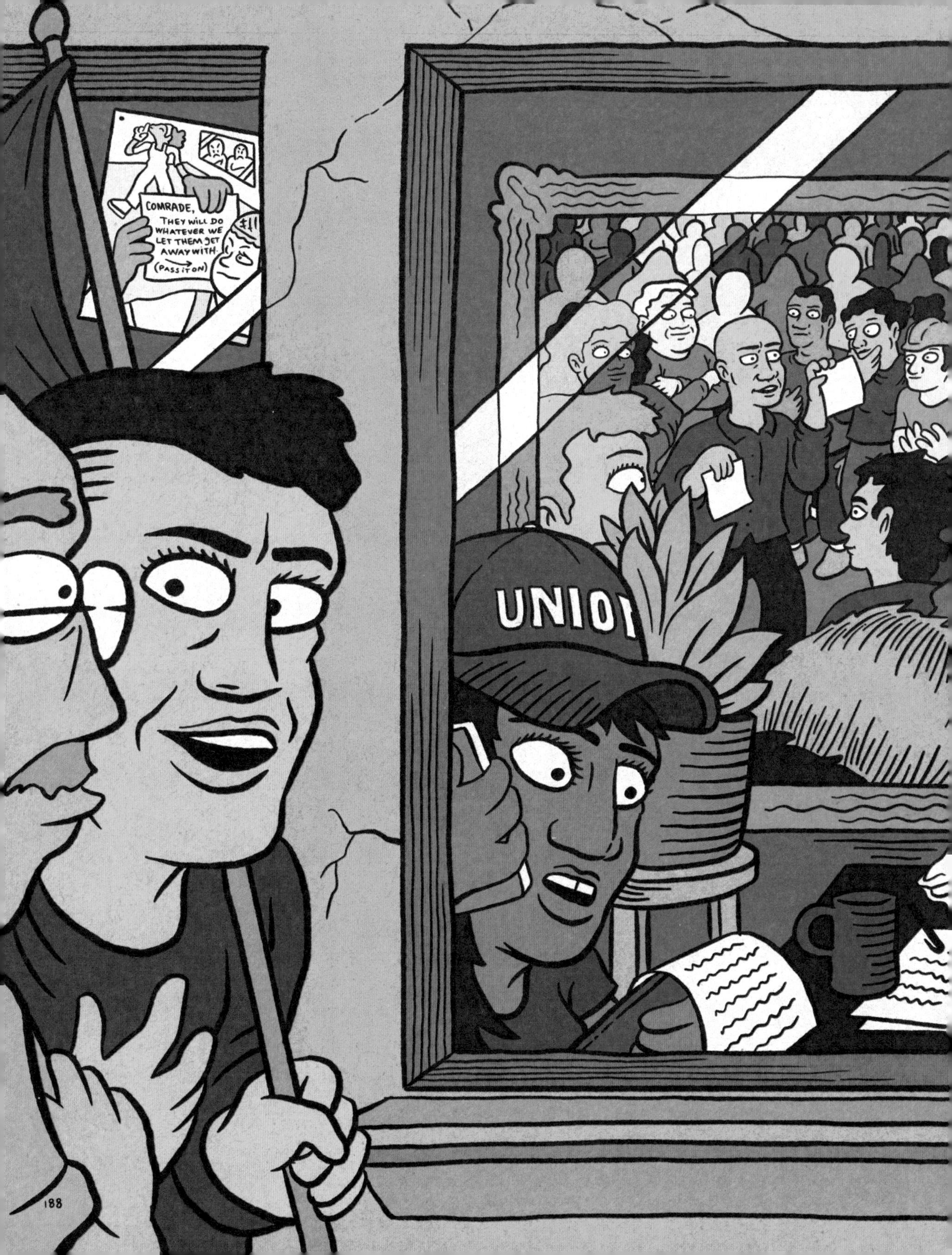
COMRADE,
THEY WILL DO WHATEVER WE LET THEM GET AWAY WITH.
(PASS IT ON)
UNIO

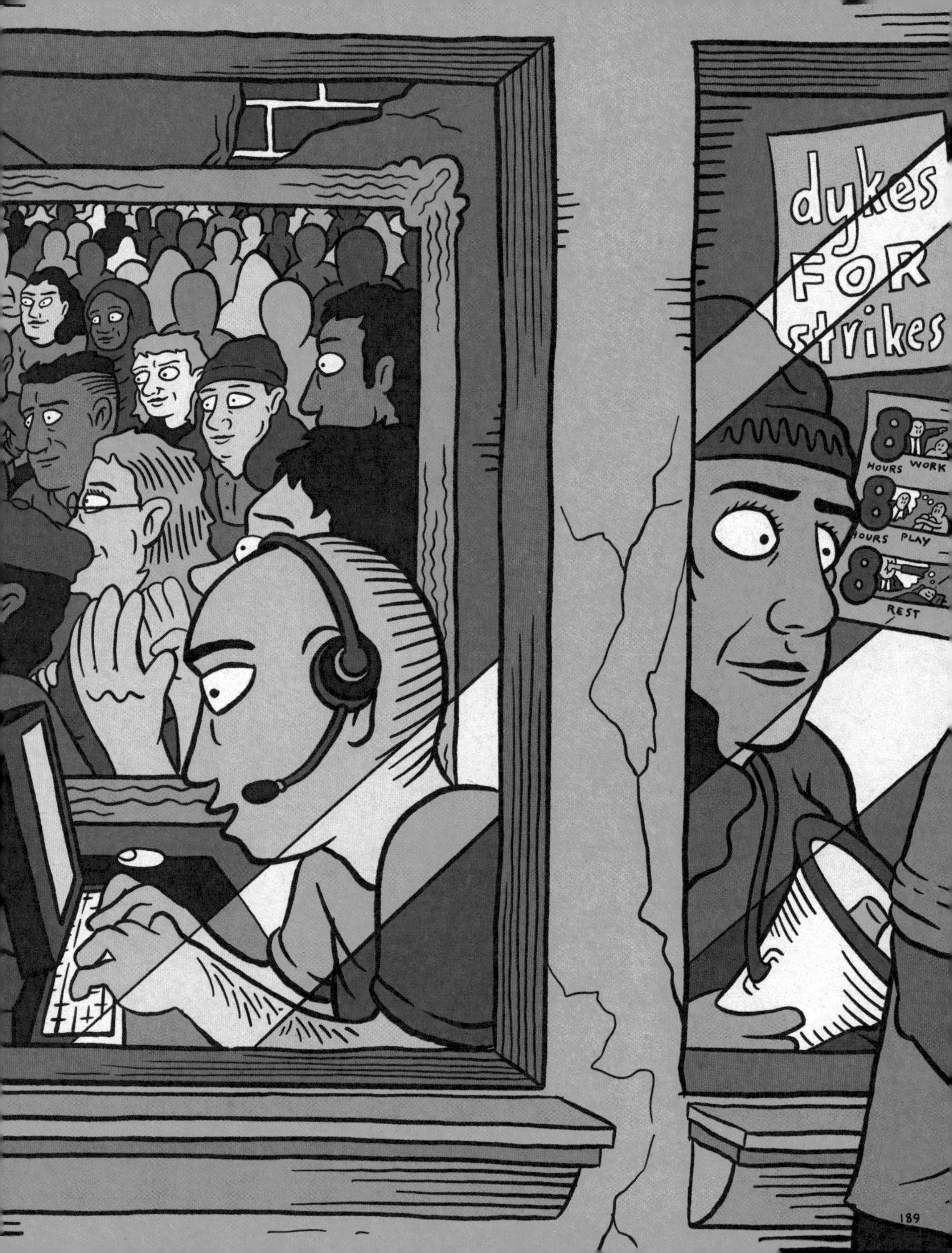
dykes
FOR
strikes
8 HOURS WORK
8 HOURS PLAY
8 REST

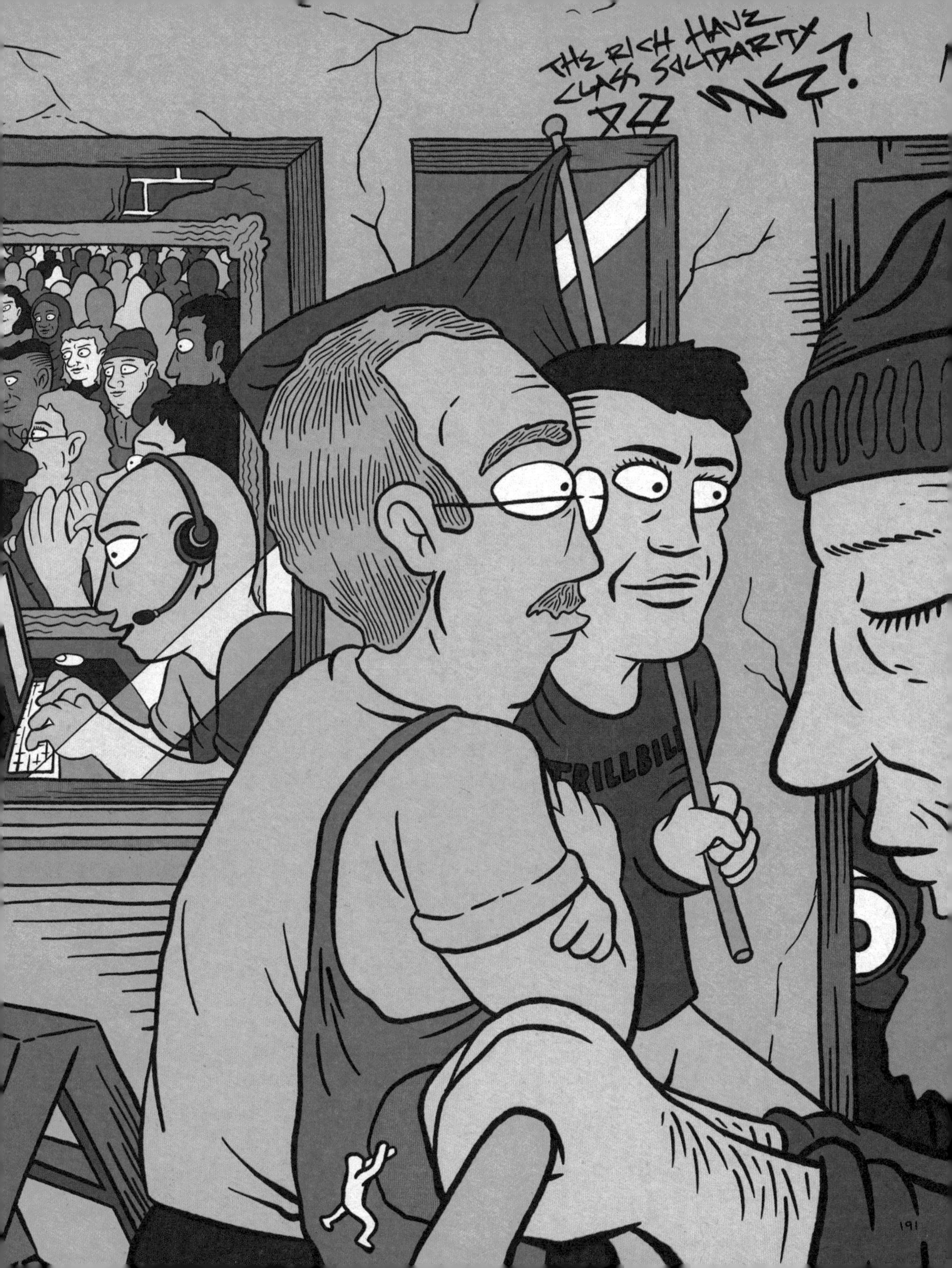
THE RICH HAVE CLASS SOLIDARITY
TRILLBILL

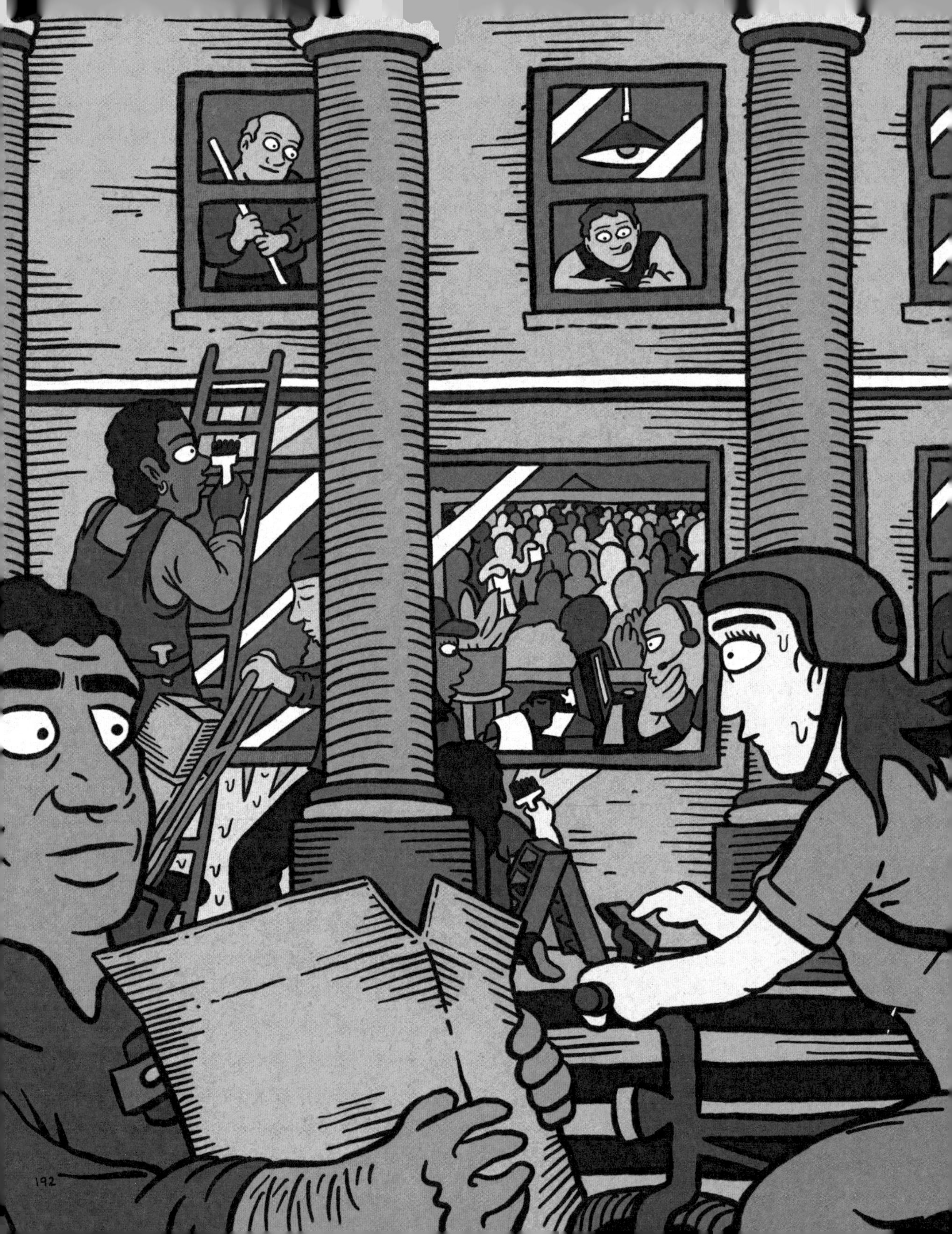

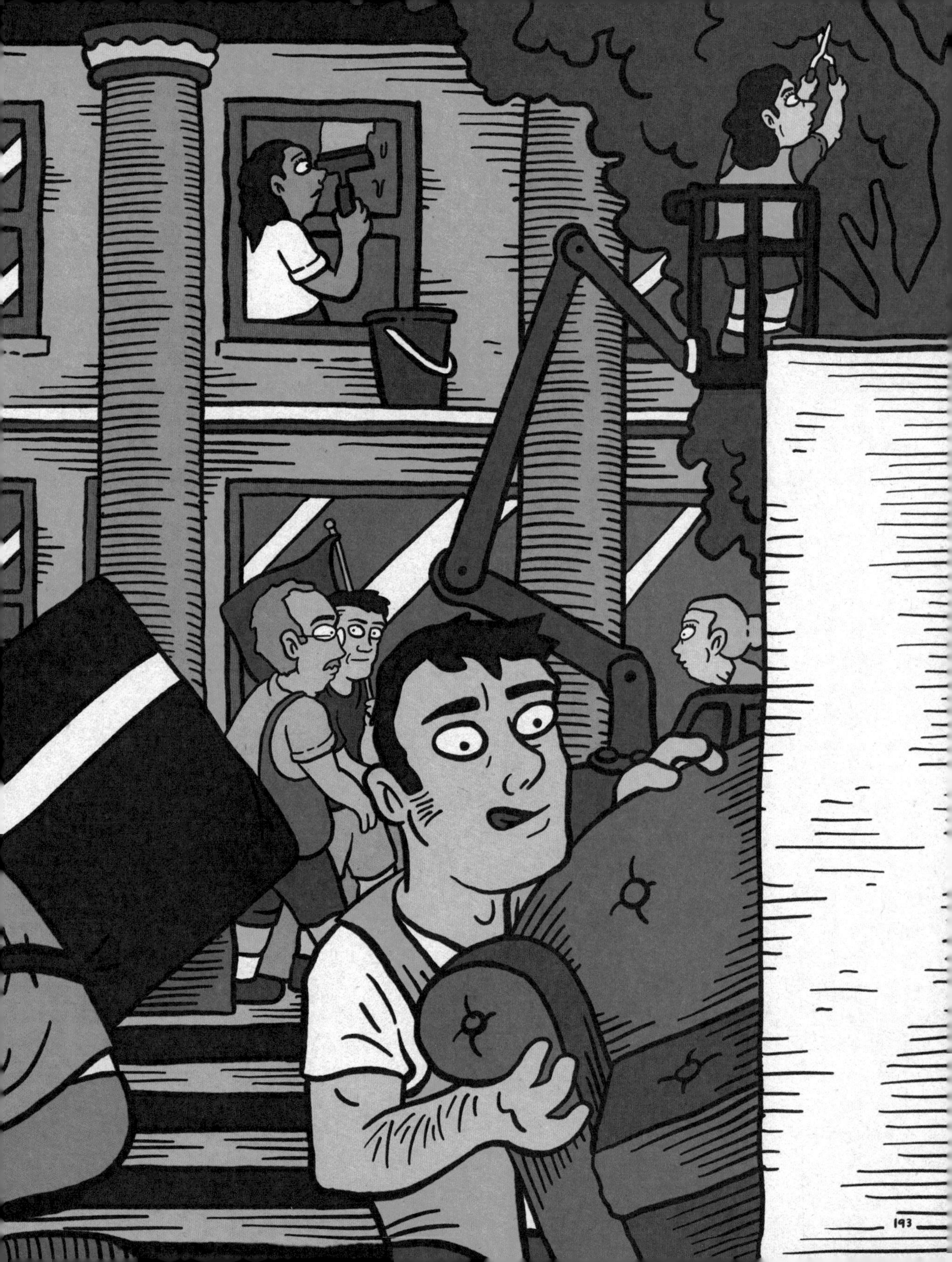

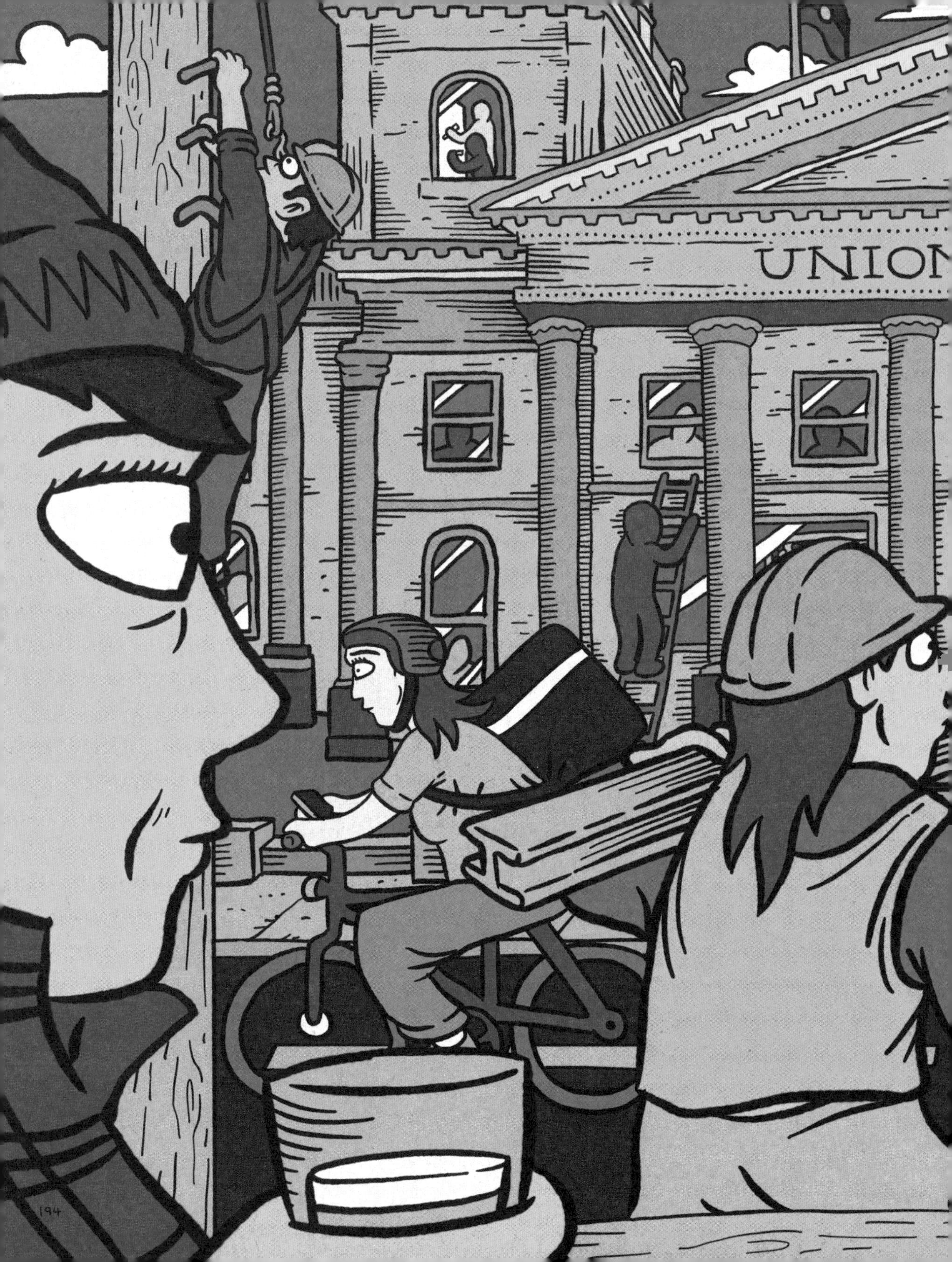
UNION

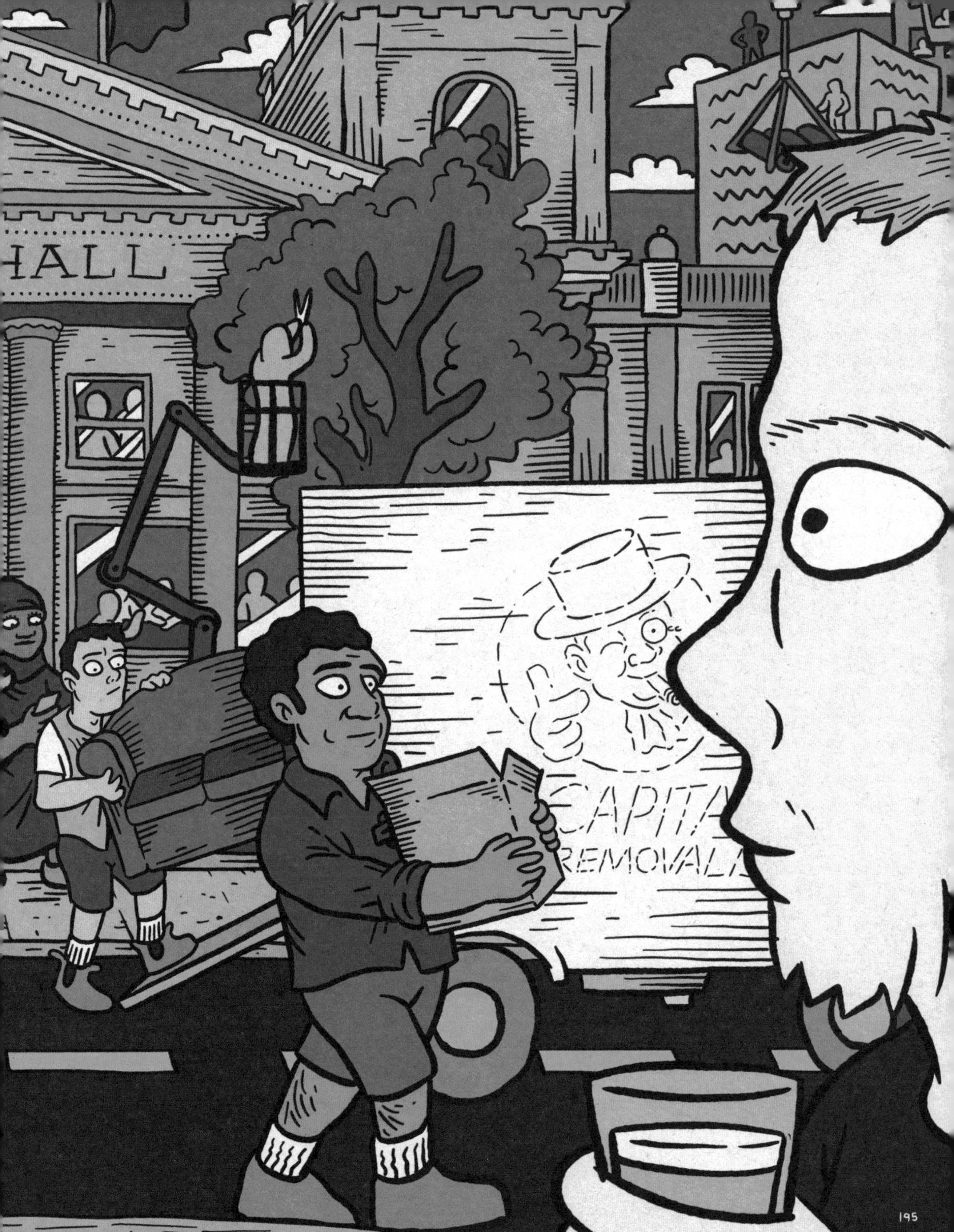
HALL
CAPITA
REMOVAL

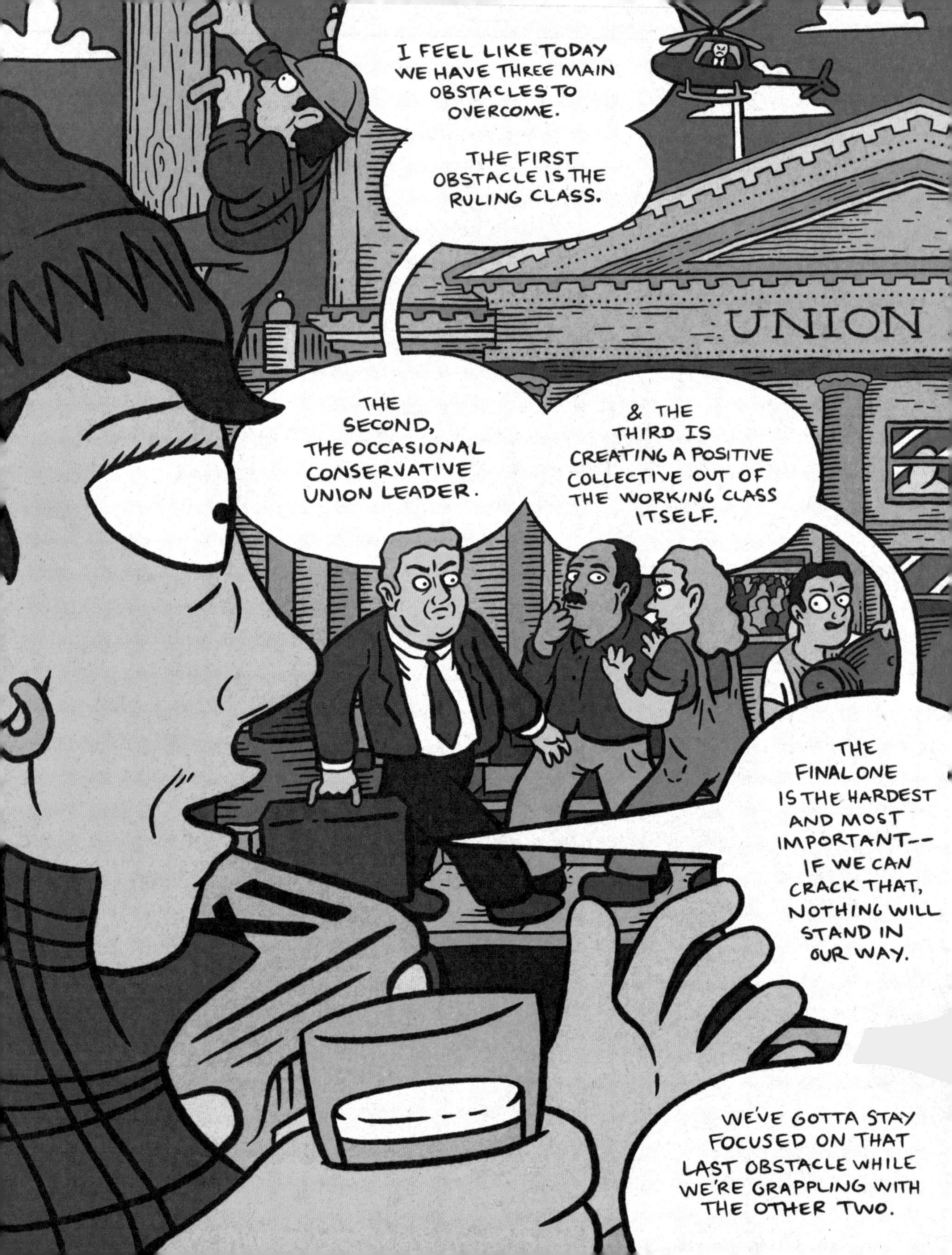
I FEEL LIKE TODAY WE HAVE THREE MAIN OBSTACLES TO OVERCOME.
THE FIRST OBSTACLE IS THE RULING CLASS.
UNION
THE SECOND, THE OCCASIONAL CONSERVATIVE UNION LEADER.
& THE THIRD IS CREATING A POSITIVE COLLECTIVE OUT OF THE WORKING CLASS ITSELF.
THE FINAL ONE IS THE HARDEST AND MOST IMPORTANT-- IF WE CAN CRACK THAT, NOTHING WILL STAND IN OUR WAY.
WE'VE GOTTA STAY FOCUSED ON THAT LAST OBSTACLE WHILE WE'RE GRAPPLING WITH THE OTHER TWO.

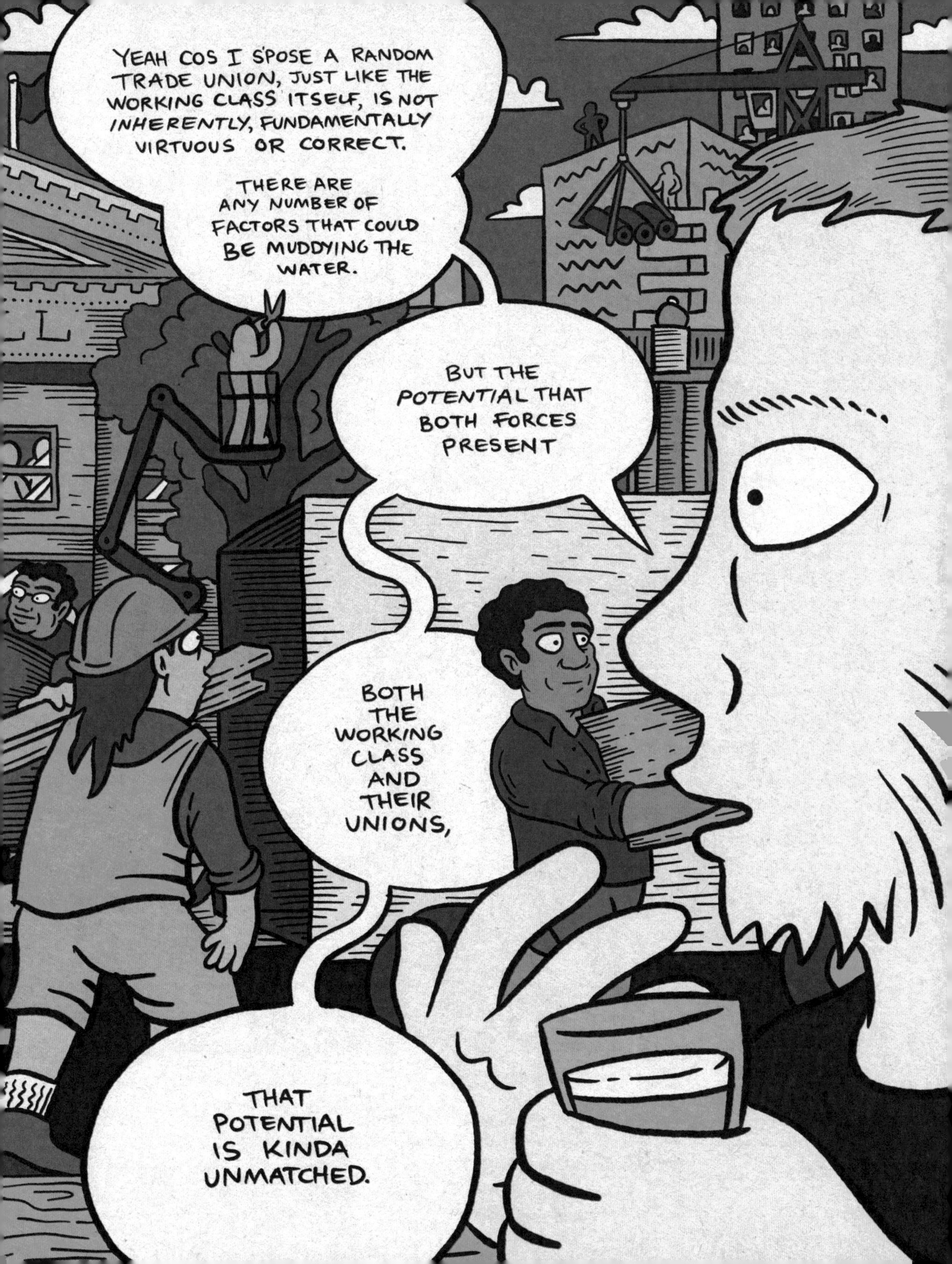
YEAH COS I S'POSE A RANDOM TRADE UNION, JUST LIKE THE WORKING CLASS ITSELF, IS NOT *INHERENTLY*, FUNDAMENTALLY VIRTUOUS OR CORRECT.
THERE ARE ANY NUMBER OF FACTORS THAT COULD BE MUDDYING THE WATER.
BUT THE *POTENTIAL* THAT BOTH FORCES PRESENT
BOTH THE WORKING CLASS AND THEIR UNIONS,
THAT POTENTIAL IS KINDA UNMATCHED.

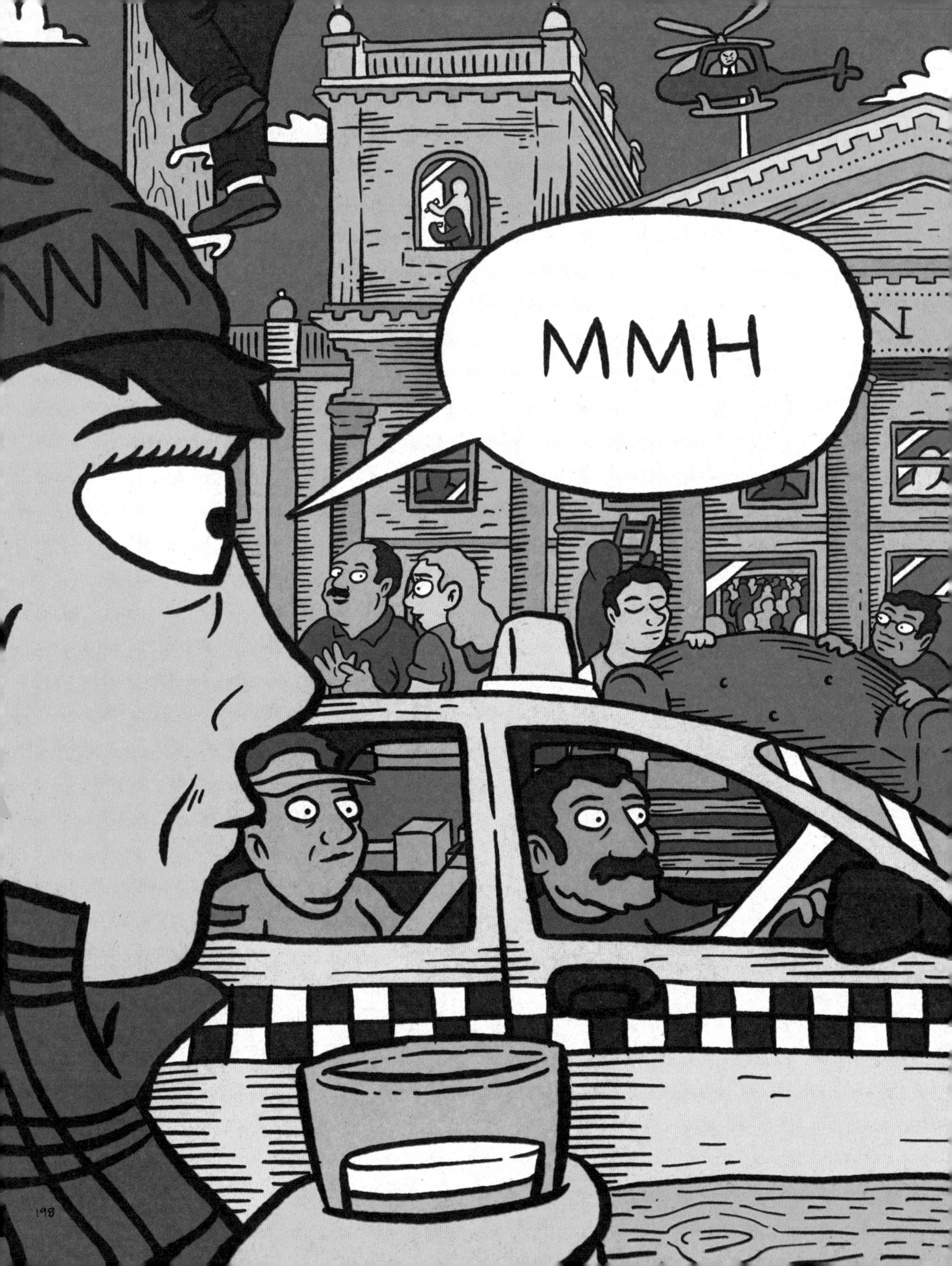
MMH

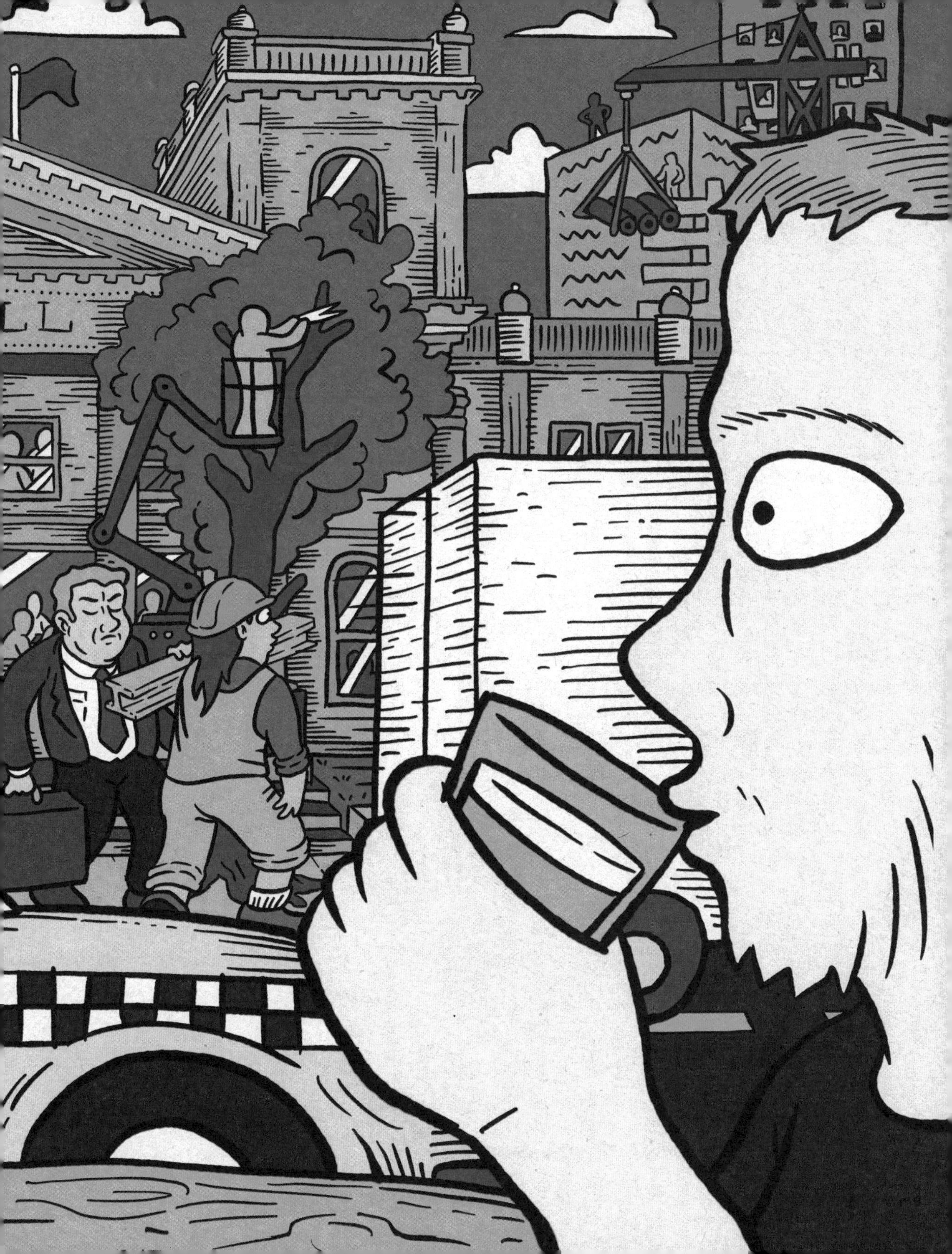

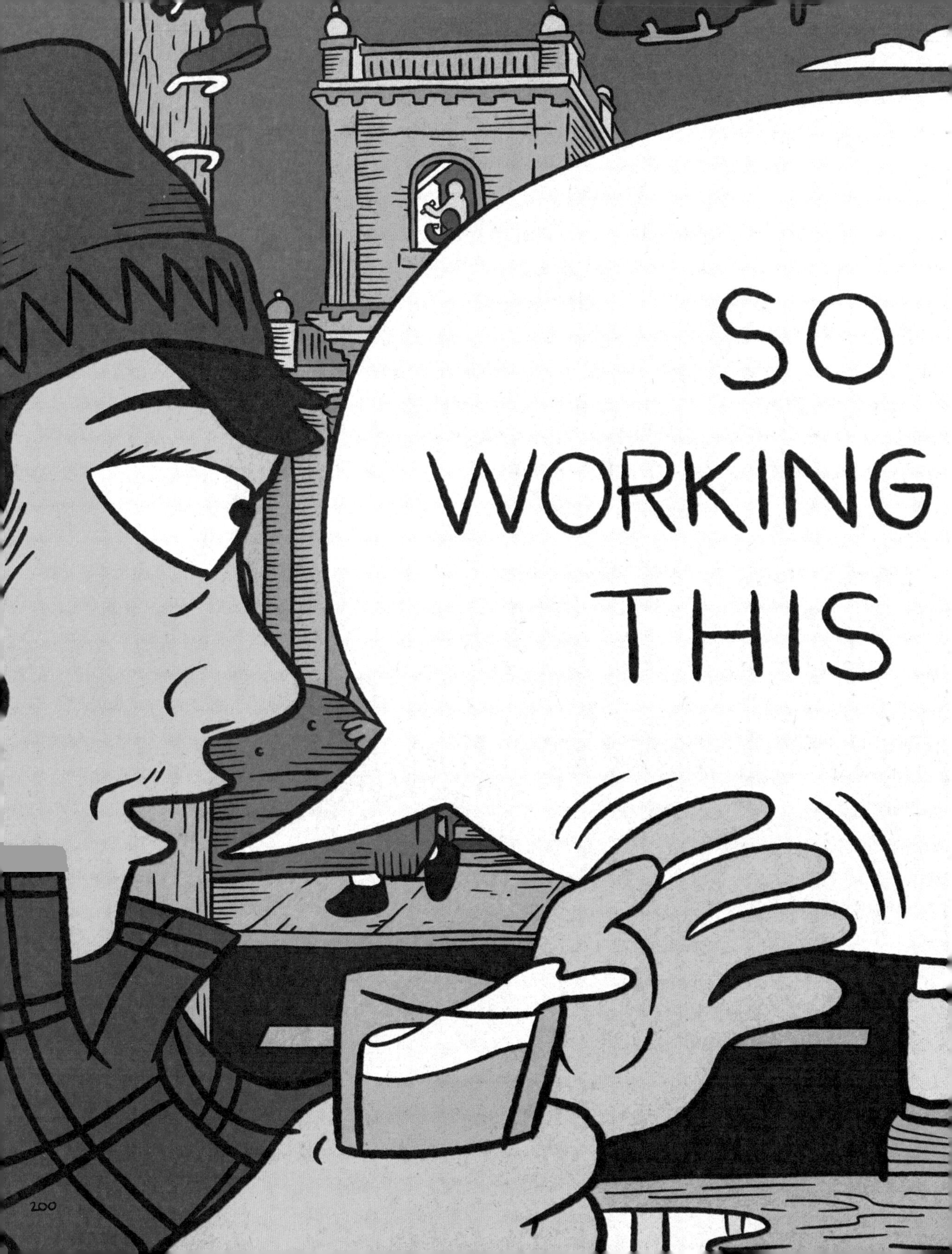
SO WORKING THIS

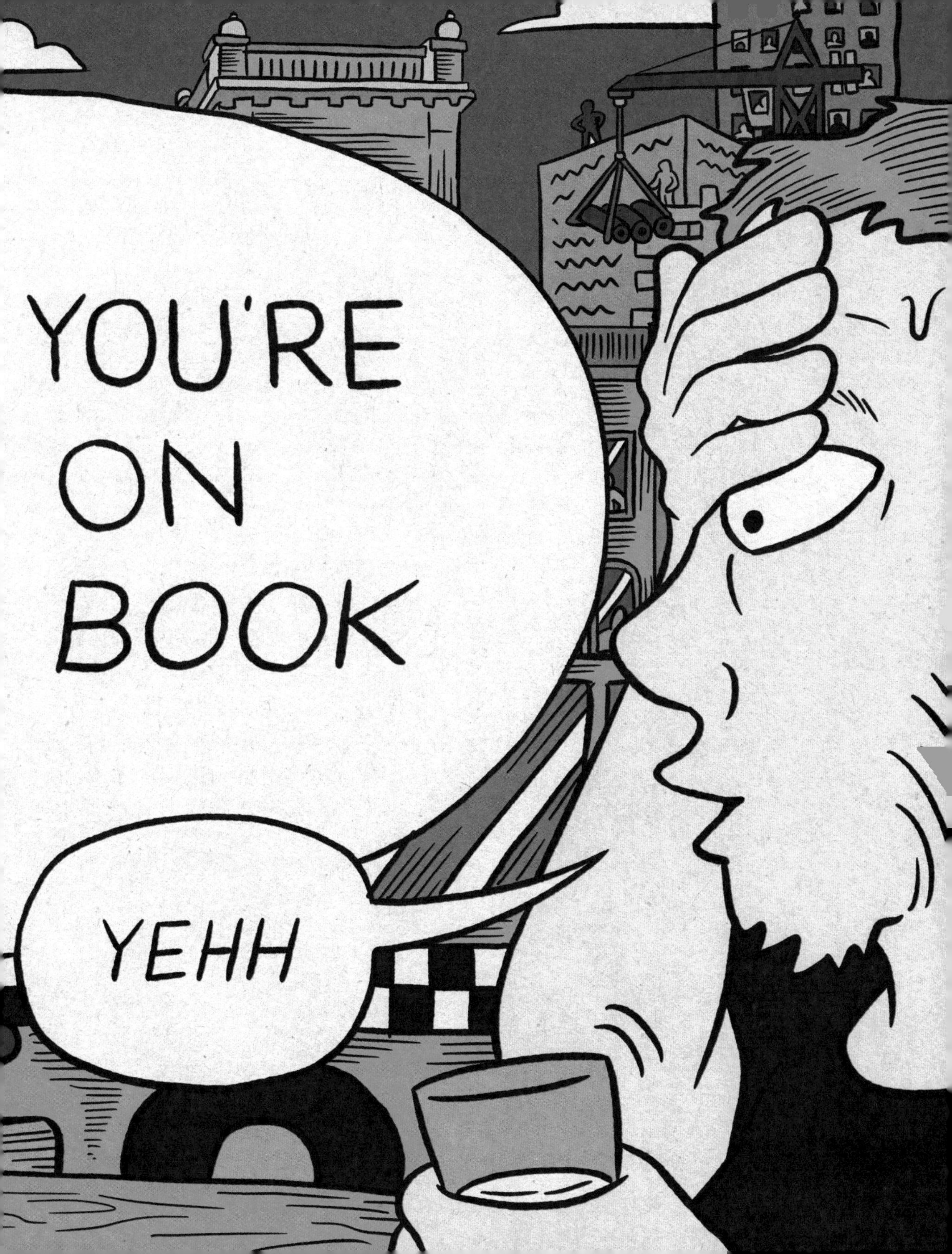
YOU'RE ON BOOK
YEHH

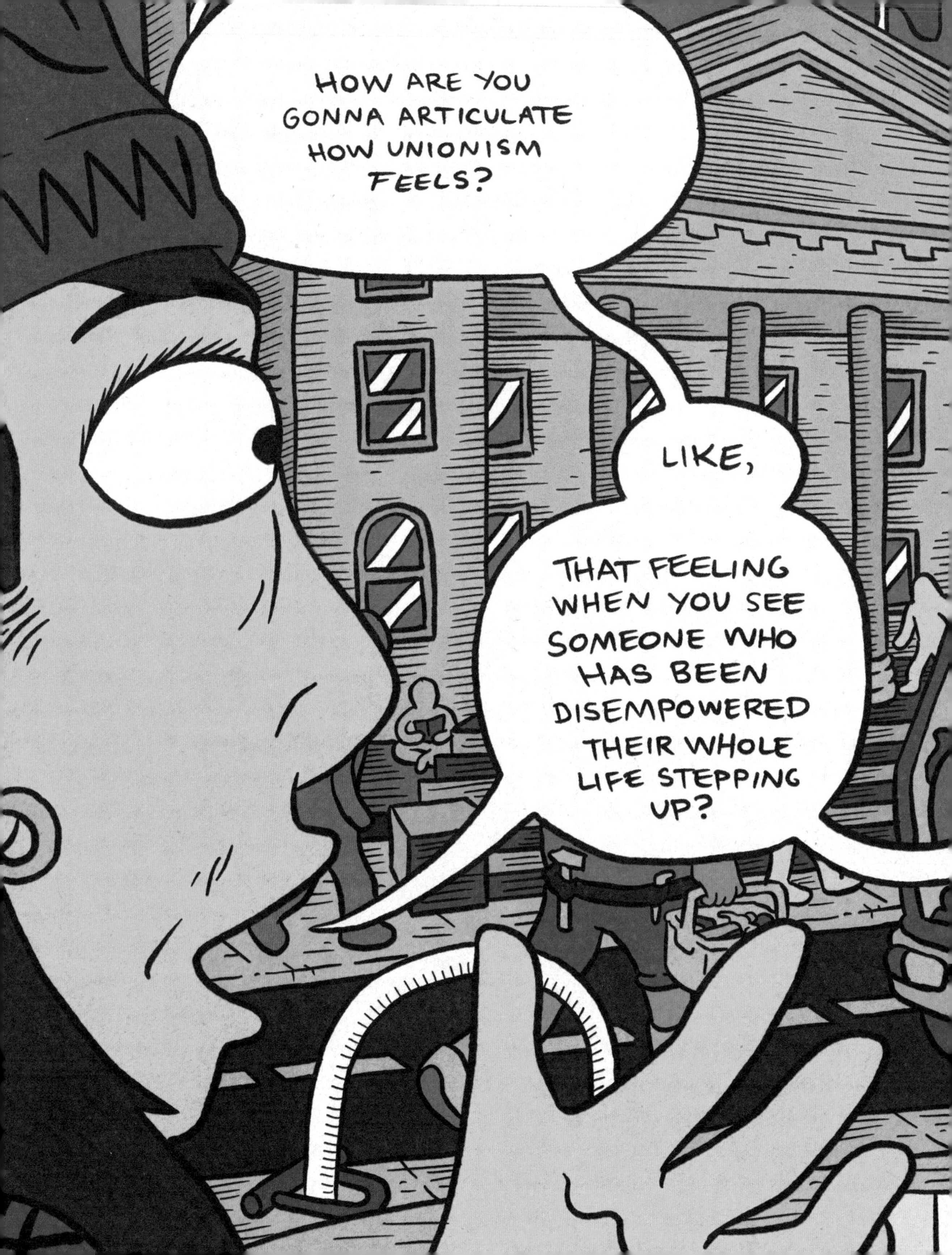
HOW ARE YOU GONNA ARTICULATE HOW UNIONISM FEELS?
LIKE,
THAT FEELING WHEN YOU SEE SOMEONE WHO HAS BEEN DISEMPOWERED THEIR WHOLE LIFE STEPPING UP?

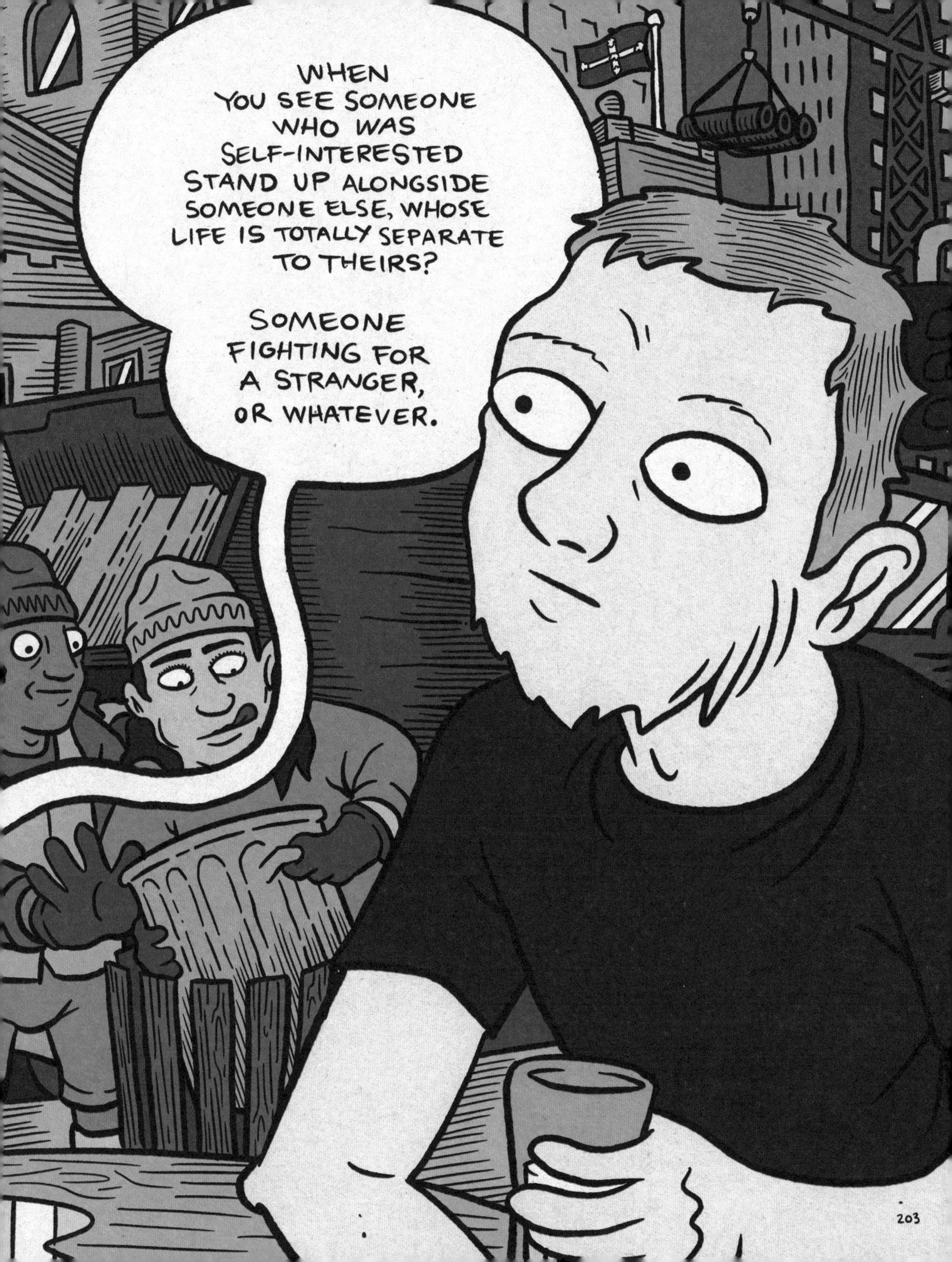
WHEN YOU SEE SOMEONE WHO WAS SELF-INTERESTED STAND UP ALONGSIDE SOMEONE ELSE, WHOSE LIFE IS TOTALLY SEPARATE TO THEIRS?
SOMEONE FIGHTING FOR A STRANGER, OR WHATEVER.

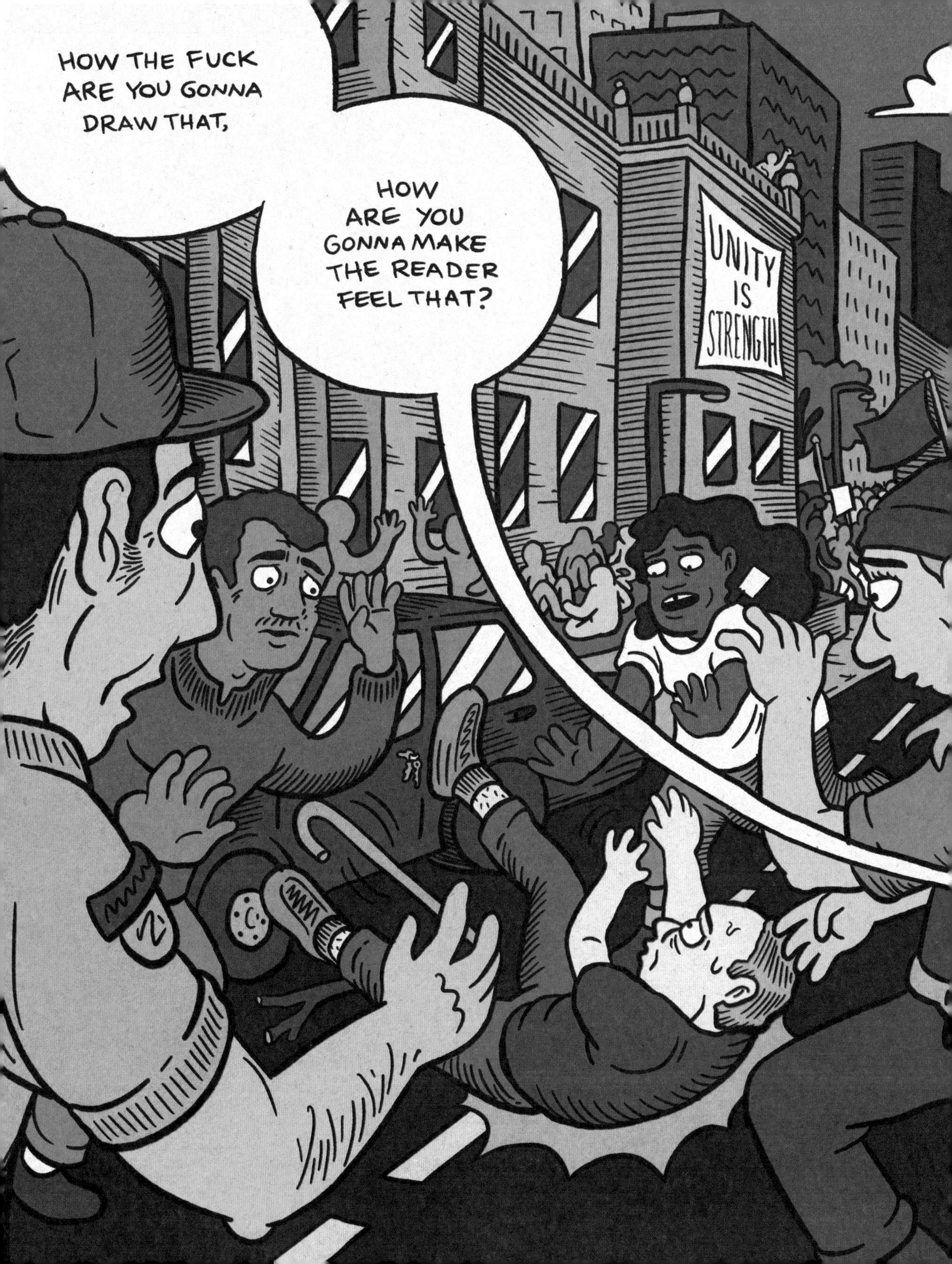
HOW THE FUCK ARE YOU GONNA DRAW THAT,
HOW ARE YOU GONNA MAKE THE READER FEEL THAT?
UNITY IS STRENGTH

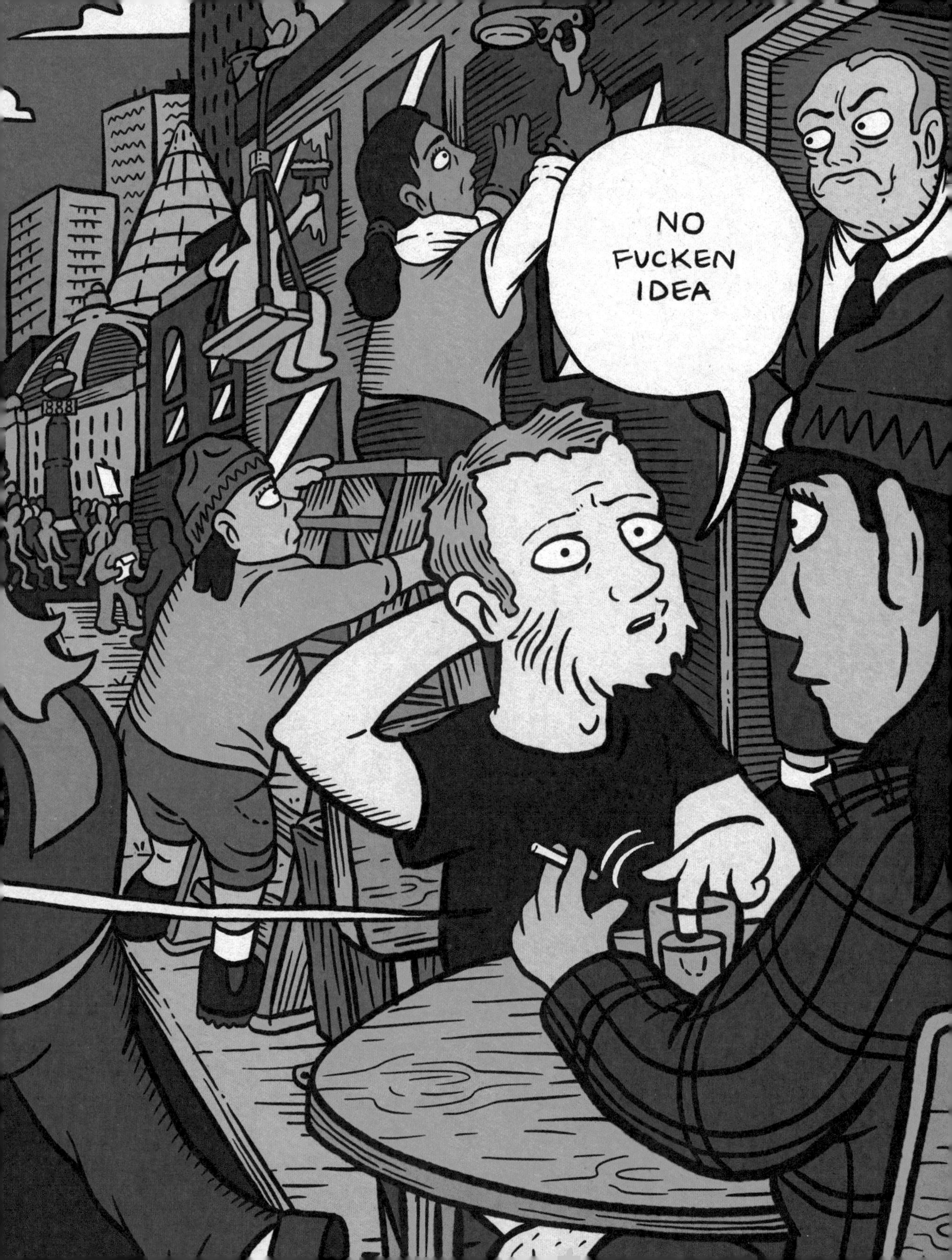
NO FUCKEN IDEA

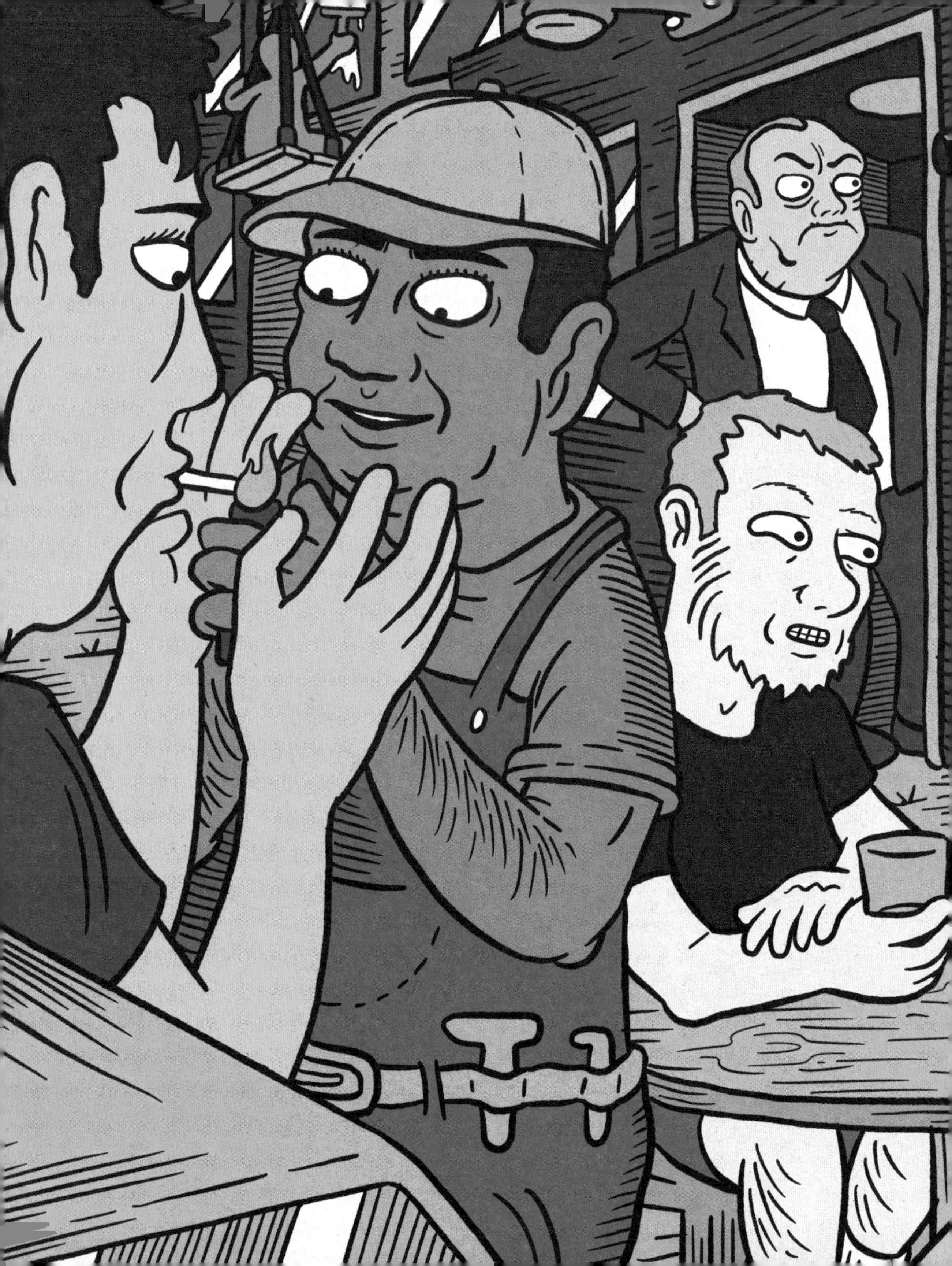

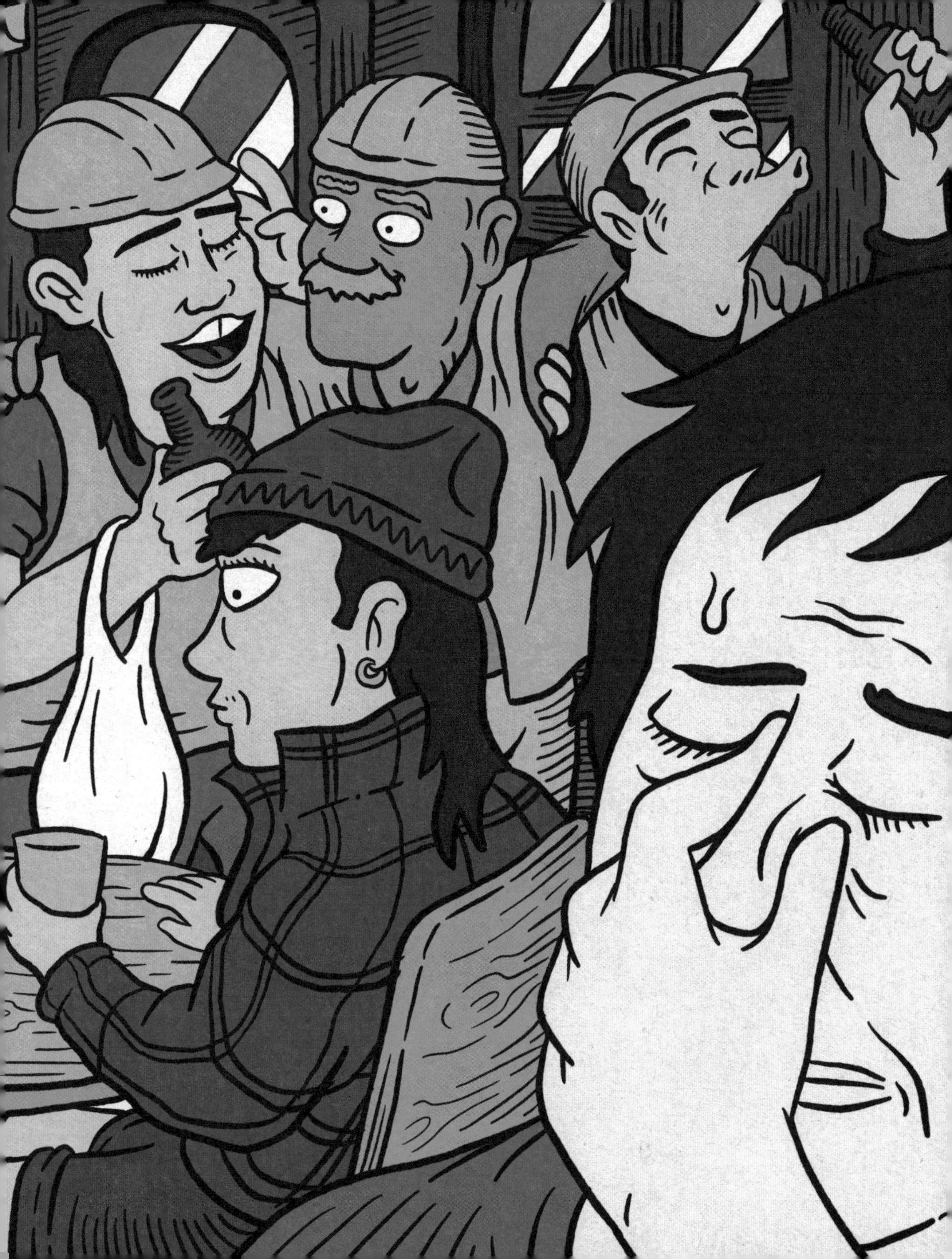

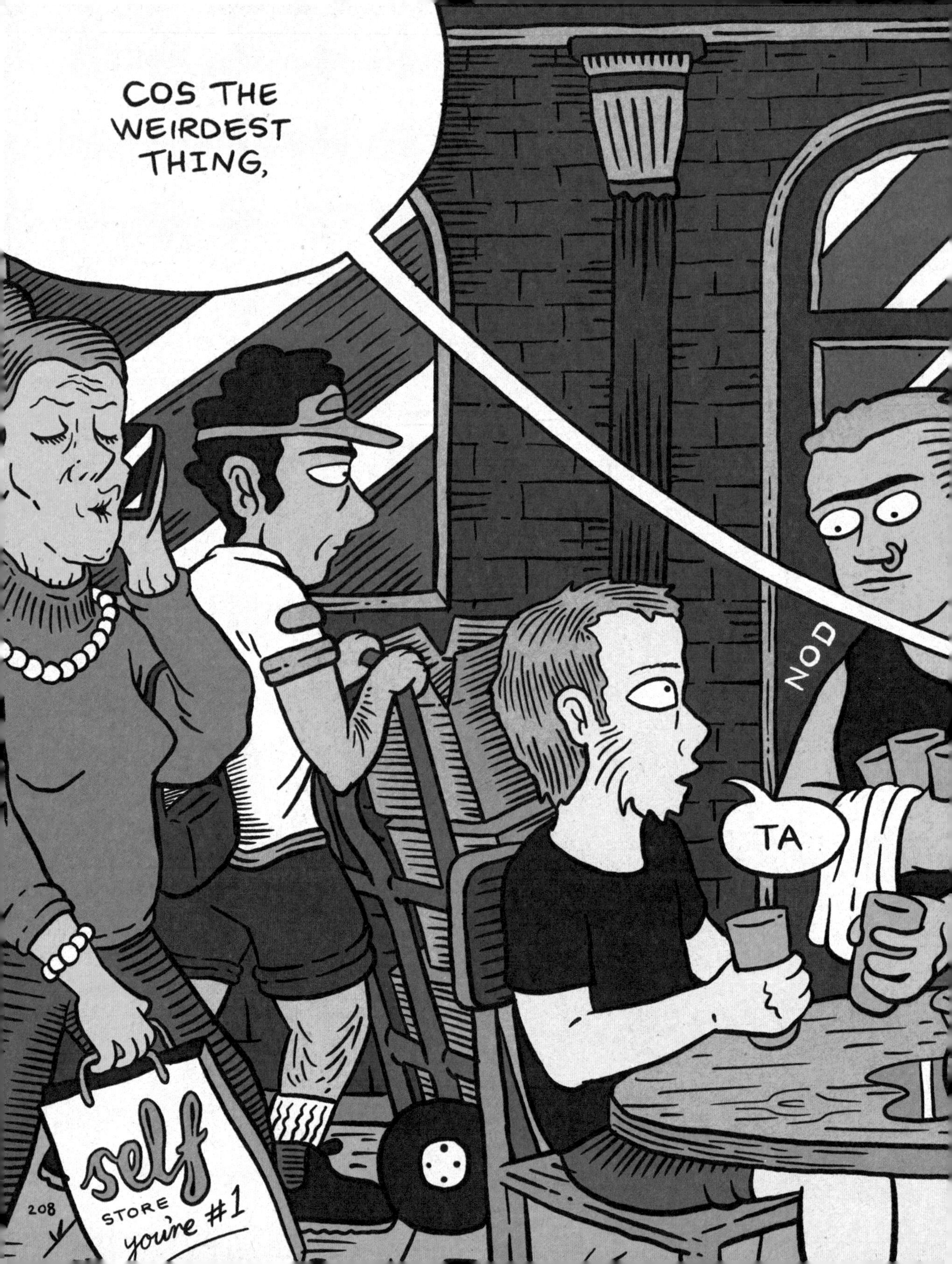
COS THE WEIRDEST THING,
NOD
TA
self
STORE
you're #1

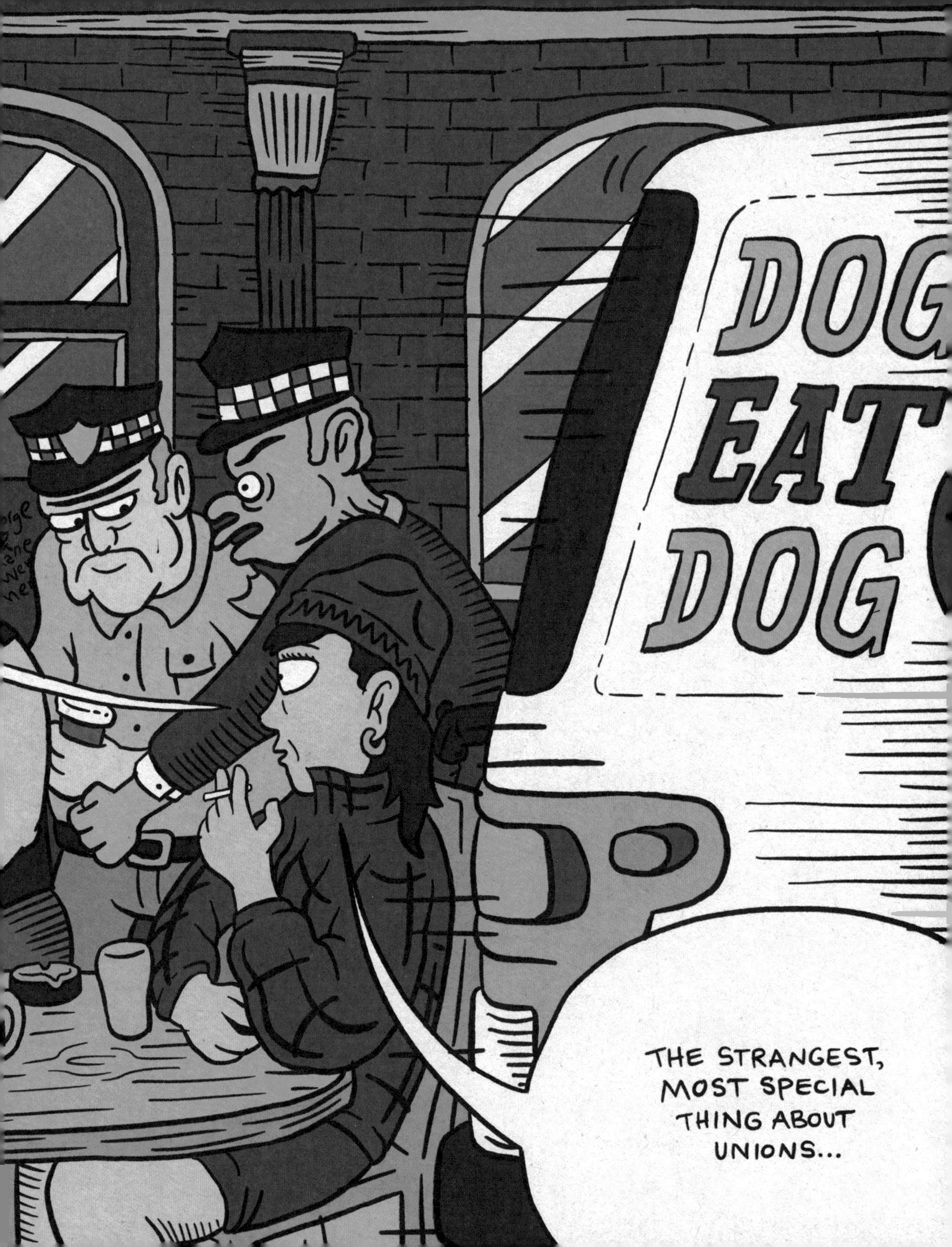
DOG EAT DOG
THE STRANGEST, MOST SPECIAL THING ABOUT UNIONS...

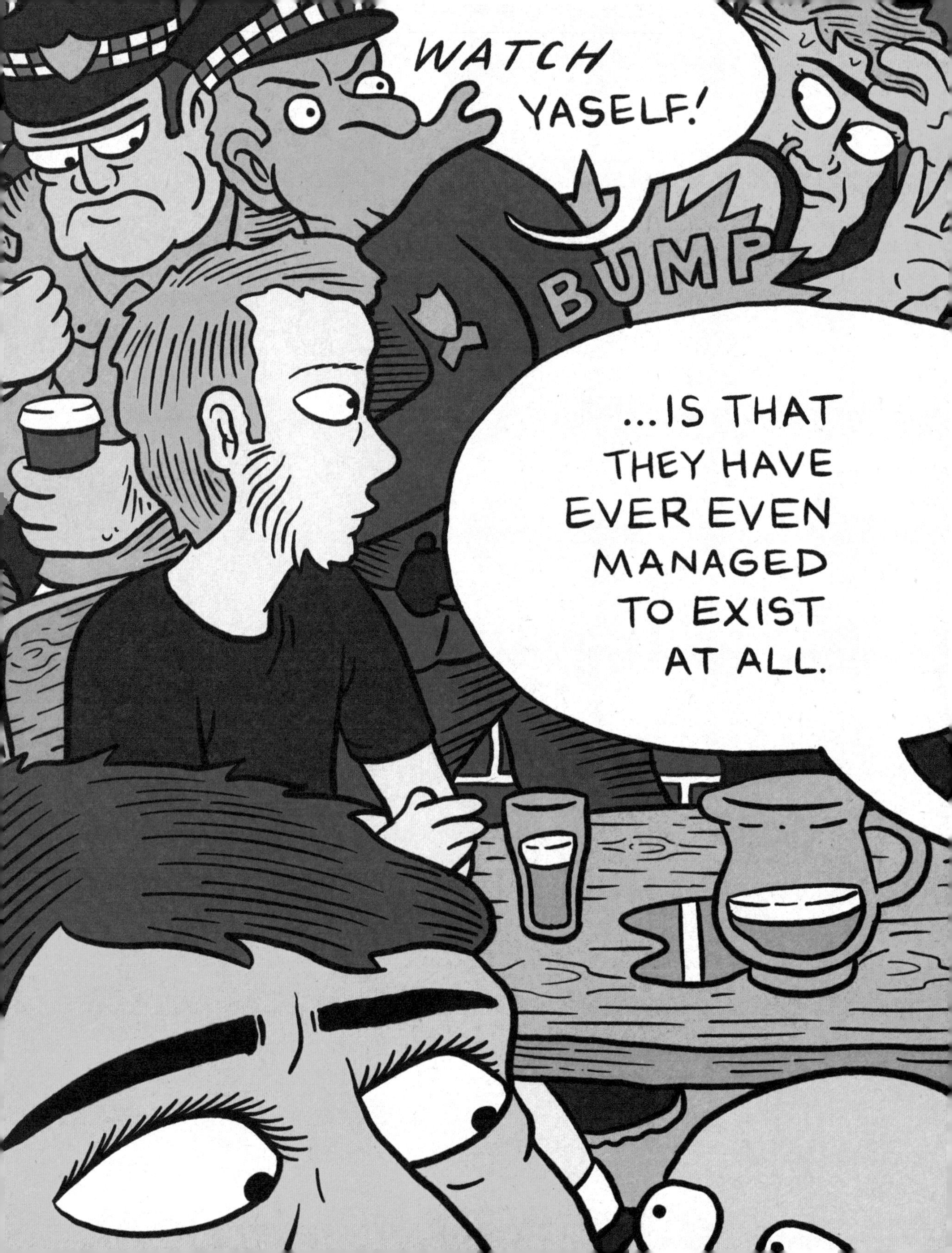
WATCH YASELF!
BUMP
...IS THAT THEY HAVE EVER EVEN MANAGED TO EXIST AT ALL.

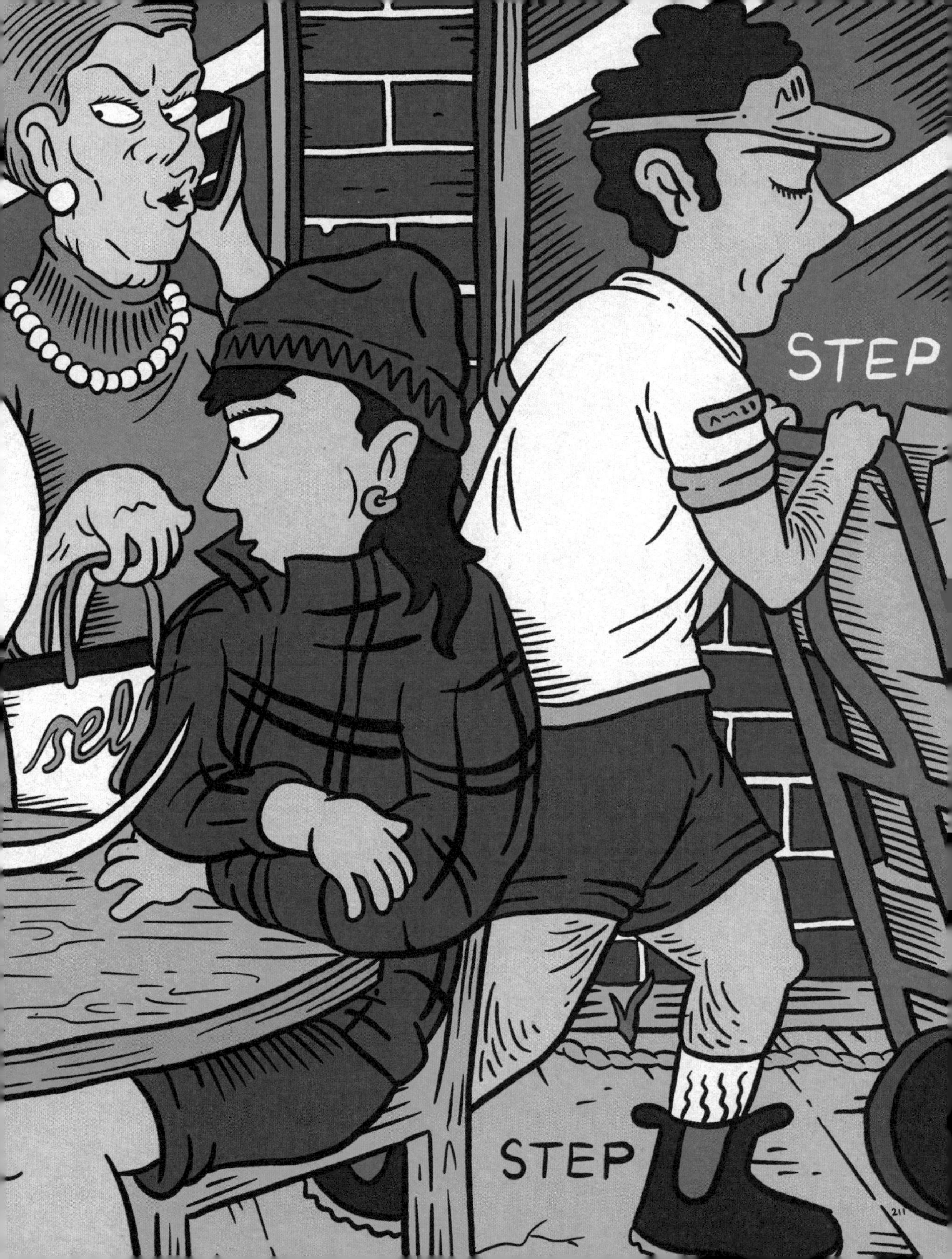
sel
STEP
STEP

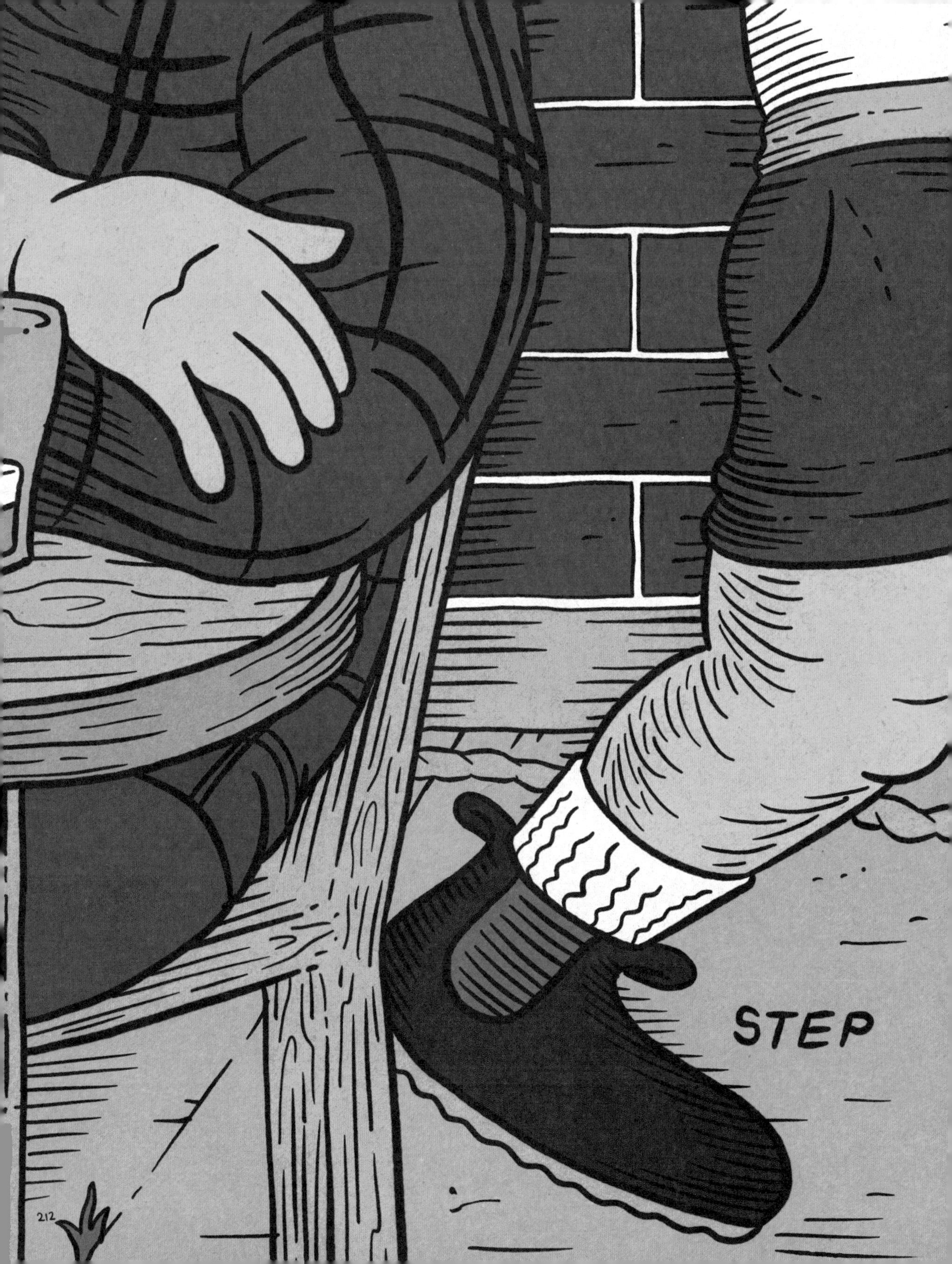
STEP

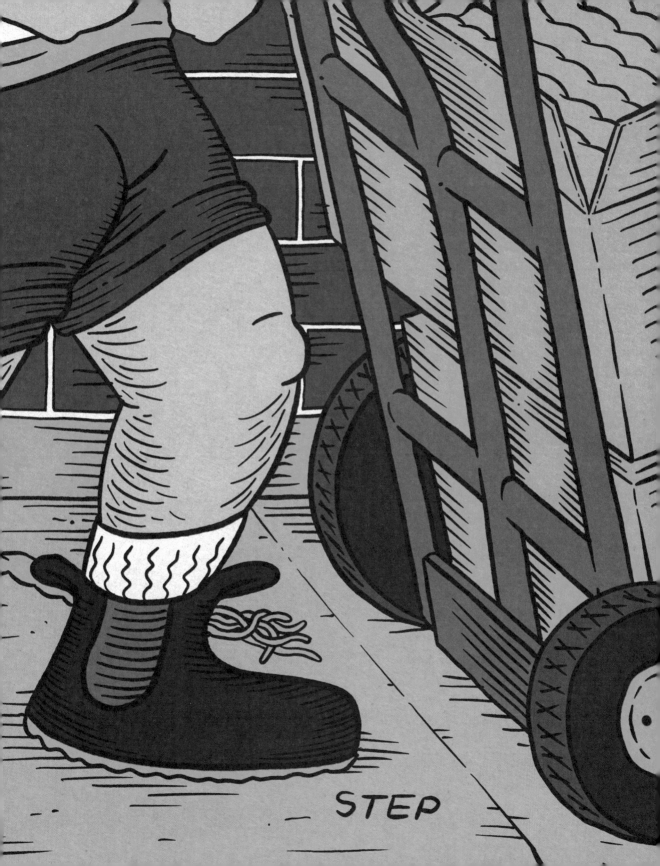

STEP

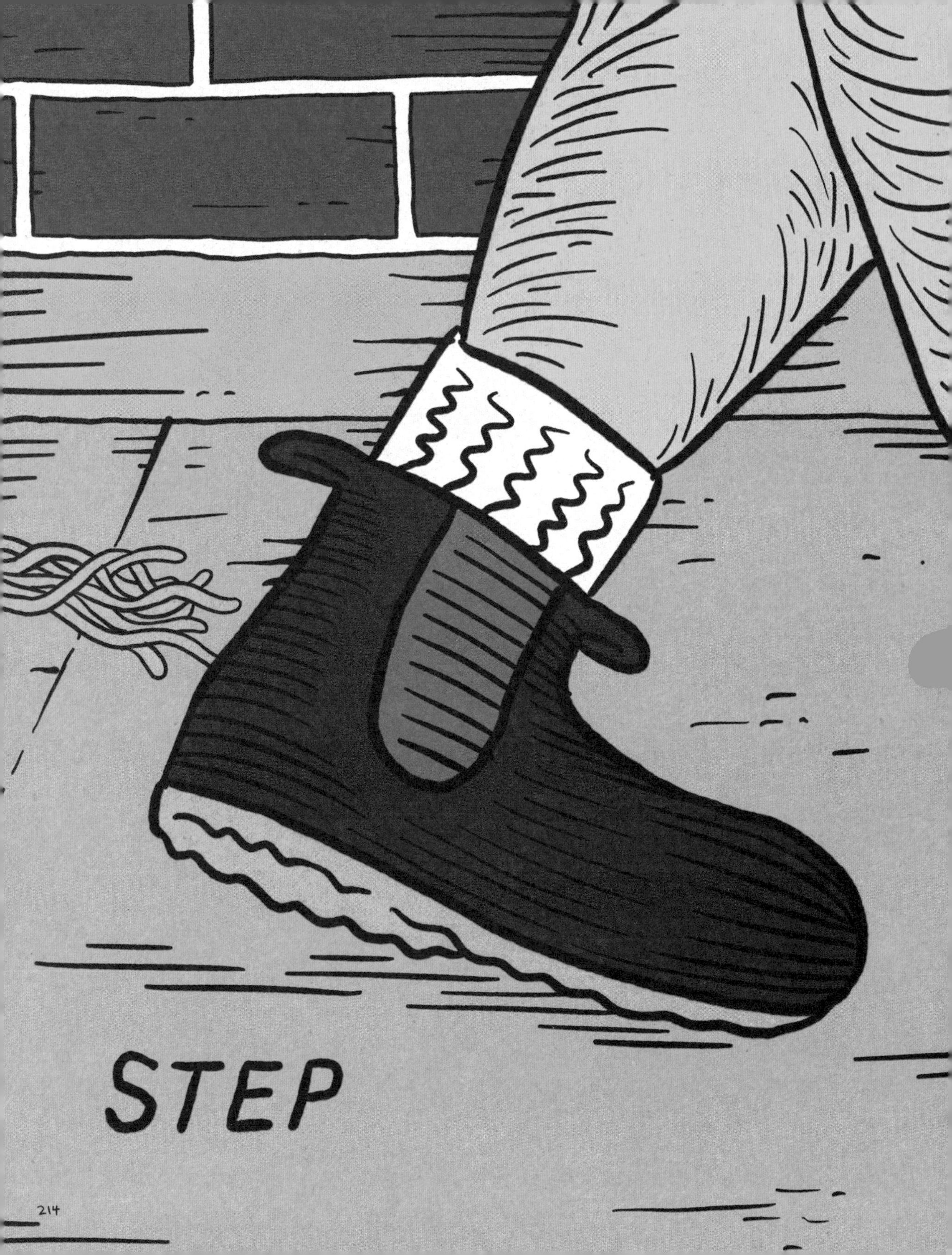
STEP

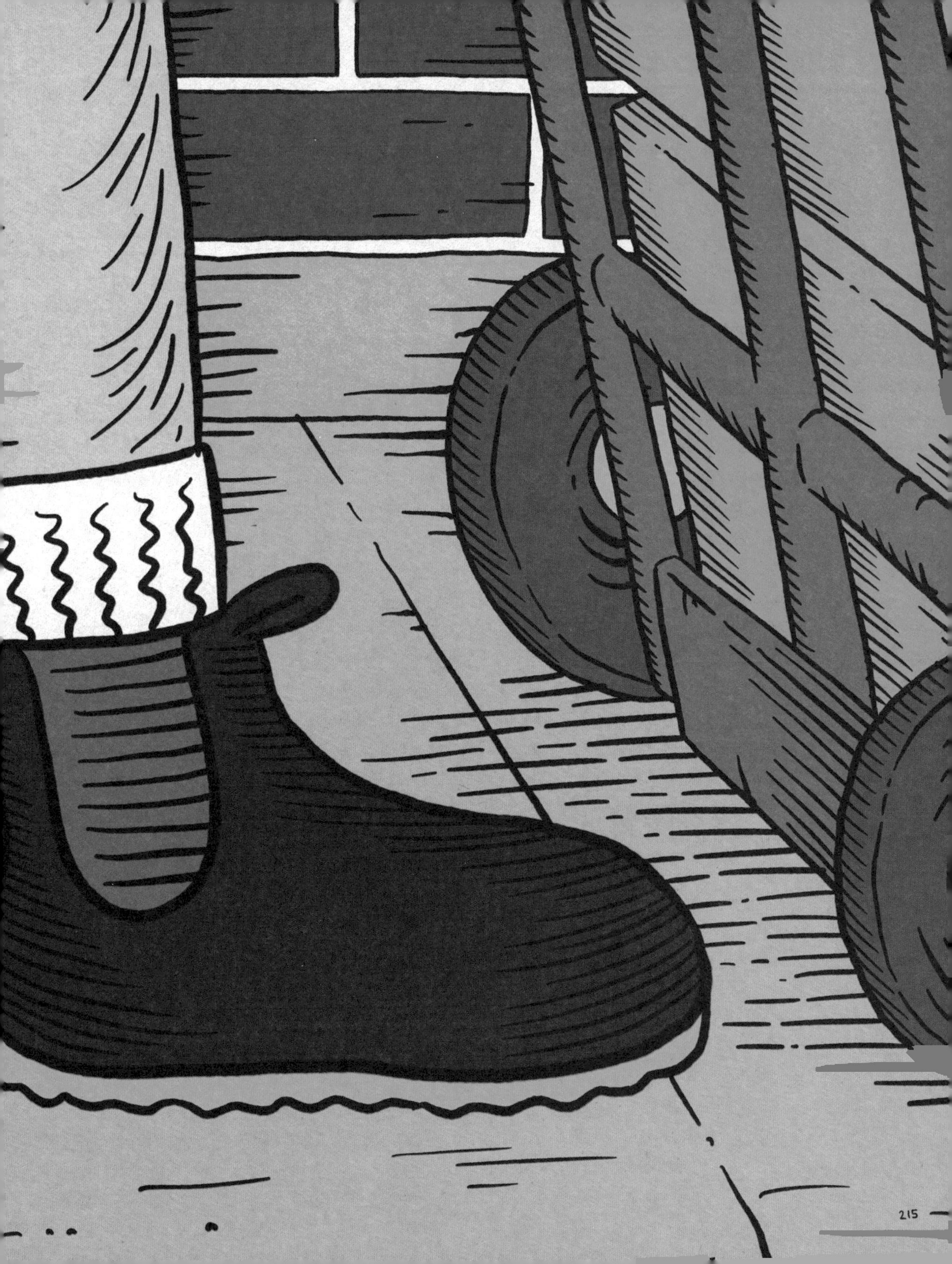

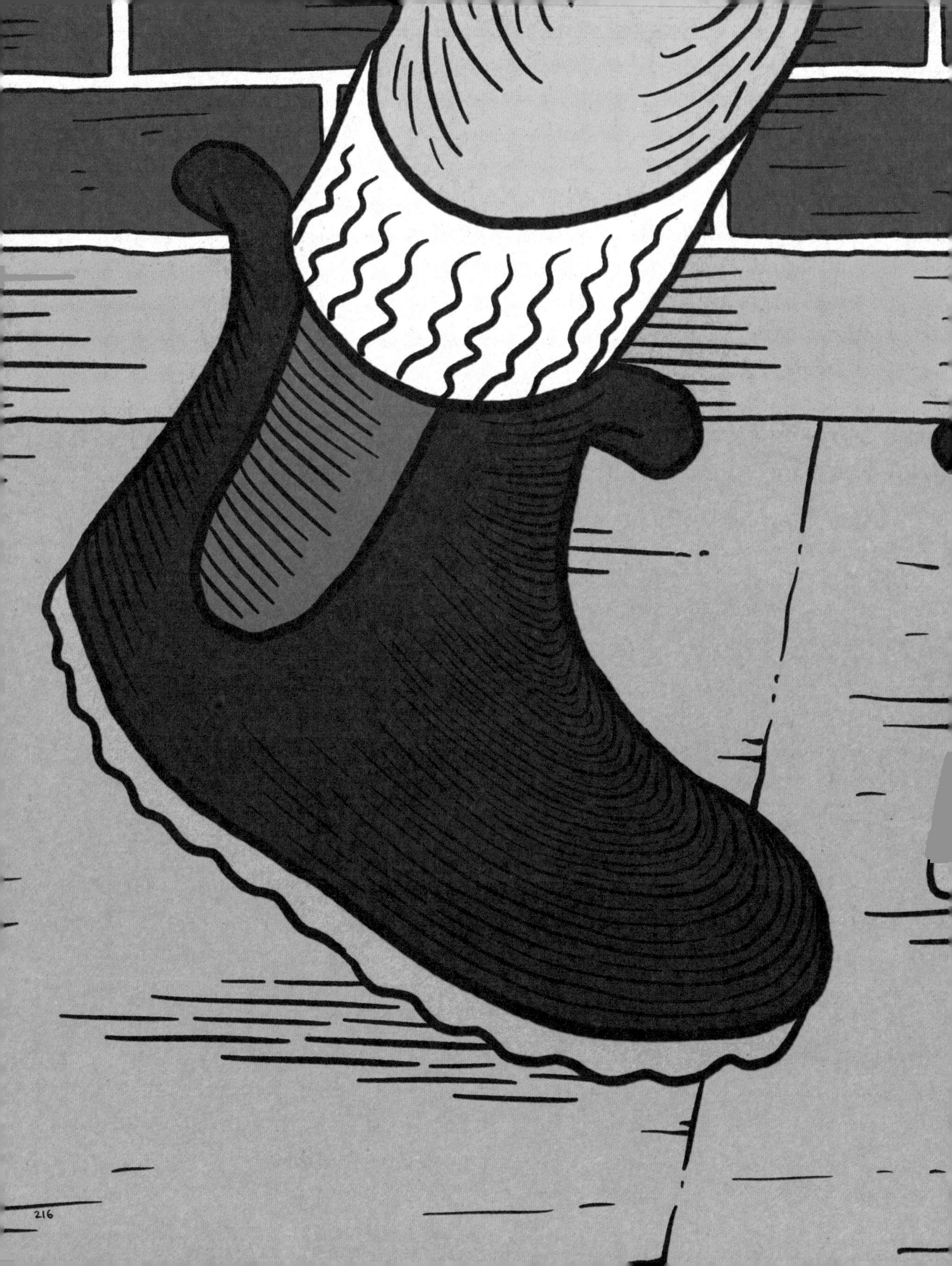

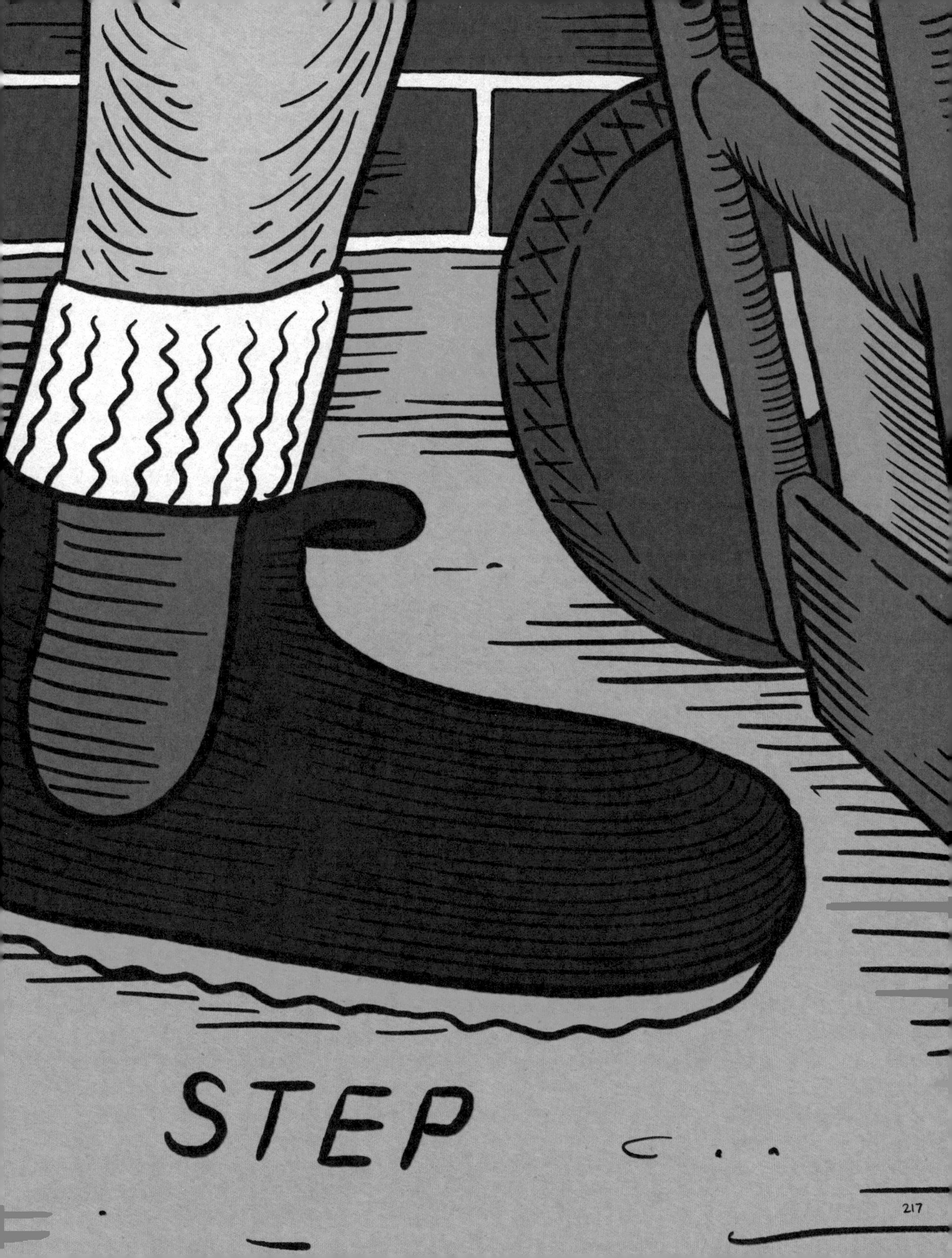
STEP

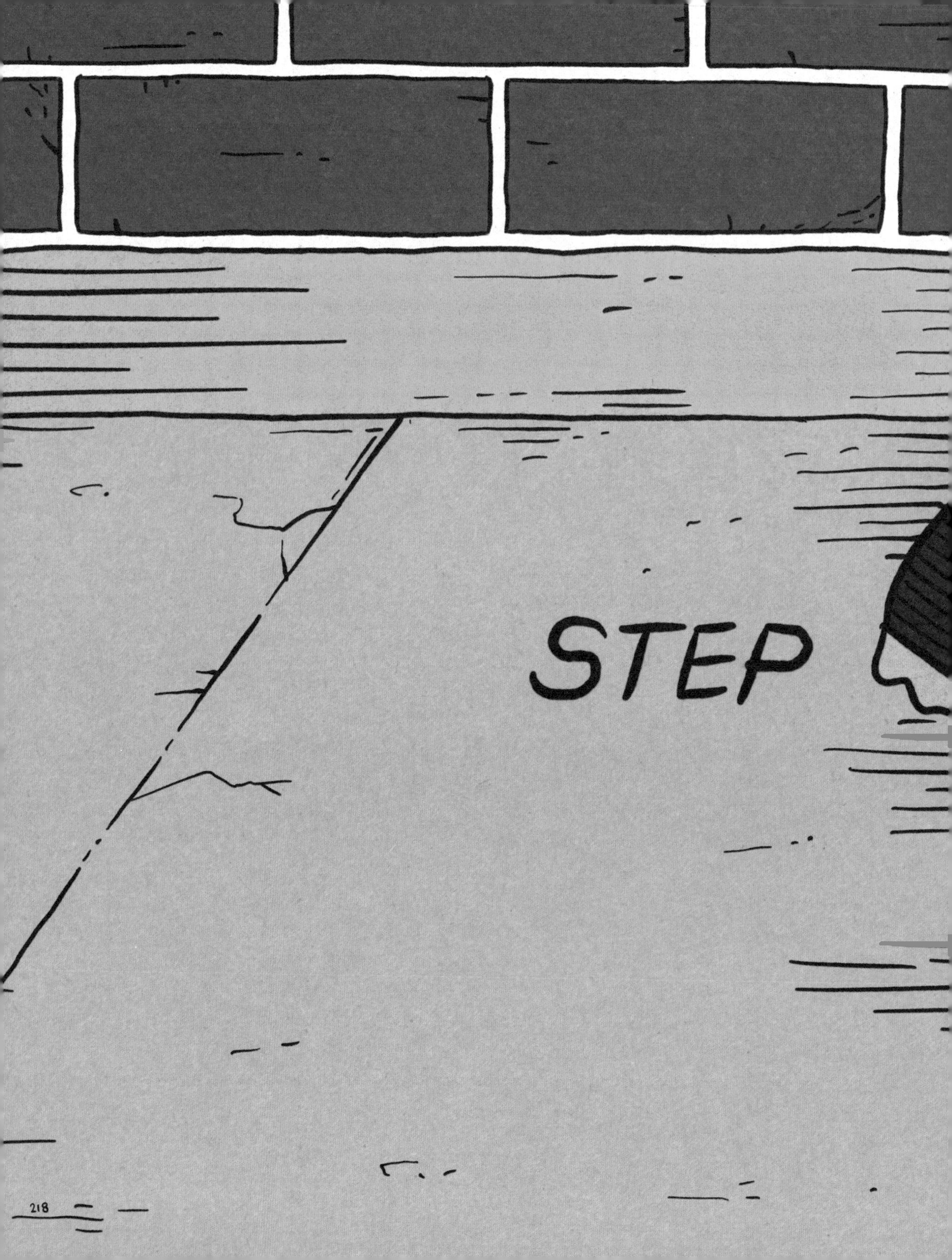
STEP

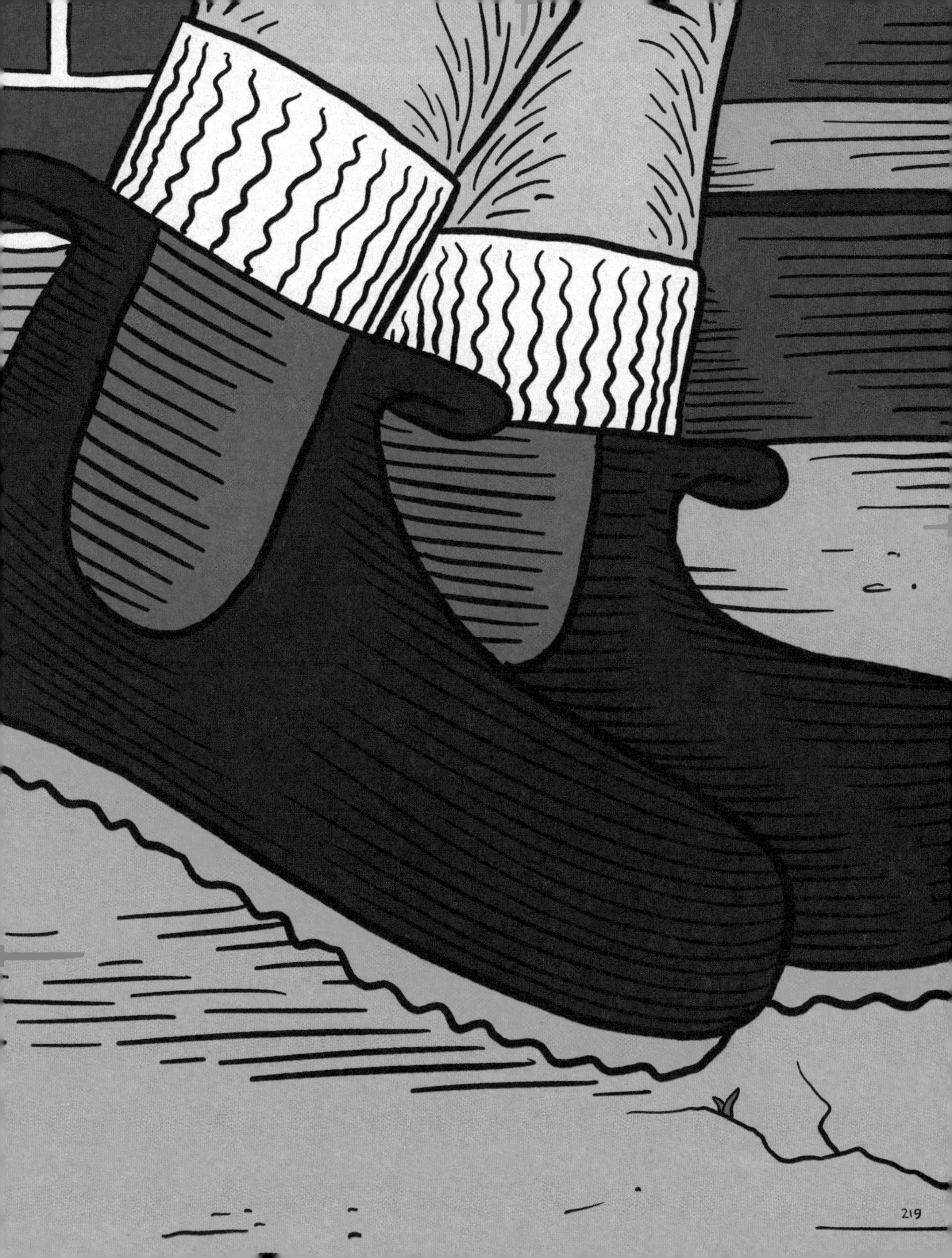

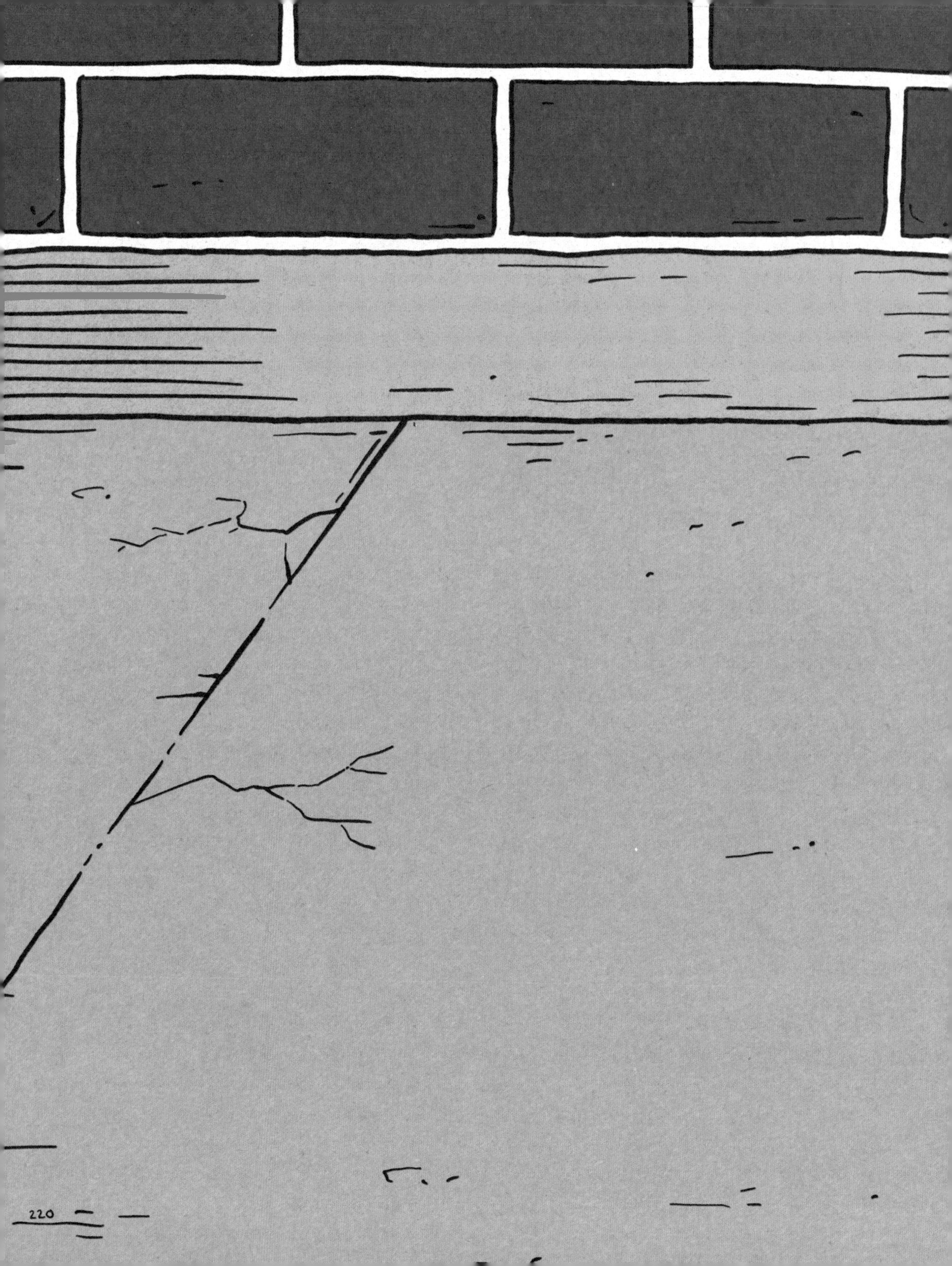

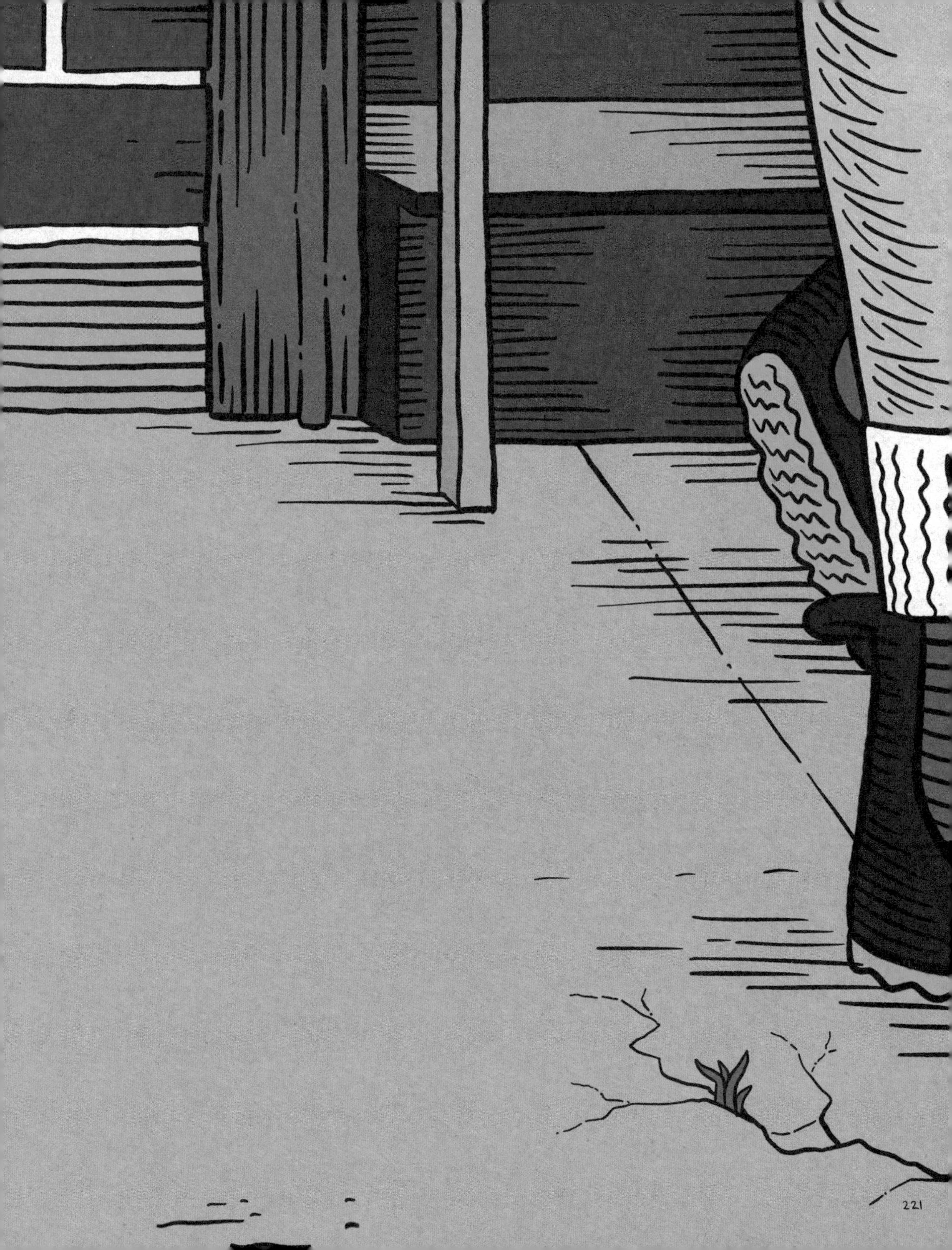

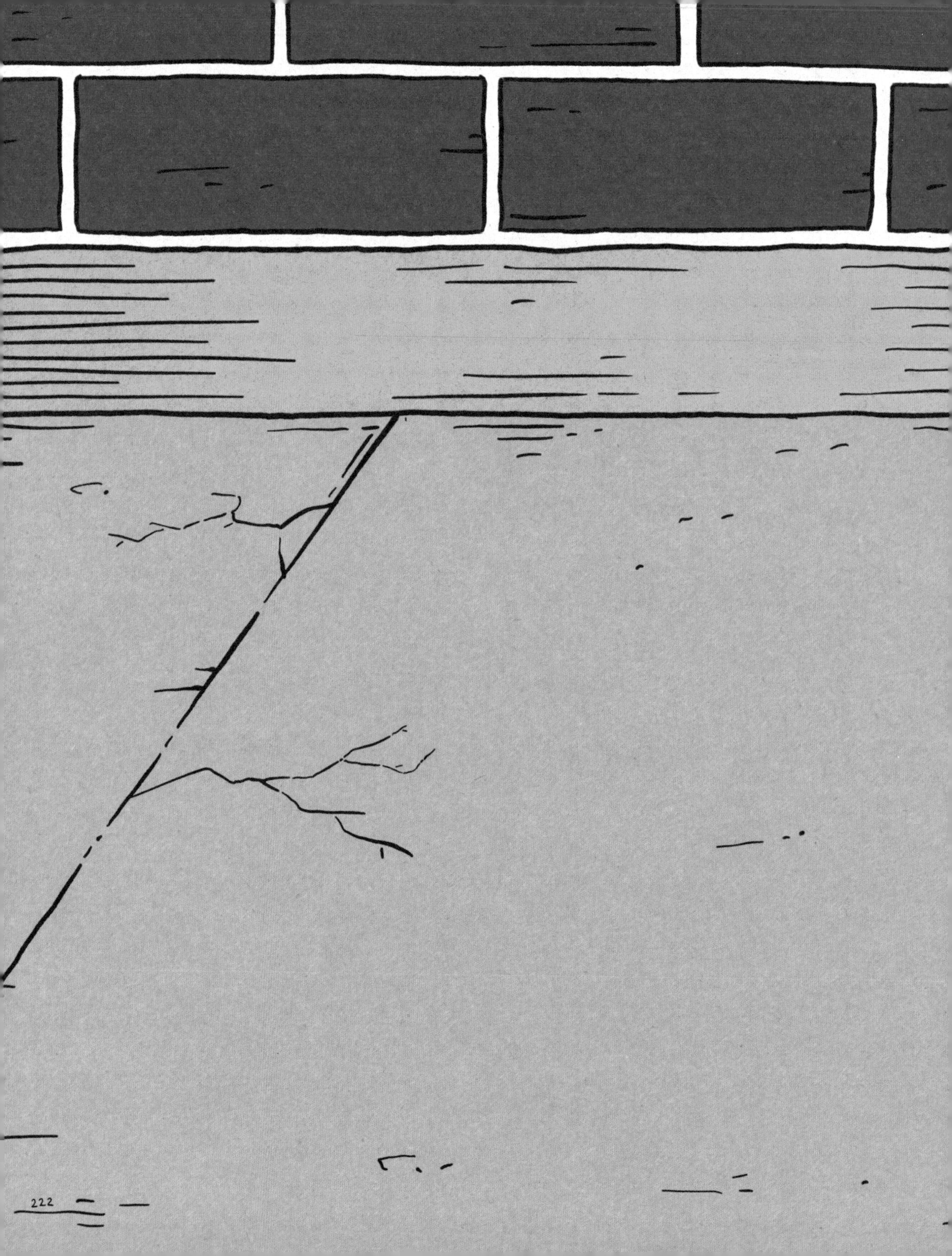

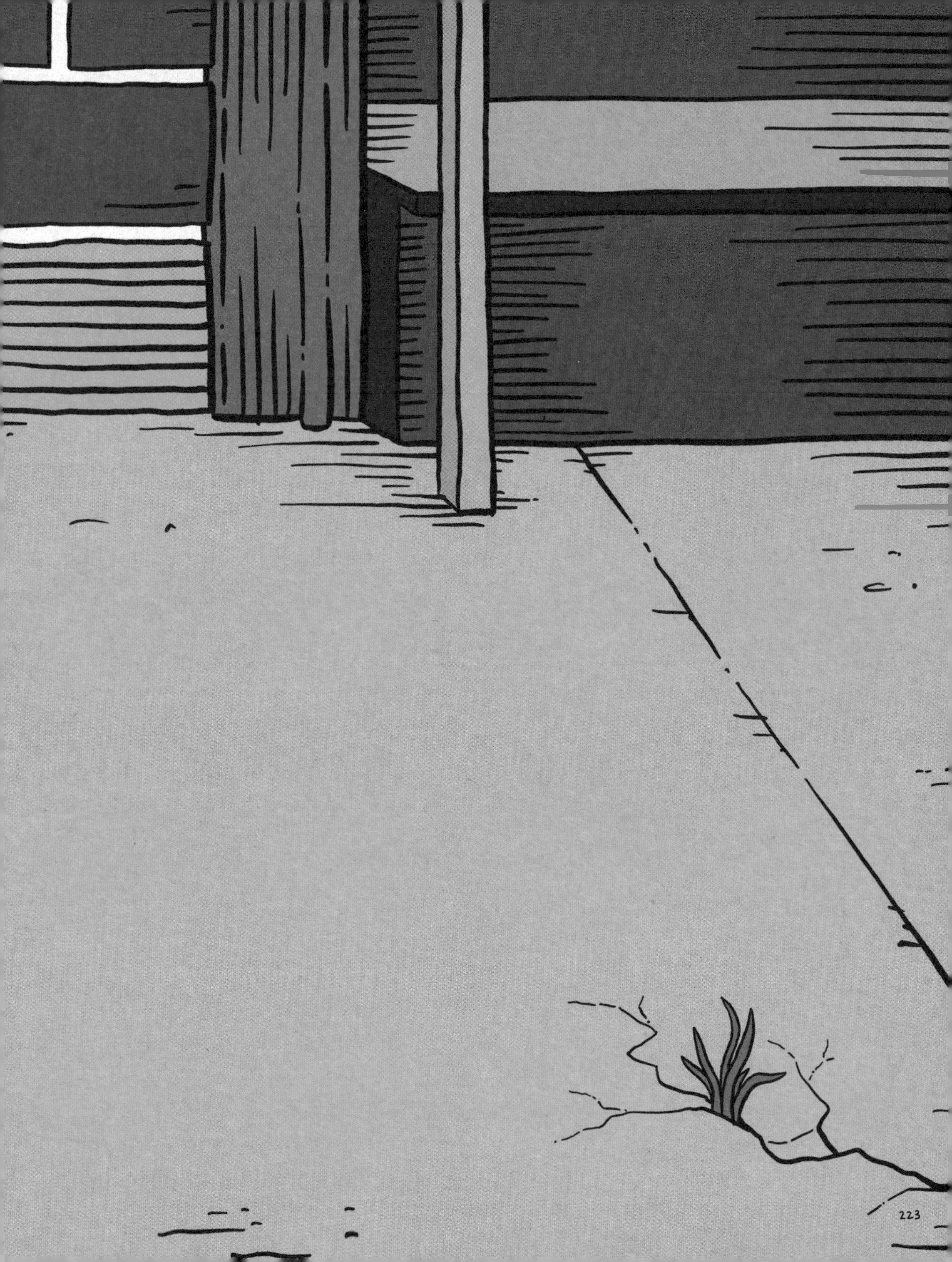

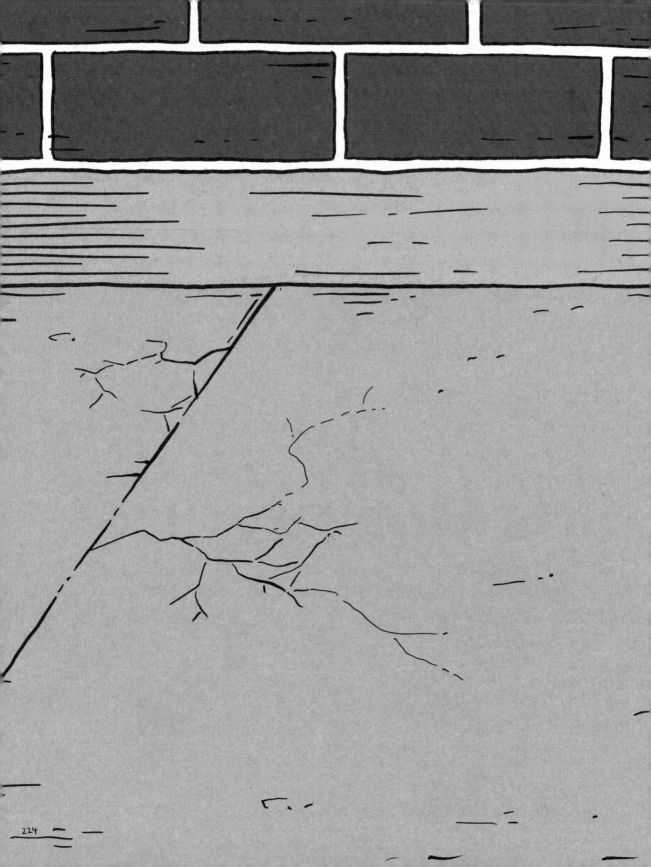

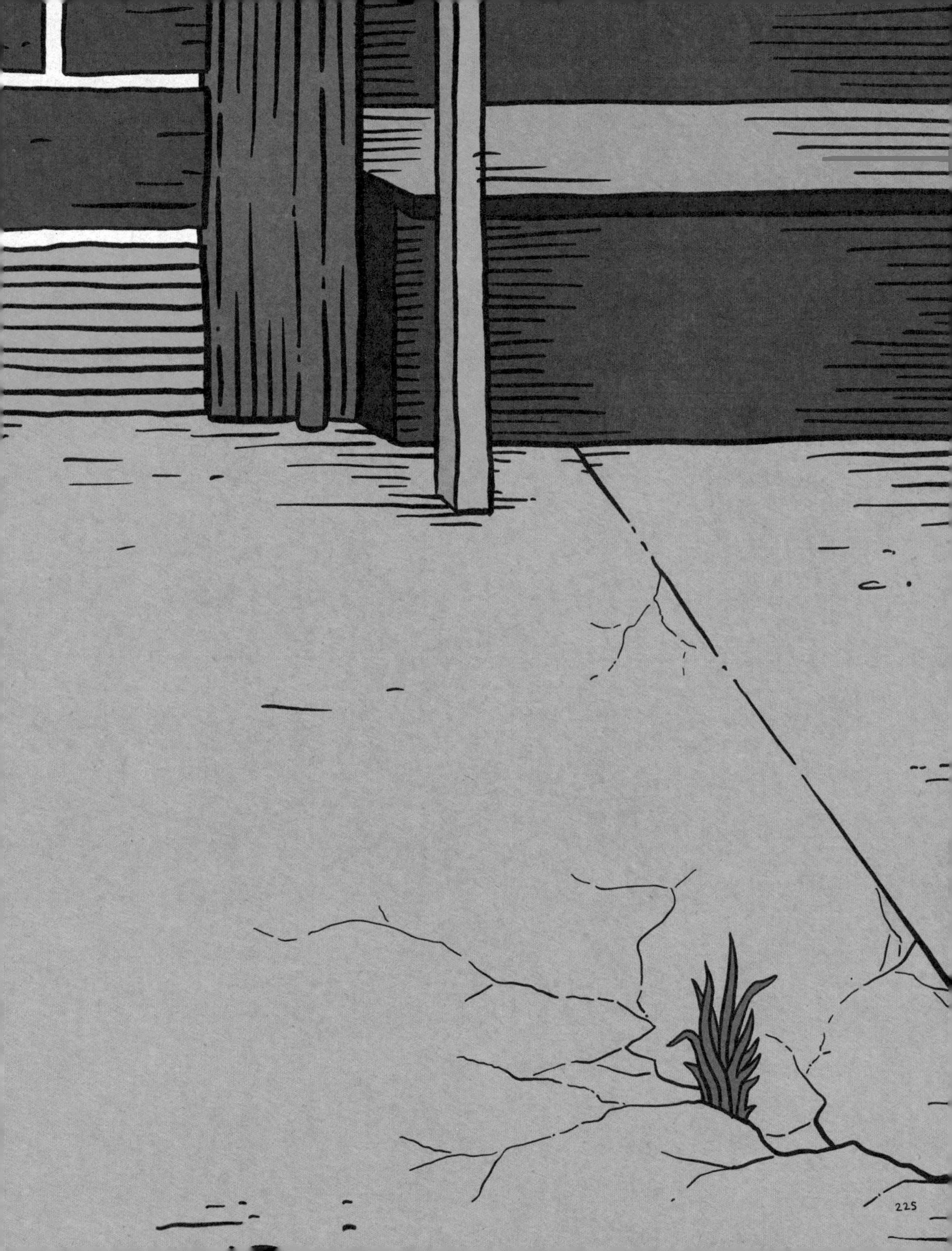

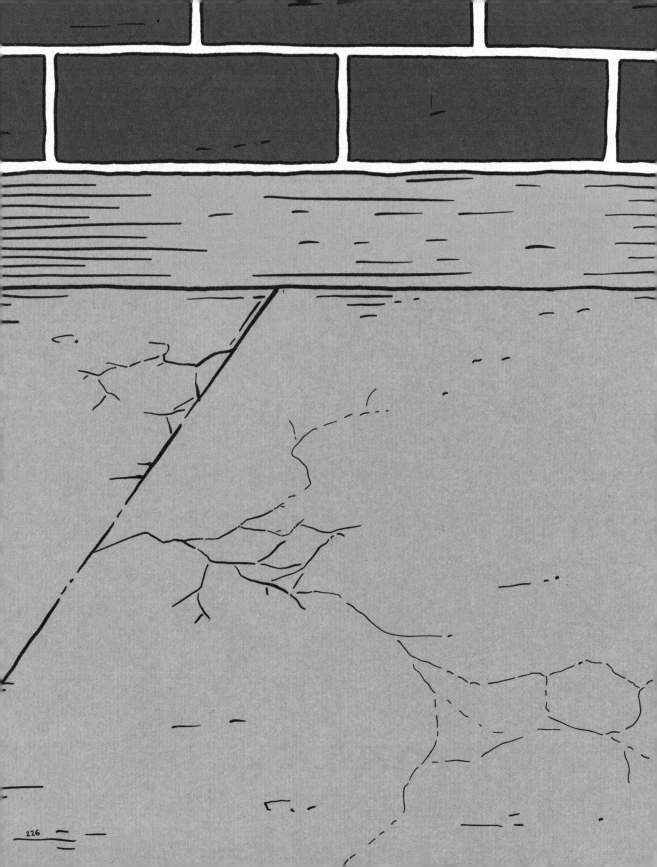

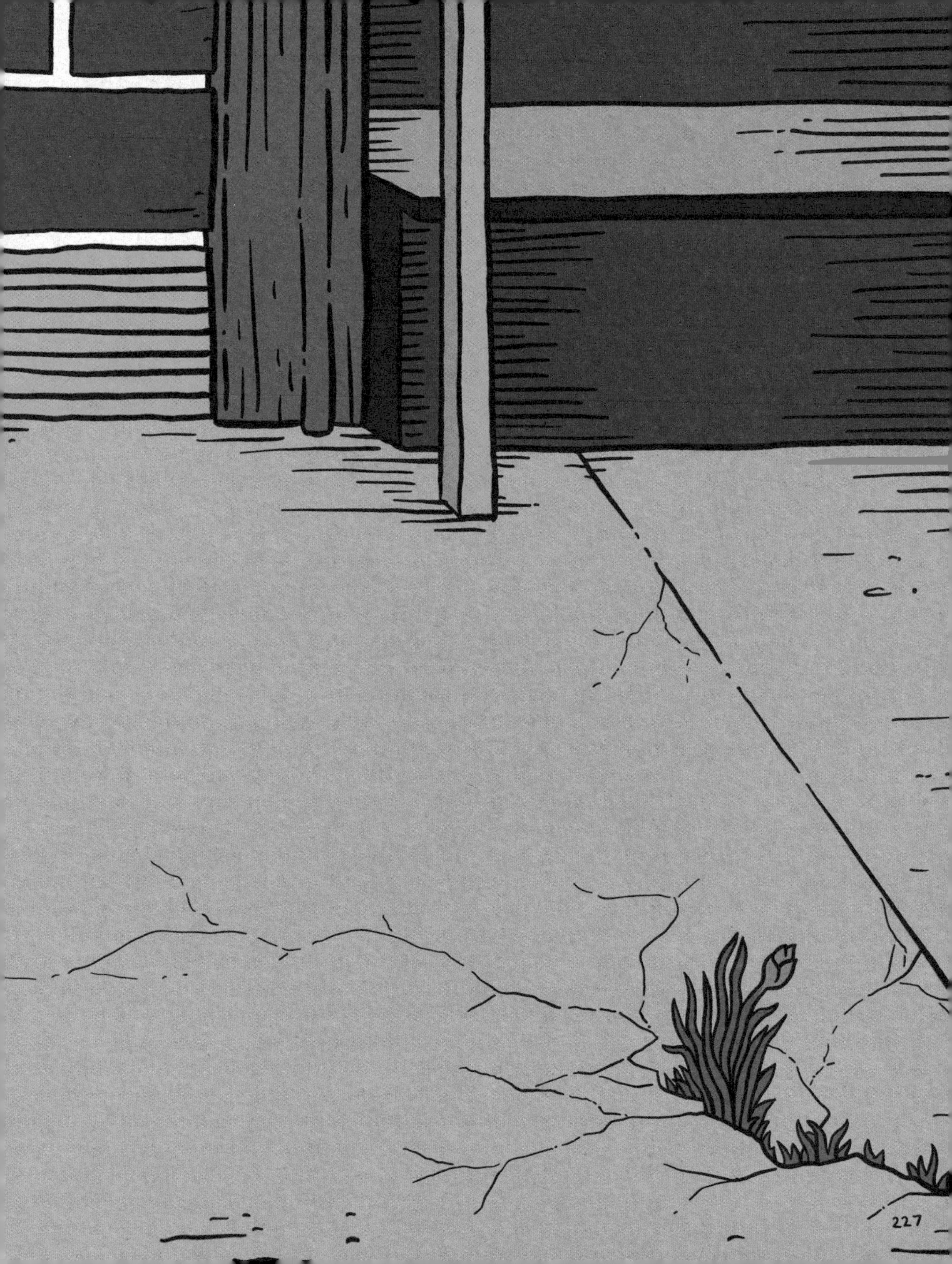

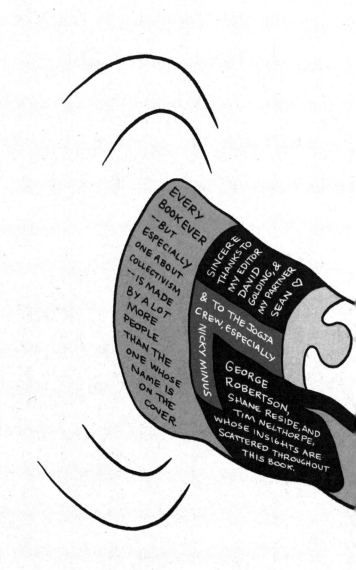

EVERY BOOK EVER --BUT ESPECIALLY ONE ABOUT COLLECTIVISM -- IS MADE BY A LOT MORE PEOPLE THAN THE ONE WHOSE NAME IS ON THE COVER.

SINCERE THANKS TO MY EDITOR DAVID GOLDING & MY PARTNER SEAN ♡ & TO THE JOGJA CREW, ESPECIALLY NICKY MINUS GEORGE ROBERTSON, SHANE RESIDE, AND TIM NELTHORPE, WHOSE INSIGHTS ARE SCATTERED THROUGHOUT THIS BOOK.

FOR THEIR GUIDANCE & COMPANIONSHIP:
YUGE THANKS TO EACH PERSON THAT SUPPORTED ME ON PATREON AS I PLUGGED AWAY AT THIS
ESPECIALLY
ELISABETH & CHRIS P
LACHLAN MUSICMAN
JOSH ANDREWS
AMY LEHPAMER
ALEXANDER NAPOLITANO
LAURA BIENIAK
ALYCIA ECONOMIDIS
ZOE R
PAT A
JEFF
ROSIE
JACINDA
KIERAN
MARC
BAILEY
CHRISTIAN
BEN
UNITED WORKERS UNION
VICTORIAN TRADES HALL
WORKERS ART COLLECTIVE
JAVED
AARIN
NICK & ALGA
TOM & TARENCE
EMMA
AMEDEO
MUM
ALEX, FOR HELP EARLY ON
CAW
DAD
THIS BOOK WAS WRITTEN & DRAWN ON ABORIGINAL LAND, PRIMARILY THAT OF THE WURUNDJERI PEOPLE. THE AMAZON WAREHOUSE IS ON THE LAND OF THE BOON WURRUNG. JUSTICE FOR WORKERS WILL NEVER BE SEEN WITHOUT JUSTICE FOR INDIGENOUS PEOPLE.

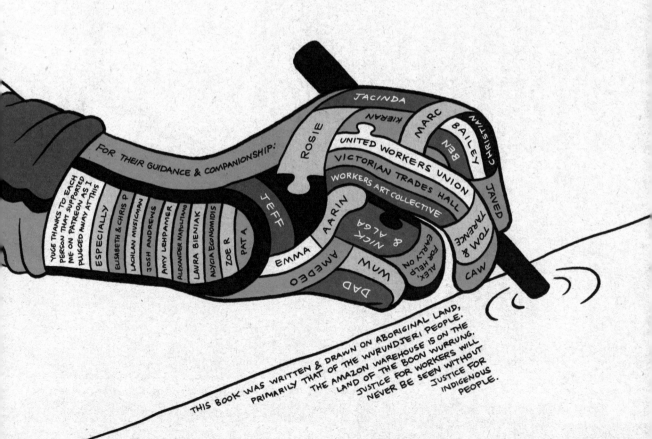

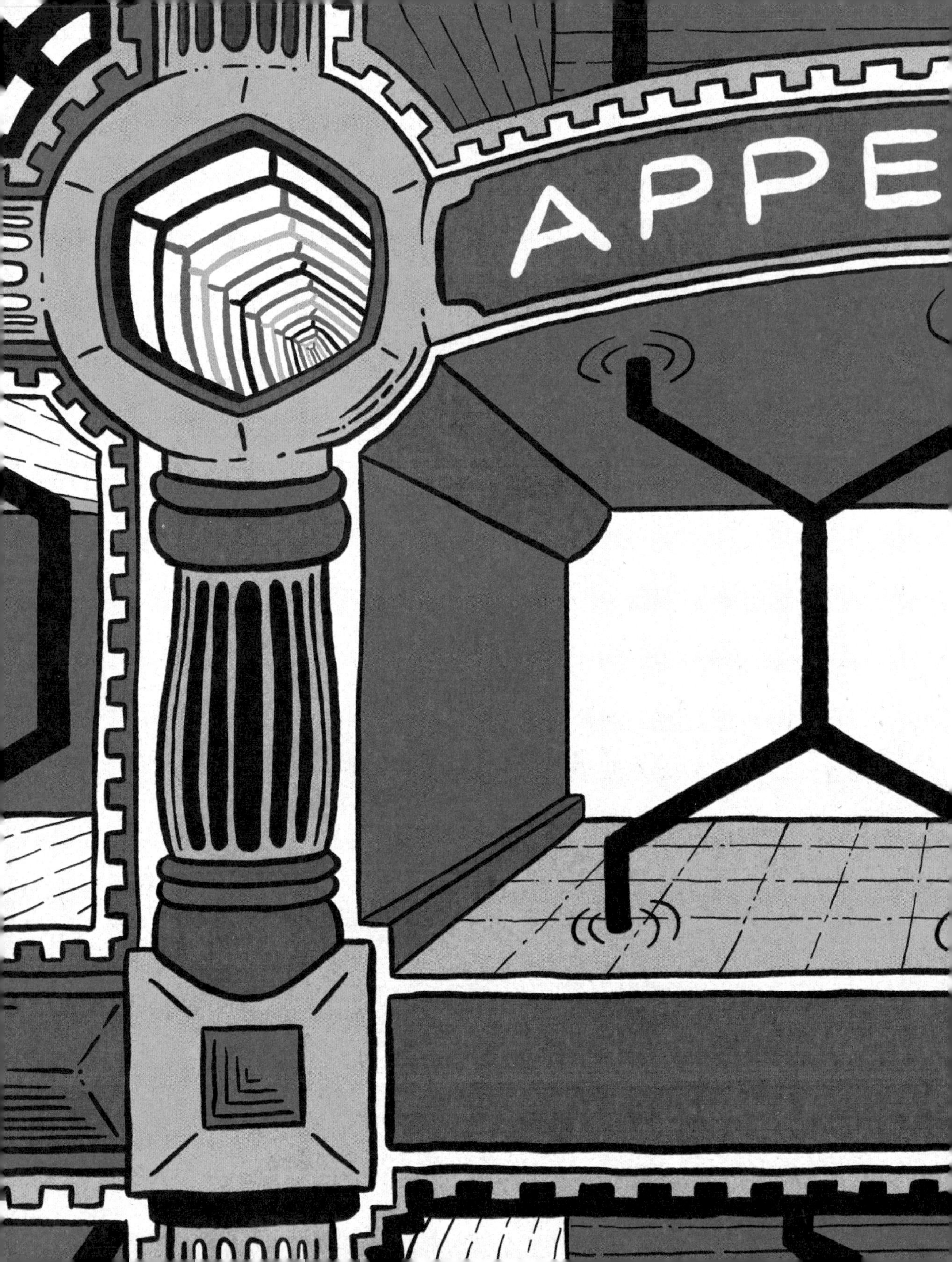
APPE

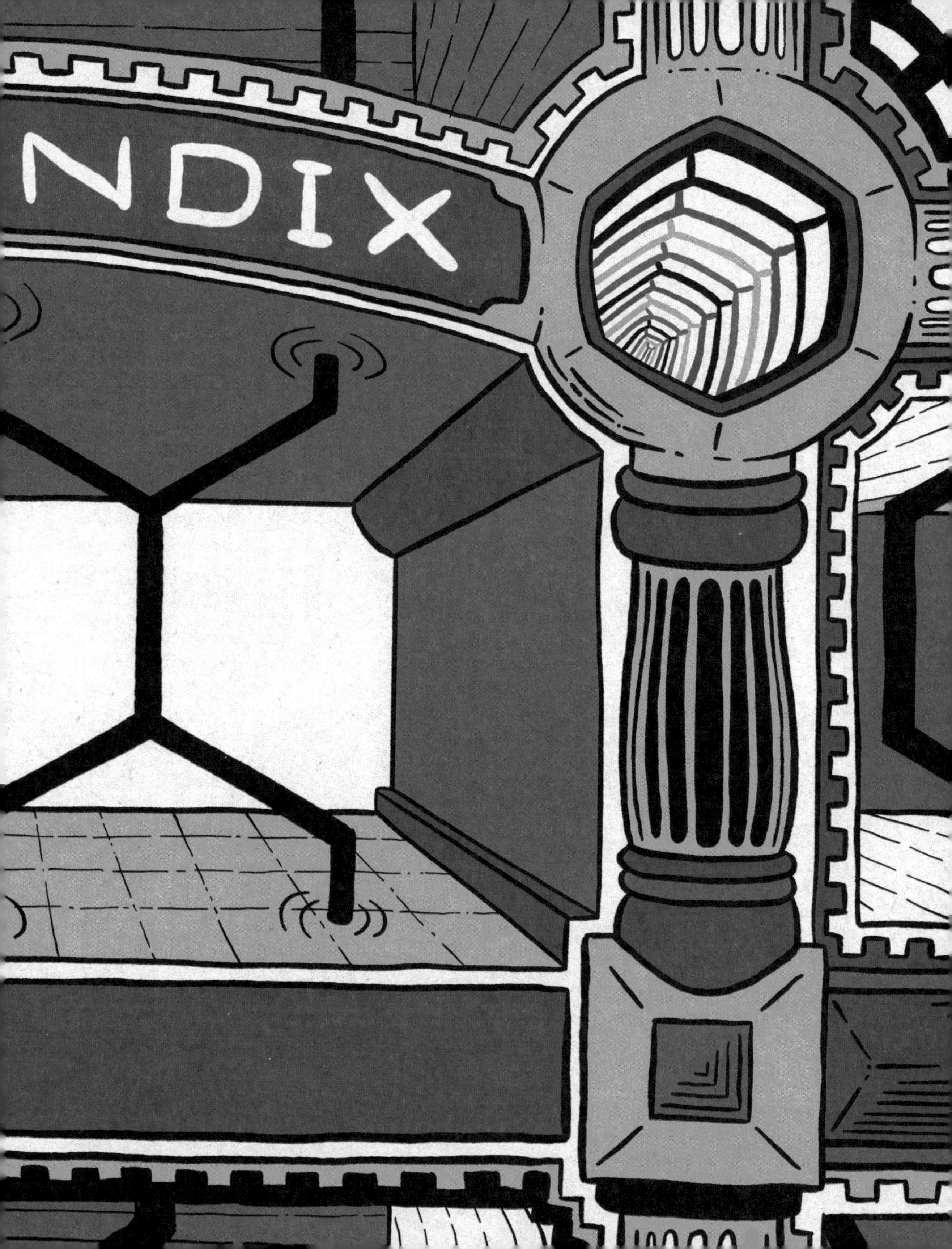
NDIX

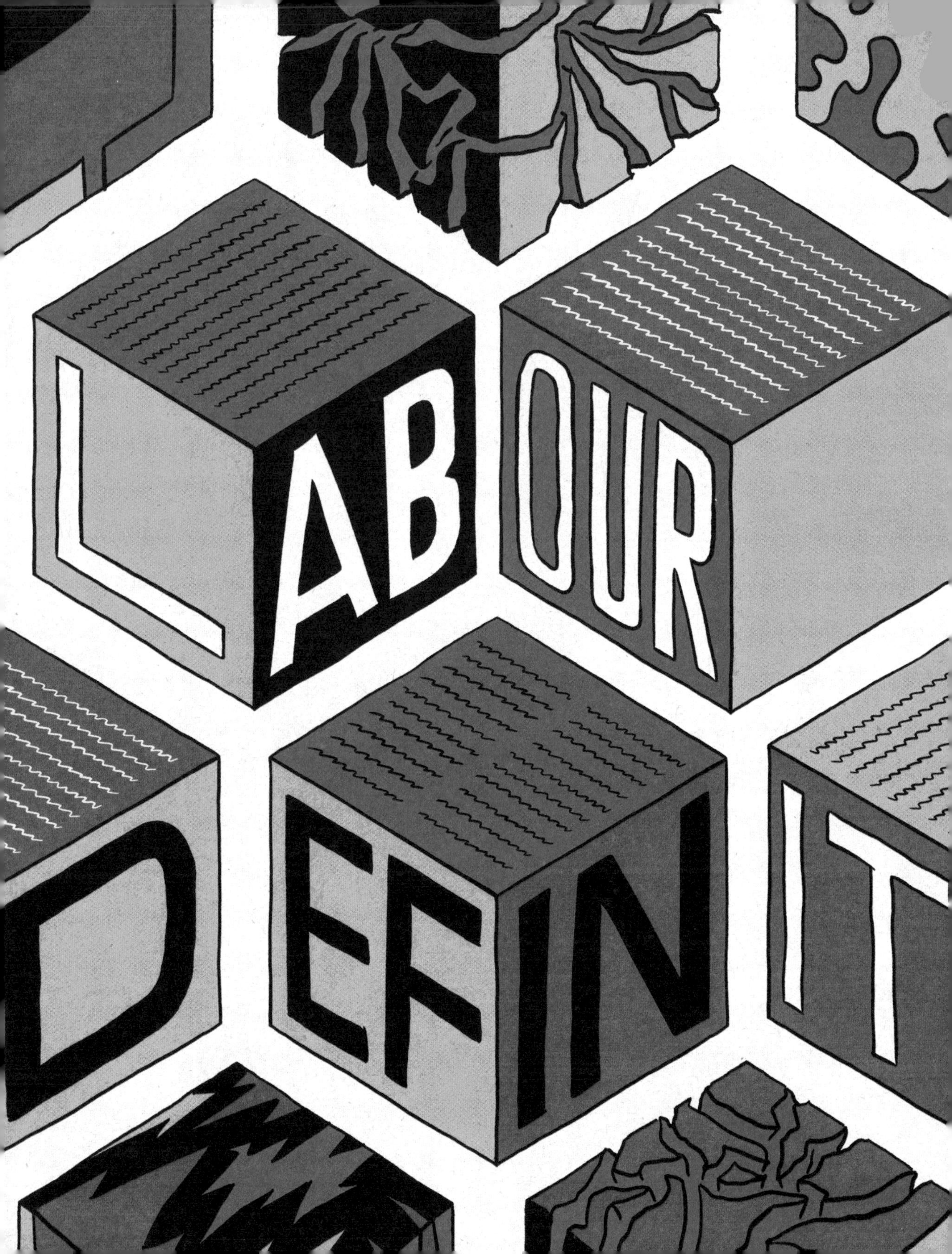
LABOUR
DEFINIT

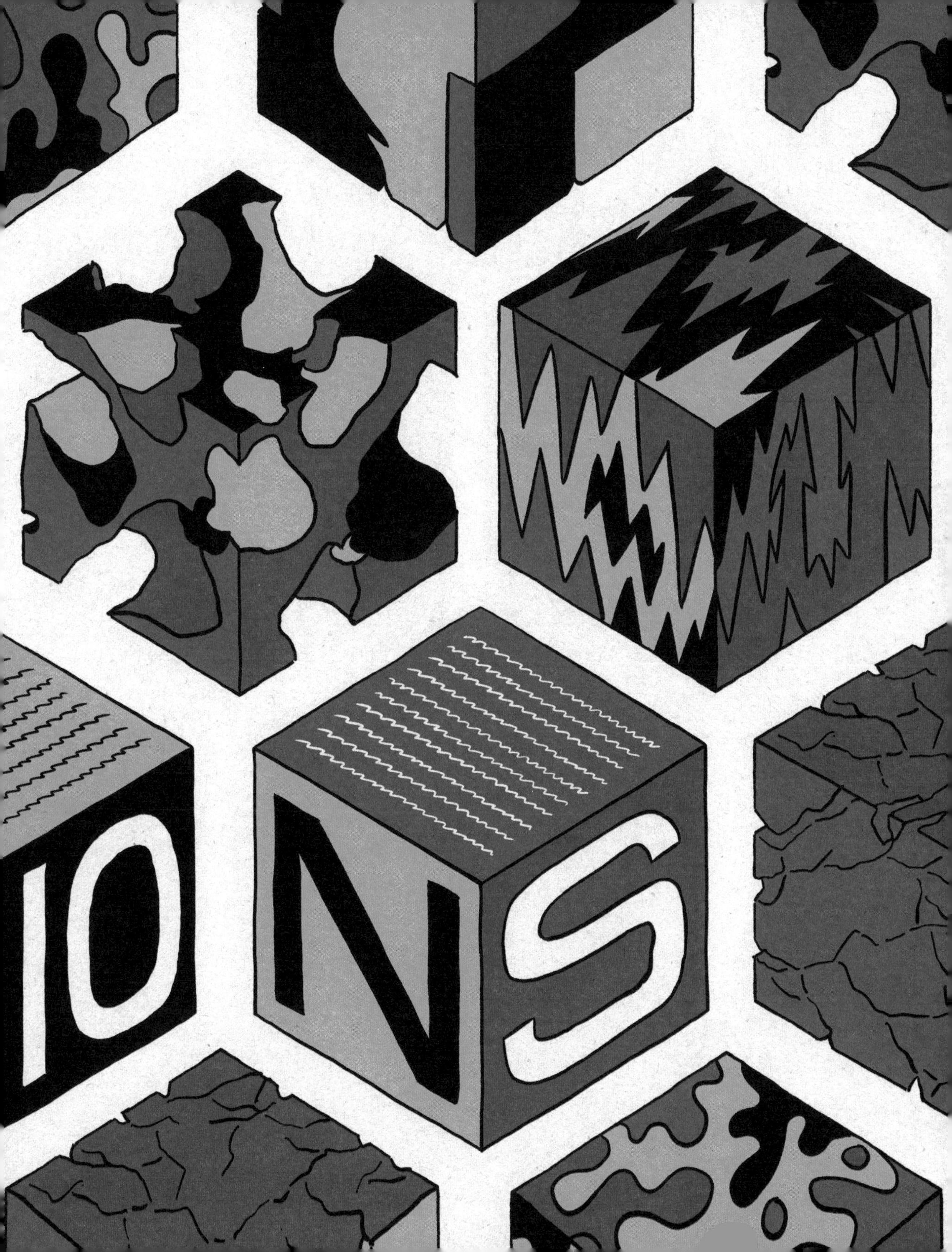
IO
N
S

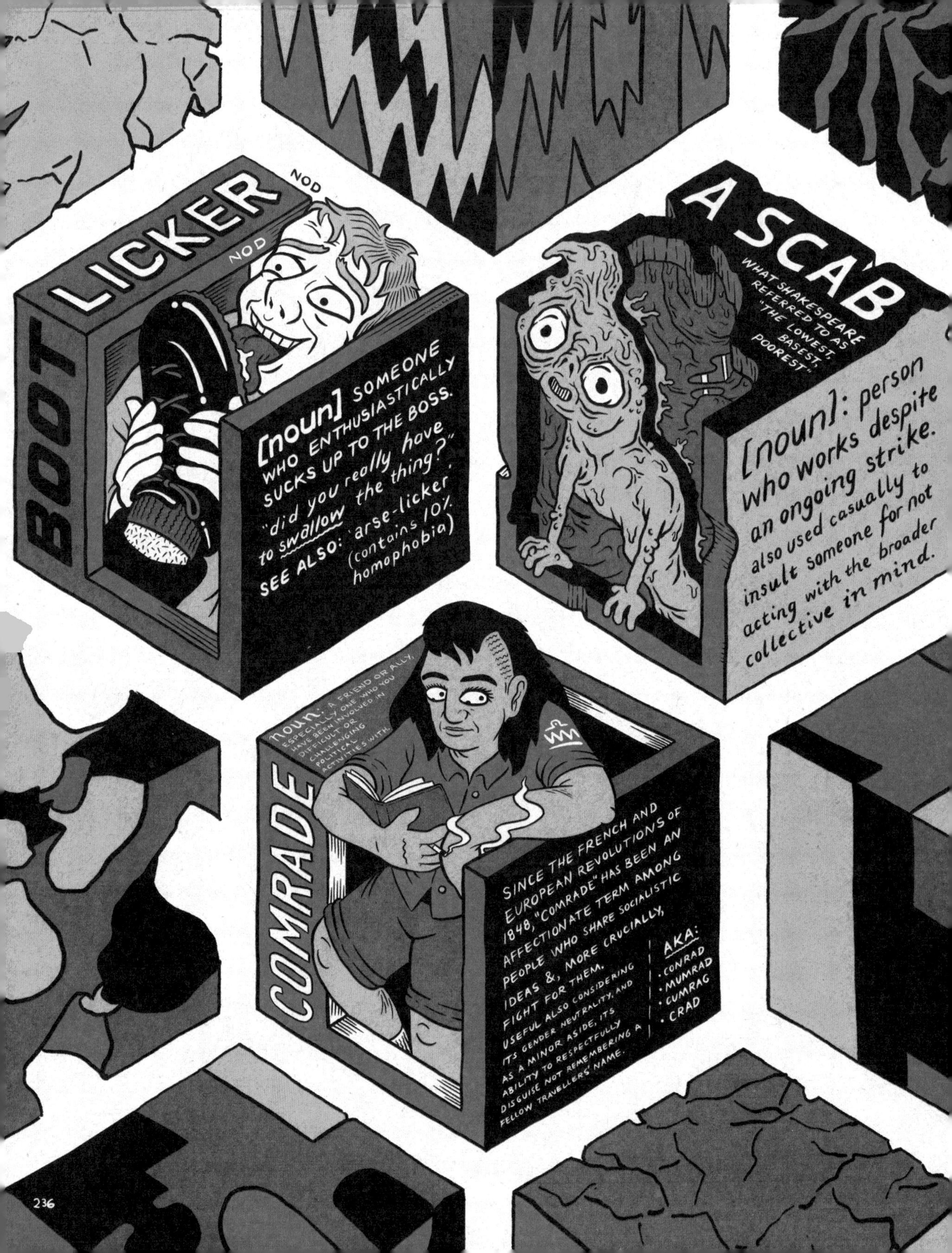
BOOT LICKER
NOD
NOD
[noun] SOMEONE WHO ENTHUSIASTICALLY SUCKS UP TO THE BOSS.
"did you really have to swallow the thing?"
SEE ALSO: 'arse-licker' (contains 10% homophobia)
A SCAB
WHAT SHAKESPEARE REFERRED TO AS "THE LOWEST, BASEST, POOREST".
[noun]: person who works despite an ongoing strike.
also used casually to insult someone for not acting with the broader collective in mind.
COMRADE
noun: A FRIEND OR ALLY, ESPECIALLY ONE WHO YOU HAVE BEEN INVOLVED IN DIFFICULT OR CHALLENGING POLITICAL ACTIVITIES WITH.
SINCE THE FRENCH AND EUROPEAN REVOLUTIONS OF 1848, "COMRADE" HAS BEEN AN AFFECTIONATE TERM AMONG PEOPLE WHO SHARE SOCIALISTIC IDEAS &, MORE CRUCIALLY, FIGHT FOR THEM.
USEFUL ALSO CONSIDERING ITS GENDER NEUTRALITY, AND AS A MINOR ASIDE, ITS ABILITY TO RESPECTFULLY DISGUISE NOT REMEMBERING A FELLOW TRAVELLERS' NAME.
AKA:
· CONRAD
· MUMRAD
· CUMRAG
· CRAD

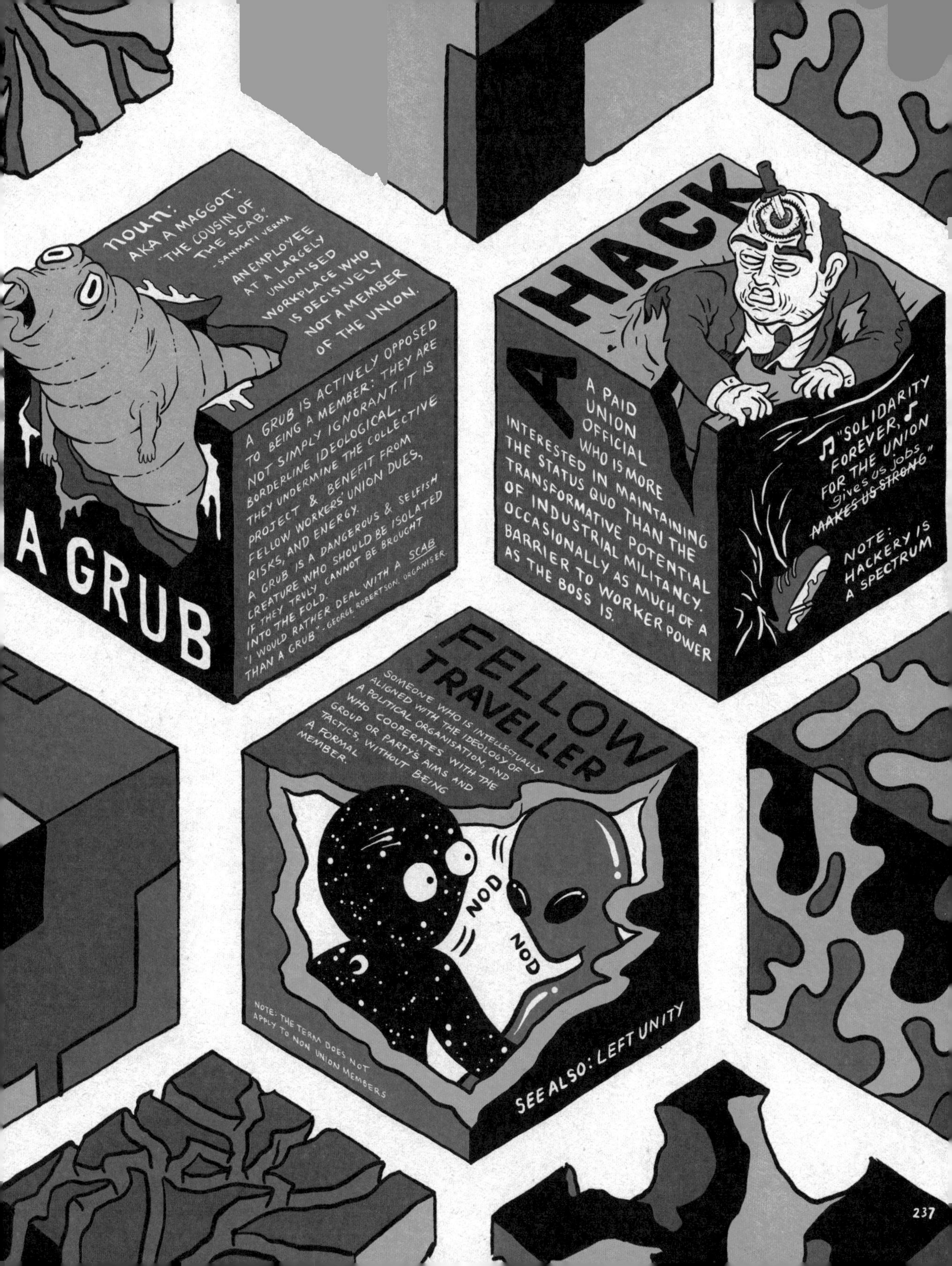

noun:
AKA A MAGGOT.
"THE COUSIN OF THE SCAB."
-SANMATI VERMA
AN EMPLOYEE AT A LARGELY UNIONISED WORKPLACE WHO IS DECISIVELY NOT A MEMBER OF THE UNION.
A GRUB
A GRUB IS ACTIVELY OPPOSED TO BEING A MEMBER: THEY ARE NOT SIMPLY IGNORANT. IT IS BORDERLINE IDEOLOGICAL. THEY UNDERMINE THE COLLECTIVE PROJECT & BENEFIT FROM FELLOW WORKERS' UNION DUES, RISKS, AND ENERGY.
A GRUB IS A DANGEROUS & SELFISH CREATURE WHO SHOULD BE ISOLATED IF THEY TRULY CANNOT BE BROUGHT INTO THE FOLD.
"I WOULD RATHER DEAL WITH A SCAB THAN A GRUB" - GEORGE ROBERTSON, ORGANISER.
A HACK
A PAID UNION OFFICIAL WHO IS MORE INTERESTED IN MAINTAINING THE STATUS QUO THAN THE TRANSFORMATIVE POTENTIAL OF INDUSTRIAL MILITANCY. OCCASIONALLY AS MUCH OF A BARRIER TO WORKER POWER AS THE BOSS IS.
♫ "SOLIDARITY FOREVER, ♪ FOR THE UNION gives us jobs MAKES US STRONG"
NOTE: HACKERY IS A SPECTRUM
FELLOW TRAVELLER
SOMEONE WHO IS INTELLECTUALLY ALIGNED WITH THE IDEOLOGY OF A POLITICAL ORGANISATION, AND WHO COOPERATES WITH THE GROUP OR PARTY'S AIMS AND TACTICS, WITHOUT BEING A FORMAL MEMBER.
NOD
NOD
NOTE: THE TERM DOES NOT APPLY TO NON UNION MEMBERS
SEE ALSO: LEFT UNITY

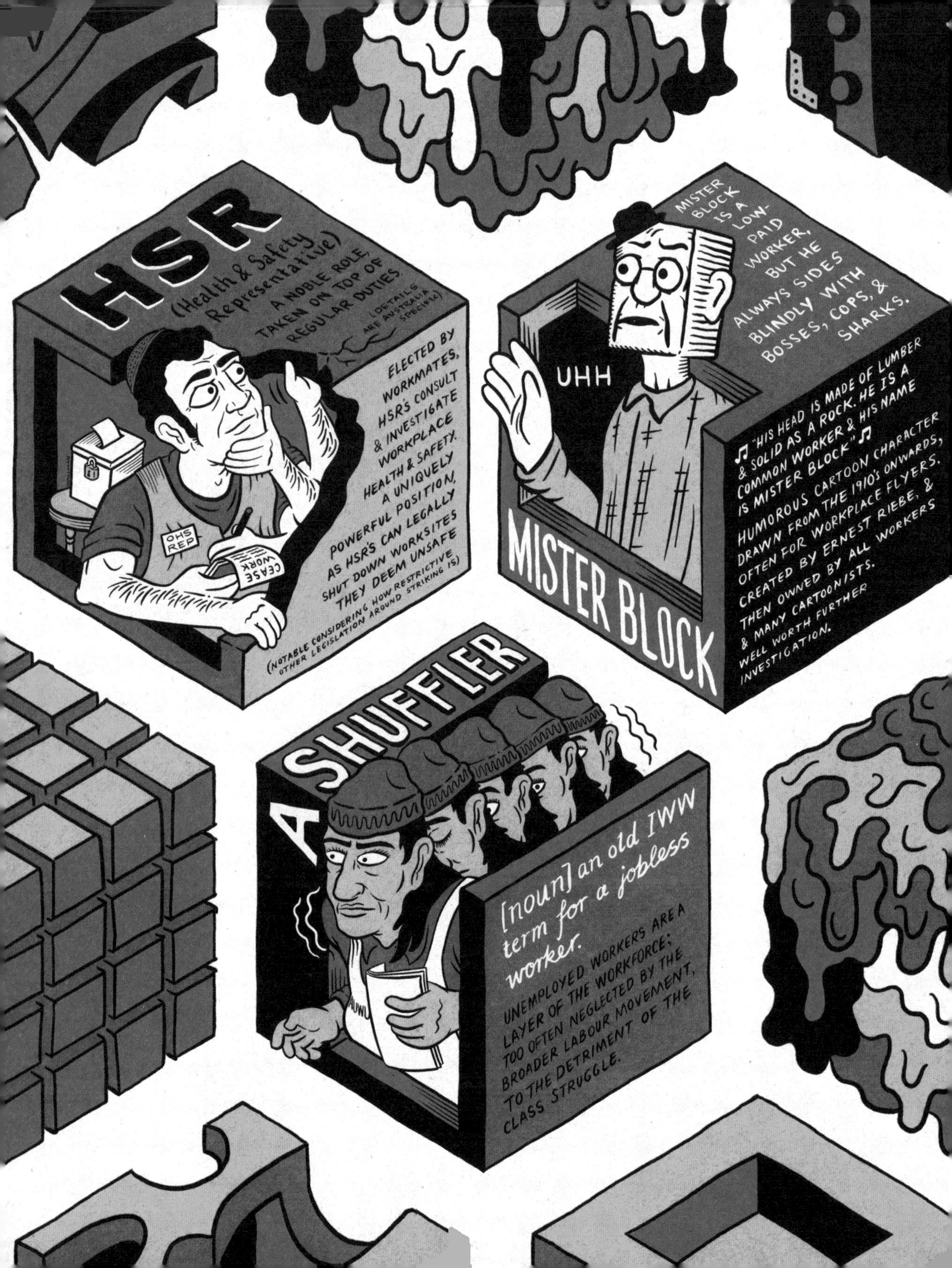

HSR
(Health & Safety Representative)
A NOBLE ROLE, TAKEN ON TOP OF REGULAR DUTIES
(DETAILS ARE AUSTRALIA SPECIFIC)
ELECTED BY WORKMATES, HSR'S CONSULT & INVESTIGATE WORKPLACE HEALTH & SAFETY. A UNIQUELY POWERFUL POSITION, AS HSR'S CAN LEGALLY SHUT DOWN WORKSITES THEY DEEM UNSAFE
(NOTABLE CONSIDERING HOW RESTRICTIVE OTHER LEGISLATION AROUND STRIKING IS)
OHS REP
CEASE WORK
MISTER BLOCK IS A LOW-PAID WORKER, BUT HE ALWAYS SIDES BLINDLY WITH BOSSES, COPS, & SHARKS.
UHH
♫ "HIS HEAD IS MADE OF LUMBER & SOLID AS A ROCK. HE IS A COMMON WORKER & HIS NAME IS MISTER BLOCK" ♫
HUMOROUS CARTOON CHARACTER DRAWN FROM THE 1910'S ONWARDS, OFTEN FOR WORKPLACE FLYERS. CREATED BY ERNEST RIEBE, & THEN OWNED BY ALL WORKERS & MANY CARTOONISTS. WELL WORTH FURTHER INVESTIGATION.
MISTER BLOCK
A SHUFFLER
[noun] an old IWW term for a jobless worker.
UNEMPLOYED WORKERS ARE A LAYER OF THE WORKFORCE; TOO OFTEN NEGLECTED BY THE BROADER LABOUR MOVEMENT, TO THE DETRIMENT OF THE CLASS STRUGGLE.
AUWU

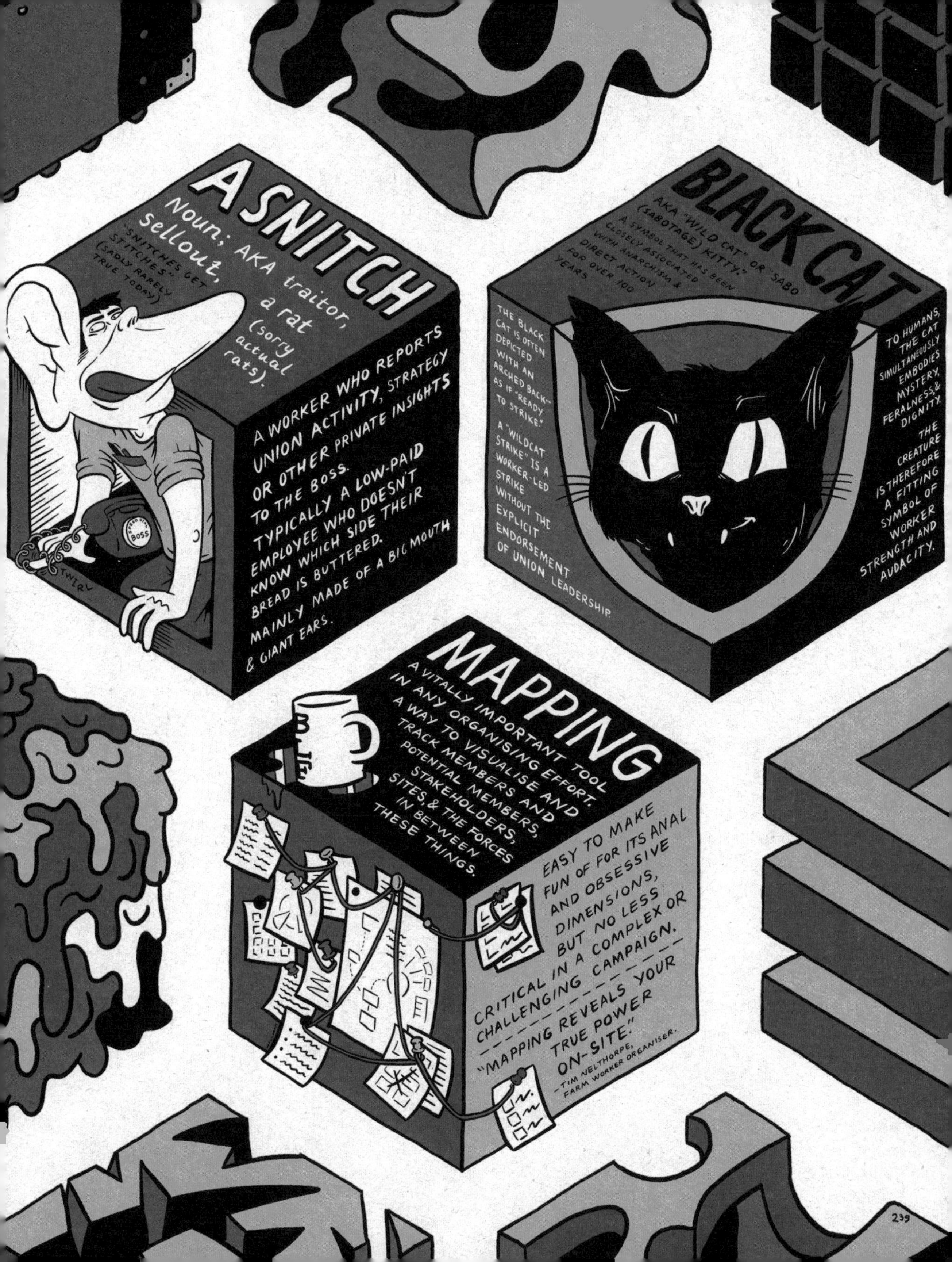
A SNITCH
Noun; AKA traitor, sellout, a rat (sorry actual rats).
"SNITCHES GET STITCHES" (SADLY RARELY TRUE TODAY)
A WORKER WHO REPORTS UNION ACTIVITY, STRATEGY OR OTHER PRIVATE INSIGHTS TO THE BOSS.
TYPICALLY A LOW-PAID EMPLOYEE WHO DOESN'T KNOW WHICH SIDE THEIR BREAD IS BUTTERED.
MAINLY MADE OF A BIG MOUTH & GIANT EARS.
BOSS
TWIRL
BLACK CAT
AKA "WILD CAT" OR "SABO (SABOTAGE) KITTY."
A SYMBOL THAT HAS BEEN CLOSELY ASSOCIATED WITH ANARCHISM & DIRECT ACTION FOR OVER 100 YEARS.
THE BLACK CAT IS OFTEN DEPICTED WITH AN ARCHED BACK— AS IF "READY TO STRIKE."
A "WILDCAT STRIKE" IS A WORKER-LED STRIKE WITHOUT THE EXPLICIT ENDORSEMENT OF UNION LEADERSHIP.
TO HUMANS, THE CAT SIMULTANEOUSLY EMBODIES MYSTERY, FERALNESS, & DIGNITY.
THE CREATURE IS THEREFORE A FITTING SYMBOL OF WORKER STRENGTH AND AUDACITY.
MAPPING
A VITALLY IMPORTANT TOOL IN ANY ORGANISING EFFORT.
A WAY TO VISUALISE AND TRACK MEMBERS AND POTENTIAL MEMBERS, STAKEHOLDERS, SITES, & THE FORCES IN BETWEEN THESE THINGS.
EASY TO MAKE FUN OF FOR ITS ANAL AND OBSESSIVE DIMENSIONS, BUT NO LESS CRITICAL IN A COMPLEX OR CHALLENGING CAMPAIGN.
"MAPPING REVEALS YOUR TRUE POWER ON-SITE."
-TIM NELTHORPE, FARM WORKER ORGANISER.

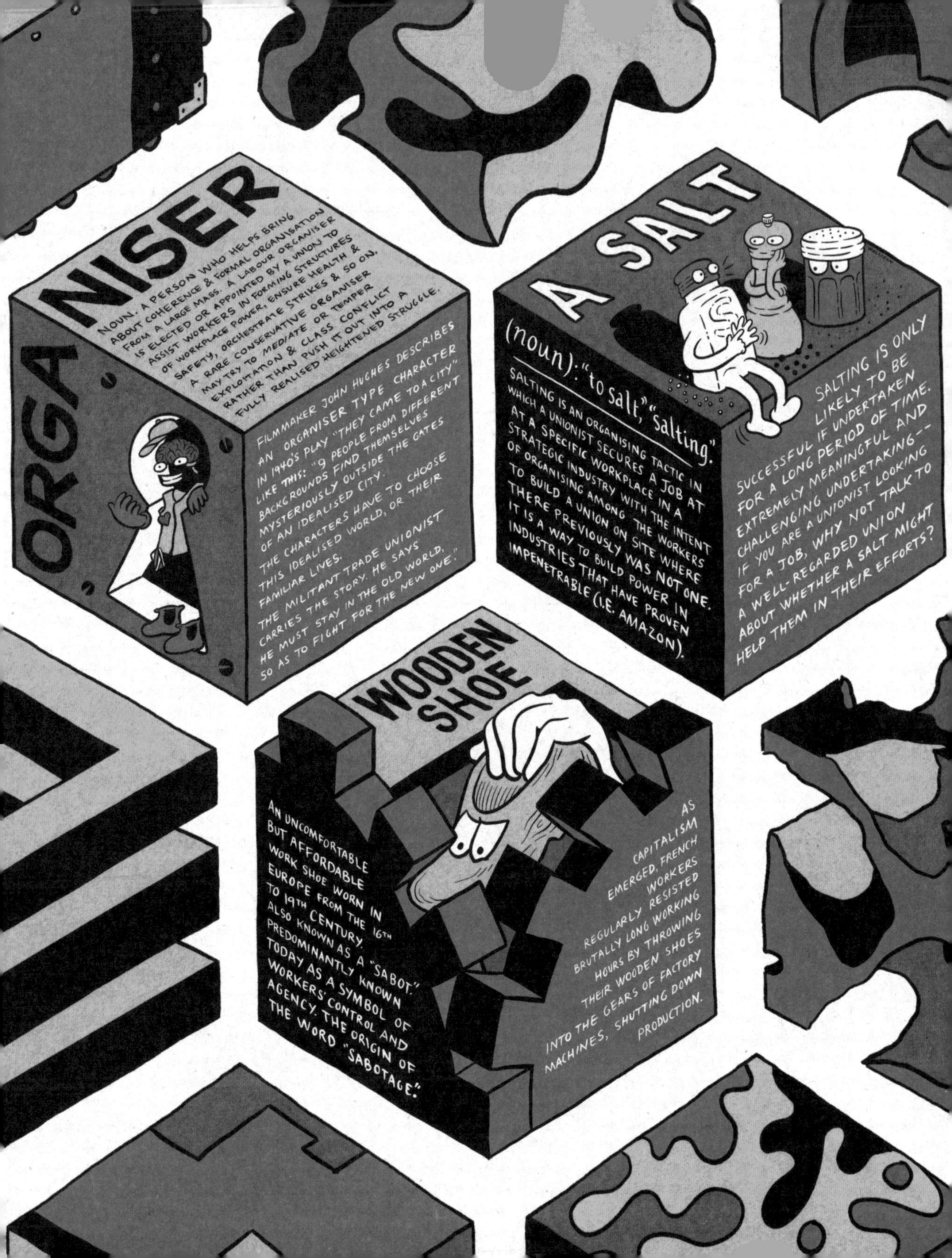
ORGANISER
NOUN. A PERSON WHO HELPS BRING ABOUT COHERENCE & FORMAL ORGANISATION FROM A LARGE MASS. A LABOUR ORGANISER IS ELECTED OR APPOINTED BY A UNION TO ASSIST WORKERS IN FORMING STRUCTURES OF WORKPLACE POWER, ENSURE HEALTH & SAFETY, ORCHESTRATE STRIKES & SO ON. A RARE CONSERVATIVE ORGANISER MAY TRY TO MEDIATE OR TEMPER EXPLOITATION & CLASS CONFLICT RATHER THAN PUSH IT OUT INTO A FULLY REALISED HEIGHTENED STRUGGLE.
FILMMAKER JOHN HUGHES DESCRIBES AN ORGANISER TYPE CHARACTER IN 1940'S PLAY "THEY CAME TO A CITY" LIKE THIS: "9 PEOPLE FROM DIFFERENT BACKGROUNDS FIND THEMSELVES MYSTERIOUSLY OUTSIDE THE GATES OF AN IDEALISED CITY. THE CHARACTERS HAVE TO CHOOSE THIS IDEALISED WORLD, OR THEIR FAMILIAR LIVES. THE MILITANT TRADE UNIONIST CARRIES THE STORY. HE SAYS HE MUST STAY IN THE OLD WORLD, SO AS TO FIGHT FOR THE NEW ONE."
A SALT
(noun): "to salt," "salting."
SALTING IS AN ORGANISING TACTIC IN WHICH A UNIONIST SECURES A JOB AT A SPECIFIC WORKPLACE IN A STRATEGIC INDUSTRY WITH THE INTENT OF ORGANISING AMONG THE WORKERS TO BUILD A UNION ON SITE WHERE THERE PREVIOUSLY WAS NOT ONE. IT IS A WAY TO BUILD POWER IN INDUSTRIES THAT HAVE PROVEN IMPENETRABLE (I.E. AMAZON).
SALTING IS ONLY LIKELY TO BE SUCCESSFUL IF UNDERTAKEN FOR A LONG PERIOD OF TIME. EXTREMELY MEANINGFUL AND CHALLENGING UNDERTAKING-- IF YOU ARE A UNIONIST LOOKING FOR A JOB, WHY NOT TALK TO A WELL-REGARDED UNION ABOUT WHETHER A SALT MIGHT HELP THEM IN THEIR EFFORTS?
WOODEN SHOE
AN UNCOMFORTABLE BUT AFFORDABLE WORK SHOE WORN IN EUROPE FROM THE 16TH TO 19TH CENTURY. ALSO KNOWN AS A "SABOT." PREDOMINANTLY KNOWN TODAY AS A SYMBOL OF WORKERS' CONTROL AND AGENCY. THE ORIGIN OF THE WORD "SABOTAGE."
AS CAPITALISM EMERGED, FRENCH WORKERS REGULARLY RESISTED BRUTALLY LONG WORKING HOURS BY THROWING THEIR WOODEN SHOES INTO THE GEARS OF FACTORY MACHINES, SHUTTING DOWN PRODUCTION.

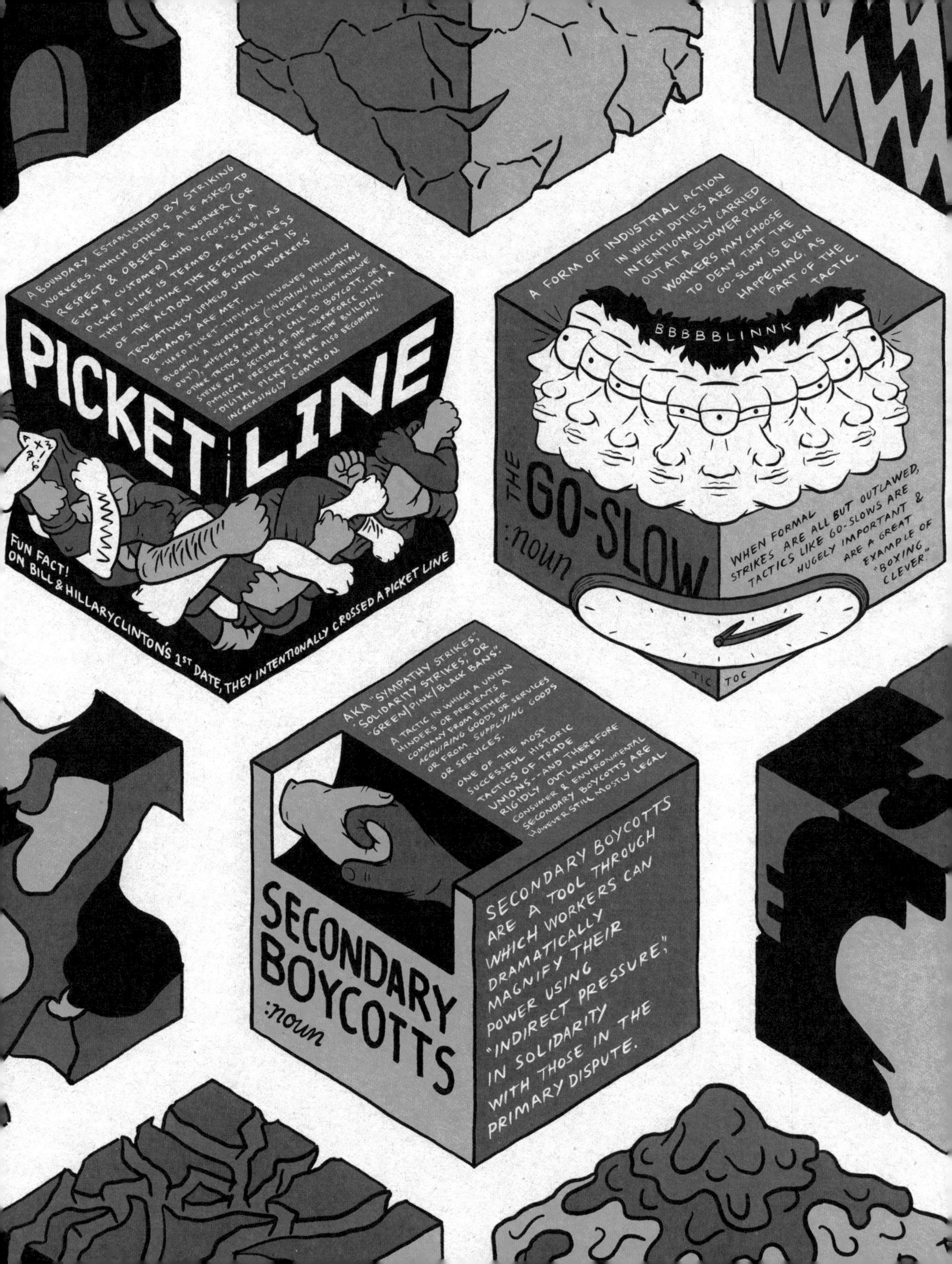
PICKET LINE
A BOUNDARY ESTABLISHED BY STRIKING WORKERS, WHICH OTHERS ARE ASKED TO RESPECT & OBSERVE. A WORKER (OR EVEN A CUSTOMER) WHO "CROSSES" A PICKET LINE IS TERMED A "SCAB," AS THEY UNDERMINE THE EFFECTIVENESS OF THE ACTION. THE BOUNDARY IS TENTATIVELY UPHELD UNTIL WORKERS' DEMANDS ARE MET.
A "HARD PICKET" TYPICALLY INVOLVES PHYSICALLY BLOCKING A WORKPLACE ("NOTHING IN, NOTHING OUT"), WHEREAS A "SOFT PICKET" MIGHT INVOLVE OTHER TACTICS SUCH AS A CALL TO BOYCOTT, OR A STRIKE BY A SECTION OF THE WORKFORCE WITH A PHYSICAL PRESENCE NEAR THE BUILDING. "DIGITAL PICKETS" ARE ALSO BECOMING INCREASINGLY COMMON.
FUN FACT! ON BILL & HILLARY CLINTON'S 1ST DATE, THEY INTENTIONALLY CROSSED A PICKET LINE
A FORM OF INDUSTRIAL ACTION IN WHICH DUTIES ARE INTENTIONALLY CARRIED OUT AT A SLOWER PACE. WORKERS MAY CHOOSE TO DENY THAT THE GO-SLOW IS EVEN HAPPENING, AS PART OF THE TACTIC.
BBBBBLINNK
THE GO-SLOW :noun
WHEN FORMAL STRIKES ARE ALL BUT OUTLAWED, TACTICS LIKE GO-SLOWS ARE HUGELY IMPORTANT & ARE A GREAT EXAMPLE OF "BOXING CLEVER."
TIC TOC
AKA "SYMPATHY STRIKES," "SOLIDARITY STRIKES," OR "GREEN/PINK/BLACK BANS."
A TACTIC IN WHICH A UNION HINDERS OR PREVENTS A COMPANY FROM EITHER ACQUIRING GOODS OR SERVICES OR FROM SUPPLYING GOODS OR SERVICES.
ONE OF THE MOST SUCCESSFUL HISTORIC TACTICS OF TRADE UNIONS--AND THEREFORE RIGIDLY OUTLAWED. CONSUMER & ENVIRONMENTAL SECONDARY BOYCOTTS ARE HOWEVER STILL MOSTLY LEGAL.
SECONDARY BOYCOTTS :noun
SECONDARY BOYCOTTS ARE A TOOL THROUGH WHICH WORKERS CAN DRAMATICALLY MAGNIFY THEIR POWER USING "INDIRECT PRESSURE," IN SOLIDARITY WITH THOSE IN THE PRIMARY DISPUTE.

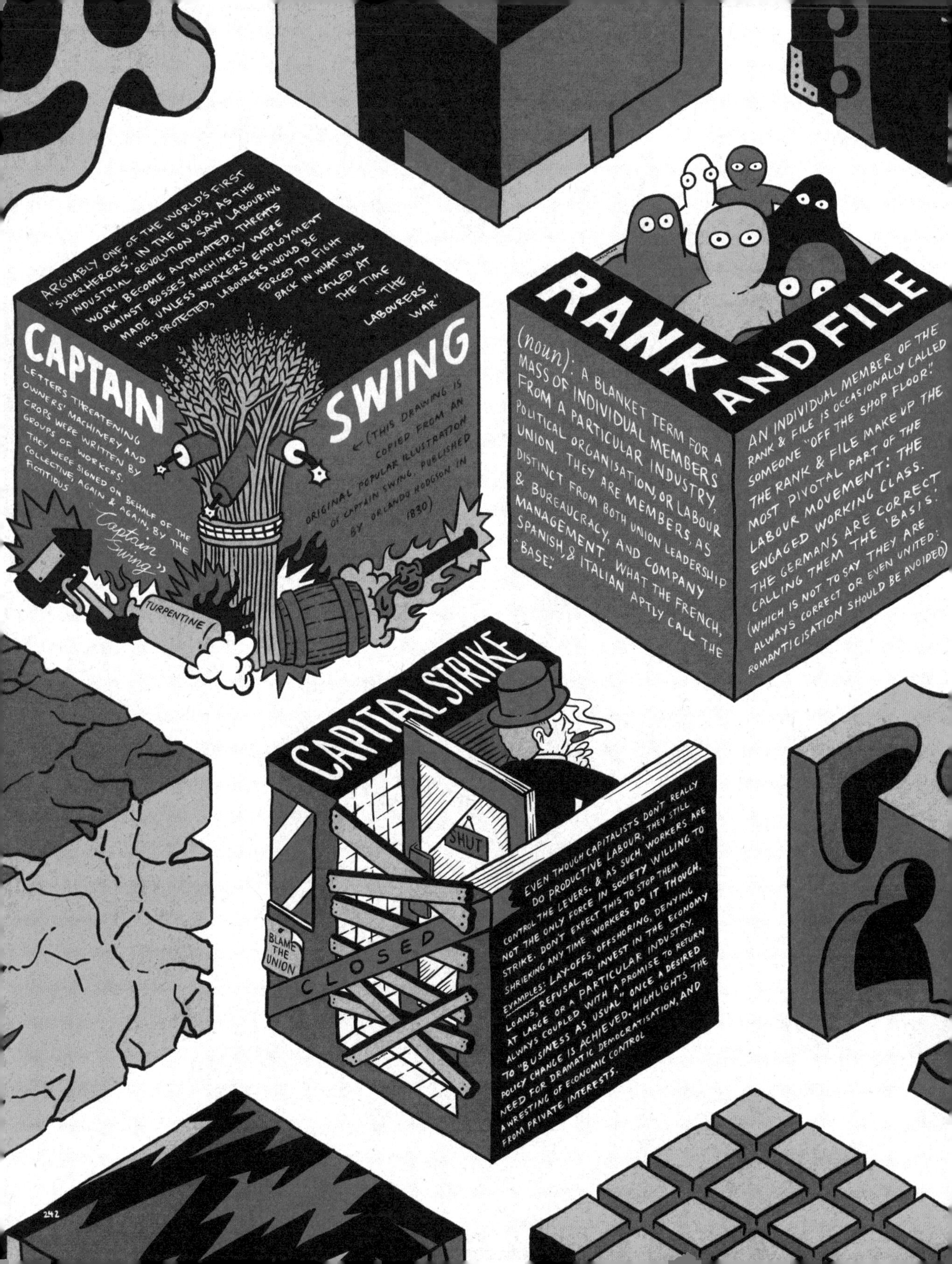

CAPTAIN SWING
ARGUABLY ONE OF THE WORLD'S FIRST "SUPERHEROES". IN THE 1830'S, AS THE INDUSTRIAL REVOLUTION SAW LABOURING WORK BECOME AUTOMATED, THREATS AGAINST BOSSES' MACHINERY WERE MADE. UNLESS WORKERS' EMPLOYMENT WAS PROTECTED, LABOURERS WOULD BE FORCED TO FIGHT BACK IN WHAT WAS CALLED AT THE TIME "THE LABOURERS' WAR".
LETTERS THREATENING OWNERS' MACHINERY AND CROPS WERE WRITTEN BY GROUPS OF WORKERS. THEY WERE SIGNED ON BEHALF OF THE COLLECTIVE, AGAIN & AGAIN, BY THE FICTITIOUS "Captain Swing"
← (THIS DRAWING IS COPIED FROM AN ORIGINAL POPULAR ILLUSTRATION OF CAPTAIN SWING, PUBLISHED BY ORLANDO HODGSON IN 1830)
TURPENTINE
RANK AND FILE
(noun): A BLANKET TERM FOR A MASS OF INDIVIDUAL MEMBERS FROM A PARTICULAR INDUSTRY, POLITICAL ORGANISATION, OR LABOUR UNION. THEY ARE MEMBERS, AS DISTINCT FROM BOTH UNION LEADERSHIP & BUREAUCRACY, AND COMPANY MANAGEMENT. WHAT THE FRENCH, SPANISH, & ITALIAN APTLY CALL THE "BASE".
AN INDIVIDUAL MEMBER OF THE RANK & FILE IS OCCASIONALLY CALLED SOMEONE "OFF THE SHOP FLOOR." THE RANK & FILE MAKE UP THE MOST PIVOTAL PART OF THE LABOUR MOVEMENT: THE ENGAGED WORKING CLASS. THE GERMANS ARE CORRECT CALLING THEM THE 'BASIS.' (WHICH IS NOT TO SAY THEY ARE ALWAYS CORRECT OR EVEN UNITED: ROMANTICISATION SHOULD BE AVOIDED)
CAPITAL STRIKE
SHUT
BLAME THE UNION
CLOSED
EVEN THOUGH CAPITALISTS DON'T REALLY DO PRODUCTIVE LABOUR, THEY STILL CONTROL THE LEVERS. & AS SUCH, WORKERS ARE NOT THE ONLY FORCE IN SOCIETY WILLING TO STRIKE. DON'T EXPECT THIS TO STOP THEM SHRIEKING ANY TIME WORKERS DO IT THOUGH. EXAMPLES: LAY-OFFS, OFFSHORING, DENYING LOANS, REFUSAL TO INVEST IN THE ECONOMY AT LARGE OR A PARTICULAR INDUSTRY. ALWAYS COUPLED WITH A PROMISE TO RETURN TO "BUSINESS AS USUAL" ONCE A DESIRED POLICY CHANGE IS ACHIEVED. HIGHLIGHTS THE NEED FOR DRAMATIC DEMOCRATISATION, AND A WRESTING OF ECONOMIC CONTROL FROM PRIVATE INTERESTS.

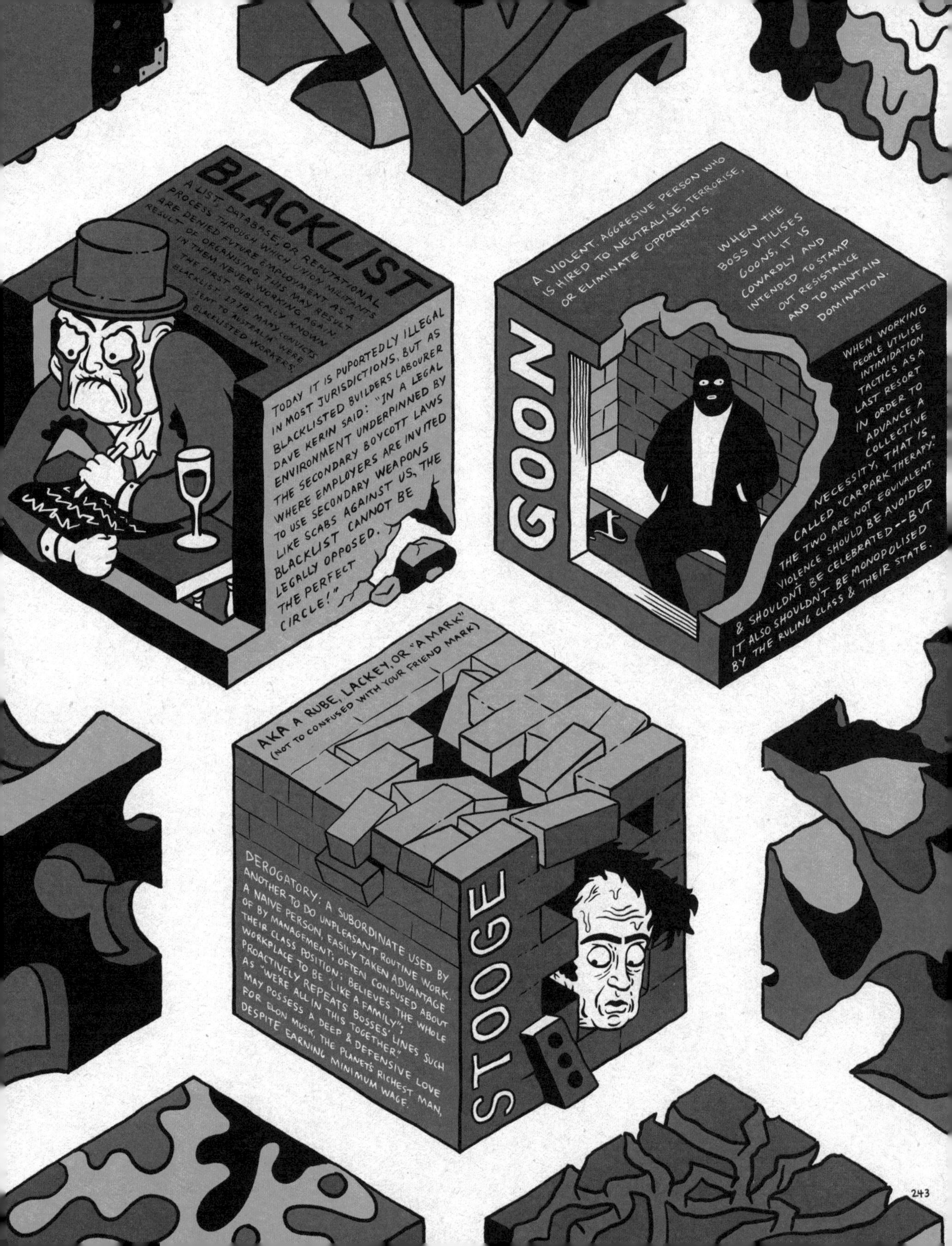
BLACKLIST
A LIST, DATABASE, OR REPUTATIONAL PROCESS THROUGH WHICH UNION MILITANTS ARE DENIED FUTURE EMPLOYMENT AS A RESULT OF ORGANISING. THIS MAY RESULT IN THEM NEVER WORKING AGAIN. THE FIRST PUBLICALLY KNOWN BLACKLIST, 1779. MANY CONVICTS SENT TO "AUSTRALIA" WERE BLACKLISTED WORKERS.
TODAY IT IS PUPORTEDLY ILLEGAL IN MOST JURISDICTIONS, BUT AS BLACKLISTED BUILDERS LABOURER DAVE KERIN SAID: "IN A LEGAL ENVIRONMENT UNDERPINNED BY THE SECONDARY BOYCOTT LAWS WHERE EMPLOYERS ARE INVITED TO USE SECONDARY WEAPONS LIKE SCABS AGAINST US, THE BLACKLIST CANNOT BE LEGALLY OPPOSED. THE PERFECT CIRCLE!"
GOON
A VIOLENT, AGGRESIVE PERSON WHO IS HIRED TO NEUTRALISE, TERRORISE, OR ELIMINATE OPPONENTS.
WHEN THE BOSS UTILISES GOONS, IT IS COWARDLY AND INTENDED TO STAMP OUT RESISTANCE AND TO MAINTAIN DOMINATION.
WHEN WORKING PEOPLE UTILISE INTIMIDATION TACTICS AS A LAST RESORT IN ORDER TO ADVANCE A COLLECTIVE NECESSITY, THAT IS CALLED "CARPARK THERAPY." THE TWO ARE NOT EQUIVALENT. VIOLENCE SHOULD BE AVOIDED & SHOULDN'T BE CELEBRATED--BUT IT ALSO SHOULDN'T BE MONOPOLISED BY THE RULING CLASS & THEIR STATE.
AKA A RUBE, LACKEY, OR "A MARK" (NOT TO CONFUSED WITH YOUR FRIEND MARK)
STOOGE
DEROGATORY: A SUBORDINATE USED BY ANOTHER TO DO UNPLEASANT ROUTINE WORK. A NAIVE PERSON, EASILY TAKEN ADVANTAGE OF BY MANAGEMENT; OFTEN CONFUSED ABOUT THEIR CLASS POSITION; BELIEVES THE WHOLE WORKPLACE TO BE "LIKE A FAMILY"; PROACTIVELY REPEATS BOSSES' LINES SUCH AS "WE'RE ALL IN THIS TOGETHER." MAY POSSESS A DEEP & DEFENSIVE LOVE FOR ELON MUSK, THE PLANET'S RICHEST MAN, DESPITE EARNING MINIMUM WAGE.

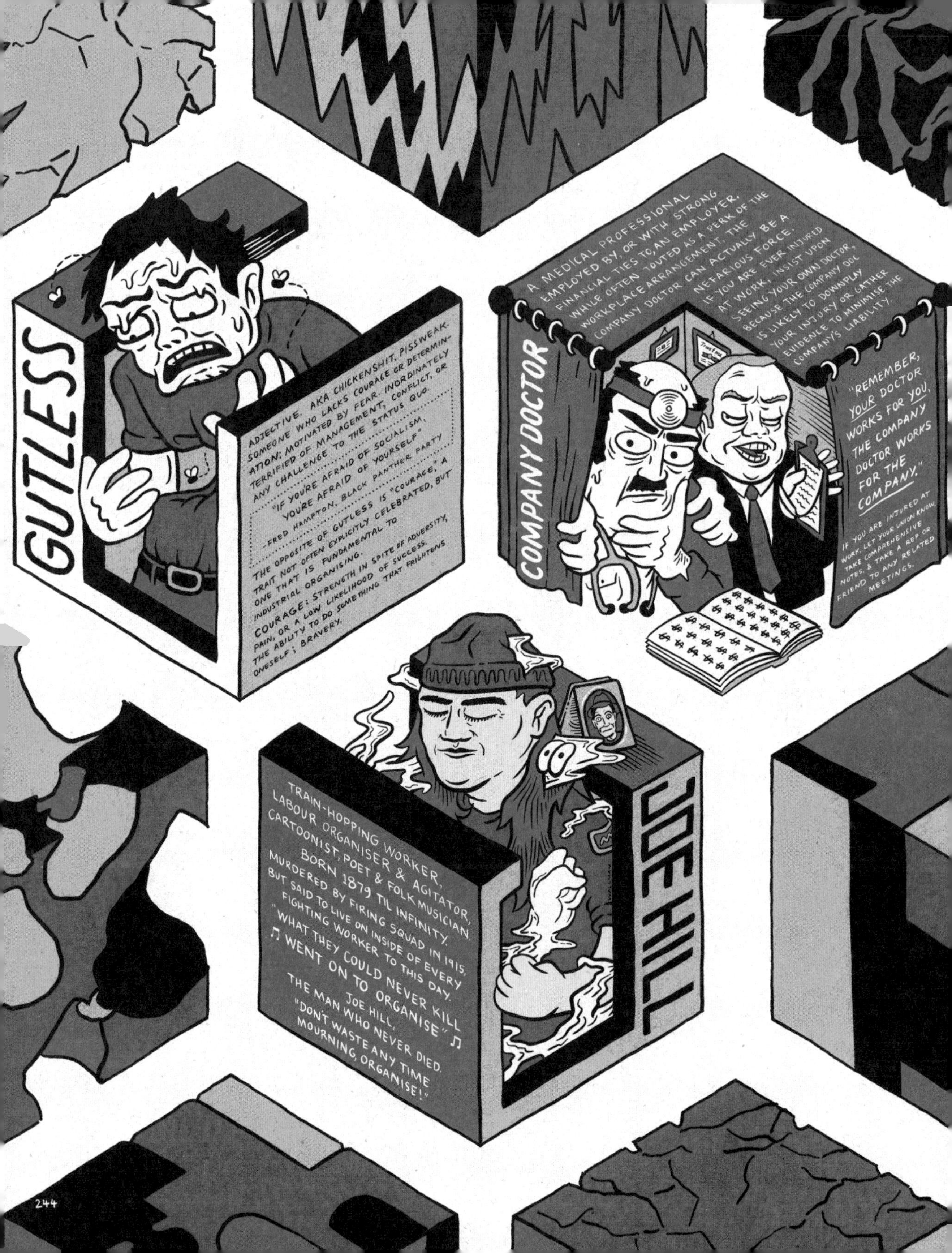

GUTLESS
ADJECTIVE. AKA CHICKENSHIT, PISSWEAK. SOMEONE WHO LACKS COURAGE OR DETERMINATION: MOTIVATED BY FEAR. INORDINATELY TERRIFIED OF MANAGEMENT, CONFLICT, OR ANY CHALLENGE TO THE STATUS QUO.
"IF YOU'RE AFRAID OF SOCIALISM, YOU'RE AFRAID OF YOURSELF"
-FRED HAMPTON, BLACK PANTHER PARTY
THE OPPOSITE OF GUTLESS IS "COURAGE," A TRAIT NOT OFTEN EXPLICITLY CELEBRATED, BUT ONE THAT IS FUNDAMENTAL TO INDUSTRIAL ORGANISING.
COURAGE: STRENGTH IN SPITE OF ADVERSITY, PAIN, OR A LOW LIKELIHOOD OF SUCCESS. THE ABILITY TO DO SOMETHING THAT FRIGHTENS ONESELF; BRAVERY.
COMPANY DOCTOR
A MEDICAL PROFESSIONAL EMPLOYED BY, OR WITH STRONG FINANCIAL TIES TO, AN EMPLOYER. WHILE OFTEN TOUTED AS A PERK OF THE WORKPLACE ARRANGEMENT, THE COMPANY DOCTOR CAN ACTUALLY BE A NEFARIOUS FORCE.
IF YOU ARE EVER INJURED AT WORK, INSIST UPON SEEING YOUR OWN DOCTOR, BECAUSE THE COMPANY DOC IS LIKELY TO DOWNPLAY YOUR INJURY OR GATHER EVIDENCE TO MINIMISE THE COMPANY'S LIABILITY.
Trust me
"REMEMBER, YOUR DOCTOR WORKS FOR YOU, THE COMPANY DOCTOR WORKS FOR THE COMPANY."
IF YOU ARE INJURED AT WORK, LET YOUR UNION KNOW, TAKE COMPREHENSIVE NOTES, & TAKE A REP OR FRIEND TO ANY RELATED MEETINGS.
JOE HILL
TRAIN-HOPPING WORKER, LABOUR ORGANISER & AGITATOR, CARTOONIST, POET & FOLK MUSICIAN. BORN 1879 TIL INFINITY. MURDERED BY FIRING SQUAD IN 1915, BUT SAID TO LIVE ON INSIDE OF EVERY FIGHTING WORKER TO THIS DAY.
"WHAT THEY COULD NEVER KILL WENT ON TO ORGANISE" ♫
JOE HILL, THE MAN WHO NEVER DIED.
"DON'T WASTE ANY TIME MOURNING, ORGANISE!"

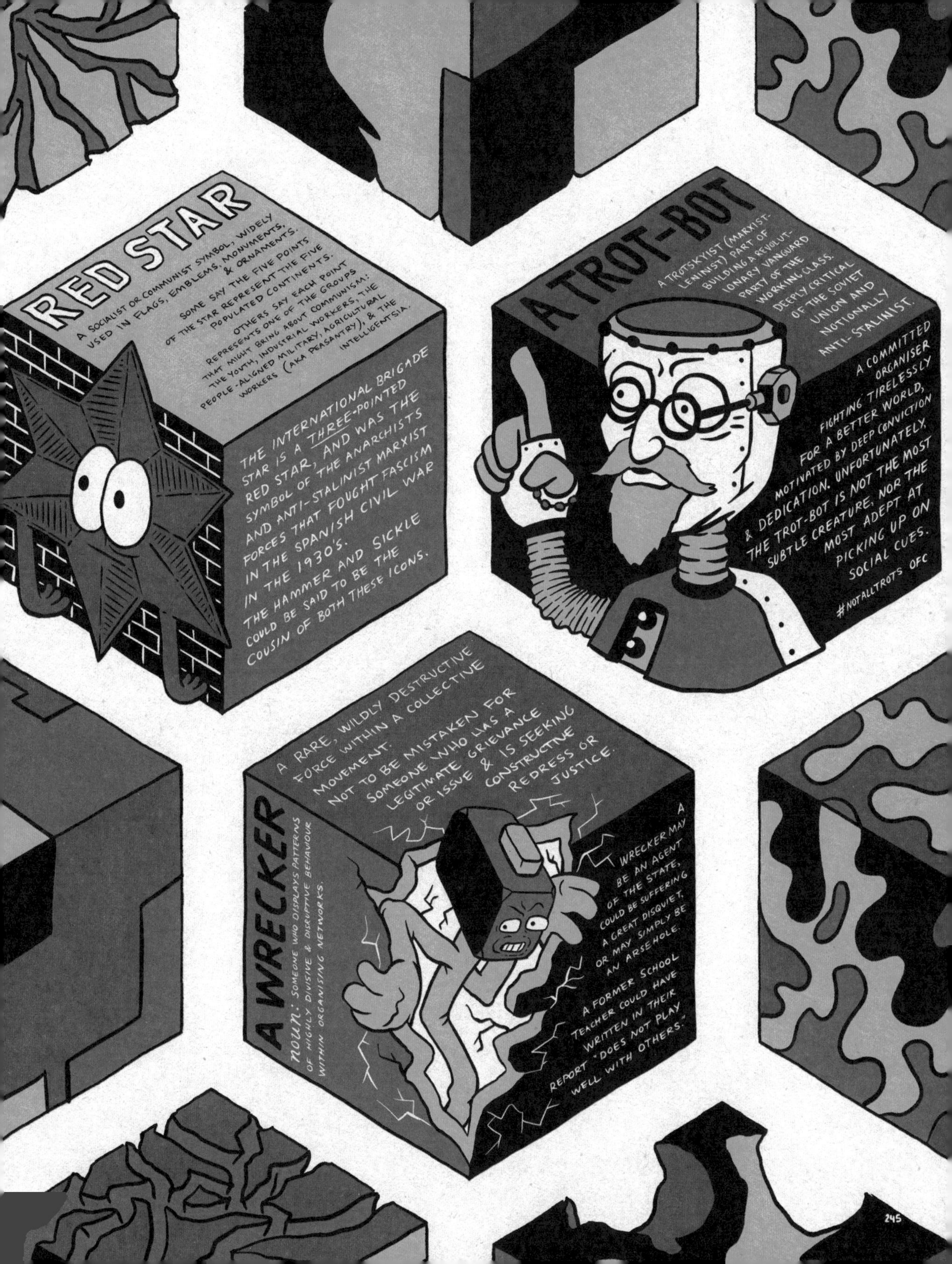
RED STAR
A SOCIALIST OR COMMUNIST SYMBOL, WIDELY USED IN FLAGS, EMBLEMS, MONUMENTS, & ORNAMENTS.
SOME SAY THE FIVE POINTS OF THE STAR REPRESENT THE FIVE POPULATED CONTINENTS.
OTHERS SAY EACH POINT REPRESENTS ONE OF THE GROUPS THAT MIGHT BRING ABOUT COMMUNISM: THE YOUTH, INDUSTRIAL WORKERS, THE PEOPLE-ALIGNED MILITARY, AGRICULTURAL WORKERS (AKA PEASANTRY), & THE INTELLIGENTSIA.
THE INTERNATIONAL BRIGADE STAR IS A THREE-POINTED RED STAR, AND WAS THE SYMBOL OF THE ANARCHISTS AND ANTI-STALINIST MARXIST FORCES THAT FOUGHT FASCISM IN THE SPANISH CIVIL WAR IN THE 1930'S.
THE HAMMER AND SICKLE COULD BE SAID TO BE THE COUSIN OF BOTH THESE ICONS.
A TROT-BOT
A TROTSKYIST (MARXIST-LENINIST) PART OF BUILDING A REVOLUT-IONARY VANGUARD PARTY OF THE WORKING CLASS. DEEPLY CRITICAL OF THE SOVIET UNION AND NOTIONALLY ANTI-STALINIST.
A COMMITTED ORGANISER FIGHTING TIRELESSLY FOR A BETTER WORLD, MOTIVATED BY DEEP CONVICTION & DEDICATION. UNFORTUNATELY, THE TROT-BOT IS NOT THE MOST SUBTLE CREATURE, NOR THE MOST ADEPT AT PICKING UP ON SOCIAL CUES.
#NOTALLTROTS OFC
A WRECKER
noun: SOMEONE WHO DISPLAYS PATTERNS OF HIGHLY DIVISIVE & DISRUPTIVE BEHAVIOUR WITHIN ORGANISING NETWORKS.
A RARE, WILDLY DESTRUCTIVE FORCE WITHIN A COLLECTIVE MOVEMENT.
NOT TO BE MISTAKEN FOR SOMEONE WHO HAS A LEGITIMATE GRIEVANCE OR ISSUE & IS SEEKING CONSTRUCTIVE REDRESS OR JUSTICE.
A WRECKER MAY BE AN AGENT OF THE STATE, COULD BE SUFFERING A GREAT DISQUIET, OR MAY SIMPLY BE AN ARSEHOLE.
A FORMER SCHOOL TEACHER COULD HAVE WRITTEN IN THEIR REPORT "DOES NOT PLAY WELL WITH OTHERS."

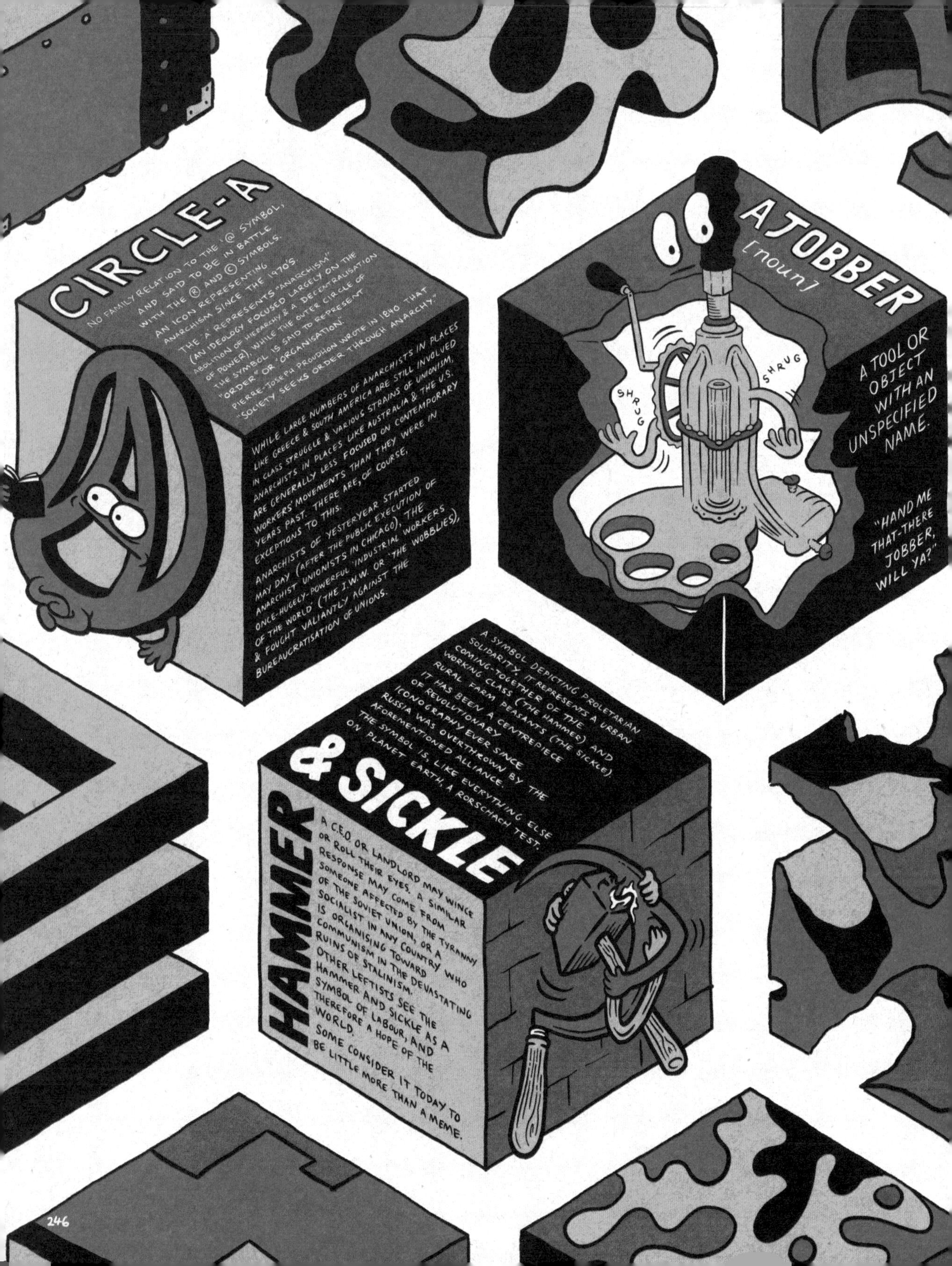
CIRCLE-A
NO FAMILY RELATION TO THE '@' SYMBOL, AND SAID TO BE IN BATTLE WITH THE ® AND © SYMBOLS.
AN ICON REPRESENTING ANARCHISM SINCE THE 1970'S.
THE 'A' REPRESENTS "ANARCHISM" (AN IDEOLOGY FOCUSED LARGELY ON THE ABOLITION OF HIERARCHY & A DECENTRALISATION OF POWER), WHILE THE OUTER CIRCLE OF THE SYMBOL IS SAID TO REPRESENT "ORDER" OR 'ORGANISATION.'
PIERRE-JOSEPH PROUDHON WROTE IN 1840 THAT "SOCIETY SEEKS ORDER THROUGH ANARCHY."
WHILE LARGE NUMBERS OF ANARCHISTS IN PLACES LIKE GREECE & SOUTH AMERICA ARE STILL INVOLVED IN CLASS STRUGGLE & VARIOUS STRAINS OF UNIONISM, ANARCHISTS IN PLACES LIKE AUSTRALIA & THE U.S. ARE GENERALLY LESS FOCUSED ON CONTEMPORARY WORKERS' MOVEMENTS THAN THEY WERE IN YEARS PAST. THERE ARE, OF COURSE, EXCEPTIONS TO THIS.
ANARCHISTS OF YESTERYEAR STARTED MAY DAY (AFTER THE PUBLIC EXECUTION OF ANARCHIST UNIONISTS IN CHICAGO), THE ONCE-HUGELY-POWERFUL 'INDUSTRIAL WORKERS OF THE WORLD' (THE I.W.W. OR 'THE WOBBLIES'), & FOUGHT VALIANTLY AGAINST THE BUREAUCRATISATION OF UNIONS.
AJOBBER
[noun]
A TOOL OR OBJECT WITH AN UNSPECIFIED NAME.
"HAND ME THAT-THERE JOBBER, WILL YA?"
SHRUG
SHRUG
HAMMER & SICKLE
A SYMBOL DEPICTING PROLETARIAN SOLIDARITY. IT REPRESENTS A URBAN COMING-TOGETHER OF THE WORKING CLASS (THE HAMMER) AND RURAL FARM PEASANTS (THE SICKLE).
IT HAS BEEN A CENTREPIECE OF REVOLUTIONARY ICONOGRAPHY EVER SINCE RUSSIA WAS OVERTHROWN BY THE AFOREMENTIONED ALLIANCE.
THE SYMBOL IS, LIKE EVERYTHING ELSE ON PLANET EARTH, A RORSCHACH TEST.
A C.E.O. OR LANDLORD MAY WINCE OR ROLL THEIR EYES. A SIMILAR RESPONSE MAY COME FROM SOMEONE AFFECTED BY THE TYRANNY OF THE SOVIET UNION, OR A SOCIALIST IN ANY COUNTRY WHO IS ORGANISING TOWARD COMMUNISM IN THE DEVASTATING RUINS OF STALINISM.
OTHER LEFTISTS SEE THE HAMMER AND SICKLE AS A SYMBOL OF LABOUR, AND THEREFORE A HOPE OF THE WORLD.
SOME CONSIDER IT TODAY TO BE LITTLE MORE THAN A MEME.

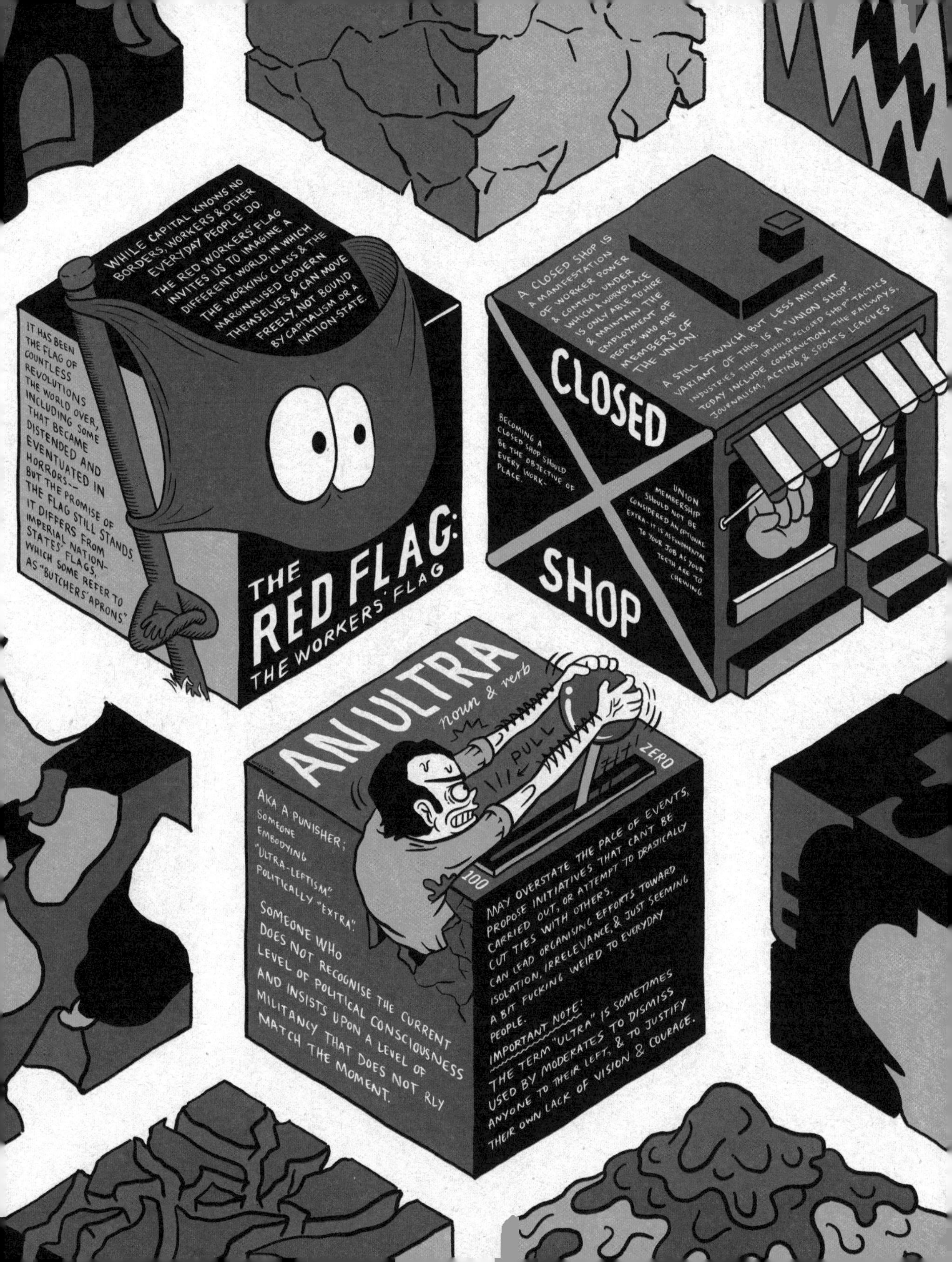
WHILE CAPITAL KNOWS NO BORDERS, WORKERS & OTHER EVERYDAY PEOPLE DO. THE RED WORKERS' FLAG INVITES US TO IMAGINE A DIFFERENT WORLD, IN WHICH THE WORKING CLASS & THE MARGINALISED GOVERN THEMSELVES & CAN MOVE FREELY, NOT BOUND BY CAPITALISM OR A NATION-STATE.
IT HAS BEEN THE FLAG OF COUNTLESS REVOLUTIONS THE WORLD OVER, INCLUDING SOME THAT BECAME DISTENDED AND EVENTUATED IN HORRORS-- BUT THE PROMISE OF THE FLAG STILL STANDS. IT DIFFERS FROM IMPERIAL NATION-STATES' FLAGS, WHICH SOME REFER TO AS "BUTCHERS' APRONS".
THE RED FLAG:
THE WORKERS' FLAG
A CLOSED SHOP IS A MANIFESTATION OF WORKER POWER & CONTROL UNDER WHICH A WORKPLACE IS ONLY ABLE TO HIRE & MAINTAIN THE EMPLOYMENT OF PEOPLE WHO ARE MEMBERS OF THE UNION.
A STILL STAUNCH BUT LESS MILITANT VARIANT OF THIS IS A "UNION SHOP". INDUSTRIES THAT UPHOLD "CLOSED SHOP" TACTICS TODAY INCLUDE CONSTRUCTION, THE RAILWAYS, JOURNALISM, ACTING, & SPORTS LEAGUES.
CLOSED
SHOP
BECOMING A CLOSED SHOP SHOULD BE THE OBJECTIVE OF EVERY WORK-PLACE.
UNION MEMBERSHIP SHOULD NOT BE CONSIDERED AN OPTIONAL EXTRA- IT IS AS FUNDMENTAL TO YOUR JOB AS YOUR TEETH ARE TO CHEWING.
AN ULTRA
noun & verb
PULL
ZERO
100
AKA A PUNISHER; SOMEONE EMBODYING "ULTRA-LEFTISM". POLITICALLY "EXTRA".
SOMEONE WHO DOES NOT RECOGNISE THE CURRENT LEVEL OF POLITICAL CONSCIOUSNESS AND INSISTS UPON A LEVEL OF MILITANCY THAT DOES NOT RLY MATCH THE MOMENT.
MAY OVERSTATE THE PACE OF EVENTS, PROPOSE INITIATIVES THAT CAN'T BE CARRIED OUT, OR ATTEMPT TO DRASTICALLY CUT TIES WITH OTHERS. CAN LEAD ORGANISING EFFORTS TOWARD ISOLATION, IRRELEVANCE, & JUST SEEMING A BIT FUCKING WEIRD TO EVERYDAY PEOPLE.
IMPORTANT NOTE: THE TERM "ULTRA" IS SOMETIMES USED BY MODERATES TO DISMISS ANYONE TO THEIR LEFT, & TO JUSTIFY THEIR OWN LACK OF VISION & COURAGE.

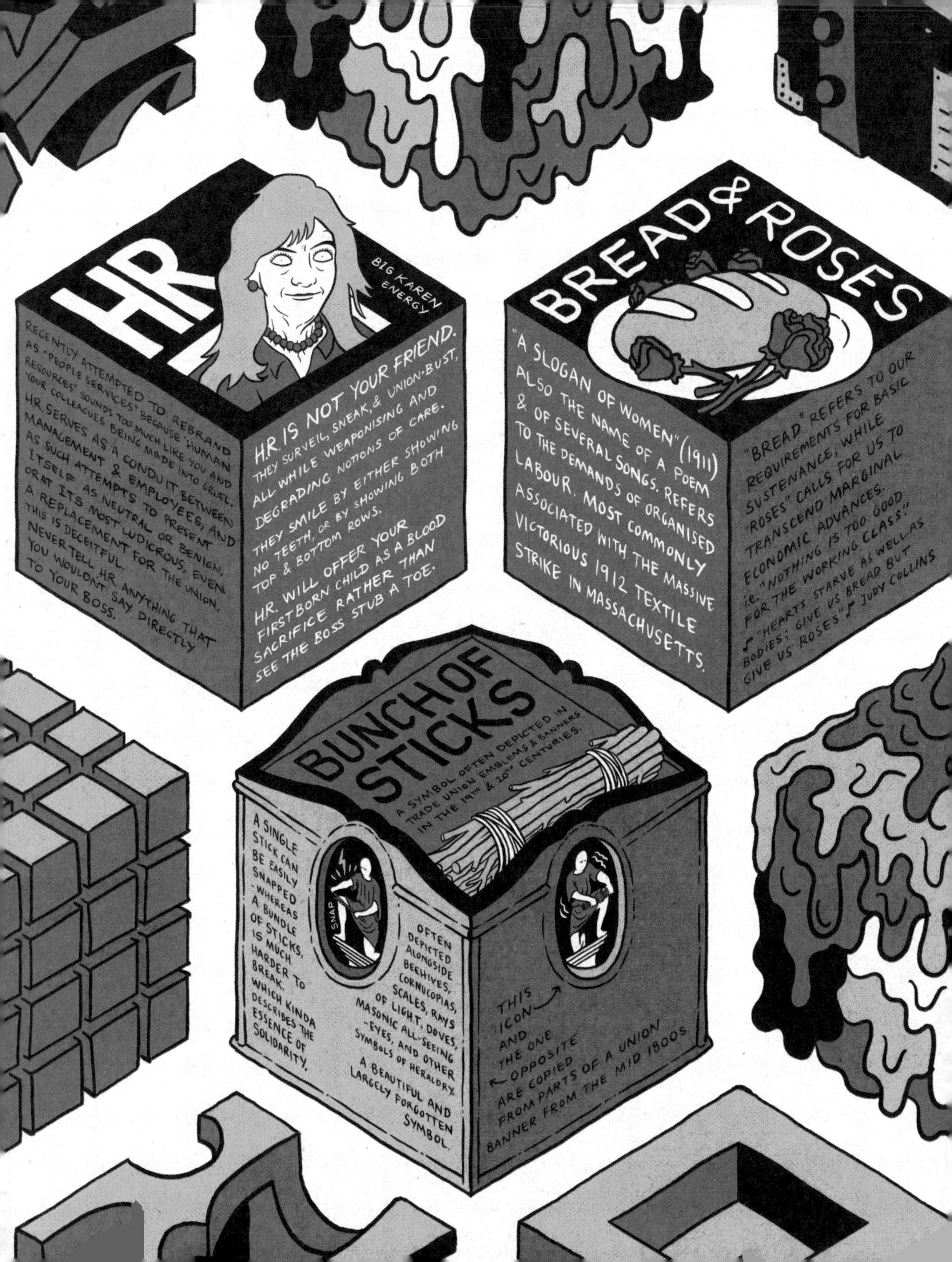

HR
BIG KAREN ENERGY
RECENTLY ATTEMPTED TO REBRAND AS "PEOPLE SERVICES" BECAUSE "HUMAN RESOURCES" SOUNDS TOO MUCH LIKE YOU AND YOUR COLLEAGUES BEING MADE INTO GRUEL. HR SERVES AS A CONDUIT BETWEEN MANAGEMENT & EMPLOYEES, AND AS SUCH ATTEMPTS TO PRESENT ITSELF AS NEUTRAL OR BENIGN, OR AT ITS MOST LUDICROUS, EVEN A REPLACEMENT FOR THE UNION. THIS IS DECEITFUL. NEVER TELL H.R. ANYTHING THAT YOU WOULDN'T SAY DIRECTLY TO YOUR BOSS.
H.R. IS NOT YOUR FRIEND. THEY SURVEIL, SNEAK, & UNION-BUST, ALL WHILE WEAPONISING AND DEGRADING NOTIONS OF CARE.
THEY SMILE BY EITHER SHOWING NO TEETH, OR BY SHOWING BOTH TOP & BOTTOM ROWS.
H.R. WILL OFFER YOUR FIRSTBORN CHILD AS A BLOOD SACRIFICE RATHER THAN SEE THE BOSS STUB A TOE.
BREAD & ROSES
"A SLOGAN OF WOMEN" (1911) ALSO THE NAME OF A POEM & OF SEVERAL SONGS. REFERS TO THE DEMANDS OF ORGANISED LABOUR. MOST COMMONLY ASSOCIATED WITH THE MASSIVE VICTORIOUS 1912 TEXTILE STRIKE IN MASSACHUSETTS.
"BREAD" REFERS TO OUR REQUIREMENTS FOR BASIC SUSTENANCE, WHILE "ROSES" CALLS FOR US TO TRANSCEND MARGINAL ECONOMIC ADVANCES. i.e. "NOTHING IS TOO GOOD FOR THE WORKING CLASS!"
♪ "HEARTS STARVE AS WELL AS BODIES; GIVE US BREAD BUT GIVE US ROSES" ♪ JUDY COLLINS
BUNCH OF STICKS
A SYMBOL OFTEN DEPICTED IN TRADE UNION EMBLEMS & BANNERS IN THE 19TH & 20TH CENTURIES.
A SINGLE STICK CAN BE EASILY SNAPPED -WHEREAS A BUNDLE OF STICKS, IS MUCH HARDER TO BREAK. WHICH KINDA DESCRIBES THE ESSENCE OF SOLIDARITY.
SNAP
OFTEN DEPICTED ALONGSIDE BEEHIVES, CORNUCOPIAS, SCALES, RAYS OF LIGHT, DOVES, MASONIC ALL-SEEING -EYES, AND OTHER SYMBOLS OF HERALDRY.
A BEAUTIFUL AND LARGELY FORGOTTEN SYMBOL.
THIS ICON AND THE ONE OPPOSITE ARE COPIED FROM PARTS OF A UNION BANNER FROM THE MID 1800S.

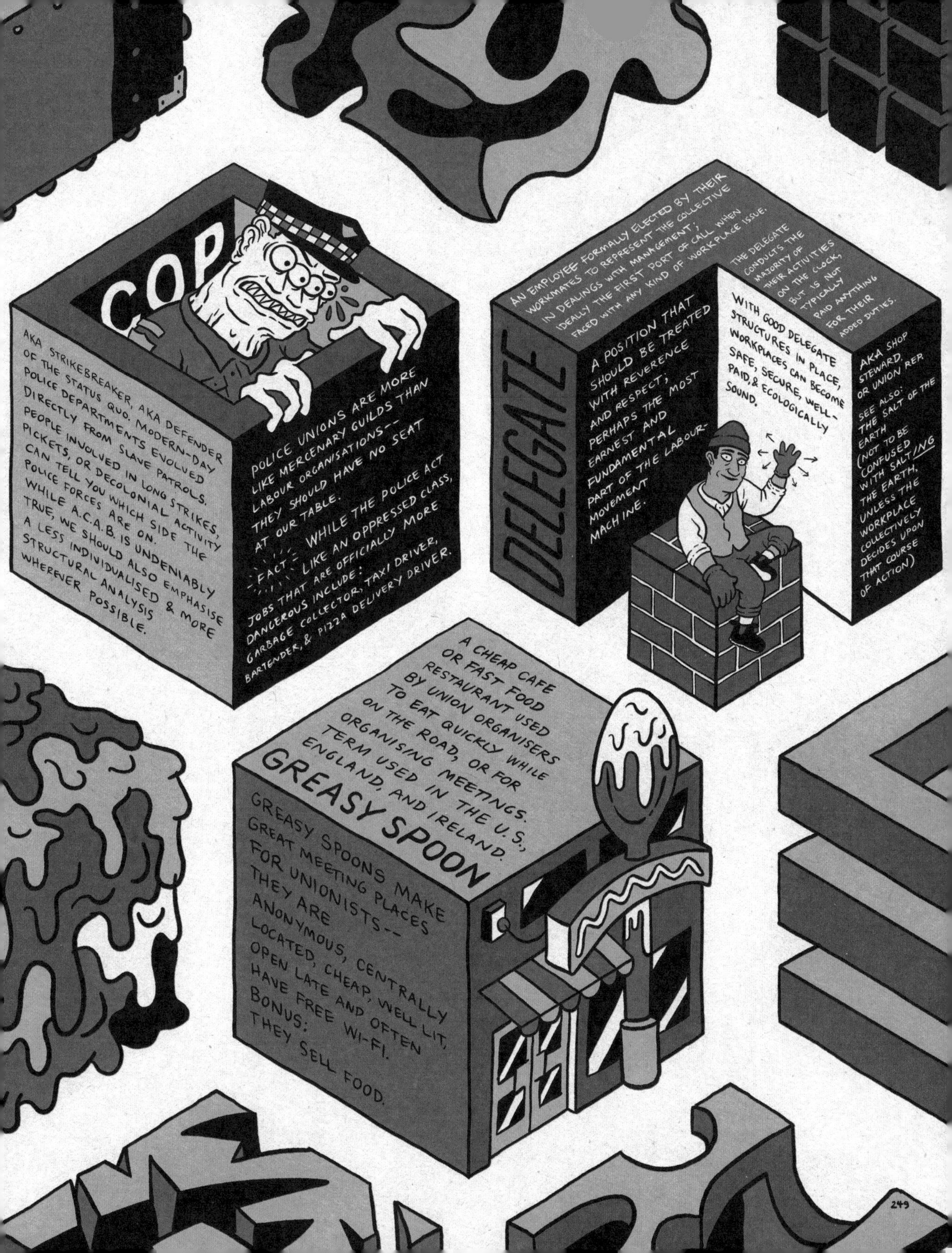
COP
AKA STRIKEBREAKER, AKA DEFENDER OF THE STATUS QUO. MODERN-DAY POLICE DEPARTMENTS EVOLVED DIRECTLY FROM SLAVE PATROLS. PEOPLE INVOLVED IN LONG STRIKES, PICKETS, OR DECOLONIAL ACTIVITY CAN TELL YOU WHICH SIDE THE POLICE FORCES ARE ON. WHILE A.C.A.B. IS UNDENIABLY TRUE, WE SHOULD ALSO EMPHASISE A LESS INDIVIDUALISED & MORE STRUCTURAL ANALYSIS WHEREVER POSSIBLE.
POLICE UNIONS ARE MORE LIKE MERCENARY GUILDS THAN LABOUR ORGANISATIONS-- THEY SHOULD HAVE NO SEAT AT OUR TABLE.
FACT: WHILE THE POLICE ACT LIKE AN OPPRESSED CLASS, JOBS THAT ARE OFFICIALLY MORE DANGEROUS INCLUDE: GARBAGE COLLECTOR, TAXI DRIVER, BARTENDER, & PIZZA DELIVERY DRIVER.
DELEGATE
AN EMPLOYEE FORMALLY ELECTED BY THEIR WORKMATES TO REPRESENT THE COLLECTIVE IN DEALINGS WITH MANAGEMENT; IDEALLY THE FIRST PORT OF CALL WHEN FACED WITH ANY KIND OF WORKPLACE ISSUE.
THE DELEGATE CONDUCTS THE MAJORITY OF THEIR ACTIVITIES ON THE CLOCK, BUT IS NOT TYPICALLY PAID ANYTHING FOR THEIR ADDED DUTIES.
A POSITION THAT SHOULD BE TREATED WITH REVERENCE AND RESPECT; PERHAPS THE MOST EARNEST AND FUNDAMENTAL PART OF THE LABOUR-MOVEMENT MACHINE.
WITH GOOD DELEGATE STRUCTURES IN PLACE, WORKPLACES CAN BECOME SAFE, SECURE, WELL-PAID, & ECOLOGICALLY SOUND.
AKA SHOP STEWARD, OR UNION REP.
SEE ALSO: THE SALT OF THE EARTH (NOT TO BE CONFUSED WITH SALTING THE EARTH, UNLESS THE WORKPLACE COLLECTIVELY DECIDES UPON THAT COURSE OF ACTION)
GREASY SPOON
A CHEAP CAFE OR FAST FOOD RESTAURANT USED BY UNION ORGANISERS TO EAT QUICKLY WHILE ON THE ROAD, OR FOR ORGANISING MEETINGS. TERM USED IN THE U.S., ENGLAND, AND IRELAND.
GREASY SPOONS MAKE GREAT MEETING PLACES FOR UNIONISTS-- THEY ARE ANONYMOUS, CENTRALLY LOCATED, CHEAP, WELL LIT, OPEN LATE AND OFTEN HAVE FREE WI-FI. BONUS: THEY SELL FOOD.

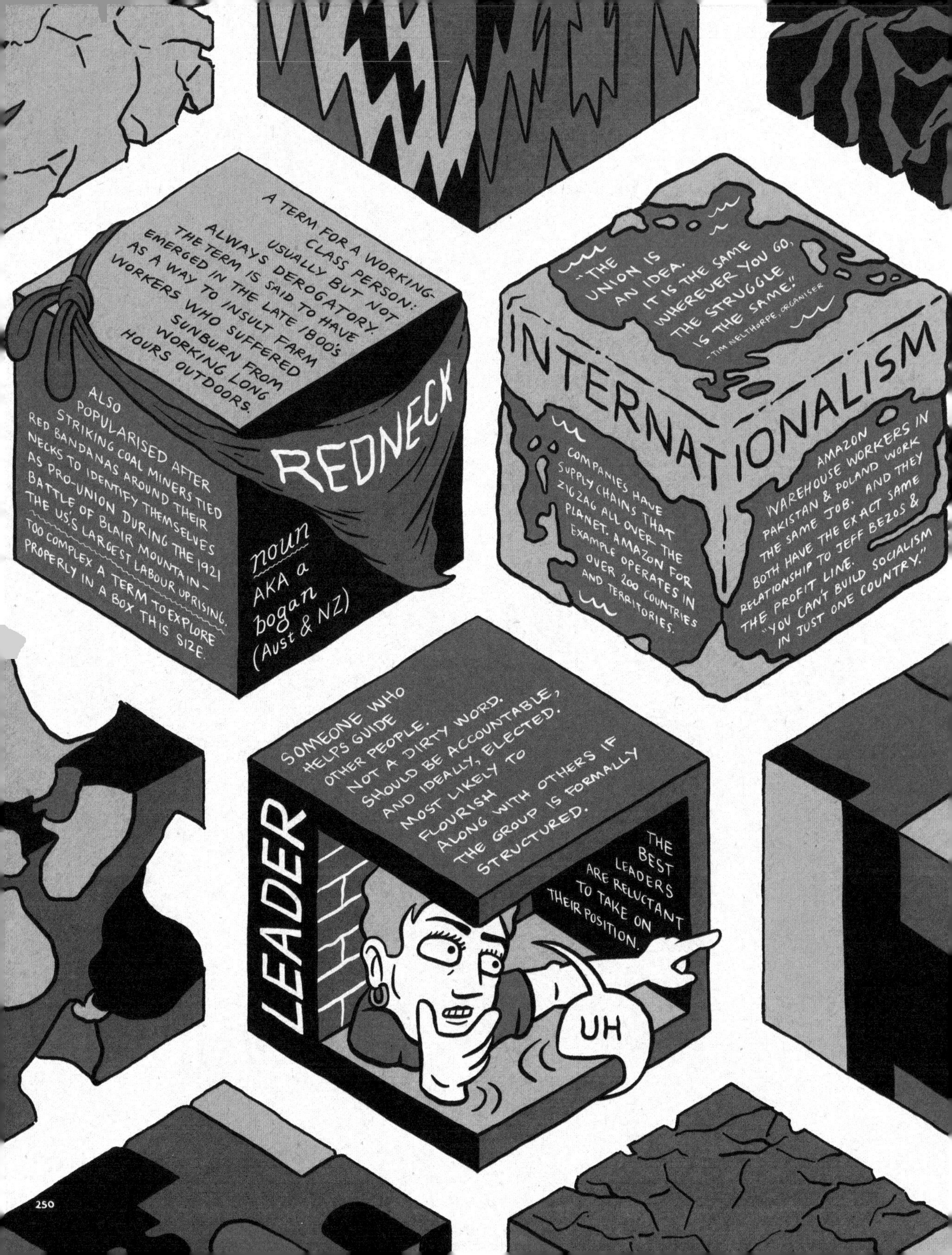
REDNECK
A TERM FOR A WORKING-CLASS PERSON: USUALLY BUT NOT ALWAYS DEROGATORY. THE TERM IS SAID TO HAVE EMERGED IN THE LATE 1800'S AS A WAY TO INSULT FARM WORKERS WHO SUFFERED SUNBURN FROM WORKING LONG HOURS OUTDOORS.
ALSO POPULARISED AFTER STRIKING COAL MINERS TIED RED BANDANAS AROUND THEIR NECKS TO IDENTIFY THEMSELVES AS PRO-UNION DURING THE 1921 BATTLE OF BLAIR MOUNTAIN – THE U.S.'S LARGEST LABOUR UPRISING. TOO COMPLEX A TERM TO EXPLORE PROPERLY IN A BOX THIS SIZE.
noun
AKA a bogan (Aust & NZ)
INTERNATIONALISM
"THE UNION IS AN IDEA. IT IS THE SAME WHEREVER YOU GO. THE STRUGGLE IS THE SAME!"
-TIM NELTHORPE, ORGANISER
COMPANIES HAVE SUPPLY CHAINS THAT ZIGZAG ALL OVER THE PLANET. AMAZON FOR EXAMPLE OPERATES IN OVER 200 COUNTRIES AND TERRITORIES.
AMAZON WAREHOUSE WORKERS IN PAKISTAN & POLAND WORK THE SAME JOB. AND THEY BOTH HAVE THE EXACT SAME RELATIONSHIP TO JEFF BEZOS & THE PROFIT LINE. "YOU CAN'T BUILD SOCIALISM IN JUST ONE COUNTRY."
LEADER
SOMEONE WHO HELPS GUIDE OTHER PEOPLE. NOT A DIRTY WORD. SHOULD BE ACCOUNTABLE, AND IDEALLY, ELECTED. MOST LIKELY TO FLOURISH ALONG WITH OTHERS IF THE GROUP IS FORMALLY STRUCTURED.
THE BEST LEADERS ARE RELUCTANT TO TAKE ON THEIR POSITION.
UH

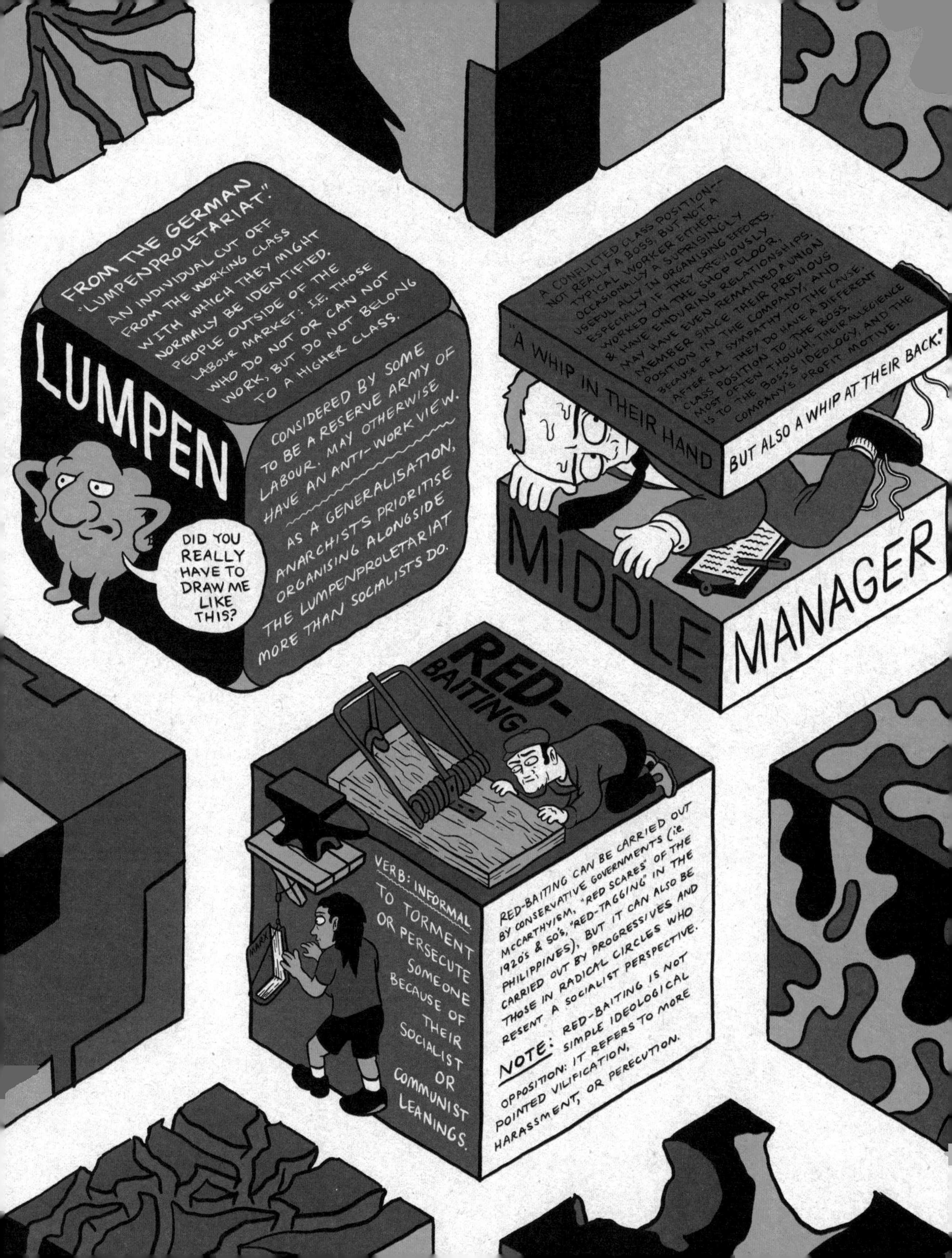

LUMPEN
FROM THE GERMAN "LUMPENPROLETARIAT": AN INDIVIDUAL CUT OFF FROM THE WORKING CLASS WITH WHICH THEY MIGHT NORMALLY BE IDENTIFIED. PEOPLE OUTSIDE OF THE LABOUR MARKET: IE. THOSE WHO DO NOT OR CAN NOT WORK, BUT DO NOT BELONG TO A HIGHER CLASS.
CONSIDERED BY SOME TO BE A RESERVE ARMY OF LABOUR. MAY OTHERWISE HAVE AN ANTI-WORK VIEW.
AS A GENERALISATION, ANARCHISTS PRIORITISE ORGANISING ALONGSIDE THE LUMPENPROLETARIAT MORE THAN SOCIALISTS DO.
DID YOU REALLY HAVE TO DRAW ME LIKE THIS?
MIDDLE MANAGER
A CONFLICTED CLASS POSITION-- NOT REALLY A BOSS, BUT NOT A TYPICAL WORKER EITHER. OCCASIONALLY A SUPRISINGLY USEFUL ALLY IN ORGANISING EFFORTS, ESPECIALLY IF THEY PREVIOUSLY WORKED ON THE SHOP FLOOR, & HAVE ENDURING RELATIONSHIPS. MAY HAVE EVEN REMAINED A UNION MEMBER SINCE THEIR PREVIOUS POSITION IN THE COMPANY, AND BECAUSE OF A SYMPATHY TO THE CAUSE. AFTER ALL, THEY DO HAVE A DIFFERENT CLASS POSITION TO THE BOSS. MOST OFTEN THOUGH, THEIR ALLEGIENCE IS TO THE BOSS'S IDEOLOGY, AND THE COMPANY'S PROFIT MOTIVE.
"A WHIP IN THEIR HAND
BUT ALSO A WHIP AT THEIR BACK."
RED-BAITING
VERB: INFORMAL. TO TORMENT OR PERSECUTE SOMEONE BECAUSE OF THEIR SOCIALIST OR COMMUNIST LEANINGS.
MARX
RED-BAITING CAN BE CARRIED OUT BY CONSERVATIVE GOVERNMENTS (i.e. McCARTHYISM, "RED SCARES" OF THE 1920'S & 50'S, "RED-TAGGING" IN THE PHILIPPINES), BUT IT CAN ALSO BE CARRIED OUT BY PROGRESSIVES AND THOSE IN RADICAL CIRCLES WHO RESENT A SOCIALIST PERSPECTIVE.
NOTE: RED-BAITING IS NOT SIMPLE IDEOLOGICAL OPPOSITION: IT REFERS TO MORE POINTED VILIFICATION, HARASSMENT, OR PERECUTION.

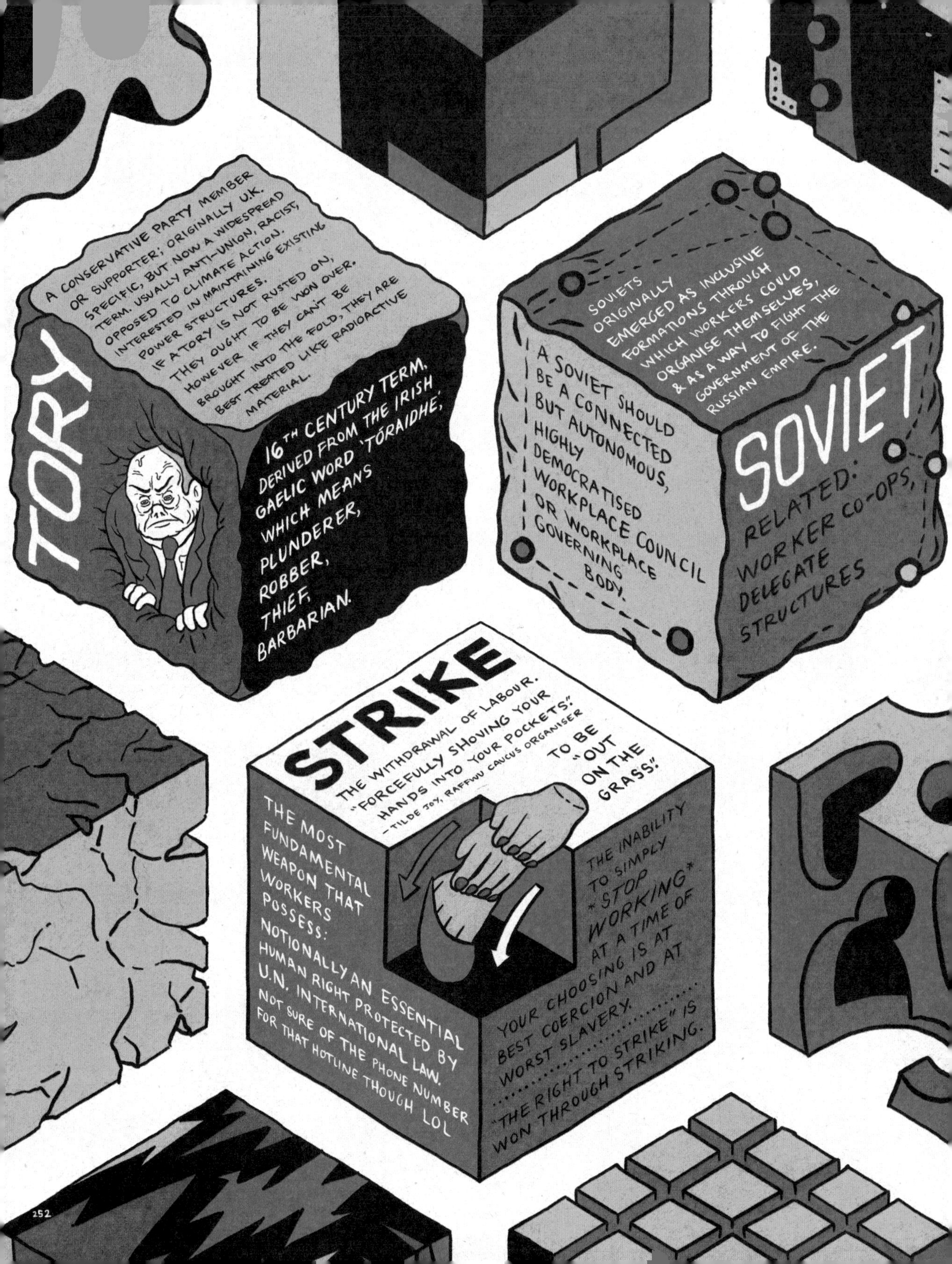

TORY
A CONSERVATIVE PARTY MEMBER OR SUPPORTER; ORIGINALLY U.K. SPECIFIC, BUT NOW A WIDESPREAD TERM. USUALLY ANTI-UNION, RACIST, OPPOSED TO CLIMATE ACTION, INTERESTED IN MAINTAINING EXISTING POWER STRUCTURES.
IF A TORY IS NOT RUSTED ON, THEY OUGHT TO BE WON OVER. HOWEVER IF THEY CAN'T BE BROUGHT INTO THE FOLD, THEY ARE BEST TREATED LIKE RADIOACTIVE MATERIAL.
16TH CENTURY TERM, DERIVED FROM THE IRISH GAELIC WORD 'TÓRAIDHE', WHICH MEANS PLUNDERER, ROBBER, THIEF, BARBARIAN.
SOVIET
SOVIETS ORIGINALLY EMERGED AS INCLUSIVE FORMATIONS THROUGH WHICH WORKERS COULD ORGANISE THEMSELVES, & AS A WAY TO FIGHT THE GOVERNMENT OF THE RUSSIAN EMPIRE.
A SOVIET SHOULD BE A CONNECTED BUT AUTONOMOUS, HIGHLY DEMOCRATISED WORKPLACE COUNCIL OR WORKPLACE GOVERNING BODY.
RELATED: WORKER CO-OPS, DELEGATE STRUCTURES
STRIKE
THE WITHDRAWAL OF LABOUR.
"FORCEFULLY SHOVING YOUR HANDS INTO YOUR POCKETS" - TILDE JOY, RAFFWU CAUCUS ORGANISER
TO BE "OUT ON THE GRASS."
THE MOST FUNDAMENTAL WEAPON THAT WORKERS POSSESS: NOTIONALLY AN ESSENTIAL HUMAN RIGHT PROTECTED BY U.N. INTERNATIONAL LAW. NOT SURE OF THE PHONE NUMBER FOR THAT HOTLINE THOUGH LOL
THE INABILITY TO SIMPLY *STOP WORKING* AT A TIME OF YOUR CHOOSING IS AT BEST COERCION AND AT WORST SLAVERY.
"THE RIGHT TO STRIKE" IS WON THROUGH STRIKING.

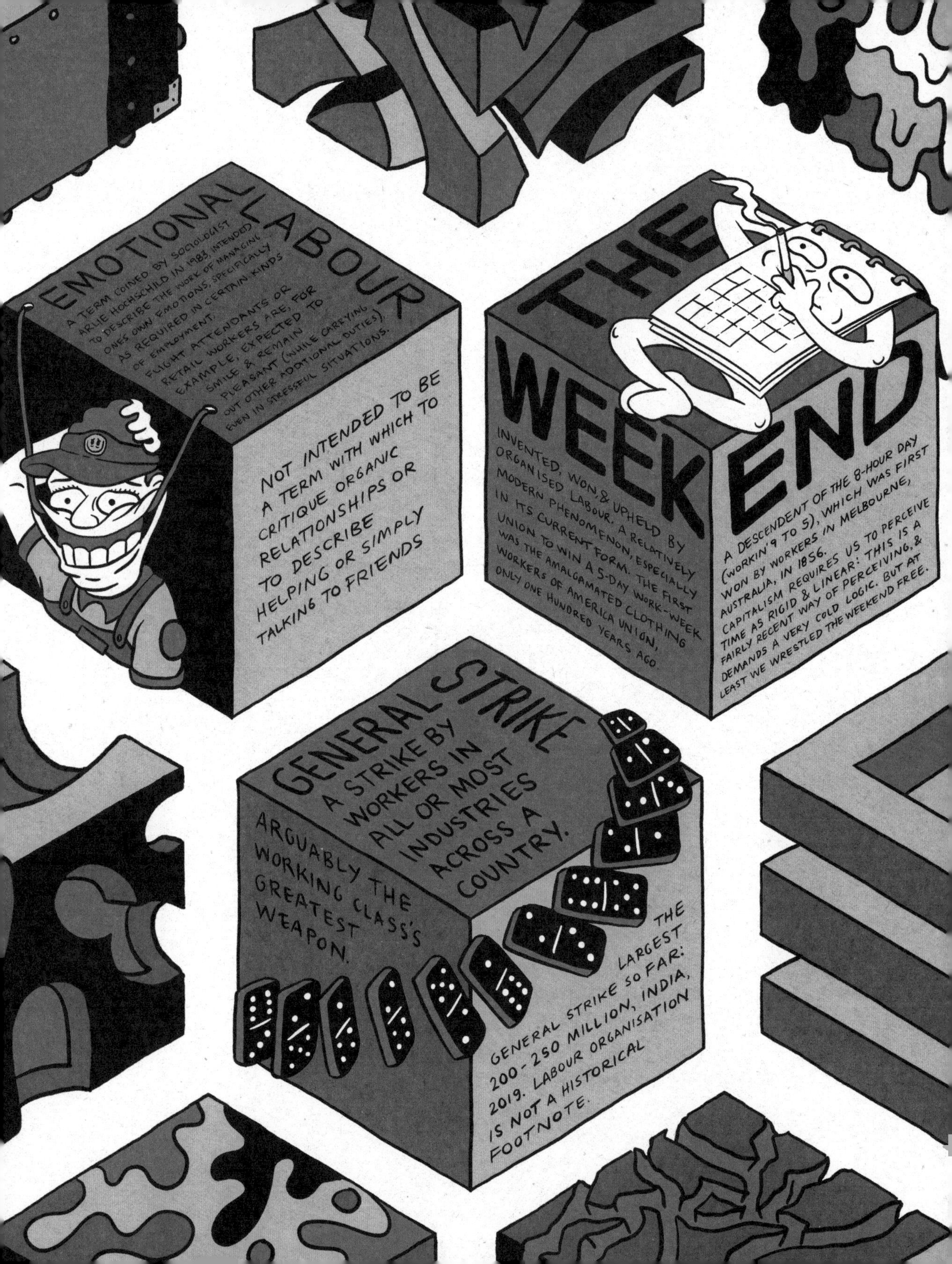
EMOTIONAL LABOUR
A TERM COINED BY SOCIOLOGIST ARLIE HOCHSCHILD IN 1983 INTENDED TO DESCRIBE THE WORK OF MANAGING ONES OWN EMOTIONS, SPECIFICALLY AS REQUIRED IN CERTAIN KINDS OF EMPLOYMENT.
FLIGHT ATTENDANTS OR RETAIL WORKERS ARE, FOR EXAMPLE, EXPECTED TO SMILE & REMAIN PLEASANT (WHILE CARRYING OUT OTHER ADDITIONAL DUTIES), EVEN IN STRESSFUL SITUATIONS.
NOT INTENDED TO BE A TERM WITH WHICH TO CRITIQUE ORGANIC RELATIONSHIPS OR TO DESCRIBE HELPING OR SIMPLY TALKING TO FRIENDS
THE WEEKEND
INVENTED, WON, & UPHELD BY ORGANISED LABOUR. A RELATIVELY MODERN PHENOMENON, ESPECIALLY IN ITS CURRENT FORM. THE FIRST UNION TO WIN A 5-DAY WORK-WEEK WAS THE AMALGAMATED CLOTHING WORKERS OF AMERICA UNION, ONLY ONE HUNDRED YEARS AGO.
A DESCENDENT OF THE 8-HOUR DAY (WORKIN' 9 TO 5), WHICH WAS FIRST WON BY WORKERS IN MELBOURNE, AUSTRALIA, IN 1856.
CAPITALISM REQUIRES US TO PERCEIVE TIME AS RIGID & LINEAR: THIS IS A FAIRLY RECENT WAY OF PERCEIVING, & DEMANDS A VERY COLD LOGIC. BUT AT LEAST WE WRESTLED THE WEEKEND FREE.
GENERAL STRIKE
A STRIKE BY WORKERS IN ALL OR MOST INDUSTRIES ACROSS A COUNTRY.
ARGUABLY THE WORKING CLASS'S GREATEST WEAPON.
THE LARGEST GENERAL STRIKE SO FAR: 200-250 MILLION, INDIA, 2019. LABOUR ORGANISATION IS NOT A HISTORICAL FOOTNOTE.

SCRIBE PUBLICATIONS
18-20 EDWARD ST, BRUNSWICK, VICTORIA 3056, AUSTRALIA
3754 PLEASANT AVE, SUITE 100, MINNEAPOLIS, MINNESOTA, 55409, USA

PUBLISHED BY SCRIBE 2022.

TEXT AND ILLUSTRATIONS COPYRIGHT © SAM WALLMAN 2022

PRINTED AND BOUND IN SINGAPORE BY C.O.S. PRINTERS PTE LTD

SCRIBE IS COMMITTED TO THE SUSTAINABLE USE OF NATURAL RESOURCES
AND THE USE OF PAPER PRODUCTS MADE RESPONSIBLY
FROM THOSE RESOURCES.

SCRIBE ACKNOWLEDGES AUSTRALIA'S FIRST NATIONS PEOPLES—
THE FIRST AND CONTINUING CUSTODIANS OF THE LAND ON WHICH
OUR BOOKS ARE CREATED. SOVEREIGNTY HAS NEVER BEEN CEDED.
WE PAY OUR RESPECTS TO ELDERS PAST AND PRESENT.

978 1 925713 05 3 (AUSTRALIAN EDITION)
978 1 950354 99 3 (U.S. EDITION)
978 1 922586 40 7 (EBOOK)

CATALOGUE RECORDS FOR THIS BOOK ARE AVAILABLE
FROM THE NATIONAL LIBRARY OF AUSTRALIA.

SCRIBEPUBLICATIONS.COM.AU
SCRIBEPUBLICATIONS.COM

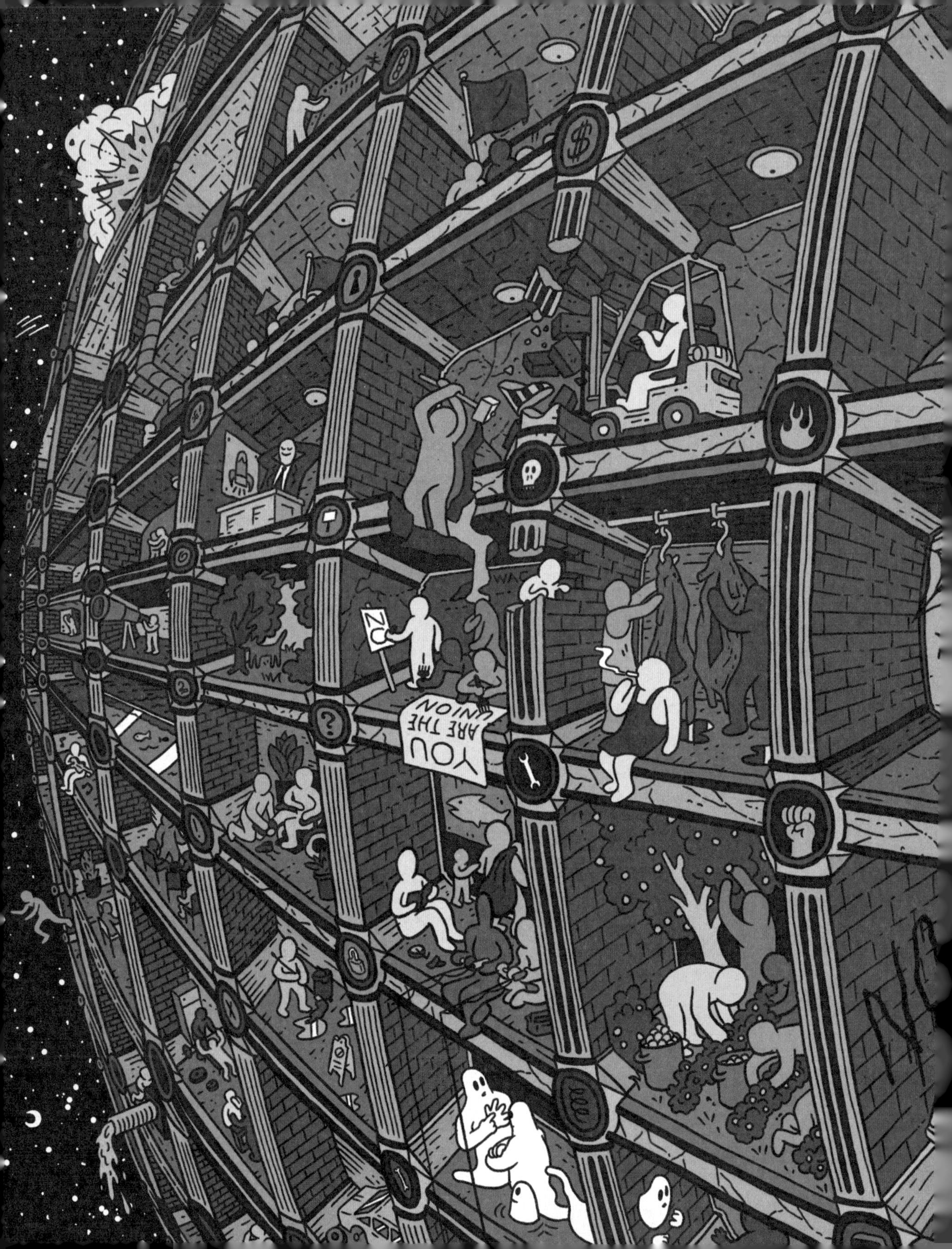
YOU ARE THE UNION